IBM SanFrancisco Developer's Guide

IBM SanFrancisco Developer's Guide

Ron Ben-Natan and
Ori Sasson

McGraw-Hill
New York • SanFrancisco • Washington, D.C.
Auckland • Bogotá • Caracas • Lisbon • London
Madrid • Mexico City • Milan • Montreal • New Delhi
San Juan • Singapore • Sydney • Tokyo • Toronto

McGraw-Hill

*A Division of The **McGraw-Hill** Companies*

1 2 3 4 5 6 7 8 9 0 AGM/AGM 9 0 4 3 2 1 0 9

P/N 0-07-135183-3
PART OF ISBN 0-07-135177-9

The sponsoring editor for this book was Simon Yates and the production supervisor was Claire Stanley. It was set in New Century Schoolbook by Keyword Publishing Services Ltd.

Printed and bound by Quebecor/Martinsburg.

Dedication

—to Ruthy, Danny, and Tal

—to Yael

CONTENTS

PREFACE

The world of Information Technology (IT) is in the midst of a paradigm shift unlike anything seen since the PC revolution. The Internet and the World Wide Web have completely changed the way we look at computer systems. In fact, this change is deeper and more fundamental than the PC revolution since it is affecting a much larger number of people and creating more opportunities than ever before. In addition, these opportunities are not only business-related but often community-related. The Web revolution is unique in that it has the potential to change the day-to-day activities of almost anyone and as such it should be viewed as a sociological phenomenon as opposed to a technology change. It is the best example that we are aware of in which technology is a real enabler of business.

Since the technologies forming this paradigm shift are viewed as the most important factors in the creation of new business models, no major vendor can afford to be oblivious to this shift. The two most important vendors today, and the two in which this can be best seen, are Microsoft and IBM. Microsoft, who has the most to lose if this shift moves too far away from the dominance of the PC, tried initially to fight this shift, but Microsoft is not stupid. A few years ago, it saw that this emerging market would not simply go away nor be reduced to a niche and jumped head-on into battle. It has since managed to transform itself into one of the two major players in the market, and in the process created a lot of really good products. IBM comes from the other extreme. After losing ground in almost all IT domains and being reduced from the mightiest IT empire to a "mainframe maker", IBM saw very early on that e-business (a term coined by IBM) has the potential to be the next decisive area on which empires can be built. And so, it has subsequently managed to realign a great many of its business units with the singular goal of becoming the dominant vendor in the world of e-business – with much success.

While these two giants share the same goal, each has taken radically different approaches. Microsoft had the ability to take a lot of its core technologies and realign them to fit the world of e-commerce. IBM on the other hand initially had less to work with. While this is a subjective issue, we believe that IBM currently leads in innovation and product breadth, which is not to say they lead in the market, nor that they provide the most complete environments. IBM has excelled in creating a large number of products and technologies that together form a coherent roadmap for building e-business applications and has used every advantage afforded by its sheer size to enable an environment in which real solutions are provided and not only tools.

The offerings that come under IBMs e-business umbrella are staggering. They includes Web servers, Java application servers (WebSphere), development environments such as VisualAge, NetObjets Fusion, and WebSphere Studio, TP monitors, databases (DB2 UDB), business intelligence solutions, XML tools and libraries, etc. The list goes on and on. It is true that not all initiatives originated from the same group at IBM, but IBM is doing a great job at consolidating all the bits and pieces into one amazing combination.

While IBM is now approaching individuals and companies (small, midsize, and large), it has a distinct advantage in its relationships with large corporations. As such, it is in a unique position to offer these companies a distinct advantage by coupling technology with domain expertise. This is what the SanFrancisco initiative is all about. The SanFrancisco frameworks are the largest Java-based frameworks initiative to date. They contain an enormous amount of functionality that is mandatory when building complex server-oriented systems with intricate business processing. This, coupled with the fact that IBM has an answer to every piece of the puzzle, makes IBM very attractive in such development projects.

But while the SanFrancisco frameworks can save a lot of time, they have one inherent problem: the frameworks are amazingly complex and have a very long learning curve. They involve conceptual understandings that are hard to come by, are based on advanced (and new) technologies, have built in patterns that must be well understood if they are to be used correctly, and involve many many details. As is often the case, intricate products have less documentation (at least proportionally), and a smaller set of experts that can help. SanFrancisco is no exception. While the SanFrancisco manuals and reference guides are excellent (all of what we have learned is based on these guides and we highly recommend them), they are nowhere sufficient to fully describe all of the frameworks' potential. As the first book to be written on the subject outside of the formal release we hope that it helps in shortening the time it takes to get up and running with SanFrancisco. While we are not vain enough to believe that any reader finishing this book will be an expert in using the SanFrancisco frameworks, we think it is a great way to start.

—Ron Ben-Natan
—Ori Sasson

PART 1

Technological Background

CHAPTER 1

Distributed Object-Oriented Programming using Java

The Java programming environment originated within Sun Microsystems and is currently marketed by JavaSoft, a Sun Microsystems company. Java started out as a Sun research project that aimed to develop a language suitable for supporting an environment of networked machines and embedded systems (remember—*the network is the computer*—Sun's motto for almost a decade—which has turned out to be amazingly correct). It was designed to be used for secure, distributed, network-based applications that will be architecture independent and portable yet small and fast enough to be useful for real-time systems and system programming.

In many respects Java can be viewed as "yet another object oriented programming language" that owes much of its success to good timing, phenomenal marketing, and to the World Wide Web. The explosive growth of the internet and the World Wide Web caught everyone by surprise, including Sun. However, Sun already had Java—and so, Java got a facelift. The characteristics of Java (including its threading, security features, and architecture neutrality) made it the perfect candidate for becoming the language of choice for Web applications. Java was instantaneously the preferred choice for interactive Web applications that must support such features as software distribution and electronic commerce, and that require more than simple processing and static display of information.

In an effort to position Java as the programming language for the Web, Sun created HotJava—a Web browser that runs on the client and looks like any other Web browser but that can also load Java code and run application segments on the client's machine. This allowed Sun to demonstrate applications written using a full-blown programming language running on the client. This feature distinguished Java from other object-oriented programming languages and started the big "Java rush."

The code segments forming these mini-applications, which were downloaded over the internet and started within the client, were called Java Applets (from the word application). In addition, HotJava itself was completely written in Java, showing that Java was not only good for little code snippets but rather that it was a general-purpose development language with which complex applications could be developed. The support for applets demonstrated the amazing potential of bringing the browser to life with application code. Finally, Sun launched an incredible marketing effort—and the rest is history; Java is the hottest language around today—certainly for Web applications.

Since Java was (and still is) available as free downloads, it was accessible to all, and by early 1998 there were over 800,000 developers using

Java. Sure, many of these were toying with the technology, but programming languages and development environments grow "bottom up" (i.e. from developers up to organizations—case in point C, C++, Perl, etc). Most developers today would prefer learning Java than any other programming language, and more books are written about Java than any other programming language.

Although initially Java was used primarily for writing little snippets of applet code, its features as general-purpose object-oriented programming language were soon recognized and a shift began. This shift consisted of using Java for server-side programming and for general application development. In all fairness, Java deserves this repositioning. When Java came to light the battle for programmer preference was over; object-orientation and component-based development had won out. The dominant language by far was C++ and the Java object and programming model is vastly superior and simpler than that of C++ (personal opinion obviously). Smalltalk and Objective-C —the forefathers of Java— and probably superior to Java (another one of those personal opinions), have never achieved enough of a market share to survive the Java rush and it was clear that they would not survive in the long term. For example, Smalltalk's primary vendor—ParcPlace—got a face lift, a new name, and started building Java development environments in parallel to continuing Smalltalk support. IBM's VisualAge development environment, which started out of a Smalltalk environment, was quickly converted to support Java.

Java is a great general-purpose object-oriented programming language. It has a modern object model with classes and interfaces, it has convenient memory management and a garbage collector, threading, networking, blah, blah, blah. Most importantly, the rate at which new libraries, frameworks, and specifications were emerging was incredible. Serious Java developers really have to visit the Java home site (http://java.sun.com) once a week to make sure they do not miss anything new which can be of use.

This book is all about the IBM SanFrancisco frameworks written completely in Java. This chapter does not intend to teach Java since this is a prerequisite of this book. The purpose is merely to remind the reader of some of the fundamentals underlying the Java programming environment and Java runtime.

Java—The Language

Java is defined (e.g. in [GoMc]) to be a *portable and interpreted, distributed, reliable, robust and secure, high-performance and threaded, simple, dynamic, and object-oriented programming language supporting runtime environments*. This list, which would not shame any software offering today, describes the characteristics of Java as a language capable of delivering and deploying applications in a completely heterogeneous and distributed environment where one has no control over the platforms and where performance and security are of major importance.

Java is portable and interpreted. The Java source code is compiled by the Java compiler into a pseudo-code representation called *bytecodes*. This is a semi-compiled, architecture-neutral representation of the application code. The notion of bytecodes is in no way a new concept introduced by Java; it was, for example, already used by Smalltalk in the late 1970s and early 1980s. These bytecodes are interpreted by a Java virtual machine (VM) [or, if a "Just-In-Time" (JIT) compiler is used, compiled directly to machine code] when running the application. Java bytecodes can be run on any architecture for which a Java VM (JVM) is available. The virtual machine encapsulates all the platform-specific services (including user interface, file system operations, and networking). Bytecodes use the common API defined by the Java VM specification and implemented by every JVM using native system calls. Java applications can, therefore, be deployed on any platform for which a Java VM has been implemented. This is of major consequences for corporate developers who need to support multiple groups within the organization, which may be using different platforms, and to independent software vendors (ISVs) who need to develop software that will be later bought by multiple clients, each with its own installed base. The importance of this to the emerging e-commerce (or i-commerce) market is even greater since such applications need to service customers that use an "uncontrolled environment"—i.e. one in which all we can assume is a browser—the killer app. of the 1990s. Since all of the common Web browsers today embed Java, Java is the idea programming language to use for e-commerce.

Java is distributed. The distributed nature of Java can be categorized as two groups. Java as a language and environment is open and portable; the market forces have caused Java to be available on a multitude of platforms, and many vendors provide Java toolsets. This allows developing cooperative systems that run in a distributed environment. The second part of the distributed picture involves the many built-in features that are useful when constructing distributed applications; all of which will be discussed in later chapters.

Java is reliable, robust, and secure. It provides many built-in features to ensure that security is not compromised (both in terms of language constructs as well as in the low-level runtime system). Since Java was designed to serve as a language for implementing applications, such as electronic commerce and Web-wide financial transactions, and since Java applications are loaded and run on client machines, these features are of major importance. Since Java is not the most mature environment, security holes and compromises have already been found (and will probably continue to pop up). Fortunately, the market ensures that these are quickly fixed. In addition, third-party solutions are constantly being introduced with the specific goal of "fortifying" Java environments against all sorts of attacks.

Java is threaded, small, and designed for high-performance applications. The threading features of Java are designed into the language using the `Thread` class, the `Runnable` interface and threading interfaces, which allows application segments to be defined as separate threads. All Java libraries have been written to be thread-safe, and the runtime system itself is multi-threaded.

Finally, Java is a dynamic object-oriented language. Java is syntactically closest to C++, and although marketed as being very close to the C++ programming model, it is actually closer to such object-oriented languages as Objective-C and Smalltalk. The syntactic similarity to C++ makes Java accessible to C++ programmers, while the fact that Java uses a more dynamic and simpler object model similar to those of Objective-C and Smalltalk means that programming Java is much easier than using C++. Like all object-oriented languages, Java uses dynamic (late) binding of implementation to interfaces that support polymorphic behavior. Java uses the *interface* concept (introduced in Objective-C) to associate implementation with interfaces in addition to the more conventional *class*-based model.

Java Language Features

Java was designed to be a *simple* object-oriented language. While maintaining syntactic similarity to C++ (which makes Java very accessible to the hordes of C and C++ developers), it uses a considerably simpler and more elegant object model. While supporting all the important object-oriented concepts (and actually providing a richer object model than C++), it omits many of the more complex and less used programming constructs. This allows Java to be simple to learn, accessible to a larger developer population, and more robust for application and system development.

Java does not use pointers. Memory references are not allowed in Java and the physical memory is hidden from the developer. This is a very important security feature of Java; it is also a major factor where simplicity is concerned. Most of the complex C and C++ bugs are related to pointers and their use (or misuse). By eliminating the pointer concept completely, simplicity and robustness were dramatically increased. To provide an environment in which memory-related issues are eliminated, Java uses a garbage collector that completely removes the memory management burden from the developer and makes Java even easier to use.

Java is a strongly typed language. All typing resolution is done at compile time assuring that many typing bugs that can be discovered at compile time do not evolve into hard-to-find problems. Java does away with casting loopholes common in C++, which are a part of C++'s legacy from C. While casting is still performed, the runtime components of Java check for casting legality and raise exceptions (error conditions) upon failure. Type checking is performed during linkage and during loading of the bytecodes—this is part of the Java security support features of Java.

Java is an object-oriented programming language. Java classes form the basic software construct for supporting all object-oriented features. Classes define a Java type and serve as a template from which objects are instantiated. The class defines the data that each object will have, the data that will be shared by all objects of that type, and the methods associated with the class. Access restrictions may be placed on the data or the methods, allowing classes to form the primary encapsulation and data hiding support mechanism.

Objects are created by specifying a class name and by using the `new` operator. When an object is created, memory is allocated and a constructor is called. The constructor is a special method of the class that is used to initialize the newly created object. Different constructors may be defined in the class to provide different initializations.

Java uses a garbage collector paradigm (similar to Smalltalk). This (together with the fact that Java has no pointers) makes development much simpler since memory management issues can be ignored until application optimization time. The garbage collector will reclaim any object to which there are no active references, i.e. objects that are no longer being used. The developer does not have to make explicit calls such as `delete` in C++. Even though memory freeing is handled by the garbage collector, Java supports a construct similar to C++ destructors for object clean-up (a notion that is not readily available in Smalltalk). The `finalize()` method (if defined in the class) will be called by the runtime system for the object just before the garbage collector decides to free the object.

Java supports class inheritance both as a code reuse mechanism as well as for raising abstraction levels for API users. Single inheritance is used because multiple inheritance adds too much complexity (both in implementation and in usage) and provides little benefit (which is solved by Java in another way). While multiple inheritance may not be necessary for design usages, it is very convenient as an implementation tool. Instead of multiple inheritance, Java supports the notion of interfaces. Interfaces are protocol specifications that define an API without an implementation. Classes are used to implement the interfaces. Because interface specifications are Java types, they can be used as method parameters to solve many of the problems for which multiple inheritance has been found to be useful.

Java defines a rich access model in which classes, members, and methods may be restricted in their use and in their visibility. As in (almost) every object-oriented programming language, Java supports public and private members, methods, and classes. In addition, Java provides some more advanced features, among which are the following.

- *Abstract* methods. These allow definition of an interface without an implementation; subclasses must implement these methods in order to be used for instantiating objects (i.e. trying to instantiate a class with abstract methods produces a compiler error). This is similar to C++ pure virtual functions and to the Smalltalk's use of the `subclassResponsibility` message.
- *Final* classes, methods, and variables. Final classes cannot have subclasses, final methods cannot be overridden by subclasses, and final variables have a constant value.
- *Native* methods. These allow a method to be declared in Java but implemented in another language. The runtime system will link in the native routine (usually implemented in C). Naturally, only languages for which linkage support is provided may be used.

- *Synchronized* methods. These allow specification that a set of methods cannot run concurrently in different threads.
- *Threadsafe* variables. These imply that a synchronizing construct should be used to enforce a critical section around access to the variable, ensuring that one thread cannot modify the variable if another thread is currently using it. This is the variable's equivalent to the method's *synchronized* modifier.
- *Transient* variables. These allow the runtime system to ignore the variable when creating a persistent representation of the object.

Classes are themselves first-class objects in Java. Given an object, one can determine what its type is, i.e. what class it was created from. An object is instantiated using the Java class `Class` for each Java class being used. These objects form the runtime representation of the class information and can be used at runtime for various lookups and services. Class objects are created both for classes and for interfaces. The `isInterface()` method (returning a Boolean value) may be used to distinguish between objects representing classes and objects representing interfaces. Instantiation of an object is internally done using the `newInstance()` methods defined in the class `Class`. Not surprisingly, most methods of the class are defined to be *native* (meaning that they are actually implemented in C—similar to primitives in Smalltalk) because they are really part of the runtime system.

In addition, as of JDK1.1 Java supports the notion of reflection. Classes, interfaces, and other programming constructs support sets of APIs that allow them to be queried. For example, a class object may be asked for a list of all data members or a list of all public methods. This notion allows programs to deal with a very generic abstraction of objects and classes, and is very useful—as users of Smalltalk have learned. At a higher abstraction level, this feature is used by JavaBeans' introspection abilities (much more about reflection and introspection in later sections and in Chapter 3).

Java solves the *fragile superclass problem* by delaying method resolution until the last possible moment. The fragile superclass problem appears in languages such as C++, where adding a new variable or a new method to a class requires that all compilation units involving this class, and that any subclass and references to the class, be recompiled. Java solves this problem by performing name lookup the first time it is referenced, allowing changes to be made without requiring constant recompilation.

Java provides an additional encapsulation construct similar to modules. A Java package is an encapsulation of a set of classes and a set of interfaces. Every class and every interface must belong to a Java package. Packages do not enforce a programming model; they are used for modularization purposes and provide a convenient way to organize related components together. They are used to enforce a namespace organization avoiding naming conflicts that could occur if a single global namespace was used. Package-naming conventions use a sequence of words separated by periods. As we will see throughout this book, a typical application will be using classes from a large number of sources, making namespace control extremely important.

The Java System Architecture

Java uses a virtual machine (VM) architecture making it architecture neutral and portable. This means that Java code can be run on any platform for which a JVM is available. Java code, when passed through the Java compiler (e.g. javac) is not compiled directly into machine code by the compiler; instead, bytecodes are created. Bytecodes are a high-level version of machine code; actually, they can be viewed as being the machine code of the virtual machine. Since these bytecodes comprise the Java program's execution instructions, any environment that has a JVM can be thought of as a Java-enabled environment.

The virtual machine is a program that takes the bytecodes and interprets them into native processor instructions. Therefore, the bytecodes are really a binary code format used by Java to solve the binary distribution problem. A bytecode stream can be sent over the network to any machine on which a JVM is available. When Java applets are used, they are run by the Java VM embedded in a Java-enabled Web browser. There is no re-compilation involved since the bytecodes are interpreted by the VM. The interpretation process ensures that name and reference resolution is done at the last possible moment.

While the initial versions of Java environments were relatively slow because of its interpreted nature, newer versions use "Just-In-Time" (JIT) compilers that dramatically improve performance. These architectural components compile bytecodes directly into the native machine language upon first reference and run this compiled version instead of interpreting the bytecodes. In addition, these machine-level instructions are cached so that additional usage of the same code does not require additional compilation. By using such compilers, Java environments can come close to the performance provided by compiled object-oriented programming languages.

Java does not suffer from any strong linkage problems, which have been the major deficiency documented in languages such as C++. Name resolution is performed when classes are linked as a result of the first reference to the object or method. Once a name is resolved, the reference is rewritten as a numeric value enabling compile-like performance.

The Java environment itself is very portable. The runtime system is written in ANSI-C with no platform-dependent extensions and has specifically been written to be easily ported to any POSIX-compliant platform. This was done in the hope that many ports will be created by third-party vendors thus assuring the popularity of Java, and has proven to be successful. Other components such as the Java compiler were written in Java itself assuring instant portability because of the basic architecture.

As Figure 1-1 shows, the Java classes run on top of the JVM. While all classes are written in Java, some are provided by the JVM vendor, whereas others will be written by an organization as components in applications. The initial set of classes provided by JavaSoft (or other vendors) is usually called the *Java Base Classes*. Together with the JVM this forms the *Java Base Platform*. Classes belonging to the Java base expose an API called the *Java Base API*. Additional functionality may be provided in the form of extension classes and extension APIs. Finally, application-level classes are built using features provided either by the base or by the extension APIs.

The Java base API provides the basic language features required to write any applications. It provides the core language functionality, basic I/O, networking, Applet support, and basic graphical user interface pro-

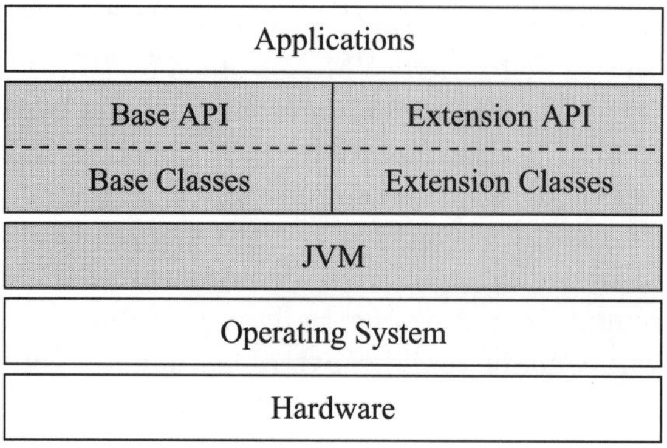

Figure 1-1 Java system architecture.

vided by the Advanced Window Toolkit (AWT). It provides all base functionality such as class loaders, Java security, and access control. In Figure 1-1 the textured boxes are provided by the vendors; the base classes (providing the base API) are provided within the Java Developer's Kit (JDK). Additional modules and APIs may be provided for specific purposes. For example, extensions are/will be provided for handling telephony, 3D graphics, or audio. The distinction between base classes and extension classes was never fully formally defined. Therefore, it is possible (and in fact intended) that a set of classes and APIs will start out as extensions and, as time progresses (and with increasing maturity), they will find their way into the base.

While extensions may be added to support more and more capabilities from within Java, JavaSoft defines a set of extensions as the *Java Standard Extensions*. These extensions form a set of published extensions that, together with the base, form a standard and open API set that can be assumed by all Java developers. Since Java is a relatively new and evolving language, this published set tends to change with time. For example, the Java Database Connectivity (JDBC) API is a standard SQL database access interface that provides a uniform API for accessing relational databases. This module (released as part of the JDK 1.1) is now considered to be one of the standard extensions.

Just-In-Time Compilers

As mentioned, the Java compiler only compiles Java source code into the intermediary bytecode format. Traditionally, the JVM would use the resulting *.class* files (containing the bytecodes) and function as an interpreter. As for abstraction elegance, this is all very well. The JVM is viewed as a machine (hence the term *virtual machine*) and the bytecodes are formed in this machine's language. But when the "rubber meets the road" this interpreted architecture had a serious performance problem, as do most interpreted environments.

The JIT compilers, introduced into second-generation JVMs (e.g. JDK 1.1.6 includes Symantech's JIT) were not invented by Java; for example, they were used by ParcPlace to solve many of Smalltalk's performance problems. The fundamental idea behind JITs is that it will often be more efficient to compile the bytecodes on the fly and run the native machine code than to use the interpreter.

The basic runtime cycle in a JVM, which includes a JIT, is to read the *.class* file and, instead of handing the bytecodes to the interpreter, compile the bytecodes into native machine code and run the resulting binary code. This is all done transparently within the JVM and by the JVM. In fact, apart from various verbose information provided by some vendors (e.g. vendor information printed to the Java console by Netscape Navigator's JVM), the user has no way of knowing whether a JIT is present or not.

Additionally, since the same method may be used many times, JITs use a code cache to cache compiled methods. If a method is activated once more while the machine code compiled for these bytecodes is still within the code cache, no recompilation will be required and a further performance improvement will be made.

Recently, another performance booster has been introduced into the Java world—the bytecode-to-native compiler. These compilers take sets of *.class* files and compile them down to native machine code. Such a compiler approach is preferable over the source code to native machine code approach for three reasons.

1. These compilers allow taking *.class* files that belong to libraries, which were not internally developed, and running them through the compiler as well.
2. These compilers delay the "platform-lock-in" phase to a later time.
3. These compilers are easier to use.

Examples of such commercial products include IBM's High Performance Compiler (HPC) and Tower Technology's TowerJ.

The JavaOS

When Java was originally created, it was intended to be used not only for large-scale, enterprise-wide development of applications but also for runtime environments such as embedded systems, real-time processors, etc. As part of this goal, JavaSoft announced the JavaOS—a highly compact operating system running Java applications directly and efficiently on a multitude of processors. Such processors may be embedded not only in PCs and Network Computers (NCs), but also in fax machines, printers, and (ultimately) even in home appliances.

Java chips, targeting the embedded processor market, is another part of the Java "grand scheme." Java microprocessors (called picoJava, microJava, and ultraJava) take Java to the next stage—inclusion at the hardware level.

A layered approach allows the JavaOS to be modular and support incremental updates. The actual components of the JavaOS are somewhat similar to other operation systems (e.g. architectural components in the JavaOS include a microkernel, a memory manager, and device drivers). However, in addition to these components, the JavaOS includes a JVM as part of the operating system. This, along with the JavaOS graphics and windowing system primitives, is what distinguishes JavaOS as an operating system that natively supports the running of Java applications.

The JavaOS is written in a combination of machine code and Java. The machine-dependent parts (which include the JVM and the Java kernel) are written in native machine code while the machine-independent parts are written in Java itself. This is the meaning of the statement that the "JavaOS is written in Java." Even low-level components such as JavaOS device drivers are written in Java; a feature that makes device drivers much less of a domain reserved for hackers and "bit gurus."

The JavaOS is only one strategy by which Java will be embedded into the operating system. Sun Microsystems intends Java to be ubiquitously available on almost all operating systems, and this seems to be the trend. Most of the operating system vendors have already announced that they will license Java and embed it directly into their operating systems. This includes Apple, HP, IBM, Microsoft, Novell, Silicon Graphics, SunSoft, SCO, and Tandem.

The Java Virtual Machine

The JVM is the central component of any Java execution environment. It is the virtual machine (implemented in software or as ROM chips) that enables Java to be portable by defining its own instruction set, which is used no matter what the underlying operating system or hardware may be. Therefore, the JVM allows Java source code to be compiled (into bytecodes) and run on any JVM-enabled platform, hence the "write once—run anywhere" slogan.

Java bytecodes (the JVM's "machine language") are created by running Java source code through a Java compiler (e.g. *javac*). These bytecodes are stored in the *.class* file in a format called the *Java class format*.

Each class file, therefore, defines a class or interface in terms of its bytecodes.

Whereas bytecodes are the JVM's machine code, they may actually be decompiled to produce Java source code. This fact involves a highly controversial program named *Mocha*, which converts *.class* files into *.Java* source files. The program actually produced readable Java code and created a serious problem for developers who did not want their code to be copied. We will discuss Mocha and scramblers while dealing with issues related to Java security.

Java bytecodes form a set of VM machine instructions. These instructions assume a certain structure regarding the "software machine;" this structure is defined by the JVM specification (see [LiYe]). The JVM structure includes a stack (the JVM is stack oriented), a small set of registers, a heap (where the garbage collector has its way), and an area where the bytecodes are stored. A program counter always points at the next bytecode to be performed.

The heap is used for allocating dynamic memory. Each time a `new` call is made the created object is placed on the heap. The heap is where the garbage collector works (since stack memory is freed when it goes out of context, e.g. when the function or block in which it was defined is removed from the call stack). While the garbage collector works in an independent thread and is activated by the JVM autonomously, developers can explicitly invoke the garbage collector (GC) by calling `Runtime.gc()` or `System.gc()`. Whereas historically garbage collection was thought to be hazardous to performance, garbage collection algorithms have improved to the point that it is worthwhile to forgo a little in execution speed in order to support a *much* simpler programming model (by removing memory management issues from the developer's realm or concerns).

Java Bytecodes

Bytecodes are packaged as one byte stream per method. A bytecode stream is a sequence of instructions that is either interpreted or JIT-ed by the JVM. The bytecode format includes an operation code (opcode) and a sequence of zero or more operands (arguments).

The JVM is stack based. Like many other stack-oriented architectures, it has a relatively small number of opcodes, many of which deal with the stack. Since it is stack based and does not use registers for storing intermediate results, arguments and results are always pushed into the stack. Since the stack is so central to the design of the JVM, many opcodes are dedicated to pushing values onto the stack. For example, almost 20 opcodes are dedicated to pushing constants onto the stack.

In addition to the simpler and more conventional opcodes provided by the JVM, it also provides advanced bytecode support for advanced features of the JVM. Examples include support for exception handling, support for *finally* clauses, synchronization using monitors, etc.

JVM Execution

JVM execution involves two main categories. Once a class is linked to the JVM, execution follows the instructions stored in the JVM's method area per the location of the program counter. However, for the JVM to be ready to execute these instructions a process must be followed that involves loading, linking, and initialization. Figure 1-2 shows a schematic view of this process; the rest of the section describes the different stages in the procedure.

JVM execution begins with an invocation of the `main` method for some class; this is a `public static` method with an array of strings as its only parameter and a `void` return type. This method is provided by the developer if running a Java application, or by the applet framework if running an applet.

Before activating the method, the JVM must load the class. This is accomplished by using a Java *ClassLoader*. The loading stage locates the bytecodes of the relevant class or interface and then creates the class representation from these bytecodes. This loading process can involve the local disk or a remote site, which depends on the context in which the JVM was invoked.

Once the class bytecodes have been loaded, linking occurs. The linking phase provides full access to the class bytecodes form within the JVM. The linking phase is a complex process involving bytecode verification, preparation, and symbolic resolution.

Bytecode verification is the JVM's first line of defense against attacks. The verifier ensures that the bytecode streams to be linked to the JVM are well formed. It will verify that opcodes are legal, that each instruction is well formed, and other such syntactic tests. In addition to structural verification, the verifier performs some more advanced tests.

Figure 1-2
JVM execution of a class.

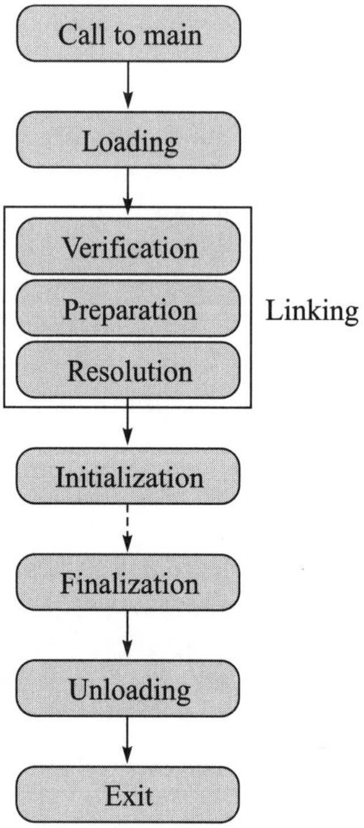

Once the bytecodes have been verified, the preparation process allocates and initializes the data locations required by the class. Default values will be created wherever relevant. Finally, symbolic resolution replaces each symbolic reference with a physical reference in the JVM. The resolution process might well involve the initiation of the loading phase for other classes (because of the original class referencing them or their methods).

Once linking has completed, the JVM goes on into the class initialization phase. This involves the (recursive) initialization of the superclass and the initialization of static members. Once initialization is complete, new instances may be created and used.

At this stage, execution in the JVM continues as defined in the main method. Execution might involve another loading–verifying–linking cycle whenever a new class is accessed. Each of these cycles is performed transparently and managed by the JVM using its own daemon threads.

Once an object is no longer in use (i.e. has no references to it), the garbage collector may decide to reclaim the memory. Before doing so however, it must allow the object to be finalized. Each class may implement a method by the name of `finalize`, which has a default implementation (doing nothing) in the class `Object` (from which all classes inherit). Finalization methods are used to free up resources used by objects and perform other clean-up routines. Note that it is the JVM's responsibility to call this method for each object before the garbage collector gets its hands on it.

JVM Threads

The JVM is a multi-threaded environment. Every JVM supports the notion of threads whether or not the native operating system does. Each thread is an independent execution path that may share memory with other threads. Threads may be synchronized using built-in primitives that manipulate in-VM monitors (a mechanism used to define a critical section, i.e. a section of code which is being run at most one thread of execution).

Java threads are categorized into two groups. Daemon and non-daemon threads. Daemon threads usually serve the correct functioning of the JVM whereas non-daemon threads are created and used by the Java application. When a thread is created, it is created as a daemon thread only if its creator was itself a daemon thread; hence the JVM threads will create additional daemon threads if they require additional threads. The `setDaemon` method can be used to change the daemon-ness property of a thread.

When a JVM starts its operation it has exactly one non-daemon thread. This is the thread that calls the `main` method. When there are no more non-daemon threads the JVM exists (since the non-existence of such a thread implies that the application has completed; since only JVM threads are running when this occurs, a new application thread will not be born).

The Class File Format

As mentioned, the Java compiler compiles Java source code into bytecodes and packages them in *.class* files. These files are then read by the JVM; they include all the information required to use the classes and interfaces. The Java class file format is a published format that must be adhered to; all JVMs know how to read this (and only this) format. The class file has the following sections:

- Magic number. A constant bit pattern occupies the first four bytes (202, 254, 186, 190) together, 0xCAFEBABE . This serves as a simple way to identify files as having the class file format.
- Version number. Four bytes specify a version number because it is possible that the class file format may change with time.
- Constant pool. An array of elements holding constant strings, literals, names, etc. This pool is used throughout the rest of the class file, which will typically hold pointers into the pool; pointers are implemented as indexes into the pool. The actual pool contents is preceded by the number of elements it stores and since each element may be of a different length, some elements also specify their own length (other elements do not require a length specification since they are always of a constant length; the first byte in each element encodes the element type).
- Access flags. Two bytes hold a set of flags that identify whether the file holds a class or an interface, and whether public, abstract, or final modifiers have been used in the definition.
- *this class* index. Two bytes represent an index into the constants pool. The indexed spot in the constant pool, which itself has another index into the constants pool into which the class or interface name is kept (as a constant string).
- *super class* index. Similarly, an index through which the superclass (or super interface) name can be retrieved.
- Interfaces. A variable size section of indexes into the constants pool where all interfaces implemented by the class are kept.
- Fields. A variable length structure with information regarding the instance and class members. Each structure comprises actual data as well as indexes into the constants pool table.
- Methods. A similar variable length structure describing the methods (only the ones defined at this level; not the inherited methods).
- Attributes. A variable length array of properties regarding the class file. Among these are the *code attributes* that embody the JVM instructions.

Class File Verification

Before a set of bytecodes are actually used, they pass through a rigorous verification process for ensuring (as much as possible) that the class file being loaded contains bytecodes that will not misbehave. Since bytecodes embody the information defining classes, interfaces, and methods, errors appearing within the bytecodes can cause execution to fail or to be incorrect. It is the verifier's task to try to eliminate as many such possibilities as possible.

The verifier is especially necessary since the JVM interpreting (or JIT-ing) the bytecodes does not know who created the bytecodes. While the Java compiler, which is part of the JDK distribution, could probably be trusted to create legal bytecodes, a JVM cannot know that the compiler is indeed the creator of the bytecode. For all the JVM knows, the creator could be a malicious attacker intending to cause as much damage as possible. Add to this the fact that the bytecodes could have come from anywhere on the Internet and the "verification process paranoia" is well deserved.

The verification process occurs during many parts of a class lifecycle. For example, parts of the verification are delayed until runtime whereas other parts are performed after loading. Most of the process is performed as part of the linking process. In general, this not only ensures that bad classes are rejected as early as possible but also improves performance as runtime verification can involve multiple tests whereas static verification can sometimes provide the same assurance using a single test. Static tests are even more important when JITs are involved because native machine code will be cached and reused once it is compiled.

The actual class file verification process that occurs within class linkage involves a number of phases:

- Class file format verification. The verifier makes sure the format of the class file is conformant to the specification.
- Structural verification. The verifier inspects the class file structure, and especially the constants pool, and tests for errors. All constant pool references are checked for valid format, valid names, and valid types. Class hierarchies are also tested to make sure each class has a superclass and that *final* classes do not have derived classes.
- Each of the code attributes (which define the instructions for the JVM in performing the methods) is tested using a complex

"prover" that analyzes the bytecodes. This phase of verification ensures that code will not misbehave. Once the code has been approved for linkage, the JVM can run at full speed since it is assured, for example, that typing is enforced, that opcodes use the stack appropriately (and with the correct types), that branches are within bounds of the code array, etc. For more information regarding the functioning of the verifier the reader is referred to [LiYe].

The Java Thread Model

Multi-threading is a necessity in today's applications. Environments that have only one thread of control (i.e. can only do one thing at a time) are no longer sufficient. Although single-threaded architectures can simulate any multi-threaded application, the programming model is much more complex and the developer resources required to implement such a simulation are inappropriate.

Networked, distributed applications and windowing applications are among the domains in which multi-threading is most useful. These applications require a number of control threads—one for network management, one for application access, one for user interfaces, etc. In addition, the same code segments in such systems will often be accessed from multiple threads, requiring a re-entrant approach to be used. All these make language and runtime system support for multi-threading an advantage, if not a necessity.

Java supports multi-threading both at the language level and in the runtime system, thus supporting fast, lightweight concurrency within a single address space. The Java language introduces the `Thread` class supporting an API for spawning, running, and stopping threads. The runtime system supports a pre-emptive thread model based on Java language threads. It schedules threads, manages them, and provides synchronization primitives for monitor sections, locking, and semaphores. The actual behavior of Java threads and their timing can depend on the threading model implemented by the VM and can depend on operating system features. In addition, the Java base libraries themselves are written in a thread-safe manner ensuring correct behavior in a threaded environment.

Java supports threading using the `Thread` class and the `Runnable` interface. `Thread` inherits from `Object` and implements the `Runnable` interface; it belongs to the `java.lang` package. Table 1-1 shows the major methods defined by the class. Creating a specialized thread class requires subclassing from the class `Thread` and overriding some of its methods. Under one scenario, one would subclass the `Thread` class and

TABLE 1-1

Methods of the class `Thread`

Method	Description
Constructors	One of: Thread(), Thread(Runnable), Thread(ThreadGroup, Runnable), Thread(String), Thread(ThreadGroup, String), Thread(Runnable, String), Thread(ThreadGroup, Runnable, String)
static Thread currentThread()	Return the currently executed thread object.
static void yield()	Causes the active thread to yield control.
static void sleep(long)	Causes the active thread to sleep for a number of
static void sleep(long, int)	milliseconds (and nanoseconds).
static int activeCount()	Answers the number of threads in the thread group.
static void dumpStack()	Prints the active thread's stack trace.
static int enumerate(Thread[])	Places a reference to all threads in the thread group in the array.
static boolean interrupted()	Answers whether the active thread has been sent an interrupt.
void run()	Run the thread's algorithm.
void stop()	Stops the thread.
void interrupt()	Sends an interrupt to the thread.
boolean isInterrupted()	Answers whether the thread has been sent an interrupt.
void suspend()	Suspend the thread.
void resume()	Resume the thread's execution.
void destroy()	Destroy a thread without cleaning up (e.g. without releasing monitors).
boolean isAlive()	Answers whether the thread is active.
int getPriority()	Get the thread's priority.
void setPriority(int)	Set the thread's priority.
String getName()	Get the thread's name.
void setName(String)	Set the thread name.
ThreadGroup getThreadGroup()	Get the thread's thread group (see constructors).
boolean isDaemon()	Answers whether the thread is a user or a daemon thread.
void setDaemon(boolean)	Marks the thread as a user thread or a daemon thread. When there are no user threads the system exists.
String toString()	Answers a string representation of the thread.
int countStackFrames()	Answers the number of stack frames in the thread.
synchronized void start()	Starts the thread.
synchronized void join(long)	Waits for the thread to die (possibly with a timeout).
synchronized void join()	Similar to the Unix `wait` system call.

override the `run()` method with the application-specific behavior required of the thread. For example, if we wanted a thread to print "*Hello World*" to the standard output stream we would create the following subclass:

```
class HellWorldThread extends Thread {
  public void run() {
    System.out.println(''Hello World'');
  }
}
```

and we would kick off this thread by calling:

```
HelloWorldThread aThread = new HelloWorldThread();
aThread.start();
```

However, new subclasses of the thread class are not often the best approach. Often all we want to do is to spawn off an application-specific behavior in a new thread; this does not mean that we want to introduce a new type into the system. This is precisely what the *interface* concept is all about, and specifically, what the `Runnable` interface is used for. Hence, the class `Thread` is defined to implement the `Runnable` interface:

```
class Thread extends Object implements Runnable { ... }
```

Instead of creating a new subclass we would use our application class as follows:

```
class HelloWorldApp implements Runnable {
  public void run() {
    System.out.println(''Hello World'');
  }
}
```

and we would spawn this off using a thread simply by calling:

```
anApp = new HelloWorldApp();
aThread = new Thread(anApp);
aThread.start();
```

causing a thread to be spawned activating `HelloWorldApp`'s run method.

Thread Synchronization

Monitor (critical) sections are supported using the language's `synchronized` modifier. Monitor sections are defined as code segments that are guaranteed to run exclusively, i.e. there may only be one copy of the code segment running at any time. This ensures that there cannot be two or more activations of the same code fragment and is necessary for assuring consistency in many threaded applications.

For example, assume that we are building a reservation system. A typical method implementation would be to check what the number of vacancies is and, if larger than zero, reserve the ticket. However, if two reservation threads could run concurrently we risk the scenario in which there is only one vacancy, but each of the threads would check the number of vacancies, see that there is one available and issue the ticket. We would then have committed the same (single) vacancy twice.

This is where critical sections come in. If we had a way to assure that each activation of the reservation method would be the only one running at a single time, we would eliminate this race condition scenario. Java provides exactly this feature using the `synchronized` modifier. By declaring a method to be synchronized, e.g.:

```
public synchronized boolean reserve(int numberToReserve) { ... }
```

we are assured that there is only one active instance of this method at any time. Alternatively, we could use the *threadsafe* variable modifier. Synchronization actually supports multiple methods allowing shared variables in an object to be exclusively accessed. The precise definition of synchronized ensures that among all methods in a class defined using `synchronized`, there is only one running at any time.

Thread Groups

Thread groups are aggregations of threads that provide a convenient mechanism through which a set of threads may be manipulated. Many thread operations can be performed on thread groups—for example, a thread group can be started, suspended, or resumed.

Every thread is a member of a thread group. The association of a thread with a thread group is done during thread creation by specifying which thread group a thread belongs to in the thread constructor. If a thread group is not specified during thread creation it will belong to the default thread group. Once this association is made, it cannot be changed—threads cannot migrate between thread groups during the course of their lives.

The association between threads and thread groups is bi-directional. Each thread knows its thread group and can return it using the method `getThreadGroup`. A thread group can enumerate all threads in the group using the `enumerate` method.

Java Exceptions

Java supports an exception model similar to that being used in Smalltalk [ST1, ST2] and in C++ [ElSt]. Exceptions can be viewed as a general-purpose error-handling mechanism but are especially useful in object-oriented systems where the code identifying the error and the code that can handle the error are not created by the same developer (e.g. where the error is identified in some third-party library but can only be handled by the application code). In this case, the function that identifies the error throws an exception. The handler catches the exception and activates an error recovery code segment. The library provider can therefore distribute functionality using a general-purpose error-handling mechanism allowing application developers to provide the customized handling behavior.

Exceptions are object in Java. They are instantiated from classes just like any other object. The Java base system defines a set of exceptions that are used by the runtime system to signal error conditions (Table 1-2 lists some Java runtime exceptions). Developers can create exception classes by subclassing from the `Exception` class. Once an exception object is instantiated it can be thrown using the `throw` statement. This invokes the exception mechanism causing the control flow to change; instead of continuing with normal execution, the system will progress

TABLE 1-2

Some Java runtime exceptions

Exception Name	Description
ArithmeticException	Divide by zero, or zero modulo.
NullPointerException	Attempt to access a variable or method in a null object or attempt to access an element from a null array.
IncompatibleClassChangeException	Mismatch between a class definition and a class usage.
ClassCastException	Illegal cast of an object to a type.
NegativeArraySizeException	Array with a negative size.
OutOfMemoryException	System is out of memory.
NoClassDefFoundException	The runtime system can't find a referenced class.
IncompatibleTypeException	Attempt to instantiate an interface.
ArrayIndexOutOfBoundsException	Index is out of range.
UnsatisfiedLinkException	The runtime system cannot link to an external function.
InternalException	Runtime consistency check failure.

to unwind the stack looking for an appropriate handler. A handler is defined using a `catch` statement specifying the appropriate class of exceptions to be handled (as a parameter of the `catch` statement). If a handler is found, the handling code is initiated. If no handler is found, an error message will typically be written to the standard error stream and the thread will terminate.

Exception handling is based on typing. The thrown object is matched against the handler parameter; if the object's class is derived from the parameter (which is a type name), or implements the parameter (when the type is an interface), the handler will be invoked. In Figure 1-3 two exception classes are defined; `BaseException` is derived from `Exception`, and `DerivedException` is derived from `BaseException`. The handler is defined as a handler of all exception of the base type. Therefore, when an exception of the derived type is thrown, it will be caught by the handler (since any object of type `DerivedException` is also an object of type `BaseException`). Therefore, it is typical to see code segments of the form shown in Figure 1-4 in which different handlers provide different specialization levels in handling error conditions.

Instead of using "catch all" handlers, the `finally` expression can be used. This has the added advantage that blocks defined using these statements are always invoked—whether an exception condition occurs or not (similar to the `valueNowOrOnUnwindDo:` message in Smalltalk).

Figure 1-3
Exception derivation.

```
class BaseException extends Exception {

     //.......

}

class DerivedException extends BaseException {

     //.......

}

try {

     /* Assume some error occurs here */
     throw new DerivedException();

} catch (BaseException ex) {

     /* Handler code */

}
```

Figure 1-4
Handling exceptions at various levels.

```
try {

      /* Some error condition will be signaled here
*/

} catch (DerivedException ex) {

     /* Specialized handler code */

} catch (BaseException ex) {

     /* General Application handling */

} catch (Exception ex) {

     /* Exception objects catch all */

} catch (Object ex) {

     /* Since any object may be thrown! */

}
```

This is important for ensuring that clean-up procedures are invoked whether the code completes or whether an exception occurs. For example, assume we open a file for processing. While processing an error may occur, in which case we would want to handle an exception. However, whether an error occurs or not, we want to close the file before continuing.

The Java Reflection API

Java Reflection, available as of JDK 1.1, provides an API through which Java programs can inspect structures of their own code. Classes can be asked to retrieve their members, methods, and constructors. The term reflection is used since the API allows objects to reflect on their own structures or let other objects use "reflections" of other objects or classes. Reflection creates a very abstract model in which all classes are simply structures aggregating members and methods; viewing objects and classes at this abstraction level is often very useful for writing very generic code that can handle all object types.

The reflection API adds a set of new classes as well as new methods in the class `Class`. Some of the new classes added as part of the `java.lang.reflect` package are:

- `Field`. Instances of this class represent data members of a class. For example, calling the method `getFields` defined in the class `Class` returns an array of `Field` objects—one per datum member (field) in the original class. Each of these describes properties of the field. For example, it may be used to retrieve the field modifiers, the type, or its name. Field objects are used both for instance side methods as well as (static) class side objects and are distinguished by the modifier information available to the field object.
- `Method`. Similarly, a class may be asked to return an array of objects each representing a method of the class.
- `Costructor`. Constructors are somewhat different than methods (e.g. they have no return type) and, therefore, have their own reflective class. Instances of this class can also be used to create and initialize objects of the class they reflect upon.
- `Member`. `Member` is an interface implemented by all of the above reflective classes. It aggregates the reflective methods that are relevant for all members (be they data members or methods) such as the class name, modifiers, etc. This interface is used when using a structural abstraction level, in which case the actual type of the class' components is irrelevant.

In addition to these classes, the reflection API adds an `Array` class (providing methods to dynamically construct and access arrays), a `Modifier` class (which encapsulates modifier information), and utility classes and instances for working with Java primitive types.

Reflection enriches the programming model and extends the things a program can do. Therefore, security must be addressed so as not to create new opportunities for code to misbehave. In general, the reflection extension specifies that API access is controlled on a class-by-class basis by the security manager. For example, in the JDK 1.1 applet security manager (used for example in the applet viewer), the following policy is used.

- Public members of a class are accessible to all classes within the same class.
- Trusted code may access all members, even those that are not public.

Methods Added to Class `Class`

- `getFields` returns an array of `Field` objects, one per public field of the class or interface. The array includes inherited fields as well as those declared by the class. `getDeclaredFields` is used to access all fields instead of only public ones (pending authorization).
- `getMethods` returns an array of `Method` objects, one per public method of the class or interface. The array includes inherited methods as well as those declared by the class. Use `getDeclaredMethods` to access all methods instead of only public ones (pending authorization).
- `getConstructors` returns an array of `Constructor` objects, one per public constructor of the class. `getDeclaredConstructors` returns all constructors instead of only public ones (pending authorization).
- `getField` provides access to a single `Field` object by name.
- `getMethod` provides access to a single `Method` object by name.
- `getConstructor` provides access to a single `Constructor` object by name.

Important Methods in the `Member` Interface

- `getDeclaringClass` returns the class object owning the field, methods or constructor.
- `getName` returns the member's name (as a `String`).
- `getModifiers` returns an integer that encodes the modifier information of the member. The class `Modifier` can be used to interpret this value.

CHAPTER 2

CORBA and Internet Inter-ORB Protocol (IIOP)

During the second half of the 1980s and throughout the 1990s, distributed objects have become a turnkey technology in most information technology (IT) organizations. The spawn of distributed objects has its root in three developments: the reliance on networks for connectivity as well as computation, the need for remote access to services and collaboration, and the Internet/World Wide Web (WWW) revolution. Although each of these developments emerged at different times and from different technology-clients, they all required distributed access to objects, data, and services in order to enable truly powerful applications to be constructed.

While the quest for distributed objects was magnified by the need for integrating disparate applications and services over the Web, it did not start there. In fact, when the Web phenomenon was finally recognized as the primary area of growth in IT and solutions geared toward solving Web application problems, the solution to distributed objects was ready. The Common Object Request Broker (CORB), an industry-wide standard for distributed object-oriented architectures developed by the Object Management Group (OMG), already fully defined how applications running on different platforms and using different development environments and programming models can interoperate. CORBA is in many respects the global object middleware—perfect for the requirements of internet applications.

The OMG was founded to work within the software industry to provide an open architecture to support multi-vendor, global, heterogeneous networks of object-based software components. The Object Management Architecture (OMA) Guide ([OMG1]) was published as an architecture, which is to serve as the foundation for the development of detailed specifications and infrastructure in order to form the future of object-based systems. The OMA defines many components that together enable the implementation of the OMG's vision. The most important architectural piece defined in the OMA is the Object Request Broker (ORB). This component is the main mechanism that facilitates the workings of the OMA. The ORB is the facilitator for sending and receiving messages between different objects and components. The ORB environment was defined in the Common Object Request Broker Architecture and Specification (CORBA). The architecture was completed at the end of 1991 and published at the beginning of 1992 (version 1.1) as [OMG2]. It defines the architecture that enables the interoperation of the participants in the OMA. It is responsible for the seamless interaction of different and diverse object systems and, as such, it is the central component in any OMA environment.

The CORBA (Revision 1.0) was adopted from a joint proposal produced by Digital Equipment Corporation, Hewlett–Packard Company, Hyperdesk Corporation, NCR Corporation, Object Design, Inc., and SunSoft Inc. It was published as OMG Document Number 91.12.1, and as a book published by the OMG and by X/Open [OMG2], and was the first widely available specification describing the adopted ORB technology. Revision 2.0 was published in mid-1995 and updated in mid-1996 ([OMG4]).

In this chapter we outline the fundamentals of the Common Object Request Broker Architecture. This includes a description of the common components interacting in a CORBA-based system and their roles. The chapter then goes on to describe CORBA 2.0 with a focus on ORB interoperability in general and the Internet Inter-ORB Protocol specifically (IIOP).

The Object Management Architecture

The OMG technology process is driven by user requirements; a user-driven approach is seen by the members of the OMG to be the best mechanism by which systems will succeed in the market. For example, many vendors in the past (and some even today) have opted for proprietary systems. In this way their users would be tied to their offerings and a continuous flow of acquisitions could be guaranteed. However, the user community has been steadily moving away from proprietary systems and most corporations today refuse to be too coupled with one vendor. The OMG's primary goals are portability and interoperability. These goals provide enormous benefit to the end user community. Even though the primary forces in the OMG are the major vendors, it has been recognized that tomorrow's technology must be open and that software consumers must be allowed to change the way their systems are developed and used.

The Object Management Architecture (OMA) is a general architecture and a taxonomy of necessary components enabling a portable and interoperable environment. The OMA outlines general technical guidelines that should be followed by every component within the OMA. These include the necessity for object-oriented interfaces, distribution transparency, a common object model forming a common base for all components, full support for all stages of the software's life cycle, a flexible and dynamic nature, high performance, robust implementations, and conformance with existing standards within the software industry.

The OMA Reference Model

The OMG Reference Model for the Object Management Architecture is shown in Figure 2-1. The Reference Model provides the underlying framework that guides the OMG technology adoption process. It defines the categories of necessary components to realize the OMG's goals and vision. The Reference Model is used as a road map to provide a direction for components that must be developed. Once this architecture has been defined, the OMG's work can be seen as providing detailed specifications for the components identified within the Reference Model.

As shown in Figure 2-1, the model is comprised of four component categories: The Object Request Broker, Object Services, Common Facilities, and Application Objects. Application Object components represent the actual software being developed for solving domain-specific problems or for providing off-the-shelf products. These objects make use of the other three categories providing them with a very rich development environment. Using the other three categories, application developers can create portable interoperable code rapidly that can later be reused by other application components. In this respect, the entire architecture is primarily targeted to provide the best possible environment for objects in this category.

The architecture's heart is the Object Request Broker, which provides the capabilities for allowing objects to interact and work together to

Figure 2-1 The OMA reference model.

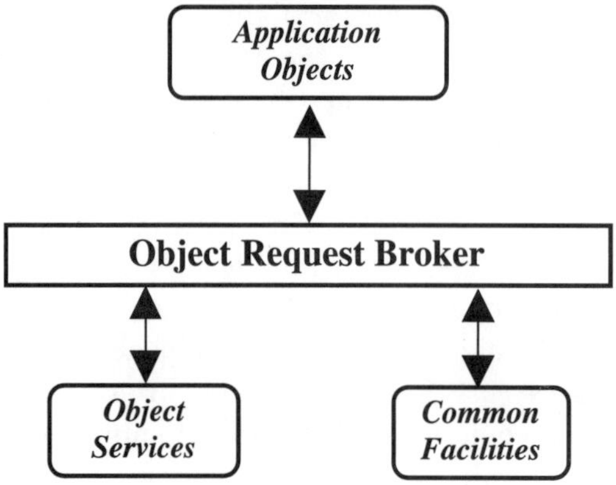

achieve a common goal. Object Services provide low-level system-type services that are necessary for developing applications such as object persistence, transaction capabilities, and security. Common Facilities provide higher-level services that are semantically closer to the application objects such as mailing and printing facilities.

Object Services define a collection of services that are necessary for any application to be constructed at a reasonably high level without requiring the application developers to "reinvent the wheel" for every application (or as many cases where application programmers design software for which they do not have the right qualifications, "reinvent the flat tire"). Common Facilities provide an even higher level of functionalities that define general capabilities required in many applications. The difference between Object Services and Common Facilities might seem a little obscure; in reality it is much clearer. Object Services have a "system orientation" whereas Common Facilities have an "application orientation." Another important difference is that while Object Services must be supported by all ORB environments on all platforms, support for Common Facilities is discretionary.

The OMA is composed of objects. Every component in the architecture is defined in terms of an object-oriented interface (although it does not necessarily have to have an object-oriented implementation). Objects request services from any other object by accessing such object-oriented interfaces. Any object can, therefore, provide services to any other object. Therefore, the architecture transcends so-called "client–server" architectures since every object is both a client and a server in potential. In fact, every request invocation defines a client and server object in the context of a single invocation. The same object can, therefore, service a request (making it a server) whereas the implementation invokes a request to get some information from another object (making it a client). Any object (including Application Objects, Object Service objects, and Common Facilities objects) will be involved in such relationships (both as clients and as servers). The taxonomy of which of the four categories an object belongs to is more a semantic definition based on domain and functionality.

Interaction uses object-oriented interfaces. Any implementation, including non-object-oriented implementations and "legacy" software, can be made to provide object-oriented interfaces. These are often called object-oriented wrappers or adapters and are easily defined for the vast majority of software. In this way the Object Management Architecture can provide an underlying model for all software components; including those that were previously developed or that are not necessarily object oriented. In addition, since any non-distributed application is a special case of a distributed application (which simply uses only one machine) the architecture can truly embed all software developments.

The Object Request Broker

The Object Request Broker (ORB) is the central component that allows the Reference Model to function. It provides the basic object interaction capabilities that are necessary for any of the components to communicate. It is, therefore, no wonder that this component was the first to be defined by the OMG (as [OMG2]). It allows client objects to issue requests for objects to provide required services. These service requests are issued by the client in a location, language, and platform-independent way. The ORB is, therefore, the primary vehicle delivering interoperability and portability as well as the enabler of building true distributed applications.

Requests are issued by objects using an object-oriented interface as defined by the service provider. The client constructs a request by specifying a reference to the object that the request should be sent to, an operation name, and any other information that is necessary. This will typically include the parameters to be sent, but can also include such things as an environment context.

Object Services

The ORB provides basic interaction capability but this is insufficient for real applications to be developed. Applications need to assume certain basic services and functionalities from the underlying environment; this is the role played by the Object Services layer. For example, the ORB provides ways for request to be delivered to service providers but does not define how service providers are found. The Object Services layer may provide a "Trader Service," which provides functionality resembling the role played by Yellow Pages for locating phone numbers.

The Object Services layer is of primary importance to the success of the OMG Reference Model. If this layer is not populated with enough functionality, the OMG's vision will not be realized. Even if the ORB is fully functional and usable this will not enable applications to be built. Too much will have to be developed by the application itself since the support provided by the ORB is at a very low level. Most application developers also lack the expertise to develop such functionalities on their own. A scenario where each application needs to provide core services for itself is not feasible and is extremely wasteful.

Object Services are thus a primary component of the OMG Reference Model. In fact, once an initial ORB-based architecture was in place, the OMG (through the Object Services Task Force) began populating this layer with services such as a Naming Service, an Event Notification Service, a Relationship Service, and a Transaction Service.

Following the general concept of separation of interfaces from implementation, Object Services only define interfaces and a semantic specification of functionality. A service definition therefore supplies the developer with an API set and a description of the functional behavior that is provided. This does not place any limitations regarding implementations for the service. In fact, it is assumed that many implementations will be provided for each service. This is absolutely necessary; services are generally complex and may have different characteristics. Situations in which stressing one characteristic of the service leads to lesser support for another will be common. Since different users of the service will require different resolutions of such tradeoffs, different implementations will be necessary. This is formulated in the Quality of Service (QOS) notion introduced by the OMG, which allows different implementations stressing different attributes of the service to be provided.

Common Facilities

Common Facilities also provide services, but they are typically at a higher level. They are closer to the application levels than are Object Services. Examples of Common Facilities are compound document management, electronic mail, and help systems. Such capabilities are still in the scope of the OMA; they can be used by many applications and can allow applications to be created faster in a portable and interoperable way. Like Object Services, they reduce the complexity of writing software within the OMG framework thus achieving the overall goal. In fact, because Common Facility services are at a higher level they will often cover more functionality necessary to the application than lower-level services. For example, a compound document framework would be preferable to a service that supports generic object graph relationships.

The OMG Object Model

The OMG Object Model was defined by the Object Model Task Force (OMTF) and is the underlying object model for all OMG specifications and all OMG-compliant technologies. The OMG/OM is not part of the CORBA; it is more fundamental and is defined in the Object Management Architecture Guide ([OMG1]).

The OMG/OM provides common semantics that characterize objects in any OMG-based system. These semantics define the interfaces that are used to interact with object state and object behavior. The semantics define objects as instances of types and allow grouping of types into higher-order structures; type grouping occurs through the subtype/supertype relationship. The OMG/OM is implementation independent. However, since it serves as the object model for object system implementation, it defines the semantics of type implementations as data structures for implementing the object state and a set of procedures to implement the object behavior. However, since the OMG/OM must remain implementation neutral, it does not restrict possible implementation. It only specifies the relationship between a type and its one or many implementations.

The OMG/OM as a model must underlay a very large technology base. Object orientation is a paradigm that can be (and is) manifested in many technology categories. For example, we talk about object-oriented programming languages, object-oriented distributed systems, object-oriented databases, etc. Each of these sectors is unique in the problems it is trying to solve, and the tools that are being used. Therefore, each requires a somewhat different model, yet they all have a large commonality because they all follow the object-oriented paradigm. The OMG/OM provides this common semantic core.

Since the OMG/OM must support a large variety of technologies, it needs to deal both with this commonality as well as with the differences. As appropriate for any object-oriented solution, the OMG/OM does not attempt to provide a monolithic all-encompassing definition. Instead, the OMG/OM is composed of a *Core Object Model*, *components*, and *profiles*. The Core Object Model is a set of definitions that must be supported in any OMG/OM-based system. The core model guarantees that even systems in different technology domains will be compatible. *Components* are extensions to the core that are not necessarily supported by all systems but that are required within some technology domain. *Profiles* group sets of components to define a model that is used by sets of systems (usually a full technology domain).

Profiles are enhancements to the core model that are required for specific definitions and are the mechanism by which the OMG/OM can be the base for such a variety of systems. Different profiles can share components. Profiles can also define similar components. This could happen because different domains may not agree on the importance, or even the detailed semantics of similar notions. For example, distributed environments and ODBMS profiles may both support object relationships, although these may stress different properties. Although it is recommended that profiles share as much as possible, profiles remain a flexible way to provide different support while sharing a common base. This is especially important since profiles can also be sector-based. Thus profiles can be defined for the financial community or for the telecommunications community. These sector-based profiles have even more elaborate domain-specific semantics and thus cannot be hindered by inflexible structures.

The goal of defining a common object model is to facilitate interoperability between software components and to ensure portability of applications. Application portability means that software can be built in a way that guarantees that the construct used by the application will be available in different systems and as different vendor products. A common object model that is supported by multiple vendors in multiple system domains allows the application programmer to program to this common model so that the software will be portable across all systems supporting this model. Application portability is extremely important to application developers, but has yet to be fully realized. Such portability eliminates dependencies on vendor companies and also eliminates unnecessary multiplicity and complexity in applications that need to work with many underlying models just because they have to access many software components.

Portability is usually divided into three types: object code portability, source code portability, and design portability. Object-level portability (also called binary portability) means that the executable can be run on different platforms. Source code portability means that the source code can be moved from one platform to the other from which a new executable can be constructed (e.g. the source code compiled) to provide a version of the software on the new system. Design-level portability means that there is an underlying set of assumptions and definitions from which the design is created in a way that a transformation to another implementation set is straightforward.

The OMG/OM supports design portability. It defines a base semantics that ensures that application designs based upon this core will be portable across compliant systems. The OMG/OM is a model; it does not define syntax. Therefore, it cannot support source code portability (and since it is an abstract definition there certainly is no meaning for object code portability). Still, system designs are the fundamental architectural components in any system, and achieving design portability is a very big and necessary step towards other forms of portability. For example, there could be no source-level portability without design portability since the architectural structures are required to be the same before source ports.

Interoperability means interaction between different software components and systems from different vendors running on different platforms. The Common Object Request Broker is the mechanism to achieve interoperability and provides the necessary transport mechanisms for allowing interoperability. This, however, is not enough because semantics are required to determine exactly what it is that is being sent over the transport layer; the OMG/OM is the core of this semantic definition.

Just as it is important to understand what the goal of the OMG/OM is, it is important to understand what it was not meant to be. It is not intended to be the ultimate and only object model. It was designed to be extensible because inflexible and closed models always break. The OM was not built by trying to include everything, nor by trying to include only a least common denominator. It was designed to include the common constructs that are needed to support design portability and interoperability. Finally, it was not intended to serve as a meta-model but rather a specific object model that would be a base for the compliance of object-based systems.

The CORBA Object Model (CORBA/OM)

The CORBA/OM is a concrete object model based on the OMG/OM described in the previous section. Therefore, it provides more detailed specifications with regard to concepts defined in the OMG/OM, it maps abstract constructs to concrete concepts, and defines model restrictions to create a model that can be implemented. The OMG/OM is an abstract object model that is the basic object model for many technologies. The

CORBA/OM, on the other hand, provides the underlying definitions for a particular technology. Such an object model focuses on a particular set of constructs and on a certain view. CORBA, in general, is interested in providing mechanisms and interfaces that enable requesters of service (clients) to be separated from providers of service (servers). It is especially interested with the clients and the encapsulated interfaces that allow services to be provided. It is less interested with object implementations (apart from the notion of having servers provide services by activating implementations). Therefore, the model focuses on interactions between clients and servers, and especially in concepts meaningful to requesters of service.

Requests

Clients are entities that request services. A *request* associates a set of information with a particular point in time. The information includes the operation requested, the target object to which the request is made, parameters of the request (in the form of values), and an optional context. An *object* is an encapsulation of services that may be requested by clients. A *value* is anything that may be a parameter in a request. Values can identify an object. An *object reference* is a name that identifies a certain object in a consistent way.

The result of a request is the result of providing a certain service to the client. The client may or may not be returned a set of results. Requests may also cause the raising of exceptions to denote abnormal conditions and may also provide additional information in the request context. The model supports the notion of a *request form* as a mechanism that can be used to issue requests. Request forms are either built within a certain programming language (using the programming language mapping) or dynamically created by using the Dynamic Invocation Interface (DII).

Operations

An *operation* denotes a service that may be requested. An operation is an entity that has a name and a signature. A *signature* defines the values that can be used for parameters and results in the operation request. An operation can be represented as:

```
[oneway] <return result type> <operation name>
    (parameter1, .... , parameterN)
    [raises(exception1, .... , exceptionK)]
    [context(contextName1, .... , contextNameL)]
```

Each parameter has a mode and a type. The *mode* is one of *in*, *out*, or *inout* according to whether the value is passed in from the client to the service provider, passed out from the service provider to the client, or both. The *type* defines what the set of allowed values for this parameter is. Each exception in the optional "raises" clause is an indication that this exception may be raised while servicing the request. The raising of an exception usually means that the request was not completed successfully. Each element in the optional "context" clause specifies a context that may be passed from the service requester to the service provider; this can supply a service implementation with additional context information that may be required on an operation-specific basis.

The CORBA/OM defines two operation execution semantics. The default semantic is called *at-most-once* and means that if the operation returned successfully it was performed exactly once, and if an exception was raised then it was either executed once or not at all. The optional *oneway* specifier denotes that the *best-effort* operation semantic should be used, meaning that the operation does not return any results and the requester does not wait for the completion of the provider.

Interfaces and Attributes

An interface specifies a set of operations. The interface of an object describes the operations that may be used by clients to issue requests. Interfaces are defined using the Interface Definition Language (IDL) described in a later section. An interface may also have attributes. An attribute is modeled by a pair of accessor operations, one used to get the attribute's value and one used to set the attribute's value. An attribute may be specified to be *read-only* in which case the setting function is omitted. Interfaces are related through the interface inheritance relationship. This mechanism allows objects to support multiple interfaces by supporting an interface that inherits from multiple interfaces.

Types

Types aggregate sets of values. The *extension of a type* (sometimes also called the type extent) is the set of values that are members of the type. An *object type* is a type whose member values are objects. Types are used to define what values may be injected into operation parameters.

Implementations

Object implementations are the entities that actually perform the services requested by the clients. The implementations perform the behavior seen by the requester. The CORBA implementation model consists of an execution model that describes how services are performed and a construction model that describes how services are defined.

The execution model specifies that services are provided by executing a code that operates on sets of data. The execution can deliver back a result, change the state of the system, or both. A *method* is a code segment that is executed upon getting a request.

The implementation model includes a construction model that specifies how object implementations are constructed. In particular, it needs to specify how methods are defined and how method dispatch is performed. The construction model must also specify how objects are created and destroyed.

The Common Object Request Broker Architecture

This section details the ORB-based architecture that supports portability and interoperability. Figure 2-2 illustrates a client making a request for a service to be provided by an object implementation. The client has an object reference for the object and activates operations for this object. This reference is opaque and the client has no notion as to the location of the object implementation, the language used to implement it, or any other detail about the implementation. It only has a specification for an operation request that is part of the interface. The client issues the request and the ORB is responsible for delivering the request to the

Figure 2-2
Client request and object implementation.

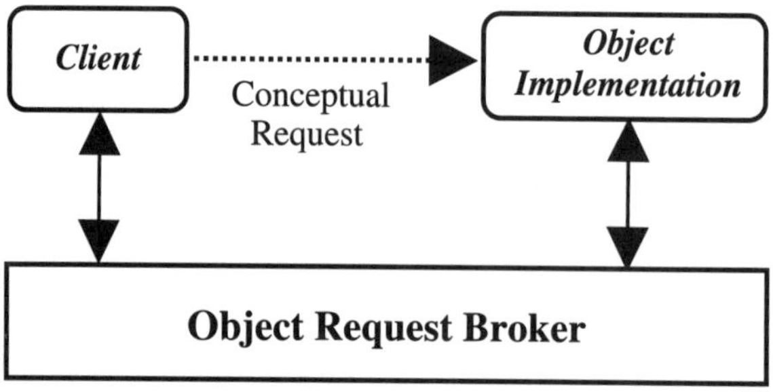

object implementation in a format that the object implementation can respond to. The client can itself be an object implementation that is being used by other clients. Thus, there is no special annotation making an object a client object or an object-providing service through the ORB.

When the client has a handle to an object implementation and desires to issue a request, two possibilities are available. If the interface was defined in IDL and the client has a definition for the type of the object implementation, a static invocation can be issued. The request is made using an IDL stub that is specific to the interface of the target object, otherwise, the DII can be used. This interface is independent of the implementation of the target object and can, therefore, be used even without thorough knowledge regarding the target object's implementation specifics. The request is constructed at runtime and makes no use of IDL stubs. Instead, the request is handled by the dynamic invocation module that uses the information stored in the interface repository. Figure 2-3 illustrates the two possible request paths. Note that when the request is delivered to the object implementation by the ORB, that object is not aware and does not care which path was taken.

Figure 2-3
Two paths for forming a request.

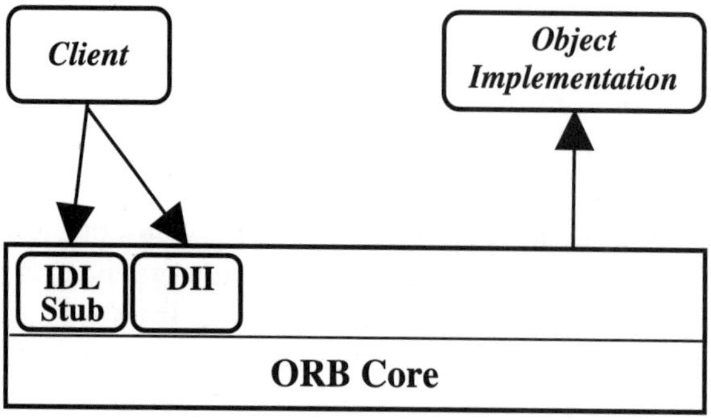

Figure 2-4 shows the delivery of the request to the object implementations. After defining the interface of an object using IDL an IDL skeleton is generated. Requests are passed from the ORB through this skeleton. An IDL skeleton will be used regardless of whether the request was issued through an IDL stub or using the DII. The object implementation is made available using information stored in the Implementation Repository provided at installation time.

CORBA defines a number of ORB subcomponents that interact to support this required functionality. Figure 2-5 illustrates a simple schematic view of these components. The schema does not mean to imply a decomposition of the ORB; in fact, CORBA does not make any assumptions or requirements regarding ORB implementations. CORBA only defines the interfaces that must be provided by every ORB.

The ORB Core

The ORB core handles the basic communication of requests to the various components. It can be seen as the underlying transport layer. CORBA is meant to support multiple systems and, thus, was separated into modular components so that different implementations can be used. This allows both different ORB cores to be used by identical layers (while hiding the differences to external components), as well as for different layered components to use the same core. The core provides basic object representation and communication of requests.

Figure 2-4 Delivering a request to an object implementation.

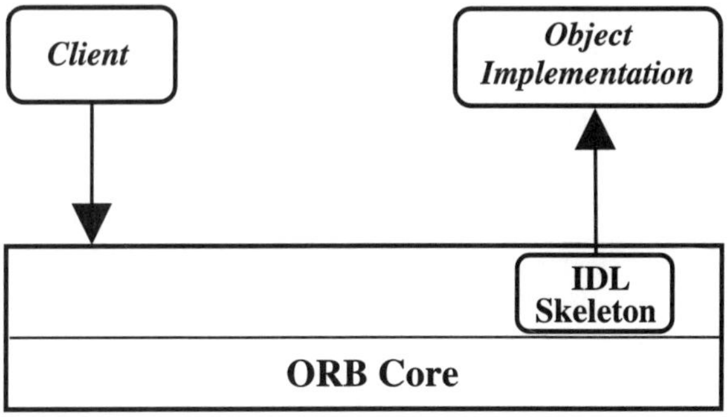

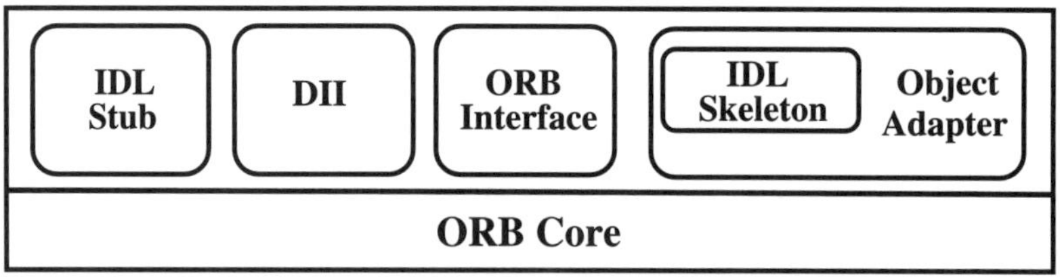

Figure 2-5 Subcomponents in an ORB.

IDL Stubs and Skeletons

The Interface definition language is used to define interfaces, types, structures, and modules. The definition of the interface is the method by which a client is informed which services are supported by an object implementation. Each interface defined in IDL specifies the operation signatures through which requests are made. It should be noted that the IDL source code is not necessary at runtime. The IDL definitions are used to create stubs and skeletons and are used to populate the Interface Repository.

Clients issue requests using their host programming language. IDL is only a definition language; CORBA does not define a manipulation or invocation language. To allow interfaces written in IDL to be used from programming languages, mappings are provided. A mapping will take an IDL definition and generate a stub for each interface within the native programming language. The stubs allow programmers to invoke operations defined as part of the target object's interface.

Implementation skeletons are generated per interface within a programming language. They are the structures that actually invoke the methods implemented as part of the object implementation. They are called implementation skeletons because they are created from the IDL definitions, yet include no implementation details. The developer of the object implementation must fill this skeleton with actual code that will be invoked when a request is received.

An IDL skeleton usually depends on the object adapter; there may be multiple skeletons for the same interface and the same language, per different object adapters. It is even possible to provide object adapters that do not make use of IDL skeletons but rather create implementations "on the fly" when requests come in.

The Dynamic Invocation Interface allows the dynamic creation of requests. This allows a client to directly specify an object, an operation, and a set of parameters and invoke this request. The interface used is common to all objects and all operations, and does not make use of the stub routines generated for each operation in each interface. Information regarding the parameters and the operation itself is usually acquired from the interface repository.

Object Adaptors and the ORB Interface

The object adaptor provides an interface to ORB services that the object implementations can use. It also provides services that may be required when a request comes in from the ORB core and delivered to the skeleton for method invocation. Since object implementations can be extremely diverse in terms of their characteristics, many object adapters are envisioned. This allows support for very diverse cases while not changing the architecture.

Other services used by object implementations are provided directly through the ORB interface. This interface is identical for all ORB implementations and does not depend on the object adapter used by the object implementations. Naturally, this interface will still be mapped to the host programming language used by the object implementation. These operations are also available to the client objects.

Repositories

The Interface Repository maintains representations of the IDL definitions. These are persistent objects that are available at runtime. The IDL information is, therefore, maintained as "live objects" which may be used at runtime. For example, the DII uses the information maintained in the IR to allow programs to issue requests on interfaces that were unknown when the program was compiled. The IR service is also used by the ORB itself to perform requests. For example, the IR information is necessary for performing marshaling and unmarshaling of parameter values. The IR is also used as a persistent store for additional information pertinent to interfaces such as annotations, debugging information, etc.

The Implementation Repository maintains information needed by the ORB to locate and startup object implementations necessary to fulfill a request. It is also used for additional information associated with object implementations such as debugging information, security specifications, etc. The Implementation Repository is specific to an operating environment since it is used in the construction and activation of object implementations—it is not standardized by CORBA.

Object References

An object reference is an opaque representation that is used for denoting an object in the ORB-based environment. Both clients and object implementations use object references. An ORB provides a mapping of object references to the programming language used. This mapping must not depend on the ORB representation of object references.

CORBA defines a distinguished object reference used for denoting no object. This reference is guaranteed to be different from any other object reference. In some environments this maps to a reference of the null (or nil) object.

Clients

A client makes a request from within the application code. The client code uses the IDL stubs as it would use any library routine. When the stub routine is called, the object reference for the target object is mapped to the object reference as represented by the ORB. The stub then calls the ORB and the client request is managed by the ORB. The ORB is responsible for locating the object implementation and for routing the request to the implementations, as well as delivering any results back to the client. If an error occurs during the method invocation, or the ORB cannot complete fulfilling the request for any variety of reasons, an exception may be delivered to the client's operating context.

If the client was compiled before the target object's interface was completed it is possible that the stubs for the target object were not available. The client code, therefore, cannot access the interface for this object. In this case, the client can name the type of object and operation to be invoked and use the DII. The client can construct the call programmatically using a sequence of calls for building up the invocation and the parameters, and then invoke the request.

A client uses object references to issue requests and as values for parameters. Clients normally receive object references as output parameters of past requests, or through requests that were sent to the client from other clients. Object references can even be converted into a string format that can be made persistent by simply storing it to disk, which can later be turned back to an object reference by the same ORB that converted the reference into the string.

Object Implementations

Object implementations encapsulate the state and behavior of the object. These are internal to the object, but the behavior is used by the skeletons to provide services for the clients. CORBA only defines the necessary mechanisms for invoking operations. It does not define specifically how these objects are activated or stopped, how they are made to persist, or how access control is handled, etc. However, since these object implementations must function in a real environment, all these issues must be addressed. The implemented is free to make choices regarding these issues.

Object Adaptors

Object adaptors are the primary ORB-related functionality providers to object implementations. The ORB itself also publishes an interface that may be used by the object implementation but the object adapter provides most of the ORB-related services that are commonly used by the object implementation. Object adapters publish a public interface that is used by the object implementation, as well as a private interface that is used by the interface skeleton. The adaptors themselves make use of the ORB-dependent interface. The following are examples for services provided by object adaptors.

- Method invocation used in conjunction with the skeleton.
- Object implementation activation and deactivation.
- Mapping of object references to object implementations, generation of object references.
- Registering object implementations so that they may be found when a request comes in.

CORBA does not require all object adaptors to support the same functionality, nor the same interface. Object adaptors may be specialized because they are a primary service provider for object implementations, as well as a major player in the request delivery mechanism. The CORBA specification itself only defines the Basic Object Adapter. Any CORBA-compliant implementation must provide a Basic Object Adapter (BOA). However, the CORBA specification does not place any limitations on definitions of additional object adapters; in fact, the specification itself provides some examples where additional object adapters will probably prove useful. Still, since object implementations rely on the object adapter interface it is not recommended that a very large number of object adapters exists. This is not restrictive because different object adapters should be used only when different services or different quality of service is required. Thus, each object adapter will typically be able to support a large set of object implementations.

An example presented in the CORBA specification is the Library Object Adapter (LOA). The BOA starts up a processing thread per request, or even a separate process per object invocation. This may be unacceptable for library implementations that may be shared by multiple clients. In addition, library objects may actually be running within the client's context so that activation and authentication are not required, thus greatly improving performance. If these object implementations were supported through the BOA all these possible optimizations would not be possible. By providing the LOA, the improved behavior can be attained.

The Interface Definition Language

CORBA is an architecture that allows the development of portable and interoperable applications. It provides for systems to be built using multiple programming languages in a way that objects written in one programming language can make use of objects written in other programming languages. This usage is transparently handled by the ORB and none of the participating objects is ever aware that the "other side" talks a different language; it is the universal translator of the objects world.

Translating objects and invocations between different programming languages can be viewed as some sort of bridging—in this case the bridging involves the translation of the object model in one programming language to the (same) object model in another programming language.

Bridging can involve two fundamental architectures: immediate bridging and mediated bridging. In the context of programming language interoperability, immediate bridging implies the translations of each relevant programming language directly into every other relevant programming language whereas mediated bridging introduces a single language (and runtime format) that describes the object model and is used as the intermediate format into which every other programming language is translated.

CORBA was intended to be ubiquitously available and support interoperability from a large set of programming languages. Already, products are available that allow CORBA interoperability in C, C++, Smalltalk, Ada, Objective-C, Java, and COBOL. Because of this large (and constantly growing) set of programming languages, the fact that a programming language may change, and the fact that different development environments may support slightly different dialects of the language, it is impossible to support programming language immediate bridging. Such an approach would not only make CORBA extremely cumbersome, but it would also require too many vendors to work too closely together to create CORBA-enabled products (for example, it would require that vendors of development environments in various languages that are used to build CORBA applications be synched up in pairs so that immediate translation occurs correctly for their own dialects). It is fairly safe to say that had the OMG taken such an approach, vendors would not have adopted CORBA at all.

Mediated bridging is the only possible solution. But what is this intermediate language? The IDL is the language used to specify the interfaces that are used by clients to issue requests. Object implementations provide methods that provide the necessary services defined by the interfaces. Interfaces are defined in IDL and used by the client programs. IDL is not used for writing code; only specifications. The client will, therefore, not be written in IDL; it will use the IDL interface specifications whereas the actual call will be done in the native programming languages. These calls will be a result of a mapping of the IDL interfaces to the programming language. The object implementations are also not written in IDL but in a (possibly other) programming language. The interface operations then map to the implementation methods.

Mapping from IDL involves the creation of stubs on the client side and skeletons on the server side. The stubs are programming language functions (or methods) that may be called by the client code. Calling such a stub (using a CORBA object) will cause an invocation to occur, even when the real object is remote and implemented in a different programming language. All this is transparent to the client. When such a call takes place, the object implementation skeleton is invoked. This is the skeleton that was created as a result of mapping the IDL to the object implementation's programming language. Because such invocations require application-specific behavior to be performed, it is the developer's task to provide programming language implementations for each of the skeletons created as a result of the IDL mapping. All this is performed within the normal development environment used by the object implementation developer.

As defined in the CORBA specification, any mapping of the IDL to a host programming language must include the following.

- A mapping of all IDL data types, constants, and object references. This includes providing a means of expressing basic data types, constructed data types, and constants in the target programming language. The mapping must also specify how an object is represented in the target programming language. Because the mapping must respect the host programming language semantics, the object representation is not dependent on the ORB's representation. The representation can either use an opaque handle to the ORB representation or a real programming language object. In the second case, the mapping must support identical object semantics of inheritance, operation signatures, etc.
- A mapping of operation signatures and invocations. The mapping includes definitions for how input parameters are handled, how return values are handled, how operations map to the programming language functions, etc. The mapping not only has to define how IDL constructs are mapped but also how they are used. This may involve dealing in memory management and lifecycle issues.
- A mapping of the exception model. If the target programming language's exception-handling mechanism (when such a mechanism exists) is being used, the mapping should describe how this mechanism is used for implementing IDL exceptions. Otherwise, the mapping should describe how operations are extended to support exceptions and what management functions are required.
- A mapping of IDL attributes. Attributes are modeled by two accessor operations (i.e. a get and a set function).

- A mapping of the ORB interface and other pseudo interfaces. This is necessary to allow programmers using the target programming language to access interfaces implemented by the ORB or one of the related components (the interface repository, the object adapter, the dynamic invocation interface, etc.). One approach might be to define these as a set of services packaged as a library. Another approach could involve pseudo-objects. A pseudo-object has an interface defined in IDL but is not implemented as an ORB managed object. Operations can only be invoked using the Static Invocation Interface (SII) and the ORB may intercept such calls and handle them. In this approach, the ORB interfaces would actually be defined as IDL interfaces. These interfaces would be part of a pseudo-object. The advantage is that the ORB interfaces can then be mapped into many programming languages using the same mechanisms developed for application interfaces. Since it is just another interface, it is handled by the mapping procedures and the case of ORB interfaces defaults to the general case.

IDL Preprocessing

IDL supports preprocessing as defined by ANSI for C++. This support for preprocessing includes:

- macro substitution;
- source file inclusion;
- conditionals;
- line-numbering diagnostics; and
- pragma directives.

IDL Modules

IDL modules form the primary name-scoping mechanism in IDL. Modules solve the namespace problem by scoping names relative to the module they are defined in. Other IDL constructs (e.g. interfaces, structures, and exceptions) also provide scoping—all within the module they are defined in. Modules also serve as the primary tool for correct modularization of an IDL specification; an IDL module should always be an encapsulated modularized component with a clear contractual obligation to other software components.

In addition to user-defined modules, a special module named `CORBA` is defined; any construct defined by the CORBA specification is implicitly a part of this module. This eliminates name clash problems that might otherwise have occurred when interacting CORBA with other development environments. For example, CORBA defines an interface called `Object`; the name `Object` would certainly clash with other classes by that name. Since this interface is defined within the CORBA module, this name is used as `CORBA::Object` instead.

IDL Interfaces

Interfaces form the backbone of CORBA APIs. An interface defines the contract between CORBA objects by defining the functionality that is available through an object reference. Since IDL is not an implementation language, interfaces do not define implementation but rather APIs. While most programming language mappings map an IDL interface to a class, this is because an interface defines a type. However, this is not always true; for example, an IDL interface (in the context of a client-side mapping) is mapped to a Java interface rather than a class.

An interface contains other IDL constructs such as type definitions, constants, exception declarations, attributes, structures, and operations. An IDL interface creates a naming scope and a legal IDL type. Forward declarations of interfaces are allowed for bi-directional naming references.

IDL supports the notion of multiple interface inheritance. An IDL interface may inherit from zero, one, or more than one interface. An interface can reference declarations made in its base interfaces using the naming resolution operator `::`. IDL inheritance does not allow a name to be redefined.

IDL Types

IDL provides interface definers with a rich type system, which is comprised of basic types, template types and a number of constructs useful in constructing user-defined types. Basic IDL types are:

- integer value types such as `short`, `long`, unsigned short, and `unsigned long`;
- `char` type;
- floating point types such as `float` and `double`;
- `boolean` type;
- `octet` used for creating general-purpose byte stream that can be used to pass uninterpreted bytes for various purposes; and
- the type `any` which can be used to represent any type. An `any` is made of a type and a value; the value is an object of the specified type. There are no restrictions as to what an object of type `any` may be.

In addition to these basic types, CORBA 3.0 will support wide characters and wide strings. This will allow CORBA to be used in multi-character set environments and internationalized systems.

IDL defines a number of ways in which constructed types may be created. The `struct` specifier is used to create data structures comprised of a number of elements. The `union` keyword may be used to construct discriminated unions and `enum` is useful for declaration of enumeration types. `Typedefs` are used to simplify code and make it more readable.

IDL arrays are similar to C arrays and include a fixed dimension and a type. IDL also supports definitions using the `sequence` element, which allows defining IDL template types as sequences of other types.

IDL sequences are one-dimensional arrays with a maximum size and a length. The maximum size is determined at compile time whereas the length can change dynamically at runtime. Sequences can be bounded (i.e. defined with a maximum size) or unbounded. More runtime operations are necessary within the language mapping code to support unbounded sequences (since marshaling needs to determine the current maximal size. This can get quite complicated with `inout` parameters because the returning size may be different than the size sent).

IDL `strings` are defined as sequences of `char`; unfortunately, the current version of the CORBA specification does not address the notion of multiple bytes character sets and is, therefore, very limited in its support for internationalization.

IDL Exceptions

Exceptions are an important part of any object-oriented environment and especially of distributed object-oriented environments. CORBA is no exception (sic) and, as such, IDL includes exception constructs that allow the definition of exception types and the specification of which operations may raise which exceptions.

An exception definition includes an exception name and a data structure that allows the passing of relevant data from the party raising the exception to the party handling the exception. Exception names are scoped by module name and interface name as other IDL constructs; this allows namespace partitioning in exceptions as well.

The CORBA specification defines a set of standard IDL exceptions. These standard exceptions are defined per ORB and must be mapped to native exceptions by any conformant CORBA product. These exceptions will normally be raised by the ORB implementation and not by application code. Whereas normally an operation must explicitly mention that a certain exception may be raised as a result of its activation, standard exceptions do not need to be explicitly defined; they may be raised as a result of any invocation. This is because these exceptions enumerate error conditions and problems that may occur as a result of the actual ORB's work.

Each of the standard exceptions has the following identical structure:

```
enum completion_status {
  COMPLETED_YES,
  COMPLETED_NO,
  COMPLETED_MAYBE
};

exception <a standard exception> {
  unsigned long      minor;
  completion_status  completed;
}
```

IDL Attributes

An attribute specifies a member in the interface and takes the general form of:

```
attribute <type> <name>;
```

An IDL attribute should not be confused with a data member; while semantically an attribute might be used to imply that such data are maintained, an attribute is a more general concept that may cover computed values as well. An attribute merely specifies that there are accessors by that name; therefore, an attribute declaration of the form

```
attribute short age;
```

means only that the IDL mapping result will produce the following two operations:

```
short get_age();
void set_age(short);
```

These operations are used for changing the object's attribute value. If an attribute is specified to be `readonly` the setting accessor is omitted.

IDL Operations

IDL operations specify the functionality exposed by objects through their interfaces. An operation has a name, a return type (or void if there is no result), and a parameter list. Each parameter has a type, a name, and a mode specifier. Mode specifiers are either `in` for parameters that are sent from the client to the server, `out` for parameters that are sent from the server to the client, or `inout` for both. In addition to these, an IDL may also include the following:

- An IDL operation may have a `raises` clause in which exceptions (other than system exceptions) that may be raised during the invocation are listed.
- An IDL operation may be defined to be `oneway`. Operations defined as such are invoked using *best effort* semantics. This means that the caller does not wait for a result (and, therefore, the operation must have no return type), delivery of the request is not guaranteed, and the operation is invoked at most once. Oneway operations have a `void` type, can have no `out` or `inout` parameters, and may not have a `raises` expression (i.e. they cannot raise application exceptions—they may still cause a system exception to be raised).
- An IDL operation may include an optional context clause. A context clause is a series of string literals. The context of the caller is a dictionary of key-value pairs. The keys of the context are strings; when an invocation occurs the runtime system will extract the values for the keys mentioned in the context clause of

the operation definition and package them as part of the invocation. In this way, context information may be implicitly passed from the caller context to the object implementation.

With CORBA 3.0, additional pass-by-value semantics will be provided for object arguments. Currently, only the reference itself may be passed. This is very restrictive in that it requires that any data that have to be passed (usually because of performance) be packaged in a structure.

The Dynamic Invocation Interface

The Dynamic Invocation Interface allows requests to be built up and invoked dynamically by clients. The client need only know interface-related information at the invocation time; no prior knowledge (e.g. at compile time) is necessary. Although the structure and process of performing requests are very different, the semantics of DII requests is identical to the semantics of requests issued using mapped IDL stubs. A DII request, like a static request, is composed of an operation name, an object reference, and a parameter list. Parameters are inserted into a name-value list, which is then used in the invocation. Because the DII always accepts a parameter list (as an object), it doesn't matter how many parameters there are; this allows the DII interface to support any invocation. These structures are built and used at runtime (these parameters may still be type checked at runtime as well as compared with the information in the Interface Repository).

DII Structures

The basic structure that supports the DII is the `NamedValue` structure (used to associate a name with a value of type *any*). This structure represents a single parameter. An `NVList` is used to hold all the parameters sent in an operation invocation. An instance of the NamedValue structure contains the argument name, an argument value, the length of the argument, and mode flags (which are similar to the mode specifiers in-out-inout in IDL and are called ARG_IN, ARG_OUT, and ARG_INOUT). The value is inserted into a variable of type *any*, which consists of a type code and the actual data.

Requests

A Request pseudo-object is used for the actual construction and invocation of requests. The operations available in the Request interface are:

```
Interface Request {
    ORBStatus add_arg(......);
    ORBStatus invoke(......);
    ORBStatus delete();
    ORBStatus send(......);
    ORBStatus get_response(......);
  };
```

The DII separates the creation of requests from actual invocation. Requests are first constructed and only then sent. The first step is actually creating a request; the call is made using the object that will be invoked. The operation `create_request` is not part of the Request interface since it is sent to the object. It is, therefore, part of the `Object` interface. Arguments are associated by either inserting an NVList object (that was pre-built) or using successive calls of `add_arg`. Each call to add_arg specifies all the information required for that argument (its name, its data type, its value, its length, and flags). Only the value and length must be provided; other information that is provided is used for type checking and validation of argument order, names, and modes. This is checked by comparing it with the arguments that are expected for the operation.

The context information is passed to the object implementation that will service the request, and the result is returned using the result argument. The operation name itself is a string and conforms to IDL identifier rules.

After the request has been created and built, and all the necessary information (target object, operation name, and parameters) embodied within the request, it can be invoked using the `invoke` operation. The DII also supplies facilities for issuing a group of requests simultaneously (without any guarantee on order). Finally, `delete` reclaims all resources taken up by the request once it has been completed.

The Deferred Synchronous Model

Calling `invoke` per a request blocks the caller until the result comes back from the object implementation. This synchronous model is the standard CORBA model but the DII supports a deferred synchronous model as well. By using the `send` operation, the request is issued and the caller does not block. Control is returned immediately and processing may continue. The caller can later use the `get_response` operation to determine whether the request has completed. This call determines whether the request has completed; if indeed the request has completed, the out parameters and return values of the request. `get_response` will block until the request completes unless the RESP_NO_WAIT flag is used. If the request issued was defined using the `oneway` specifier or if a flag of INV_NO_RESPONSE was used while sending the request, get_response need not be used.

Context Objects

Context objects are aggregations of 2-tuples each one consisting of a name and a string value. These properties allow information to be passed from the client to the object implementations. Context properties are usually composed of information about the client's environment that the object implementation might find useful. It is the client's decision as to exactly what context information is to be passed to the server. Since all request invocations go through the ORB, the ORB may also use this contextual information.

Context objects can be dynamically created or destroyed and may be chained together to provide environment context support. Each search for a context value will always start at the nearest context object and so overriding in the usual sense can be used. In this way very elaborate context structures can be built by different applications.

The Interface Repository

The Interface Repository (IR) is, as its name suggests, a persistent repository for interface-related information. It is a central component to the operation of the ORB as it is the central manager of the IDL definitions.

The two methods for creating and invoking requests are either using IDL stub routines or using the DII. In both cases the interface definitions are a prerequisite. In both cases the ORB itself is involved in the request fulfillment, and must know the structure of the request. This is for type-checking reasons as well as for marshaling and unmarshaling operations. The ORB must, therefore, have access to the interface definitions; the IR provides these facilities.

The IR is also a central component in allowing the interoperability of different ORBs. It is also an excellent source of information for other systems and environments such as CASE tools (which may provide browsers and editors of types and interfaces), IDL-to-programming languages compilers, etc.

The IR maintains information as objects. This makes it very easy and natural for programs that need the information to get at it and use it. Interface definitions are represented as sets of objects that contain descriptions for the operations, exceptions, context objects, and parameter types. Constant values and typecodes (describing types as structures) are also maintained. Modules are used as grouping mechanisms, i.e. objects such as constants, exceptions, type definitions, interfaces, and other modules may be grouped as a module in the IR.

The IR provides an interface through which the objects are accessible. It provides operations for managing and accessing the objects maintained in the IR. Although these operations and the conceptual framework of the IR manages an object representation of the interface information, the implementation of the IR is not restricted in any way and may choose to use a non-object-based implementation; the interface to the users of the IR remains object oriented. For example, the information may not be organized as persistent objects but as a set of relational tables. However, when this information is accessed, appropriate objects are created for the use of the IR clients.

ORBs may access multiple IRs, and IRs may be accessed by multiple ORBs. Typecodes are central to ensuring consistency of different IRs because the types are described in structural terms. Various systems may also provide IR interfaces if they desire to internally maintain type information yet collaborate in an ORB-based environment.

The Structure of an Interface Repository (IR)

IR operations are defined for retrieval of information objects maintained in the IR. The specification, however, does not define what operations are available for inserting and creating the information objects maintained in the IR, as well as the IR administration operations. This was intentionally left unresolved to allow maximal flexibility for IR implementations because such issues are dependent on operating systems, development environments, and administration policies. The specification gives examples for different ways in which the IR can be populated, for example, extraction from IDL definitions, using DII calls, or cloning of informational objects from another IR.

The CORBA specification does not place limitations on the implementation of the repository. Because different implementations may be radically different in many characteristics with regard to distribution and replication, the IR definition in the CORBA specification does not provide additional specifications or characteristics regarding the repository, the management and availability of the IR, or the repository characteristics. Important issues such as security-related topics (What is the security mechanism used? How does it relate to operating system security? What granularity is used for security? etc.) are not discussed in the CORBA specification. Only the retrieval interface is fully specified. This allows differing implementations that range from flat file structures to complex object database systems. Such different implementation strategies will naturally have very different attributes, and will affect the way the IR can be used in different CORBA-compliant products. This is a good example of how different implementations of the CORBA specification can have very different characteristics, and why it is very important to know details about the different products when making a selection of a preferred environment; it is not enough to know that it is "CORBA compliant."

The IR is basically a collection of objects. Each object maintained in the IR can be one of the following types:

`AttributeDef`: An object representing an attribute.

`ParameterDef`: An object representing a parameter of an operation.

`ExceptionDef`: An object representing an exception that may be raised by an operation.

`OperationDef`: An object representing an operation.

`TypeDef`: An object representing a type definition (other than interfaces).

`ConstantDef`: An object representing a constant.

`InterfaceDef`: An object representing an interface definition. This object will contain a collection of objects representing attributes, operations, types, constants, and exceptions.

`ModuleDef`: An object corresponding a module definition. May contain a collection of objects representing interfaces, types, constants, exceptions and, other ModuleDef objects.

`Repository`: A top-level organizational object that maintains a collection of definition objects.

IR Containers

The IR interface includes two base interfaces called *Container* and *Contained*. All *XXXDef* interfaces inherit from one or both of these interfaces. The Contained interface is inherited by all of the IR structures except the Repository interface; i.e. by all types that may be contained in other objects. The Container interface is a super interface for Repository, ModuleDef, and InterfaceDef, i.e. by all types that have collections of other objects. These interfaces mainly define navigational operations and are used to locate objects within the IR.

The *Container* interface provides operations for locating objects that are contained within a particular object. The `contents` operation returns a list of such objects and can be used to recursively traverse the containment hierarchy starting from the Repository root object, through module and interface objects, culminating with objects whose interfaces derive from the Contained interface. The operation can be used in various filtered modes. For example, the operation can return only contained objects of a certain type. The `lookup_name` operation accesses a named object within a containment sub-tree. Various flags may be set to allow this operation to provide filtering and search options. Finally, the `describe_inherited` operation returns a description for each of the object's contained objects.

All interfaces except the Repository interface inherit from the Contained interface. Attributes include a name, an id, and an id of the enclosing object. Each object meaningful to the programmer that is maintained in the IR has these three attributes. The id of the enclosing object may have two meanings. If the contained object is defined within the containing object (e.g. an operation is defined in an interface or a constant is defined in a module) then the enclosing object is the object in which it was defined. However, contained objects may be inherited. For example, an operation object may be defined in an interface named *interfaceA* and another interface (*interfaceB*) may derive from interfaceA. The Contained object representing the operation in the interfaceB object will have the `defined_in` id of interfaceA. This represents the fact that the object is contained through inheritance and uses the semantic of identifying the object from which it was inherited. This is consistent with the enclosing object identifier of the same object, as contained in the interfaceA object. Although the meaning is different (representing the object in which it was defined), it is still the same identifier.

The Contained interface defines two operations. The `within` operation returns a list of objects in which the object is contained and the `describe` operation.

The ORB Interface

Clients, and especially object implementations, may request services that are provided by the ORB base environment. The interface to such services is provided either by the ORB interface or the object adapter (OA) interface. The operations provided by the ORB interface are those operations that are independent of the object implementation (and the object adapter it uses) and that can be used by both clients and object implementation (the object adapter interface is only accessible by the object implementation). The ORB interface must be supported by any ORB no matter what its implementation strategy.

The operations provided in the ORB interface are all implemented by the ORB. However, for model consistency, these operations can appear to be implemented by the objects themselves. The ORB interface provides additional operations for creating lists and for retrieving the default context to be used by requests issued using the DII.

Object References and Strings

Object references are opaque types. Therefore, they may not be readily exported from one ORB to another and are not a convenient persistent value representation. Other than direct ORB-based invocations they cannot be passed from one application to another. To facilitate such communication of object references the ORB interface provides operations for converting object references to strings and back. Strings may be conveniently stored and communicated. The two operations used for these conversions are defined as part of the ORB interface as:

```
string  object_to_string ( in Object obj );
Object  string_to_object ( in string str );
```

Operations on Object References

The two conversions between object references and strings are operations that can be applied to any object reference. The ORB interface supports additional operations that can be applied to any object reference. The operations described in this subsection have the additional characteristic that the operations seem to be services provided by the object references themselves; they are, however, implemented directly by the ORB and not by the object implementations. These operations are, therefore, defined in the Object interface. This is called in CORBA vernacular a pseudo-interface whereas the actual implementation is intercepted by the ORB. The operations provided by the `Object` interface include:

```
boolean              is_nil();
Object               duplicate();
void                 release();
InterfaceDef         get_interface();
ImplementationDef    get_implementation();
```

The `is_nil` operation tests an object reference for referencing no object (a value of OBJECT_NIL). The `duplicate` operation allows an additional object reference to the same object to be created. This operation is necessary because object references are opaque and ORB dependent. Neither clients nor object implementations can create object references. The `release` operation reclaims the storage used up by the object reference. Note that the object implementation is not involved in any of these operations and is totally unaware of their occurrence. Thus the object implementation can have no way to distinguish between requests delivered through an "original" object reference or a duplicated object reference. The object implementation is also not affected by the release of an object reference (since it may be referenced by other clients).

The `get_interface` operation returns the IR object associated with this object and can be used to extract meta-information regarding the object type. The `get_implementation` operation returns an object that describes the object implementation from the Implementation Repository.

The Basic Object Adaptor

CORBA defines object adaptors (OAs) as the primary way that object implementations access services provided by the ORB. The OA defines interfaces for generating object references, implementation registration, and request authentication. The object adaptor also serves as a service layer between the IDL skeleton (above which the object implementation works) and the ORB core, and is primarily responsible for activating the object implementations. The authors of CORBA predict that there will be a number of object adaptors since the architecture will be required to support a wide variety of objects with differing characteristics. Different granularities, lifetimes, policies, and usage attributes will require various adapters that will be custom tailored to provide the necessary functionality for each group. A number of examples such as the Library Object Adapter (LOA) and the Database Object Adapter (DOA) are envisioned.

CORBA also provides a concrete and full definition of an object adapter called the Basic Object Adapter (BOA). This means that any CORBA-compliant ORB environment must provide an implementation of a BOA. The BOA is the most generic object adapter. This means that it can support any object implementation but is, therefore, less suited for very specialized requirements. It does the job, but specialized adapters may do the job much more efficiently.

The BOA functionality can mostly be expressed in IDL and is packaged as the BOA interface. Functionalities that cannot be expressed in IDL are those that must map directly to the programming language of the object implementation (e.g. operations that bind the object implementation). The functionalities provided by the BOA are:

- creation of object references;
- translations of object reference (in addition to the ORB functions to translate object references to strings and back);
- activation and deactivation of the object implementation;
- activation and deactivation of other objects;
- invocation of methods of the object implementation through the IDL skeleton; and
- authentication of the client making the request.

CORBA 2.0

Although CORBA 1.0 and CORBA 1.1 were a big success in defining a standard architecture for distributed object-oriented systems, they did not achieve all the goals related to interoperability that their creators had envisioned. Users were reluctant in selecting ORBs as the central middleware component in their mission-critical systems. While this was partly because of the relative immaturity of some of the products and to non-technical issues, such as the lack of acquaintance with these products, the initial versions of the CORBA specification has a fundamental flaw.

In their effort to create a flexible and open specification, the creators of CORBA 1.x did not address the issue of *interORBability*, i.e. the notion of interoperability among different ORBs. One of the main goals of CORBA as an architecture is to define mechanisms by which application and service objects can be constructed in such a way that any object can be used by any other object. The ORB is defined as the primary enabler of this architecture by delegating requests between objects. However, CORBA 1.x did not address issues regarding how ORBs interact with other ORBs. Therefore, the result of CORBA 1.x was an open architecture so long as a single ORB type was used. Systems utilizing ORBs from a single vendor could indeed accomplish what CORBA intended; unfortunately, if one attempted to use multiple ORB products within the system, interoperability was not achieved.

This fact was a major hurdle in the adoption of CORBA as an enterprise-wide solution by many corporations (and hence in the adoption of CORBA in general because CORBA primarily targets the corporate market). This was not only because CORBA 1.x was seen to be incomplete but also because of many pragmatic reasons. Since ORBs could not interoperate and an ORB-based architecture could only be constructed using a single vendor, corporations felt that they would not be achieving a vendor-independent and open solution (which, as you might recall from the previous chapter, was one of CORBA's goals). Also, because different ORB products stressed support for different programming languages and environments (e.g. Iona's Orbix initially for C++ and HP's DST for Smalltalk—now owned by ParcPlace), it was only natural to have a mix of ORBs.

Once CORBA 2.0 was published, ORB vendors immediately embraced the standard and CORBA 2.0 products started appearing at an impressive rate. CORBA 2.0 was also the turning-point as far as corporate (user) adoption was concerned.

While there is not doubt that CORBA has truly taken off as a primary enabler of distributed object-oriented systems over the past couple of years, it is always difficult to assess how much of this was because of CORBA 2.0 and how much because CORBA, as a concept, has been around for more than 5 years, a period that was necessary for a certain comfort level to be reached. In addition, the phenomenal growth of the Internet and the WWW was definitely an important catalyst in the use of CORBA as a foundation for application-level communication.

First-generation applications offered on the Web were no more than form-based information accessors with little-to-no application functionality. The Web as a delivery platform, however, quickly proved itself as having infinite possibilities as far as audience and client base were concerned. This made IT organizations think of using the Web to deliver applications to a very large client base. The emergence of the corporate intranet as *the* application delivery mechanism accelerated this trend.

While Web technologies quickly emerged to allow applications to be written for deployment within Web-based software (e.g. Java applets running within Web browsers), it became apparent that while it was feasible to write small application from scratch, it was impossible to rewrite entire systems in which years' worth of work was invested just so that application functionality could be run using a different technology base (be it popular as it may be—someone still had to pick up the bill). Instead, corporations began looking into solutions that would allow them to use these "old" systems as components in the "new" technological world (probably the only true way to define "new" and "old" in this context is by saying that "old" = "anything we know really works and can use" and "new" = "everything we keep hearing about but really have no clue about; we really need some highly paid consultants here").

CORBA, and specifically CORBA 2.0, emerged as an obvious candidate to fill this gap. CORBA, as an architecture, was from the outset meant to solve precisely such interoperation problems. Luckily, the battle over CORBA 2.0 was won by the TCP/IP Internet backers (it is quite certain that had the decision been to base CORBA interoperability on Distributed Computing Environment (DCE), CORBA would not be where it is today—in fact, it would probably have become one more good, but unused technology). This positioned CORBA perfectly for being used as *the* interoperable architectural standard for Web-based systems and allowed CORBA to ride the Internet wave.

ORB Interoperability

CORBA 2.0 deals with many issues not dealt with by CORBA 1.x. Among these topics, interoperability is by far not only the most important, but also the one single area in which more work has been invested and more results have been produced than any other. The CORBA 2.0 specification not only defines the GIOP and IIOP protocols, but also addresses DCE-based interoperability and interoperation with the Microsoft Component Object Model and OLE Automation.

In addition to being a concrete specification, CORBA 2.0 also addresses interoperability architectures as a design-level abstraction. By providing an in-depth discussion on what interoperability architectures should provide, how bridges should work, and what solutions should be used in different cases, CORBA 2.0 becomes central to the underlying technologies of distributed systems [no matter whether these are locally distributed systems or systems being distributed on the Wide Area Network (WAN)]. The CORBA 2.0 specification is certainly one of the cornerstone documents in the field of distributed computing.

CORBA 2.0 addresses interoperability between objects running in different ORB environments (after all, even CORBA 1.x addressed interoperability of objects running within an ORB environment). ORB interoperability is defined as "... the ability for a client on ORB A to invoke an OMG IDL-defined operation on an object on ORB B, where ORB A and ORB B are independently developed" (see Figure 2-6). ORB interoperability is a difficult task (as seen by the set of solutions that were required of CORBA 2.0). The inherent complexity of ORB interoperability is the result of the following points.

- CORBA is a specification defined at the behavioral and architectural level. It does not enforce implementation-level properties. Different ORBs can, therefore, be very different in terms of their inner workings. Since the definition of ORB interoperability makes no assumptions on the participating ORBs,

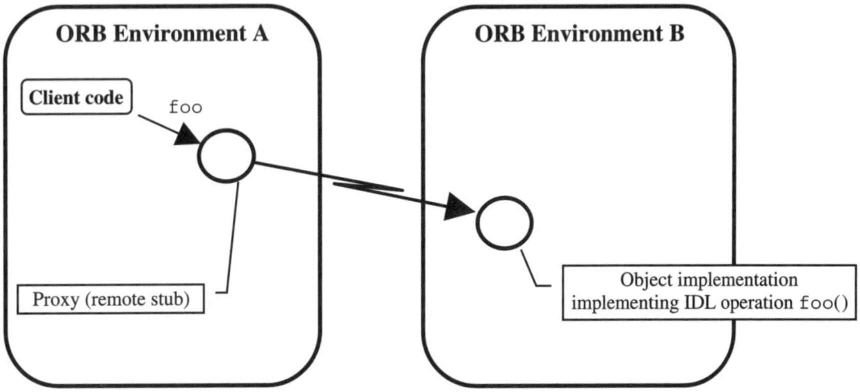

Figure 2-6
ORB interoperability.

the specification ensuring interoperability must take into account any possible implementation of the spec.

- The CORBA world (i.e. the core ORB, object services, and object facilities) is a very complex environment that supports a whole lot of functionalities. The set of properties forming the semantic context of an object and of a request can, therefore, be very large and complex. These semantics must be correctly managed and maintained when a request or object reference passes an ORB boundary. In addition, CORBA as an architecture is continuously evolving. The specifications for interoperability must ensure that future services or facilities are supported with little or no additional work—and certainly must make sure that future additions are in no way compromised by a limited architectural view taken today.
- Interoperability is and must be bi-directional. It is not enough for one ORB environment to have access to another. An invocation often includes an object reference that is passed as an argument and is then used by the object implementation to invoke another operation on the referenced object (thereby reversing the role of client and server). An invocation in which an object in one environment has access to an object in a second environment implicitly implies that every reference passed into the first environment is available to the second environment.

Since interoperability between ORBs must handle many cases, The CORBA 2.0 specification defines two distinct approaches to bridging between two environments. The first, called *mediated bridging* and shown in Figure 2-7, asserts that each internal ORB environment may adhere to its own internal representations and requires that an interoperable format be used externally to communicate between the two ORB environments. Elements that need to cross ORB boundaries are transformed into the interoperable format and then into the other ORB's representation. IIOP for example (for ORBs that do not use IIOP internally) is an example of a protocol used for mediated bridging.

In the second approach, called *immediate bridging* and illustrated in Figure 2-8, entities are converted directly between the two internal forms. Naturally, immediate bridging is more efficient but less flexible as transformation routines are required for each pair of differing environments.

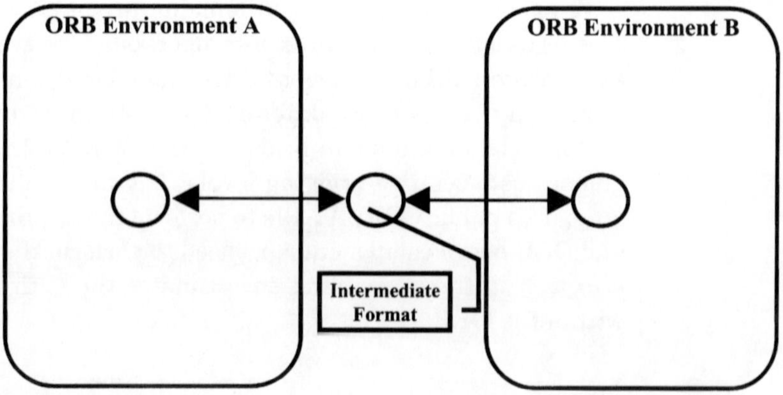

Figure 2-7 Mediated bridging.

Domains

A domain is an organizational unit that aggregates a set of components with similar characteristics. This is a very broad term that can be used both for physical partitioning as well as for functional-related partitioning. Recall from the previous chapter that the OMA defines a core set of characteristics and a set of profiles that add semantic properties to objects. These profiles can define characteristics that distinguish objects in one domain from other domains.

Characteristics of domains are important when interoperability is concerned because bridging between domains requires a mapping from one set of characteristics to another. It is not always possible to define a mapping between two domains that will not lose information because some domains are semantically richer than others.

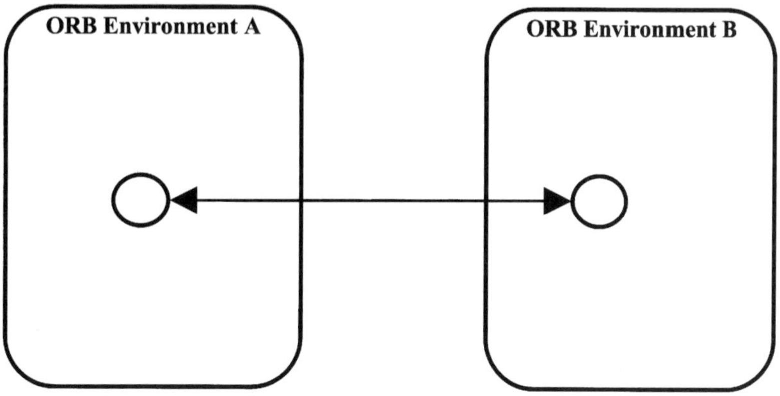

Figure 2-8 Immediate bridging.

Physical or administrative domains are relatively well understood. The focus of this chapter is interoperability between domains defined as separate ORB environments. The notion of domain bridging is limited to bridging between two different ORB environments.

When defining domain bridging, the CORBA 2.0 specification distinguishes between two bridging levels. The first, called *request level bridging*, uses public CORBA APIs to perform the required translations. ORB and ORB-based components are used to perform the translations. *In-line bridging* on the other hand encapsulates the entire translation process within the ORB.

The Dynamic Skeleton Interface

A major component defined in CORBA 2.0 for use in request-level bridging is the Dynamic Skeleton Interface (DSI). The DSI resides alongside implementation skeletons generated by IDL as shown in Figure 2-9. The difference between the DSI and an IDL skeleton is that the DSI can serve as a skeleton for any object implementation without knowing what the actual interfaces are.

The DSI magic is somewhat similar to the DII magic. The DII allows a client to create a request by specifying the target object reference, the operation name, and the parameters. It provides a mechanism by which this request can be fired off after its construction. The DSI provides the implementation-side counterpart to this process—but in reverse. No matter which request comes in, the DSI is invoked with the same method. This method is called the Dynamic Implementation Routine (DIR) and

Figure 2-9
The dynamic skeleton interface.

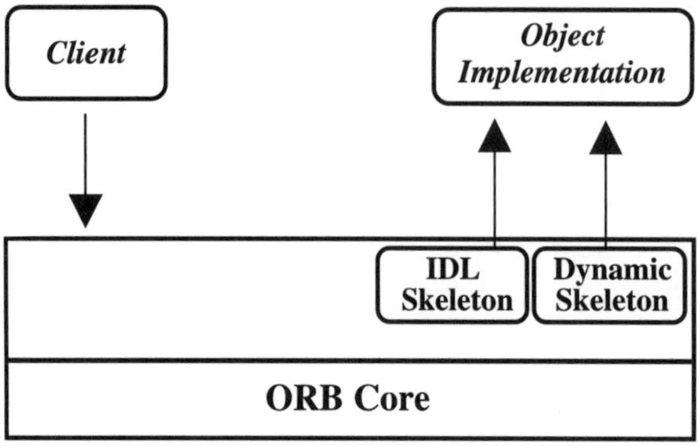

receives the same structures created within the DII that represent any operation request (i.e. a structure that specifies the target object, the operations, and the parameters). The DSI is defined as a pseudo-object (i.e. its interface is defined using an IDL interface but not necessarily implemented as a CORBA object, e.g. can be embedded as part of the ORB). The PIDL (pseudo IDL) representing a server request is shown by the following IDL:

```
module CORBA {

  pseudo
  interface ServerRequest {

    Identifier  op_name();
    Context     ctx();
    void        params(inout NVList params);
    any         result();

  };

};
```

Just as the object implementation is not aware of how a request was generated when servicing it (i.e. whether the DII or an IDL stub was used), so is a client issuing a request (and receiving results) oblivious to whether a request was serviced through an IDL skeleton or through the DSI.

This transparency allows the DSI to be used for request-level bridging. In such a scenario, the request (issued on an object reference managed by another ORB) is delivered to the bridge using the DSI (which can handle any request without requiring any compile-time information). On the other side of the bridge, the DII will be used to deliver to request to the real object in the second ORB environment. This is shown in Figure 2-10. The combination of these two components, which deal with an abstract and generic model of a request, makes such bridges relatively simple to build.

Inter-Domain Referencing

The issue of how object references are represented is perhaps the single most important issue in interoperability. As long as both the client and the object implementation reside within the same ORB environment, references are legal—but what happens if they reside in different domains and use different representations? Observe, for example, the

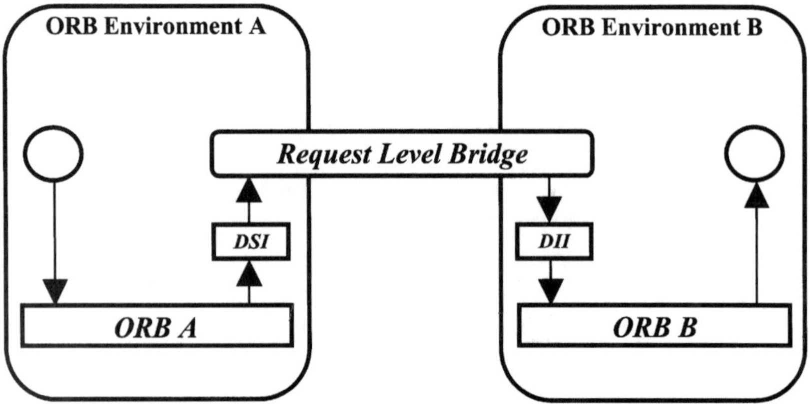

Figure 2-10
Request-level bridging.

scenario depicted in Figure 2-11. The client invokes an operation on an object in another ORB environment. The operation call has another object as a parameter; the actual object used is within the client's environment. When the object implementation services the request, it may need to use the object reference passed as an argument, i.e. send it a message. This implies that the inter-domain call (the first one in our example) must manage the object reference translation such that the object implementation may transparently use the argument to make additional calls. As an even more elaborate example, the object reference serving as the operation argument could reside in a third (different from both the client's and the object implementation's) ORB environment.

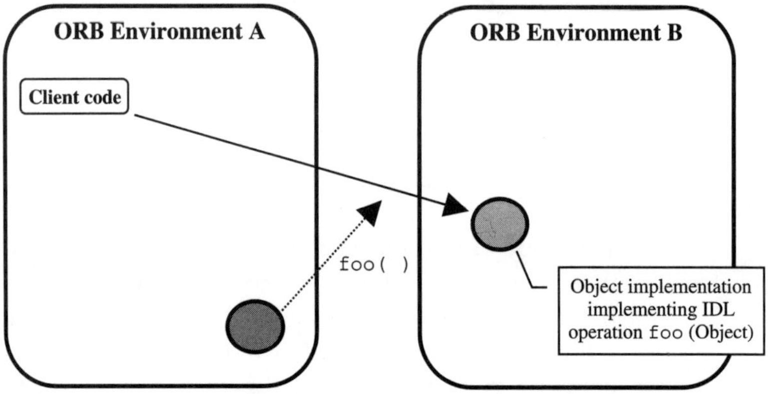

Figure 2-11
Inter-domain referencing.

The CORBA 2.0 specification identifies the following information as being necessary for object reference representation and translation.

- Is the object being referenced a *null* object?
- What is the object's type?
- What protocols are supported within the environment?
- What ORB services are available?

These data, which are required to correctly represent an object reference, comprise the structure of the Interoperable Object Reference (IOR), which is so critical to ORB interoperability.

Interoperable Object References (IOR)

IORs represent object references as a data structure useful to bridges in order to support ORB interoperability. The data structure is defined in IDL for convenience but is not intended to be directly used by components other than bridges.

An IOR consists of a type specifier and a set of tagged profile specifiers, one per supported protocol. Although many cases will have a single protocol (e.g. ORB environments that use IIOP as the internal protocol), the specification supports multiple environments with multiple protocols. A tagged profile contains an identifier and an octet stream that holds all the information required to identify the object being referenced within that particular protocol (i.e. hold the "opaque" representation of the object in the appropriate protocol). The fact that an IOR holds this identifying information for multiple protocols allows the same IOR to be passed around, even when the underlying protocol changes (as long as the underlying profiles have corresponding octet streams defined within the IOR). Null objects are represented by an IOR with a special type ID as well as an empty set of profiles.

IORs may be stringified (i.e. a string representing the IOR can be created) using the `object_to_string` operation defined in the ORB interface. This string representation can be later used to create an IOR for direct usage using the `string_to_object` call. This implies that the string representing the IOR is encoded with all of the data contained in the IOR. A typical stringified representation will, therefore, be quite a long string similar to:

```
IOR:000000000000002849444c3a4a4f4d6573736167696e674c6179
65722f4a4f4d65737361676551756575653a312e3000000000020000
000100000064000000000000000040000000a000000107d48e77d8ceb
000002500312cd0000000000000b000000107d48e77d8ce600000250
0312cd0000008104000000000000c4453543a352e363a0113057b0810
400300000001038302e332e31382e3230353b33343630000000000000
002c00010000000000c38302e332e31382e323035000d840000000000
00107d48e77d8ceb000002500312cd000000
```

The stringified representation of an IOR is very important for allowing systems to have a common starting-point. The first object reference from which others are accessed has always been problematic to agree upon. Although name services are already prevalent, the fact that simply passing a string in some way can create a common starting-point is used extensively. For example, a string that can be embedded in an applet parameter is a very convenient way to start an ORB-based interaction.

ORB Services

The ORB Service is a new concept defined by the CORBA 2.0 interoperability specification and should not be confused with the term CORBA Services or Object Services (although they are related). ORB Services are ORB-level modules that support special interoperability transformations required to support CORBA Services.

CORBA Services provide various application level functionalities, such as support for transactions, security, relationships, and more. Services can be partitioned into two groups (relevant to the discussion of ORB Services): those that require no support at the ORB level and are completely defined through a set of IDL interfaces, and those that do require ORB-level awareness. In order to support this second group, ORB Services were defined.

For example, the transaction service and security service both require ORB-level support. Transactions bracket code must be atomically performed (i.e. either all code is performed or nothing is). Since a transaction may include a remote invocation, the transaction bracket may span more than one process on more than one machine. It is, therefore, necessary for the transaction context information to be passed along with the remote invocation. This management of transaction context, however, must not be visible to the application programmer and must, therefore, be supported by the ORB service.

Assume now that the environment in which the application runs is different than the environment in which the object implementation resides. In such a case, the call is made in one ORB environment and must be transformed into the second ORB environment. Because this call must include appropriate transaction context information, this part of the request must also be translated into the new environment; the ORB Service created to provide interoperability support for the Transaction Service is the component responsible for performing such translations.

The Security Service is another good example for the necessity of ORB Services. Security information (such as authorization, signatures, etc.) is propagated along with a request in a secure environment. This information must be transformed when a call crosses domain boundaries—a transformation handled by the appropriate ORB Service.

Since the CORBA specification does not directly deal with CORBA Services, ORB Services are defined as architectural components. The specification does not address any particular service and how it can be supported; rather, it puts a framework in place for dealing with these services with the intent that such support can be extended later to any other service that will be added. It tries to identify the various areas in which such support may be required and what hooks are required from within the ORB layers. It also defines how negotiation between different ORBs occurs when each supports a (possibly) different set of ORB Services.

In order to support translation for any service-related information that might be required for various services the interoperability spec defines an IDL type that encapsulates service-related information in a sequence of structures, each one composed of a service identifier and an octet stream holding onto the service-related context information:

```
module IOP {

  // Each CORBA Service will define its own constant
  typdef unsigned long ServiceID;

  struct ServiceContext {

    ServiceID         context_id;
    sequence<octet> context_data;

  };

  typedef sequence<ServiceContext> ServiceContextList;

};
```

These additional context structures are sent by the communicating ORBs as part of the requests, thus allowing the propagation of service context.

The General Inter-ORB Protocol

The General Inter-ORB Protocol (GIOP) is an ORB interoperability protocol that can be mapped onto any connection-oriented transport layer. The GIOP associates a request with a connection and assumes that the connection provided by the transport layer is reliable and maintains message ordering. It also assumes that the transport layer provides some form of connection-less notification and acknowledgment of delivery. While the GIOP is a generalized protocol, and these assumptions are not very limiting as far as connection-based transport protocols, the GIOP was constructed with TCP/IP as the reference transport level model; the mapping to TCP/IP—code-named IIOP—is, therefore, very natural.

The GIOP specification consists of the Common Data Representation and the GIOP message specifications. The Common Data Representation maps IDL types into a wire-level representation forming the GIOP transfer syntax. The GIOP also defines which set of messages may be exchanged between the participators in a session and how these messages are formatted.

The Common Data Representation

The Common Data Representation (CDR) defines how IDL types are packaged into byte streams. CDR was designed to be simple, efficient, and flexible (yeah yeah, these definitely do contradict each other—but one has to try). The CDR is a wire-level transfer syntax that defines what actually goes over the wire and how IDL is packaged into these byte streams.

CDR not only maps IDL types, it maps the entire contents that will have to be passed in order for a request to be performed correctly. For example, CDR also defines the mapping of pseudo-objects, such as typecodes as well as data types, that are not fully specified by the CORBA core specification.

CDR places everything in an octet stream (i.e. a byte stream for our purposes). It deals with how these streams are created and how they may be unpacked. In doing so it distinguishes between two types of streams; streams that are used to package a GIOP message and streams that package *encapsulations*. An encapsulation is a stream that packages any IDL data structure into an independent byte stream (having an IDL type of `sequence<octet>`). This can later be used as a module for insertion into other streams, be they message streams of other encapsulations. Encapsulations are useful in creating a containment hierarchy of streams and supporting a "divide-and-conquer" approach for marshaling and unmarshaling data onto streams.

CDR's approach to byte ordering is called *receiver-makes-right*. CDR does not enforce and maintain a certain byte ordering (i.e. big endian or little endian). Instead, CDR packaging of data types may be either way. The CDR stream encodes which of the two byte orderings were used when the stream was packaged. It is the receiver's responsibility to either use the bytes as they are packaged or to reverse them if the packaging ordering does not match its own ordering. This approach has the advantage that, if the two endpoints use the same byte ordering, no conversions are necessary. Note that encapsulation streams also have an ordering tag and that it is quite possible for an enclosing stream to have a different byte ordering than an encapsulation stream that is embedded in it.

Other than IDL data types and typecodes, the CDR also defines how the following are encoded.

- Context: Recall that the context is a list of name-value pairs that holds information that forms the context in which a request was made. The context is passed to the object implementation by writing it to a CDR stream as a sequence of strings—a sequence in which there must be an even number of strings.
- Principal: The principal identifies a caller and is used in security-related mechanisms. CDR merely defines that the principal is packaged as a byte stream; it does not associate any semantics with this stream at this level.
- Exceptions: Exceptions are packaged as a string identifying the exception followed by members of the exception structure.
- Object references: Object references are packaged using the IOR structure.

GIOP Messages

GIOP supports all functionality required by CORBA using a small set of simple messages. The core set consists of only seven messages; these support all invocation models, exception raising and propagation, context passing, and reference management.

A typical GIOP session starts out with a `Request` type message being sent from the client to the server (the client being the ORB through which the application client holding the object reference invokes the operation, and the server being the ORB through which the object implementation will be activated). If all is well, his server will respond with a `Reply` message. To close the session the server sends the `CloseConnection`. At any time, both the client and the server may issue a `MessageError` message.

Request messages are used by clients to encode an operation invocation. The request message contains a header and a body. The header contains such information as the service context (see the section regarding ORB services), an indication of whether the request requires that a response be sent back to the client, and the name of the operation for which the request message was issued. The body of the request message encapsulates the `in` and `inout` parameters (i.e. the parameters that are passed from the client to the object implementation) and an optional encoding of the context object.

Replies are sent in response to a request (where appropriate—for example, oneway operations do not require a response). *Reply* headers contain a context list, a request id, and a reply status. The reply status can be one of the following:

- NO_EXCEPTION—the request processing was completed normally. In this case the reply message body encodes the return value and values for the `out` and `inout` parameters.
- USER_EXCEPTION or SYSTEM_EXCEPTION—an exception occurred while processing the request. In this case the body of the message will encode the exception that occurred.
- LOCATION_FORWARD—the server is indicating to the client that the operation should be re-sent to a different object reference (for various possible reasons, e.g. the object may have been relocated). The message body will encode the IOR that should be used for resending the message.

CancelRequest messages are sent by clients to servers and encode within their headers the request id that should be canceled. *LocateRequest* and *LocateReply* are useful for querying about a particular object reference. A client can issue a *LocateRequest* for determining whether the object packaged in the message is legal, whether it is managed by the server, etc. The server replies with a *LocateReply* message in which the locate status is either UNKNOWN_OBJECT, OBJECT_HERE, or OBJECT_FORWARD. In the case where the status is LOCATE_FORWARD the body of the message contains the new IOR to be used for accessing the object.

During a request session, both server and client may send a *MessageError* message to indicate inconsistencies in version number or unrecognized message structures. The last message type, *CloseConnection*, is sent by the server to indicate that it will not respond to further requests.

The Internet Inter-ORB Protocol

The Internet Inter-ORB Protocol (IIOP) is a specific version of the GIOP mapped to the TCP/IP transfer protocol. Since TCP/IP is so ubiquitous, the name IIOP has become a code-name for CORBA 2.0 and for GIOP. TCP/IP and the Internet (which is mostly comprised of networks running TCP/IP) have made IIOP *the* ORB protocol.

The IIOP can serve two roles in ORB environments. The IIOP was built as an interoperability protocol in that it can be used as the common representation to which ORB environments convert when crossing ORB boundaries. Since the IIOP is a published format owned by the OMG it is a perfect candidate for the various ORB vendors to convert to.

While the IIOP's goal was to serve as the common interoperability protocol over the most common transport protocol (TCP/IP), it is being used in a far more encompassing way. IIOP is an interoperability protocol; however, it is also an ORB protocol that can represent all that is required within an ORB environment. Therefore, IIOP is not only being used as an interoperability protocol; it is also being used as an ORB protocol for many of today's commercial ORBs. IIOP is not only being used within ORB boundaries; it is also being used internal to an ORB's domain.

Since IIOP is merely an implementation of GIOP over TCP/IP, it only requires a specification of the IIOP profile that will be the "IIOP representative" in IORs. Since TCP/IP supports the abstraction in which a communication channel is formed using a host identifier and a port number, the profile body contains these along with the additional byte stream, which represents an opaque data structure used by the managing ORB to denote the object. This structure is put within request messages by the ORB software; because the receiver ORB is the owner and creator of the opaque structure, it can interpret it and service the request.

CHAPTER 3

JavaBeans

JavaBeans is a component model defining the structure of Java components. Software component models in general, and JavaBeans in particular, aim at defining a simple yet powerful model that will allow the creation of reusable pieces of code and their packaging in a way that others may easily use the functionality provided by these components. Component models aim at specifying a very strict structure that is well known both by creators of software components and users. By adhering to such structures, developers can guarantee that their components will be well understood and will be compatible with development environments, frameworks, etc.

The purpose of any component model is to allow a component-based industry to evolve. In order for that to happen, it is not enough to create a component model; it is necessary to achieve a certain "critical mass" in terms of integrated development environments (IDEs), packaging tools, and third-party components. While JavaBeans is certainly not the first component model to be created [among the prestigious list of component models we can find Microsoft's highly successful Component Object Model (COM) and Apple/IBM's not-so-successful OpenDoc], JavaBeans certainly holds the record in terms of the rate at which it has been embraced. JavaBeans is currently part of the base JDK distribution (the package `java.beans` is part of the JDK 1.1.x) and forms the base for almost any Java library on the market today. It also forms the base for the Enterprise Java Beans (EJB) specification, which will be the topic of the next chapter.

This chapter provides an overview of the JavaBeans specification as defined in [JB]. The JavaBeans component model specifies the structure of Java components in terms of properties, events, and methods. In addition to this basic structure, the issues of persistence, introspection (which is akin to Java reflection), customization, and packaging will be discussed. Readers who are familiar with JavaBeans may skip this chapter. If you are not familiar with JavaBeans you should definitely not skip this chapter since the SanFrancisco frameworks will be much easier to understand once you have the Java component model under your belt.

Definition of a JavaBean

A JavaBean (or bean) is a reusable Java component that has a very specific structure as defined by the JavaBeans specification. This structure forms a common ground between components developed by many organizations, doing different tasks, and using different resources. As such, it can be manipulated both at development time and at runtime by tools and programs that were written well before the bean was written, and without any specific knowledge of the bean's particulars. These tools don't have to know anything special about our bean; instead they can handle all beans since all beans will have the same fundamental structure. The abstraction level at which these tools and programs can perform is at the component-abstraction level. Much like software hierarchies in object-oriented programming allow many different implementations to be viewed by external users as being similar, by providing a common inheritance root, JavaBeans does this—to a greater extent—by defining a common structure. The fundamental principle behind JavaBeans (and any component model) is:

> JavaBeans defines an abstraction level which unifies software entities and allows each such entity to become a *component*. By allowing disparate code from multiple origins to "look the same" in terms of its handling—both at the time of development and at runtime—JavaBeans elevates software reuse within the Java world.

The structure that defines the common base for all beans includes the following three categories:

- *Properties*. Properties are the attributes of a bean. Each attribute has a name and a type and is accessed through accessors (get and set methods). Attributes usually map to the functionality that the bean implements; much can be learned about a bean by its set of properties. Examples of properties can include attributes such as size, color, and shading for visual beans, or domain-specific attributes such as pager type, pager number, and retry policy in a `PagerRequest` bean. (You may be asking why we would want to package such an object as a bean. Packaging objects as beans allows tools that are being used within your system to be used with all these objects. For example, property editors may be written—or even bought—that can be used to edit any bean so that we can use the editor for creating page requests, part orders, or almost any other domain object. What this means is that you can often create extremely generic software by doing very little else but "follow the standard").
- *Methods*. Methods are an object's main functional interface. A bean's public methods comprise its normal API which reflect what

this object knows to do. A bean developer may decide to export only a partial set of the public methods as the bean's API in which case she will have to build a special "descriptor" for the bean.

- *Events*. The third category that affects how a bean behaves in a runtime environment is the set of events that the bean may raise. Events are the preferred mechanism for one software component to notify another thereby supporting component interaction by allowing one component to react to events created by another component. The JDK 1.1 (and onward) relies heavily on the notion of components raising events and other components being registered on these events using listeners. JavaBeans stresses this architecture by requesting that each bean define the set of events it may raise by a set of subscription methods through which other components may be notified of the bean's events.

A bean's life is slightly more complicated than the life of an "ordinary" piece of reusable Java code. This complication arises from the fact that a bean is built to be "very reusable." A bean is "very reusable" because it knows how to behave within an IDE during development time. It must therefore not only provide a set of APIs for use at runtime but also provide APIs and structures which are useful during development time. For example, it must work along with the IDE so that the IDE can know about the bean's properties, methods, and events. It must also provide enough information about itself so that it can plug into the tools available within an IDE (e.g. property editors and visual connection managers). It must allow developers the opportunity to customize and set its attributes and must provide the mechanisms for saving itself once it has been customized. All these additional complexities are necessary for a component to be a true bean. Once this complexity has been managed, the bean's value grows as a reusable component since the effort involved in using it in one's own program is much smaller.

A bean developer must be aware of the following issues in order for the bean to behave correctly at development time as well as at runtime:

- *Persistence*. A bean must provide the functionality required so that it can be serialized and de-serialized. This is required because a bean user will typically set some of the bean's properties and then want to save these settings until runtime. The mechanisms afforded to beans under the JavaBeans model is that of serialization; i.e. a bean should provide methods for writing itself on a stream and reading itself from a stream; these methods are then used by IDEs and/or programs using the bean.

- *Introspection.* A bean must provide enough information about itself so that an IDE can help a developer in understanding what the bean can do and defining how it interacts with other code segments in the system. JavaBeans defines two ways in which this can be done. The first relies on a set of conventions. For example, if a `PagerRequest` bean has a property called `TelephoneNumber` of type String then the bean developer should provide two methods of the form:

```
String getTelephoneNumber()
void setTelephoneNumber(String aString)
```

  These are the canonical accessors for a property. Often, a bean developer will not need to do much more than follow these conventions in order for the bean to perform correctly within an IDE. However, this is not true in cases of complex beans. For example, the conventions state that all public methods are viewed as the JavaBeans methods of the component. If a bean developer wants to shield some of these methods (yet cannot change the access category to anything but public), she/he will have to work a little harder. In this case, a `BeanInfo` object must be defined and implemented. This object describes the bean structure and is used by the IDE in the introspection process (it is a meta-data object).

- *Customization.* Beans can define customizers. Customizers are specialized editors that are tailored to allow the bean to be more easily used within an IDE. Customizers often involve building wizards and attractive user interfaces that guide a bean user through the process of customizing and using a bean.
- *Packaging.* Since beans are components written by one party and used by another, the JavaBeans specification defines how beans are packaged by bean developers so that users of the bean are not faced with unnecessary difficulties when trying to use the bean within their development environment.

Before delving into the details of JavaBeans, a simple example is presented. In this example we will look at a simple "Juggler" bean and a simple button bean and how they look inside Sun's BeanBox. (The BeanBox is part of the Bean Developer Kit (BDK) available at

Figure 3-1
The BeanBox canvas.

http://java.sun.com:80/beans/software/bdk_download.html). We will create a very simple application involving two buttons that control the juggler: one starts the juggling and one stopping it. All of the "programming" will be done within the BeanBox by visually hooking events. Both of the beans used are part of the BeanBox distribution and are provided as examples for bean development.

The BeanBox is composed of three tools: The canvas shown in Figure 3-1 is the work area in which beans are placed. The ToolBox shown in Figure 3-2 is the palette from which beans may be dragged off. Upon startup, the BeanBox startup procedure analyzes a set of JAR files (the package format for beans) and places all available beans in the ToolBox. All you have to do in order to add a new bean to your palette is to place

Figure 3-2
The BeanBox toolBox.

Figure 3-3
The BeanBox property editor.

the JAR file in the right directory (%BDK_HOME%jars by default). Finally, Figure 3-3 shows the property editor. The editor allows you to set the values of a bean's properties. The editor will always reflect the properties of the current selection; in Figure 3-3 the editor shows the property of the default container that is also part of the BDK distribution.

First, we drop the three beans on the canvas (as shown in Figure 3-4). Then we notice that the juggler is juggling too fast; we want to change the rate at which the juggling is performed. We click on the Juggler bean and look at the property sheet for the Juggler (Figure 3-5). One of the juggler's properties is the juggling rate. The introspection mechanism allows the BeanBox to know this and place this property in the editor. Since we want to slow the rate down, we select 125 instead of the original 250. Also, we need to set the labels of the button to "Stop" and "Start" respectively; one of the button bean's properties is its label so we use the property editor for setting the right labels.

Now we need to hook up the events. Buttons may be pressed. When a button is pressed an action event is generated. What we would like to do is hook up this event (which occurs within the buttons) to call methods in the juggler (specifically the `startJuggling` and `stopJuggling` meth-

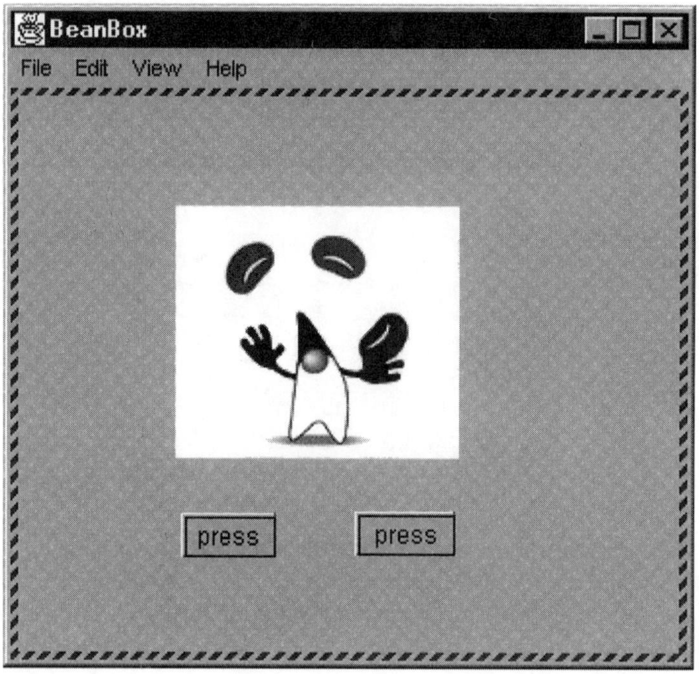

Figure 3-4
Placing the beans on the canvas.

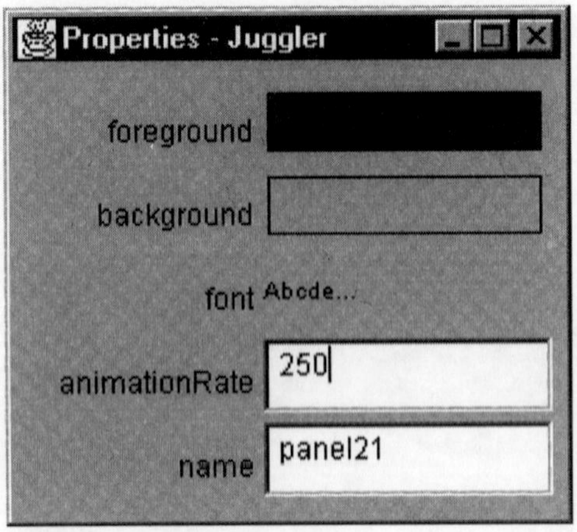

Figure 3-5 Juggler property sheet.

ods). The BeanBox allows us to do all this visually (as do many other modern IDEs). Under the covers what occurs is that an adaptor is placed between the juggler and the button. The adaptor is added as a listener on the action performed event (generated by the button) and when fired—calls the appropriate juggler method (which is part of the API defined by the juggler).

For us, the job is much simpler. The BeanBox allows us to do all of this without writing a line of code. First, we select the button we have designated to be the start button. Then we select `Edit → button push → actionPerformed`; this defines the event we are interested in (Figure 3-6). Then we drag the line to the juggler bean. A list of methods forming the juggler's public interface pops up (Figure 3-7); we select `startJuggling` and the adaptor is created and compiled. The process is repeated for the Stop button. That concludes our little experiment. We have a small working application that we can save and run; isn't technology wonderful?

Introspection

Introspection is the process through which a development environment discovers what properties, events, and methods a bean supports. In the example in the previous section we saw the effect of this discovery process. By knowing about a bean's properties the BeanBox is able to provide the correct property sheet, which lists the events—allowing us to

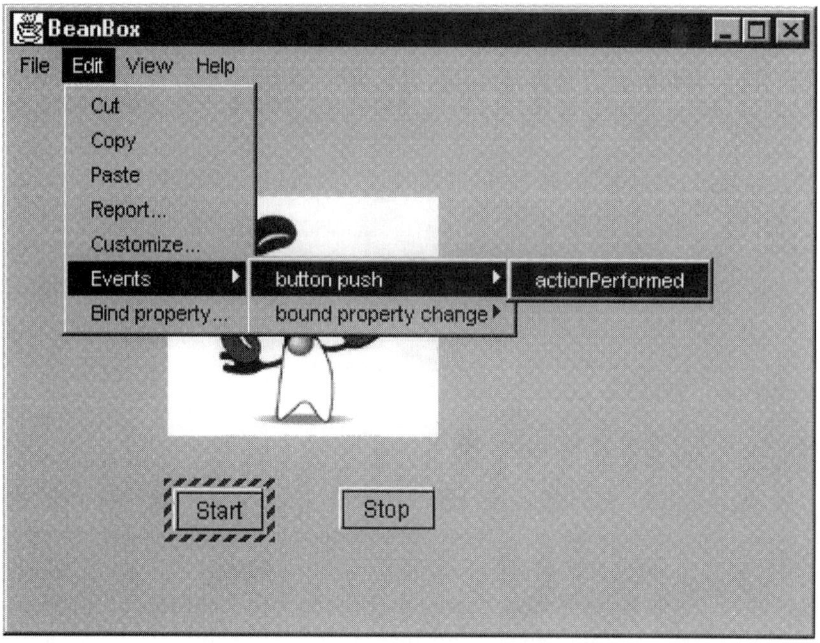

Figure 3-6
Selecting the push button event.

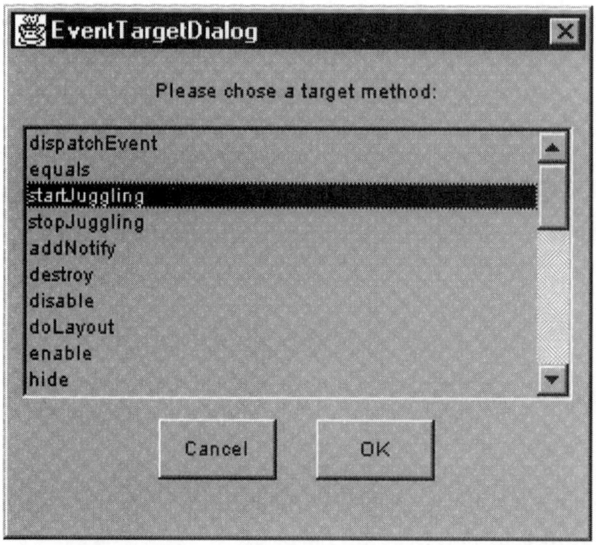

Figure 3-7
Selecting the method to be activated.

choose an action to be registered on, and knowing the methods we can select control what happens when the event occurs. The BeanBox uses introspection, both for the button bean and for the Juggler bean, in order to enable this visual programming.

The fundamental purpose of JavaBeans introspection is to provide a means through which a bean's capabilities can be inspected. This is not a totally new concept; there are many environments in which a definition or specification language is used for defining capabilities. For example, IDL is a specification language, and the information embodied within an IDL specification is stored as live objects within the IR—accessible to tools that provide browsing capabilities. JavaBeans introspection makes use of the Java language itself so as not to introduce a new language and allow the entire definition to be completely phrased in Java.

Java introspection can be achieved through one of two mechanisms. The low-level approach relies on conventions. The JavaBeans specification defines a set of conventions (which we will discuss in later Sections) for naming methods that provide access to properties, events, and methods. The low-level introspection mechanism uses Java reflection to access these names, and based on the set of conventions, ascertain what properties, events, and methods a bean supports.

The default low-level mechanism is very useful for most simple beans. For more complex beans it is often not enough because a complex bean may have been built to provide different services in different environments, or may contain too rich an interface to be useful for simple programming tasks. JavaBeans' introspection defines a second mechanism that, while requiring more work from a bean developer, provides fine control over what a bean will show to the outside world. JavaBeans defines a `BeanInfo` interface (whose methods are explained in the JavaDoc page shown in Figure 3-8) which provides methods for describing properties, events, and methods of a bean. A bean developer can create a class that implements the `BeanInfo` interface for describing the capabilities of his/her bean. Figure 3-9 shows a simple class implementing the `BeanInfo` interface for our `PagerRequest` bean. The `PagerRequestBeanInfo` class extends `SimpleBeanInfo`—a utility class in the `java.beans` package that has a null implementation for each of the required methods. Our bean will have three simple properties (telephone number, PIN, and message), a method for paging the number, and an event that will be raised when the pager gets the message. Note that we did not explicitly define the methods, showing that you can use an explicit `BeanInfo` definition for some aspects of the bean yet rely on the default naming conventions for others.

Figure 3-8
The `BeanInfo` interface.

- **getBeanDescriptor**

```
public abstract BeanDescriptor getBeanDescriptor()
```

Returns:

A BeanDescriptor providing overall information about the bean, such as its displayName, its customizer, etc. May return null if the information should be obtained by automatic analysis.

- **getEventSetDescriptors**

```
public abstract EventSetDescriptor[] getEventSetDescriptors()
```

Returns:

An array of EventSetDescriptors describing the kinds of events fired by this bean. May return null if the information should be obtained by automatic analysis.

- **getDefaultEventIndex**

```
public abstract int getDefaultEventIndex()
```

A bean may have a "default" event that is the event that will mostly commonly be used by humans when using the bean.

Returns:

Index of default event in the EventSetDescriptor array returned by getEventSetDescriptors.

Returns -1 if there is no default event.

- **getPropertyDescriptors**

```
public abstract PropertyDescriptor[] getPropertyDescriptors()
```

Returns:

An array of PropertyDescriptors describing the editable properties supported by this bean. May return null if the information should be obtained by automatic analysis.

If a property is indexed, then its entry in the result array will belong to the IndexedPropertyDescriptor subclass of PropertyDescriptor. A client of getPropertyDescriptors can use "instanceof" to check if a given PropertyDescriptor is an IndexedPropertyDescriptor.

- **getDefaultPropertyIndex**

```
public abstract int getDefaultPropertyIndex()
```

A bean may have a "default" property that is the property that will mostly commonly be initially chosen for update by humans who are customizing the bean.

Returns:

Index of default property in the PropertyDescriptor array returned by getPropertyDescriptors.

Returns -1 if there is no default property.

- **getMethodDescriptors**

```
public abstract MethodDescriptor[] getMethodDescriptors()
```

Returns:

An array of MethodDescriptors describing the externally visible methods supported by this bean. May return null if the information should be obtained by automatic analysis.

- **getAdditionalBeanInfo**

```
public abstract BeanInfo[] getAdditionalBeanInfo()
```

This method allows a BeanInfo object to return an arbitrary collection of other BeanInfo objects that provide additional information on the current bean.

Figure 3-8
(Cont'd)

If there are conflicts or overlaps between the information provided by different BeanInfo objects, then the current BeanInfo takes precedence over the getAdditionalBeanInfo objects, and later elements in the array take precedence over earlier ones.

Returns:

an array of BeanInfo objects. May return null.

- **getIcon**

```
public abstract Image getIcon(int iconKind)
```

This method returns an image object that can be used to represent the bean in toolboxes, toolbars, etc. Icon images will typically be GIFs, but may in future include other formats.

Beans aren't required to provide icons and may return null from this method.

There are four possible flavors of icons (16x16 color, 32x32 color, 16x16 mono, 32x32 mono). If a bean chooses to only support a single icon we recommend supporting 16x16 color.

We recommend that icons have a "transparent" background so they can be rendered onto an existing background.

Parameters:

iconKind - The kind of icon requested. This should be one of the constant values ICON_COLOR_16x16, ICON_COLOR_32x32, ICON_MONO_16x16, or ICON_MONO_32x32.

Returns:
An image object representing the requested icon. May return null if no suitable icon is available.

Since beans take the form of classes, and since a class may inherit from another class, the introspection process is a multi-phased process that walks up the inheritance tree. For every superclass of a bean, JavaBeans' introspection will try to determine if a `BeanInfo` object can be retrieved. If so, it will merge this information into the bean's complete description. If not, it will activate the low-level reflection mechanism and add the convention-based definitions to the bean merged description.

Properties

Properties are named attributes of beans. Properties have a name and a type and are defined by providing accessor methods in a bean. If the property is read/write, two accessors (a `get` and a `set`) will be implemented. Read-only properties require only a `get` method. Just as in CORBA IDL attributes, a property does not necessarily imply that the bean has a data member (although typically it does); a property may be derived (or computed) and can involve complex business logic.

```
import java.beans.*;


public class PagerRequestBeanInfo extends SimpleBeanInfo {


    public BeanDescriptor getBeanDescriptor() {
            BeanDescriptor _descriptor =
                  new BeanDescriptor(PagerRequest.class);
            return _descriptor;
    }


    public PropertyDescriptor[] getPropertyDescriptors() {
            try {
                  PropertyDescriptor _propertyDescriptors[]
= {
                        new PropertyDescriptor(
                              "Telephone Number" ,
                              String.class),
                        new PropertyDescriptor(
                              "PIN" ,
                              String.class),
                        new PropertyDescriptor(
                              "Message" ,
                              String.class)
                  };
                  return _propertyDescriptors;
            } catch (IntrospectionException e) {
            e.printStackTrace();
                  return null;
        }
    }


    public int getDefaultPropertyIndex() {
            return 0;
    }


    public EventSetDescriptor[] getEventSetDescriptors() {
            try {
                  EventSetDescriptor _eventDescriptors[] =
{
                  new EventSetDescriptor(
                        PagerRequest.class,
                        "Acknowledge Received",
                        java.awt.event.ActionEvent.class,
                        "acknowledgeReceived"
                        )};
                  return _eventDescriptors;
            } catch (IntrospectionException e) {
            e.printStackTrace();
                  return null;
```

Figure 3-9 The `PagerRequestInfo` class.

Figure 3-9
(Cont'd)

```
            }
        }


        public int getDefaultEventIndex() {
                return 0;
        }


          public java.awt.Image getIcon(int iconKind){
                java.awt.Image img =
    loadImage("PagerRequest.gif");
             return img;
        }


    }
```

The convention regarding properties for low-level introspection is that for a property by the name of `<PropertyName>` of type `<Property Type>` two accessors should be defined:

```
public <PropertyType> get<PropertyName>()
public void set<PropertyName>(<PropertyType> arg)
```

If the property is read-only, only the `get` accessor should be defined. When a `BeanInfo` class is not provided and the low-level introspection mechanism discovers a pair of public methods, as described above, it will know about the bean's property.

Special handling is defined for a number of common cases. If a property is of a Boolean type (which is very common) the get method should be defined as:

```
public boolean is<PropertyName>()
```

If a property has an array type (i.e. `<PropertyType>`[]) then the pattern to be followed is:

```
public <PropertyType> get<PropertyName>(int index)
public void set<PropertyName> (int index, <PropertyType> arg)
```

JavaBeans defines two more categories of properties called bound and constrained properties. Bound properties support automated notification upon a property value change, and constrained properties allow subscribers to perform validation on property value changes. Bound and constrained properties will be fully discussed in Sections 3.5.1 and 3.5.2 as they require an understanding of events.

Methods

By default, all public methods of a bean are exposed as the bean's API. This also includes all property accessors and event listener subscription methods; therefore, it is usually wise to define the method signatures within a `BeanInfo`.

Events

The JavaBeans event model follows the JDK 1.1 event model and defines a framework for propagating notifications from a source object to a set of listeners. Propagation means the activation of Java methods defined in the listener objects that follow a set of naming conventions. The Java methods that handle the events are grouped in interfaces called event listener interfaces whose signatures correspond to the naming conventions.

Hooking up an event subscriber to an event producer requires that both the source (the producer) and the listener (subscriber) follow the JavaBeans event pattern. The source must provide methods that the subscriber can use to register interest in a certain event. These are the `add` and the `remove` methods. For example, if an object wishes to support publishing an `ActionEvent` then that object should implement an `addActionListener` and a `removeActionListener`. Using these methods, subscribers can register their interest on this event type on the source object. In order to complete the cycle, the subscribers must implement a method defined in the appropriate listener interface (the argument to the `addActionListener` method); this is the method that will be called by the source object when firing the event.

The implementation specifics of how an event is raised and how it is propagated to the listeners is less important and is not limited by the JavaBeans' specification to one implementation. For example, most implementations of beans will maintain a collection of dependents (subscribers) and use the `add` and `remove` methods to manage this collection;

firing an event in this case implies iterating over this collection and calling each subscriber. However, nothing in the JavaBeans specification requires such a collection to be managed and many alternative implementations are possible. The only truly important specification is the protocol between the publisher and the subscriber.

Firing an event by a source object means creating an event object (an instance of a class inheriting from java.util.EventObject), inserting information regarding the state change into this event object, and invoking a method in every one of the interested listeners. Event objects are immutable and should not be changed by individual listener objects. Since the same event object will be passed to all listeners, any such change may affect correct processing in other listeners.

As in properties and methods, low-level JavaBeans introspection uses reflection and naming conventions to determine which events may be fired by a source object. A pair of methods of the form:

```
public void add<EventListenerType>(<EventListenerType> ev)
public void remove<EventListenerType>(<EventListenerType> ev)
```

imply that the bean creates <EventType> events that notify listeners implementing the <EventListenerType> interface. A special case supported in JavaBeans defines the naming convention to be used for unicast event sources. The default event-handling paradigm allows handling multiple subscribers on a single event source. If the event source model should only support a single listener then the method definition should be of the form

```
public void add<EventListenerType>(<EventListenerType> ev)
  throws java.util.TooManyListenersException
```

Finally, when an event source raises an event, it iterates over all the subscribed listeners and for each one calls a method of the form

```
public void <EventOccurrenceMethodsName>(<EventStateObjectType> ev)
```

The event object used encapsulates the information regarding the state change.

The event delivery semantics defined in the JavaBeans model is one of synchronous delivery with respect to the event source. The call made by the source object on the subscriber is performed within the caller's thread. If one listener fails (in a way that fails the thread) the following listeners will not get notification.

The synchronous event delivery semantics is fundamental to the notion of constrained properties. Constraint properties are an enhancement on bound properties—both being constructs that couple properties with events and are so common that they receive special status in JavaBeans. A bound property is a property that is of interest to another object—usually the container of the bean. This feature is useful for "binding" customized behavior to a change of a property value. Constrained properties are similar to bound properties in that an object may be interested in a property change, but they go even further in supporting validation by allowing the interested object to reject the change if it thinks it inappropriate. Synchronous semantics are important for implementing constrained properties because a listener may reject a change by simply raising an exception, thereby stopping normal processing of the event handler thread.

Bound Properties

As mentioned, bound properties allow coupling a property with an "OnChanged" notification type. In order to provide a bound property, a bean supports a pair of multicast listener registration methods for the PropertyChangeListener type:

```
public void addPropertyChangeListener(PropertyChangeListener l)
public void removePropertyChangeListener(PropertyChangeListener l)
```

When a change occurs, the bean calls the listener's propertyChange method—passing it a PropertyChangeEvent object. The Property ChangeEvent object includes the property name that has changed, its old value, and its new value. If one wants to register precisely on a single named property the following methods are also supported by JavaBeans (and are preferred):

```
public void addPropertyChangeListener(
    String propertyName, PropertyChangeListener l)
public void removePropertyChangeListener(
    String propertyName, PropertyChangeListener l)
```

The call to the listeners' propertyChange methods is performed only after the change has been made—the subscribers have no say regarding the change. Figure 3-10 shows a simple example of using a bound property of internal frame in the Swing (JFC) library (com.sun.java.swing.JInternalFrame); when an internal frame is maximized the property will change and we will be notified of the change.

Constrained Properties

Constrained properties extend bound properties with support for validation. Instead of being called after the property changes, subscribers are called before the change is made and are given a chance to veto the change. A subscriber can stop the change from being made by raising a PropertyVetoException; because of the synchronous event semantics, it is possible for the bean to ensure that the change will not be performed

```
//
// When the screen is opened set up the listener to get
// notified when the internal frame's properties change.
// One of these properties is the isMaximized property which
// is of interest.
//

public void postOpenWindow(com.sun.java.swing.JInternalFrame win) {

      OnMaximizeOrMinimize aListener = new OnMaximizeOrMinimize();
      win.addPropertyChangeListener(aListener);

}


//
// When called, check whether this is the property of
// interest to us in and if so, call the handling routine
// (not showed here)
//

class OnMaximizeOrMinimize implements java.beans.PropertyChangeListener
{

      public void propertyChange(java.beans.PropertyChangeEvent ev) {
         if (ev.getPropertyName().compareTo(
         com.sun.java.swing.JInternalFrame.IS_MAXIMUM_PROPERTY) == 0) {
            boolean aBoolean =
                  ((Boolean)ev.getNewValue()).booleanValue();
                        setBasedOn(aBoolean);
            }
      }

      public void setBasedOn(boolean aBoolean) {
            // ….
      }

}
```

Figure 3-10
Using a bound property.

until all listeners have been called and given a chance to veto the change. The naming conventions used for constrained properties include `add` and `remove` methods of the form:

```
public void addVetoableChangeListener(VetoableChangeListener l)
public void removeVetoableChangeListener(VetoableChangeListener l)

public void addVetoableChangeListener(
     String propertyName, VetoableChangeListener l)
public void removeVetoableChangeListener(
     String propertyName, VetoableChangeListener l)
```

The handling method in the listener interface is defined to throw a `PropertyVetoException`.

One of the complexities involved with a constrained property is the fact that if one subscriber vetoes the change, it may be possible that other subscribers have already been notified of the change and accordingly have taken some actions. Since this may cause incorrect application behavior, the subscribers must be notified when the property is being changed back to the old value (when a veto occurs). Therefore, when a bean handles a veto exception raised by one of its subscribers it must fire another vetoable change event for reverting back to the old value.

Event Adaptors

Event adaptors are objects that interpose between the source objects and the subscribers (or between the event producer and the event consumer). Event adaptors are not necessary for the correct propagation of events but they are often very convenient to use. This convenience may be attributed to two issues:

1. Event adaptors allow decoupling the subscriber from the source. Instead of forcing the subscriber to implement the correct set of methods necessary for the event to be passed from the source, the adaptor can form a "translator" of sorts, allowing the source and subscribers to remain unaware of each other. Because the different components are often developed by third parties it is even possible that such a coupling may not be possible; in this case, event adaptors are a must. Figure 3-11a shows the basic setup of an event adaptor and Figure 3-11b shows what happens at runtime. In this example the paging system is a subscriber that has been purchased by a third party. It has an API for paging by using a phone number and a PIN. Our source is a

dispatch queue that raises an event whenever a dispatch request should be issued. The event adaptor implements the listener API required in order for it to be added as a listener, and calls the API translation for the paging system.

2. Event adaptors may perform additional operations required by the application, such as filtering events, implementing security policies, implementing queuing (for example, the CORBA Event Service has a notion called the Event Channel, which could be partially implemented within an application as an event adaptor), etc. Another example of the usefulness of adaptors involves transactions. Suppose we have multiple subscribers on the same node that must all perform some operation when the source fires an event. Also, suppose that all of these operations need to occur within the same transaction bracket (i.e. either they all complete successfully or none is performed). Someone must coordinate this transaction. The coordinator will usually not be the source object (either because it was not developed

Figure 3-11
(a) Event adaptor setup. (b) Event adaptor at runtime.

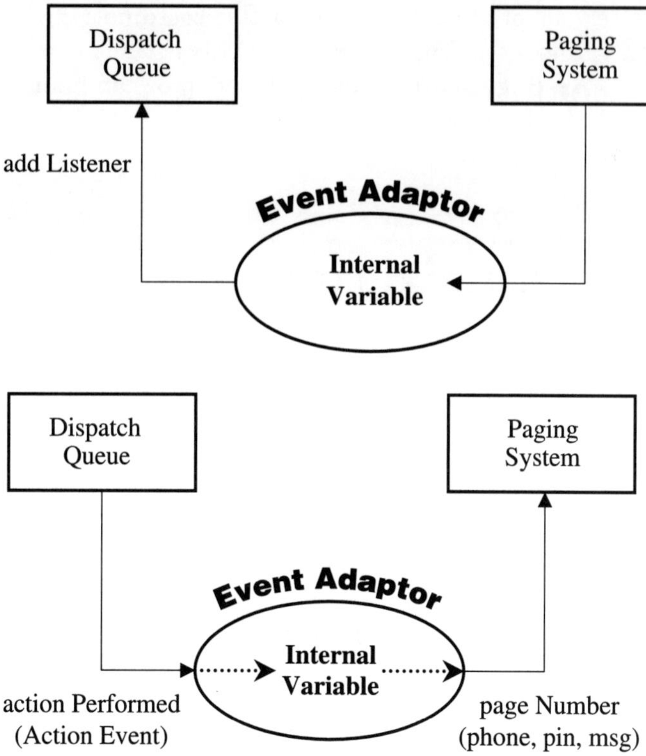

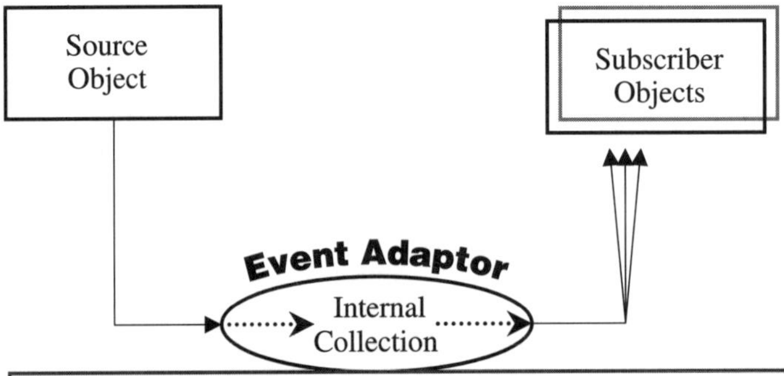


```
getCurrentTC.begin();
for (Enumeration e = iCol; e.hasMoreElements();) {
      e.nextElement().invoke();
  }
getCurrentTC.commit();
```

Figure 3-12 An event adaptor as a transaction coordinator.

internally, i.e its source cannot be changed, or because other users of the same component care nothing about transactions). It certainly can't be one of the subscribers because we can't rely on notification ordering (any implementation trying to make use of one of the subscribers for this coordination will almost surely be messy and non-reentrant). This is obviously a job for an adaptor. As Figure 3-12 depicts, the adaptor can manage the transaction for its subscribers.

Customization

Property editors, such as the one shown in Figure 3-3, are useful for simple beans. For complex beans or for beans with complex data types as properties, the default property editors may not be enough. For such cases, JavaBeans defines the notion of a customizer for a class. A customizer is a class that provides a way for a user of a bean to provide values for properties of a bean at design time. This can include wizards, specialized user interfaces, or editors that allow complex data types to be entered.

Customizers need to inherit (directly or indirectly) from `java.awt.Component` since they are used by the bean IDE as a GUI. They must also implement the `java.beans.Customizer` interface (whose methods are shown in Figure 3-13). These methods are used for

Figure 3-13
The `java.beans.Customizer` interface.

setObject

```
public abstract void setObject(Object bean)
```

Set the object to be customized. This method should be called only once, before the Customizer has been added to any parent AWT container.

Parameters:

bean - The object to be customized.

addPropertyChangeListener

```
public abstract void addPropertyChangeListener(PropertyChangeListener
listener)
```

Register a listener for the PropertyChange event. The customizer should fire a PropertyChange event whenever it changes the target bean in a way that might require the displayed properties to be refreshed.

Parameters:

listener - An object to be invoked when a PropertyChange event is fired.

removePropertyChangeListener

```
public abstract void removePropertyChangeListener(PropertyChangeListener
listener)
```

Remove a listener for the PropertyChange event.

Parameters:

listener - The PropertyChange listener to be removed.

managing the interaction with the rest of the IDE—by using property change events.

Attaching a customizer to a certain bean involves going through the `BeanInfo` object. The customizer for a bean is retrieved by calling the `getCustomizerClass()` method after getting the bean description from the `BeanInfo` object (using the `getBeanDescriptor()` method).

Persistence

When using a bean within an IDE, the user will typically customize it by setting properties, attaching events, etc. This information must be externalized to some persistent store in order for the system to function correctly at runtime. JavaBeans use Java object serialization as the mechanism for storing out and reading in beans. While the specification defines other alternatives for making a bean persistent (including allowing the tool to control the process and allowing specialized formats to be used), the current state of the market is such that you should use serialization and/or externalization only.

Packaging

JavaBeans are packaged within JAR files. JAR files were introduced in JDK 1.1 as a generic and very useful packing and distribution mechanism. JAR files were not produced specifically for beans but rather to solve issues involving cohesive packaging of code, bitmaps, help information, etc. However, because JAR files can contain Java bytecodes, serialized objects, help files, icons, and more—JAR was an obvious candidate for packaging beans. Details regarding the JAR manifest file and the precise use of JAR files for bean packaging are beyond the scope of this book and may be reviewed in [JB].

CHAPTER 4

Enterprise JavaBeans

The IT industry has gone through a series of revolutions in the underlying architecture of large-scale applications. Before the 1980s, the primary computing platform used for mainstream applications was the mainframe with its set of "networked computers"—its so-called "dumb" terminals. These were hardwired to a central mainframe in the back office and provided no processing capabilities at all (or almost none at all). This disadvantage, along with their inherent lack of a graphical user interface, helped bring about the first revolution.

In the 1980s, and especially towards 1985, the Wintel revolution began. The availability of relatively cheap PCs that had impressive processing power, along with the release of early Windows by Microsoft, helped push the client/server revolution (which had already started before with the Unix workstations). The system model that emerged on this platform involved an application architecture consisting of data stored in database servers and application logic performed mostly by the client. The shift in terms of architecture was that the client became more and more central to application functionality, and code migrated from the server to the client (see Figure 4-1). The client became a "fat" client while the server only provided data services and limited management services (later, with the advent of database stored procedures, application logic began migrating back to the server). Like anything in life, the client/server architecture provided many advantages but also some serious disadvantages. The administration of these applications turned out to be difficult, deployment was painful, and integration with other systems became a major issue; the total cost of ownership did not fall (as was promised initially by client/server vendors).

The next revolution started in the mid-1990s with the rise of the Internet. Although the Internet is a networked environment similar to common client/server environments, it has some additional characteris-

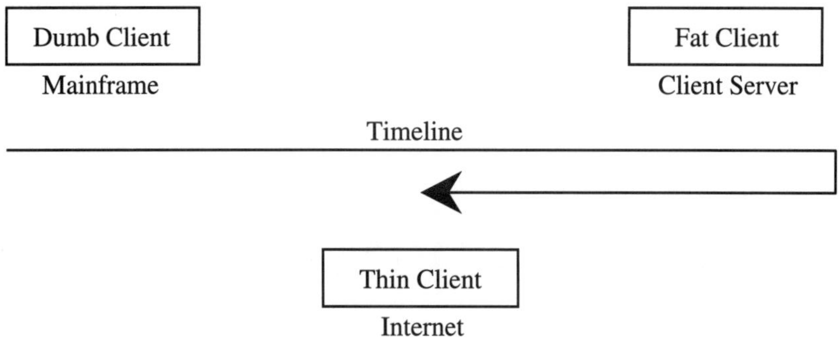

Figure 4-1 Evolution of application architectures.

tics. It is ubiquitous and supports a very high degree of distribution. Basically, the big difference is that of scale—the Internet is such a large network that even though it uses the same protocols as do LANs and corporate networks, it is fundamentally different. While the Internet is certainly an amazing phenomenon, it poses some very difficult security problems while relieving other management problems common to client/server systems. As the Internet began gaining ground as a deployment environment, it became apparent that there was a mismatch between this deployment environment and the client/server model. This mismatch brought about the next architectural shift—back to a server-centric architecture in which the server manages the core business processes, yet client processing is still available for performing some application functions. The Web browser has become the universal client application; the application model is currently called "thin" client architecture (it is after all much nicer to be "thin" than "fat" or "dumb"). While the browser provides a common application platform, it can also embed applications in a very wide variety of "thinness". Application clients can be "really dumb" (as in the various package tracking applications, for example) or provide an environment where the application client has considerable application logic (even to the point where the client is written in Java and performs business logic). This flexibility in capabilities allows a correct balance for many applications. In addition, it does not enforce a single model, and allows different applications to have slightly different structures based on the application needs.

The fact that the application is run within a browser is certainly a major factor in what makes the Web-based model so compelling. However, from an application architecture point of view, this correct balance and the allowance for tailoring what processing is performed on the client and which is on the server—is the underlying motivator that will, in the long term, help this architecture become mainstream.

In the push toward a balanced thin client, Java plays an important role. Java's characteristics as a language make it an ideal candidate for building both Web-based clients as well as servers. Its portability, architecture neutrality, security policies, and networking support give it an advantage in becoming a dominant language for writing complex Web client applets. Because Java bytecode files may be placed on the server and downloaded by the client, applications may be managed and distributed in a relatively simple manner. Application upgrades can be distributed simply by putting the new class files on the server; the client will simply download these during the next access. And because the market is steadily moving toward the integration of Java with CORBA, robust and mission-critical applications can be built in an architecture that can make use of the best in both the mainframe and client/server worlds.

But Java's strengths are as important to the server side of applications as it is to the client side. Its strengths as a good object-oriented language, security capabilities, portability, and networking features, should have immediately made it an important player in the enterprise software market (on the server). However, because of Java's immaturity, application server developers were (and to a great extent still are) hesitant to use Java in this central role. This immaturity takes two forms: Java is slow and needs some major performance upgrades, and Java does not have a good environment within the server. The performance issues are constantly being addressed and hopefully by the time you read this book it will already have been solved. As for the server-side framework, it was clear by the end of 1997 that unless some structure was put in place for supporting issues such as transactions, security, distribution, etc., Java was going to become a language for writing applets (after which it was certain to go away).

Enter Enterprise JavaBeans (EJB). Just like building client software requires frameworks and standards to ensure that one can make use of others' tools and services, so do server-side components. Business logic on the server should focus on building domain functionality and not on systemic features such as transaction management and coordination, security policy enforcement, etc. Since no serious application can do without a solution to each of these issues, a standard API set was required to ensure that application components on the server can select solutions for system and architecture problems without limitations and without being locked into a single solution. This is what EJB is all about.

> *Enterprise JavaBeans defined a component model for the development and deployment of Java applications based on a multitier, distributed object architecture... Java currently has a component model called JavaBeans. Enterprise JavaBeans extends the JavaBeans component model to support server components. Server components are components that run on the server. In a multitier application architecture, most of an application's logic is moved from the client to one or more server. A server component model simplifies the process of moving the logic to the server. The component model implements a set of automatic services to manage the component.*
>
> *Enterprise JavaBeans:*
> *Server Component Model for Java,*
> by Anne Thomas, Patricia Seybold Group, December 1997.
> Prepared for Sun Microsystems, Inc.

The importance of EJB stems from the fact that when building real systems, the work can be partitioned into two primary categories: domain-level application programming and system-level issues. Every software system developed at the department or enterprise level has two types of programmers: developers faced with the need to implement business logic and domain-specific functionality and developers who build "infrastructure" that deals with issues such as transactions, security, naming etc. EJB tries to separate these two categories and provides a framework in which application developers can focus on the domain functionality while using servers and containers built by specialists to solve their needs at the system level. In this form, not only can enterprise software developers save a lot of time, but they can also get solutions that are potentially far superior to those they would have received had they built the entire system themselves. EJB allows "infrastructure" developed by "infrastructure vendors" to have a standard API and standard framework so that it can be used by multiple domain-level applications. The goals of the EJB architecture, as defined in the EJB specification, are:

- To define a component architecture for the development of Java-based distributed business applications.
- To allow mixing components built by different vendors in providing an enterprise-level solution.
- To facilitate scenarios in which experts provide solutions for transactions, security, distribution, multi-threading, and other system-level issues in a way that can be easily used by domain experts building business applications.
- To address the entire software lifecycle and provide definitions by which EJB components can be used within tools during development time (much like JavaBeans addresses both the runtime and the design time issues).
- To define aspects of interoperability. Specifically, EJB relies on CORBA for distributed object interoperability; this does not mean that EJB interoperability is only related to CORBA—many other API mappings and transports are possible.

And why is the EJB so important in the context of the SanFrancisco frameworks? SanFrancisco is written in Java and primarily targets large-scale server-side application development. It is only natural that it will be compatible with the EJB standard. By doing so, SanFrancisco objects will have even greater reusability characteristics making SanFrancisco components reusable within multiple deployment environments. In addition, IBM as a vendor of enterprise tools, such as transaction monitors and Web servers, will profit by supporting EJB.

All of these factors have created a reality in which IBM has not only embraced EJB, it is a leader in the EJB initiative. As part of this initiative IBM has announced that SanFrancisco will fully support and follow the EJB standard; therefore, all SanFrancisco objects will be EJB components. Because the SanFrancisco frameworks were developed before EJB was released, the current version (1.2)—the version on which this book is based—is not yet EJB compatible. However, as this chapter explains, EJB is all about containers that provide the interfaces and APIs that allow a component to make use of EJB services. Therefore, while keeping in mind that your SanFrancisco components may need to be slightly modified in the future, knowing about EJB will help you write today's components in a way that future modifications will be minimal.

IBM has already committed to make the necessary changes in the SanFrancisco Common Business Objects and the Core Business Process layers. The first stage will be to enable the Common Business Objects to be used as enterprise beans within any EJB server (all these terms will be fully discussed in the following sections). Then, Core Process components will be EJB-enabled, completing the push to ensure that SanFrancisco components can run within any EJB server.

EJB Components

The EJB architecture provides a framework for building distributed transaction-oriented components. Like JavaBeans, EJB is a component model and, as such, defines what the structure of an EJB component is as well as describing the world in which it lives. This second point is extremely important. A well-known thesis in philosophy is that in order to fully describe an entity one must describe its surroundings and how it interacts with its environment. This is also the approach taken by the EJB architecture. An EJB component is a Java component that implements business logic. As a component living within the EJB world, it must assume a very well-defined environment and a set of interactions that it must participate in. For example, the EJB architecture defines the notion of a container. In describing containers, the EJB specification defines the responsibilities of containers and the responsibilities of EJB components in the context of containers. It also fully defines the interaction between the container and the EJB component, thereby defining a very structured world that an EJB builder can rely on. This brings the task of building EJB components and EJB-based systems a little closer to being an engineering discipline than an art—the ultimate purpose of the computer science field called software engineering.

The EJB architecture is inherently difficult in that it attempts to create a balance between various contradictory requirements. On the one hand, it attempts to create a very strict framework for distributed object-oriented systems so that many components can be easily created and assembled into larger systems. In this respect the framework must be simple, clear, concise, and easy to use. On the other hand, the EJB architecture aims at very large, robust, mission-critical systems; systems that often have very specialized requirements, and systems that push the envelope in many issues such as customization, performance, throughput, etc.

The balance afforded by the EJB architecture relies on the divide-and-conquer approach. The EJB architecture divides responsibilities typically found in systems into a number of roles. It then defines a modular architecture in which different entities fill these roles (the word "entities" was used instead of "components" simply because this is a very overloaded word in the context of this chapter). Finally, it defines the interaction between these entities and the contracts each must conform to in order for the entire architecture to function correctly. The fundamentals of the definition of an EJB component's environment are:

- An enterprise bean is developed to implement business functionality.
- An enterprise bean is not an island of its own. An enterprise bean lives within a container deployed within a server. The enterprise bean is never accessed directly; the container manages access to the enterprise bean functionality. This allows the responsibility of managing things, such as transactions and security, to be moved from the enterprise bean to the container and the server. For example, instance creation of the enterprise bean type is performed exclusively by the container. This allows the container to manage lifecycle and transaction issues for this class. Figure 4-2 illustrates the high-level relationships between an enterprise bean and a container.

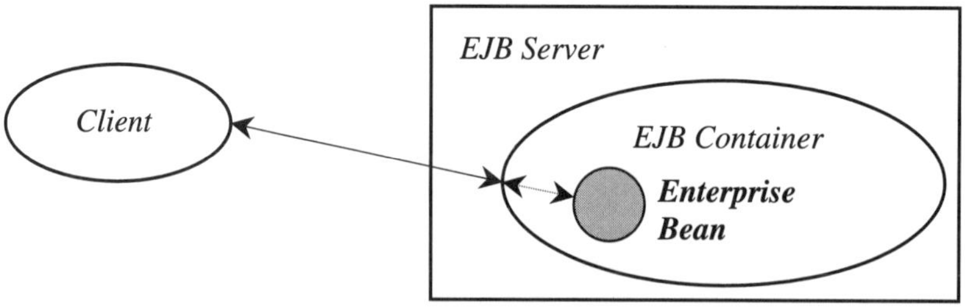

Figure 4-2
High-level overview of an enterprise bean's environment.

- Enterprise beans and containers are fully de-coupled. This means that multiple EJB-compliant containers can be used to manage instances of an enterprise bean. All services provided to the enterprise bean by the container are well defined in the EJB specification. The specification allows for EJB containers and EJB servers to provide extended services. Enterprise beans that rely on such services may be limited in the range of EJB containers and servers they may run in.
- An enterprise bean defines sets of properties that affect its runtime behavior. These properties are separated as meta-data, or descriptors in order to allow customization at setup and deployment time. This is similar in nature to the notion of design time customization in JavaBeans; the difference is mostly in the nature of the properties. While JavaBeans properties are usually user interface related, enterprise beans' properties involve control over transaction, distribution, security, and persistence.

In order for an EJB component to be used by client software it must provide support for the following implementation issues.

- *Object Identity*. The unique identifier that can be used to identify an object (not all enterprise beans have an object identity visible at the application level).
- *Method Invocation*. Business methods form the contract between the enterprise bean and, ultimately, the client. The methods are grouped into an interface that forms the contract that must be satisfied by the bean developer.
- *Home Interface*. Home interfaces are defined per EJB type. Within a home each bean can be identified using the primary key (if the bean has an application-level identity). Object lookup therefore involves two stages: locating the home interface and

then using the primary key for locating a specific object. The home interface is stored by a naming service and the client can access it using the standard Java Naming and Directory Interface (JNDI). An enterprise bean's home interface extends the `javax.ejb.EJBHome` interface.

In fact, client software never actually uses the enterprise bean directly and never accesses the bean's functionality without first going through an intermediary container. The container is involved because it is responsible for managing most of the system-level issues and must, therefore, constantly know what is happening to the enterprise bean. The effect is that each container of an enterprise bean must also support the API categories mentioned. This support usually requires some work of the container (for example, determining what the transaction bracket is and possibly changing it) and then delegating to the appropriate method in the enterprise bean.

A client using an enterprise bean can rely on the fact that it has a unique identifier. The responsibility for actually creating this identifier is sometimes that of the enterprise bean and sometimes that of the container. For example, if the bean represents a persistent domain object, it will provide the object identifier and the container will simply propagate this identity to the clients when asked. On the other hand, a bean can be a transient object that is used by the client for performing some tasks. Such an enterprise bean may be an extension of the client on the application server and may expire when the client is no longer using it. In this case, the bean's lifetime is cohesive with the client's and its identity is undefined as a property of the bean itself; the container may generate the object identity for use by the client (usually when it constructs the bean for the client).

Home interfaces define one or more `create` methods and zero or more `find` methods. Creation methods allow clients to create new instances of EJB components and finder methods allow clients to look up a specific EJB. Both of these sets of methods must obviously be supported by the enterprise bean itself; for example, an enterprise beans developer must provide an `ejbCreate` method for each of the `create` methods, and an `ejbFind` method for each of the `find` methods defined by the home interface. In addition, the container provides system-level functionality that is accessed by the client; some of these require work to be done by the enterprise bean developer.

Because an enterprise bean lives within an EJB container, the EJB specification also defines precisely the APIs used by the container when managing the enterprise bean. The notion of a container is an important part of EJB as it allows an enterprise bean developer to rely on standard services that are taken care of by the container. The most important of these is lifecycle management. Although lifecycle management is the container's responsibility, it cannot do this without the full cooperation of the enterprise bean. This "cooperation" (or contract between the enterprise bean and its container) is defined in a set of interfaces that must be implemented by the enterprise bean. Specifically, an enterprise bean must implement a set of state management callbacks that are called by the container in order to notify the enterprise bean of important changes made as part of lifecycle operations. These interfaces are either `javax.ejb.SessionSynchronization` or `javax.ejb.EntityBean` depending on whether the enterprise bean is a session bean or an entity bean. Other elements of this contract between an enterprise bean and its container include APIs through which a container can inform a bean what its current context and environment are.

Finally, because EJB aims at the high-end market for component development, a standard mapping of enterprise beans' interfaces to CORBA exists. This opens up the EJB architecture making it truly a multi-vendor, multi-language, and multi-platform architecture. It is difficult to exaggerate how important this mapping is both to adopters of EJB and to EJB itself. The current world of software is divided into two camps: the Microsoft world, and everyone else. The Microsoft camp is bigger. In fact, when you go out to speak to CIOs and CTOs, more often than not you will hear that the only viable platform for enterprise software today is Microsoft. This is definitely bad news for many firms in the industry but it is also bad news (we think) for users of technology. Who are the other companies—the ones that do not view the Microsoft platform as being the only possible solution? Mostly they are large organizations with a very large install base of differing operating systems, hardware, and architectures. These organizations cannot afford to fall in line with a single (and often limited) set of tools. These are the organization that EJB must appeal to; otherwise it will quickly become another standard that never emerged as an implementation (another good idea that belongs to the history books). Since CORBA is certainly a de-facto standard within these organizations, it is only fitting that EJB inherently map to CORBA for providing an architecture for distributed enterprise solutions.

A mapping for EJB to CORBA includes a number of important categories: the mapping of interfaces to CORBA IDL, the propagation of an EJB transaction bracket as an Object Transaction Service (OTS) transaction context, support for the Naming Service, and the propagation of security information within a security context. By defining the mapping in terms of these categories, EJB elevates itself to full semantic as well as wire-level interoperability.

Session Enterprise Beans

Enterprise beans are categorized into two groups: session enterprise beans and entity enterprise beans. The major distinguishing feature between these two groups is the notion of persistence. Session beans represent server-side components that implement business logic but are not persistent whereas entity beans guarantee full persistence of their state. This section focuses on session beans; the next section discusses entity beans at length.

A session bean implements business logic on behalf of a client. The session bean is not persistent and is not shared by multiple clients; in this respect it is a convenience mechanism for providing correct application partitioning. Application partitioning is an important concept in distributed computing that recognizes that business logic should often be performed at differing locations while continuing to support location transparency to the client software. A primary example of this is application partitioning as a facilitator of improved performance. Assume, for example, that a certain business function receives a small set of inputs and produces an output but is very database-intensive while performing the function. Obviously, the application partition shown in Figure 4-3b will perform better than the partition shown in Figure 4-3a. Session beans allow an application developer to partition the application in a way that some of the business logic processing occurs on the server *on behalf* of the client; the session bean is, therefore, a logical extension of the client processing.

A session bean does have an object identity, but as a non-persistent entity its object identity is also not persistent. A session bean might therefore live for a while, providing service to some client, and later be reborn with a different identity. Therefore, the object identity of a session bean is never an application-meaningful descriptor; at best it might be used by the client for temporary convenience functions (such as placing it within a hash table managed by the application). Please note that while the session bean may logically be reborn to provide services to the same

Figure 4-3
Implications of application partitioning on performance.
(a) Application partitioning – Option 1;
(b) application partitioning – Option 2.

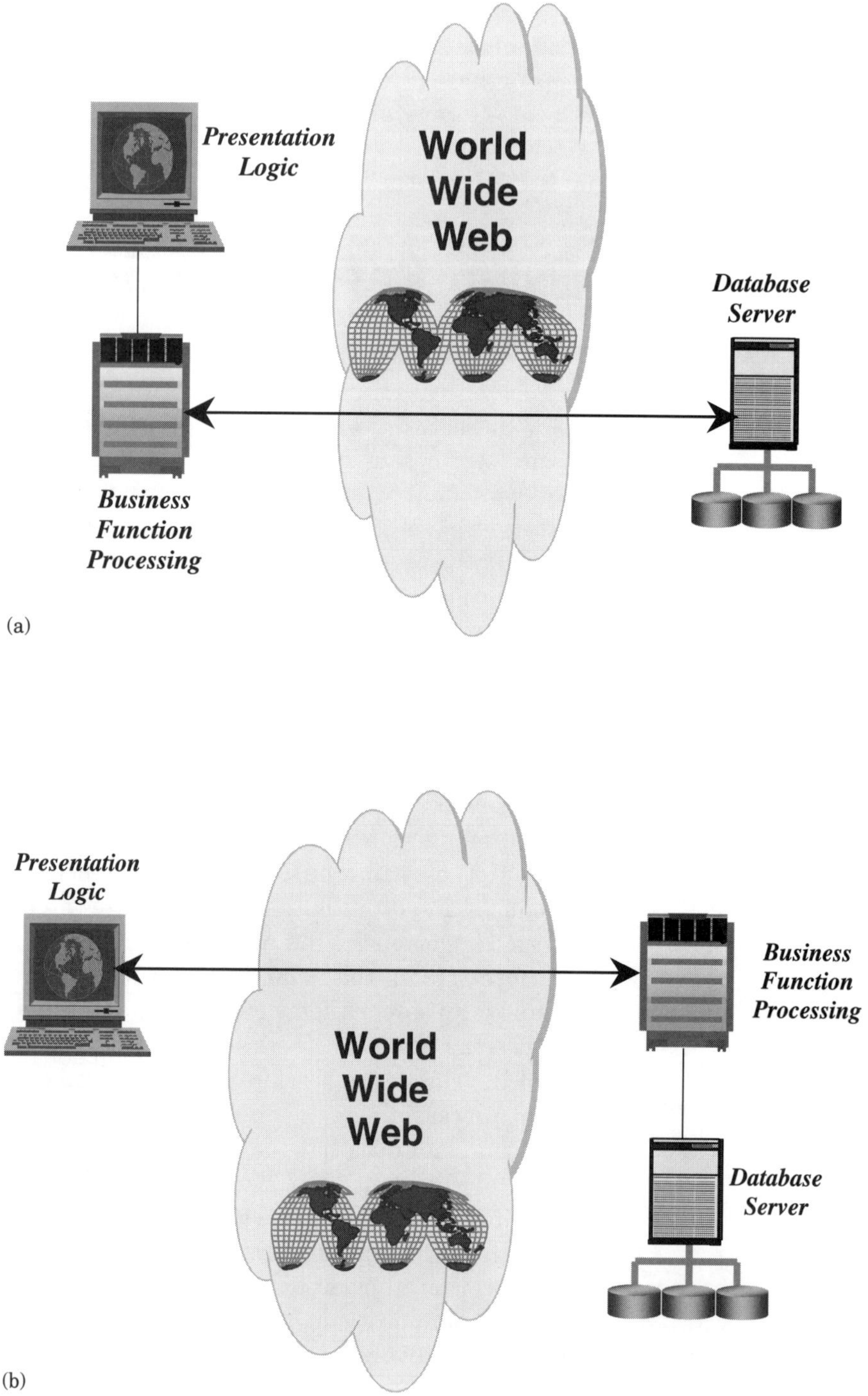

client, it is in fact a different object with a different identity; it should not be confused with an entity object that can support a complex lifecycle. The session bean's identity cannot be used as a key and should, in principle, not be exposed to the client.

Access to a session bean's functionality is always through an object called an EJB Object. The EJB Object exposes a session bean's interface as a remote interface using Java RMI, possibly layered over CORBA IIOP. All calls made on the EJB Object are delegated to the enterprise bean. A user of a session bean's functionality does not have to be concerned with regard to the precise location of the bean; RMI and CORBA will make the remote nature of the invocations transparent. In addition to delegating the domain-level method calls to the enterprise bean, an EJB Object provides a few methods for managing the EJB Object itself such as object comparison.

Like all enterprise beans, a session bean too lives within an EJB container. The container manages the bean's lifecycle, access to the bean's methods, security, transactions, and more. The container also supports lookup via JNDI. Using a container's lookup function, a client can access the home interface of the enterprise bean. The home interface provides functions for creating new EJB Objects, removing an EJB Object, and accessing meta-data information (implementing the `javax.ejb.EJBMetaData` interface) of the enterprise bean that is useful for tools during design time (similar to the `BeanInfo` object). For example, the code fragment required to create a new `PartOrder` object is shown in Figure 4-4. Note that the actual creation method (the constructor) is specific to the part order but that all creation methods are

```
Context clientContext = new InitialContext();

PartOrderHome partOrderHome = javax.rmi.PortableRemoteObject.narrow(
      clientContext.lookup("applications/services/parts/orders"),
      PartOrderHome.class);

PartOrder aPartOrder = partOrderHome.create(
      new Date(),               // creation date
      "AT&T",                   // company name
      "Jane Doe",               // person ordering
      ...);
```

Figure 4-4
Creating a new `PartOrder` object.

called using the home interface; the actual creation is always managed by the EJB container.

Figure 4-5 depicts a schematic view of the states a session bean will typically go through during its lifetime. A session bean is created when one of the home interface's creation methods is invoked. The enterprise bean is created on the server and an object (possibly remote) reference is returned to the caller (this is the EJB Object). The client can then start invoking methods using the bean's handle.

When the client is through with using the bean and wants to release it, one of the removal methods should be called to destroy the bean. Removal methods may be called either using the EJB Object or by using the home

Figure 4-5
A session bean's Lifecycle.

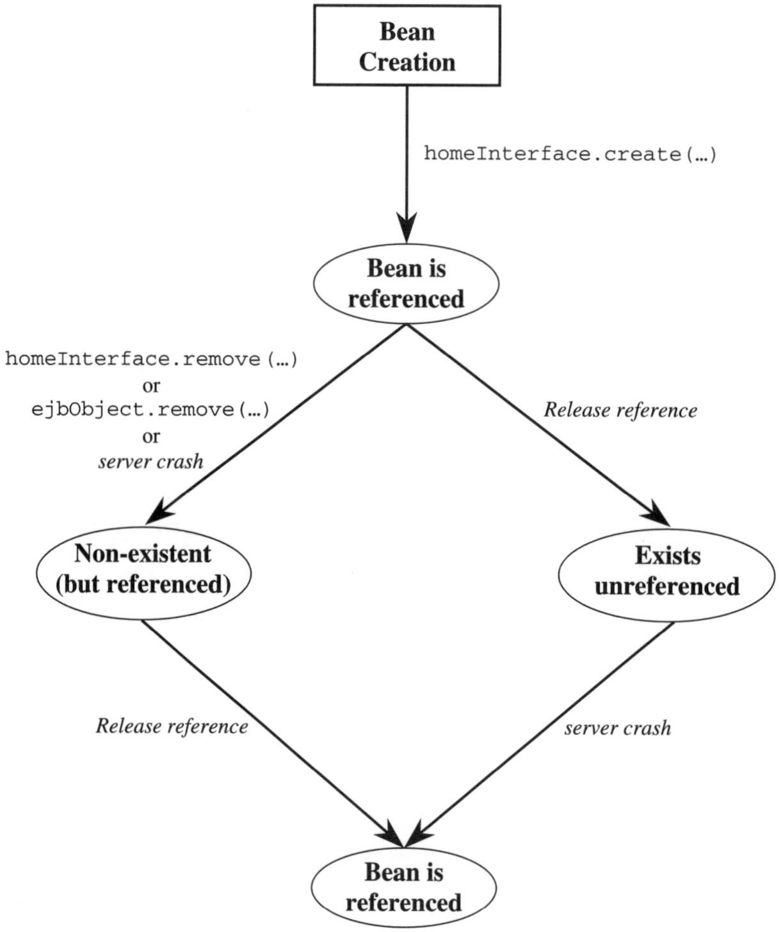

interface. In both cases, the result is the state in which the enterprise bean no longer exists but is still referenced by the client; the client should then release the reference. If the client uses the handle when the enterprise bean no longer exists, a `NoSuchObjectException` will be raised. If the client releases the reference before it calls one of the removal methods then the enterprise bean will continue to exist until the server exits (either through a normal shutdown or a system crash). During that time, the client can reclaim the handle using a `getEJBObject` call to the EJB Object (the handle), which returns our state machine to the state in which the enterprise bean exists and is referenced.

Calls made through the EJB Object and through the container will ultimately reach the enterprise bean. A session enterprise bean should implement the following methods defined in the `SessionBean` Java interface:

- `setSessionContext`. Used by the container to set a bean's context; the context is managed by the container. The `SessionContext` object provides the following functions that are used by the enterprise bean.
  - `getEJBObject`. Returns the handle object.
  - `getHome`. Returns the home interface.
  - `getEnvironment`. Returns the environment properties.
  - `getCallerIdentity`. Returns the identity of the invoking client. This is a very convenient function allowing the bean to possibly configure its reply based on the identity of the calling object. For example, pricing information may differ based on whether the ordering entity is an internal or external customer. A price book bean may therefore wish to know details regarding the object that requested pricing information.
  - `isCallerInRole`. Provides a bean with a testing method for matching a caller with a certain role.
  - `setRollbackOnly`. Allows the bean to guarantee that the current transaction may not be committed and that any changes made within this transaction bracket must eventually be discarded by a rollback.
  - `getRollbackOnly`. A testing method that returns a Boolean value indicating whether the transaction is marked as rollback only.
  - `getUserTransaction`. Returns the `javax.jts.UserTransaction` providing direct access to the

transaction and allows for manual handling of transaction bracketing.

- `ejbRemove`. The container is responsible for managing the lifecycle for a bean. When the container removes a bean it calls the `ejbRemove` method allowing the bean to perform any clean-up or finalization procedures. Since a session bean is not a persistent entity, such clean-up is usually very simple.
- `ejbPassivate`. Called by the container when it intends to passivate a bean, which allows it to close resources or do miscellaneous preparations so that after re-activation its state will be correct.
- `ejbActivate`. Called by the container when a bean is activated. The bean can then perform any inverse operations required to prepare its state.

A session bean may also implement additional methods defined in the `SessionSynchronization` interface. These methods provide synchronization hooks allowing a session bean to tune its behavior in the context of a transaction.

- `afterBegin`. Called when a transaction begins.
- `beforeCompletion`. Called before the commit stage begins but after the client has completed its work. This allows the bean to do any preparations before the commit.
- `afterCompletion`. Called after the transaction completes—whether by rollback or by successful commit (a flag is passed as an argument).

While a session bean is not a persistent entity, it can still manage state on behalf of its client; its non-persistent nature simply implies that this state will not persist after the bean is destroyed. Distributed object applications can be generally classified as conforming to one of two models: the stateless model and the state-full model. In a stateless model, the server does not maintain state on behalf of the client; during each invocation, the client must pass enough information to the server in order for the server to successfully perform the operation on behalf of the client. The HTTP Web model is stateless—each request made by a browser for information served by a Web server is independent and does not rely on previous requests. In a state-full model the server maintains a session for the client and is aware of some state parameters regarding this client.

Both models of distributed interaction are legitimate, each being more appropriate in different cases. Enterprise JavaBeans, therefore, supports both models. When a session bean is deployed it defines how it should be managed by its container. By specifying that the bean is STATELESS, the container is told that no conversational state needs to be maintained and that it is possible for the same bean to be used by multiple clients (none of the clients need be aware of this fact since no state is managed within the server). Alternatively, the container may be told that the bean is STATEFUL, in which case the container will manage the bean's conversational state on behalf of the client. Conversational state is defined as the bean's field values and every object that is reachable from one of these fields. Obviously, since object-based applications manage quite complex object graphs, this definition of the conversational state can easily include a very large number of objects. Therefore, conversational state is not coupled with transaction support. A session bean's conversational state is not transactional and is not rolled back when a bean's transaction is rolled back. The bean developer is responsible for correctly managing conversational state in the context of transactions. Please note that while session beans are not persistent, they may be transactional in the sense of operations being atomic—the only difference being that the transaction outcome is not guaranteed to be persistent (or durable—the fourth word in the transaction-defining acronym ACID—Atomicity, Consistency, Isolation, and Durability).

Stateless beans should be viewed as workers belonging to a pool of service providers. The assignment of workers to clients is arbitrary, and creating a new instance of a stateless bean will simply add to the pool. The only allowed creation method in the home interface for a stateless session bean is a creation method taking no arguments. The size of the worker pool is controlled by the container and is based on load parameters and availability times.

State-full session beans have a much more elaborate lifecycle as shown in Figure 4-6. A bean is created when a client invokes a `create` method on the home interface. The container then calls `newInstance` to create the bean and sets the context using `setSessionContext`. Finally, `ejbCreate` is called and an EJB Object is returned to the client. The bean is then ready for use by the client.

As long as the client makes non-transactional calls, the bean stays in a non-transactional state. When a transactional method is called, the bean is included in a transaction and `afterBegin` is called, allowing the bean to perform any bean-specific handling. As long as other transactional methods are called, the bean stays in the transactional state. If a non-transactional method is called while the bean is in the transactional state an error is flagged.

If the transaction is about to commit, the container makes the `beforeCompletion` call (which is guaranteed to be delivered before the actual commit). The same is true when the transaction is about to

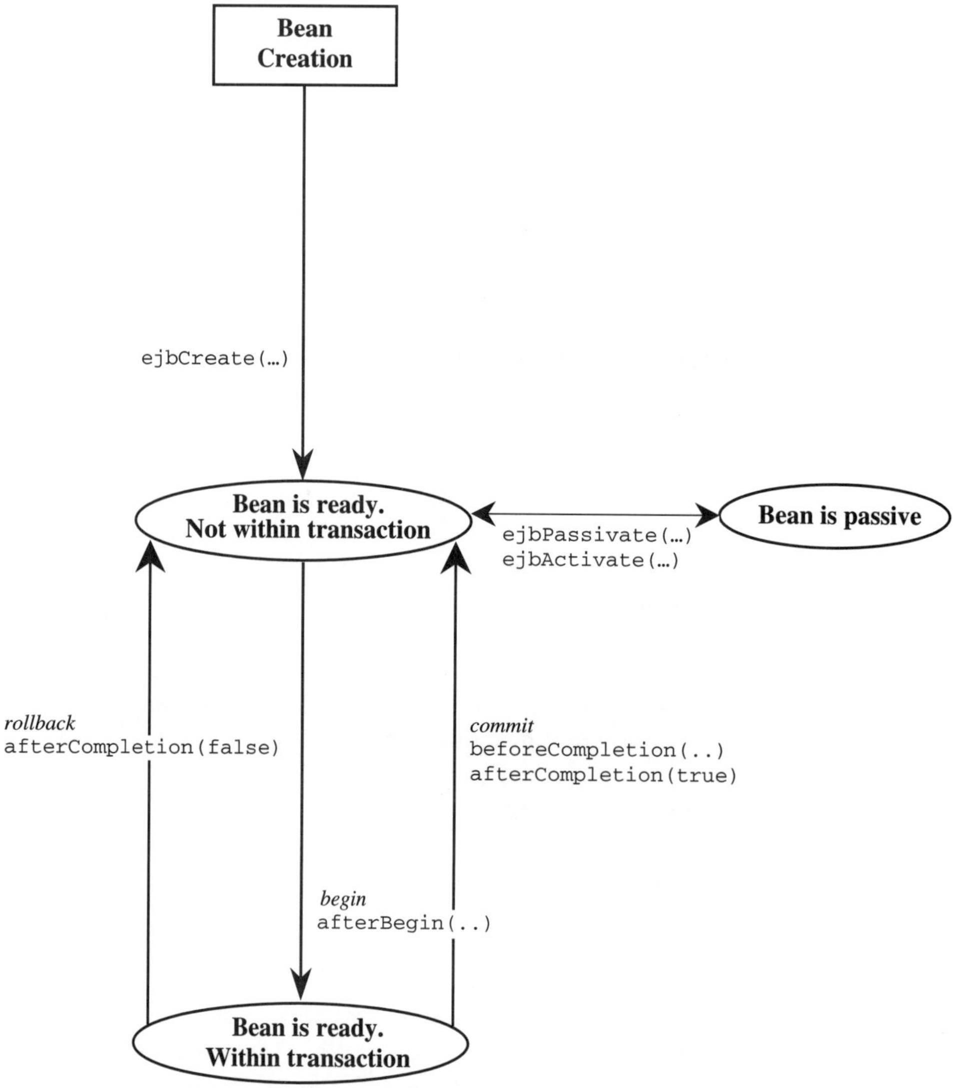

Figure 4-6
The lifecycle of a STATEFUL session bean.

be rolled back. The end transaction status is passed as an argument to the `afterCompletion` call.

While the bean is in a non-transactional state, the container may decide to evict the bean from memory. In this case it will call `ejbPassivate` to allow the bean to free up any resources it may be currently holding and prepare for its eviction. When the client later requests a service to be provided by this bean (recall that we are talking about state-full beans), the container will re-activate the bean and call the `ejbActivate` method giving the bean a chance to prepare itself.

Entity Enterprise Beans

Entity enterprise beans represent an object stored in some form of persistent storage. Entity beans include state that can be saved between different uses of the object. As a persistent object, an entity bean has an object identity which is created at the same time that the object is created and is fixed throughout the object's lifetime. The identity can be used to look up the object and serves as a primary key through which objects can be identified and compared.

Entity beans live within EJB containers that manage lifecycle, transactions, security, etc. In addition, containers manage the entity bean's persistence. Multiple clients may use the same entity bean concurrently. Synchronization is managed by the container in which the entity bean lives. A client accesses the entity bean by using the home interface that returns an EJB object that serves as the handle to the bean. In this respect the framework for entity beans is identical to session beans. Therefore, the rest of this section will focus on the differences introduced by entity beans and will not reiterate on what is common to session beans.

Like session beans, entity beans require a home interface that provides access to creation methods and finder methods. Unlike session beans, a home interface of an entity bean must implement the method `findByPrimaryKey`. This method provides access to entity beans using a primary key; this is possible since an entity bean is a persistent object that is uniquely identified by the primary key. Typical examples include an account number, a part order number, a country name, etc. A key is itself an object and can be of any type so long as it is serializable. Please note that a primary key is unique only within a home interface. The combination of a home interface and a primary key value is what uniquely identifies an object; in fact if two objects have the same home interface and have the same key value they are considered to be identical. The key is accessible by calling the `getPrimaryKey()` method implemented by the EJB object. Given two EJB objects one can use the following to determine if they are identical:

```
obj1.isIdentical(obj2)
```

As mentioned, an entity bean represents a persistent entity and is an application extension to an object residing in another system—the system that takes care of the persistence details. Examples include an object that is stored within a relational database as a set of records, or an object that interfaces with a legacy application that is responsible for the persistence details (see Figure 4-7).

There are two possibilities for entity bean persistence: bean-managed persistence and container-managed persistence. In the case of bean-managed persistence, the bean itself is responsible for implementing object persistence. For example, the bean developer may use JDBC or JSQL calls to implement load and save capabilities directly into the bean. In container-based persistence, the container performs database access on behalf of the bean. In order for the container to construct the appropriate

Figure 4-7 An entity bean's persistence.

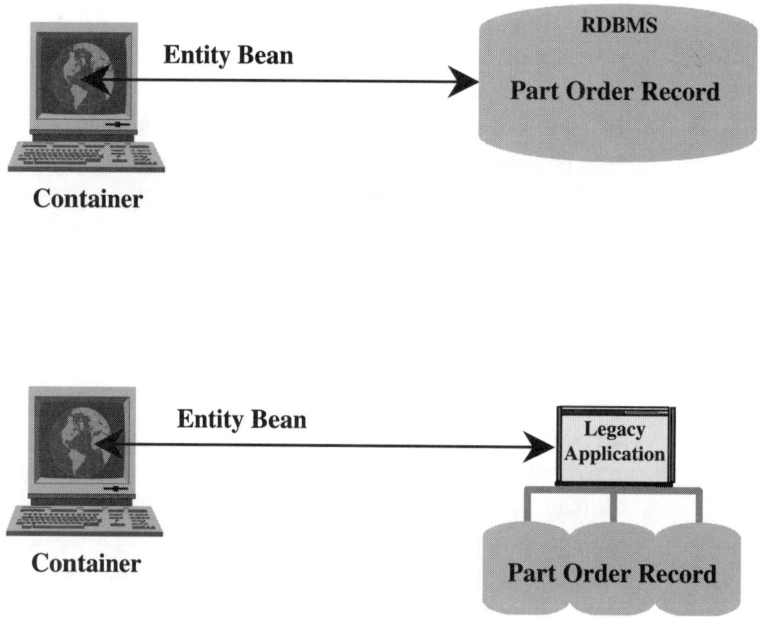

data access calls it requires descriptive meta-data from the bean. The entity bean protocol calls for a `containerManagedFields` deployment descriptor to be provided by the entity bean.

There are advantages and disadvantages to each of the persistence mechanisms. Bean-based persistence is obviously simpler to implement and conceptually clearer (anything involving two entities is inherently more complex than tasks that are performed by one party). However, bean-based persistence is hard coded into the bean and cannot remain persistence-neutral. Container-based persistence delays the coupling with the data store until the bean is deployed in some container, thus making the entity bean inherently more reusable.

Figure 4-8 depicts the lifecycle of an entity enterprise bean. An entity bean is created when the container calls the `newInstance` method (after which the context is set by calling the `setEntityContext` method). At this point the instance is part of a pool; it has been created but has not been associated with an EJB Object nor does it have any distinguishing data—all instances in the pool are equivalent. The next transition is to the ready state—this can be performed either by using an `ejbCreate` method or by calling an `ejbActivate` method following an `ejbFind` method invocation. Immediately after calling an `ejbCreate` method, the container calls the `ejbPostCreate` method. At the time the `ejbPostCreate` method is called the object identity is already available; the call allows the bean to take further action that may require the object identity. The first case creates a new object to service the client whereas the second allows for using an existing object. Once having entered the ready state, the container will activate the `ejbLoad` method to retrieve the bean's data from its persistent store; after that the container may periodically save the data using `ejbStore` or refresh the data using `ejbLoad`. When the work is complete the bean will transition back to the pooled state using one of `ejbPassivate` or `ejbRemove`. Once back in the pool the entity bean no longer has the object identity; the next time around it may be assigned to a new object.

Since entity beans represent domain objects, an entity bean may be accessed by two concurrent clients. Synchronization of concurrent access is one of the services provided to the bean user and bean developer by the container. It is the responsibility of the container to ensure correct synchronization between concurrent clients using the same entity bean. Figure 4-9 illustrates the two possible management strategies. In the first case the container manages two entity beans accessed through the same EJB object. Each of the two beans lives within a different transaction context—each transaction belonging to a different client. Ultimate

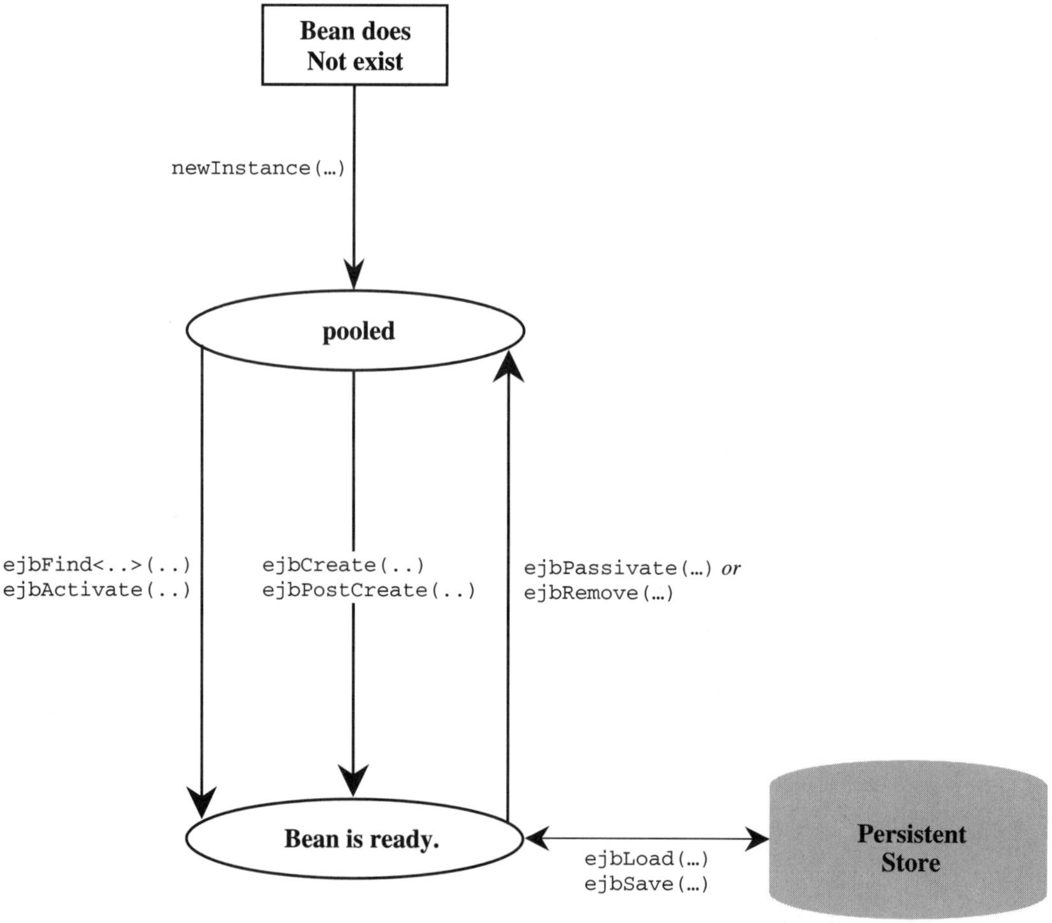

Figure 4-8
The lifecycle of an entity bean.

synchronization is performed by the data store when calling the `ejbLoad` and `ejbStore` methods. In the second case, the container manages exclusive access to the bean through the EJB Object. Only one bean exists and access to its functionality through the EJB Object is serialized. In most cases the first scenario is preferable for the following reasons.

- Better performance can be achieved.
- Database synchronization is usually more robust and has more features than container synchronization.

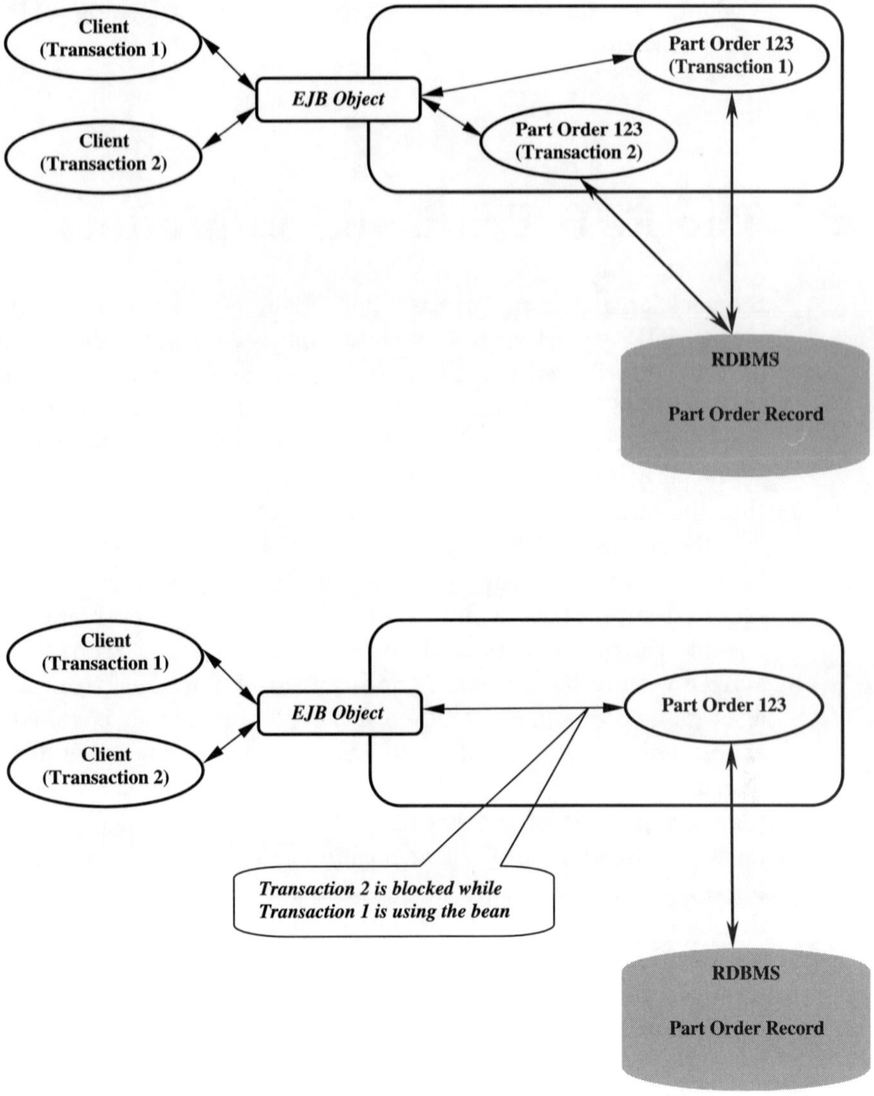

Figure 4-9
Managing concurrent access to an entity bean.

- In complex applications the database is often used by additional modules such as the reporting module, data extraction procedures, etc. It is, therefore, much safer to rely on transaction and locking management at the database level than within the EJB world.

- Containers do not need to incorporate complex locking and serialization code.

The EJB Transaction Model

Support for distributed transaction is one of the primary features that makes EJB attractive to enterprise software developers. Building support for distributed transactions into an application is a difficult task that is alleviated when using EJB. By moving the responsibility for managing transactions from the bean developer to the container and server provider, EJB simplifies application development and ensures that the difficult issues involving transactions are handled by experts.

EJB transaction support mirrors the CORBA Object Transaction Service (OTS) and supports the flat transaction model. OTS defines required support for a flat transaction model and optional support for nested transactions. Nested transactions allow for transactions to be started within the context of another transaction. Each transaction manages its own change set. When a nested transaction is rolled back, all changes made within that nested transaction are discarded. If the nested transaction is committed the changes made within the nested transaction become part of the enclosing transaction's change set (to be committed or rolled back by the enclosing transaction). In a nested model the top-level transactions often correspond to the database transactions. In this case the nested transactions are limited in that they are often not durable (i.e. persistent) because, right up to the moment in which a top-level commit occurs, the information is not stored in the database. EJB transaction support stays with the flat transaction model; this decision is based on the fact that today's database systems and transaction monitors support the flat transaction model.

EJB uses the Java Transaction Service (JTS), and specifically the Java Transaction API. JTS maps the OTS API to the Java programming language (i.e. it maps the OTS IDL definitions to Java using the IDL-to-Java language mapping). In addition, JTS is a Java mapping for the X/Open XA interface standard. The Java Transaction API provides a convenient set of Java interfaces to be used for transaction processing. Such conformance to standards ensures that JTS will remain the standard as far as transaction handling in Java.

The JTS `javax.transaction` package defines the application-level demarcation APIs, and allows transaction bracketing to be defined by the application developer. EJB relies on this interface, and more specifically on the `javax.transaction.UserTransaction` interface shown in Figure 4-10 (the EJB container provider only needs to implement this interface). Bean developers and clients make demarcation calls using APIs in this package.

Transaction demarcation may be performed by the client, by the bean, or by the container. Demarcation performed by the container is the simplest because both client and bean are oblivious to transactions. Obviously, the container must use policy information defined by the bean because the container is a generic entity that must adapt its behavior to the bean. In the case of transactions, the bean defines a demarcation policy through the transaction attribute. The container uses the fact that access to bean functionality must go through the container in order to manage transaction demarcation. The actual decision of what to do is based on the transaction attribute defined by the bean. Note that the policy may be defined globally for the entire bean or for one bean method at a time; therefore, it is possible for different transactional behaviors to occur for different methods. For example, a bean can set its transaction attribute to say that every method invocation must reside within its own transaction. In this case the container will start up a new transaction for every call made on the bean and manage the propagation of that transaction context if the bean makes additional calls during the processing of the original invocation. This scenario is shown in Figure 4-11.

Possible transaction attribute values are:

- TX_NOT_SUPPORTED. By using this value the bean notifies the container that it does not support transactions. Invocations coming through the container will not be within a transaction. The container guarantees this by suspending any transaction that is active during calls made on the bean.
- TX_BEAN_MANAGED. This attribute is used by the bean when it intends to use explicit demarcation and wants to notify the container that it should not manage transactions on its behalf.
- TX_REQUIRED. Used by beans that wish to ensure that any processing is performed within a transaction. If the call is made within a transaction started by a client, the bean invocation is performed within this transaction. Otherwise, the container is responsible for starting a transaction before handing control over

Interface javax.transaction.UserTransaction

public interface **UserTransaction**

The UserTransaction interface defines the methods that allow an application to explicitly manage transaction boundaries.

Field Index

•**STATUS_ACTIVE**

A transaction is associated with the target object and it is in the active state.

•**STATUS_COMMITTED**

A transaction is associated with the target object and it has been committed.

•**STATUS_COMMITTING**

A transaction is associated with the target object and it is in the process of committing.

•**STATUS_MARKED_ROLLBACK**

A transaction is associated with the target object and it has been marked for rollback, perhaps as a result of a setRollbackOnly operation.

•**STATUS_NO_TRANSACTION**

No transaction is currently associated with the target object.

•**STATUS_PREPARED**

A transaction is associated with the target object and it has been prepared, i.e.

•**STATUS_PREPARING**

A transaction is associated with the target object and it is in the process of preparing.

•**STATUS_ROLLEDBACK**

A transaction is associated with the target object and the outcome has been determined as rollback.

•**STATUS_ROLLING_BACK**

A transaction is associated with the target object and it is in the process of rolling back.

•**STATUS_UNKNOWN**

A transaction is associated with the target object but its current status cannot be determined.

Figure 4-10
The `javax.transaction.UserTransaction` interface.

Method Index

•**begin**()

Create a new transaction and associate it with the current thread.

•**commit**()

Complete the transaction associated with the current thread.

•**getStatus**()

Obtain the status of the transaction associated with the current thread.

•**rollback**()

Roll back the transaction associated with the current thread.

•**setRollbackOnly**()

Modify the transaction associated with the current thread such that the only possible outcome of the transaction is to roll back the transaction.

•**setTransactionTimeout**(int)

Modify the value of the timeout value that is associated with the transactions started by the current thread with the begin method.

Figure 4-10
(Cont'd)

to the bean. The container is also responsible for committing the transaction before returning control over to the caller.

- TX_SUPPORTS Used by beans that want to be invoked within the same scope as the client. If the client has a transaction open when calling the bean then the bean will perform within the transaction of the caller, otherwise it will perform without an active transaction.
- TX_REQUIRES_NEW. Beans using this value inform their container that they need to be invoked within the scope of a new transaction. No matter what the transaction state of the client, the container will always open a new transaction that will be active throughout the operation of the bean. When the bean completes, the container commits the transaction and resumes the suspended client transaction.
- TX_MANDATORY. Similar to TX_SUPPORTS in that the bean is activated within the transaction of the client. However, if a client without an open transaction tries to make the call, a

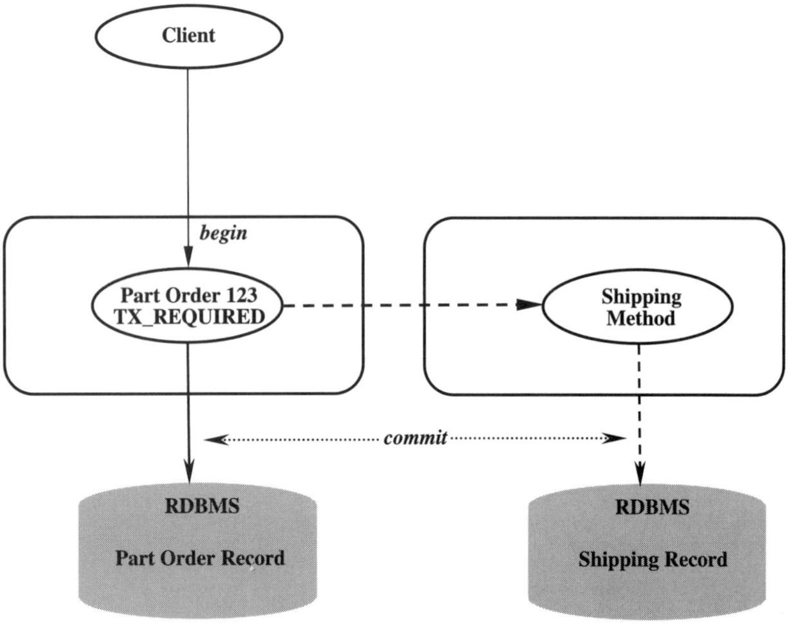

Figure 4-11 An example for container demarcation.

`TransactionRequired` exception is raised. This attribute is used by beans that need to be invoked within the context of the client transaction but wish to guarantee that they cannot be invoked without a transaction.

Another attribute that must be defined by beans in order for the container to manage transactions on its behalf is the transaction isolation level that controls the locking options for reads. These values mirror the options available in the `java.sql.Connection` interface. Possible values for transaction isolation levels are:

- TRANSACTION_READ_UNCOMMITTED. It is possible to read data that is marked as dirty (i.e. dirty reads); uncommitted data can be read.
- TRANSACTION_READ_COMMITTED. Dirty reads are prevented; only committed data can be read.
- TRANSACTION_REPEATABLE_READ. Dirty reads and non-repeatable reads are prevented.
- TRANSACTION_SERIALIZABLE. Transactions are serialized; one transaction must complete in order for another to proceed.
- TRANSACTION_NONE. No transaction is used.

Although container demarcation is certainly the simplest model for the client and bean developers, sometimes the set of possible values assigned and allowed as transaction attributes does not provide fine enough control over transaction demarcation. Both bean-managed and client-managed demarcation is allowed under the EJB transaction model. For bean-managed demarcation the bean will be defined using the TX_BEAN_MANAGED transaction attribute (informing the container that it should not manage transactions on behalf of the bean). The bean can then use the `javax.transaction.UserTransaction` interface. Beans that do not define TX_BEAN_MANAGED as their transaction attribute are not allowed to make direct calls to the underlying transaction manager. Alternatively, the client itself can use the `javax.transaction.UserTransaction` interface to *begin*, *commit*, and *rollback* transactions.

Since transactions may be managed by the container and the server, exceptions related to transactions may be raised—specifically, `TransactionRolledbackException`, `TransactionRequiredException`, `InvalidTransactionException`. Any exception-handling mechanism is, in general, a mechanism designed for situations in which the error detector (the object that raises the exception) may be a different object than the error handler (the object that catches the exception and can possibly try to take corrective measures). Therefore, raising an exception within the context of a container-managed transaction cannot automatically mean that the transaction must be marked for rollback only. It is quite possible that the client having caught the exception can fix the problem and continue with a follow-up call to the business method. The only case in which the client can assume that the current transaction has been marked for rollback is if the `TransactionRolledbackException` exception is raised. Alternatively, the exception handler can use the explicit test of `getRollbackOnly()` to verify the status of the active transaction. Beans that manage their own transaction processing (i.e. that use TX_BEAN_MANAGED) should use the `setRollbackOnly()` call before raising the exception depending on whether the error that they have discovered is such that it should not allow the changes made thus far to commit.

The EJB Distribution Model

EJB targets large-scale distributed object applications. Therefore, distribution is fundamental to the definition of EJB. Application programming in the EJB world involves building the enterprise beans and the clients using the business functionality implemented by the beans. The containers, servers, and other EJB infrastructure objects are provided by vendors and are used to simplify building the distributed applications. Therefore, the EJB distribution model must be simple enough that application programmers can use it, yet powerful enough to build mission-critical and large-scale applications.

In order to do so the EJB distribution model uses a proven distribution technology based on proxies and object stubs. The EJB distribution model is not a new model; it uses standard Java RMI based on the CORBA distribution model. Distribution transparency is complete from both sides. Enterprise bean functionality may be accessed locally or remotely and clients can access enterprise beans with no regard to their actual physical location. Neither the client nor the enterprise bean is aware of its peer's location.

The Java RMI stubs created involve the EJB Object and the home interface object. Since the EJB Object is the interface object through which functionality is accessed, it is only natural for it to be the object for which a Java RMI stub is created. In addition, the home interface gets its own RMI stub; this is necessary to initiate the connection with the enterprise bean (either through creation or through a finder process). Figure 4-12 depicts the RMI stubs used to support location transparency in EJB.

Using Java RMI as the stubs and interfaces for supporting distribution in EJB does not infer on the underlying wire-level protocol. In fact, the preferred solution for EJB in terms of the network protocol is CORBA IIOP. By using IIOP, EJB ensures that its distribution model remains interoperable and open to interfacing with non-Java objects and legacy systems. The basing of EJB on CORBA IIOP is quite natural; after all, the distribution model is identical, EJB transactions are based on the CORBA OTS model, and both use the same object model. Even the naming issue is resolved by mapping the CORBA naming service (part of the Common Object Services—COS) to the JNDI API. Finally, EJB security (discussed in the next section) is mapped to CORBA security (using `CORBA::Principal` for mapping the user ID, IIOP over SSL for client

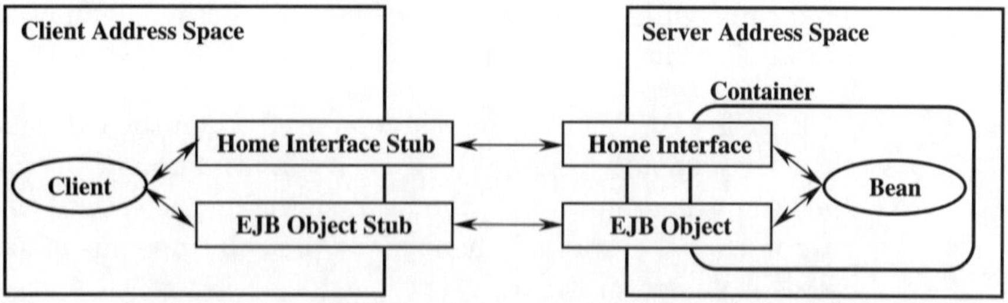

Figure 4-12
EJB stubs.

authentication and encryption, and the SECIOP—Secure IIOP—for mapping to a specific security mechanism such as GSSKerberos).

EJB Security

As in transactions, the primary goal of EJB in terms of its security infrastructure is to provide a set of interfaces that allow the responsibility for implementing security to be moved from the enterprise bean developer to the container and server implementor. This does not mean that an enterprise bean cannot control security; it means that mechanisms are provided so that the typical enterprise bean can declaratively define what its security attributes are, allowing the implementation details to be handled by the server and container. As in transactions, this is achieved through a set of security attributes used at deployment time.

Through the `AccessControlEntry` attribute, a bean defines rules for defining an access control policy. An `AccessControlEntry` can be defined per method or for the entire bean. Methods that do not have their own access control entries assume the access control value associated with the bean as a whole. Each access control entry defines a list of authorized users; each authorized entry being of type `java.security.Identity`, the standard interface in Java used for access control identification and authorization.

Additional deployment attributes related to security include the `RunAsMode` and `RunAsIdentity` attributes. The `RunAsMode` defines the security identity that will be propagated when the bean makes additional calls while servicing a client request. Possible values that may be assumed by this attribute are:

- CLIENT_IDENTITY. This value is used when the call made by the bean should assume the security information of the client making the original call; the bean servicing the second call will think that the original client made the call (in terms of security). This is shown in Figure 4-13.
- SYSTEM_IDENTITY. The call will use the identity of a privileged system account.
- SPECIFIED_IDENTITY. The call will be made using a specific user account.

The `RunAsIdentity` attribute is relevant only when the `RunAsMode` attribute has a SPECIFIED_IDENTITY; in this case it defines the actual user identity to be used when making the second call.

SanFrancisco and EJB

As already mentioned, Release 1.2 of the SanFrancisco frameworks is not yet EJB compliant (and neither is Release 1.3). However, as part of IBM's continuous commitment to EJB, the SanFrancisco marketing and development organization released a paper in April of 1999 that defines the proposed migration of the SanFrancisco frameworks to EJB technology. This includes a very general time line (the migration plan is expected to take between 12 and 24 months!). In a sense, this migration aligns all of the different IBM initiatives including the SanFrancisco frameworks, the WebSphere server family, and the VisualAge development environment to form what is certainly one of the most powerful offerings for developing large-scale three-tier Java-based enterprise systems.

Figure 4-13
CLIENT_IDENTITY.

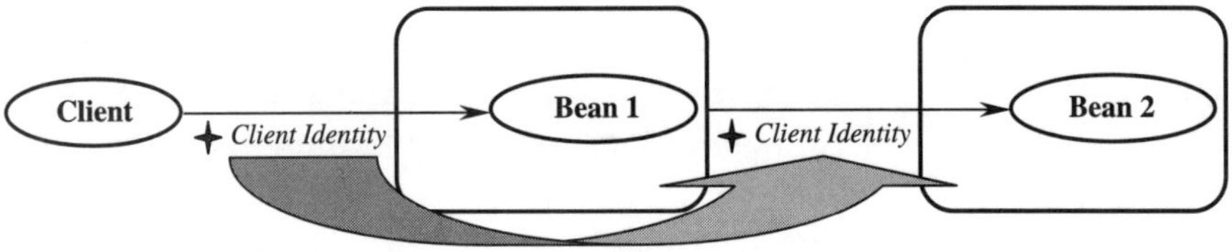

The commitment made by the SanFrancisco marketing and development organization consists of the following points:

- The Common Business Objects and the Core Business Process frameworks will be migrated to become EJB components.
- The initial migration will make CBO and CBP components run within the WebSphere Application Server—Advanced Edition. Other EJB servers will be supported at a later time although only WebSphere Enterprise Edition has been explicitly named.
- IBM will provide tools that will aid in porting applications based on SanFrancisco Version 1 to the EJB-based SanFrancisco frameworks. The estimate is that these tools will automate 90 percent of the conversion effort.
- A new client framework will be provided in Release 1.4. This client framework aims as decoupling the client code from server functionality and enables a smoother migration to an EJB-based design.

In terms of the actual migration process for applications using the current versions of the SanFrancisco frameworks, the following activities should be expected:

- Code created from models using the SanFrancisco code generator will need to be regenerated. The initial generator will not provide for automated merging of added code; this can be expected later with the introduction of the Merge-Free Forward Generation (MFFG) generator.
- Client code will need to be rebuilt to make use of the new client architecture; this will facilitate an automated conversion process to the EJB frameworks. The new client architecture will be part of the 1.4 release, allowing application developers to migrate their client code in advance.
- Persistence schemas will be converted to EJB persistence using a schema definition migration tool. An additional tool will convert the actual data stored in relational databases to the format required for EJB entity objects.

In terms of the time line, the suggested migration path will begin as of Version 1.4 with the introduction of a set of tools, porting instructions, a new client architecture, and a technology preview for the EJB frameworks. This technology preview will include ports of several CBOs and foundation services and will be used to validate the concept of repackaging the SanFrancisco frameworks as EJB components. The major effort to be done in this release is the migration to the new client architecture. The defined time frame for this stage is end-1999. The second stage, to be completed sometime in the year 2000, will include a significant subset of CBOs and CBPs. The final stage will include all frameworks and services and is slated for 6 to 12 months after stage two.

PART 2

A SanFrancisco Primer

CHAPTER 5

An Overview of the SanFrancisco Frameworks

Project SanFrancisco started out when several large IBM customers came up to IBM and asked for assistance in upgrading a set of enterprise-level, mission-critical applications to new technologies. These companies had large application suites in various business domains and were interested in replacing the old technology base (often COBOL running on a mainframe) to object-oriented, network-centric architectures. The implications of a widespread technology migration and application rewrite were such that these companies requested guidance and assistance from their large vendor—IBM.

As the relationship with IBM around the technology migration was formulated, a few areas in which IBM could assist were defined. Technology adoption, retraining, and knowledge transfer were areas in which IBM could clearly help. Help in analysis and design was another area; skilled developers and analysts from IBM could be involved with internal development projects to bootstrap processes and make sure that designs were done correctly. But as the relationships formed, it became clear that more was necessary. As is always the case with new technologies, they hold much promise, but initially lack many infrastructure components that come with years of use and market maturity. Multitier software architectures and network-centric application infrastructure are no exception. The companies working with IBM (along with IBM itself) identified fairly early on that they would all benefit greatly if some infrastructure components were put in place that could then be reused throughout the business systems being created. And so project SanFrancisco was born.

Project SanFrancisco started with wide-scale analysis of the business systems for which it would be used. It was then constructed as a set of business process components that could be reused within multiple business systems and multiple domains. Quite early on, the fundamental structure of project SanFrancisco was set to make use of the notion of object-oriented frameworks (as opposed to class libraries, for example). As such, SanFrancisco provides an infrastructure, a consistent design and programming model, along with default business logic that can be changed and extended. Although reusable object-oriented software components are certainly not new to the software industry, and even in terms of frameworks the market has already seen some excellent implementations, SanFrancisco is certainly the largest, most complete set of frameworks to date. In addition, SanFrancisco is one of the first examples of a framework that includes high-level business functionality; most frameworks used today solve low-level system issues and user interface functionality only.

So what is the state of SanFrancisco? SanFrancisco is currently in its third public release (Release 1.3 as of October 1998). It is a collaborative effort led by IBM, involving hundreds of international independent software vendors (ISVs) who are willing to base their system architecture on the SanFrancisco frameworks, and are willing to help stabilize and form the ultimate structure of SanFrancisco. In addition, a number of tool vendors are working with IBM in order to create a functional-rich development environment for developing with the SanFrancisco frameworks.

This chapter provides an introduction to the SanFrancisco frameworks. It provides a very high-level overview of the different pieces of the framework in order to ensure that the scope of SanFrancisco is clear. Along with the next chapter (which provides a little more insight into the architecture of the SanFrancisco frameworks), it provides a "big picture" before we delve down into the details.

Object-Oriented Frameworks

SanFrancisco is structured as a set of object-oriented frameworks. So, before we can discuss SanFrancisco, we should make sure we all agree on what is an object-oriented framework and why IBM (and most of the industry today) believes that frameworks can dramatically improve the software development process.

Software is amazingly complex. It is very difficult to build large software systems. The software crisis is well documented—but less so solved. While software engineering has made many advances over the past two decades, it is still in its infancy and has yet to actually affect day-to-day development. Probably the most pragmatic approach to improving the development process has been the widespread adoption of object-oriented technologies that promote componentization and software reuse. The fundamental concept here is simple—code that is not written cannot break; therefore, instead of writing code, let's use code written by someone else. If that code is stable and well tested, we may be able to save ourselves a lot of time and money.

Sounds simple doesn't it? Well, it's not! The principle of reuse is sound and it does actually work. Scale and flexibility are the problems. Modern enterprise software systems need to deal with a plethora of issues. They are usually interactive and need to have a good graphical user interface. They interface with other systems. They provide networking features.

They need to run on multiple platforms. They need to exhibit some form of fault tolerance. They need to be customized by the user, etc. etc. Therefore, even if software components and libraries are available for all (or most) of infrastructure issues, just combining them and adding the business logic may be (and usually is) a daunting task. If the libraries are large, just learning them requires considerable effort, and reaching the point in which they can be utilized to their fullest extent is never accomplished. The fact that reusable components and libraries usually follow different programming models (since they are created by independent parties) does not help one bit.

Let's look at the life of a typical corporate or enterprise software vendor developer. One day, management decides that a new system needs to be built; obviously they want all the latest and greatest technologies. A team is formed and two tasks commence: domain analysis is started to form requirements and analysis documents for the system and a process begins for defining the system architecture and the tools to be used. Nothing simpler—right? Wrong! Suppose you are tasked with leading the process for evaluating and selecting tools and for defining some system architecture aspects. You've read all the hype and the future looks just peachy—just pick a lot of off-the-shelf components and 80 percent of the system will be done. Not so fast—which components do you pick? How do you evaluate them? You make a list of the relevant libraries you will use. You then grab hold of every periodical you can get your hands on, surf the Web, and read a lot of technology rags; the number of component libraries you need to evaluate turns out to be around 20. Every review you read seems to imply that the discussed library is excellent. You start evaluating the possibilities and quickly find out that it will take you longer to complete a serious evaluation of these libraries than you have allocated for the entire project!! So instead, you end up picking almost randomly. If you're lucky, you picked well and get a usable set of libraries. If not, you'll spend a lot of time learning about the deficiencies and will end up throwing the library away and converting to something else.

In any case, even if you're lucky, you haven't quite finished yet. Each of these libraries provides you with a very large set of reusable building blocks. The problem is that software building blocks are not quite like Lego blocks. Each one is different and it takes a long time to learn how to put them together in the right ways. In fact, mastering a component library is something that takes a lot of time. There is a lot of knowledge that is not apparent from the component library structure; knowledge that is similar to design patterns in the field of software engineering. The patterns are crucial to correct usage of the libraries—they form the glue that differentiates between a set of disparate API calls and between consistent and efficient use of the reusable components. In fact, we believe that one of the best definitions for a framework is a set of reusable components and operational patterns that are directly formulated as code.

Object-oriented frameworks promise to dramatically improve the software development process by integrating a set of reusable and extensible classes that provide well-defined sets of functionalities. Frameworks are not building blocks; they are fully functional out-of-the-box, yet they can be extended through delegation or subclassing. They are best viewed as well-designed structures and templates of a working system providing well-defined behavior along with pre-built dimensions in which this behavior can be extended. Frameworks provide infrastructure and design. The internal wiring between the reusable components making up the framework ensures that the architectural model and the design of the framework are preserved. Since good design is the most crucial element in the fight for superior software, frameworks promise much in elevating software development to a greater height. In addition, since frameworks provide more working code than do component libraries, frameworks typically require even less code from application developers constructing a system. Application developers typically change only things that deviate from the framework code and are specific to their own organization.

Most frameworks to date are system-level frameworks such as application management frameworks and user interface frameworks. Domain-level frameworks (such as SanFrancisco) are potentially even more important. Since a framework embodies working functionality, a domain-level framework can embody a design for a complete business application, which allows specifics to be added by application developers. Since "a framework is a set of classes that embodies an abstract design for solutions to a family of related problems" [JOOP1_2], the solutions provided by domain-level frameworks are extremely valuable.

What are the distinguishing features of frameworks? Frameworks solve problems and, as such, they have at least the structure than an application would have. Therefore, frameworks include the so-called "main loop" that forms the main event loop. As opposed to the use of class libraries in which the application controls the flow and calls the library components, a framework controls the main application processing and calls out to the custom code added by the extending developer. The code added by the application developer must conform to the framework design, ensuring that the end result is a well-designed system. Actual extension of behavior takes one of two forms: derivation from framework classes or creation of aggregations of instances from custom classes that are called upon from within the framework. Both have their advantages and disadvantages. Derivation-based frameworks are more flexible in their ability to extend behavior but require considerable work to do so. Composition-based frameworks use a data-driven approach that makes customization easier but is more limited since the degrees of freedom are fixed while designing the framework. Obviously, combining the two approaches (and using the best of both worlds) ensures the best results.

Project SanFrancisco is a melding of three of IBM's dominant commitments to the software industry—two of which are technology oriented and one driven by a client-centric approach. IBM is fully dedicated to Java and is backing this commitment with a large set of tools and solutions—one of these being SanFrancisco. SanFrancisco not only illustrates the commitment to Java but also to e-commerce (or e-business as advertised by IBM). The SanFrancisco foundation implements all that is needed to build robust mission-critical applications in a Web environment, including support for multiple users, multiple platforms, transaction processing, etc. In addition, IBM (through its investment in Taligent) views object-oriented frameworks as the preferred approach to translating functionality provided by Java components to useful business systems. Hence, the SanFrancisco project was structured as a set of interrelated frameworks that together bring much more to the table than would each of its components separately. The third commitment made by IBM was to its customer base; the SanFrancisco frameworks do not stop at the system level as do other frameworks but rather provide many components that are useful at the business level, including core business objects and domain-specific business processes. So what does SanFrancisco bring to the table as domain-level frameworks?

> *... offering solution developers business process components, designed as frameworks that provide an object-oriented infrastructure, a consistent programming model, and some default business logic that can be used to start building applications. The frameworks make it easier to move to object-oriented technology because developers use well-tested services instead of building their own. They can design their solutions using a proven programming model instead of developing their unique approach. ... The frameworks provide some basic business logic that can be enhanced and extended instead of having to build the entire application*

from scratch. Developers can build their application by modifying and extending the default business objects and logic instead of having to start their application from raw requirements statements. This allows developers to apply more development resources on the functions that will give them a competitive advantage since much of the basic application function is supplied by the framework. ... Feedback from companies that tested early versions of the code shows that the frameworks provide about 40% of a typical working application within the supported domains (SanFrancisco Project Technical Summary).

The Layers of SanFrancisco

Although SanFrancisco includes many frameworks, services, and utilities, the core of the environment are three software layers with increasing proximity to business applications: the foundation layer, the Common Business Objects (CBO) layer, and the Core Business Processes (CBR) layer. Each of these layers relies on the previous layer (see Figure 5-1). The foundation layer implements the infrastructure and services available for all objects participating in the SanFrancisco environment. It supports the notion of object persistence, transaction processing, distribution and location transparency, naming, security, ownership, etc. It is the largest layer and the one providing context-free infrastructure-related support that is surely useful for all applications. The Common Business Objects layer implements a set of elementary business objects that are common to a very large set of business domains. These objects include addresses, money-related objects, customer and location, etc. The final layer, the Core Business Processes, provides complete sets of business objects and processes that form sets of mini-applications, and includes working functionality that is useful in the relevant domains. This layer is actually not one layer but rather a set of vertical layers, each one providing support in a certain domain. Naturally, the first verticals to be selected were those most relevant to IBM customers and, as time goes on, additional verticals will be added. By understanding and using both the Core Business Processes and the Common Business Objects, one can customize the SanFrancisco frameworks, either through derivation or composition (or a combination of both), making the end result extremely attractive. The simplest reuse scenario involves the use of business objects and processes out of the box while setting proper-

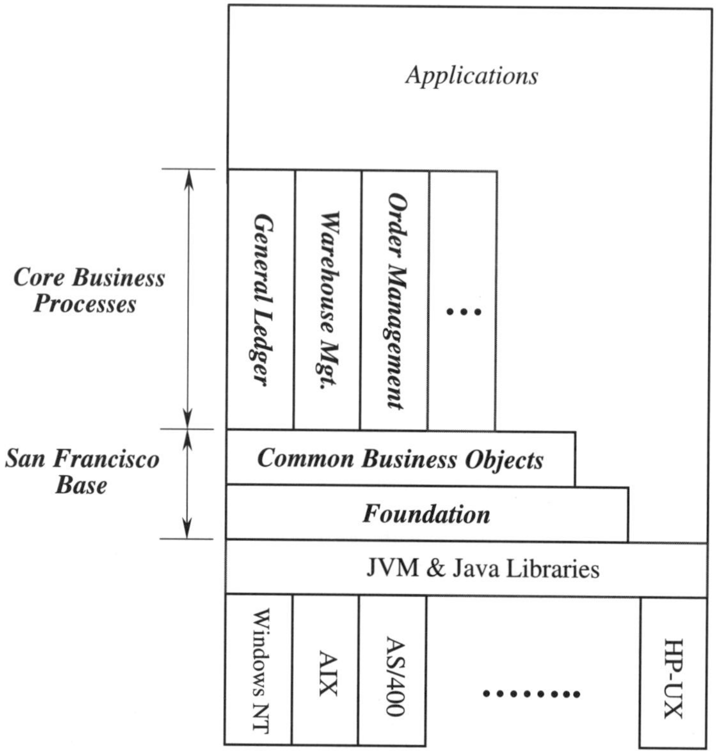

Figure 5-1 SanFrancisco framework layers.

ties that are built-in parameters of the business objects. The next level of complexity allows you to alter the way in which objects are created and define which class to be used for instantiating a certain business concept. By supplying your own extension to the business class you can customize behavior while remaining within the framework. Alternatively you can fully extend a domain's class through substitution or through derivation and modification of functionality.

As shown in Figure 5-1, the foundation layer and the Common Business Objects layer form the SanFrancisco Base. The base layers provide the services and underlying object support required for building multitier, distributed, object-oriented applications along with a fundamental set of objects that conform to the SanFrancisco patterns. This not only allows the application builder to be semi-oblivious to the difficulties involved with complex application architectures, it also helps to jump-start the development process. The Core Business Processes complement the base with rich functionality in various domains, with all building occurring at the base. As Figure 5-1 shows, an application builder is not limited in how the frameworks may be used. Applications can be built within one (or more) of the Core Business Processes (in which case SanFrancisco can provide the most bang for the buck). If the domain is not covered by one of the process frameworks, or the functionality provided is too different from the one required, the application can make use of the Common Business Objects layer as a set of reusable business objects that function within the SanFrancisco environment. This use will save a lot of development time and even more testing time, but will still require more work than the use of a Core Business Process layer. Finally, new business objects will sometimes be created directly over the foundation. In this case the new business objects will make use of the underlying services only—which solve the most complex of issues in the system architecture. Obviously, any combination of the described alternatives are possible; an application may use parts of the Core Business Processes, some of the Common Business Objects directly, combined with a set of objects using foundation services. Once all pieces of the application use the foundation services, the objects will work in tandem.

We mentioned that as long as objects are built over the foundation layer, they form a coherent application structure. Building objects that are external to the foundation and work at the application level is much more difficult and is not suggested. As long as objects use the foundation services and conform to the SanFrancisco patterns they can participate in the SanFrancisco world and thus make use of the benefits. Objects not built in this way need to solve many difficult problems such as persistence, transactions, etc. Even worse, if you do decide to do so you will have to synchronize and maintain the two models. For example, if you have a single business transaction that includes objects using the base, and objects that require self-management for transactions, you will somehow have to synchronize all of this into one transaction—something that you really should not attempt without serious "adult" supervision.

The SanFrancisco base, and especially the foundation layer, are extremely important in the sense of implementation neutrality and may be viewed as an extension to Java and CORBA in terms of the level in which neutrality may be achieved (see Figure 5-2). Java provides hardware and operating system neutrality by basing all application code on Java bytecodes that drive the Java virtual machine. By building your application using Java you attain one level of platform neutrality and portability. CORBA provides an additional level of portability and interoperability by supporting location transparency. By using CORBA you can hide details regarding physical location and support application functionality that

Figure 5-2 Levels of independence.

San Francisco Base	*Application Infrastructure*	**Transactions, security, persistence, concurrency, synchronization, error handling, and much more.**
CORBA	*Distribution*	**Object references, invocations, primitive services (through CORBA Services), ...**
Java	*Operating System*	**User interface widgets, files, communication protocols, ...**

can be distributed across various configurations. The SanFrancisco foundation layer allows you to achieve another level of portability by encapsulating capabilities and services in application infrastructure areas such as persistence, transactions, security, etc. By building on the SanFrancisco base you ensure that any vendor product conforming to SanFrancisco and supporting its APIs will be an option for you to use in your application. The extent in which neutrality and independence is achieved is considerably greater because the abstractions you can rely on are closer to the application level.

The Foundation Layer

The foundation layer is part of the SanFrancisco base and is perhaps the layer that is functionally the most important. It supplies the underlying infrastructure necessary for building SanFrancisco applications including a set of services and utilities. The foundation layer is the lowest level at which SanFrancisco may be used and in most practical scenarios some application components will be built directly over the foundation (as opposed to a reuse of higher levels of the framework).

The foundation layer encapsulates application services. This means two things: it means that it provides these services, but also that it hides many implementation details regarding these services. Therefore, by basing the entire application over the foundation layer, an application can remain independent from the implementation of these services. In a world that is constantly moving towards standards-based products (be they formal standards or de-facto standards), this is of great benefit to the application developer. Many of the services provided by the foundation layer are based on the CORBA Services specification defined by the Object Management Group (OMG). Examples include the transaction service, security, persistence, and more. See Cutout 5-1 for more details regarding CORBA Services.

Although SanFrancisco is certainly CORBA based and CORBA Services based, a word of caution is in order. SanFrancisco is not dependent on CORBA and does not include an ORB in its distribution. The communication infrastructure is based on Java Remote Method Invocation (RMI—see Cutout 5-2) and not directly on CORBA; through the integration between Java and CORBA (and specifically between RMI and IIOP), CORBA is enabled for the SanFrancisco foundation layer. As for services, most of the SanFrancisco implementations of CORBA Services are compatible. For example, SanFrancisco supports optimistic and pessimistic locking as defined by the CORBA Concurrency Control Service specification. Cutout 5-3 details the differences between optimistic and pessimistic locking.

Services provided by the foundation layer are encapsulated and abstracted within a set of base classes called the Object Model Classes. These classes form an object model that is the basic structure of SanFrancisco objects and provide the consistent programming model within SanFrancisco applications. The Object Model Classes include a number of classes that form the basic types in the systems—types not in terms of a certain application domain but rather in terms of structural types. These types categorize objects into a set of fundamental behaviors that differ in how they are managed within the application frameworks and especially in the overall lifecycle. For example, objects can be categorized into objects that represent a distinguished entity and may be referenced by many other objects, or to objects that are contained in other objects and have no existence outside their container. The Object Model Classes include a base class called `Entity` for the first category and a base class called `Dependent` for the second. The most important classes forming the Object Model Classes are:

- `Entity` and `Dependent`. These base classes represent the business objects in the system. Domain-level business objects and support objects used for managing a user interface will typically be implemented by a class that inherits from one of these two classes. These two classes form the primary hierarchy for business objects and objects supporting application functionality. A common base class is very common in object libraries because it allows definition of framework functionality at the root level. Both

Cutout 5-1
CORBA services.

ORBs provide the mechanism for making requests and performing operations in a platform-independent way; they are the fundamental component in any OMG-based technology. However, CORBA is but the foundation of a usable object-centric technology; it does not provide capabilities that will be required by application developers. CORBA provides the messaging facility that is the base of any object-oriented distributed environment; however, this is not enough. Based upon this foundation, the OMG Reference Model goes on to define other component categories that must be populated to ensure a technology that is usable for building applications. This includes *CORBA Services* (also called *Object Services*), which are low-level support functions that are used by applications, and *CORBA Facilities* (also called *Common Facilities*), which are higher-level functions such as I/O, mail, compound document architectures, work groups, etc. As with other architectures, the OMG Reference Model takes a layered approach. First CORBA was defined. Once the underlying messaging facility was available, the low-level service functionalities can be defined. After that, higher service functions can be defined. The most important category and the one where most work has been done (outside of CORBA itself) within the OMG is the Object Services sector. Object services are a collection of services that any software component may rely upon. These services comprise a basic set of functionalities that may be assumed by application developers.

Object Services provide a set of functionalities that are available to application developers regardless of their platform or environment. Therefore, object Services form (with CORBA) an architecture for allowing the creation of portable object-based systems. As a set of basic functionalities available to all developers, object services must be available in a platform, language, and environment-independent way. Object services must also be defined in a way that allows multiple implementations, each assuming slightly different traits. The same service could be provided in multiple ways, each one being most suitable for different sets of applications. Thus, object services are typically specified as sets of interfaces; this allows them to be both independent of the environment as well as allow multiple mappings to various implementations. These interfaces are expressed as IDL interfaces. Note that this does not imply anything about the implementations of the services; the implementations need not be object oriented at all.

The definition of services follows a development plan defined by two documents: the Object Services Architecture (OSA) document ([Thompson]) and the Object Service Roadmap (OSRM) document ([Lewis1]). The OSA details the goals of the Object Services and the role they perform. It then goes on to list the architectural goals and the requirements that services should address. It outlines a set of conventions and guidelines that should be followed by services. The OSRM is a companion document to the OSA that provides additional details regarding the Request for Proposal (RFP) process. It specifies the general structure required of RFPs, the process that will be followed, and the criteria to be used for evaluation of proposals submitted to the Object Services Task Force (OSTF). The OSA and the OSRM define a framework that is followed by all object services. This framework includes a specification of architectural requirements, policies, and guidelines, and includes the following points:

- Object Services should define functionality, not implementation. This allows multiple implementations to be provided for a service. The OSA uses a concept called "Quality of Service." Quality of service (QOS) is used to distinguish between different implementations for the same service. For example, a direct tradeoff may exist within some services between performance and flexibility. Therefore, the same service can be provided by

Cutout 5-1
(Cont'd)

an implementation that stresses performance at the cost of dynamic flexibility, whereas another implementation can stress flexibility at the cost of additional indirection levels (translating into reduced performance). These differing implementations of the same service are both justified; different applications may require the same functionalities but have different considerations—thus stressing different goals.

- Services are defined by sets of interfaces. This is the Application Programming Interface (API) by which they are used. A specification of an object service is primarily the specification of the interfaces supporting it. Interfaces are provided in IDL and are object oriented.
- Services contain multiple sets of interfaces. A service typically supplies three sets of interfaces: functional interfaces, management interfaces, and construction interfaces. Functional interfaces are used by application developers and by Object Facilities developers (accessing the service functionality). Management interfaces provide administrative functions that might be needed for correct operation of the service, and construction interfaces are used by the service itself for internal management.
- Although it may be possible for certain services to require extensions to CORBA (e.g. the Security Service), such extensions should be minimized. CORBA 2.0 introduces the notion of ORB Services to support a common structural alternative to such extensions.
- Services should provide a single and focused set of functionalities. Services should not be cohesive but rather modular. Users will then be able to use different services to achieve higher-level functionalities. It is preferable that such dependencies and coupling are formed at higher levels while the services remain as independent and encapsulated as possible.
- Services should have a consistent style.

The following service definitions are part of the CORBA Services specifications:

Naming Services allow a name to be bound to an object within a certain naming context. This name can then be used to provide access to the object. This supports basic capabilities for name-based object management, which is extremely important in most object-based systems. Naming contexts allow different name space scopes to be used. Naming contexts make up a graph of name spaces that can be managed in a distributed and scaleable manner. The naming model itself is designed to be generic, and to support many implementation decisions and commercially available naming facilities in object-based systems.

The Event Notification Service provides a distributed and scaleable facility for delivering event information from event suppliers to event consumers. The service is designed as a collection of building blocks that can be composed in various ways to provide multiple behaviors (e.g. point-to-point or multicast, reliable or unreliable, synchronous or asynchronous, and various push or pull models). Different levels of support can be provided through the use of different building blocks and models that are part of the Event Notification Service. The provided interfaces may be subtyped by users that require functionalities not provided in the base service.

Lifecycle Services include the creation, deletion, copying, and moving of objects. These are fundamentally important to any working object-based environment. CORBA defined how requests are issued to objects, but it never specified how objects were created (except that they could be returned from invocations). Therefore, dif-

Cutout 5-1
(Cont'd)

ferent commercial implementations were forced to come up with their own support for such issues. The Lifecycle Service fills this void with a design, a set of services, and a set of conventions for lifecycle operations in a distributed environment. The Lifecycle Service uses a concept called a *Factory Object*. These objects are used to create other objects. Factory Objects are not special in any way; they are defined by an IDL interface and have no special characteristics. Many commercial implementations of first-generation ORBs had a similar concept of factories.

The Persistence Service is implemented by the Persistent Storage Manager (PSM), which provides for the management of a CORBA object's persistent state. The service is often called the PSM because it is not directly accessed through the ORB, but rather uses a separate API. In this respect it is similar to a pseudo-object. The PSM is a lightweight mechanism. It is not intended to replace Object Database Management Systems (ODMSs). Actually, the PSM was designed to be consistent with the ODMG specifications so that an application using the PSM could later replace it with a full ODBMS. Therefore, the PSM does not handle such issues as concurrent access or multi-user transactions.

Relationships (often also called Associations; see [RBPEL]) are constructs that are used for representing semantically meaningful relationships between objects. Object references are useful in implementing such relationships when a first-class mechanism is not available. However, real relationship structures (as defined by the Relationship Service) provide many added benefits. For example, the relationship itself can have attributes and is responsible for ensuring referential integrity and the elimination of dangling pointers. In addition, the Relationship Service may cooperate with other services to provide higher-level functionalities (e.g. cooperation between the Lifecycle Service and the Relationship Service for supporting distributed object graphs).

Externalization of an object means creating an external representation of the object's internal state. This representation can then be saved (possibly to disk). The Externalization service implies support for internalization; therefore, the representation that was the result of the externalization process could be used to reconstruct the internal state of the object. This combination can be used for a variety of lifecycle-type and persistence-type operations. For example, an externalization/internalization combination can be used to copy objects or to save an object's representation for later use.

Controlling concurrent access to objects is the goal of the Concurrency Control Service; basically, the Concurrency Service deals with locks. Since everything in the OMA Reference Model will have an object-oriented interface, this service will provide the necessary mechanisms for building multi-program and multi-user environments. Without such a service any environment is extremely limited since it may be difficult to enforce consistent behavior. The Concurrency Service is not intended to enforce a certain concurrency model. There are many concurrency models, each used in certain scenarios. The goal is to provide interfaces for such a service yet allow multiple implementations that focus on different requirements. Because a concurrency control mechanism is especially relevant in any transaction-based environment, this service must also address requirements of the Transaction Service.

Any real world information system of sizable responsibility requires transaction-based functionalities. This is the responsibility of the Transaction Service. Transactions provide ACID properties to applications:

- *Atomicity*. A transaction is a collection of operations that are performed as one atomic unit of work. This means that either all these operations are

Cutout 5-1
(Cont'd)

completed or none of them is performed. When a transaction commits we are guaranteed that all of its operations have been performed. If a user aborts a transaction or if it is aborted for other system-related reasons (such as lack of resources), then the transaction is rolled back and none of its operations is performed.

- *Consistency*. A transaction takes the underlying resource manager from one consistent state to another. The consistency of the state is guaranteed as a result of the transaction properties.
- *Isolation*. Transactions typically run concurrently with other transactions. The Isolation property guarantees that the result of completing a set of concurrent transactions is identical to the result of a serial execution of the transactions. This is necessary to ensure the consistency property of transactions. This requirement of the Transaction Service is the reason that the Transaction Service will have some form of dependency on the Concurrency Control Service because isolation requires locks.
- *Durability*. The actions of a transaction cause a new state to be formed. Once the transaction commits this state is assured to be durable, i.e. persistent. Therefore, the Transaction Service will have some dependency on the Persistence Service and will have access to persistent storage, e.g. databases.

The Transaction Service defines how CORBA objects can make use of ACID properties and how these properties are interpreted in an ORB-based environment. Transaction services need a way to handle concurrency; therefore, the description of the Transaction Service in the next chapter also includes issues pertinent to concurrency.

The Query Service defines a set of query-based functionalities that may be used within an object model that conforms to the OMA. Queries are defined as the manipulation of a set of objects that returns another set of objects that conform to the defined predicates.

The property Service allows associating named attributes with objects in a dynamic way. While attributes are useful for representing object state, they are static and form the IDL definition of objects.

The Licensing Service defines a mechanism by which producers of objects can control the way in which their objects are used. Access control, authorization, and compensation are all addressed by the Licensing Service, which promises to be a corner-stone service in implementing a component-based world.

The Time Service specification defines how a user can obtain the current time value along with an estimated error. The concept of time synchronization and event ordering is a complex and crucial concept in the construction of distributed systems in which multiple computers (each with its own notion of the current time) must cooperate in a single computation; the Time Service addresses some of these issues.

The Trading Service offers services for locating objects based on complex condition sets. Although passing of object references and the use of the Naming Service was a first step towards distributed object access, the Trading Service increases the ease in which object spaces may be managed and used. ◇

Cutout 5-2
Java remove method invocation (RMI).

Remote Method Invocation (RMI) and Object Serialization are two offerings from Sun (JavaSoft). RMI adds RPC capabilities to Java whereas serialization is another name for externalization/internalization and allows objects to be flattened onto a stream that can later be used to reconstruct the object. Both RMI and Object Serialization are part of the core Java libraries as of JDK 1.1.

RMI allows a Java object in one Java virtual machine to invoke methods of another Java object in another virtual machine (including on a different host). Therefore, it implements a Java-specific RPC mechanism (that is tightly optimized for Java). Although a CORBA interface provides a more complete and standardized solution, RMI is the preferred technology when two strictly Java systems in different virtual machines must interact.

For a Java object to be accessible to remote clients it must implement a new interface called `java.rmi.Remote`. The steps required for providing remotely accessible services are:

- create an interface that extends `Remote` for your application-specific functionality;
- each method declared in the new interface must declare that it may throw the `RemoteException`;
- create a class that implements the new interface;
- implement or use a marshaling mechanism for references to objects instantiated from the new class: the RMI package provides one such class—`UnicastRemoteServer`; and
- use the `rmic` utility to generate stubs and skeletons (similar to an IDL compiler in CORBA) that are used as the RPC end-points.

When an RMI call is made, arguments must be correctly marshaled on the caller's side and unmarshaled by the remote object. RMI arguments are passed from one virtual machine to another using Object Serialization. Object serialization allows an object to be stored as a byte stream that can then be used to reconstruct an equivalent object by the remote virtual machine. RMI arguments are physically passed as byte streams that, using Object Serialization, create the application-level capability of object migration and pass-by-value. ◇

classes can be used for persistent or transient objects, and for objects used primarily to manage a user interface process. The difference between the two classes involves the notion of ownership and dependence. Entity objects are objects that have an independent being and do not depend on another object for their existence. Dependent objects, on the other hand, live within another object (typically within an Entity object) and have no existence outside their owner. This may seem like a philosophical discussion but it has many practical consequences. A dependent object is not referenced from any object other than the dependent's container. The dependent object's lifecycle is

Cutout 5-3
Optimistic and pessimistic locking.

Most systems require some form of locking in order to ensure data integrity. The classic example illustrating why locking is necessary involves an airline reservation system that allows multiple reservation agents to book seats on a flight. Unless some form of locking is performed, the same seat can be potentially sold twice (or even more times). In the problematic scenario, two reservation agents would be (almost) simultaneously looking at the status of a certain flight and, seeing that a certain seat is vacant, sell it to the customer they are dealing with.

In order to solve this problem, locking at some level is required. Locking policies typically involve a number of attributes but the two important ones are the locking granularity and the locking policy (i.e. pessimistic or optimistic). Locking granularity defines the entity that will be locked. For example, one extreme solution in the airline reservation example would be to lock the entire system. This would surely ensure that only one reservation agent can perform a booking at a time. Obviously, this is not a feasible solution. In general the tradeoff involving locking granularity is that larger locking granularity (i.e. large entities being locked) results in less concurrency whereas smaller granularity allows for more concurrency (since conflicts are less likely), but is more difficult to implement. In modern RDBMS systems the two common alternatives are locking at the table or at the row levels.

The locking policy defines how locking is performed. Pessimistic locking is the classic locking policy. In such a policy the caller acquires a lock on a certain entity and holds it until completion. When it completes it frees the lock. Any caller that wants to use the entity must first acquire the lock; if the lock has already been acquired by another process, the caller blocks until the lock is free (or proceeds otherwise without using the entity). In the airline reservation example locks may be available on seats of a flight and in order to go ahead and perform the reservation the lock must be acquired. Acquiring a lock is an atomic operation, so when the second reservation agent wants to make the reservation she will need to acquire the lock on the seat, but will fail because the first reservation agent is already holding the lock.

Pessimistic locking has two major problems that have caused optimistic locking to become dominant in modern systems. Pessimistic locking causes locks to be held for long periods of time and inherently causes less concurrent access to data. In addition, because locks need to be held by applications, deadlocks can occur. A deadlock is a situation in which one caller is holding lock number 1 and needs to acquire lock number 2, while a second caller is holding lock number 2 and needs to acquire lock number 1. Both of these callers cannot proceed and so they deadlock.

Optimistic locking promotes a method that does not really acquire locks in the traditional sense. In optimistic locking an application performs the changes it requires within a transaction as if it solely has all the locks it needs—without actually acquiring anything. The policy is called optimistic because the application behavior optimistically assumes it has everything it needs to complete its operations. Upon commit this is checked; each change made within the transaction context is verified by making sure that the value that is to be changed has not been changed since the beginning of the transaction. If it has, the entire transaction will fail; otherwise it will succeed. In the airline reservations example, both reservation agents will proceed with selling the seat. Since committing a transaction is an atomic operation, one agent will commit first—and succeed. When the second agent attempts to commit the system will see that the availability status of the seat has been changed since the beginning of the transaction (because of the reservation made by

Cutout 5-3
(Cont'd)

the first agent) and the transaction will fail. The agent will then look for a different seat to sell to the customer.

Optimistic locking provides for better concurrency because conflicts have a much lower frequency than locks do. The issues of locking policy and locking granularity are very strongly related. If locking granularity could be made to be very small and many lock types were developed (e.g. read locks, write locks, etc.) then pessimistic locking conflicts would not be so common. However, most systems do not support small locking granularities very well and so optimistic locking is the preferred choice for most systems today. ◇

completely dependent on the container's lifecycle; for example, when the container ceases to exist so does the dependent. Finally, a dependent that is persistent will define its mapping to persistent storage through the container; for example, if persistence mechanism uses a mapping to a relational database then the dependent object will be mapped to the container's tables.

The answer to the question of which classes are dependents and which classes are entities is a complex one that sometimes has an objective answer and is sometimes specific to the domain or application in question. Most classes that represent important concepts in the real world will be entities. Thus, many classes of the Common Business Objects and the Core Business Processes layer are already categorized as either dependent classes or entity classes (or both—through two classes). It is almost certain that this categorization will fit almost all applications (which is very fortunate because if it was not, these classes would be useless for many application developers). On the other hand, the fact that the conceptual difference between dependents and entities is based on the subjective notion of existentialism, it is very possible that a concept will be a dependent in one application and an entity in another. For example, the notion of a zip code is usually represented simply as a string in many applications and may be modeled as a dependent of an address object. On the other hand, in an application that manages addresses and zip codes and performs geographical inference based on zip codes (such as various systems offered by Lucent Technologies or Bellcore), a zip code will certainly be an entity.

Figure 5-3 shows the root of the SanFrancisco class hierarchy including the classes `Entity`, `Dependent`, and `DynamicEntity` (along with snippets from the `javadoc` documentation pages).

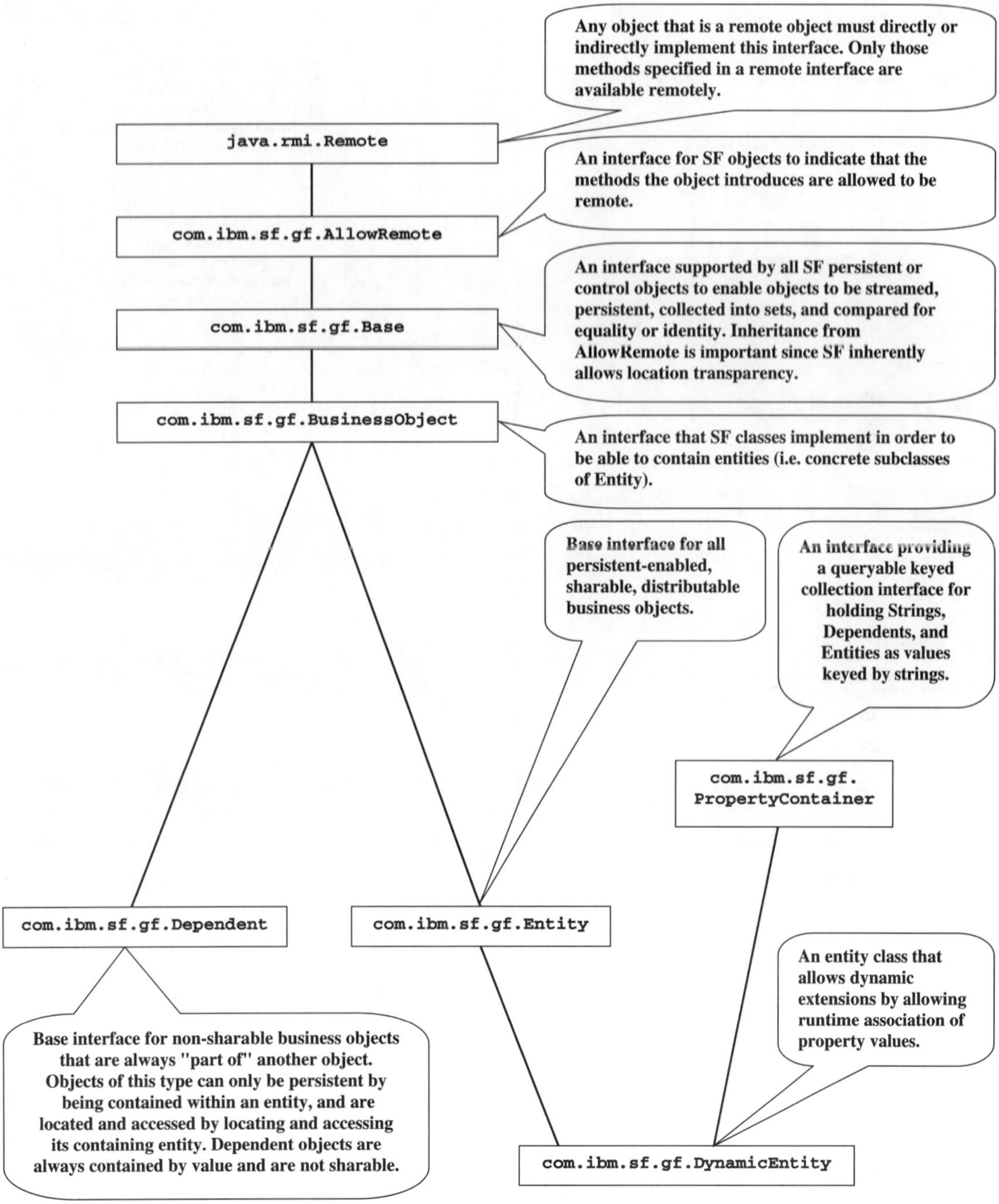

Figure 5-3
The SanFrancisco base hierarchy.

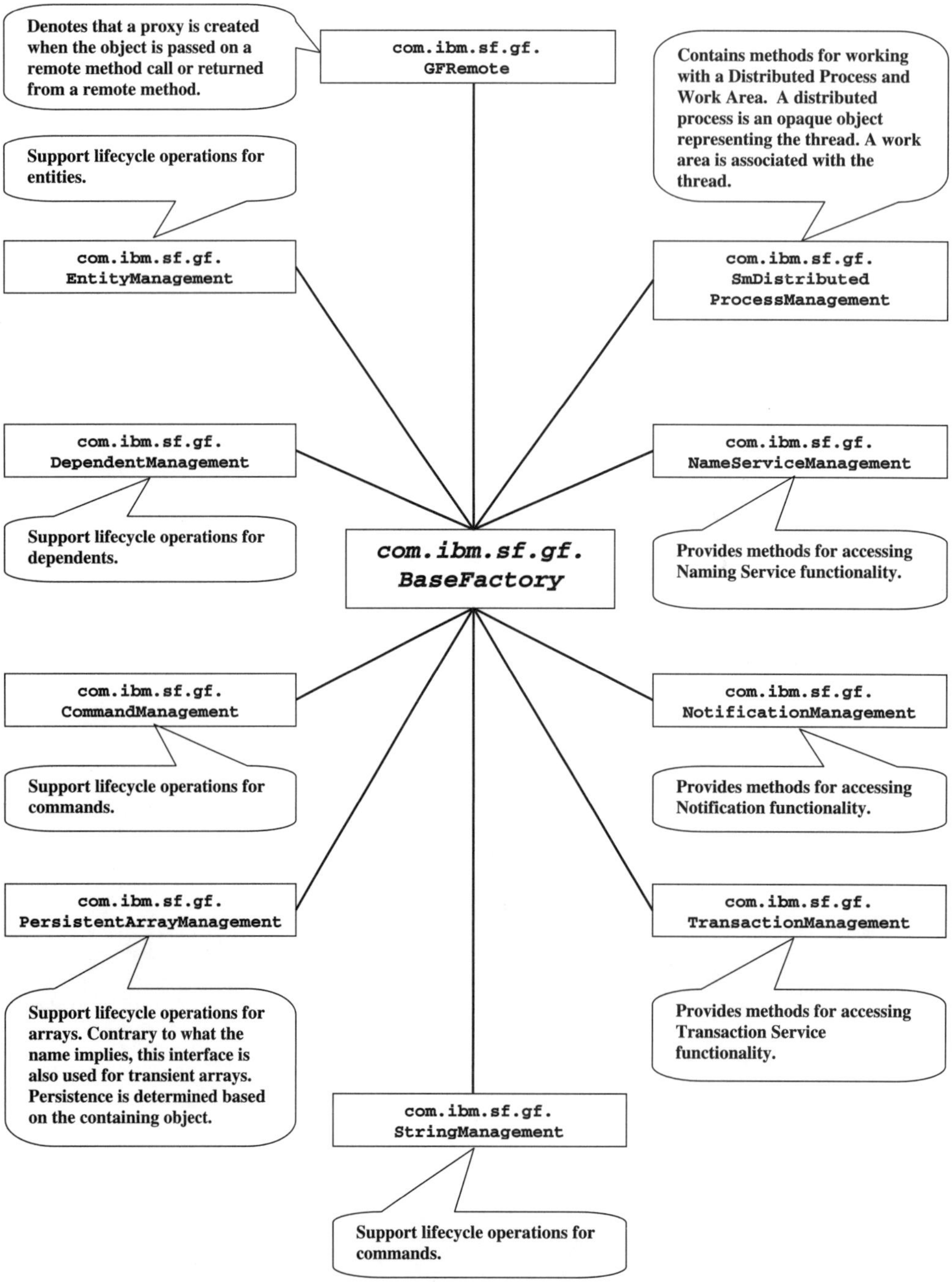

Figure 5-4
Interfaces aggregated by `BaseFactory`.

`DynamicEntity` is an `Entity` class that also support runtime binding of named properties. This provides additional flexibility because attributes can be dynamically attached at runtime without requiring code changes to the class definition. Addition of property values is not only supported at runtime but supported per object—therefore, different objects of the same type can have different properties associated with them (allowing some form of instance-based programming). Note that the API for binding property values is defined in the `PropertyContainer` interface.

- `BaseFactory`. Factory objects are responsible for lifecycle operations. They are used to create objects, delete them, etc. Factories are certainly not a new concept in object-oriented systems and are present in Java and in CORBA. The `BaseFactory` interface denotes objects in SanFrancisco that are responsible for lifecycle issues, in addition to many other issues—it is also involved with handling transactions, security policies, distributed access, and more. `BaseFactory` as an interface does not directly define APIs—it is merely an aggregation of numerous other interfaces each responsible of an important aspect of object management—this is shown in Figure 5-4. Each of the interfaces in Figure 5-4 represents a system-level category supported by the foundation layer.
- `Collection/Iterator`. Like any object-oriented type system, SanFrancisco supports collections of objects and iterators used to traverse these collections.
- `Command`. The command object encapsulates a set of operations on an object, or a group of objects that are to be performed together. It is an important feature of SanFrancisco, both in terms of performance (if the set is moved to a remote process and performed there) as well as in terms of an abstraction of business logic, which involves more than one object or more than one operation.

The base classes forming the Object Model Classes are inherited from and are used in two ways. They implement behavior that is assumed by the inheriting class. In addition, the base classes define interfaces that are implemented by the inheriting classes as specific implementations of abstract concepts. By supporting the two, the base classes provide the overall object architecture assumed by each SanFrancisco application (something that is crucial in any development project and is always very hard to accomplish) while leaving enough flexibility for customization. The benefits of a consistent object architecture that has been designed and built by experts are enormous. A good object model (assuming it is used correctly) is difficult to build but almost always produces superior application designs. This is not only because the design patterns are somewhat embedded in the fundamental object models but also because decisions that are always hard to make (and therefore may be made with little or no understanding of the consequences) are made by experts.

In addition to the services and base classes provided within the foundation layer, a set of utilities aid in developing SanFrancisco applications. These utilities are part of the foundation layer because they are useful for every application and do not depend on certain business objects or domains. Utilities are provided for managing application security, for managing configuration information, for synchronizing between operations that should not be performed concurrently, for creating installation procedures, and for creating audit trails.

Common Business Objects

The Common Business Objects layer provides classes that are useful in almost any domain. Examples include `Company`, `Currency`, `Address`, `BusinessPartner`, `FiscalYear`, `PaymentMethod`, `PaymentTerms`, `Project`, `UnitOfMeasure`, etc. While it is clear that such entities are certainly common to many domains and applications, it is also clear that different systems will have slightly different data structures and behavior associated with these concepts. Therefore, the Common Business Objects layer defines the interfaces and APIs to these entities, and how they interact with other central entities. However, in order to support differing functionality in different systems, SanFrancisco patterns allow for the common portions to be provided by the Common Business Objects layer while allowing application segments to extend and provide custom structures and behavior.

Even within one concept, there are a number of classes and interfaces involved. For example, `com.ibm.sf.cf.Company` is an interface defining the behavior of the basic organization structure of the "owning" entity of the application (the company providing the service in a customer service application, the bank in a financial application, or the manufacturing company in a manufacturing application). `com.ibm.sf.cf.CompanyImpl` is a class implementing the `Company` interface, which can be used to instantiate `Company` objects. `com.ibm.sf.cf.CompanyFactory` is the factory object for the `Company` class. `com.ibm.sf.cf.ComanyController` and `com.ibm.sf.cf.CompanyControllerImpl` are an interface and a class used for creating a singleton (a single object of that type) used for managing the extent of all `Company` objects. `com.ibm.sf.cf.CompanyContext` adds some static methods that help clients to work with companies, the controller and the active `Company`. These form the basic `Company`-related classes and interfaces (a few more exist but are of no interest at this point).

You may have noticed that the classes and interfaces forming the examples of the Common Business Objects layer have all been in the `com.ibm.sf.cf` package—CF for Common Functions. The Common Business Objects layer includes an additional package—the `com.ibm.sf.cffi`, which includes all the common financial objects. Examples include the bank abstraction, accounts, invoices, etc.

Core Business Processes

The Core Business Process frameworks provide the highest abstraction levels in SanFrancisco by supplying not only classes and services for certain domains, but by providing processes and collaborations that supply working application structures. The Core Business Process frameworks rely on the Common Business Objects—including the financial objects—as depicted in Figure 5-5.

The Core Processes are impressive in that they are working sets of behaviors that provide real application structures while incorporating enough extension points in order to allow application developers to customize behavior with business rules, country-specific requirements and functions, a user interface, etc.

The current release of SanFrancisco provides the General Ledger (`com.ibm.sf.gl` package), Warehouse Management (`com.ibm.sf.whs` package), and Order Management (`com.ibm.sf.om` package) processes, with Release 1.3 adding the Accounts Receivable and Accounts Payable Ledger process (`com.ibm.sf.le` package)—it was in beta status in 1.2. The General Ledger framework provides behavior that

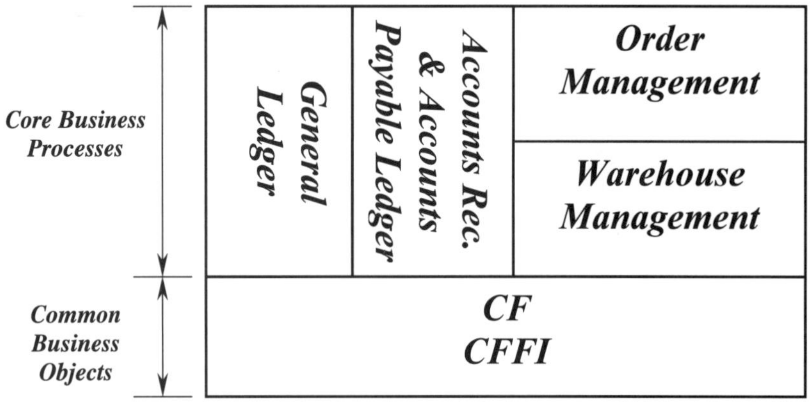

Figure 5-5
Layering of the Core Business Processes.

is common in applications managing the general ledger of sets of companies, including journal operations and book closing. The Account Ledger framework supports functions for processing account receivable items and account payable items, including all payments and item transfers to business partners. The Warehouse Management framework supports stock logistics and inventory management, including replenishments, stock movements between warehouses, and both bin and bin-less management of inventory tracking. The Order Management framework builds on the Warehouse Management framework and provides for sales-order management, sales-order quotes and contracts (including pricing, costing, and discounts), purchase-order management (including back-to-back processing), and more.

CHAPTER 6

The SanFrancisco Architecture

This chapter continues the overview of the SanFrancisco frameworks started in the previous chapter. In this chapter we go into a little more detail regarding the three layers of frameworks and explain how this architectural approach helps in providing a manageable environment for developing distributed, transaction-oriented applications. We also give more detail as to what are the abstractions defined in each of these layers. Our hope is that, together with Chapter 5, you will have a good top-level understanding of what SanFrancisco is and how its different components should be used. This high-level understanding will give the right context when we start delving down into code examples using features belonging to each of the different layers.

The SanFrancisco architectural design was depicted in the previous chapter by Figure 5-1 and is based on a layered approach. The first two layers—the operating system and the JVM—are not part of SanFrancisco, but are used by it to provide multi-platform support with no re-coding—the famous "write once, run everywhere."

Next comes the Foundation layer, which is the core technological layer of SanFrancisco, and provides services and infrastructure for supporting all the goodies—transactions, security, persistence, lifecycle, naming, notification, etc. Most importantly, the Foundation layer defines an object model and related usability patterns that form the base for all other layers of SanFrancisco and applications written over any of the SanFrancisco layers. The Foundation layer's set of base classes are responsible for two objectives of utmost importance—they define the basic structure assumed by all SanFrancisco objects as well as a portability layer by which an application is decoupled from the underlying vendor services used during deployment.

As mentioned, the Foundation layer supports a set of services such as security, persistence, and configuration control. Support for such services implies a number of issues.

- Models, APIs, and infrastructure components are provided for access to the services. For example, SanFrancisco supports notions of users, user groups, user profiles, etc., which are used for maintaining access control and security.
- Tools for managing instances of the infrastructure components. For example, a user interface is provided for managing users and user groups, and a reporting utility is provided for building reports and printing them.
- Interfaces to external products. An example involves object persistence. SanFrancisco supports data store independence.

Objects can be made persistent using more than one data store mechanism. This independence has two forms. Like most development environments, SanFrancisco supports multiple products within relational database technology (i.e. multiple RDBMS products) by supporting ODBC and client-side libraries. However, SanFrancisco goes one step further by supporting more than one storage paradigm, e.g. POSIX files and RDBMSs. In this category, like other categories, this implies that SanFrancisco must implement interfaces to the underlying products.

The Common Business Objects (CBOs) form the first layer of reusable business objects and are grouped into three categories. The general business objects category includes classes such as address, business partner, currency, project, etc. The second category is the financial business objects category that includes objects such as bank accounts, invoices, financial calendar, etc. Finally, the CBO layer also includes common functions that are closer to services provided by functional libraries than object libraries, but are useful across domains and layers. An example includes the notion of a cached balance that maintains a summary of elements for efficient access to aggregate data.

The highest abstractions in SanFrancisco are provided by the Core Business Processes (CBRs). These frameworks are domain-level frameworks that embody real business processes out-of-the-box. Figure 6-1

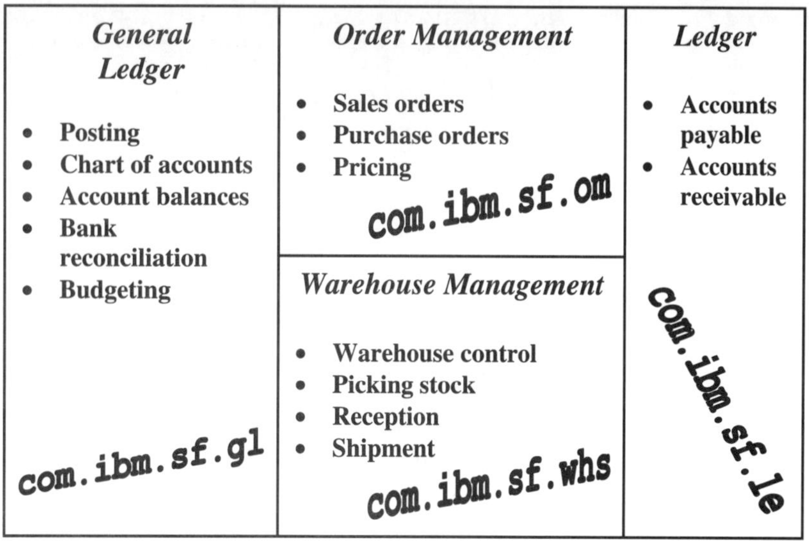

Figure 6-1 Core business process functions and package names.

shows the primary functions provided by each of the core business processes along with the Java package names to which the classes belong. These frameworks make SanFrancisco less of an object library and more of a pseudo-application. An application belonging to a domain in which a Core Business Process exists is extremely easy to build.

Foundation Architecture

Everything in SanFrancisco is built on the foundation layer and, to us, it is the most important layer (but then again—we are programmers). It is the technological layer that forms the underlying software architecture assumed by any application running over SanFrancisco. This software architecture then goes on to infer on the application architecture. Therefore, it is very important to understand the architectural choices made by the foundation layer.

The basic premise of the SanFrancisco foundation layer is that of creating a robust environment for developing large-scale, transaction-oriented, distributed applications. It is not a development environment for small, user interface-centric data-access applications. The architectural requirements for supporting applications in such an environment are stringent and complex and it is now an accepted assumption that "normal" application programmers cannot provide "correct" architectures without the assistance of experts. The goal of the foundation layer architecture is to capture this expertise and provide a solid architecture for all applications to rely on. As such, the foundation layer creates an architectural structure that inherently takes care of the following issues:

- persistence,
- transactions,
- distribution,
- naming,
- notification,
- queries, and
- security.

Persistence

We have already mentioned that SanFrancisco supports persistence of object state in both relational databases and POSIX files. The intent is that storage mechanism independence will be one of the features of the SanFrancisco foundation layer (as you know, in software the "0,1, many" rule implies that you either don't support a feature, you support it in one certain way, or you support it in many ways). While this is all very nice, the POSIX file feature is only useful for demos and for proof-of-concepts; it is not a mechanism that can serve as the underlying data storage for any real application. The relational database layer, on the other hand, abstracts away the details of different Relational Database Management Systems (RDBMSs) and provides for application independence of the actual product used. At this time SanFrancisco supports DB2 for Windows NT, Oracle for Windows NT, and DB2 Common Server for AIX. We are assuming that in the event that SanFrancisco becomes widely accepted and used, more RDBMS vendors will provide adaptors. Because the interface to RDBMS is based on ODBC, and since almost all vendors provide ODBC interfaces, this should prove to be a no-brainer.

As documented by the SanFrancisco manuals:

> It is important to understand that choosing the persistence model is a purely administrative task that can be performed without influencing the application coding. You can configure your persistent data stores with an administrative utility. If you later need to modify your choices in terms of persistent stores, you can do it without modifying a single line of code. This extremely powerful feature allows you to configure the same application in completely different ways as far as persistence is concerned. Install an application for a small customer who only uses a single database server, and later install the same application at a larger customer's site where multiple distributed databases are used. In the first case, you may choose to concentrate all the persistent data on a single database; in the latter case, you can distribute objects across multiple data stores. All this does not require a single change to the application code.

The concept is depicted in Figure 6-2. Database independence in SanFrancisco means two things: vendor independence and deployment configuration independence. Vendor independence is a common feature in today's tools and is almost assumed of new frameworks like SanFrancisco. It is accomplished by adding an abstraction layer that is product independent and forms the interface to the application levels.

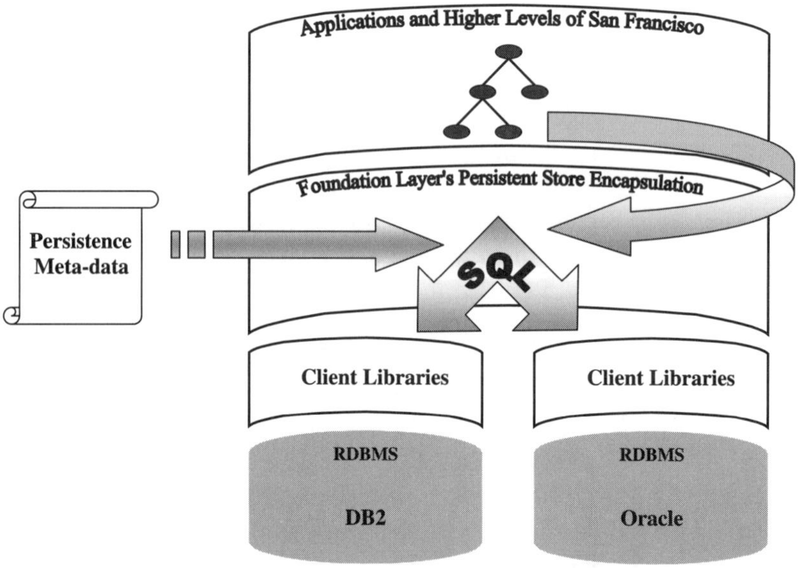

Figure 6-2 Database independence.

This abstraction layer uses sets of product-specific interfaces to the product client libraries.

The configuration independence is part of a more complex feature that uses persistence meta-data. This meta-data contains data regarding the mapping between objects to tables as well as data regarding the actual database deployment. This independence is much harder to support and can, theoretically, produce very elegant system architectures. So why "theoretically," and why did we quote the SanFrancisco manual as opposed to just explaining the notion of configuration independence? Our experience has shown that the issues involving the mapping between object structures and database schemas, as well as the issues involving how the databases are used by the application, have an extensive effect on application performance. This effect on performance can be so radical that it can make the difference between an application being viable, and an application being a bad joke. In our opinion, the decoupling of object models and database schemas is a very nice academic exercise that does not hold up in the real world. In real applications the tension between the object model and the relational model is something that has to be balanced—meaning that the relational schema must sometimes give way to the object model, and the object model will sometimes have to be changed to accommodate efficient use of the database.

Transactions and Locking

Transactions allow concurrent access to objects. They form the backbone of any system that needs to service multiple clients (or requesters). Without transactions we could not have multiple processing threads that are shielded from one another—any processing would be non-deterministic and unusable. The fact that transactions provide a protected environment for completing operations is mandatory to any multi-user application sharing data. In addition, transactions ensure persistence of changes made within a transaction scope.

The Foundation layer supports object-level transactions that map to database-level transactions. The SanFrancisco transaction model is flat—nested transactions are not supported. Changes made to business objects should only be made within a transaction context. The notion of attaching an object to a transaction context relies on locking policies that define the constraints placed on the shared business objects and affects their behavior in other transactions. The Foundation layer defines an extensive set of locks to provide for numerous access methods that control object locking.

SanFrancisco transactions follow the conventional transaction API. The API can be used programmatically by accessing a `BaseFactory` object (using the `Global.factory()` call) and then using the interface methods defined in `com.ibm.sf.gf.TransactionManagement`, which is one of the base interfaces of `com.ibm.sf.gf.BaseFactory` (shown in Figure 6-3). In addition, the `Command` object may be activated using the `doTransaction()` method, which performs all the operations of the `Command` object within a transaction block.

Although most changes and accesses to business objects will be made from within a transaction, SanFrancisco also provides a feature for accessing business objects outside of a transaction. This mode, called the NO_LOCK mode, creates a copy of the business object. Any change made to the copy will not be performed on the real object and so this feature is useful in cases where read-only access is performed and we wish to minimize overhead. This mode is also useful in another pattern that we call the "Draft" pattern (shown in Figure 6-4). This pattern supports changes made to business objects using short-lived transactions, while allowing work to be performed on an object that appears to be the real object. Instead of opening a transaction, by making changes directly on the object, and then either performing a commit or a rollback based on whether the user accepts the changes, we actually work on a copy (effectively making a draft of the changes). Since changes

Figure 6-3 com.ibm.sf.gf.TransactionManagement.

Interface com.ibm.sf.gf.TransactionManagement

This class provides an interface for San Francisco applications to manage transactions.

- **begin**()

  Begins a new transaction.

- **commit**()

  Commits the current transaction.

- **getTransactionStatus**()

  Indicates the status of the current transaction.

- **rollback**()

  Performs rollback on the current transaction.

- **rollbackOnly**()

  Marks current transaction to ROLLBACKONLY.

made in the NO_LOCK mode will not persist, when asked to accept the changes made we need to perform all the changes on the real object—this time within a transaction bracket.

Lock options are defined in the class `LockMode`. This class has static values used to specify the desired lock when accessing an Entity through the factory. The lock types provided are:

- NO_LOCK. Provides access to the Entity with no lock by making a copy of the object. During creation of the copy, a READ lock is acquired and released once the copy has been created. Thus, this mode will conflict with WRITE locks while those are being held on the entity.
- OPTIMISTIC. Synchronization is performed at commit time—at which point the transaction may fail if the object has been changed since the entity was locked. When the lock is acquired the entity is copied using a READ lock and may conflict with any existing WRITE locks. The READ lock is released once the copy has been made. When the transaction is committed, Entity

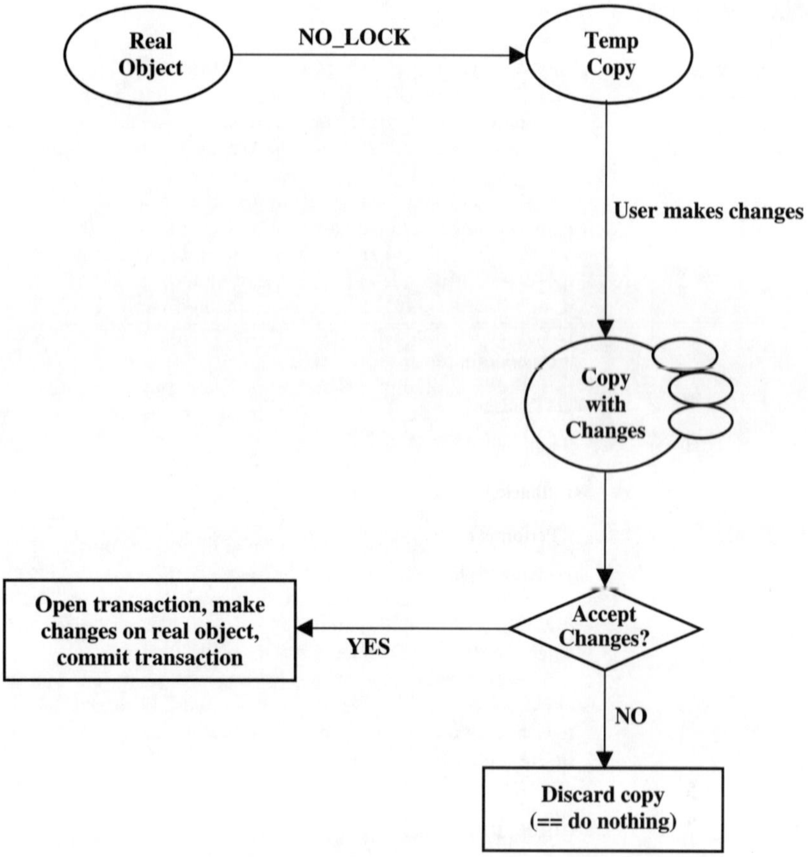

Figure 6-4
The draft pattern.

version checking is performed to determine if the Entity has changed since the optimistic lock was acquired and, if so, an `OptimisticLockException` is raised.

- OPTIMISTIC_CLEAN. This lock type is a variation on the optimistic lock in that checks performed on entities at transaction commit time are performed even on objects that have not been changed inside the current transaction. This can be useful when you wish to signal that the processing of the current transaction relies on the value of the entity (see Cutout 6-1 for more details).
- READ. Pessimistic read lock conflicting with existing write locks.
- WRITE. Pessimistic write locks conflicting with existing read or write locks.

Cutout 6-1
Locking objects.

Transactions and locking have traditionally been associated with databases and have only recently begun to capture the attention of developers of object-oriented applications. Therefore, the understanding of the implications that locking and transactions have on object design is very much in its infancy and the interaction between operations on objects and transactions are not always well understood. Sure, accessing and changing data is precisely that—whether it's called "data access" or whether it's called "object methods accessors"—but it is wise to try to formulate the locking and transaction behavior in terms of object manipulation.

Objects methods are used for many things. Methods can be used to implement behavior required of the object, can be used to change the state of the object, can be used to access state of the object, and can be used for navigation of the object space. Let's discuss the last category since it is fairly clear how the first three categories of methods should interact with transactions and locking.

Object-oriented programs are designed to form an object graph that represents the real world entities and the relationships existing among them. The graph is formed using pointers or references that exist between the objects. These references are encapsulated as variables within the objects themselves (or using some other data structure associated with the objects). In order to traverse such a link, one uses an accessor method (a `<get>` method). The accessor method is often no different from an accessor method that returns a value that is part of the state of the object. This is no coincidence—the set of references are viewed as part of the object's state. For example, when using a PartOrderLine object as shown in Figure 6.5 there is no difference at the object model level whether we access the quantity variable in the object or the PartOrder object that it references.

However, when discussing locking, we must distinguish between access methods activated in order to access data as opposed to access methods used purely for navigation purposes. Since object navigation is one of the most common occurrences in an object-oriented program's life (it is common to see code such as `aTask.getOwner().getQueue().size()`), we need to specify what we are relying on in terms of our transaction.

At first glance it would seem that methods that access object state are equivalent to read locks—if we are "reading" the information, we must require a read lock on it. But since object navigation cannot be distinguished from state access, this is not so simple. Going back to our part order line example, suppose that we need to display the address the order will be shipped to (maintained at the header) and the quantity being shipped. Obviously, accessing the quantity variable should cause a read lock to be placed, but what about the navigation to the header, `this.getPartOrder().getHeader()`?

What is it that we need to lock? We certainly should not be locking the part order object—for example, we don't really care whether another line object is added to the part order object. What we do care about is the navigation path—we must make sure that the part order line continues to reference the same part order object, and that the part order object continues to reference the same header object. Therefore, when navigation through accessors is performed the implication on locking is that the actual reference needs to be locked and not the object being referenced. The state of the part order line object includes the pointer only, and the pointer specification (equivalent to the values of a foreign key in a relational database) must be locked when performing the navigation.

Distribution

Every entity in SanFrancisco may be distributed anywhere in the Logical SanFrancisco Network, and every object may be remotely referenced from any other object in a location-transparent manner using a `Handle` to the object (`Handle` being one of the infrastructure classes the Foundation layer provides). Any object may be uniquely situated at any node in the logical network

However, the notion of distribution in SanFrancisco does not stop with providing location-transparent access to objects (as do most environments supporting distributed processing). The Foundation layer supports both the reference model and the replication model (see Cutout 6-2). When creating an object, one can pass an `AccessMode` object to the `BaseFactory`. `AccessMode` objects allow programmers to control characteristics of the object created in the local address space—one of them being a specification of whether Local Mode or Home Mode is desired (other characteristics include lock types, lock wait timeout, and more—see Figure 6-7). When selecting Home Mode, the Foundation layer is told

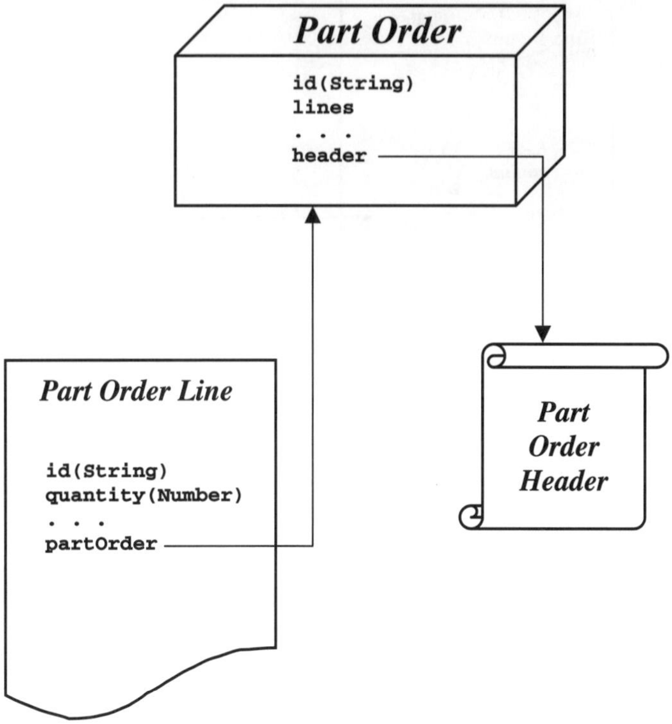

Figure 6-5 A `PartOrderLine` object.

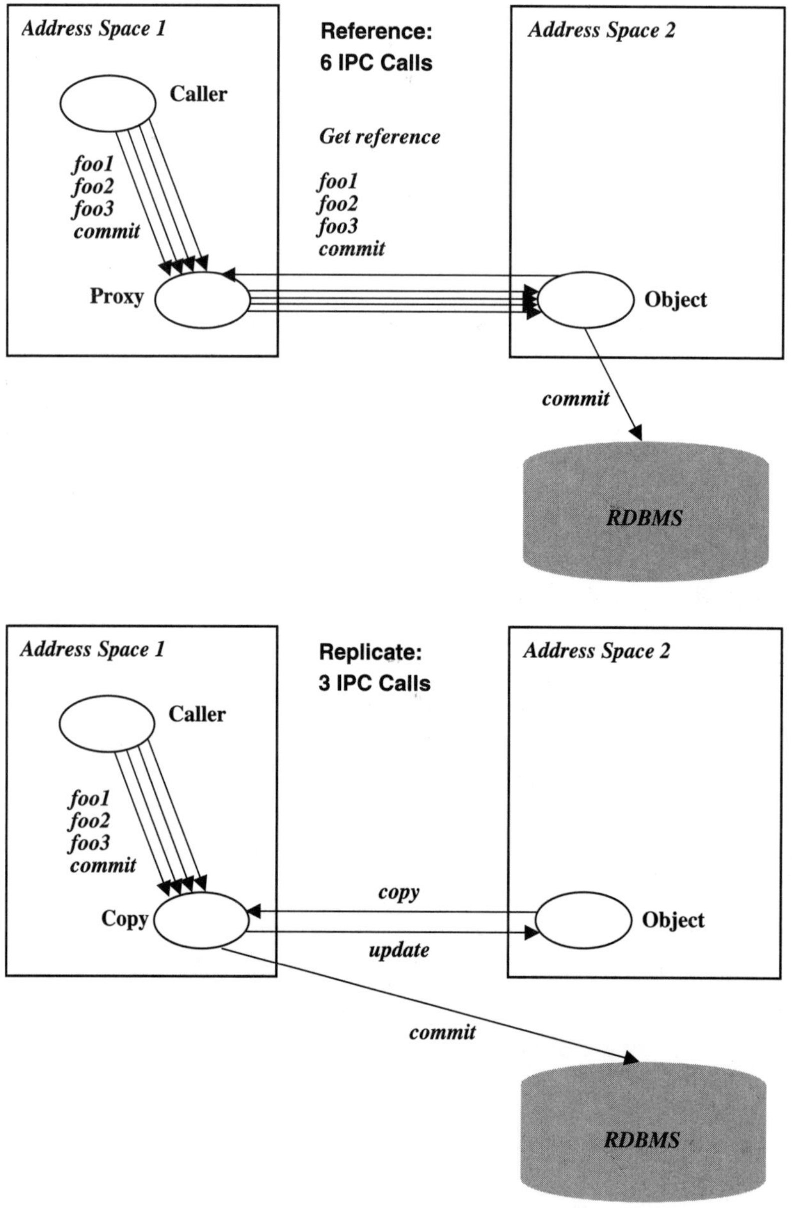

Figure 6-6 The reference model and the replication model.

that we want to use the object in its home environment. If the object lives in a separate address space than the caller then a proxy will be created pointing at the real object. If, on the other hand, Local Mode is specified, we are telling the Foundation that we want a local copy of the object to be

Figure 6-7 `Access Mode` and `Access Location`.

Class com.ibm.sf.gf.AccessMode

```
java.lang.Object
   |
   +----com.ibm.sf.gf.AccessMode
```

AccessMode objects are passed as parameters to the factory to indicate the type of access desired to new or existing entities. Controls access related to the lock applied to the entity, desired Entity location, compatibility of the desired location, and lock wait time. Static methods of this class provide a set of tailorable characteristics for use in application programs.

●create

```
public static AccessMode create(int entityLock,
                                int entityLocation,
                                int entityCompatibility,
                                int elementLock,
                                int elementLocation,
                                int elementCompatibility,
                                long startingElement,
                                int elementsEachAccess,
                                int waitTime) throws GFException
```

Create a new instance of an AccessMode initialized to the specified state.

Parameters:

entityLock - Type of lock to obtain on the entity. Valid values defined in LockMode

entityLocation - Desired location of the entity. Valid values defined in AccessLocation

entityCompatibility - How access of the object is allowed. Valid values defined in CompatibilityMode

elementLock - The type of lock to obtain on entity elements contained in the collection when they are later accessed through the collection. Only applies if the entity being accessed is a collection. Valid values defined in LockMode

elementLocation - Desired location of entity elements contained in the collection when they are later accessed through the collection. Only applies if the entity being accessed is a collection. Valid values defined in AccessLocation

elementCompatibility - How access to the collections entity elements is allowed when they are later accessed through the collection. Only applies if the entity being accessed is a collection. Valid values defined in CompatibilityMode

startingElement - The collection element to start with when performing iterations over the collection. Only applies if the entity being accessed is a collection

elementsEachAccess - The number of elements to retrieve when performing iterations over the collection. Only applies if the entity is a collection

waitTime - The length of time that will be spent waiting for a lock on the entity. Valid values defined in Timeout

Figure 6-7 (Cont'd)

Class com.ibm.sf.gf.AccessLocation

```
java.lang.Object
   |
   +----com.ibm.sf.gf.AccessLocation
```

This class has static values used to specify the desired location for the Entity being accessed. Location refers to which process space that the Entity should be accessed in.

LOCAL

```
public static final int LOCAL
```

The Entity will be accessed in the local address space of the calling process. A "working" copy is made in the local address space which is written back to the "home" address space during commit().

HOME

```
public static final int HOME
```

The Entity will be accessed in the address space that the entity is configured to persist in. An RMI proxy is returned to the actual sharable Entity in its home process.

Cutout 6-2 Reference and replication as distributed processing models.

The primary issue concerning distributed computing involves how objects are shared among multiple address spaces in order to collaborate in a task. Distributed computing can be broadly categorized into two models—the reference model and the replication model. The categorization is based on the approach used for sharing objects. The reference-based model assumes that each object exists only in one address space and all other address spaces using the object need to get an object reference. The proxy (or surrogate) is merely a stub, forwarding all requests to the real object. The replication model takes a different approach, creating copies of the object in every address space where the object is used extensively. The different copies need to be synchronized, or locks need to be used to eliminate the danger of inconsistent states on the same conceptual object.

Both models are important tools for distributed computing, and each has its advantages and disadvantages. The replication model can provide for increased performance because most operations on the object can be local as opposed to requiring inter-process communication (as shown in Figure 6.6). On the other hand, the replication model is more complex and requires more work for copying and synchronizing information and for ensuring that duplicates do not get out of sync. As a framework that has placed distributed computing as one of its primary goals, the SanFrancisco Foundation supports both models.

created in our address space. Using the locking specification we can even request any changes committed on the local object to be propagated to the real object—in effect supporting a replication model. Obviously, the fact that the Foundation layer supports both models for distributed computing is a very important advantage for enterprise software developers.

Naming

The Naming Service is one of the cornerstones of the SanFrancisco architecture both in allowing distribution and location transparency as well as supporting correct application structure. Figure 6-8 shows the primary functions of the Naming Service as defined in methods of the `com.ibm.sf.gf.NameServiceManagement` interface (from the javadoc API definition). This interface allows:

- Binding, unbinding, and replacing user aliases with entity objects (i.e. associating a name—a string—with a handle to an entity).
- Retrieval of a handle to a container of a class which can then be used for creating entities.
- Access to special factories associated with classes.
- Control over which concrete instance will be created when a factory is used. This is performed using class replacement that allows a class name to be mapped to the concrete instance that will be created. This mapping can be changed dynamically using configuration tools, thereby allowing the software to follow a design that can have multiple installed deployments—each having slightly different behavior based on the concrete class used for instantiation.

Notification

In the past 5 years, the notification function has become central to many modern applications. The publish/subscribe model in which one party defines what they are interested in, and one party publishes information that is ultimately dispatched to all parties that expressed interest in that information type, solves many application problems. The decoupling afforded by this model is extremely important for robust scaleable application architectures. The Foundation layer fully supports notification using two possible delivery mechanisms—asynchronous or on-demand. Asynchronous notification follows the Observable pattern (also known as the Model-View pattern). On-demand notification used a mailbox paradigm.

Asynchronous notification is supported by the `com.ibm.sf.gf.NotificationManagement` interface that provides an API for adding

Figure 6-8
com.ibm.sf.gf.
NameService
Management

Interface com.ibm.sf.gf.NameServiceManagement

public interface **NameServiceManagement**

extends AllowRemote

This class provides an interface for factory to manage naming services.

---

addUserAlias

```
public abstract void addUserAlias(String entityUserAlias,
                                  Handle handleOfEntity) throws GFException
```

Defines the given userAlias to be associated (bound) with the entity referred to by the input handle. When a userAlias has been added through this interface, applications may then use this alias (in addition to its handle) to access the persistent entity. Any single entity may be referred to by multiple userAliases (as defined by the application).

getContainer

```
public abstract Handle getContainer(String classNameToken) throws
GFException
```

Returns a handle containing the default persistent container location information as specified in the configuration information for the specified class name token (must correspond to an Entity, or a class which extends from Entity). This Handle can then be used as the locationHandle argument in a createEntity() call to place the new entity in the container according to the configured default persistent container.

getContainerByName

```
public abstract Handle getContainerByName(String containerName) throws
GFException
```

Returns a handle containing the default persistent container location information as specified by the container name as specified in the naming data priming source file (e.g. Global Name). This method is intended to provide a bootstrap mechanism for creating top-level hierarchical objects (therefore no persistent objects exists for which to create near with). This Handle can then be used as the locationHandle argument in a createEntity() call to place the new entity in the container according to the configured persistent container.

getSpecialFactory

```
public abstract Object getSpecialFactory(String classNameToken) throws
GFException
```

Returns an instance of any special factory class configured for the specified class name token. Null is returned when there is no special factory class associated with this class name token and the normal Factory class methods should be used for creation. Special factories are intended to be called from within class factories and provide functions relative to legacy data bases.

removeUserAlias

```
public abstract void removeUserAlias(String entityUserAlias,
                                     Handle handleOfEntity) throws
GFException
```

Removes the existing user alias (which has been previously associated) for the Entity referred to by the input Handle (handleOfEntity).

Figure 6-8
(Cont'd)

replaceUserAliasEntity

```
public abstract void replaceUserAliasEntity(String entityUserAlias,
                                             Handle handleOfSourceEntity,
                                             Handle handleOfTargetEntity)
throws GFException
```

Re-assigns the specified user alias from the source Entity referred to by the source handle to the target Entity referred to by the target handle.

getRealClassName

```
public abstract String getRealClassName(String classNameToken) throws
GFException
```

Returns the real class that should be instantiated, given a class name token. The class name token is looked up in the configuration information. If there is a substitute class name mapped to this token, that is used. If there is a substitute interface name that has a corresponding ...Impl class, that class is used. If there is no substituted interface or class name in the configuration information, and the class name token is an actual class that class is used. If there is no substituted interface or class name in the configuration information, and the class name token is an interface with a corresponding ...Impl class, that class is used. The classNameToken "String" mapping is fixed to "java.lang.String", no SF-Class substitution is allowed.

and removing `Observers`. A typical interface call includes the following arguments:

- `observerEntity`. The entity expressing interest (to be notified upon events).
- `notificationInterest`. An `Interest` object (part of the Foundation layer), which is an abstract class that should be inherited by application-specific classes to define the events that cause notification.
- `access`. For application control over how the asynchronous notification is performed.
- `observable`. A handle to the entity upon which the interest is being expressed.

On-demand notification is supported by the `com.ibm.sf.gf.NotificationMailbox` interface that acts as an intermediary between the observer and the observable and serves as a "mailbox" in which events (placed by the observable) wait until they are pulled by the observer. The two notification patterns follow the CORBA Event Service in that the functionality supported by the `com.ibm.sf.gf.NotificationManagement` interface resembles conventional event dispatch, whereas the functionality supported by the `com.ibm.sf.gf.NotificationMailbox` interface is similar to the features of the Event Channel.

Queries

Queries are central to any business application. As a result, the SanFrancisco Foundation layer provides mechanisms for phrasing queries in the object world. Generally, queries have historically been associated with relational databases and SQL. SQL databases form the benchmark for querying in terms of ease-of-use, availability, and performance.

The SanFrancisco approach to querying is based on the notion of query commands that are applied to collections of objects. Each application of the query command acts as a filter that determines whether the object in the collection satisfies the query; if so, then it will be part of the collection returned from the call applying the query command to the original collection.

The syntax for defining a query command in SanFrancisco is a subset of the SQL92 syntax with additions allowing accessors to objects to be used. Therefore, it is easy to retrieve all part orders that include more than 10 part order lines using a syntax that is close to the object world; one would simply phrase it as `getLineNumber() > 10` and be done with it. In general, most collections can be used as starting-points for queries and, as much as possible, the resulting collection (the collection of the objects satisfying the query) will have the same attributes (so, for example, applying a query to a Set will in general produce a Set). The one important difference is that the resulting collection is always transient and never owns the objects it contains. In addition, since the `EntityOwningExtent` collection is closely related with the underlying relational database—it can provide important performance enhancements by using the underlying store's query engine and optimizer.

The Foundation layer provides two interfaces for creating query commands—the `com.ibm.sf.gf.QueryCmd` interface and the `com.ibm.sf.gf.AdhocQueryCmd` interface that extends the `QueryCmd` interface. `QueryCmd` defines the query activation mechanism, requiring subclasses to implement the specifics for performing the query as a command object. The actual work is performed by the subclasses of the abstract class `QueryCmdImpl` whose methods are shown in Figure 6-9. Another class that is of use is the `AdHocQueryCmdFactory` that creates `AdHocQueryCmd` objects. These ad-hoc query objects take any select statement and perform queries on collections of objects following the SanFrancisco syntax (which we will discuss at length later in the book).

Figure 6-9
com.ibm.sf.gf.
QueryCmdImpl

Class com.ibm.sf.gf.QueryCmdImpl

public abstract class **QueryCmdImpl**

extends CommandImpl

implements QueryCmd

```
protected QueryCollection query(String selectStatement,
                                String bindNameOfCollectionInSelect,
                                SelectCompare selectCompareObject,
                                String bindNameOfSelectCompare,
                                SortCompare orderbyCompareObject,
                                String bindNameOfOrderbyCompareObject,
                                QueryCollection collectionToQuery,
                                boolean accessResults,
                                String specificationKeyId) throws
SFException
```

Performs an object level query .

Parameters:

selectStatement — the String which contains the Select statement

bindNameOfCollectionInSelect — the String which contains the bindNameOfCollectionInSelect

selectCompareObject — the SelectCompare object used to query

bindNameOfSelectCompare — the String which contains the bindNameOfSelectCompare

orderbyCompareObject — the SortCompare used to sort

bindNameOfOrderbyCompareObject — the string which contains the bindNameOfOrderbyCompareObject

collectionToQuery — the QueryCollection object to query

accessResults — boolean indicating whether to drop access of the elements of the result collection

specificationKeyId — the string which contains the specificationKeyId

Returns:

QueryCollection (transient)

Throws: SFException

from query Engine.

Figure 6-9
(Cont'd)

```
 protected QueryCollection query(String selectStatement,
                                 String bindNameOfCollectionInSelect,
                                 SelectCompare selectCompareObject,
                                 String bindNameOfSelectCompare,
                                 SortCompare orderbyCompareObject,
                                 String bindNameOfOrderbyCompareObject,
                                 QueryCollection collectionToQuery,
                                 boolean accessResults) throws SFException


 protected QueryCollection query(String selectStatement,
                                 String bindNameOfCollectionInSelect,
                                 SelectCompare selectCompareObject,
                                 String bindNameOfSelectCompare,
                                 SortCompare orderbyCompareObject,
                                 String bindNameOfOrderbyCompareObject,
                                 QueryCollection collectionToQuery,
                                 boolean accessResults,
                                 String hostVariableNames[],
                                 Object hostVariableValues[]) throws
SFException


 protected QueryCollection query(String selectStatement,
                                 String bindNameOfCollectionInSelect,
                                 SelectCompare selectCompareObject,
                                 String bindNameOfSelectCompare,
                                 SortCompare orderbyCompareObject,
                                 String bindNameOfOrderbyCompareObject,
                                 QueryCollection collectionToQuery,
                                 boolean accessResults,
                                 String specificationKeyId,
                                 String hostVariableNames[],
                                 Object hostVariableValues[]) throws
SFException
 public QueryCollection getResult()
```

Returns the result of the query.

```
 public void initialize() throws SFException
 protected void destroy() throws SFException
 public void setEqual(Dependent object) throws SFException
 public boolean equals(Object object)
 public String toString()
 public int hashCode()
 public void externalizeToStream(BaseStream stream) throws IOException
 public void internalizeFromStream(BaseStream stream) throws IOException
 public Handle getResultHdl()
```

Security

Support for application-level security is built into the Foundation layer. Features supported include user management, user passwords, and authorization. User logins and passwords are managed through a security policy that controls authentication in SanFrancisco. While an installation of SanFrancisco can disable authentication, if the system administrator defines that authentication is to be performed then, before accessing any resource on the SanFrancisco network, a user will have to provide a login and a password with which authentication is performed. This authentication process will usually also involve authentication at the database level — although specifics may change through the usage of specialized security policy objects that can be configured to be used by any SanFrancisco installation. The default `LogonController` object in SanFrancisco even ensures that only a single logon is necessary from any client using resources within the same Logical SanFrancisco Network (LSFN)—so long as all accesses are performed from within a single JVM.

Authorization in SanFrancisco follows a paradigm of Actor–Resource–Action. An *Actor* represents a user of the system that has been authenticated and, therefore, can be given a system identity (to which authorization specifications may be linked). *Resource*s can be one of two things: servers in the LSFN or functional entities controlled by the `Company` object (part of the Common Business Objects). The `Company` object is a central manager for all system-wide entities—one of the categories being the secure entities. An `Action` is any usage that may be attempted using a resource by an actor. Authorization in such a model is naturally defined by associating access right definitions with linkages between actors, and actions on resources.

Authorization to functional entities is managed through a concept called *secure tasks*. Secure tasks are built into the Foundation layer and a partial API is shown in Figure 6-10. Forming a secure task involves the following steps:

- An application developer creates a `SecureTask` instance. Code that needs to be performed before or after authentication is performed, is placed within the `beginSecureTask` method and the `endSecureTask` method, respectively. Note that the secure task bracketing is performed by the application developer—the secure task merely provides a place holder for associating access control information. Figure 6-11 provides an example.
- Access control lists that specify which actors can perform which secure tasks are defined.
- At runtime, when a secure task begins, the `beginSecureTask` verifies that the user has the appropriate access rights, and if not then an authorization exception is called.

Figure 6-10
`com.ibm.sf.gf.SecureTask`

Class com.ibm.sf.gf.SecureTask

•**ACTOR_ANY_USER**

Used for setActorType() to indicate that this SecureTask can be executed for any user.

•**ACTOR_USER**

Used for setActorType() to indicate that the user must be specifically authorized to this SecureTask.

•**ivActorType**

The type of Actor that may be authorized to this task.

•**ivDescription**

Detailed descriptive information for this task.

•**ivName**

A unique identifier for the task within a naming service context.

•**ivNameServerPermissions**

Vector to hold NameServerPermissions

•**ivPermissions**

Hashtable to hold Permissions

•**ivResourceType**

The type of resource that may be associated with this task in an AccessRight.

•**RESOURCE_COMPANY**

Used for setResourceType() to indicate that this SecureTask requires a Company object to be specified on the beginSecureTask() method and for an AccessRight.

•**RESOURCE_NONE**

Used for setResourceType() to indicate that this SecureTask does not require any resource to be specified on the beginSecureTask() method or for an AccessRight.

•**createSecureTask**(String, String)

Creates a new SecureTask transient object.

•**getActorType**()

Gets The type of Actor that may be authorized to this task.

•**getDescription**()

Gets the detailed descriptive information for this task.

Figure 6-10
(Cont'd)

•**getName**()

Gets the name for the secure task.

•**getResourceType**()

Gets the type of resource that may be associated with this task in an AccessRight.

•**setDescription**(String)

Set detailed descriptive information for this task.

•**setName**(String)

Set a unique identifier for the task within a naming service context.

•**setResourceType**(int)

Set the type of resource that may be associated with this task in an AccessRight.

•**toString**()

Generates a string to contain information about this object

Figure 6-11
Using a secure task.

```
try {

    Global.security().beginSecureTask(
         "Close a part order",
         "com/rts/ServiceSuite4/Call",
         partOrderHandle);

    // If we get here then we are authenticated and are
   // allowed to change the status of the part order

   partOrderHandle.close();

    Global.security().endSecureTask
         "Close a part order",
         "com/rts/ServiceSuite4/Call",
         partOrderHandle);

 }
 catch (NotAuthorizedException ex)
 {
    // No permissions associated with this
   // particular secure task object
 }
 catch (SFException ex)
 {
    // General exception
 }
```

Localization

SanFrancisco targets the global market. As such, it supports the notion of internationalization and localization. Internationalization means building software in such a way that location-specific and cultural-specific issues are decoupled from the code. If this is performed, at deployment time the software can be localized according to local conventions.

Well-known examples of internationalization and localization include date formats, number formats, and language. A program that has been internationalized (or globalized) will have displays pertaining to dates, and numbers that are formatted based on external policy objects (which are called locales—as we will shortly see). Texts and messages are displayed using an additional level of indirection. Instead of having code that hard codes the message text to be shown to the user, the code uses a symbolic name (or a numeric code) that is then mapped to various message texts in various languages based on the localization of the program. Obviously, there are many other issues pertaining to localization—some of them much more difficult to deal with (for example, languages that are written from right-to-left or top-to-bottom, sorting of strings, maintaining application data in various languages, etc.).

The Foundation layer supports locales as a specifier for a geographic and cultural selection. Many classes in the SanFrancisco distribution are locale-sensitive. A class is locale-sensitive if its behavior is affected by the locale being used when that class' functionality is invoked. Thus the locale is merely a specifier whereas the locale-dependent behavior is encapsulated in a set of classes forming the Foundation. For example, date objects are locale-sensitive because their formatting features depend on the current locale.

SanFrancisco follows the accepted representation of locales as strings of the form:

```
LA_CO_XXX
```

where LA is a two-letter encoding of the language (such as `en` for English and `fr` for French), CO is an encoding of a country name (such as US or CA for Canada) and XXX is called the variant code (such as WIN for Windows or MAC for Macintosh).

Locales are managed within a LSFN by the `LocaleController` and `LocaleContext` classes. The `LocaleController` maintains all the available locales in the LSFN—starting with the locales available in the native JDK1.1. There is only one instance of the `LocaleController` possible in a LSFN, maintained by the `LocaleContext`. Trying to create an additional `LocaleController` will result in an error. All applications running in a LSFN share the same controller through the `LocaleContext` that is used for retrieving locales.

SanFrancisco provides very broad support in terms of locale-sensitive classes. Obviously, time zones are fully supported as well as date and time formats. Message catalogs are used to implement string mappings based on locales. Message catalogs include both `StaticMessageCatalogs` and `DynamicMessageCatalogs`—the later allowing runtime modifications. Static message catalogs are normally used for error and informative messages that are fully bound at development time. Dynamic message catalogs are usually used for maintaining messages encapsulated using a `DescriptiveInformation` object. A `DescriptiveInformation` is returned by objects implementing the `Describable` interface.

We know this sounds confusing—but actually it is very simple. Most classes in the Common Business Object and the Core Business Process layers implement the `Describable` interface (or an interface extending it such as `DynamicDescribableEntity`). As such, they implement a method returning a `DescriptiveInformation`:

```
public abstract DescriptiveInformation
getDescriptiveInformation() throws SFException
```

This is then used as an entry point into the dynamic message catalogs, allowing entities to describe themselves differently based on differing locales. This is depicted in Figure 6-12.

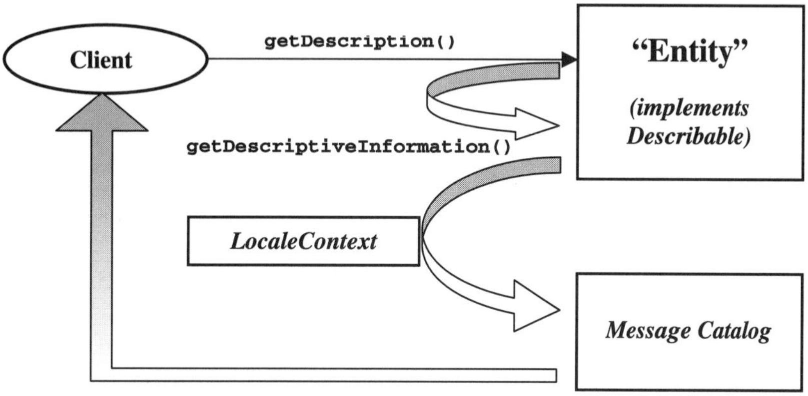

Figure 6-12 Interaction between locales, describables, and message catalogs.

Foundation Class Architecture

Apart from supporting the infrastructure services described above (and certainly not less important), the foundation layer defines the basic software architecture assumed by applications using SanFrancisco by providing the base classes that must be used by all applications. These classes ensure that applications conform to the architectural rules defined by the foundation layer. They also introduce a few fundamental concepts such as dependency, ownership, and references.

Dependency is an important notion that was already covered in the previous chapter (a class inheriting from the `Dependent` class is wholly contained and has no existence outside its container). Dependency is somewhat related to another important notion of the SanFrancisco foundation called ownership. One object is owned by another if its lifecycle fully depends on the lifecycle of its owner. For example, a part order object may be modeled as a part order header and a collection of part order lines (see Figure 6-13). The part order header and the part order lines are fully owned by the part order. This means, for example, that when a part order is deleted, so is the part order header and the part order lines. The notion of ownership is wider than the notion of dependence. Instances created from a dependent class are always fully contained—they are always fully owned. On the other hand, objects created from an entity class can be wholly owned or not. There will be cases where they will be shared and have multiple references to them

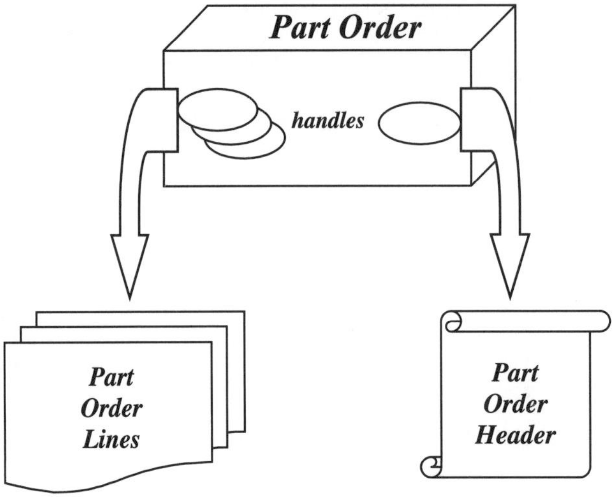

Figure 6-13
A possible part order model.

whereas in other systems they may be fully owned. In our example, a part order line may be fully owned by the part order object in a Help Desk system (which only cares about the customer's view of the part order) and as an independent entity driving the supply process in a Warehouse/Logistics application. The notion of ownership allows more flexibility in that control over lifecycle is based on how the objects are used and not on how they are defined.

CBO Architecture

Architecturally, the Common Business Objects are organized as an object library. This layer provides reusable classes used by application code as well as by the various Core Business Processes. A partial list of interfaces in the Common Business Objects layer:

- `com.ibm.sf.cf.Address`. Encapsulates an address for SanFrancisco objects.
- `com.ibm.sf.cf.Area`. Structurally, this interface merely provides accessors for a code and a description, but semantically, it represents an arbitrary area such as a geographic area, a shipping area, or an organizational area.
- `com.ibm.sf.cf.BusinessPartner`. Represents a business partner of the `Company` in a SanFrancisco application. The concept of a business partner is an important one in the SanFrancisco framework and additional support classes (such as business partner types—representing a supplier, customer, subcontractor, etc.).
- `com.ibm.sf.cf.BusinessPartnerBalance`. Maintains a balance of a business partner.
- `com.ibm.sf.cf.BusinessPartnerCached Balances`. Encapsulates the mechanism of caching a balance for business partners. It is useful when many transactions affect the bottom line and while we can always recalculate the result from the individual transactions, the balance will often be cached. This is an important mechanism used by almost every business application for performance and convenience reasons.

- `com.ibm.sf.cf.BusinessPartnerController`. Manages the business partners for a company in terms of accessing them.
- `com.ibm.sf.cf.BusinessPartnerGroup`. Supports the grouping of business partners.
- `com.ibm.sf.cf.CalendarPeriod`. Encapsulates a period within a calendar. Many operations in the business world must be associated with a period. Examples include services provided to customers, arrivals on site, etc. Other SanFrancisco operations—such as transactions in the General Ledger Core Business Process—require an association with a calendar period.
- `com.ibm.sf.cf.Company`. Encapsulates any part of the organization structure for the organization for which the application is written (for example, in a field service management system the company is the service company as opposed to the customers of the service companies). Each independent organizational unit may be represented by such an object, and these objects may be grouped in some structure.
- `com.ibm.sf.cf.Country`.
- `com.ibm.sf.cf.Currency`. Encapsulates all attributes for currencies in the system; these are referenced by monetary values in the system.
- `com.ibm.sf.cf.CurrencyController`. The manager for currency objects.
- `com.ibm.sf.cf.DatedCalendarPeriod`. A *from-to* type calendar period.
- `com.ibm.sf.cf.DatedFiscalPeriod`. Encapsulates a fiscal period covering a specific date range.
- `com.ibm.sf.cf.Day`
- `com.ibm.sf.cf.DocumentLocation`
- `com.ibm.sf.cf.Enterprise`. The root of the `Company` organizations.
- `com.ibm.sf.cf.ExchangeRateType`. Used for conversion between currencies.
- `com.ibm.sf.cf.FiscalCalendar`. Encapsulates the fiscal calendar and is used by the General Ledger and Accounts Payable/Receivable Core Business Processes.

- `com.ibm.sf.cf.FiscalPeriod`. The primitive element comprising the fiscal calendar.
- `com.ibm.sf.cf.FiscalYear`. A fiscal year that can be separated into mutually exclusive periods.
- `com.ibm.sf.cf.HierarchyLevelInformation`. One of the various interfaces and classes useful for creating and using hierarchical structures.
- `com.ibm.sf.cf.Initials`. Represents a signature of a person or a group.
- `com.ibm.sf.cf.NaturalCalendar`
- `com.ibm.sf.cf.NumberSeries`. Used for creating number series such as systems that generate numbering of application objects.
- `com.ibm.sf.cf.PaymentMethod`. Defines details relevant to verification and validation performed in payment processes.
- `com.ibm.sf.cf.PaymentTerms`. Involved in defining payments for items.
- `com.ibm.sf.cf.PeriodizedCalendar`. A calendar that is made up of years, which are themselves made up of periods.
- `com.ibm.sf.cf.Project`. Used as a handle to projects and used for associating properties with a project.
- `com.ibm.sf.cf.SupplementaryCharge`. Encapsulates additional charges that may be associated with contracts, quotes, etc.
- `com.ibm.sf.cf.UndatedCalendarPeriod`. A calendar period with no dates associated with it.
- `com.ibm.sf.cf.UnitOfMeasure`. Encapsulates the properties of a physical unit used to measure items.

CBR Architecture

The SanFrancisco Core Business Processes form the top-most layer in the SanFrancisco architecture. The Core Business Processes are a set of domain-specific frameworks that provide very high abstraction levels for application developers. These frameworks are very close to being quasiapplications out of the box, in that they not only provide sets of reusable classes, but rather complete sets of classes along with processes and structural information that can support complete application segments.

Version 1.3 of SanFrancisco provides four high-level frameworks: The General Ledger framework, the Accounts Payable/Accounts Receivable framework, the Warehouse Management framework, and the Order Management framework. Each of these frameworks provides functionality specific to a certain domain. As such, these frameworks are not architected with the goal of providing building blocks to be used for building applications in other domains. For example, the Warehouse Management framework provides interfaces and classes supporting costing policies and costing calculations. Among other interfaces it defines the `com.ibm.sf.whs.DCostingPolicy` interface for defining handling common to various costing policies. While it would be reasonable to think that costing as a concept is not specific to warehouse management and could be used in other types of applications (such as field service dispatching, service outsourcing, etc.), this is contrary to the SanFrancisco architecture. The positioning of the Core Business Processes is such that they are not constructed to provide reusable objects used in multiple application domains—this is the intent of the Common Business Objects. Each of the Core Business Processes provides a complete set of classes that operate together, aiming to completely solve a certain application domain. So while the Core Business Processes do not add to the number of common reusable objects, they can focus on providing extremely high reusability levels that could not have been achieved using Common Business Objects.

Core Business Processes are architected to allow for multiple implementations in the specific domain to use the same base code. So while each Core Business Process is fully functional out-of-the-box, it has many built-in customization features (called extension points) that are used to customize and adapt the framework to the specific need of the application developer. In other words, the Core Business Processes were designed and developed to be a cross between a shrink-wrapped application and a template for applications. The formidable goal of the Core Business Processes is to allow creating applications extremely quickly with very limited changes or code additions while allowing for advanced usage of these frameworks in more elaborate schemes. Therefore, the Core Business Processes will typically be used in one of three methods:

- The Core Business Process may in some cases provide the complete functionality required by your application. In this case all you will need to do is study the framework, and make use of its structures (and make no mistake about it—this in itself can be a very lengthy task).

- The Core Business Process definitely supports the general functionality, but there are differences between how your application handles various issues and how the framework does. In this case you will use the framework extension points to adapt the framework—making it compliant with your functionality requirements.
- The Core Business Process provides only a limited set of the functionality you require. In this case you will need to make use of all architectural tools at your disposal, using perhaps some of the Core Business Process together with Common Business Objects, and even home-grown objects directly above the Foundation Layer. You may need to subclass some classes or create delegation structures—in any case, your task will obviously be more complex and require higher skill levels.

Since a core business process usually requires some up front customization to allow for differences between different applications and business rules, the use of a Core Business Process involves two stages:

- setup; and
- activities.

Setup is the process in which an application designer uses the built-in classes and extension points provided by the framework to define the correct structures and data required for correct operation of the framework in the context of the specific application. Any application framework implementing functionality in a way that can accommodate multiple implementations will have many parameters (both in terms of values and algorithms). These extension points are necessary to support the customization of the framework. However, in order to customize the framework the correct structures and parameters need to be set up before the framework can be used within the application. This setup stage is often the most difficult part in a reuse process because it assumes a good understanding of the semantic structures used by the frameworks—once this understanding is attained, the rest is downhill.

Activities are the actions or business transactions performed in the system. They form the dynamic entities that are responsible for moving the system from one state to the next—they are the lifeline of the system.

Any information regarding the system can be attained through analysis of the activities. Generally, activities are classified as either being day-to-day activities or being periodic activities. For example, in the context of a field service management system, a day-to-day activity may be a part order, or a service fix—anything that needs to be recorded in the context of a service call. A periodic activity may be the creation of invoices to be mailed to the customers every month for collecting payments for services and contract maintenance.

The General Ledger Framework

The purpose of the General Ledger framework is to track and report on the flow of money within a Company. The General Ledger framework—as with other Core Business Processes—requires a setup phase in which the structures are formed. In the case of the General Ledger, the structures being created are the "Chart of Accounts"—basically this is the collection of accounting structures that will later be used as buckets that aggregate transactions. Setting up the account structure involves four steps (bottom-to-top).

- Setting up analysis codes.
- Setting up analysis groups.
- Setting up posting compositions.
- Setting up accounts.

Analysis codes and analysis groups form the primitive elements of a Chart of Accounts. `AnalysisCodes` form validation structures that define the appropriate values, types, and units of measures for each primitive piece of the accounting structure. `AnalysisGroups` aggregate `AnalysisCodes` into higher-level structures; the codes themselves are owned by `AnalysisGroupCodeController` objects, which are themselves aggregated in a hierarchical structure with a root of type `AnalysisGroupCodeControllerRoot`. This hierarchy forms the analysis structure for the Chart of Accounts for the entire company. Since the creation of the structure is completely data driven, it can accommodate differences in companies, countries, etc.

The next concept used in the General Ledger framework is that of a Posting Combination and a Dissection. A `PostingCombination` is usually an account in the general ledger—it forms one of the serialized categories managed by the ledger. The term `PostingCombination` is a generalization of the account since it represents the basic entity for which activities or transactions can be reported. Therefore, it allows for a very high degree of flexibility in that no restrictions are placed on what can aggregate transactions. Structurally, a `PostingCombination` holds sets of `AnalysisCodes` from one or more `AnalysisGroups`. A Dissection is the actual object that associates a value with a `PostingCombination`.

Once the valid structures for posting combinations and dissections have been defined, the accounts for the company may be defined. Valid account types and the account structures for the company are all that is required for activities to be reported within the General Ledger.

Once the setup has been defined for the application, activities may be reported. Activities are categorized as being either day-to-day activities or as being periodic activities. Day-to-day activities are the business transaction recordings that detail money transfers involving the company whereas periodic activities include accounting operations that occur when closing a year or generating reports. So once a chart of accounts has been set up, the journal will be continuously updated with transactions that associate value with a transaction and even transactions that associate quantities (with an arbitrary unit of measure) with dissections (using a `com.ibm.sf.gl.DQuantityDissection`), thereby documenting the transfers recorded by the journal. Obviously, individual transactions may invalidate a journal temporarily. Additional offsetting transactions will normally correct the journal making it a valid one for posting. Day-to-day activities normally end with an activity that makes the journal valid and ready for posting. Note that the definition of the validation business rule for a journal in a Core Business Process extension point allows different applications to redefine what a valid journal is. In fact, almost any entity in the framework has some validation policy, and these policies may be changed by different applications—for example, the interface `com.ibm.sf.gl.DDissectionValidationPolicy` defines how dissections and quantity dissections are deemed to be valid, and allow different applications to provide their own concrete implementation of the validation rules.

Finally, the General Ledger framework supports all periodic processes regarding journals. This includes activities related to the end of a fiscal year, activities run when a period is closed, and the generation of reports such as profit and loss (P&L) statements and balance sheets. Support for reports includes only the processing of the data and not the formatting—this should be handled by the application using an external report generator. The fact that the Core Business Processes are based on Common Business Objects and on the Foundation layer is very apparent and provides a very clear and convenient structure, which aids understanding and proficiency in the frameworks. For example, closing a journal is performed using a `Command` object of the form:

```
public interface interface com.ibm.sf.gl.GLClosingCmd extends
Command

Purpose: This command performs the GL Closing processing.
Description: This command calculates the overall balance for
profit and loss accounts within the first period of the year and
the given endPeriod. Then it adds dissections to a final profit
and loss journal or it sets the zeroProfitAndLoss attribute to
TRUE. Note: Before running the command, the posting combinations
in GLClosingParameters used for year end processing have to be
set by the application.
```

The Accounts Payable/Accounts Receivable Framework

The Accounts Payable/Receivable framework records transactions between parties in the context of sets of accounts, ledgers, and logs in order to provide an accurate and up-to-date snapshot of a company's assets and liabilities. This framework is an important addition to the General Ledger framework in the management of a company's financials. It includes support for the following topics.

- Enter values for payments and receipts.
- Assign a payment or a receipt to an account or accounts.
- Validate a value of a payment or receipt in the context of assigning it to an account or set of accounts.
- Support for the full lifecycle of payment of a receipt, including logging, cancelling, etc.
- Support for all aspects of payment and receipts in the context of a debt, including adjustments, discounts and fines, and currency rates.
- Management of associations between various documents and Accounts Payable/Receivable objects such as ledgers, transactions, payments, debts, accounts, etc.

Following the general spirit of the Core Business Processes, the Accounts Payable/Receivable framework also involves initial setup for use within an application after which activities (both day-to-day and periodic) manipulate the defined structures. The setup stage involves setting up business partners, account structures, analysis codes and groups, dissections, payments types, etc. Day-to-day activities involve payments and receipts, all performed as transactions, which affect accounts, ledgers, and logs. Posting combinations and dissections are fully supported—making use of similar concepts from the General Ledger framework. Periodic activities include ledger reconciliation, debt management and collection, and reevaluations. The objects of the framework are ready built, allowing information to be extracted for periodic reports and letters to business partners.

The Warehouse Management Framework

The Warehouse Management Framework supports the management of inventory and stock items. Processes supported include product and part ordering, sourcing, replenishment, warehousing (both binned and not), transfer of inventory between warehouses, creation of follow-up activities, etc. The primary entities forming the Warehouse Management Framework include:

- `Warehouse`. The `com.ibm.sf.whs.Warehouse` interface represents the warehouse abstraction in the system, associating inventory with a location. Organization of inventory within a warehouse is also supported using stock zones (`com.ibm.sf.whs.StockZone`), which can contain multiple stock locations (`com.ibm.sf.whs.StockLocation`). Each stock location may contain more than one product type. Lots are also fully supported by the Warehouse Management framework.
- `Inventory`. Inventory represents goods that are in stock. An instance of an implementation class for `com.ibm.sf.whs.Inventory` holds the balance of one product in a warehouse. The inventory may be maintained for serialized or non-serialized inventory; if the goods are serialized, the collection of serial numbers may be maintained.
- `Product`. Product is the main entity managed by the framework. Structurally, a product maintains the descriptive information of the entities in the warehouse. Functionally, many of the methods required to manipulate goods in a warehouse are implemented

Figure 6-14 Methods of com.ibm.sf.whs.Product

- **addCost**(Cost, Warehouse, Lot, UnitOfMeasure)

  Adds the passed Cost to the appropriate internal collection of Costs held by the corresponding ProductWarehouseLink.

- **addFutureReception**(FutureReception)

  Adds the passed future reception for a product warehouse relation, the received balances are updated.

- **addProductReservation**(ProductReservation)

  Adds the reservation for a product warehouse link and updates the cached balances, if any.

- **assignStockLocation**(Warehouse, StockTypeValue, UnitOfMeasure, StockZone, Lot, DMeasurement, DProductTransactionQuantity, DStockLocationValidationSelectionPolicy, DStockLocationAssignerSelectionPolicy)

  Assigns a valid StockLocation for a product in a warehouse that is location controlled.

- **chooseLot**(DProductTransactionQuantity, Warehouse, StockTypeValue, DTime, DTime, DTime, DLotChooserSelectionPolicy, DLotValidationSelectionPolicy)

  Returns a set of DLotChooserResult instances.

- **chooseSerialNumbers**(Warehouse, DProductTransactionQuantity, StockTypeValue, DTime, Lot, StockLocation, DSerialNumberChooserSelectionPolicy, DSerialNumberValidationSelectionPolicy)

  Interface to the SerialNumberChooserPolicy.

- **chooseStockLocation**(Warehouse, DProductTransactionQuantity, StockTypeValue, DTime, Lot, DStockLocationChooserSelectionPolicy)

Returns a set of ChooseStockLocationResult objects.

- **getAvailableQuantity**(DProductTransactionQuantity, ProcessTokenValue, Warehouse, StockTypeValue, Lot, StockLocation, SerialNumber, DTime, BusinessPartner, MannerOfTransport)

  Calculates available quantity of the product based on input arguments.

- **getBalance**(DProductBalanceAccessKey)

  Returns available balance for this product based on passed access key.

- **getBaseUnitOfMeasure**()

  This method retrieves the base unit of measure for the product.

- **getCost**(CostTypeValue, Warehouse, Lot, UnitOfMeasure)

  Returns a Cost for the passed CostTypeValue object from Product if warehouse is null or from ProductWarehouseLink if a warehouse is specified.

- **getCostPrice**(DCostingPolicyNonTransactionBased, CostTypeValue, Warehouse, UnitOfMeasure, Lot)

  Returns the cost price for the passed in costingPolicy.

- **getLotValidationSelectionPolicy**()

  Gets LotValidationSelectionPolicy

- **getProductGroup**()

  Returns the ProductGroup for the current Product

- **getSerialNumberValidationSelectionPolicy**()

  Gets SerialNumberValidationSelectionPolicy

- **getStockLocationAssignerSelectionPolicy**()

  Gets StockLocationAssignerSelectionPolicy

- **getStockLocationChooserSelectionPolicy**()

  Gets StockLocationChooserSelectionPolicy

Figure 6-14
(Cont'd)

•**getStockTransactions**()

Returns a copy of the Collection of StockTransaction, used by framework - NOT FOR CLIENT USE

•**getWarehouses**()

Returns the set of warehouses for this product.

•**initialize**(ProductController, String, DescriptiveInformation, boolean, boolean, ProductPolicyFactory, Initials, ABCClassification, DEntityOwningMap, DTime, DLotChooserSelectionPolicy, DLotValidationSelectionPolicy, DSerialNumberChooserSelectionPolicy, DSerialNumberValidationSelectionPolicy, DStockLocationChooserSelectionPolicy, DStockLocationAssignerSelectionPolicy, boolean)

This method is invoked by the Factory after Construction of an instance of this class to ensure proper initialization

•**isFictitious**()

Gets flag to indicate whether this Product is fictitious.

•**isLocationControlled**(Warehouse)

Returns true if this product is location controlled in the passed in warehouse

•**isLotControlled**()

Gets flag to indicate whether this Product is lot controlled

•**isRelatedToUnitOfMeasure**(UnitOfMeasure)

Checks whether the product is related to the passed in unit of measure

•**isRelatedToWarehouse**(Warehouse)

Checks whether this product is related to the specified warehouse.

•**isSerialNumberControlled**()

Gets flag to indicate whether this Product is serial number controlled

•**isStockControlled**(Warehouse)

Returns true if this product is stock controlled in the passed in warehouse

•**isStockControlledInAnyWarehouse**()

Returns true if this product is stock controlled in any warehouse related to the product

•**validateLotMandatory**(Lot)

Validates that if lot controlled product, lot is mandatory and must exist.

•**validateLotOptional**(Lot)

Validates that if lot controlled product, lot is optional, but if passed it must exist.

•**validateProductWarehouseLink**(Warehouse)

Validates if the passed in warehouse is valid for the product.

•**validateSerialNumberMandatory**(SerialNumber)

Validates that if the Product is serial number controlled, the SerialNumber is mandatory and must exist.

•**validateSerialNumberOptional**(SerialNumber)

Validates that, if the Product is serial number controlled, the SerialNumber passed exists for the Product.

•**validateStockLocationMandatory**(Warehouse, StockLocation)

Validates that if locationControlled product warehouse relation, stockLocation is mandatory and must exist.

•**validateStockLocationOptional**(Warehouse, StockLocation)

Validates that if locationControlled product warehouse relation, stockLocation is optional, but must exist if passed.

DBackToBackHandlingPolicy	DBackToBackHandlingPolicyDefault	DBuildCommonOrderPolicy
DBuildCommonOrderPolicyDefault	DBuildCommonOrderPriceDetailPolicy	DBuildCommonOrderPriceDetailPolicyDefault
DBuildFullOrderPolicy	DBuildOrderPolicy	DBuildCommonOrderRequestedDetailPolicy
DBuildFullOrderPolicyDefault	DBuildFullOrderPriceDetailPolicy	DBuildFullOrderPriceDetailPolicyDefault
DCreditHandlingPolicy	DBuildFullOrderRequestedDetailPolicy	DBuildCommonOrderRequestedDetailPolicyDefault
DBuildOrderPolicyDefault	DBuildOrderPriceDetailPolicy	DBuildOrderPriceDetailPolicyDefault
DBuildOrderRequestedDetailPolicy	DBuildOrderRequestedDetailPolicyDefault	DBuildFullOrderRequestedDetailPolicyDefault
DCreditHandlingPolicyDefault	DDeliveryTimeHandlingPolicy	DFullPurchaseOrderRequestedDetailExtension
DDiscountDefinitionChooserPolicy	DDiscountDefinitionChooserPolicyDefault	DDiscountDefinitionChooserSelectionPolicy
DExchangeRateHandlingPolicy	DExchangeRateHandlingPolicyDefault	DDiscountDefinitionChooserSelectionPolicyDefault
DFullPurchaseOrderExtension	DFullPurchaseOrderCreateableExtension	DFullPurOrderRequestedDetailCreateableExtension
DFullSalesOrderExtension	DFullPurchaseOrderPriceDetailExtension	DFullPurchaseOrderPriceDetailCreateableExtension
DFullSalesOrderCreateableExtension	DDeliveryTimeHandlingPolicyDefault	DFullSalesOrderPriceDetailCreateableExtension
DFullSalesOrderPriceDetailExtension	DFullSalesOrderRequestedDetailExtension	DFullSalesOrderRequestedDetailCreateableExtension
DInventoryValidationPolicy	DInventoryValidationPolicyDirectSalesDebit	DOpenOrderBalanceValueProductExtension
DInventoryValidationPolicySalesDebit	DInventoryValidationPolicySalesCredit	DOpenOrderBalanceValueChargeExtension
DOrderBackorderHandlingPolicy	DInventoryValidationPolicyPurchaseDebit	DOrderBackorderHandlingPolicyUpdatePicking
DOrderBackorderHandlingPolicyUpdatePlanning	DOrderBackorderHandlingSelectionPolicyDefault	DOrderBackorderableDetailExtension
DOrderDeletePreparationPolicy	DOrderDeliveryGroupDetailExtension	DOrderDeliveryGroupDetailHandlingPolicy
DOrderDeliveryGroupDetailHandlingPolicyDefault	DOrderDeliveryGroupPolicy	DOrderDeliveryGroupPolicyDefault
DOrderDeliveryTimeHandlingExtension	DOrderDeliveryTimeHandlingPolicy	DOrderDeliveryTimeHandlingPolicyDefault
DOrderDeliveryValidationPolicy	DOrderDeliveryValidationPolicyDefault	DOrderExtension
DOrderInvoiceAttributesChangePolicy	DOrderInvoiceChangePolicyDefault	DOrderInvoiceDissectionCreatorPolicyDefault
DOrderInvoiceGenerationPolicyDefault	DOrderInvoiceGroupPolicy	DOrderInvoiceGroupPolicyDefault
DOrderInvoiceableDetailChargeExtension	DOrderInvoiceableDetailExtension	DOrderInvoiceableDetailProductExtension
DOrderInvoicingDetailChargeCreatorPolicyDefault	DOrderInvoicingDetailChargeExtension	DOrderInvoicingDetailDeletePreparationPolicy
DOrderInvoicingDetailExtension	DOrderInvoicingDetailProductCreatorPolicyDefault	DOrderInvoicingDetailProductExtension
DOrderInwardOutwardBoundExtension	DOrderIsBackorderExtension	DOrderPaymentAttributesChangePolicy
DOrderPaymentChangePolicyDefault	DOrderPickCommitPolicyDefault	DOrderPickCommittableDetailExtension
DOrderPickConfirmableDetailExtension	DOrderPickableDetailExtension	DOrderPickingDetailDeletePreparationPolicy
DOrderPickingDetailDeletePreparationPolicyDefault	DOrderPickingDetailExtension	DOrderPlannableDetailExtension
DOrderPlanningDetailCreatorPolicyBackToBack	DOrderPlanningDetailDeletePreparationPolicy	DOrderPlanningDetailDeletePreparationPolicyDefault
DOrderPlanningDetailExtension	DOrderPriceAndDiscountCalculationPolicy	DOrderPriceDetailDeletePreparationPolicy
DOrderPriceDetailDeliveryValidationPolicy	DOrderPriceDetailDeliveryValidationPolicyDefault	DOrderPriceDetailExtension
DOrderPriceDetailInvoiceAttributesChangePolicy	DOrderPriceDetailInvoiceChangePolicyDefault	DOrderPriceDetailPaymentAttributesChangePolicy
DOrderPriceDetailPaymentChangePolicyDefault	DOrderPriceDetailPriceDiscountHandlingPolicy	DOrderPriceDetailPriceDiscountHandlingPolicyDefault
DOrderPriceDetailQuantityHandlingPolicy	DOrderPriceDetailQuantityHandlingPolicyDefault	DOrderReceivableDetailExtension
DOrderReceivingDetailDeletePreparationPolicy	DOrderReceivingDetailDeletePreparationPolicyDefault	DOrderReceivingDetailExtension
DOrderReceptionCommittableDetailExtension	DOrderReceptionConfirmableDetailExtension	DOrderRequestedDetailDeletePreparationPolicy
DOrderRequestedDetailDeletePreparationPolicyDefault	DOrderRequestedDetailExtension	DOrderRequestedDetailInvoiceAttributesChangePolicy
DOrderRequestedDetailInvoiceChangePolicyDefault	DOrderRequestedDetailPaymentAttributesChangePolicy	DOrderRequestedDetailPaymentChangePolicyDefault
DOrderRequestedDetailQuantityHandlingPolicy	DOrderRequestedDetailQuantityHandlingPolicyDefault	DOrderSupplementaryChargeExtension

Figure 6-15
Policy and extension-related classes and interfaces of the Order Management framework.

DOrderSupplementaryChargeHandlingPolicy	DOrderSupplementaryChargeHandlingPolicyDefault	DOrderSupplementaryChargeableExtension
DPriceAndDiscountChooserPolicy	DPriceAndDiscountChooserPolicyDefault	DPriceDefinitionChooserPolicy
DPriceDefinitionChooserPolicyDefault	DPriceDefinitionChooserSelectionPolicy	DPriceDefinitionChooserSelectionPolicyDefault
DReplacingOrderProductUnitChooserPolicy	DReplacingOrderProductUnitChooserPolicyDefault	DReplacingOrderProductUnitValidationPolicy
DReplacingOrderProductUnitValidationPolicyDefault	DReservationAndFutureReceptionDirectOrderPolicy	DReservationAndFutureReceptionFullOrderPolicy
DReservationAndFutureReceptionHandlingPolicy	DStockTypeHandlingPolicy	DStockTypeHandlingPolicyDefault
DSubstituteOrderProductUnitChooserPolicy	DSubstituteOrderProductUnitChooserPolicyDefault	DSubstituteOrderProductUnitValidationPolicy
DSubstituteOrderProductUnitValidationPolicyDefault		

Figure 6-15
(Cont'd)

either directly on the `Product` hierarchy, or are related to its methods. Figure 6-14 shows a partial list of some important methods (from the javadoc page) used to manipulate product in a warehouse.

- `Stock Transaction`. Stock transactions form the lifeline of a warehouse application and record all stock movements in a warehouse. Obviously, the types and effects of stock transactions are important extension points of the framework.

The Order Management Framework

The Order Management framework implements functionality related to order-processing systems, including creation and processing of orders, order types, purchases, prices, etc. The framework provides many extension points that allow any types of orders to be processed and customization of the processes used. Products on order, and business partners performing the order, are encapsulated by the `com.ibm.sf.om.OrderProduct` and the `com.ibm.sf.om.OrderPartner` interfaces, respectively. Prices and discounts are fully supported along with various extension points for different calculation methods. The entire framework is built around sets of policy objects that make the framework very flexible in the processing of orders; in fact, of approximately 350 interfaces comprising the framework, almost 150 (shown in Figure 6-15) are policy and extension related.

As for the actual business processes supported by this framework, the Order Management framework builds on (and uses classes from) the Warehouse Management framework. In addition, the framework supports invoicing and supplementary charges using Common Business Object support, and new business processes involving order capture, order acknowledgment, and details requests.

CHAPTER 7

Downloading and Installing SanFrancisco

This chapter will walk you through the installation process for the SanFrancisco frameworks. Since SanFrancisco is built to solve highly complex problems, its architecture, and, therefore, installation is quite intricate. By reading this chapter before attempting the SanFrancisco installation you will hopefully be spared some of the little installation pitfalls involving SanFrancisco.

Extracting SanFrancisco

The SanFrancisco frameworks evaluation kit CD is available from IBM. If you do not hold a copy of this CD, the best place to start would be the SanFrancisco Website `http://www.software.ibm.com/ad/sanfrancisco`.

The SanFrancisco developer kit is available for Windows 95/98/NT, AS/400 and some of the more common UNIX flavors. The remainder of this chapter will be limited in scope to the Windows version, but the process is similar for the other versions.

Before you start the installation, make sure that the resources available on your computer are adequate. Once installed the evaluation version takes up approximately 200 MB of disk; quite a lot of code out there! Version 1.2 (and above) also requires the JDK 1.1.6 and Swing 1.0.2 (or Swing 1.0.3 because 1.0.2 is not in use any more). These are provided on the SanFrancisco Evaluation kit CD, but can also be downloaded directly from `http://java.sun.com`. All in all, you should reserve about half a gigabyte of disk space for the SanFrancisco installation. Another consideration is memory—you should have at least 128 MB of memory. Theoretically you can do with less, but then the performance you get is quite agonizing.

There are a couple more things to verify, but these are only if your machine is not hooked up to the Internet. You should verify that your system has TCP/IP networking support. This is usually the case, but you can verify it by taking a look at the "Protocols" tab in the "Networks" entry in the Control Panel. Last but not least, you should have a Web-browser installed, either Netscape Navigator® 4.0 (or later) or Microsoft Internet Explorer 4.0 (or later).

Once the SanFrancisco CD is placed in your CD-ROM drive, installation may begin (see Figure 7-1). The installation instructions are located at `$SFINSTALL/SFEval120/com/ibm/sf/doc/Install.htm` and

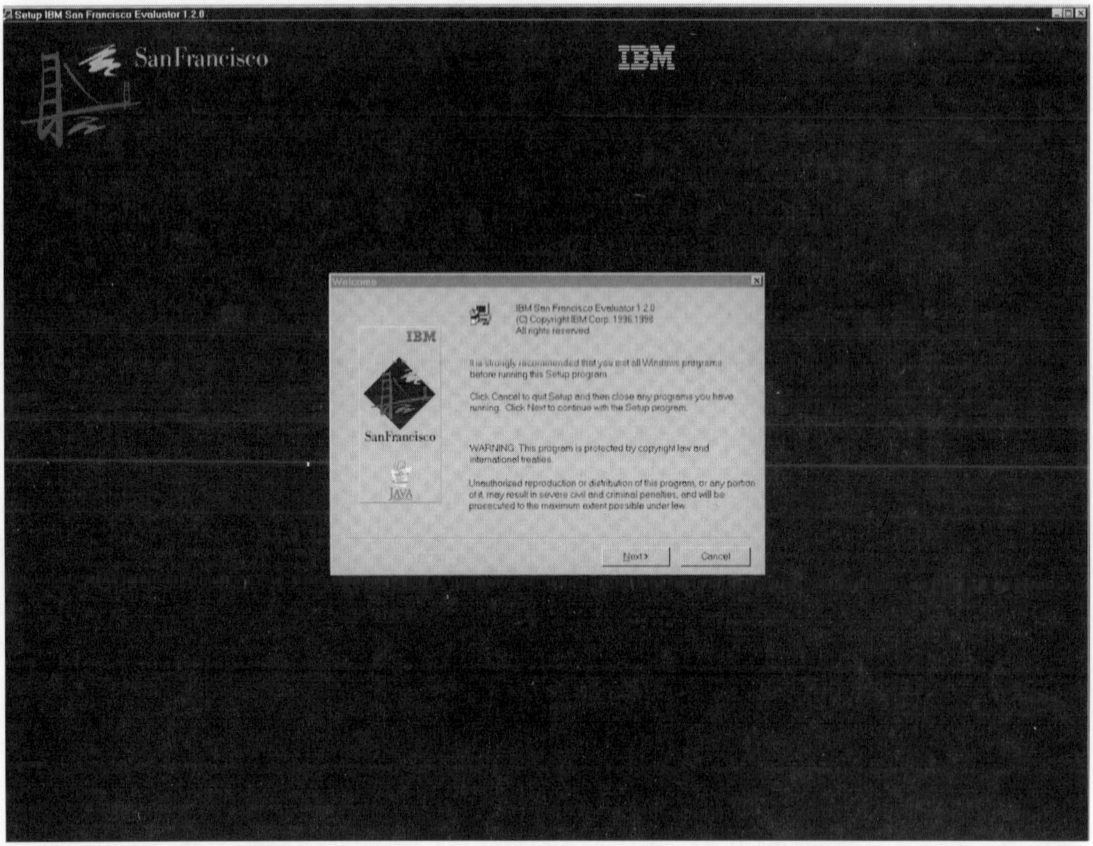

Figure 7-1
SanFrancisco installation.

should be read carefully before running the installation; since you can't read the file until after the installation (duh ?!?) you should proceed according to the following stages:

1. Run the self-extracting file and install the files; *do not* restart the computer when asked to.
2. Read the installation instructions.
3. Restart the computer.

Unfortunately, installation in many cases can be a pain; not enough effort has been invested in making this process a smooth one. For example, the JDK installed on our machine was JDK 1.1.5. After reading the installation notes, we went ahead to install JDK 1.1.6. However, just installing it was not enough for the SanFrancisco installation to succeed. In fact, the installation succeeded only after we changed the PATH variable and the registry information to match the JDK 1.1.6 installation. What was really annoying was not necessarily that we had to do all of these (it is obviously questionable whether IBM or Sun is at fault); what really bothered us was that the error dialog that comes up during the installation in case the wrong JDK version is used is very hard to interpret and occurs late in the installation process. In order to successfully install SanFrancisco we had to wait through the lengthy copying procedure at least four times until we finally got it right. But then again, "no pain, no gain."

To make sure that you have the right JDK version and the right JFC version, take a look at the "Environment" tab under the "System" icon in the Control Panel (see Figure 7-2). You should make sure that the CLASSPATH and PATH environment variables are correctly set. Note that if either the JDK or JFC is not installed and included in the CLASSPATH the installation will fail. Figure 7-3 shows an example of an error message caused by missing JFC.

One other peculiarity we discovered in the SanFrancisco installation procedure; the installation script places a batch file called `sfpic.bat` in the Startup Folder. The contents of this batch file are shown in Figure 7-4. The rationale behind this file is that a certain process needs to be invoked once before SanFrancisco is usable. This batch file makes the right calls and then deletes the batch file making sure that it is only called once. The only problem is that often the installation does not produce an environment that runs smoothly (as happened in our case). Therefore, when the batch file was run, it did not succeed in getting to the point of deleting the batch file and we were left with a configuration that called the batch file whenever we started the computer (whether we wanted to work with the SanFrancisco frameworks or not!). We kept getting a bunch of DOS windows that are very annoying. Needless to say, we removed this file very early on—as should the SanFrancisco people responsible for packaging the product.

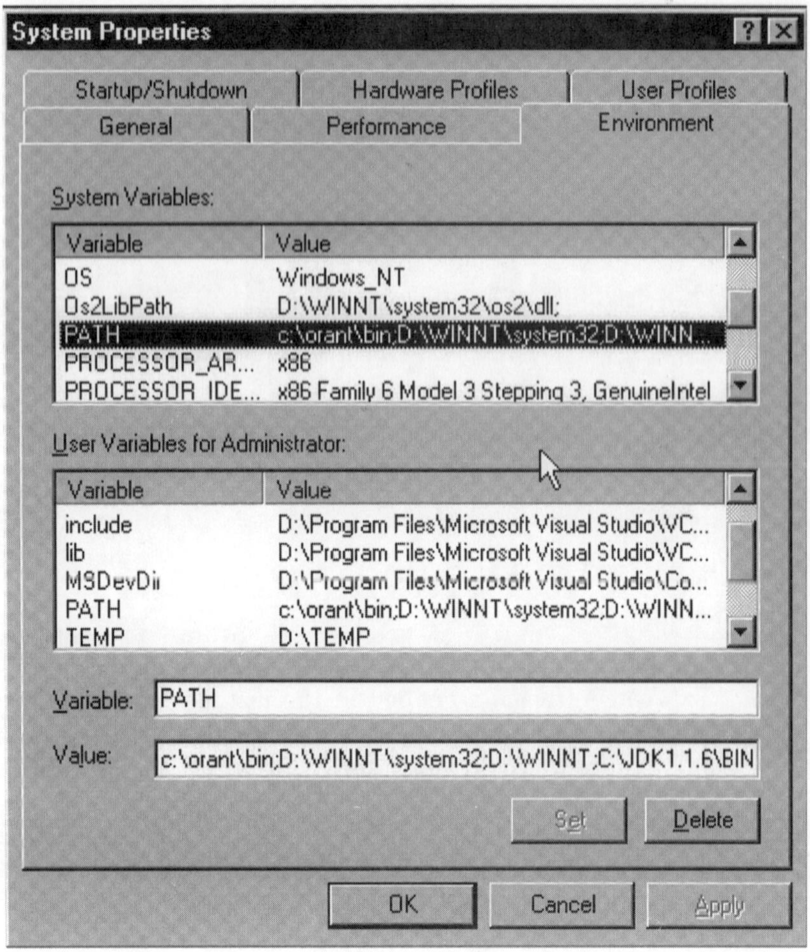

Figure 7-2
Environment settings.

Figure 7-3
Missing JFC error.

```
@echo off
JAVA com.ibm.sf.util.PrimeBase
JAVA com.ibm.sf.util.PrimePMSamples
JAVA com.ibm.sf.util.PrimeGL
JAVA com.ibm.sf.util.PrimeWM
JAVA com.ibm.sf.util.PrimeOM
JAVA com.ibm.sf.util.PrimeLE
JAVA com.ibm.sf.util.StartGSM
JAVA com.ibm.sf.util.PrimeSecurity
JAVA com.ibm.sf.util.PrimeConflictControl
START JAVA com.ibm.sf.util.DeleteFile "C:\WINNT\Profiles\All
Users\Start Menu\Programs\Startup\Sfpic.bat"
```

Figure 7-4
`sfpic.bat`

The Priming Process

Having finally succeeded in making our environment consistent with the requirements defined in the installation file (which in our case meant making sure we had the right versions for the Java libraries and making sure we could run stand-alone without a network), we finally proceeded to run the `sfpic.bat` file. We later learned that this is called the Priming Process since it creates the primary setup and configuration required to run the SanFrancisco architecture.

A word of caution regarding the priming process. The process takes a *very* long time to complete (25 minutes on our 200-MHz machine with Windows NT and 128 MB of memory!!). Naturally, no warning is given to hint at the fact that the process will take so long, so for the first three times we figured that there was still something wrong with our configuration and halted the DOS batch process. During the fourth try we waited long enough to see meaningful messages appear on our DOS windows. Figure 7-5 shows the printout of the main priming process and Figure 7-6 shows one of the steps performed in the priming process (startup of some of the main services). As illustrated, apart from setting up the main SanFrancisco business process frameworks, the priming process starts the main services. The main services include:

- The Global Name Service
- The Security Service

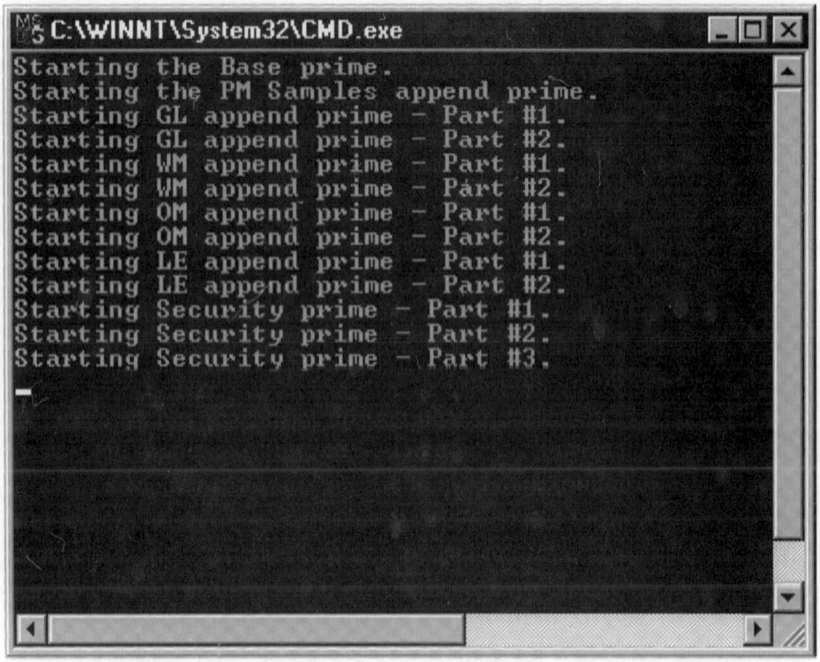

Figure 7-5
The main priming process.

- The Local Server Manager
- The Transaction Service
- The Factory Service

At the end of the process you will be left with two running processes as shown in Figure 7-7. These two processes are the Global Server Manager (GSM) process and one business process in the SanFrancisco network.

Priming in SanFrancisco includes the initiation of the naming service. Many sets of configurations are stored by SanFrancisco using a namespace mechanism managed by the Global Name Service. This service is used at runtime to access all sorts of configuration information required for the operation of an application within the SanFrancisco environment. Obviously, before this namespace may be accessed, it must be created. This creation occurs once after installation, as described above. Later, changes can be made by modifying configuration data and rerunning parts of the priming process. This will be discussed at length when we deal with the Global Name Service.

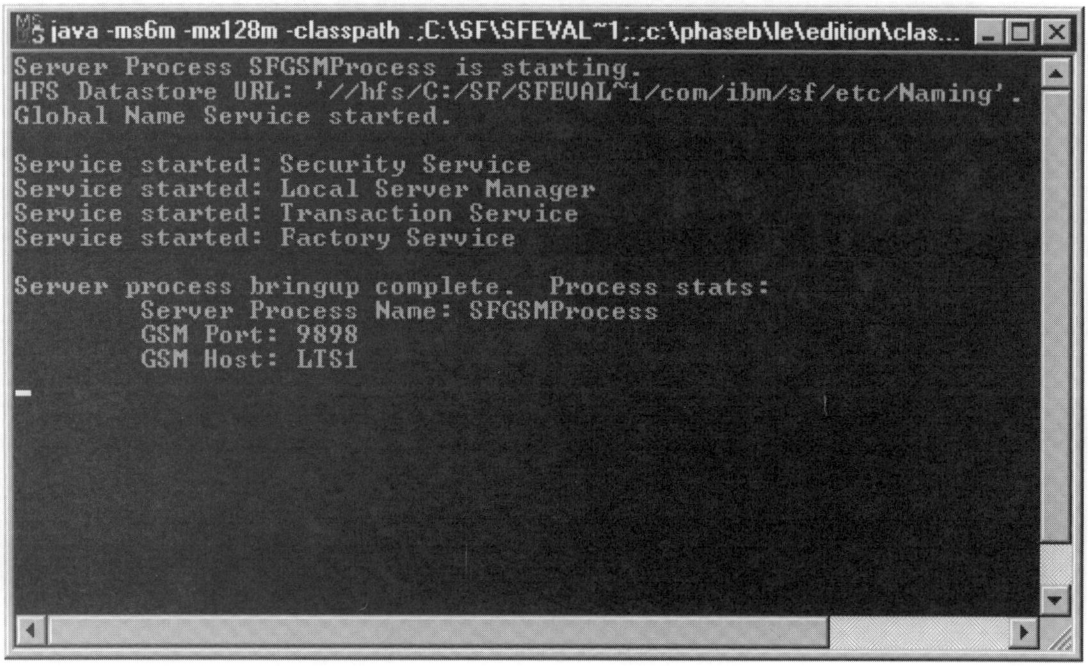

Figure 7-6
A stage in the priming process.

Checking the Installation

The next stage is to check whether the installation succeeded. For this purpose, the SanFrancisco environment provides a simple sample application that can be executed; if the installation is correct the sample should run properly. The sample is the `GUI CheckBook` sample and is located off the SanFrancisco programs category (see Figure 7-8). When started, a window should come up as shown in Figure 7-9. This window allows you to create an account by typing in your name and an account number. Then, hit the submit button. An account will be created for you (assuming this is the first time you are running the program). Once an account exists, you can start depositing and withdrawing, each within a SanFrancisco transaction. Once finished, exit the sample—you have successfully completed the SanFrancisco installation and are ready to start working.

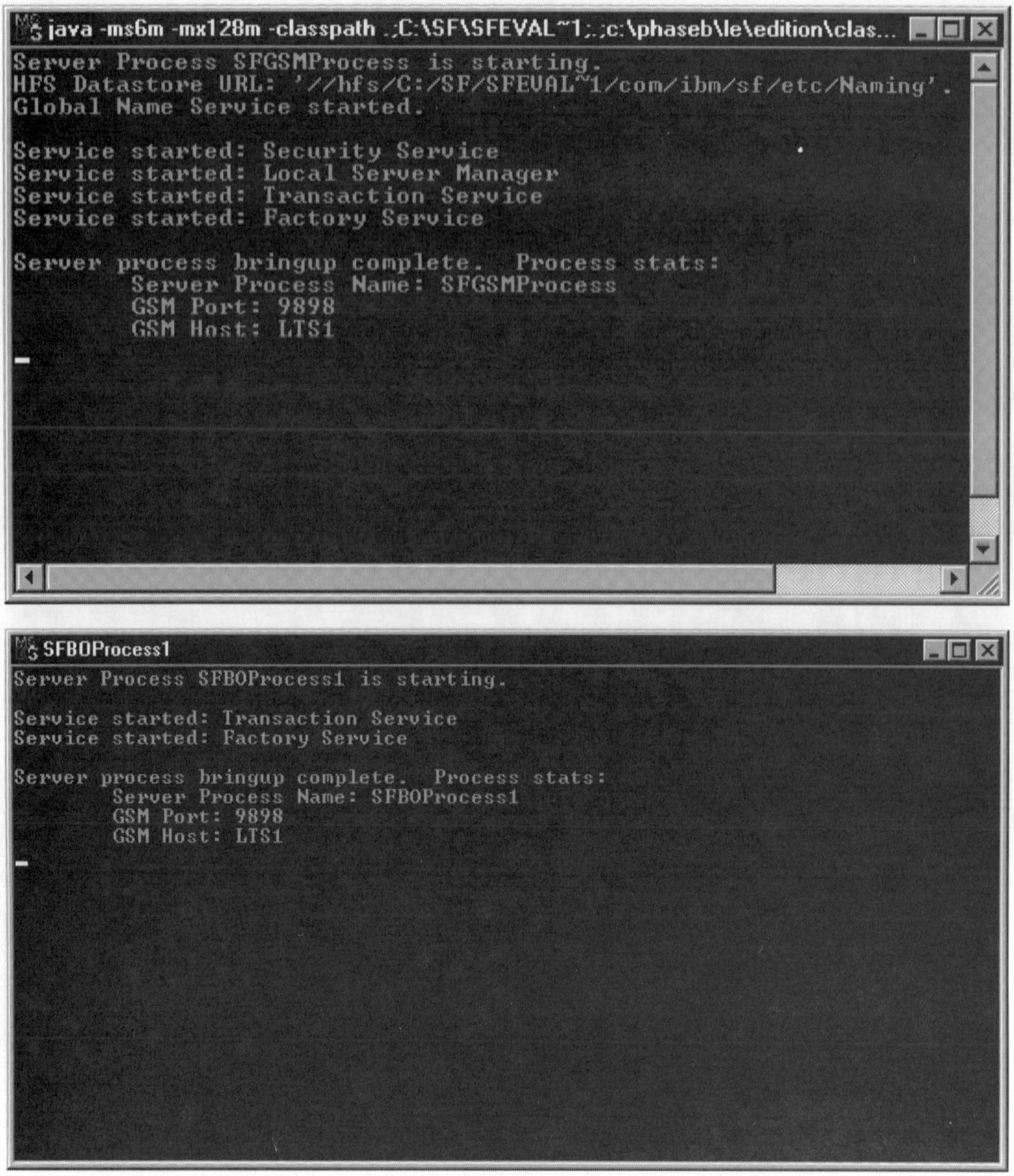

Figure 7-7
Running processes after priming.

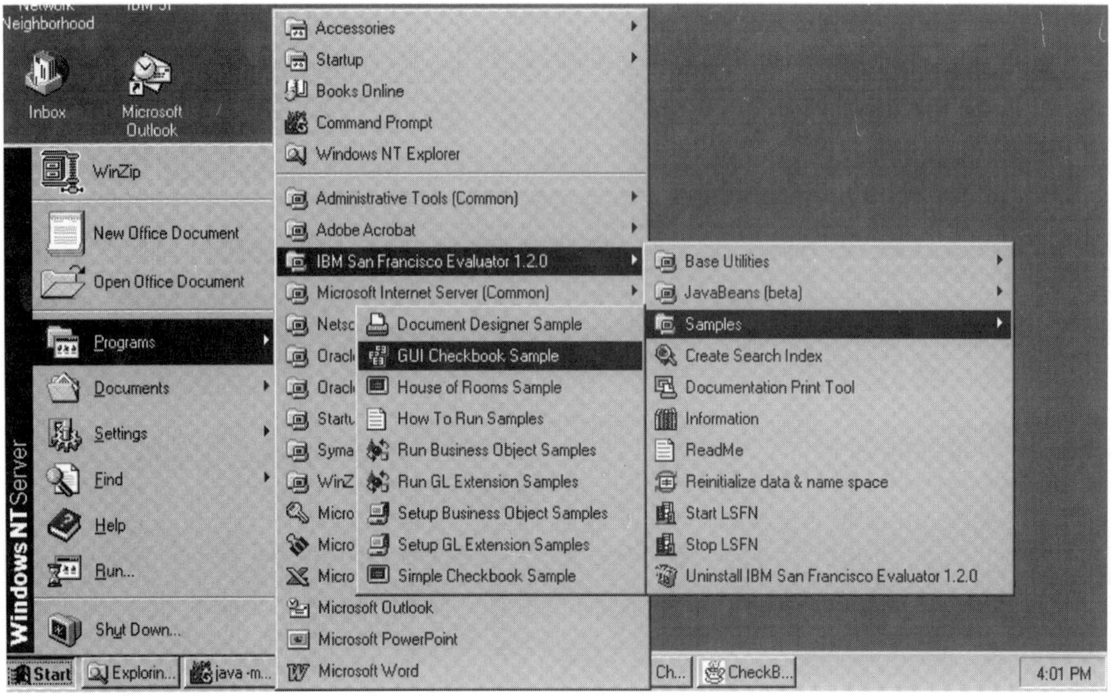

Figure 7-8
Running the `GUI CheckBook Sample`

The process described above is relevant if you are running the sample immediately after installing SanFrancisco; the installation and priming process ensures that the Logical SanFrancisco Network (LSFN) is up and running and that the GSM is awaiting client connections. If this is not the case (e.g. you've decided to check the installation later and have shut down your machine), you will need to start up the LSFN and the GSM. This is depicted in Figure 7-10. This startup procedure also takes quite a bit of time so don't start hitting the ctrl-alt-del keys.

Obviously, a number of things can go wrong—we are *checking* the installation aren't we? This means that there is a possibility that it won't work, right? Well, the possibility certainly exists—in fact, it did happen to us the first time around. The problem is that when something doesn't work the `GUI CheckBook` sample's error messages are not very helpful. For example, Figure 7-11 shows the error message you will almost always get when something goes wrong. Well, as far as we

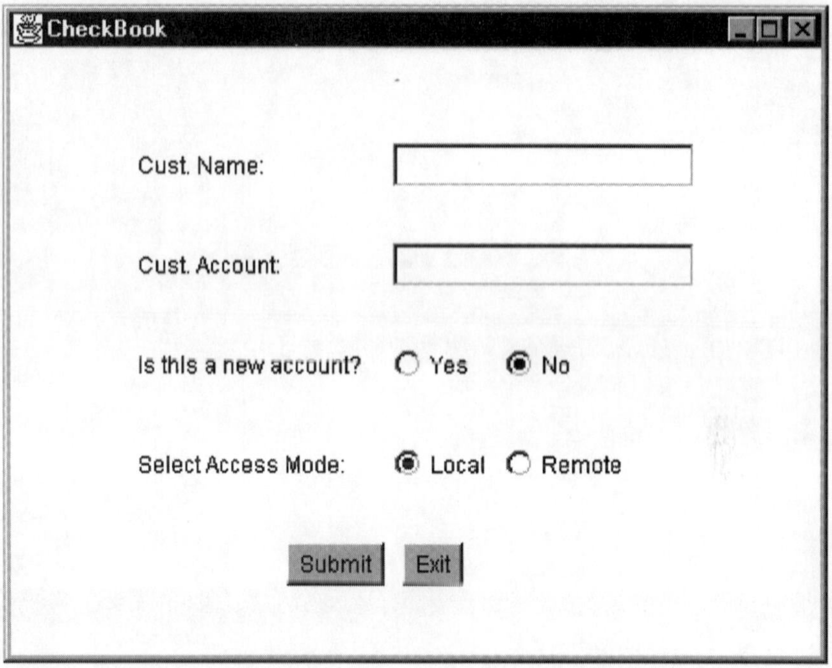

Figure 7-9 The GUI `CheckBook Sample`

remember we did start up the LSFN so what is the problem? To see what the real problem is you should take a look at the command prompt window—this shows the stack trace created by the exception thrown. As Figure 7-12 shows, the problem seems to be that the Naming Server is not up. By the way, the samples also include a `Simple CheckBook Sample` that is non-GUI and simpler. This sample is often useful in determining what the problem is. Figure 7-13 shows the exception in the `Simple CheckBook Sample`.

It was very unclear to us what was happening and unfortunately, the error messages didn't help one bit. It seemed we tried everything and were getting pretty frustrated. Eventually we did manage to solve the problem but, from our standpoint, it had very little to do with the name server (or maybe it did, but was just a symptom). The problem was eventually solved when we reset our networking parameters (eliminated the DHCP feature and selected our own TCP/IP address). Then we needed to re-prime the installation using the re-initialization feature shown in Figure 7-14. After that, we were home free—the CheckBook example finally worked.

Since we never did figure out what happened, we went back to try to understand when problems occur in the installation. We discovered that

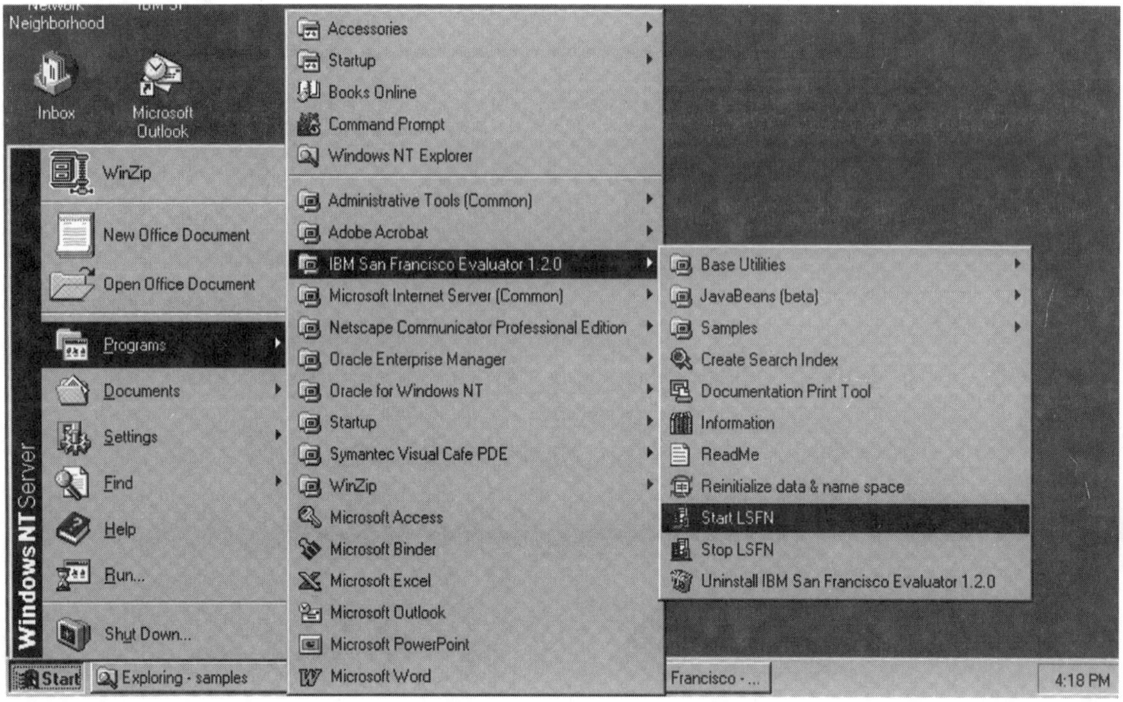

Figure 7-10
Starting the LSFN.

the SanFrancisco installation is extremely sensitive to correct network installation and that most problems are caused by networking parameters. The installation instructions provide a test for verifying that the network values are acceptable to the SanFrancisco installation. The instructions say that you should be able to ping `localhost` as well as being able to ping your machine name. Unfortunately, both

Figure 7-11
A typical GUI `CheckBook Sample` error message.

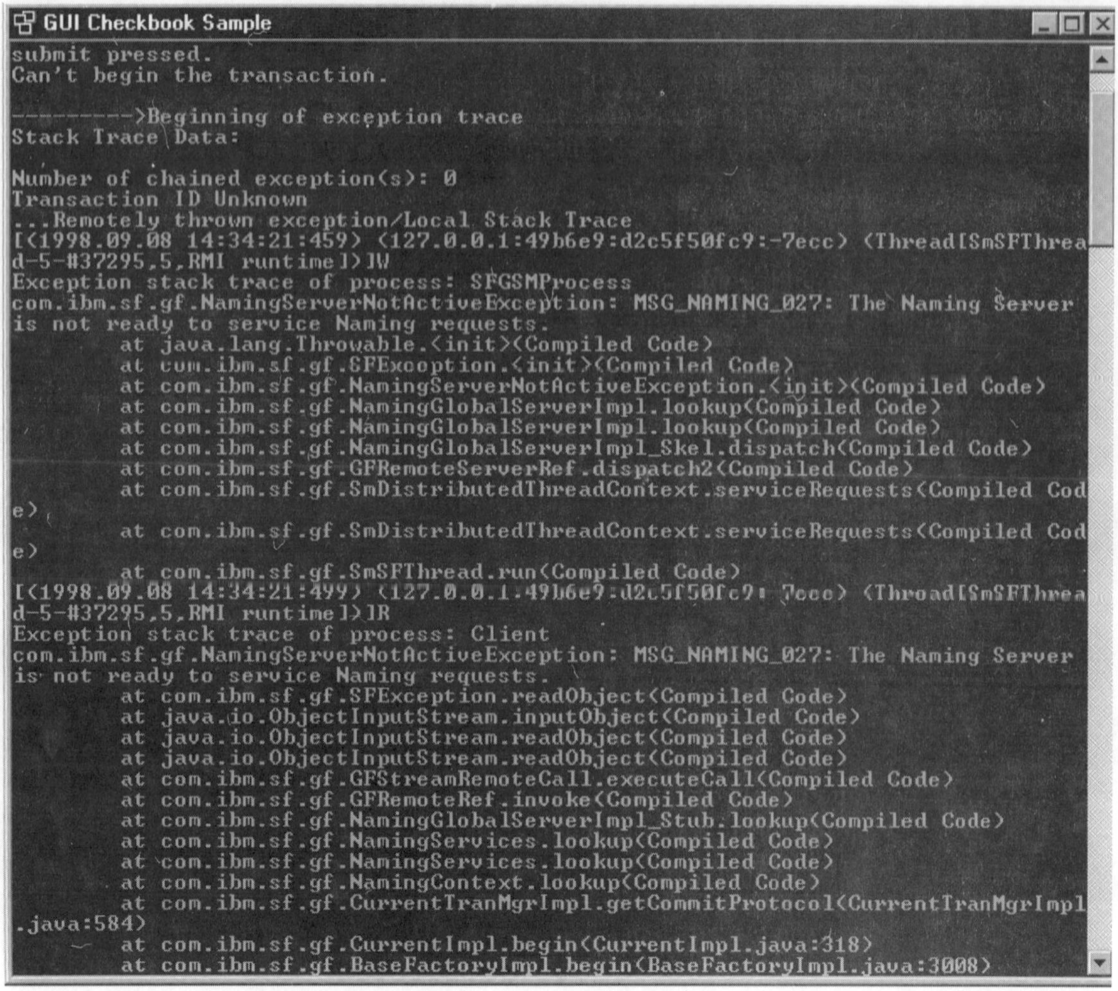

Figure 7-12
Stack trace showing the real problem.

may be true and the CheckBook sample might still refuse to work. If you do have problems with the samples, you should reconfigure your TCP/IP installation, make sure it allows you to contact the outside world and that the outside world can ping your host, *and then make sure to re-prime*. The SanFrancisco installation will not start working until you have re-primed it (after changes to TCP/IP parameters).

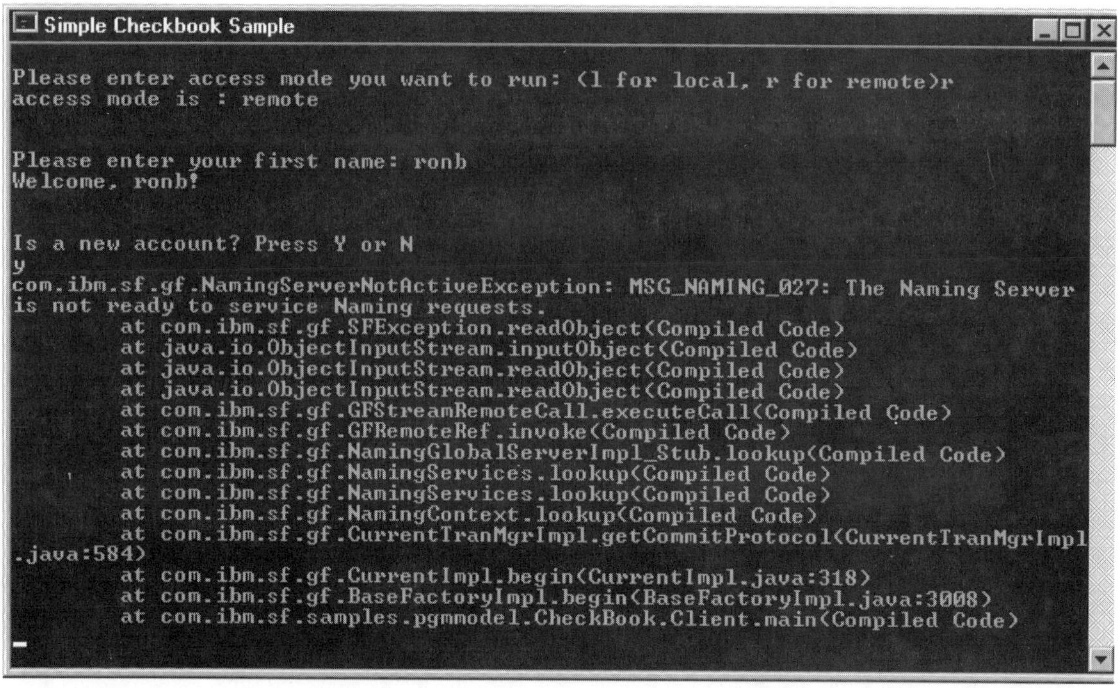

Figure 7-13
Stack trace produced by the `Simple CheckBook Sample`

Advanced Installation Considerations

Global Server Manager Port

If you intend to run multiple copies of SanFrancisco on one machine concurrently, you must choose a different number for the GSM port in the second installation. The default TCP/IP port for the GSM is 9898, but you may choose any other value which is 2000 or more. Note that you must first verify the port you choose is not in use by another TCP/IP application on your computer.

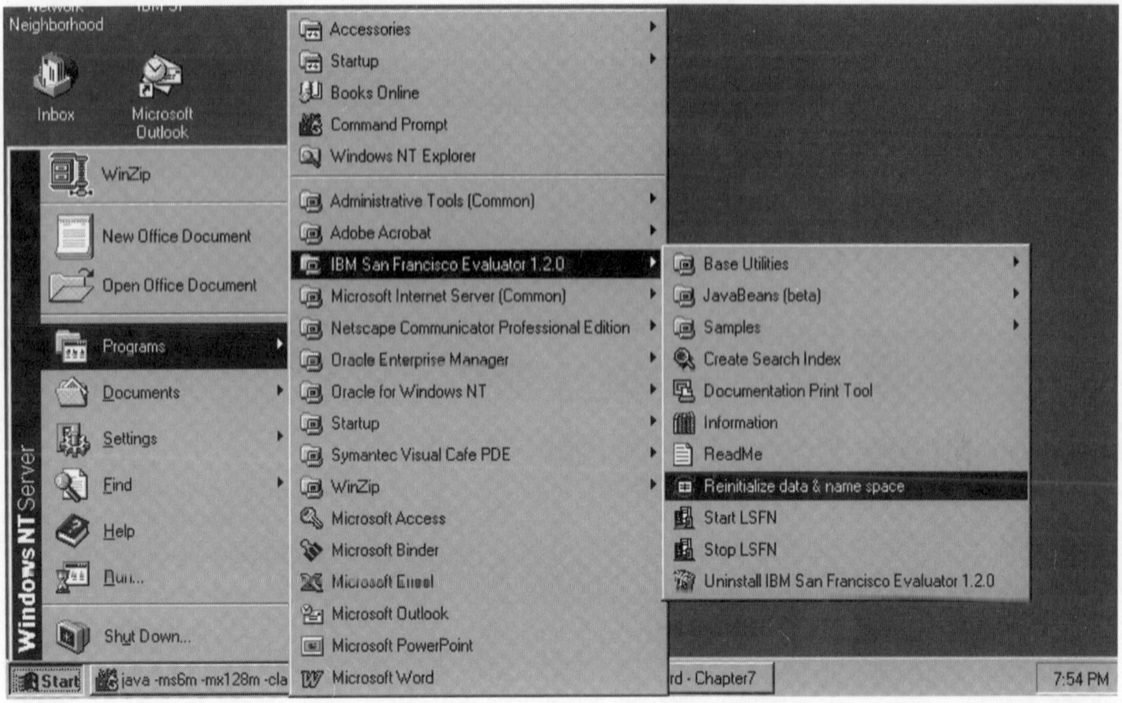

Figure 7-14
Re-priming SanFrancisco.

Primary and Additional Languages

The primary language is the language associated with documentation-related tools (Information link, Create Search Index, Documentation Print tool). It is possible to select different primary languages. Currently SanFrancisco supports the following languages:

- English
- French
- German
- Italian
- Spanish
- Japanese

In addition you may select other languages as additional languages. For these languages, the documentation is installed on your disk, but are not set as the defaults associated with the documentation-related tools. It is easy to modify that by changing the shortcut properties of the relevant icons, and by changing the PrimaryLanguage entry in the *SFconfig.ini* file.

CHAPTER 8

The SanFrancisco Samples

SanFrancisco is provided with quite a few sample programs. These programs were designed with the intention of introducing the essential concepts of SanFrancisco. In this chapter we review the sample programs and their usage. Obviously, in order to run the samples, you must have SanFrancisco installed and running, so we assume you have successfully completed the installation process described in previous chapter. All the samples appear in the "Samples" folder in your SanFrancisco folder, as shown in Figure 8-1.

The CheckBook Sample

The CheckBook application is a simple application for maintaining checkbook balances for bank accounts. The bank accounts are identified (much like in a real bank) by their owner's name and the account number. The CheckBook sample application comes in two flavors: a graphical user interface (GUI)-based version and a character mode version. In the following, we focus on the GUI-based version.

When the CheckBook application starts, you see the main window, depicted in Figure 8-2. The main window shows two text fields, one for the customer name and the other for the customer account number. In

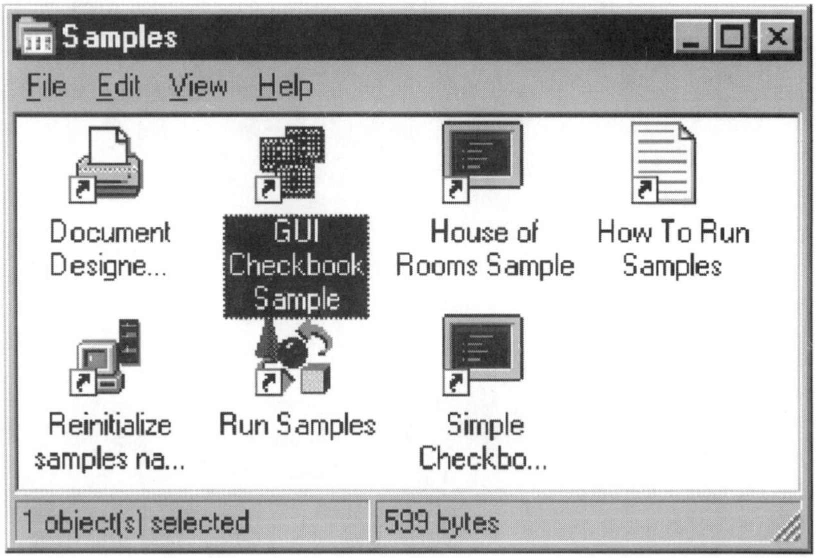

Figure 8-1 SanFrancisco Samples Folder.

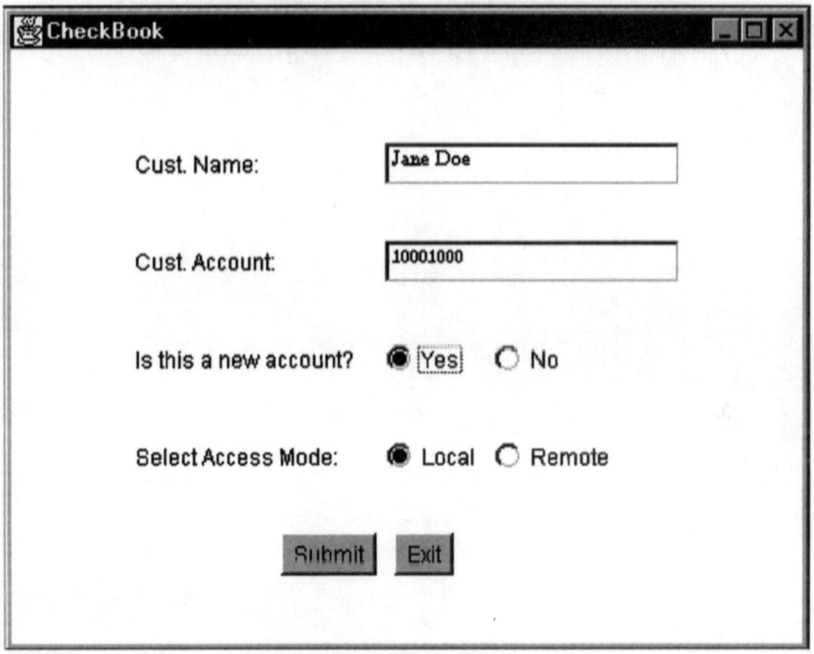

Figure 8-2 CheckBook Application Main Window.

addition it has two sets of radio button groups, one for indicating whether the account is new or not, and the other for local or remote use. The bottom of the window has "Submit" and "Exit" buttons.

The user is expected to provide input using the two text fields and the radio buttons, then push the "Submit" button. The only field whose role is not obvious is the access mode button. The terms "local" and "remote" access relate to the way the object is accessed internally. This access mode is a general SanFrancisco concept, and is not unique to the CheckBook application. If "Local" access to an object is requested from a SanFrancisco server process, then a copy of the object is supplied to the client application. In contrast, when "Remote" access is used, what happens is that the object is instantiated in the server, and the client accesses it through a proxy. Note that these access modes work in a manner that is completely transparent to the actual location of the client and server processes on the network. That is, both the local and remote modes appear to be working the same way whether the client and the server run on the same machine or on different machines.

Once you provide the required inputs and click the "Submit" button, a window appears, which says "Creating or Retrieving Account." This window, shown in Figure 8-3, disappears once account creation or retrieval is

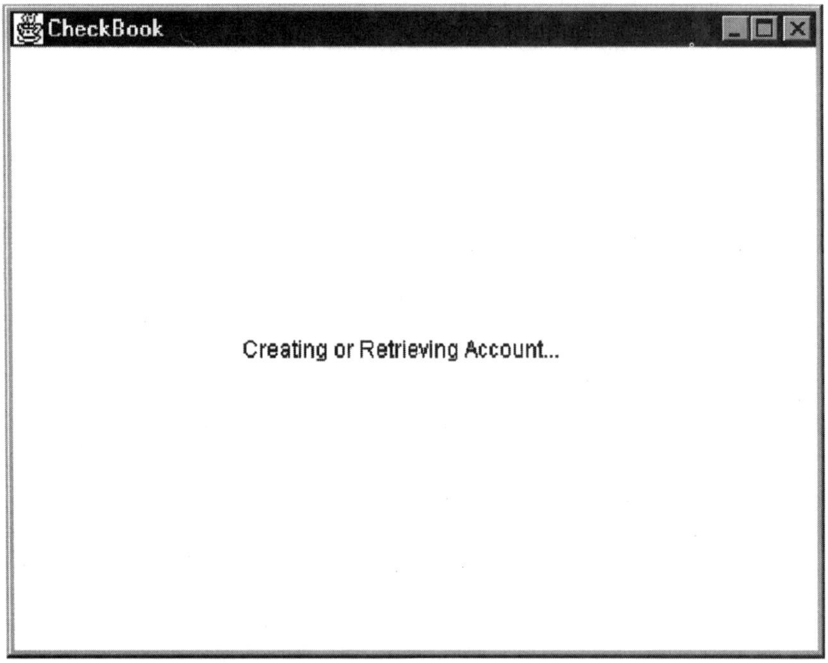

Figure 8-3 CheckBook Application Creating/Retrieving Account Window.

complete. If you attempt to create a new account with a number that is already taken, or if you attempt to retrieve a non-existent account, an error message box appears, as shown in Figure 8-4. This message box can be dismissed using the "OK" button.

Once you make it through the creation or retrieval process, you see a window for performing a transaction (shown in Figure 8-5). This window displays the current account balance, a text field for the transaction amount, a radio button group, that allows you to choose between "Deposit" and "Withdraw," and finally there are "Apply" and "OK" buttons at the bottom. The amount you key in as the transaction amount input is either deposited or withdrawn when you press the "Apply" button, depending on your selection in the first radio box. There is a transaction limit, called a "credit limit," of $50.00 for withdrawals. There is no limit on the size of deposits. To quit the transaction mode, push the "OK" button. After exiting transaction mode, you can either "rollback" or "commit" the changes made in this session, as shown in Figure 8-6. Again, these terms represent general notions in SanFrancisco applications. If you choose to commit, the account information is updated to reflect its current state. If "rollback" is selected, all changes made in the current session are discarded, including new account creation. The program

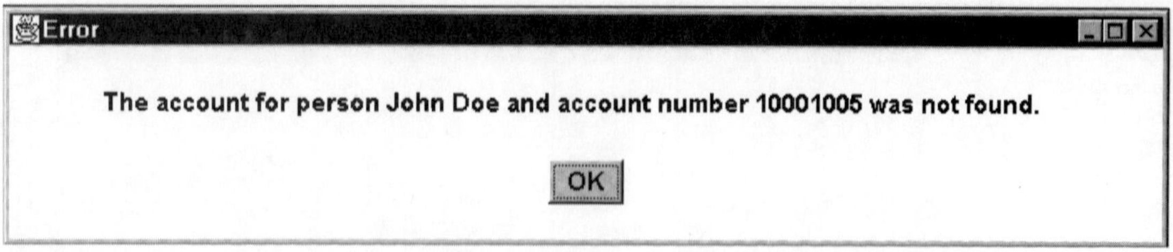

Figure 8-4
CheckBook Application Error Dialog.

Figure 8-5
CheckBook Application Transaction Window.

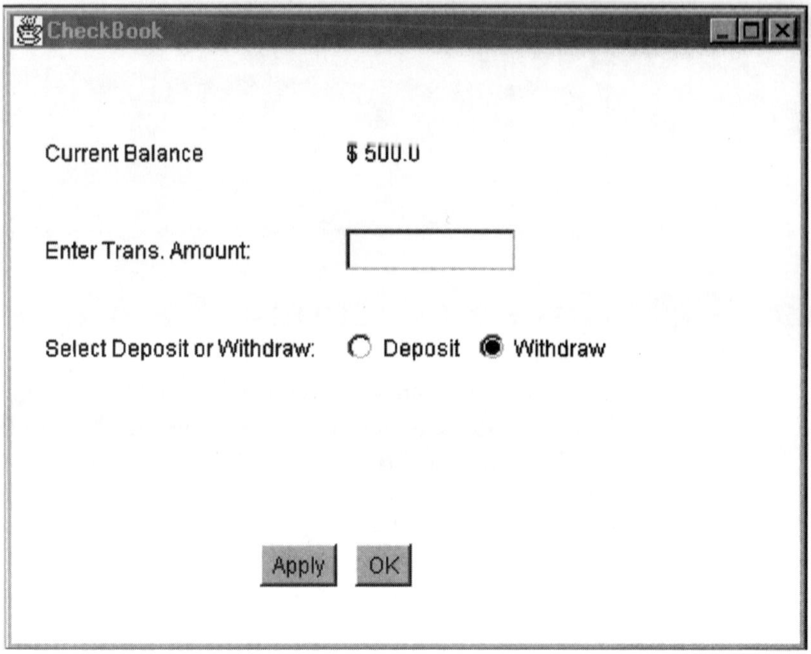

returns to the opening window for specifying account information. You may continue doing updates through additional transactions by repeating the same procedure, or just push the "Exit" button to quit the program.

The CheckBook sample illustrates the local and remote object, transaction, and persistence mechanisms available in the SanFrancisco Foundation Layer.

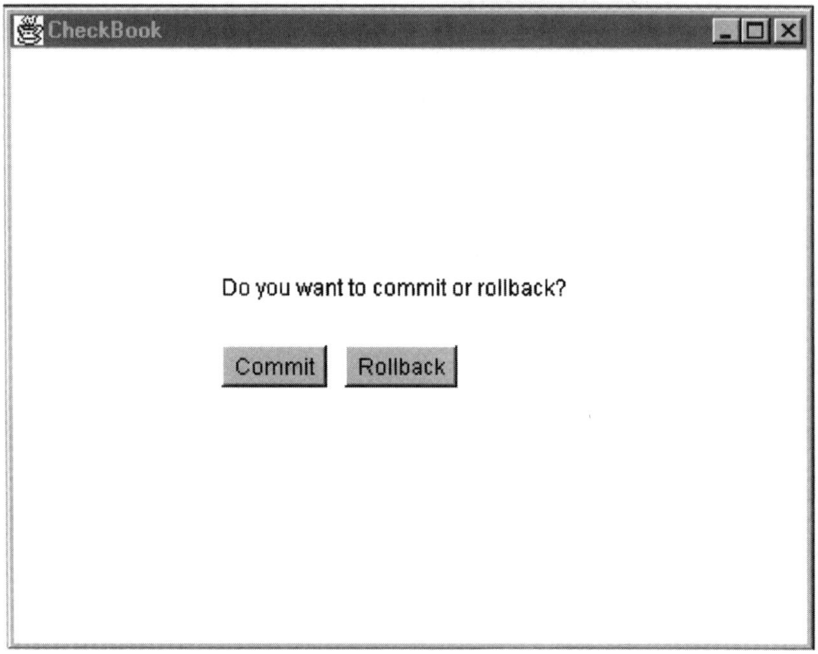

Figure 8-6 CheckBook Application Commit/ Rollback Dialog.

House of Rooms Example

The House of Rooms sample is again a simple program. However, it does make use of the major base classes in the SanFrancisco foundation. Unlike the CheckBook sample program, this program is a non-GUI (non-graphical) application. It executes in one command-prompt (MS-DOS) window, and all interaction is character-mode.

What this sample application does is keep track of houses to be built. The size of the house is fixed, and the architect divides the house into rooms, each characterized by its own size and cost. The sum of room costs determines the cost of the house. In addition to the size, cost, and room information, the application keeps the name of the architect and contact information for the owner of the house and for all subcontractors who will participate in the construction of the house.

The first thing this program does when you start it is go through an initialization and setup phase. This setup includes building a list of houses, each of which has a list of rooms contained in it. The list of houses is a persistent SanFrancisco object (a container). Once setup is complete, it shows the collection of owners of the various houses it has created, and prompts the user. Figure 8-7 shows the appearance of the

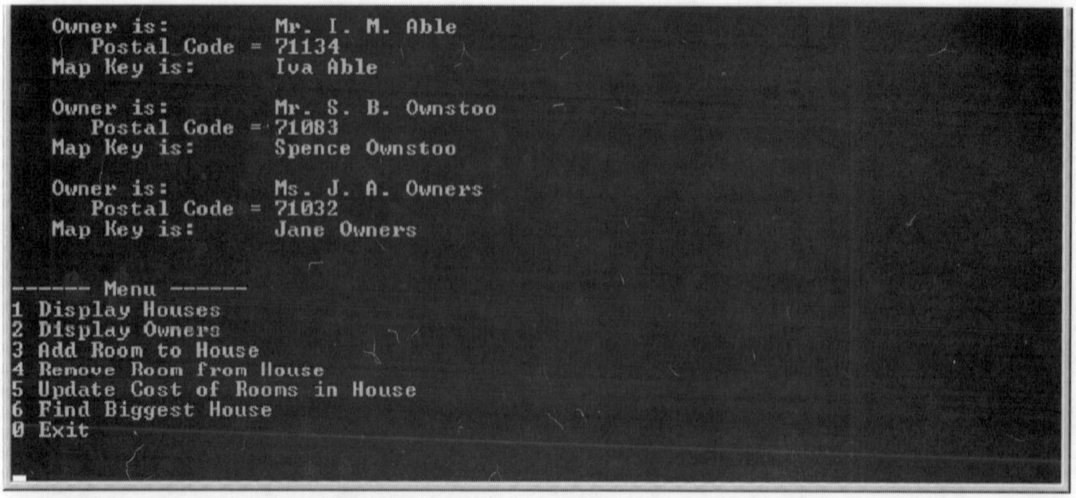

Figure 8-7
House of Rooms Application Opening Display.

display when the application has completed initialization and is waiting for user input.

The program lists three houses, and the user is prompted to select which function to perform, out of seven possible options:

- Display Houses
- Display Owners
- Add Room to House
- Remove Room from House
- Update cost of Rooms in House
- Find Biggest House
- Exit

Select option 6, titled "Find Biggest House." Figure 8-8 shows how the display should look now. Given two houses from which to select, type 1, and press Enter. Then type 2, and press Enter again. Finally, type 0 and press Enter to indicate that you selected all of the desired houses. The application finds out which one of the houses is the larger one (well, this sample program isn't that complicated). The output of the application, shown in Figure 8-9, indicates the size of the larger house followed by the name of its architect. You may select 0 at any time to quit the program.

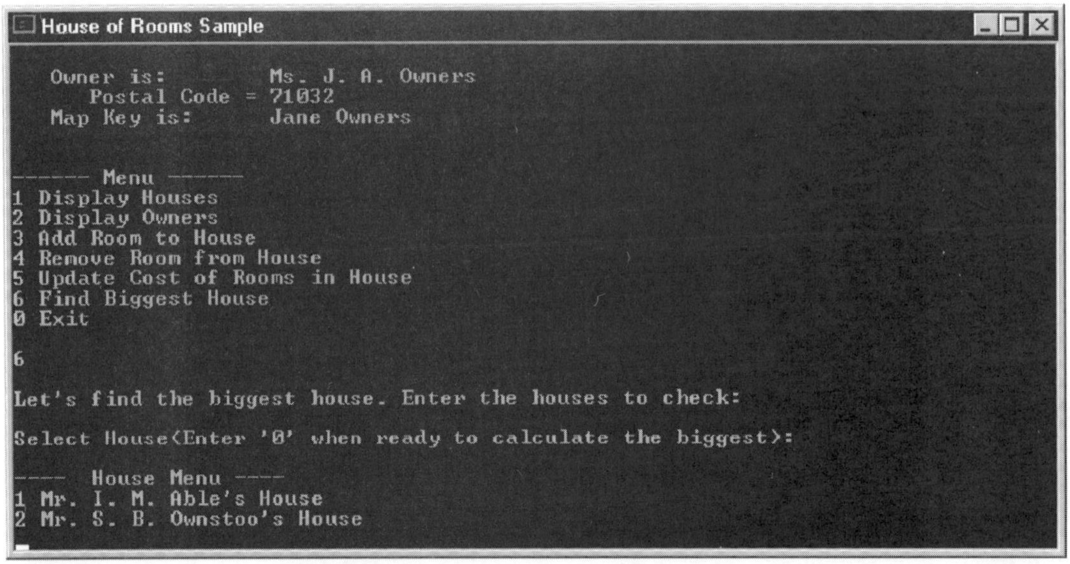

Figure 8-8
House of Rooms Application Comparison Option.

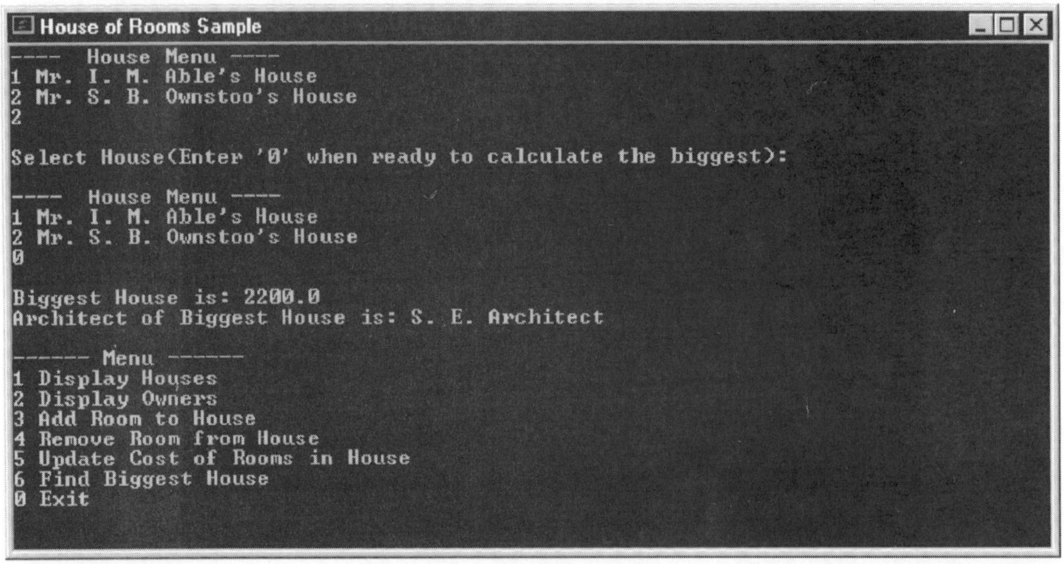

Figure 8-9
House of Rooms: finding the larger house.

Business Object Samples

The Business Object samples provide a simple way to interact with the Business Objects through the SanFrancisco GUI framework. In order to run the Business Object samples, you first have to run a special setup program, which creates the required objects on your SanFrancisco global server. To do that, just double-click on "Reinitialize samples name space" in the Samples folder under your SanFrancisco folder (shown previously in Figure 8-1). If you are using SanFrancisco 1.2 or older, you should look for an icon titled "Setup Business Object Samples".

These samples consist of seven different categories, reflecting the main components of the upper layers of SanFrancisco.

- *Common Functions (CF)*. This category includes what we refer to as "General Common Business Objects." These objects deal with the common elements to any enterprise environment. For example, the kinds of objects in this category include Companies, Business Partners, Currencies, Units of Measure.
- *Common Functions Financial Interface (CFFI)*. This category includes what we refer to as "Financial Common Business Objects." This category includes Business Objects that define financial interfaces between Common Functions and the different Core Business Processes.
- *General Ledger (GL)*. This category includes the objects that are part of the General Ledger Core Business Process (i.e. the accounting subsystem).
- *Warehouse Management (WM)*. This category includes business objects that are part of the Warehouse Management Core Business Process, and deal with the management of warehouses and their operation.
- *Order Management (OM)*. This category includes business objects that are part of the Order Management Core Business Process, and deal with the creation and lifecycle management of different kinds of orders (e.g. purchase orders, sales orders).
- *Accounts Receivable/Accounts Payable (AR/AP)*. This category includes business objects that are part of the Accounts Receivable/ Accounts Payable Core Business Process, allowing the management of ledger items. A ledger item can hold information

about an amount that was paid or that needs to be paid, including the time of payment.

- *General Ledger Extensions (GLExtn).* This category includes business objects that demonstrate how the SanFrancisco Core Business Processes can be extended. Specifically, this category deals with extending the General Ledger Core Business Process.

Running the Business Samples

In order to start using these samples, double-click the "Run Samples" icon in your samples folder. What you get is a small window (as shown in Figure 8-10), referred to as the "LaunchPad." The LaunchPad shows the sample applications in a tree-like structure, similar to the way other GUI file managers work. The LaunchPad first shows you the seven categories mentioned above, each of them associated with a folder. You may expand each of them by clicking on the small plus ("+") sign on the right of the category folder. Figure 8-11 shows the result of expanding the first folder, the one for the CF category.

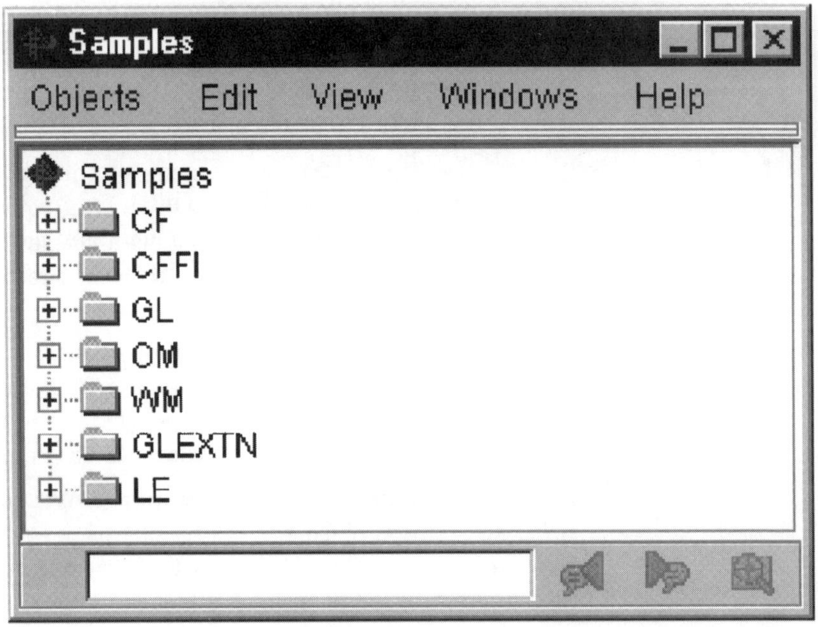

Figure 8-10 Business Objects Samples LaunchPad.

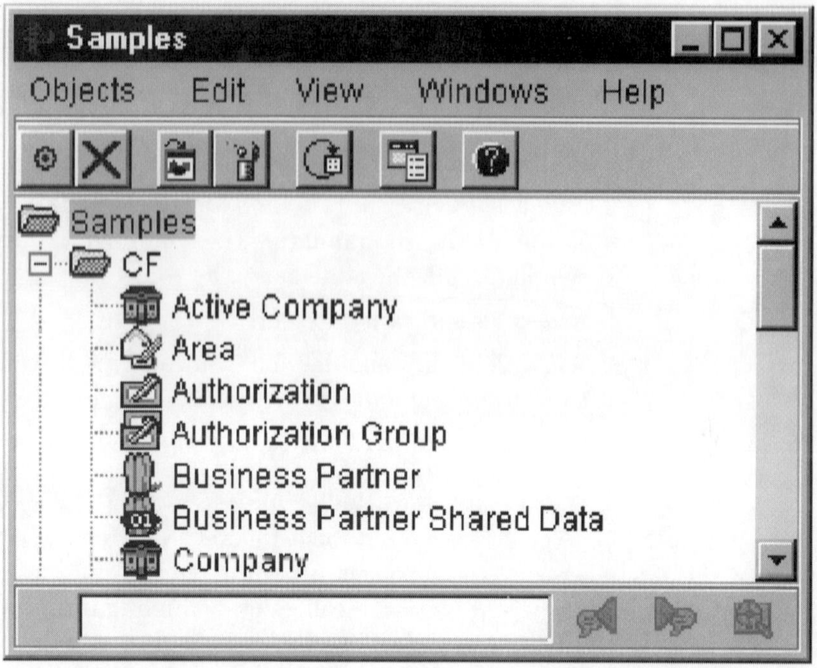

Figure 8-11 Business Objects Samples LaunchPad with CF expanded.

Note that once you expand one of the folders you see specific sample applications, referred to as "tasks" in the LaunchPad. Each of these tasks has a different icon, and you can explore its attributes by double-clicking it, or by selecting "Open" out of the "Edit" menu after highlighting the object.

It is interesting to note that some of these attributes are actually references to other business objects or even collections. When editing an attribute of a business object that is a reference to another business object, the edit dialog includes four components (two of which are optional).

- Text field indicating the identifier of the object currently referenced.
- Selection button for changing the currently referenced object; you may click it to select a new object.
- An optional edit button that allows you to change the attributes of the referenced object. When you click on it you get a separate form for the referenced object.

- An optional label (read-only text field) with a textual description of the referenced object.

When you edit the attributes of an object (e.g. after pressing the edit button), the user interface color-codes the fields to help you navigate through them.

- *Yellow* fields are mandatory, i.e. you have to correctly and completely fill these fields.
- *Red* fields indicate an error.
- *White* fields are enabled, i.e. you can type in your input there, but they are not mandatory.
- *Grey* fields are read-only, and you cannot modify them.

If you encounter a collection of objects, the way you edit them is similar. You can add a new object using "New" entry in the "Object" menu, or delete an existing object using the "Delete" in the same menu. Otherwise, you edit objects in the collection by highlighting them, and then clicking "Edit" in the "Object" menu. This brings up a dialog with the attributes (and referenced objects) of the edited object.

List of Business Object Samples

Table 8-1 shows the list of Business Object Samples for the CF and CFFI categories, each with a short description of its purpose (as described by the SanFrancisco documentation). The General Ledger samples (as described by the SanFrancisco documentation), listed in Table 8-2, are grouped into subcategories on the LaunchPad:

- Daily Activities
- Periodic Activities
- Maintenance

Table 8-3 shows the list of Business Object Samples for the OM and WM categories (as described by the SanFrancisco documentation).

The AR/AP Ledger samples allow you to manage ledger items. Ledger items can be created for invoices, credit notes, and payments. A detailed discussion of the AR/AP Ledger is deferred to Chapter 29.

TABLE 8-1

CF and CFFI Business Object samples

Category	Name	Description
CF	ActiveCompany	SanFrancisco has the notion of the currently active company. This sample application lets you switch the currently active company. This in turn may affect other Business Object Sample programs.
	Area	This sample application allows the user to manipulate SanFrancisco `Area` objects (see Chapter 21 for a detailed description of these objects).
	Authorization	This sample application allows you to manipulate signatory abilities, representing a certain authority. Signatory ability objects are associated with `Initials` objects.
	AuthorizationGroup	This sample application deals with manipulating signatory ability groups in an enterprise. A signatory ability group is associated with an `Initials` object, and is a collection of single signatory ability objects.
	BusinessPartner	This sample application allows the user to manipulate BusinessPartner objects. In SanFrancisco, this class is used to represent any other element with which the company is doing business, including suppliers, customers, and distributors. A single BusinessPartner object can be treated differently by different parts of the company, and this application allows you to create, delete, and update information about a business partner which is relevant only to the relationship between the business partner and a particular operating unit of the company. For example, one division of the company may view the business partner as a customer whereas another view the business partner as a supplier.
	BusinessPartnerSharedData	This sample application allows the user to create, delete, and update information about a business partner that is common across the application (i.e. it is shared between different components). For instance, the company name and address should be shared data.
	Company	This sample application allows the user to create, delete, and update `Company` objects. Companies are organized in a tree-like hierarchy, where the root is an enterprise (which has no parent company), and each other company in the hierarchy has exactly one parent and any number of sub-companies. A Company object includes, in addition to the parent company, registration ID, address, description, and default locale.
	Country	This sample application lets you create, delete, update countries (doesn't that sound quite powerful?). `Country` objects are used in SanFrancisco for `Address` objects, and they include the description of a country.
	Currency	This sample application allows you to manipulate `Currency` objects. `Currency` attributes include name, fractions (e.g. cents to dollars), symbol, editing rules (what decimal precision to use internally and externally).

TABLE 8-1

continued

Category	Name	Description
CF	DateBasedExchangeRate	This sample application allows you to manipulate date-based exchange rates. These objects are specified by the source and destination currencies, date range, along with the exchange rate.
	Initials	This sample application lets you create, delete, and update Initials objects. These objects hold a description and signatory abilities and a signatory ability group.
	Locale	This sample application lets you add and remove locales from the list of available locales. A locale represents a specific geographical, political, or cultural region. A locale-sensitive operation is an operation that requires a locale. Usually such operations involve customizing information for the user. See Chapter 20 for more details on locales in SanFrancisco.
	NaturalCalendar	This sample application allows you to maintain the natural calendar object that has been set up in the setup process. This is a simple GUI and so it does not reflect all the abilities of the NaturalCalendar class. This user interface allows you to maintain the set of default working days (e.g. for each weekday specify whether or not it is a working day), and to define dates for which these defaults are overriden (e.g. because of holidays).
	NumberSeries	This sample application allows you to create, delete, and update a number series and define the existence of number series, subseries, and their respective attributes.
	PaymentMethod	This sample application allows you to determine in what way a bill owed to you is paid, out of the list of payment methods available (e.g. cash, check, credit card).
	PaymentTerms	This sample allows you to define the payment schedule for an installable item. `PaymentTerm` holds a `DPaymentTerms`, which in turn holds a `DPaymentTermsDetails` and is where the payment schedule is actually defined. A term may allow a single due date or multiple due dates for an item. The number of due dates for an item determines the number of installments that are created for that item.
	PeriodBasedExchangeRates	This sample application lets you create, delete, and update period-based exchange rates. The period-based exchange rate is specified by the source and target currencies, a fiscal period, and the exchange rate.
	Project	This sample application allows you to create, delete, and update `Project` objects. A project in SanFrancisco represents an activity or group of activities with a certain objective.
	SupplementaryChargeType	This sample application allows you to add non-product-related charges and fees to any charge documents you issue (e.g. quotations, orders, invoices).

TABLE 8-1

continued

Category	Name	Description
CF	UnitCategory	This sample application allows you to create, delete, and update unit categories. It defines units of measure for a specific unit category and holds information on how to convert between these units. A unit category has a base unit, and all conversions to other units are defined in this unit category.
	UnitOfMeasure	This sample application allows you to create, update units of measure. A unit of measure supports the definition of the quantity-related information relevant to a physical unit. It supports categorizing them by their physical properties (e.g. width, length, height) and stores them by the category to which they are assigned.
CFFI	Banks	This sample application allows you to create, update, and delete banks. A `Bank` object holds general bank information, such as name and address. All banks used in the system must be defined here.
	ExternalBankAccounts	This sample application allows you to create, update, and delete external bank accounts. An external bank account includes (among other things) bank account number and bank description. External bank accounts are accounts held by external parties, such as business partners.
	InvoicingTypeValue	This sample application allows you to create, delete, and update different invoice types. The `InvoiceTypeValue` class is used as an identifier for different types of invoices.
	TransactionSource	This sample application allows you to create, delete, and update transaction sources. Financial transaction sources are used by journals for identifying the source of a transaction.
	TransactionType	This sample application lets you create, delete, and update transaction type values, which hold a description of a financial transaction type.

TABLE 8-2

GL Business Object samples

Category	Name	Description
GL	AccountType	This sample application allows you to create, update, and delete account type values. Account type value holds a description of the account type. Account type is used to determine the account type in a chart of account attributes (see the following description of AnalysisGroup).
	AnalysisGroup	This sample application allows the user to create, update, and delete analysis groups. Analysis groups are used to compose the possible parts of posting combinations to be used when creating dissections. When creating an analysis code, you need include an analysis group. If, for example, an analysis group is created for cost centers, this group holds the codes for all valid cost centers in the General Ledger. When creating a posting combination, it uses analysis codes from the analysis groups. The samples have a predefined set of analysis groups created by the setup. These are main account, cost center, and product. This sample application also allows you to create, update, and delete analysis codes. The analysis codes are held in analysis groups and used when creating a posting combination. To create a posting combination, one or zero analysis codes from each analysis group is required (for the sample application, at least a main account has to be provided). The GUI also supports creating, updating, and deleting a chart of account attributes. When creating an analysis code with the main account group, a chart of account attributes has to be created. The chart of account attributes holds accounting information for this analysis code. In addition to analysis groups and analysis codes, you can create, update, and delete analysis code subsets. An analysis code subset holds a description of the analysis code subset. It is used for reporting purposes. For example, an analysis code has a length of “3,” and an analysis code ID of “ABC.” A subset is defined to say that the description of AB is “fixed assets.”
	Balances	This sample application is responsible for the calculation of all kinds of balances based on General Ledger dissections. It holds definable “balance types” that represent “criteria” for the selection of dissections to be included in the balances, as well as specific calculative conditions. For faster access, you can have the framework cache and dynamically maintain these balances. It is also possible to use these cached balances to calculate condensed balances, defined by selection criteria that are a subset of those of the original balance type.
	BankMovement	A bank movement is a single transaction with the bank, at the lowest level. This sample application allows you to create, update, and delete bank movements and change or assign the internal bank account of a bank movement. It also displays the associated dissections and journals.

TABLE 8-2

continued

Category	Name	Description
	BankStatement	Bank statement objects are responsible for the creation and maintenance of bank statements and their statement lines. The bank normally issues a bank statement each month, containing opening and closing balances for the account. It also holds a list of statement lines.
	BanktoBankTransfer	A bank-to-bank transfer concerns the transfer of funds from one bank account to another and, therefore, two internal bank accounts (the source and target bank accounts). The GUI allows you to create and delete bank-to-bank transfers.
	BankTransaction	This sample application allows you to create, delete, and update bank transactions, add or remove bank movements to a bank transaction, and unsuspend or resuspend bank transactions. A bank transaction is equivalent to one line on a bank statement. Each bank transaction consists of bank movements, which represent each individual item of the transaction, for example, each check that is part of the payment.
	BudgetProfile	This sample application allows you to create, delete, and update budget profiles. A budget profile holds a description, an indicator if the journal is required to balance, and an indicator if the budget profile is post-inhibited. The budget profile is used when creating budgets.
	CurrencyGainAndLossAccounts	This sample application allows the user to create, delete, and update currency gain and loss accounts, which hold posting combinations for realized gain and loss, and unrealized gain and loss, along with a description. The currency gain and loss accounts are used for General Ledger revaluation, Accounts Receivable and Accounts Payable revaluation, and Accounts Receivable and Accounts Payable allocation. The accounts are set up per currency, but several currencies may share the same posting combinations.
	CurrencyRevaluation and CurrencyRevaluationInformation	These sample applications allow revaluing balances of General Ledger posting combinations ("accounts") to be specified. These applications also initiate the creation of General Ledger journals for currency profits and losses to be posted.
	FinancialBatch	The financial batch is responsible for controlling a group of items that are processed together and may differ in type. Items of a given type are distinct and dealt with separately within the batch. In the sample, the items processed within the batch are General Ledger journals. A General Ledger journal holds header details and a balancing posting journal that is used to update accounts and posting combinations in the General Ledger. You can create, update, suspend, and delete General Ledger journals within the batch. When a batch is posted, all of the General Ledger journals in the batch are validated. If the validation is successful, the journals are posted. When the batch is deleted, all the General Ledger journals in the batch are deleted. A General Ledger journal holds a number of dissections. A dissection has

TABLE 8-2

continued

Category	Name	Description
GL		a posting combination and a value in prime and base currency. It is possible to spread a dissection by adding spread information to it. The spread information spreads the dissection automatically over a set of periods as defined by the spread information, by creating new General Ledger journals and dissections. It is also possible to unspread a dissection. A dissection may hold one or more quantity dissections. A quantity dissection is connected with a quantity unit, containing the actual quantities, the associated unit of measure and, optionally, a unit category. A dissection connects a value with a posting combination (account). Posting combinations consist of analysis codes from different analysis groups. It can have quantity dissections attached. The implementation of the dissection list in the journal interface is different from all the other samples. To improve performance when loading several dissections (if defined for the journal), only the handles and the string information of the dissections are brought down from the server to the client. These strings are shown in the dissection collection list. This is done by executing the query of the dissections on the server and splitting all of the information into strings. This is done in the `DissectionsQueryCmd`.
	FinancialIntegration	This sample application allows you to create journals and dissections based on generic transactions from other subsystems (for example, warehouse). These journals and dissections can be picked up by journal maintenance for further processing.
	InternalBankAccounts	This sample application allows you to create, update, and delete internal bank accounts. Internal bank accounts hold information about bank accounts owned by the company such as bank account number, bank, description, currency, and so on.
	Journal	This sample application allows you to create and edit a General Ledger journal. A General Ledger journal contains business transactions that are recorded in chronological order.
	ReconciliationEvent	Bank reconciliation is responsible for the creation of reconciliation events, that is matching bank transactions and statement lines against each other to try to get a zero (0) result. Also, individual bank transactions may be matched against each other, or individual statement lines. The GUI does not support matching statement lines from different bank statements.
	YearEnd	This sample application demonstrates Year-end. It creates a new General Ledger journal with the financial transaction source GL_CLOSING, and adds that journal to a batch.

TABLE 8-3

OM and WM Business Object samples

Category	Name	Description
OM	Tools—FullSalesOrderHierarchy	This sample application displays the hierarchy of all full sales orders.
	Tools—OrderLifeCycleHierarchy	This sample application displays the hierarchy of all order lifecycles.
	DDiscountDefinition	This sample allows you to create, delete, and update discount definitions for sales, purchase, and internal purposes.
	DPriceDefinition	This sample program lets you manipulate price defnitions used for sales, purchase, and internal orders.
	FullSalesOrder	This sample application allows you to create a new order or change an existing order. This sample treats only the full sales order type (which is the most general type of sales order).
	OrderPartner	This sample application extends a business partner to contain additional data, in the form of attributes that are required for OM. There are three types of order partners: customers, suppliers, and internal warehouses for which we want to use the order management processes to manage internal transfers.
	OrderProduct and OrderControllerType	These sample applications define order products. An `OrderProduct` object defines an order product in the system and holds all information related to it. There are three uses for an `OrderProduct`: sales, purchase, and internal. This is handled by having three controllers, one for each use. This use is represented by an `OrderControllerType`, which gives the flexibility to add new types.
	OrderSupplementaryCharge	This sample application extends common functions of the supplementary charge by adding order management lifecycle features.
WM	ABCClassification	ABC classification allows the grouping of products (for example, expensive products, cheap products, etc.). This sample supports the creation, deletion, and modification of ABC classification types.
	BackToBackTypeValue	This sample application supports the creation, deletion, and modification of back-to-back type values.
	CostTypeValue	This sample application supports the creation, deletion, and modification of cost-type values. Cost-type values identify the different cost types for which separate cost prices or cost transactions are to be held.
	LeadTimeDefinition and LeadTimeRetrieval	These sample applications provide the mechanism to define and retrieve the lead time for a particular product. Lead time is the time it takes to obtain a product from a supplier or an internal warehouse and place that product into the specified warehouse.
	MannerOfTransport	This sample application defines the manners of transport available on the system.
	ManualStockTransaction	This sample application creates a manual stock transaction for a product. Quantities can be added or subtracted from the inventory for the product using a manual stock transaction. This is the highlight of the warehouse samples set.

TABLE 8-3

continued

Category	Name	Description
WM	Product	This sample application represents an item. This sample allows the creation, changing, and deletion of products from the company.
	ProductGroup	This sample supports the creation, changing, and deletion of product groups, each containing products. A specific product can be associated with a group through the product sample application.
	ProductWarehouseLink	A product is associated with a warehouse, through a product warehouse link. These links can be also created from the product sample application. Inventories of a product are associated with a product warehouse link, so such a link must exist before a manual stock transaction can take place.
	ReplenishmentSuggestion	This sample allows you to create, delete, and update replenishment suggestion details. Once such a suggestion is ready for further processing, it can be transformed into purchase orders or stock movements.
	StockTransactionType	This sample allows you to create, update, and delete the different types of stock transactions used in the system, such as manual stock transactions and picked stock transactions.
	StockTypeValue	This sample supports the creation, changing, and deletion of stock-type values, used as identifiers for different types of stock (e.g. on-hand stock, rejected stock, reserved stock, transit stock, stock in quality control).
	TermsOfDelivery	This sample application defines the terms of delivery available on the system.
	TransportTimeDefinition	This sample allows you to create, delete, and update the transport times available for transportation.
	TransportZone	This sample allows you to to create, delete, and update the transport zones available for transportation.
	Warehouse	This sample application supports the creation, deletion, and modification of warehouses, which are entities containing products.

The GL Extension samples are intended to provide you with some examples of how you can extend the SanFrancisco Core Business Processes. These samples will be discussed in Chapter 26.

CHAPTER 9

Utilities and the SanFrancisco Development Environment

Before delving into all the details of SanFrancisco, this chapter is intended to give you the technical introduction of how to actually use SanFrancisco. We start out by introducing the development environment and continue by briefly describing some of the utilities provided by SanFrancisco.

The SanFrancisco Development Environment

Because of the diversity of target audiences of SanFrancisco, there is no single development tool or environment that is the ultimate development platform for SanFrancisco. Instead, IBM opted for cooperation with other Java tool vendors in order to integrate SanFrancisco support in their products. Such support is provided through specific "wizards" and other enhancements. It is reasonable to expect that this kind of support will become wider and more complete as time passes.

Currently supported tools include:

- OO analysis and design tool: Rational Rose (Rose diagrams of SanFrancisco are included with SanFrancisco, Rational Rose includes a SanFrancisco Wizard)
- SanFrancisco Code Generator (Generates Java code from Rose diagrams. Provided by IBM)
- Java IDEs
  - Borland JBuilder (includes a special SanFrancisco Wizard)
  - IBM VisualAge for Java
  - Symantec Visual Cafe

In order to avoid going into the specifics of different development platforms, we will describe how to work with SanFrancisco when using the standard JDK.

Whenever you write new source code or modify existing code, you need to compile it before it can run. In order to do that, we will use the javac program that is part of your JDK. After opening a command prompt (e.g. a DOS session), you should run the command:

```
javac <class name>.java
```

For example, to compile the `HouseTest` class, which is part of the "House of Rooms" sample programs, perform:

```
javac HouseTest.java
```

Java includes support for Remote Method Invocation (RMI). Part of the support for this mechanism is through a stub and skeleton generator called *rmic*. You can think of *rmic* as a RMI class compiler. SanFrancisco developers should use *sfrmic* instead of *rmic* when creating stubs and skeletons for remotely invoked SanFrancisco objects. The command line options of *sfrmic* and its behavior are pretty much the same as those of *rmic*. You can find more information on that in the JDK documentation (e.g. at `http://java.sun.com/products/jdk`). The only difference between the way *rmic* works and *sfrmic* works is that by default, the latter generates for each SanFrancisco remote object the following methods as remote methods in both the stub and skeleton: `equals()`, `hashCode()`, `toString()`. To exclude any of these methods from being generated as a remote method in the stub and skeleton, you can add the option -x <method_name> in the command line.

Once you have your code compiled, you can run it. To start a Java class, you just need to issue the command:

```
java <class>.class
```

For example, to manually start the SanFrancisco Access Rights Administration utility, use the following command:

```
java com.ibm.sf.util.AccessRightAdmin
```

If you are interested in debugging a program, you can use `jdb` instead of `java`. The documentation for both programs can be found in the JDK documentation available from JavaSoft.

SanFrancisco Utilities

This section is intended to brief you on the different utilities that are part of the SanFrancisco distribution. Table 9-1 lists the SanFrancisco utilities along with a short description of each.

TABLE 9-1

List of SanFrancisco utilities

Icon	Name	Purpose
	Conflict Control Administration	This utility helps you define potential conflicts between certain actions in your application. See Chapter 35 for more on Conflict Control.
	Conflict Control Maintenance	This utility allows you to monitor active actions, load new conflict definitions or change existing ones, and try to troubleshoot actions that terminate abnormally. See Chapter 35 for more on Conflict Control.
	Access Rights Administration	This program allows the administrator to set a security policy requiring user-IDs and passwords for accessing specific objects, resources, or tasks. See Chapter 35 for more details on this utility.
	Configuration	This utility is used to configure SanFrancisco. You may use it to do any of the following: ■ Change the default HTML browser for SanFrancisco ■ Set the security policy ■ Determine if a user-id is required ■ Setting of administrator password ■ Changing the persistence type (POSIX, RDB) ■ Creating new containers ■ Adding new classes to containers ■ Controlling transaction operation For a full description of this utility, see Chapter 34.
	Problem Manager	This utility is used to view error messages reported by SanFrancisco components. It provides you with detailed problem information.
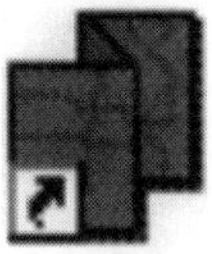	Schema Mapper Tool	This utility allows you to map SanFrancisco Business Objects to RDBMs. This utility is described in detail in Chapter 30.
	Server Access Rights Administration	This program allows the system Administrator to grant users permission to use a certain SanFrancisco server. See Chapter 34 for more details on this utility.

TABLE 9-1

continued

Icon	Name	Purpose
	User Administration	This program is used to create a new user, which can be granted access privileges using the Access Rights Administration utility. See Chapter 34 for more details on this utility.
	Server Management	The composition of the LSFN, or in other words the list of servers we have is defined through this utility, and is covered in Chapter 34. Specific object locations must be defined by configuring containers, which is covered in the same chapter.
	Start LSFN	The SanFrancisco Logical Network (LSFN) is the backbone of all SanFrancisco applications. It is described in detail in Chapter 33. We have already learned that we need to start LSFN before we can run any SanFrancisco program.
	Stop LSFN	This utility is used to stop the LSFN. This should be done before you stop using SanFrancisco, or before shutting down your system. You also must stop the LSFN and then restart it whenever you make changes in the implementation of existing methods of business objects (of course, changes in client code do not require any restart).
	Reinitialize Data & Namespace	This utility should be used when class names need to be added or removed from the namespace. It also comes in handy if your LSFN terminated abnormally and you have trouble accessing your data. Note that running this program might have significant side-effects as far as persistent storage is concerned. You risk losing all `Entity` data in POSIX files, and losing Entities in the RDBMS containers that are not stored in a special kind of container called `EntityOwningExtents`.

Reading SFException Print Stack Trace Output

As you might recall from Chapter 7, the first time we saw a SanFrancisco program crash we couldn't make much out of the output we saw. In this section, we will try to explain how to read the print stack trace output, with emphasis on the peculiarities of SanFrancisco.

The first thing to keep in mind is that SanFrancisco exceptions are derived from SFException, which extends the Java Exception class. SFException includes a method called `printStackTrace`, which collects stack trace information from any relevant SanFrancisco process in your logical SanFrancisco network, and provides you with an aggregated picture.

Just before the stack trace printout there is a header that shows the date, time, JVM ID, and thread information. The top of the stack trace shows the throw point, which is where the exception object was created. As with any Java trace output, it shows you the class, method, and source code line for each of the methods in the stack of calls when the exception was generated. When the stack trace reports a chained exception, it means the exception was caught and re-thrown without any modification. In some cases, the code might perform some actions and then throw a different exception, in which case the new exception is not considered to be chained.

Each single exception is enclosed within a block that starts with the following line:

```
--------->Beginning of exception trace
```

and ends with:

```
--------->End of exception trace
```

Let's take a look at a few examples to see how these stack traces can be read. The first example is shown in Cutout 9-1, taken from the SanFrancisco Programmer's Guide. In this example, a transaction in the SFGSMProcess catches an exception that is not handled by the program and is, therefore, sent back to the client process. In this example, you can immediately see that there are no chained exceptions (their number is 0), and that the exception originated within the SanFrancisco SFGSMProcess, which passed it along to the client process. Stack information for both processes is shown, with the respective timestamps. Also, note the SanFrancisco transaction ID that is shown.

```
--------->Beginning of exception trace
StackTraceData:

Number of chained exception(s): 0
Transaction ID 606910446947995648.-2305842996177452337
...Remotely thrown exception/Local Stack Trace
[(1998.03.06 7:52:26:497) (9.5.66.207:1ec867:cf0849d2ad:-7d26) (Thread[SmSFThread-10-
#1,5,RMI runtime])]W
Exception stack trace of process: SFGSMProcess
com.ibm.sf.gf.NamingNameNotFoundException: MSG_NAMING_004: Name
'/IBM.SF/UserAliases/johnDoeNoNameAlias' does not exist.
      at com.ibm.sf.gf.NamingHFSDataStore.readBa(NamingHFSDataStore.java:281)
      at com.ibm.sf.gf.NamingGlobalServerImpl.lookup(NamingGlobalServerImpl.java:938)
      at com.ibm.sf.gf.NamingGlobalServerImpl.lookup(NamingGlobalServerImpl.java:876)
      at
com.ibm.sf.gf.NamingGlobalServerImpl_Skel.dispatch(NamingGlobalServerImpl_Skel.java:493)
      at com.ibm.sf.gf.GFRemoteServerRef.dispatch2(GFRemoteServerRef.java:245)
      at com.ibm.sf.gf.SmDistributedThreadContext.serviceRequests(SmDistributedThreadContext.java:
530)
      at com.ibm.sf.gf.SmDistributedThreadContext.serviceRequests(SmDistributedThreadContext.java:
462)
      at com.ibm.sf.gf.SmSFThread.run(SmSFThread.java:422)
[(1998.03.06 7:52:26:544) (9.5.66.207:1ec867:cf0849d2ad:-7d26) (Thread[SmSFThread-10-
#1,5,RMI runtime])]R
Exception stack trace of process: Client
com.ibm.sf.gf.NamingNameNotFoundException: MSG_NAMING_004: Name '/IBM.SF/UserAliases/
johnDoeNoNameAlias' does not exist.
      at com.ibm.sf.gf.SFException.readObject(SFException.java:169)
      at java.io.ObjectInputStream.inputObject(ObjectInputStream.java:996)
      at java.io.ObjectInputStream.readObject(ObjectInputStream.java:287)
      at com.ibm.sf.gf.GFStreamRemoteCall.executeCall(GFStreamRemoteCall.java:438)
      at com.ibm.sf.gf.GFRemoteRef.invoke(GFRemoteRef.java:151)
      at
com.ibm.sf.gf.NamingGlobalServerImpl_Stub.lookup(NamingGlobalServerImpl_Stub.java:792)
      at com.ibm.sf.gf.NamingServices.lookup(NamingServices.java:546)
      at com.ibm.sf.gf.NamingServices.lookup(NamingServices.java:487)
      at com.ibm.sf.gf.NamingContext.lookup(NamingContext.java:353)
      at com.ibm.sf.gf.TestingHooks.userAliasExistTest(TestingHooks.java:221)
      at ibmsftest.gf.tutil.TestEntityImpl.getCustomer(TestEntityImpl.java:585)
      at
ibmsftest.gf.bvt.BVTProgrammingModelTest.runu(BVTProgrammingModelTest.java:334)
      at
ibmsftest.gf.bvt.BVTProgrammingModelTest.runTest(BVTProgrammingModelTest.java:145)
      at ibmsftest.gf.tbase.SFDriver.runOneTest(SFDriver.java:457)
      at ibmsftest.gf.tbase.SFDriver.main(SFDriver.java:217)

--------->End of exception trace
```

Cutout 9-1
First example of stack trace printout.

```
--------->Beginning of exception trace
Stack Trace Data:

Number of chained exception(s): 1
Transaction ID 399646625301991424.-2305842996177452337
...Locally thrown exception/Local Stack Trace
com.ibm.sf.gf.TransientEntityNotFoundException: MSG_GFException_002: Resource
'MSG_FACTORY_TransientEntity' not found in bundle
'com.ibm.sf.gf.resources.ContainerExceptionResources'.
      at com.ibm.sf.gf.TestingHooks.throwGFException(TestingHooks.java:202)
      at ibmsftest.gf.tutil.TestEntityImpl.getCustomer(TestEntityImpl.java:590)
      at
ibmsftest.gf.bvt.BVTProgrammingModelTest.runu(BVTProgrammingModelTest.java:334)
      at
ibmsftest.gf.bvt.BVTProgrammingModelTest.runTest(BVTProgrammingModelTest.java:145)
      at ibmsftest.gf.tbase.SFDriver.runOneTest(SFDriver.java:457)
      at ibmsftest.gf.tbase.SFDriver.main(SFDriver.java:217)
Root Exception=com.ibm.sf.gf.NamingNameNotFoundException:
[(1998.03.05 18:28:12:456)(9.5.66.207:1ec867:cf058af0c4:-7e89)(Thread[SmSFThread-6-
#1,5,RMI runtime])]W
...Remotely thrown exception StackTrace from process: SFGSMProcess
com.ibm.sf.gf.NamingNameNotFoundException: MSG_NAMING_004: Name
'/IBM.SF/UserAliases/johnDoeNoNameAlias' does not exist.
      at com.ibm.sf.gf.NamingHFSDataStore.readBa(NamingHFSDataStore.java:281)
      at com.ibm.sf.gf.NamingGlobalServerImpl.lookup(NamingGlobalServerImpl.java:938)
      at com.ibm.sf.gf.NamingGlobalServerImpl.lookup(NamingGlobalServerImpl.java:876)
      at
com.ibm.sf.gf.NamingGlobalServerImpl_Skel.dispatch(NamingGlobalServerImpl_Skel.java:493)
      at com.ibm.sf.gf.GFRemoteServerRef.dispatch2(GFRemoteServerRef.java:245)
      at
com.ibm.sf.gf.SmDistributedThreadContext.serviceRequests(SmDistributedThreadContext.java:
530)
      at
com.ibm.sf.gf.SmDistributedThreadContext.serviceRequests(SmDistributedThreadContext.java:
462)
      at com.ibm.sf.gf.SmSFThread.run(SmSFThread.java:422)
[(1998.03.05 18:28:12:690)(9.5.66.207:1ec867:cf058af0c4:-7e89)(Thread[SmSFThread-6-#1,5,RMI
runtime])]R
...Remotely thrown exception StackTrace from process: Client
com.ibm.sf.gf.NamingNameNotFoundException: MSG_NAMING_004: Name '/IBM.SF/UserAliases/
johnDoeNoNameAlias' does not exist.
      at com.ibm.sf.gf.SFException.readObject(SFException.java:169)
      at java.io.ObjectInputStream.inputObject(ObjectInputStream.java:996)
      at java.io.ObjectInputStream.readObject(ObjectInputStream.java:287)
      at com.ibm.sf.gf.GFStreamRemoteCall.executeCall(GFStreamRemoteCall.java:438)
      at com.ibm.sf.gf.GFRemoteRef.invoke(GFRemoteRef.java:151)
      at
com.ibm.sf.gf.NamingGlobalServerImpl_Stub.lookup(NamingGlobalServerImpl_Stub.java:792)
      at com.ibm.sf.gf.NamingServices.lookup(NamingServices.java:546)
      at com.ibm.sf.gf.NamingServices.lookup(NamingServices.java:487)
      at com.ibm.sf.gf.NamingContext.lookup(NamingContext.java:353)
      at com.ibm.sf.gf.TestingHooks.userAliasExistTest(TestingHooks.java:221)
      at ibmsftest.gf.tutil.TestEntityImpl.getCustomer(TestEntityImpl.java:585)
      at ibmsftest.gf.bvt.BVTProgrammingModelTest.runu(BVTProgrammingModelTest.java:334)
      at ibmsftest.gf.bvt.BVTProgrammingModelTest.runTest(BVTProgrammingModelTest.java:145)
      at ibmsftest.gf.tbase.SFDriver.runOneTest(SFDriver.java:457)
      at ibmsftest.gf.tbase.SFDriver.main(SFDriver.java:217)

--------->End of exception trace
```

Cutout 9-2
Second example of stack trace printout.

```
--------->Beginning of exception trace
Stack Trace Data:

Number of chained exception(s): 1
Transaction ID 399646625301991424.-2305842996177452337
...Remotely thrown exception/Local Stack Trace
[(1998.03.05 18:28:16:253) (9.5.66.207:1ec9bf:cf058bd335:-7f5a) (Thread[main,5,main])]W
...Remotely thrown exception StackTrace from process: Client
com.ibm.sf.gf.TransientEntityNotFoundException: MSG_GFException_002: Resource
'MSG_FACTORY_TransientEntity' not found in bundle
'com.ibm.sf.gf.resources.ContainerExceptionResources'.
      at com.ibm.sf.gf.TestingHooks.throwGFException(TestingHooks.java:202)
      at ibmsftest.gf.tutil.TestEntityImpl.getCustomer(TestEntityImpl.java:590)
      at ibmsftest.gf.tutil.TestEntityImpl_Skel.dispatch(TestEntityImpl_Skel.java:120)
      at com.ibm.sf.gf.GFRemoteServerRef.dispatch2(GFRemoteServerRef.java:245)
      at
com.ibm.sf.gf.SmDistributedThreadContext.serviceRequests(SmDistributedThreadContext.java:
530)
      at com.ibm.sf.gf.SmCommOutThread.executeCall(SmCommOutThread.java:114)
      at com.ibm.sf.gf.GFStreamRemoteCall.executeCall(GFStreamRemoteCall.java:428)
      at com.ibm.sf.gf.GFRemoteRef.invoke(GFRemoteRef.java:151)
      at ibmsftest.gf.tutil.TestEntityImpl_Stub.setEqual(TestEntityImpl_Stub.java:806)
      at
ibmsftest.gf.bvt.BVTProgrammingModelTest.runu(BVTProgrammingModelTest.java:404)
      at
ibmsftest.gf.bvt.BVTProgrammingModelTest.runTest(BVTProgrammingModelTest.java:145)
      at ibmsftest.gf.tbase.SFDriver.runOneTest(SFDriver.java:457)
      at ibmsftest.gf.tbase.SFDriver.main(SFDriver.java:217)
[(1998.03.05 18:28:16:362) (9.5.66.207:1ec9bf:cf058bd335:-7f5a) (Thread[main,5,main])]R
...Remotely thrown exception StackTrace from process: SFBOProcess1
com.ibm.sf.gf.TransientEntityNotFoundException: MSG_GFException_002: Resource
'MSG_FACTORY_TransientEntity' not found in bundle
'com.ibm.sf.gf.resources.ContainerExceptionResources'.
      at com.ibm.sf.gf.SFException.readObject(SFException.java:169)
      at java.io.ObjectInputStream.inputObject(ObjectInputStream.java:996)
      at java.io.ObjectInputStream.readObject(ObjectInputStream.java:287)
      at com.ibm.sf.gf.GFStreamRemoteCall.executeCall(GFStreamRemoteCall.java:438)
      at com.ibm.sf.gf.GFRemoteRef.invoke(GFRemoteRef.java:151)
      at
ibmsftest.gf.tutil.TestEntityImpl_Stub.getCustomer(TestEntityImpl_Stub.java:155)
      at ibmsftest.gf.tutil.TestEntityImpl.setEqual(TestEntityImpl.java:161)
      at ibmsftest.gf.tutil.TestEntityImpl_Skel.dispatch(TestEntityImpl_Skel.java:442)
      at com.ibm.sf.gf.GFRemoteServerRef.dispatch2(GFRemoteServerRef.java:245)
      at
com.ibm.sf.gf.SmDistributedThreadContext.serviceRequests(SmDistributedThreadContext.java:
530)
      at
com.ibm.sf.gf.SmDistributedThreadContext.serviceRequests(SmDistributedThreadContext.java:
462)
      at com.ibm.sf.gf.SmSFThread.run(SmSFThread.java:422)
[(1998.03.05 18:28:16:534) (9.5.66.207:1ec9bf:cf058bd335:-7f5a) (Thread[main,5,main])]R
...Remotely thrown exception StackTrace from process: Client
com.ibm.sf.gf.TransientEntityNotFoundException: MSG_GFException_002: Resource
'MSG_FACTORY_TransientEntity' not found in bundle
'com.ibm.sf.gf.resources.ContainerExceptionResources'.
      at com.ibm.sf.gf.SFException.readObject(SFException.java:169)
      at java.io.ObjectInputStream.inputObject(ObjectInputStream.java:996)
      at java.io.ObjectInputStream.readObject(ObjectInputStream.java:287)
```

Cutout 9-3

Third example of stack trace printout.

```
      at com.ibm.sf.gf.GFStreamRemoteCall.executeCall(GFStreamRemoteCall.java:438)
      at com.ibm.sf.gf.GFRemoteRef.invoke(GFRemoteRef.java:151)
      at ibmsftest.gf.tutil.TestEntityImpl_Stub.setEqual(TestEntityImpl_Stub.java:806)
      at ibmsftest.gf.bvt.BVTProgrammingModelTest.runu(BVTProgrammingModelTest.java:404)
      at ibmsftest.gf.bvt.BVTProgrammingModelTest.runTest(BVTProgrammingModelTest.java:145)
      at ibmsftest.gf.tbase.SFDriver.runOneTest(SFDriver.java:457)
      at ibmsftest.gf.tbase.SFDriver.main(SFDriver.java:217)

Root Exception=com.ibm.sf.gf.NamingNameNotFoundException:
[(1998.03.05 18:28:16:112)(9.5.66.207:1ec867:cf058af0c4:-7e6e)(Thread[SmSFThread-6-#1,5,RMI
runtime])]W
...Remotely thrown exception StackTrace from process: SFGSMProcess
com.ibm.sf.gf.NamingNameNotFoundException: MSG_NAMING_004: Name '/IBM.SF/UserAliases/
johnDoeNoNameAlias' does not exist.
      at com.ibm.sf.gf.NamingHFSDataStore.readBa(NamingHFSDataStore.java:281)
      at com.ibm.sf.gf.NamingGlobalServerImpl.lookup(NamingGlobalServerImpl.java:938)
      at com.ibm.sf.gf.NamingGlobalServerImpl.lookup(NamingGlobalServerImpl.java:876)
      at
com.ibm.sf.gf.NamingGlobalServerImpl_Skel.dispatch(NamingGlobalServerImpl_Skel.java:493)
      at com.ibm.sf.gf.GFRemoteServerRef.dispatch2(GFRemoteServerRef.java:245)
      at
com.ibm.sf.gf.SmDistributedThreadContext.serviceRequests(SmDistributedThreadContext.java:
530)
      at
com.ibm.sf.gf.SmDistributedThreadContext.serviceRequests(SmDistributedThreadContext.java:
462)
      at com.ibm.sf.gf.SmSFThread.run(SmSFThread.java:422)
[(1998.03.05 18:28:16:159)(9.5.66.207:1ec867:cf058af0c4:-7e6e)(Thread[SmSFThread-6-#1,5,RMI
runtime])]R
...Remotely thrown exception StackTrace from process: Client
com.ibm.sf.gf.NamingNameNotFoundException: MSG_NAMING_004: Name '/IBM.SF/UserAliases/
johnDoeNoNameAlias' does not exist.
      at com.ibm.sf.gf.SFException.readObject(SFException.java:169)
      at java.io.ObjectInputStream.inputObject(ObjectInputStream.java:996)
      at java.io.ObjectInputStream.readObject(ObjectInputStream.java:287)
      at com.ibm.sf.gf.GFStreamRemoteCall.executeCall(GFStreamRemoteCall.java:438)
      at com.ibm.sf.gf.GFRemoteRef.invoke(GFRemoteRef.java:151)
      at
com.ibm.sf.gf.NamingGlobalServerImpl_Stub.lookup(NamingGlobalServerImpl_Stub.java:792)
      at com.ibm.sf.gf.NamingServices.lookup(NamingServices.java:546)
      at com.ibm.sf.gf.NamingServices.lookup(NamingServices.java:487)
      at com.ibm.sf.gf.NamingContext.lookup(NamingContext.java:353)
      at com.ibm.sf.gf.TestingHooks.userAliasExistTest(TestingHooks.java:221)
      at ibmsftest.gf.tutil.TestEntityImpl.getCustomer(TestEntityImpl.java:585)
      at ibmsftest.gf.tutil.TestEntityImpl_Skel.dispatch(TestEntityImpl_Skel.java:120)
      at com.ibm.sf.gf.GFRemoteServerRef.dispatch2(GFRemoteServerRef.java:245)
      at
com.ibm.sf.gf.SmDistributedThreadContext.serviceRequests(SmDistributedThreadContext.java:
530)
      at com.ibm.sf.gf.SmCommOutThread.executeCall(SmCommOutThread.java:114)
      at com.ibm.sf.gf.GFStreamRemoteCall.executeCall(GFStreamRemoteCall.java:428)
      at com.ibm.sf.gf.GFRemoteRef.invoke(GFRemoteRef.java:151)
      at ibmsftest.gf.tutil.TestEntityImpl_Stub.setEqual(TestEntityImpl_Stub.java:806)
      at ibmsftest.gf.bvt.BVTProgrammingModelTest.runu(BVTProgrammingModelTest.java:404)
      at ibmsftest.gf.bvt.BVTProgrammingModelTest.runTest(BVTProgrammingModelTest.java:145)
      at ibmsftest.gf.tbase.SFDriver.runOneTest(SFDriver.java:457)
      at ibmsftest.gf.tbase.SFDriver.main(SFDriver.java:217)

--------->End of exception trace
```

Cutout 9-3
continued

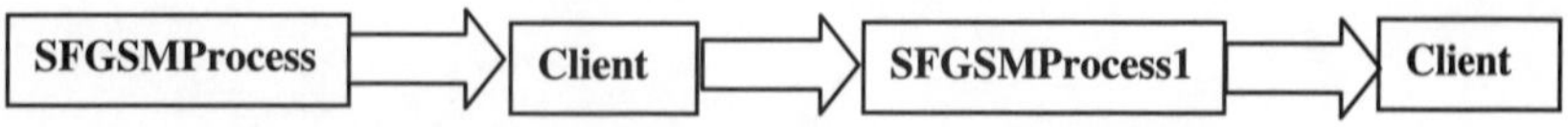

Figure 9-1
Exception flow in third example.

The second example, shown in Cutout 9-2, is quite similar to the first one, only that the exception is now caught in the SFGSMProcess and re-thrown to the calling process. As a consequence, we now can see that the number of chained exceptions is 1. The root exception (i.e. the original exception from which the whole chain of throwing and re-throwing starts) is `com.ibm.sf.gf.NamingNameNotFoundException` thrown within the SFGSMProcess. The SFGSMProcess receives it and re-throws it as `com.ibm.sf.gf.Transient EntityNotFoundException`.

The last example, shown in Cutout 9-3, is quite complicated and involves a thrown exception which is passed from one SanFrancisco process to another. The stack trace printout shows that the root exception, `com.ibm.sf.gf.NamingNameNotFoundException`, was thrown at 1998.03.05 18:28.16:112 and was received by the calling process (Client) over the network. In turn, the Client re-throws `NamingNameNotFoundException` as `TransientEntityNotFound Exception`, which is sent to SFBOProcess1 and comes back to the Client. In summary, the flow of the exception is shown in Figure 9-1.

CHAPTER 10

The SanFrancisco Object Model

This chapter reviews the SanFrancisco object model. Although all SanFrancisco objects are Java objects, they have special characteristics. Some additional attributes and constraints are required in order to allow SanFrancisco to provide all its features.

Object Model Basics

The first thing to remember when studying the SanFrancisco object model, is that all SanFrancisco objects are defined and implemented in Java. Therefore, SanFrancisco objects share all the attributes of Java objects, and specifically follow the Java object model. In other words, some of the most fundamental issues of the SanFrancisco object model are addressed through the Java object model. Examples of such issues are:

- abstraction,
- typing, and
- hierarchy (inheritance).

SanFrancisco business objects follow a special set of rules, which allows them to co-exist and make use of the SanFrancisco environment.

SanFrancisco Objects as Special Java Objects

A very important rule applied to SanFrancisco Business objects is that no public member variables are allowed. This rule is required in order to facilitate distribution.

A common software engineering practice is the separation of interface (or definition) from implementation. Java addresses this issue through Java interfaces and classes. Most SanFrancisco classes have a corresponding Java interface. This way, programmers using the object are only required to know the interface name in their code. Most SanFrancisco concepts are introduced through interfaces, and each interface is implemented in a class whose name is the same as the interface name with the suffix "`Impl`" (more on SanFrancisco naming conventions in just a little while).

Persistence and Sharing

An object is called persistent if its lifespan exceeds that of the thread (or process) creating it. So, any object stored to a file or transmitted over the network is in a way persistent. Object persistence is a considerable technical challenge in object-oriented programming languages, mainly because it is highly platform-dependent.

A non-persistent object is called transient. Transient objects are created locally in the address space of the calling process and live only until deleted or until the process terminates.

SanFrancisco supports object persistency through Relational Databases (RDB) or POSIX streams (which should not be used for anything but prototypes). Persistent objects are created according to configuration information and location preferences specified at creation time to be associated with permanent storage (i.e. a specific RDB or POSIX file). Persistent objects are associated with a "home" server process where they exist in memory when accessed by any client process.

The idea of a persistent object can sometimes lead to what might appear to be a conflict with the Java object model. In some cases, the memory image of such an object in the server process might be garbage collected by the Java Virtual Machine. Such garbage collection could take place when the object is not in use in any transaction and there are no active references to it. However, since the object is persistent, garbage collection does not destroy it. Any subsequent access through the `BaseFactory` will cause the persistent object to be again taken from its permanent store and its image to be reconstructed in memory. In order to really delete a persistent object from its permanent store and from the SanFrancisco configuration in which it was created, the `BaseFactory` must be used.

In SanFrancisco, `Entity` objects may be either transient or persistent. `String` and `Dependent` objects, including `Commands`, are persistent only if they are contained in another persistent object, and in any other case they are transient. Specifically, when a `String` or `Dependent` object is created through the factory specifying that it is contained in another object, it is transient or persistent according to whether its containing object is transient or persistent.

Since Java includes garbage collection, explicitly deleting transient business objects is not required, but it is good practice nonetheless. The reason is that SanFrancisco provides a uniform interface for deleting an object—the same factory delete method should be called on transient business objects as on persistent ones, in order to free up the storage occupied by the objects. So, instead of trying to keep track of which objects are persistent and which are not, just delete any unused objects.

Client programmers do create and access persistent `Entity` objects directly. Some transient `Entity` objects may also be created or used, for example transient collections that hold results of queries performed on persistent collections.

A business object is considered to be shared when it is in use by more than one other persistent business object. All `Entity` objects can be shared, whereas `Dependent`, `Handle`, `String` and `array` objects can never be shared. Object sharing is facilitated in a transparent manner, just by accessing Entity objects.

When invoking a method on an object it is important to remember whether the returned value is a copy of a reference.

- Methods on persistent objects that return Strings return a reference, not a copy.
- The `get<>ForRestrictedUse()` methods for `Dependent` attributes return a reference, not a copy.
- Methods on persistent objects that return `Dependents` or arrays always return a transient copy, not a reference.
- Remote method calls always pass `Dependents` and arrays by value. So a method that accesses a Dependent or array returns a copy of that object.
- Methods that take, as input, an object to persist (such as any `set<>()` method on a persistent object) always make a copy of the specified object. Therefore, subsequent operations that the caller may perform on the passed object will not affect the persistent copy.
- The Dependent returned from any get<>`ForRestrictedUse()` method must never be modified and must not be used outside the valid scope of access for the Entity it was retrieved from. Similarly, the String returned from any get<>() method must not

be used outside the valid scope of access for the Entity it was retrieved from. Everything other than NO_LOCK access means that the Dependent or String must be used only within the same transaction in which it was retrieved. If such use is needed, the receiver must make a copy of the Dependent or String and use that copy rather than the original.

Ownership vs. Containment

Containment is a very commonly used relationship between objects. Most object-oriented analysis methodologies define at least two different containment relationships between objects. One is called containment by value, or "ownership," and the other is called containment by reference. The two containment relationships are unrelated to whether the implementation of an object holds the actual object or a pointer to the object. Instead, the containment is conceptual. The decisive difference between ownership and plain containment is the responsibility for deleting the contained objects.

Owned objects are logically part of their owning object. For example, cash deposits are part of a bank account record, so a bank account record owns the cash deposits. At the implementation level, the significance of ownership is that an object that is owned by another object cannot live longer than its owner. In SanFrancisco, this is implemented by ensuring that, when an object is deleted, it deletes any object it owns. So, in this specific example, deleting the bank account record object will lead to the deletion of all the cash deposits that are part of it.

Whatever the containment relationship is, at the implementation level a business object that contains an Entity stores the Handle of the contained Entity as a reference to it. In contrast, Java uses object references for contained `Dependent`, `String`, and array objects. When a Dependent, String, or array object is contained in another object, it is always owned.

When dealing with a given business object and some `Entity` that appears to be contained in it, it is important to understand whether it owns or simply contains the other `Entity` by reference. This determines whether deleting the business object will delete the contained `Entity`. It also determines whether setting the contained Entity to "null" or removing it from a collection will delete the Entity. If it is owned, the contained

Entity will be deleted; otherwise, it will not be deleted. Entity objects can be owned by other Entities. Of course, they are never owned by `String` objects and should never be owned by a `Dependent` object that is public. It is possible for a `Dependent` object that is an implementation detail of an `Entity` to own another `Entity`, but such `Dependents` must be kept internal to the implementation.

In order to prevent confusion relating to whether a contained `Entity` will be deleted, SanFrancisco business objects provide method names for manipulating contained Entities that make it clear whether the Entity is owned, by having the word "Owned" inside the method name. For example, an unowned Entity can be set in its containing Entity with a method such as `setHomeOwner()` or `addContractor()`, whereas an owned Entity would be set in its containing object with methods such as `setOwnedAddress()` or `addOwnedRoom()`. In the same way, an Entity from a collection would use either `removeContractor()` or `removeOwnedRoom()`. The owned `Room` is deleted, but the `Contractor` is not.

Objects that contain owned Entities support either a `setOwned...()` or `removeOwned...()` method, which will delete the `Entity`, and an `orphanOwned...()` method, that removes the Entity from the containing object without deleting it.

SanFrancisco has additional support related to ownership beyond the naming conventions which help in remembering when one is dealing with owned Entities. There is a special set of collection classes that correctly implement ownership semantics for owned `Entity` objects. These collections all have "`EntityOwning`" in their names, e.g. `EntityOwningSet`. These collections support the `...Owned...` names on the relevant methods.

The regular non-owning collections (`Set`, `List`, `Map`, `DSet`, `DList`, and `DMap`) are used for elements such as `String`, `Dependent`, or non-owned `Entity` objects. Even though `String` and `Dependent` objects are owned, there is no conceptual problem using non-owning collections with them, since they are never shared and are always manipulated through "copies" just like primitive type objects (e.g. int, float).

Transparent Distribution and Multi-threading

One of the main goals of SanFrancisco is to provide transparently distributed computing on a network of heterogeneous platforms. SanFrancisco programs are implemented as Java programs that execute in a "client" process. This process accesses and uses business objects that reside in SanFrancisco "server" processes. Persistent business objects (usually part of a large business database) exist only in server processes. Working copies of them and other temporary business objects may be created both in the server process and in the client process.

The transparency of the distributed environment makes sure that neither the user nor the developer is aware (or needs to be aware) of the actual location of server processes. The processes are accessed by their "logical" name, and the actual location may vary. For example, when running a client on a Windows 98 machine that requires a certain service, the server might run on a Windows NT server in the next room as well as on an RS/6000 workstation in a different state.

Multi-threading is an essential part of the Java language. SanFrancisco supports multi-threading in both client and server programs. Client programs may start threads using the normal Java thread support. Any thread that will use SanFrancisco objects should use `SmSFThread` or create a work area that is associated with the Java thread. This class can be subclassed or used just like the Java Thread class, but its use is required because it supports passing required context information between client and server processes.

A SanFrancisco server process is a set of threads in the same Java virtual machine process, and it requires care to avoid having one thread interfere with or corrupt another.

SanFrancisco supports a variety of locking mechanisms. The simplest one is just having no locking, and this is referred to as `NO_LOCK`. When using this kind of locking, you actually receive non-transactional access to the object, which means you get a copy of the object, and any changes you make are not recorded in the persistent object. Since you get a copy of the object, and no real locking is performed, you can use the Java reference you receive outside of transaction boundaries, and across multiple transactions.

Another type of lock is a pessimistic lock. These locks offer you exclusive locking according to your access mode. In other words, if you obtain a read lock you are sure the object is not being modified (nobody else can write to it) and if you obtain a write lock, nobody else can read the object you are locking.

Optimistic locks work in a more complex way: a copy of the object is provided for the requesting transaction. At commit time, if no other changes were made to the object, then the changes made are copied to the original object. If any other changes were made to the original copy, then the commit operation will fail. When using this locking technique you increase the concurrency level for your transactions (i.e. more transactions can run concurrently accessing the same objects), but at the same time you increase the risk of commit time failures. An optimistic lock doesn't actually do any "locking" in the usual sense; when one transaction obtains such a lock, other transactions can get another optimistic lock, or even a pessimistic read or write lock.

Although SanFrancisco provides the illusion of a single network of cooperating objects, the SanFrancisco Foundation layer introduces the notion of access mode to objects. You may access distributed objects in home mode or in local mode. When using home mode, the SanFrancisco Foundation dynamically and automatically creates a proxy object in the address space of the requester. The proxy appears to be the same as the real instance. In other words, it has the same interface. The client can transparently invoke methods on the proxy and the proxy delegates the method calls to the actual (remote) instance. This mechanism is implemented on top of the Java RMI (Remote Method Invocation) software layer. If local mode is chosen, in most cases the Foundation returns a copy of the real instance to the requesting program. Depending on the lock mode you selected, the Foundation may also automatically reflect all changes back onto the real object at commit time.

The decision whether to use home or local mode can be made by the application at runtime or by using the configuration utility at installation time. This choice affects the programming logic and the programmer needs to decide whether to use home or local access and to structure the application accordingly.

The main consideration when choosing between home and local access mode is the performance consequences. Although accessing an object through a proxy is convenient, every method call translates into a remote call and has to go through the RMI mechanism, which in turn is implemented using TCP/IP communication. In contrast, if an object is accessed in local mode, every method call is local and, therefore, significantly more efficient. However, in this case, a copy is taken and if the object encapsulates a large number of data, this may degrade the performance. So, to summarize, home mode is most useful when executing a limited number of method invocations on a large object, whereas local mode should be preferred when executing a large number of method calls on a small instance.

A Word About SanFrancisco Naming Conventions

Naturally, the naming convention for SanFrancisco interface and class names follows the Java naming convention. The Java convention is that interface and class names are composed of the concatenation of one or more words, where the first letter of each word is capitalized. No spaces or underscores separate the words in a class name.

SanFrancisco introduces additional naming conventions, or actually requirements. For any distributable object, the class name should be the interface name with a "`Impl`" suffix, and the class factory name should be the interface name with a "`Factory`" suffix.

For example, in the House of Rooms sample:

- `Room.java` is the interface to the Room object,
- `RoomImpl.Java` implements this interface, and
- `RoomFactory.java` is the class factory for the Room object.

Other conventions are:

Base Class	Convention
`Entity`	First word is a noun (e.g. `House`) or adjective followed by a noun (e.g. `YellowHouse`)
`Command`	Follow the form <noun><verb>Cmd where the noun refers to the main target of the command and the verb the main task performed (e.g. `HouseUpdateCmd`).
`Dependent`	Dependent subclass names (except for Commands) start with a "D" prefix followed by a noun that is capitalized (e.g. `DDecimal`).

CHAPTER 11

SanFrancisco Base Classes

This chapter is aimed at providing a quick overview of the SanFrancisco base classes. A short description of the role of each class will be given. In-depth explanations regarding each of the classes and their usage will be provided in Chapters 14–20.

The SanFrancisco Base

The SanFrancisco Foundation layer includes a set of Java classes called Base Classes that help programmers to implement basic business objects and processes and help in supporting persistence. The base classes represent the root of the inheritance tree for the SanFrancisco business objects. In order to make use of the services offered by the Foundation layer, programmers must inherit from these classes.

The top part of the SanFrancisco inheritance tree is shown in Figure 11-1, which is derived from Figure 5-3.

Entity

As previously mentioned, and shown in Figure 11-1, `Entity` is the most frequently used type of business object. It encapsulates most of the support for shared persistent objects that can be named, locked, secured, participate in transactions, and be contained in other entities. Note that each `Entity` object has a unique identity, hence two different entities are unequal objects even if their content is identical. Although entities are intended to be persistent, it is possible to create transient entity objects to hold temporary data.

The `Entity` class is designed so it can be extended. Programmers can extend the `Entity` class whenever they need to create business objects that have the `Entity` capabilities, i.e. they are inherently persistent, they can be shared among multiple processes, and they can participate in transactions.

In accordance with the SanFrancisco object model, you do not create instances of objects derived from Entity by using the `new` Java operator. Whenever you need to create an instance, use the methods provided by a

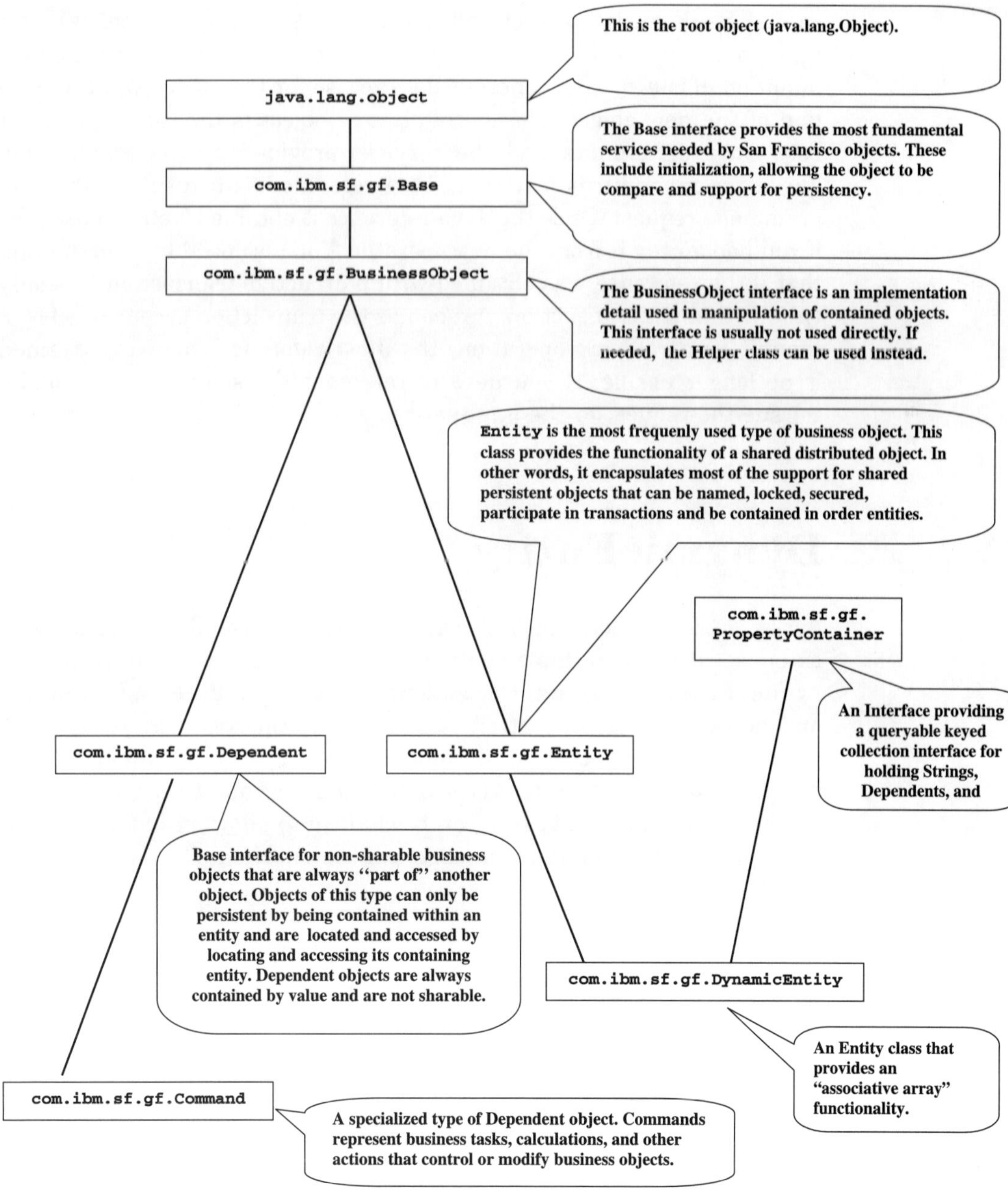

Figure 11-1
The base classes hierarchy.

special SanFrancisco object called the `BaseFactory` (see below). The `BaseFactory` provides you with a level of indirection for runtime determination of the specific concrete class to use for the object and the location of the new object. The `BaseFactory` object is the major mediator between programmers and the services provided by the Foundation. `BaseFactory` returns a normal Java reference as a result of the programmer's request. Once the Java reference is obtained, you can use it as if you had gotten it from the `new` operator. You also need to keep in mind that if the reference was obtained within an active transaction it is only valid within the transaction. As soon as the transaction is concluded by a commit or a rollback operation, the Java reference that you obtained is no longer usable. If you need to reference the same instance again, reissue the request to the `BaseFactory`.

DynamicEntity

`DynamicEntity` adds an "associative array" functionality to `Entity`. It extends `Entity` and implements a `PropertyContainer` interface. The `PropertyContainer` interface allows you to dynamically add, remove, and access user-defined attributes, called "properties," at runtime. A property is an object that is added to a property container with a name. It can later be retrieved by that name. Property containers and therefore `DynamicEntities`, can be chained to allow an instance to get some properties from other property containers chained to it.

Dependent

Dependents support business objects that encapsulate a small number of data. These objects are different from Entities in that they are not shared and are persistent only when contained in an `Entity`. Persistent `Dependent` objects are always contained in an `Entity`, but transient `Dependent` objects can be autonomous. The lifecycle of a persistent `Dependent` object can never exceed that of its containing `Entity`. When the containing Entity is deleted, all its contained `Dependent` objects are deleted. `Dependent` objects are always locked, accessed, stored, and committed in a transaction through the containing `Entity`.

`Dependent` objects do not have unique identities. Therefore, they cannot be named. If two Dependents have the same values, they are considered to be equal objects. Java references to these objects within their containing Entity are typically not returned or passed outside of their class. Rather, these objects are typically returned and passed using copy semantics.

Command

`Command` subclasses are a specialized type of `Dependent` object. Commands represent business tasks, calculations, and other actions that control or modify business objects. `Command` objects allow logging of modifications to persistent business objects. Some commands support undo and redo of actions, e.g. Commands that edit attributes of business object. Commands can be used to perform their task atomically or as part of a larger transaction. Commands can be created to execute their task in a remote server process or locally. Commands are often transient but may be persistent if contained in an Entity.

At first glance, the idea of a `Command` object appears to contradict the idea of encapsulating data and functionality inside an object. However, there are three major reasons for isolating specific business logic in Command objects.

- If business rules change, you can immediately identify which parts of the application need to be modified.
- Entity classes become more generic because some of the functionality is moved away into Commands and, hence, promote their reusability.
- Performance can be boosted using `Command` objects. If a process involves dealing with multiple Entities and invoking a relatively large number of methods, both home mode and local mode might turn out to be unsatisfactory. In these cases a `Command` that works in the remote address space and that operates the process can be used, to access the various Entities with Home access on the server.

The Query Command is a special subclass of Command that is meant to encapsulate a query request to be executed on a collection of objects. We expand on this in Chapter 19.

BaseFactory

The BaseFactory object provides and manages the services needed to operate in a distributed environment. Among these services are naming, concurrency, distribution, transactions, persistence, and object lifecyle services such as creation, deletion, and copying. One BaseFactory object exists in every client process. This object is accessed through the static class method factory() in the class Global. If the SanFrancisco environment has not been explicitly started using Global.initialize(), then the first use of Global.factory() automatically starts up the SanFrancisco environment and creates the BaseFactory object.

Although BaseFactory provides the user with a rich set of capabilities, these are actually implemented in different classes. In order to do that, BaseFactory inherits from quite a few classes. As already shown in Figure 5-4, it inherits from: EntityManagement, DependentManagement, StringManagement, NameServiceManagement, TransactionManagement, SmDistributedProcessManagement, NotificationManagement, CommandManagement, PersistentArrayManagement, and GFRemote.

The following list is a partial list of services that are accessible through the BaseFactory.

- Starting a transaction (Global.factory().begin())
- Committing/rolling back a transaction (Global.factory().commit() or rollback())
- Creating business objects (for instance, Global.factory().createEntity(...), Global.factory().createDependent(...))
- Deleting persistent business objects
- Requesting lock levels on business objects
- Accessing the notification mechanisms

When using class factories, you must use static create methods to create an instance of the corresponding class instead of calling the `BaseFactory` directly. There should be one class factory for each business object class.

Collections

A collection is a way to group objects. Any business object, as well as String objects, can be put in a collection. There are two types of collection classes: those that derive from Entity and those that derive from Dependent. Figure 11-2 shows how the Entity and Dependent collections fit into the class hierarchy shown in Figure 11-1. Among the SanFrancisco Foundation classes, there are collection classes that are intended for organizing groups of business objects in a manner that fits certain needs. From a functional perspective, the different collections offered by SanFrancisco are:

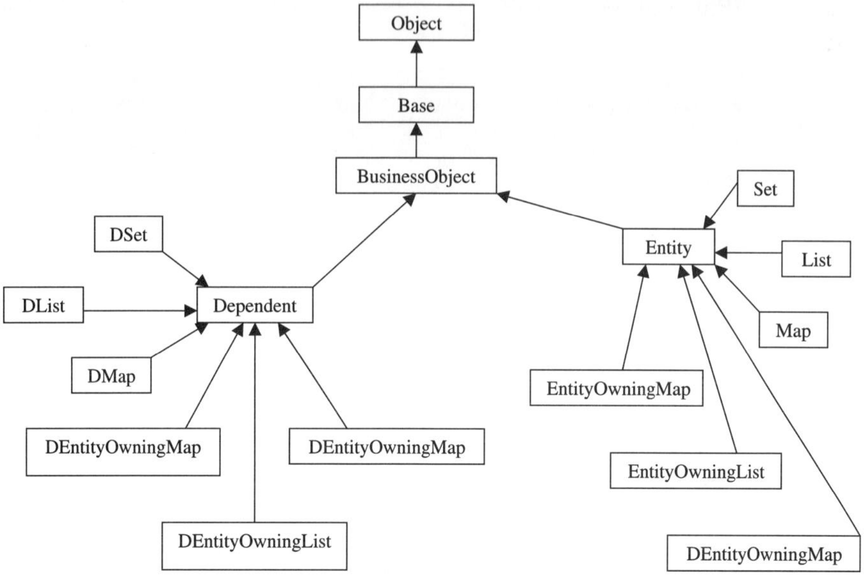

Figure 11-2
The collections hierarchy.

- *List Collections*. Collections that maintain the order of insertion and allow duplicate objects.
- *Set Collections*. Collections where no duplicates are allowed and no specific order is maintained.
- *Map Collections*. Collections that facilitate object retrieval by a specific key, and where no duplicates are allowed.

All collections support the *Iterator* pattern. An *Iterator* allows traversing the collection of objects in a way that does not depend on the implementation details of the Collection.

Entity Collections

The `Set`, `List`, and `Map` collection classes are derived from `Entity`. Special versions of these are used when the collection owns its `Entity` elements: `EntityOwningSet`, `EntityOwningList`, `EntityOwningMap`, and `EntityOwningExtent`—a class that is slightly different than the others, as we will see shortly. These collections are provided to help the programmer with special handling of owned Entities. Collections derived from `Entity` support SQL-style queries to retrieve a subset of the collection. These `Entity` queryable collections have (by inheritance) all the properties of `Entity` described above. That is, they themselves can be persistent, named, locked, and secured, and can participate in transactions.

- `Set` and `EntityOwningSet`. The `Set` and `EntityOwningSet` collections contain elements in an unordered sequence, but the elements are unique. For example, a House contains a set of Rooms. The Rooms are in no particular order, but each room can exist in the House only once.
- `List` and `EntityOwningList`. The `List` and `EntityOwningList` collections contain elements in an ordered sequence based on the sequence in which the elements were added to the collection. The elements do not have to be unique.
- `Map` and `EntityOwningMap`. The `Map` and `EntityOwningMap` collections contain not only elements, but also keys for accessing those elements. The elements are in an unordered sequence and do not have to be unique. This means that the same object can be

in the collection more than once. However, the keys must be unique.

- `EntityOwningExtent`. The `EntityOwningExtent` collection is semantically similar to a `Map`, but it does not allow `Entity` elements to be added. `Entity` elements are always owned by the `EntityOwningExtent` collection and must be created "into" the `EntityOwningExtent`. That is, at creation time, the creation location must be the `EntityOwningExtent` collection object. An `EntityOwningExtent` has been specifically designed to allow it to be mapped to a table, or to a subset of a table, in a database. This allows higher efficiency in the implementation of `EntityOwningExtents` that is not always possible with the other collections.

An `EntityOwningExtent` object can be configured in such a way that its elements match the rows of an existing database table. This is performed for you implicitly (i.e. you don't have to iterate over the rows and add each one of them to the collection). This makes `EntityOwningExtent` the only collection type that can be used to automatically map to relational data. With all other collection types, the only elements that are part of the collection are those objects that have been explicitly added to the collection.

The `EntityOwningExtent` collections are intended to be the most scalable of the collections because they can be mapped directly to the database. In many real world applications tables can hold hundreds of thousands and even millions of rows; it would be inconceivable to require collections to be fully populated with an object per row. The other `Entity` collections are designed to be more flexible in the way they are used, but cannot be as efficient for very large collections. So, to summarize—the `EntityOwningExtent` plays a key role in SanFrancisco applications when it comes to managing high volumes of data and to integrating new functions developed using SanFrancisco with legacy applications using a relational database.

One other major difference between an `EntityOwningExtent` collection and a `Map` is that an `EntityOwningExtent` supports only method keys. That is, multiple keys are supported, but they must be defined from the methods supported by the interfaces of the elements. The concrete `Map`, on the other hand, supports a single key, which can be any arbitrary `Base` object or `String`.

A small technicality that shows the ease of programming in SanFrancisco, is that SanFrancisco operations that are "pushed down" (delegated) to the database (e.g. `query()` and `getElementBy()` when performed on an `EntityOwningExtent`) always return the correct results. In other words, the results reflect any `Entity` creation, deletion, or update made in the current transaction, without the programmer needing to make any explicit calls to `syncEntity()`. Obviously, the Foundation Layer has to implicitly synchronize dirty Entities with the underlying datastore in order to accomplish this. If you need to ensure that the actual database record is updated before `commit()` is called (for example, to trigger database operations such as constraint or duplicate key checking), then you must use the `syncEntity()` method (see Chapter 14 for more details).

`EntityOwningExtents` that are accessed with `NO_LOCK` mode have the following limitations:

- An `EntityOwningExtent` accessed using NO_LOCK throws an exception when an attempt is made to insert an element or to remove an element.
- Query pushdown on an `EntityOwningExtent` accessed using NO_LOCK does not see changes made to NO_LOCK copies of the elements in the `EntityOwningExtent`.

Dependent Collections

Another set of collections derives from Dependent.

- `DSet`. Set collection holding `Dependent` objects
- `DList`. List collection holding `Dependent` objects
- `DMap`. Map collection holding `Dependent` objects
- `DEntityOwningSet`. Set collection for `Dependent` objects owned by an `Entity`
- `DEntityOwningList`. List collection for `Dependent` objects owned by an `Entity`
- `DEntityOwningMap`. Map collection for `Dependent` objects owned by an `Entity`

These collections do not support querying. By being derived from `Dependent`, they have the properties of a `Dependent` object in that they are made persistent, locked, and secured by their containing Entity. They can also participate in transactions as part of the containing

Entity. These collections have no optimizations for large numbers of elements and should be used for very small collections typically having up to 20 elements. Having a larger number of elements does not affect functionality, but will probably generate pretty poor performance.

Which Collection Class To Use?

The large selection of collection classes is confusing at first. How would one select the right collection for a specific need? The list of characteristics of the different collections, as shown in Table 11-1, might come in handy.

Other Base Classes

Figure 11-3 shows the interface inheritance among most of the remaining base classes and interfaces. Classes that do not inherit directly from classes previously described are not shown in the figure. The major purpose of each class is briefly described below. For classes and interfaces treated in detail in one of the following chapters, the chapter number appears in brackets immediately after the class (or interface) name.

- `Interest` [18]. All Entities support generation of notifications at commit time to observers that were previously registered. The `Interest` class is an abstract base class for registering interest in a particular event for which an `Entity` supports notification.
- `EntityInterest` [18]. The `EntityInterest` class is a final concrete subclass of `Interest` supported by all Entities that will cause a notification if any state of the `Entity` is changed. Notifications are delivered during commit processing by calling a method on the observer object.
- `NotificationMailbox` [18]. If a pull style of notification is desired, rather than a push style, a `NotificationMailbox` entity can be used as the observer.
- `NotificationEvent` [18]. The `NotificationMailbox` queues up notifications as NotificationEvent objects that can be accessed when desired.

TABLE 11-1

Summary of collection characteristics

Collection Classes	Characteristic
Map Dmap EntityOwningMap DentityOwningMap Set DSet EntityOwningSet DentityOwningSet EntityOwningExtent	Iteration interface provides only forward iteration
List DList EntityOwningList DentityOwningList *transient collections*	Iteration interface provides both forward and backward iteration
All entity collections	Provides SQL queries (see Chapter 19)
EntityOwningExtent	Supports query pushdown Enables holding legacy data (through RDBMS) Hold very large collections
Map EntityOwningMap Dmap DentityOwningMap EntityOwningExtent	Support keyed access
EntityOwningMap EntityOwningSet EntityOwningList EntityOwningExtent	Elements are *owned* Entities
Set List Map EntityOwningSet EntityOwningList EntityOwningMap	Aimed at holding medium-sized collections (i.e. not very small, but not too big either)
All dependent collections	Hold small collections
All list collections	Preserve the order of insertion
All set collections EntityOwningExtent	Require elements to be unique

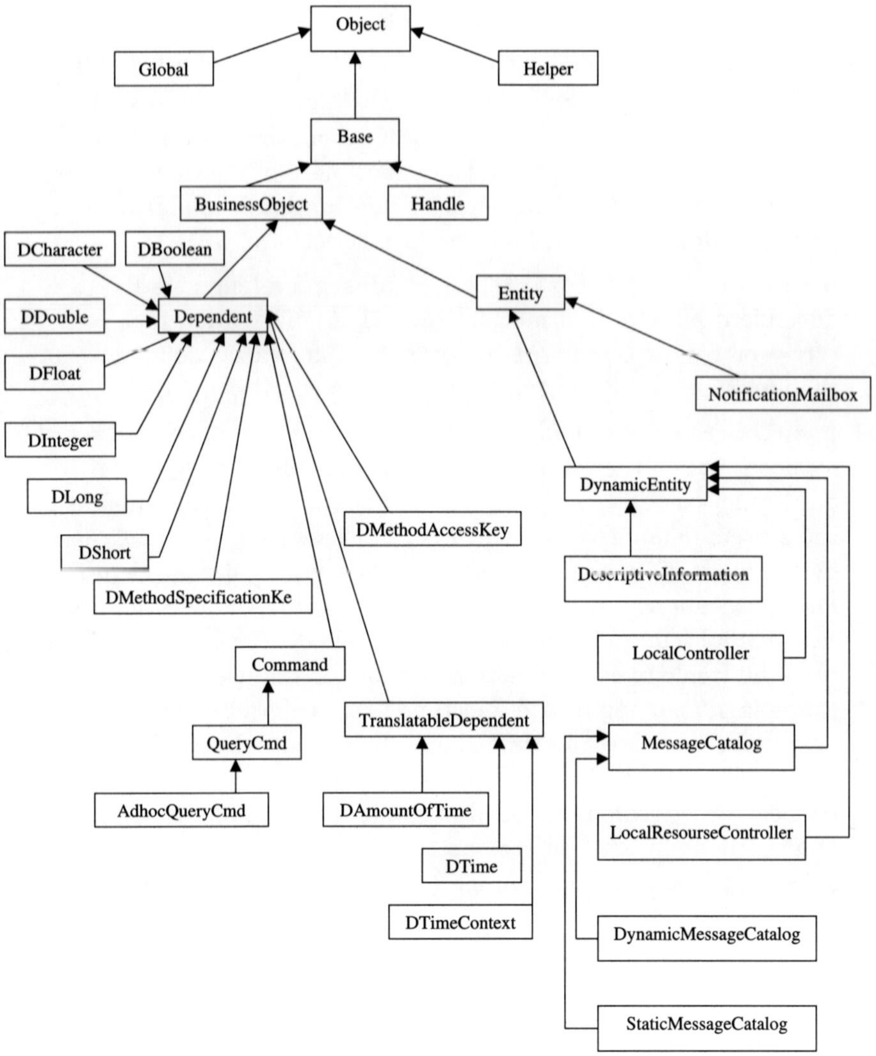

Figure 11-3
Other base classes.

- `DynamicMessageCatalog` [20]. The `DynamicMessageCatalog` is a message repository that allows updates at runtime. That is, messages can be added, removed, or replaced. It can be initialized using a messages file, and its contents can be written back to that file.

- `StaticMessageCatalog` [20]. This is a read-only message repository. It is initialized by reading messages from a file and allows only read access to those messages.
- `Describable` [20]. `Describable` defines a common interface for objects that have a language-dependent piece of information (text) associated with them. That piece of information is meant to provide a description of the object it is associated with.
- `DescriptiveInformation` [20]. Represents a language-dependent piece of information (text). The information text retrieved from a `DescriptiveInformation` varies depending on the language or locale currently used in a running application.
- `LocaleController` [20]. `LocaleController` manages the set of locales that represents the locales supported by the logical SanFrancisco network (LSFN). `LocaleController` also defines the system default locale, which is the locale most commonly used by the users of an application. A locale is essentially an identifier for a geographical, political, or cultural region. An operation that requires a locale to perform its task is called "locale sensitive" and uses the locale to customize information for the user. For example, displaying a date and time is a locale-sensitive operation. The date and time should be formatted according to the conventions of the specific country, region, or culture. Within the framework, a locale is encoded in a `String`. All running instances of a single application share one `LocaleController` object. That object must be accessed through the `LocaleContext` interface.
- `LocaleResourceController` [20]. `LocaleResourceController` is used to manage locale-dependent resources. A locale-dependent resource is an object whose behavior and state are specific to a locale. The `LocaleResourceController` has to be retrieved through the `LocaleContext` interface.
- `LocaleContext` [20]. `LocaleContext` is the main interface for accessing and defining the locale setup of the LSFN. It is also the interface to use when accessing the `LocaleController` and `LocaleResourceController`.
- *Numeric Dependent Wrappers*. `DLong`, `DInteger`, `DShort`, `DCharacter`, `DBoolean`, `DFloat`, and `DDouble` are concrete subclasses of `Dependent` that provide wrappers for the Java

primitive non-array data types so that values of these primitive data types can be held in SanFrancisco collections.

- DmethodKeys. The DMethodAccessKey and DMethodSpecificationKey dependent interfaces are used to define keys into EntityOwningExtent collections. The specification identifies the methods to use in the lookup. The access key identifies the values for those methods. Concrete key classes that support these interfaces can be used to look up elements in an EntityOwningExtent.
- QueryCmd [19]. QueryCmd is an abstract subclass of Command that provides a standard interface for querying Entity collections of objects, and also for sorting them.
- AdhocQueryCmd [19]. AdhocQueryCmd, a concrete subclass of QueryCmd, supports an arbitrary SQL-style query of an Entity collection, including ordering of the result set.
- Translatable [20]. Translatable is the common interface for objects that provide language- or locale-dependent String representations.
- TranslatableDependent [20]—Used to ensure type safety when using a Translatable object that is also a Dependent.
- DDecimal. Represents a basic numerical value of up to 18 total digits. It implements a signed decimal providing a complete set of basic arithmetic operations, along with control over the rounding or truncation behavior of these operations. Various comparison and assignment operations are available for this class. It is typically used to represent currency values. Decimal data types of this sort are commonly used in commercial applications to represent numerical values such as currency values because they guarantee that the appropriate precision is preserved in calculations (as opposed to floating-point arithmetic, for example).
- DAmountOfTime. DAmountOfTime represents an absolute amount of time that can be added to, subtracted from, or used to hold differences of DTimes.
- DTime. This class represents a timestamp. In other words, it represents a specific date and time. DTime objects store a point in time of a Gregorian calendar date (year, month, and day) and a time in that day (hours, minutes, and seconds). DTime provides basic arithmetic operations and locale-sensitive formatting. When

you create a DTime instance, you specify a *precision* that lets you ignore a certain portion of the DTime instance. For example, by specifying an hour precision, you actually ignore minutes, seconds, and milliseconds. The default is the highest possible precision—milliseconds. You can perform date and time arithmetic with DTime objects. For instance, you can determine how many days there are between two dates, or add a certain time to a date to obtain a new one. For more complex date-related calculations such as determining the number of working days between two dates, look at the `NaturalCalendar` class in the Common Business Object layer.

- `DTimeContext` [20]. The main interface for accessing and defining the `DTime` and `TimeZone` setup of an application. It should be used for the global system default `TimeZone` as well as the local active `TimeZone`.
- `SelectCompare` and `SortCompare` [19]. Abstract interfaces that can be supported by any object and used to provide special selection or sort comparison algorithms for use in query operations.
- `AccessMode` [14]. This class encapsulates all the parameters that can be used to control the way a shared, persistent Entity object is accessed.
- `Handle`. Every `Entity` object has its own network-wide unique identity, which is automatically assigned to it by SanFrancisco. This allows the `BaseFactory` to locate objects throughout the network. The `Handle` class encapsulates this unique identification of the object. Handles are extremely important in a SanFrancisco application because they allow entities to store a reference to other entities and client programs to request the retrieval of existing instances. If a SanFrancisco business object has an entity among its attributes (e.g. an invoice with a list of products), it only needs to store the `Handle` to the contained object. `Handles` can be used to retrieve entities. The `BaseFactory` can locate and access the entity based on the information contained in the `Handle`. This is the most common way for retrieving entities in SanFrancisco. You also have the option of giving entities a name (referred to as *user alias*) and to retrieve them based on this information. However, this technique should be only applied to a limited number of top-level entities. It goes without saying that

assigning, maintaining, and using user aliases is not as efficient as using `Handles`.

- `Global`. The `Global` class contains static methods that allow access to objects or primitive values that should be available to all objects and methods executing within the same process. In particular, as previously mentioned, one `BaseFactory` object per process can be obtained from the static `factory()` method in `Global`.
- `Helper`. This class contains static methods that are useful when implementing business objects that contain other business objects.

CHAPTER 12

SanFrancisco Framework Patterns

In this chapter, we look at some design patterns that are used in SanFrancisco. Design patterns are a powerful paradigm for exercising design reuse. We start this chapter by explaining what are design patterns, and then continue to see how SanFrancisco makes use of some well-known patterns and what new patterns it introduces.

What Are Design Patterns?

Design patterns are elements of reuse in an object-oriented design. A frequently cited definition of design patterns is the following one by Christopher Alexanders, a professor of architecture at the University of California at Berkeley:

> Each pattern describes a problem which occurs over and over again in our environment, and then describes the core of the solution to that problem, in such a way that you can use this solution a million times over, without ever doing it the same way twice.

Alexanders' idea was that having clear and concise definitions of repeatedly used design elements (these are the design patterns), would make them accessible to professionals (architects in his case, software developers in ours). Specifically, design patterns allow novices to quickly learn from the experience of experts. Since the whole idea of reusable software frameworks is to allow programmers to benefit from the experience of experts (or specialists in specific techniques such as networking and databases), one would expect to have quite a few design patterns appear in SanFrancisco.

The basic reference book for Design Pattern in Software is *Design Patterns: Elements of Reusable Object-Oriented Software*, by Erich Gamma, Richard Helm, Ralph Johnson and John Vlissides, sometime referred to as the "Gang of four" [GOF]. The next section reviews how some of the design patterns described in this book are used in SanFrancisco.

The description we provide for the patterns detailed in this chapter is structured as follows.

- *Intent*. States the intent of the pattern or the problem it is intended to solve.

- *Motivation*. Explains the motivation for this pattern, especially in the context of SanFrancisco.
- *Concept*. Gives a high-level description of how the pattern fulfills the intent.
- *Benefits*. Explains how the pattern promotes reusability and extensibility.
- *Usage*. Describes how this pattern is used in SanFrancisco.

The Use of Well-Known Design Patterns in SanFrancisco

Command [GOF]

Intent

Encapsulate operations in objects, thereby allowing you to parameterize clients with different requests, and manipulate these operations in different ways (e.g. queue them, log them, undo them).

Motivation

As a business environment changes over time, the application supporting this environment has to be able to react to those changes while minimizing the impact to the overall application. An additional need is to provide a way to update a group of objects at once while ensuring that, if the complete group is not updated successfully, all the changes can be undone. The business logic may span many business objects (classes), which makes the placement of this logic within any of the objects involved impractical.

Concept

Commands are objects with the sole purpose of providing a separate location for a specific piece of functionality, and in the case of SanFrancisco, business logic processing. By packaging this logic into a single object, any changes to the particular business can be implemented with minimal impact on various users.

A `Command` often affects more than one business object, and may require that all the objects affected are updated or all changes reversed. Commands support a rollback capability that allows all these changes to be reversed.

Note that a Command in the context of SanFrancisco usually encapsulates more functionality in it that what is usually done when applying this pattern. In this respect, the SanFrancisco Command has some of the attributes of the Strategy pattern (GOF).

Benefits

The implementation of business logic affecting several distinct business objects through Commands has obvious advantages as far as maintenance is concerned. In addition, it allows application designers to isolate activities from their users by encapsulating the business logic in a `Command` object. The result is that it is much easier to replace, modify, or enhance a certain piece of logic without affecting its users.

Beside the maintenance benefits, Commands can also provide performance advantages by locating the code that implements the algorithm in the most suitable process.

Usage

The Command pattern is implemented in SanFrancisco through the `Command` interface. Variations of the `Command` exist to support special requests, and developers can define their own Commands to support specific needs of their applications. The Query Command is a special type of Command that encapsulates a particular query request, which then creates a subset of the elements of a collection. The Query Command encapsulates features of an object query that is *similar* to Search Query Language (SQL), including selection and sorting (by the way, the implementation of the Query command uses the Interpreter design pattern [GOF]).

Iterator [GOF]

Intent

Provide a way to access elements of a collection without making you aware of its internal structure.

Motivation

Both persistent and transient collections are extensively used in any application, and specifically in business applications. The need to traverse the elements of a collection is a basic and obvious requirement.

Concept

An Iterator can hold the context for iterating a certain collection. This abstraction allows simple and generic interfaces for traversing different collections.

Benefits

- Simplification of the collections (containers) interface
- Support of different ways of traversing the container (e.g. forward, backward)
- More than one traversal can be performed on a container at the same time

Usage

The Iterator pattern is implemented in SanFrancisco by the `Iterator` interface. Iterating can be done using this interface or by using interfaces of the collection (which require as parameter the `Iterator`). Special iterators are provided for bi-directional iteration (using the `ReversibleIterator` interface).

Observer [GOF]

Intent

Define a dependency between two objects in a manner that when one object changes its state, the other object is notified about the change (this pattern is usually generalized to a one-to-many relationship).

Motivation

Business applications developed using Java are typically composed of a set of interacting objects. These objects require some protocol to enable them to be informed about changes in other objects. This might be required because of the need to maintain consistency, or because of pure functional reasons such as user interface considerations.

Concept

The Observer pattern is implemented by an "observer" object that is registered with an "observable" object. Note that this pattern is very common, and is actually implemented in the JDK API. SanFrancisco provides support for the observer pattern through two variants:

- *Asynchronous*. In this mode the observer registers with the observable, and a special callback method is activated when changes in the object occur
- *On-demand*. The observer informs the observable that it is interested in notifications, but that these notifications should be routed through a special "mailbox." The observer inspects the mailbox at his own will, and is not necessarily informed immediately when changes occur.

Chapter 18 goes into the details of how this pattern is implemented in the SanFrancisco Notification Service.

Benefit

The main benefit of this pattern is that it provides an elegant way to create coupling between different objects in a generic and flexible manner. The specific implementation in SanFrancisco is compatible with the Java notion of observer/observable, and also provides support for distributed and persistent implementation of this paradigm.

Usage

The notification service uses the Observer pattern and is described in detail in Chapter 18.

Strategy [GOF]

Intent

Define a family of algorithms, encapsulate each one in an object, and make them interchangeable. This pattern lets the algorithm vary independently from the clients using them.

Motivation

Each business has a set of specific business policies that define exactly how that business participates in the market environment. These policies include factors from the various layers of government, the business owners, how the company moves the product, and the types of products the business sells. In turn, these policies are applicable to employees and business partners. Specific business policies (in the form of algorithms) are incorporated into the business applications developed to support a specific enterprise. As the business environment is rapidly changing (especially these days), these business policies are often revised. In other words, these policies are "volatile." Changes to business policy impact the business application more often than not and this, in turn, requires application developers to modify software.

Concept

The Strategy pattern encapsulates the business policy (algorithm) in a certain object as the primary motivation for the object. This allows such algorithms to be managed (created, replaced, extended, and so on) independent of objects relevant to the situation. This pattern also allows the creation of families of related algorithms. For objects implementing this pattern, a user may select a suitable policy from the family of policies and dynamically associate it with a target object at runtime. Thus, the policy that is used for an operation may vary among the different instances of the class.

SanFrancisco has identified three common scopes for Strategies.

- *Instance Specific*. Implies that a Strategy is defined at object creation time, or possibly passed as a parameter to the operation affected by it. Each instance of a used class may actually implement a different Strategy.
- *Company Wide*. Implies that a Strategy (or family of Strategies) is maintained at the company level (see Chapter 21 for details relating to the `Company` class) and is used for all instances of a certain class within this company. Objects in different companies may have different Strategies. These Strategies are set up at company setup time.
- *Application Wide*. Implies that a Strategy is defined at the application level and is applicable for all instances used in all enterprises defined by this application. In this case, every object of this class in the entire application uses this Strategy. The

Strategy is set at application deployment through the configuration process.

A Strategy may have a *state* associated with it (that is, the Strategy class may have internal attributes), or it may be a pure algorithm with no state. Most of the Strategies in SanFrancisco are stateless (that is, they do not have internal attributes). This keeps the Strategies lightweight and ensures the exact algorithm that is executed for every instance of a specific Strategy class remains the same.

Benefits

The Strategy pattern allows for the isolation of volatile business logic, which makes it easier to identify and make changes to that logic while minimizing impacts to the overall application. This pattern allows for the extension of default Strategies provided by a SanFrancisco framework without impacting the classes using these Strategies.

Usage

The Strategy pattern is used extensively in the Core Business Processes for providing extension points, i.e. ways to modify and tune the behavior of the Business Processes. Refer to Chapters 25–29 for specific examples. In general, names of objects representing strategies (or policies in SanFrancisco terminology) have names ending with the suffix "`Policy`".

Cache [Grand]

Intent

Store and maintain intermediate calculation results for improved performance.

Motivation

Users often need to repeatedly calculate values that involve collecting data from multiple objects. These calculations are usually needed frequently and hence should be provided rapidly. Such calculations can be done by collecting the data from objects each time they are needed. In many cases it is more valuable to store and maintain the results of the calculation in order to get them more rapidly.

Concept

The idea behind this pattern is to build a mechanism for defining which calculation results are to be stored. When using this mechanism, you can decide what level of control should be exposed, such as providing a predefined set of calculations, or allowing the user to specify what calculations they are interested in. The most simplistic way of viewing the implementation of this pattern is as an "associative array."

Benefits

The Cache pattern provides a mechanism that can be used to provide caching of dynamic information in a flexible way. It allows playing with the classic trade-off of speed vs storage, deferring it to the application, or in some cases the end user.

Use

The Cache pattern is implemented in SanFrancisco through the `CachedBalances` interface, described in Chapter 23.

More Patterns

This section briefly describes a few more patterns which appear in SanFrancisco, without going into all the details:

- *Singleton [GOF].* The SanFrancisco `BaseFactory` implements the Singleton pattern. This is a class which has only one instance. The `BaseFactory` provides a global point of access to most of the Foundation Layer Services.
- *Façade [GOF].* The `BaseFactory` provides the interface to most of the Foundation Layer services, hence it implements the Façade pattern. This pattern is aimed at providing a unified interface based on a set of subsystem interfaces.
- *MVC [Krasner].* The SanFrancisco user interface framework is based on the Model–View–Controller pattern. This is described in more detail in the next chapter.
- *Chain of Responsibility [GOF].* The `PropertyContainer` (used extensively for Business Objects) implements this pattern. In short, this pattern connects objects in a chain, and when a certain operation needs to be performed, each object either performs the

operation or delegates it to the next object in the chain. In the case of `PropertyContainer`, the operation delegate is the lookup operation of a property. See Chapter 24 for further discussion of the `PropertyContainer` use.

- *Composite [GOF].* The composite interface involves composing objects into hierarchies (usually tree structures) in which individual objects and whole hierarchies can be treated in a uniform manner. SanFrancisco treats Company hierarchies this way (see Chapter 21 for more details on the Company interface).

SanFrancisco Patterns

This section introduces patterns specific to SanFrancisco.

Factory Class Replacement

Intent

Allow for runtime replacement of classes at instantiation time, based on external configuration files.

Motivation

Sometimes, during the lifecycle of an application, a class needs to be modified to support a particular business need. Client programs that create, access, or maintain instances of this class must be allowed to remain unaware of the modifications to the said class unless they wish to use any new capabilities introduced.

Concept

Factory Class Replacement, similar to the Abstract Factory pattern from [GOF], allows specifying a substitute class that is created instead of the one requested. When a client requests the creation of a new object it issues a request to the desired class factory. The class factory requests the `BaseFactory` class to create a new object. The `BaseFactory` determines the actual class instance to be created, which is returned to the client. This decision is based on external configuration files.

Benefits

The obvious advantage of using this pattern is the ability to replace a class without affecting any users of that class. This relieves client programs from the burden of needing to know about unrelated changes to the classes it uses.

Controller

Intent

Manage sets of objects with specific relationship to the enterprise organizational structure. Note that the name of this pattern is a little misleading.

Motivation

The average business application needs to manage multiple instances of a business object within its organizational structure. Usually this is achieved by using collections, but collections do not necessarily comply with the organizational structure. One would like to have some operations or associations that depend directly on the enterprise structure.

Concept

Controllers are objects that are used to track and manage primary business objects within a business domain. Controllers can be attached to the organizational hierarchy, and they can be attached at different levels in this hierarchy. The business objects held by the Controller in association with a particular level of the organizational hierarchy may be either shared with, or isolated from, other levels. This is managed by modifying the type of Controller that is selected to hold the business objects. SanFrancisco introduces three types of Controllers:

- *Root*. A Controller manipulating only its immediately contained objects; hence, it assumes that there is *no* higher level in the organizational hierarchy. Specifically, it has no access to objects held at a higher level in the organizational hierarchy.
- *Aggregating*. A Controller that allows sharing objects used by higher levels in the organizational hierarchy. If a Controller of this type cannot find a requested object in its immediately contained set of objects, it delegates the request to the respective

"parent" Controller (i.e. a Controller above it in the organizational hierarchy). If the parent Controller does not find the requested object, it again passes the request to its own parent Controller. This iterative process is repeated until the object is found or a root Controller is reached.

- *Hiding*. A special type of aggregating Controller that "hides" a certain set of objects. It holds a collection of object IDs for objects held by the parent Controller, which are treated as non-existent (i.e. requests for these objects return null). What this actually means is that the use of these objects is restricted to their defined level in the organizational hierarchy.

Benefits

Controllers facilitate dynamic configuration of an organizational hierarchy, at runtime, for sets of business objects, each pertaining to a business area of interest (for example, business partners, banks, currencies). These controllers enable selective sharing, overriding and restricting the use of these business objects at each level of the hierarchy. By using this pattern, the developer can ignore the complexity of the organizational hierarchy because calls to higher levels of the hierarchy are made automatically.

Another benefit of this pattern is that Controllers may be added, removed, or changed independently at any level of the organizational hierarchy without any effect on other Controllers.

Usage

SanFrancisco provides controllers for different classes of objects. For example, `AreaControllerAggregating` is an aggregating Controller for the `Area` object. Similarly, `AreaControllerRoot` is a root Controller for the `Area` object. Controllers are available for many of the different business objects.

Property Container

Intent

Hold a dynamic set of properties attached to a class or to specific objects.

Motivation

A typical application usually has to support many different users, sometimes with different needs. It is easy to image scenarios in which it is necessary to customize a certain object for a particular customer. This specific information may either affect all instances of objects of a class, or only a smaller set of a few specific objects. For example, an application user may need to track the receiver of a particular invoice for those invoices over a certain dollar amount into the associated general ledger (GL) account.

Concept

The Property Container design pattern provides a solution to the problem of customizing objects to specific needs. A property can be a single attribute (i.e an additional piece of information), a more complex object, or a relationship (i.e. an association with another object). Properties do not affect the context of the object when added to an existing object, hence they can be used to extend an object without any impact. In addition, the pattern provides additional flexibility by allowing selective extension of individual objects at runtime, as opposed to subclassing, which extends *all* objects of the class at compile time.

Each property added to a Property Container is identified by a string that is called the property name. A property can be retrieved from a Property Container by specifying its property name.

Benefits

Loose coupling is a key benefit of this pattern. Loose coupling refers to the degree of "awareness" that exists between software components. By using Property Containers, there are no changes to the classes of affected (coupled) objects. Property Containers are implemented through generic interfaces inherited by all classes implementing this pattern. These interfaces allow Property Containers to manage properties, irrespective of their usage or type. Therefore, for any class implementing the Property Container pattern, the addition, retrieval, or update of properties does not require class changes. Classes are changed only if tighter coupling is needed.

An important benefit of the Property Container pattern is that it allows concurrent extensions of the same business object by developers. Each developer can add different properties to the same business object without affecting others (as long as there are no conflicts in using property names). As previously mentioned, another benefit of Property Containers is that information does not have to be attached to every object of a particular class, but only to certain objects, possibly identified only during runtime.

It is important to remember that Property Containers cannot directly cause behavior changes, because properties cannot be methods. To do that, you should use other means, such as subclassing or class replacement.

Usage

SanFrancisco provides the interface `PropertyContainer` as part of the Foundation. This class implements the pattern. The `DynamicEntity` interface extends it, and can be used for constructing business objects implementing this pattern.

Chain of Responsibility Driven Strategy

Intent

Avoid coupling the sender of a request to its receiver. In other words, allow an object to send a request without knowing which particular object will actually handle it. This is done by passing the request to a chain of objects, each of which may handle the command, pass it on to the next object, or do both.

Motivation

In some cases in the Core Business Processes, a certain domain algorithm requires more flexibility than that provided by the standard Strategy pattern. An algorithm might need to vary based on objects involved in the processing, other than the object implementing the algorithm.

Concept

The Chain of Responsibility Driven Strategy pattern addresses this need. This pattern allows an application provider to configure a default behavior for the domain algorithm (typically on a company-by-company basis), override that default behavior on an object-by-object basis for any objects involved in the domain algorithm, and make performance vs flexibility trade-off decision on an object-by-object basis.

The Chain of Responsibility Driven Strategy design pattern is a combination of the strategy pattern with the chain of responsibility pattern. The former was described earlier in this chapter, and both patterns are described in [GOF]. The resulting design is composed of two separate Strategy class hierarchies that are combined into one. The first class hierarchy supports the specific domain algorithm through a standard Strategy class hierarchy. The second class hierarchy supports the logic for selection of which instance of the actual domain-level Strategy to use. The selection Strategy encapsulates the chain of responsibility of where to look for the former Strategy. For example, it may start looking for it in the product, if it cannot find it there it will go on to the warehouse and if no luck, then will continue to the company.

Benefits

The Chain of Responsibility Driven Strategy pattern allows the domain algorithm to be placed on the correct object. It allows the application to determine what objects should be included in the chain of responsibility when looking for the Strategy to invoke. It can easily be configured to provide the same performance as the simple Strategy pattern (since the class hierarchies combined together still include both the domain-level algorithm and the selection strategy). This is transparent to the user of the function, hence providing a very flexible design. The user simply calls the function, which then determines what algorithm to use, depending on how the Strategies were configured.

Usage

This pattern is used in various Core Business Processes. For example, the Warehouse Core Business Process needs to provide a means of choosing a particular lot of a product. It needs to make a decision based on input such as the warehouse to use, the quantity of the product required, and the date and time when the product is required. This would be used, for example, when sourcing or picking products to fulfill a sales order. A single algorithm for choosing lots of a product will often be insufficient for a particular application. For example, some products might have special requirements for choosing lots, such as choosing lots with the nearest expiration date whenever possible for products with expiration dates. Similarly, some warehouses may have special algorithms that take into account the warehouse attributes (such as its layout, available space, temperature, etc.).

CHAPTER 13

The User Interface Framework

In this chapter, we introduce the SanFrancisco GUI framework. The SanFrancisco user interface is implemented on top of the JDK and the Java Foundation Classes (JFC), previously known as Swing.

A natural question is why we need a GUI framework in SanFrancisco. There are a lot of applications out there with great user interfaces that were not built using this framework. Obviously, you could use other tools or even plain AWT to build your own interface. The advantage of using the SanFrancisco GUI framework is that it is compatible with the other parts of SanFrancisco. Building the GUI in a different way would require you to spend time integrating the GUI with SanFrancisco server objects (and you could probably think of better ways to spend your time). The SanFrancisco GUI framework includes a set of user interface components that can be composed to build the GUI of an application. These components have built-in support for working with SanFrancisco objects as their data model. The GUI framework also introduces "maintainers," which are used to manage the interaction of GUI components with SanFrancisco Business Objects. Another consideration, which led IBM to include a GUI framework in SanFrancisco, is the desire to have a standard look and feel for SanFrancisco applications.

The SanFrancisco UI Framework Philosophy

The underlying design concept for the SanFrancisco User Interface framework is one of separating the model from the view. To be more precise, the SF GUI framework is based on a *model–view–maintainer* concept in which you build your application of three kinds of building blocks.

- *Model*. Data model represented by objects encapsulating the logic of the application.
- *View*. Graphical representations of the objects in an application and graphical controls for manipulating them.
- *Maintainer*. An intermediate component maintaining the connection between models and their view.

Whereas the model is covered by other parts of the SanFrancisco Frameworks (i.e. the Foundation, the CBOs, and the Core Business

Processes), views and maintainers are dealt with in the GUI framework. Views are composed of pre-built visual components grouped together, and maintainers correspond to views in order to bridge the gap between objects and the views showing them. Maintainers are responsible for performing the actions that are triggered by the user (e.g. when a button is pressed) and for reflecting object state changes (e.g. refreshing the display in case of a change in an attribute). Figure 13-1 illustrates this design concept.

Views

A view in SanFrancisco is built of a frame that contains a sub-window called its "main form" used to display the content of the view. The standard SF GUI frame is called `UIFrame` and is an extension of `JFrame`. Such a standard frame has a title bar and system control widgets (minimize, maximize, and close). In addition, the frame can have an optional menu, tool bar, and status area, which are all standard. If you are using a visual IDE you are able to use a property editor to set these. The frame is associated with a maintainer and this maintainer is in charge of any user interaction with these optional controls.

`UIForm` is the standard SF GUI form and is an extension of `UIPanel`, which itself is an extension of `JPanel`. A form instance is always associated with a single maintainer that includes all the functionality relating to maintaining the view. Note that forms can be nested, i.e. you can

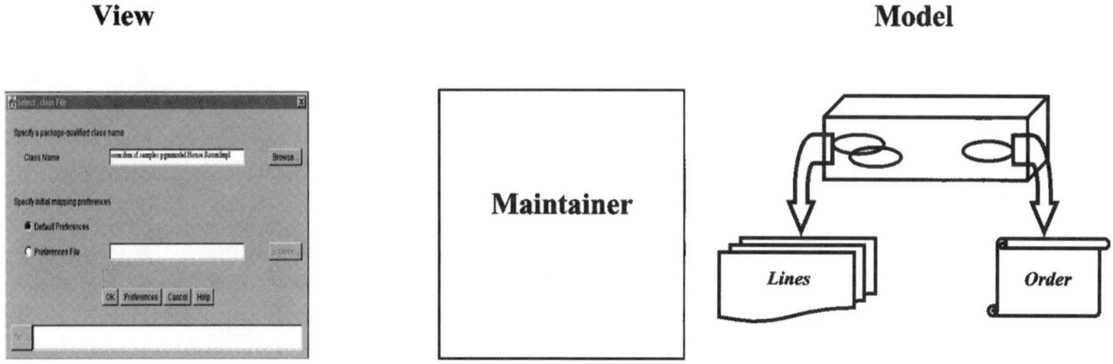

Figure 13-1
Model–view–controller.

place one form into another. This is useful when you need to have a specific form in different parts of your application (e.g. in different dialog windows). Such nested forms should have their own maintainers.

The last ingredient of the view, and the one where you have the most variability, is client-area controls. A client-area control is an on screen representation of some part of a business object (such as a text field showing a certain attribute), or a component that supports user interaction (such as a push button). Another kind of client-area control is a container used to group other controls (e.g. a tabbed-control). The GUI controls used in SanFrancisco are extensions of the corresponding JFC components.

Maintainers

Maintainers handle all interactions between views and SanFrancisco business objects. They have access to business objects on the one hand, and act as event listeners for user actions, on the other hand. Whenever a new client area control is created it passes on the maintainer information about its interaction with the business object and the way data should be formatted for presentation.

Figure 13-2 shows the hierarchy of maintainer classes. As shown in this figure, all maintainers implement the `UIMaintainerModel` interface, which defines the signatures for common methods. When providing maintainers for a specific application, you should never subclass the generic `UIComponentMaintainer`. Instead, for each form, you must provide a specific maintainer that extends `UIFormMaintainer`. In your maintainer, you should override some of the maintainer methods for objects interaction.

A direct extension of `UIFormMaintainer` is suitable for a form that contains nested forms. A form that contains one business object should be associated with a subclass of `UIObjectMaintainer`. The other two maintainer types that you must subclass are `UIReferenced Maintainer` and `UICollectionMaintainer` and should be associated with forms that contain specific GUI controls, as explained later in the chapter.

The component maintainer for each client-area control, combined with the subclassed object maintainer you provide, handles the link between the business objects attribute and the control. The component main-

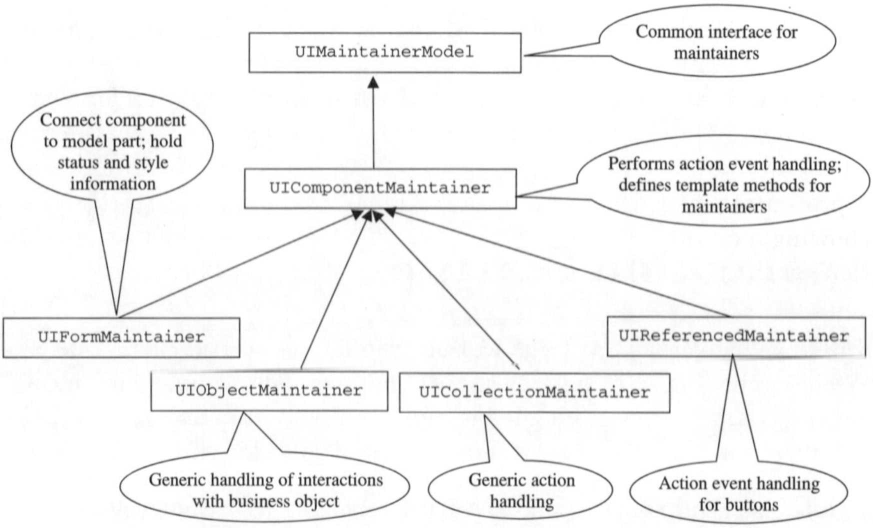

Figure 13-2
Maintainers hierarchy.

tainer initializes the control via its parent object maintainer, which is also responsible for modifying the business object attribute.

Working with the GUI Framework

Any Java development tool can be used for SanFrancisco GUI development. However, note that the GUI components in SanFrancisco are implemented as JavaBeans (see Chapter 3), which means you can use visual builder tools in order to construct the GUI of the application. All you need to do is place the SanFrancisco GUI beans into your bean palette. It is beyond the scope of this book to explain how to use specific visual builder tools, so we will leave this issue by noting that the GUI component beans reside in `com.ibm.sf.gui` and under it in `com.ibm.sf.gui.container`.

Most of the sample programs provided with SanFrancisco are GUI based. Virtually all these samples are built using the building blocks described in this chapter. To get familiar with the way maintainers, frames, and forms are built and managed, you can look at any of these samples. Most classes (and the corresponding file names) end with suffixes, which indicate the role of the class. Such typical extensions are `<>ObjectMaintainer`, `<>CollectionMaintainer`, `<>ReferencedMaintainer` for maintainer, `<>Frame` for frames, and `<>Form` for forms.

Application Startup

Unlike your average Java application, you do not start a client-side SF-based application through a `main()` method defined on your frame. Instead, a separate class should be implemented that takes care of proper initialization. Namely, the responsibilities of this class are:

- initialize SanFrancisco and the SanFrancisco GUI framework;
- instantiate the resource bundles for the application; and
- instantiate and display the application main frame.

When using the SanFrancisco GUI framework, any text or images appearing inside GUI components must be specified through resource bundles you define for your application. You may have either one or many resource bundles for your application but each of these resource bundles should be associated with properties files. A properties file is a text file whose name ends with a `.properties` extension. A properties file defines a set of text or images each of which has a key. Figure 13-3 shows an example of such a property file.

Defining the startup class can be deferred until you have designed your frames and forms. However, if you want to use a visual IDE for this design you will have a bootstrapping problem because the resource bundles should be loaded into your visual IDE (the resource bundles contain all the text and images used by your application). Therefore, you should start by preparing the resource properties files, then the startup classes, and then continue to define the frames and forms. Your initialization procedure should include, at the least, the following two steps.

- Initialization of SanFrancisco Foundation Layer through a call to `Global.initialize()` (see Chapter 14 for more details.)
- Initialization of the SanFrancisco GUI framework using the `UIInitializer` class. This class is a JavaBean, and its properties are shown in Table 13-1.

Figure 13-3
Sample properties file.

Sample properties file, taken from the Conflict Control Utility provided as part of the San Francisco distribution

```
#Conflict Control Text Resources

#================================

TXT_HANDLE=Handle

TXT_ACTION_ID=Action ID

TXT_USER_ID=User ID

TXT_REGISTRATION_TIME=Registration time

TXT_ID=ID

TXT_DESCRIPTION=Description

TXT_PARAMETER_NAME=Parameter name

TXT_PARAMETER_VALUE=Parameter value

TXT_ACTIVE_ACTION_PARAMETERS=Active Action Parameters

 •
 •
 •

CMD_CLOSE=Close

CMD_FILE=File

CMD_VIEW=View

CMD_HELP=Help

 •
 •
 •

MSG_SAVE_ERROR=MSG_CCRESOURCES_001: Error saving changes:
{0}.  Contact your system administrator.

MSG_SAVE_ERROR_CAUSE=The changes could not be saved.
A non-recoverable error occurred.

MSG_SAVE_ERROR_RECOVERY=Contact your system administrator.
Use the error message text displayed and this message to
recover from the problem.  Then make and save the changes
again.

 .
 .
 .
```

TABLE 13-1

UIInitializer properties

Property Name	Description
applicationContainerIconResource	Icon for a frame whose form contains a container control.
applicationIconResource	Application icon.
applicationName	Application name. This field is set by default to the key `TXT_ApplicationName` in the SF GUI framework `UIResourceBundle`.
applicationObjectIconResource	Icon for a frame whose form contains an object view.
factoryClassName	This holds the class name for the factory, there is no need to change this if you intend to work with business objects in your application. `UISFFactory` is for use with business objects, and `UIFactory` is for applications that do not interact with business objects.
helpContextResource	Optional base URL containing help files (in HTML format).
helpEnabled	Flag indicating whether help facilities are enabled for the application.
messageDispatcherClassName	This holds the class name of a "message dispatcher" that routes Throwables. The framework provides two implementations `UISFMessageDispatcher` and `UIMessageDispatcher`, which are used for applications that interact or don't interact, respectively, with business objects. You can subclass either of these implementations to provide your own error handling.
ValidationOnLostFocus	If this is set to TRUE, all fields losing focus are validated. Otherwise, validation is deferred until a save request.

Class `UIResourceBundle` represents resource bundles. A resource bundle object holds the path to the resource files, the path of the directory in which the image resources are placed, and a flag indicating whether this resource bundle is the default for the application. This class, too, is a JavaBean, and its properties are shown in Table 13-2.

The final action you must take before creating the application frame is to create an instance of `UIOpenFrameParameters` and place in it the name of your application frame using the `setFrameClassName` method. Note you must do this with actual code because this class is not a JavaBeans component. To create the frame call the `createFrame` method on the `UIFactory`, which is the factory object for the SanFrancisco GUI, and pass to it the `UIOpenFrameParameters` object as a parameter.

TABLE 13-2

UIResource Bundle properties

Property Name	Description
bundleProperties	Path and file name of the properties file to be associated with the resource bundle.
Default	Indicates this bundle is the default for your application.
imagePath	Path to the image resources for your application. If you do not specify a path here, the resource key. TXT_imagePath in the resource bundle is used to set the path.

Note that the argument to setFrameClassName() is the fully qualified name of your application frame relative to the CLASSPATH. You should also invoke the setObject() method on the open frame parameters if the frame is supposed to show a specific existing business object; the parameter to this method is an object handle.

Defining Frames and Forms

As mentioned, frames in the SanFrancisco GUI frameworks are represented by UIFrame, an extension of JFC's JFrame. To create a frame you need to create a new class that extends com.ibm.sf.gui.UIFrame. After you have created your frame, you can work with it in visual composition mode. The properties of UIFrame are shown in Table 13-3.

Forms in your application should be subclassed from UIForm, which is derived from JPanel. The outermost form positioned in a frame is called the main form. Other forms positioned within it or within another form are considered to be nested forms. Nested forms can be used as reusable components used in several different frames. The properties of UIForm are shown in Table 13-4. Each form, either main or nested, should have its own maintainer subclassed from the maintainers provided in the GUI framework. Maintainers are explained later in the chapter.

TABLE 13-3

`UIFrame` properties

Property Name	Description
contentPaneClassName	Class name of the main form for the frame, fully qualified with respect to the CLASSPATH used. All frames must contain an application-specific main form (extension of `UIForm`).
frameRegistered	Flag indicating whether this frame should be added to the frame list for your application. If this field is set to True, the frame title will appear in the frame list window that the GUI framework displays when the user selects the Windows item from the View menu in the frame menu bar.
helpId	Resource bundle and key that identify the HTML file to be displayed when the user presses the help key.
iconResource	Image resource for the icon to be displayed in the left corner of the frame title bar. If you do not set either this property or the iconType property, the setting for the applicationIconResource property of the `UIInitializer` is used.
iconType	Which of the application icon types, if any, that you specified as properties of the `UIInitializer`, should be used for this frame.
menuBarClassName	The class used for the menu bar in the frame, if there is one.
statusBar	Whether the frame should have a status area.
titleResource	Resource bundle and key for the frame title in the title bar. By default, a frame has a title bar.
toolBarClassName	The class used for the tool bar in a frame, if there is one.

TABLE 13-4

`UIForm` properties

Property Name	Description
attributeId	The framework uses the attribute id to get and set the form, as any other client-area control. This is useful only if this is a nested form. If this is a reusable form, specify an application-wide unique integer value in this field.
componentName	Optional; retrievable name of the form. This is the JFC name property.
helpId	Resource bundle and key that identify the HTML file to be displayed when the user asks for help
maintainerClassName	Fully qualified name, relative to the CLASSPATH used, of your own subclassed maintainer for the form.
toolTipText	Resource bundle and key for the tool-tip String, if any.

Using Client-Area Controls

The SanFrancisco GUI framework provides a set of pre-built client-area controls. Figure 13-4 lists these controls. All these controls are JavaBeans and can be instantiated and edited using a visual IDE. Table 13-5 shows the common properties applicable for most controls.

Basic Controls

One kind of control is basic control, which roughtly corresponds to the JFC component it extends. Basic controls are text field (properties shown in Table 13-6), password field (properties shown in Table 13-6), text area (properties shown in Table 13-7), combo-box (properties shown in Table 13-8), checkbox (properties shown in Table 13-9), list-box (properties shown in Table 13-10), and radio button pane (properties shown in Table 13-11).

The list-box control is slightly more complicated to set up than the other controls. This control contains a scrollable list of selectable items and its content is represented by `UIListData` object. You should provide the content of this object either when creating the form or through the maintainer. `UIListItemInfo` objects are used to represent single elements.

The GUI framework attaches the component maintainers associated with basic controls in a form as children of your own object maintainer. Through each component maintainer, the framework uses the object maintainer to associate the control with the corresponding business object attribute, and to manage the user interaction or input with the attribute value represented by the control.

The basic controls are color-coded to indicate the importance of the data they represent.

- *Mandatory*. A non-empty value (e.g. non-empty string for text controls) must to be set before the data can be committed to the associated object. Such fields are indicated by a yellow background color.
- *Enabled*. Non-mandatory field that allows tabbing and user input. The default system settings for enabled (and also disabled) controls are used for these fields.

Component	Class	Example
Button	`UIButton`	
Button List	`UIButtonList`	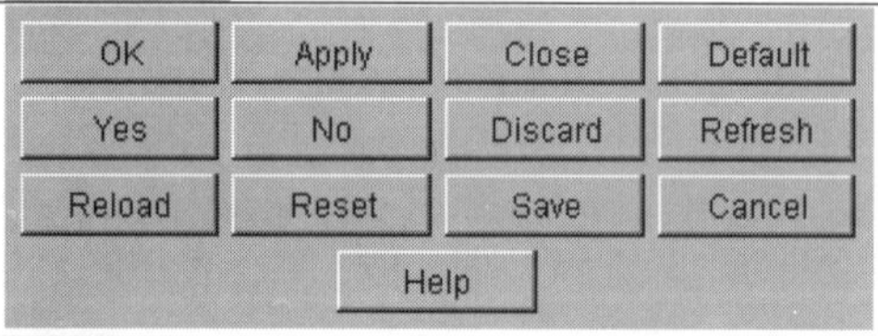
Check Box	`UICheckBox`	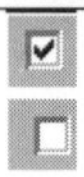
Combo Box	`UIComboBox`	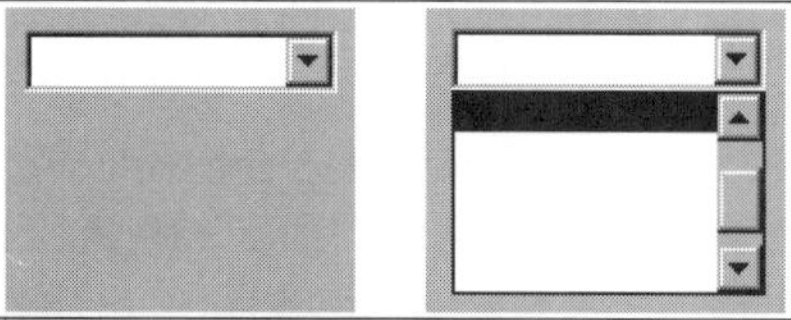
Container Control	`UIContainerControl`	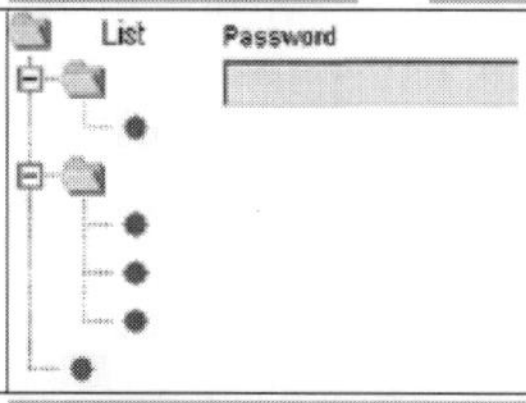
Group Box	`UIGroupBox`	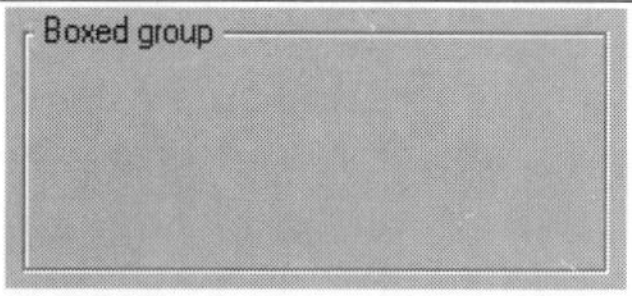
Icon	`UIIconComponent`	
Label	`UILabel`	
List Box	`UIListBox`	
Password Field	`UIPasswordField`	
Radio Button Pane	`UIRadioButtonPane`	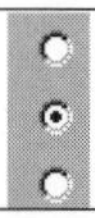

Figure 13-4
SanFrancisco GUI Framework Controls.

Referenced Object	UIReferencedObject	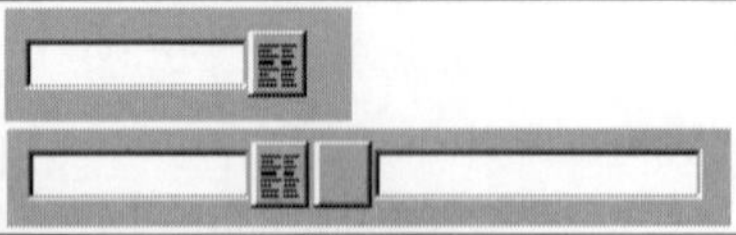
Text Area	UITextArea	
Text Field	UITextField	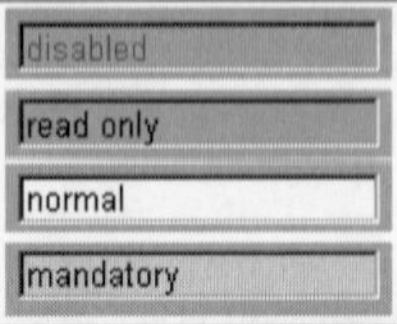
Two List	UITwoList	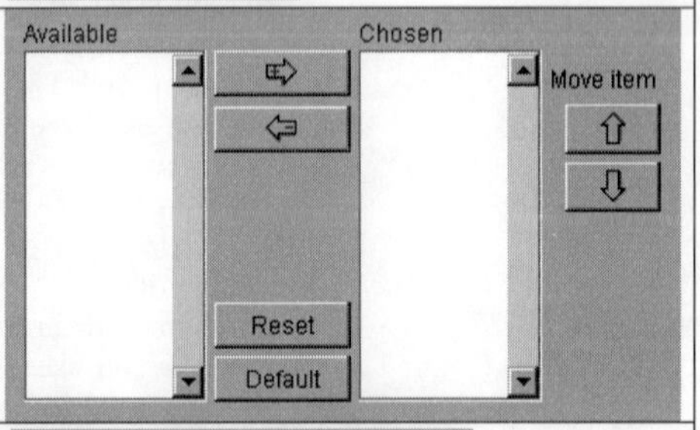
Tab Control	UITabbedPage UITabbedPane	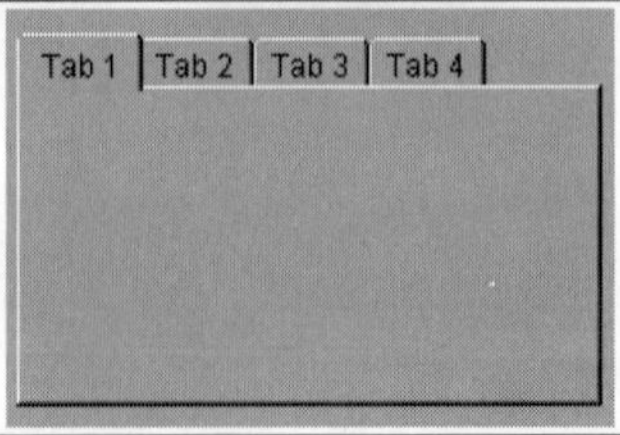

Figure 13-4
(Cont'd)

- *Read only*. No user input or even tabbing can be performed, but scrolling (when applicable) can be done. Such fields are indicated by a gray background color.

The basic controls have built-in support for working with SanFrancisco business objects:

- A control can be associated with a specific attribute of a business object. The control will then keep track of user input and

TABLE 13-5 Common control properties

Property Name	Description
attributeId	Integer constant that identifies the business object attribute represented by the control.
componentName	For use if you want to retrieve a component by its JFC component name in your subclassed maintainer for the form containing the control. If use an attribute id, you usually do not need the component name.
converter	Name of the converter class that the GUI framework will use for converting a data type between that of the business object attribute and that required for display in the control (usually a String).
enabled, mandatory, readOnly	Boolean fields that specify the graphic and functional style flag settings for the control as defined in the `UIControlSettings` helper class. There is a default style (or combination of styles) for each control, which you can change in the properties editor.
helpId	Name of the HTML help file provided for the control as context-sensitive help that the GUI framework should popup in a Help frame when the control has focus and the user presses the Help key. You specify the help Id as a help resource key in a resource bundle for your application.
setDirtyAllowed	Boolean field that allows or disallows setting of the dirty flag on user input to the control. In other words, `True` (the default) causes the GUI framework to attempt a save of the business attribute value represented by the control when the user clicks the Close button on the frame's title bar.
toolTipTextResource	Text resource for the tool-tip to be displayed when the user positions the mouse over the control.
validationGroupId	Name of the validation group to which the control belongs.

autonomously determines if the associated object attribute needs to be updated.

- A control validates the data contained in it with respect to the kind of field (i.e. mandatory vs enabled) and produces corresponding error messages.
- National language support is inherently provided with these controls.

The following sections describe other kinds of controls. These controls are also used to present views or business object attributes (the exceptions are the action and static controls). These controls all have methods for getting and setting their component maintainer, getting and setting

TABLE 13-6

`UITextField` and `UIPassword Field` properties

Property Name	Description
Common properties	Properties described in Table 13-5.
columns	Numeric value limiting the number of characters a text field contains (if more characters are required, scrolling is used).
echoChar	For the password field control only. Set the character to be displayed in the password field rather than the character the user actually types.
formatter	Formatter to be attached to the control.
formatString	Pattern String for the formatter to use, where applicable.
text	String to be displayed as the initial contents of the text field. Used only if an attribute id is not specified.

TABLE 13-7

`UITextArea` properties

Property Name	Description
Common properties	Shown in Table 13-5.
columns	Numeric value limit for the number of characters you expect the text area to contain in one line.
formatter	Optional Formatter to be attached to the control.
formatString	Pattern string for the formatter to use.
horizontalScrollBarPolicy, verticalScrollBarPolicy	When scrollbars should be shown for the control. Options are `SCROLLBAR_AS_NEEDED`, `SCROLLBAR_ALWAYS`, and `SCROLLBAR_NEVER`.
rows	Numeric value for the number of rows to be shown in the text area without scrolling.
text	String to be displayed as the initial contents of the text area. Used only if an attribute id is not specified.

TABLE 13-8

`UIComboBox` properties

Property Name	Description
Common properties	Shown in Table 13-5.
itemList	Optional list of items to be displayed as the initial contents of the dropdown list box.
maximumRowCount	Maximum number of rows shown without scrolling.

TABLE 13-9

`UICheckbox` properties

Property Name	Description
Common properties	Shown in Table 13-5.
state	Initial checkmark state of the control.
textResource	Resource bundle and the key for the label title.

TABLE 13-10

`UIListBox` properties

Property Name	Description
Common properties	Shown in Table 13-5
horizontalScrollBarPolicy, verticalScrollBarPolicy	Controls scrollbars display policy. Options are SCROLLBAR_AS_NEEDED, SCROLLBAR_ALWAYS, and SCROLLBAR_NEVER.
itemList	Optional list of items to be displayed as the initial contents of the list box.

their attribute Id (used for the maintainer), returning the value of the attribute they represent, and refreshing their contents upon request.

The four pre-built advanced controls (which are container, referenced object, two-list, and tabbed) are composite JavaBeans. The properties of the individual controls that compose an advanced control are exposed as needed.

Two-list Control

This control form allows the user to move or copy selected items between a predefined available set on the left and a chosen set on the right, using a pair of buttons. In its fullest, this control is composed of an available objects list on the left, a chosen objects list on the right, two buttons for transferring an object from one list to another, Reset and Default buttons (a pair of buttons for moving items up or down in the chosen list), and labels (see Table 13-12). All the buttons in the two-list control are optional. Actually, you can also hide the available list or the chosen list. You can even replace them with other controls of your choice. In order to specify the available items, and their placement, this control uses the `UITwoListData` object.

TABLE 13-11

`UIRadioButton Pane` properties

Property Name	Description
Common properties	Shown in Table 13-5
itemList	List of items to be displayed as labeled radio buttons.

TABLE 13-12

`UITwoList` properties

Property Name	Description
Common properties	Shown in Table 13-5
copyStyle	If True, items from the available list to be copied rather than moved to the chosen list.
defaultButtonPresent, resetButtonPresent	Flags indicating if the respective buttons should appear.
moveControlPresent	Flag indicating if the move buttons and label should appear.
addButtonIconResource, moveDownButtonIconResource, moveUpButtonIconResource, removeButtonIconResource	Keys of the image resources for the respective buttons, if applicable.
availableLabelTextResource, chosenLabelTextResource, defaultButtonTextResource, moveLabelTextResource, resetButtonTextResource	Resources controlling the text labels displayed on the respective buttons, if applicable.

Action Controls

The action controls, Button and Button List, all generate user-triggered action events. These controls do not have component maintainers. Their properties are shown in Table 13-13 and Table 13-14, respectively.

Static Controls

Static controls are used to provide the end-user with information without having any means for interaction. These controls are Label (see properties in Table 13-15), Icon (see Properties in Table 13-16) and Group Box (see Properties in Table 13-17). These controls, too, have no corresponding component maintainers.

Tabbed Control

A tabbed control is a tabbed pane that contains a number of tabbed pages, very much like the JFC tabbed pane. To set up the tabbed control, place the `UITabbedPane` bean in a form. Then place `UITabbedPage` beans into the tabbed pane. On each tabbed page, use client-area controls

TABLE 13-13

`UIButton` properties

Property Name	Description
Common properties	See Table 13-5
actionCommand	Name of the action command associated with the button. This is used to override the `actionPerformed()` method of the subclassed maintainer for the form.
componentName	Use if you want to retrieve the button by its JFC component name.
enabled	Whether the button is enabled. The default is `True`.
helpButton	Indicates if this is a help button.
helpId	Resource bundle and the key that specify the path of the HTML help file. If the button is not the help button, this is the context-sensitive help that the GUI framework pops up when the user presses the help key while the button has the focus.
iconResource	Resource bundle and the key that specify the name of the image resource for the button.
textResource	Resource bundle and the key for the button label.
toolTipResource	Resource bundle and the key for the tool-tip string.
triggerValidation	Flag indicating whether this button should trigger validation of the control that last had the focus.

TABLE 13-14

`UIButton List` properties

Property Name	Description
componentName	For use if you want to retrieve the button list by its JFC component name.
defaultButtons	Buttons to appear in your button list, which is a set of `UIButtons` with action commands constructed as CMD_ followed by the button label (that is, CMD_Apply, CMD_Close, and so on). The GUI framework registers your subclassed maintainer for the form as the action listener for the buttons. Handle action events in the `actionPerformed()` method of your subclassed maintainer.
helpId	Resource bundle and the key that specify the path of the HTML help file. The GUI framework pops up context-sensitive help for the button list in its standard help frame when the user presses the help key while one of its buttons has the focus.
style	Indicates whether the buttons are to be arranged horizontally or vertically. If you choose horizontal, a flow layout manager is used. If you choose vertical, a gridbag layout manager is used.
toolTipTextResource	Resource bundle and the key for the tool-tip string.

TABLE 13-15
`UILabel` properties

Property Name	Description
componentName	For use if you want to retrieve the label by its JFC component name.
textResource	Resource bundle and key for the label title.

TABLE 13-16
`UIIcon Component` properties

Property Name	Description
componentName	For use if you want to retrieve the icon by its JFC component name.
imageResource	Resource bundle and the key for the icon image.
preferredSize	Icon size
toolTipTextResource	Text resource for the tool-tip to be displayed when the user positions the mouse over the icon.

TABLE 13-17
`UIGroupBox` properties

Property Name	Description
componentName	For use if you want to retrieve the group box by its JFC component name.
helpId	Resource bundle and the key that specify the path of the HTML help file for context-sensitive help, if you are providing it. The GUI framework pops up context-sensitive help in its standard help frame when the user presses the help key while the group box has the focus.
titleResource	Resource bundle and the key for the group box title, if you want a title for the group box.
toolTipTextResource	Text resource for the tool-tip to be displayed when the user positions the mouse over the control.

and nested forms as needed. The properties of the tabbed pane and tabbed pages are shown in Table 13-18.

Container Control

The container control shows a list of business objects of one or more types, as a tree, details, or tree-details view. It is also possible to allow users to edit data in any of the views. You must provide a viewer that implements the `UIContainerViewer` interface, and that corresponds to the business objects and the business object attributes displayed

TABLE 13-18

`UITabbedPane` and `UITabPage` properties

Property Name	Description
Tabbed Pane	
Common properties	Shown in Table 13-5
selectedIndex	Index of the tabbed page that is to appear as the initial visible page.
Tabbed Page	
Common properties	Shown in Table 13-5
tabResource	Text resource for the tab title. This is a required property.

in the container control. In addition, you can provide a `UICollectionMaintainer` for specific action handling and for defining filter criteria for the maintainer. The container control combines the `JFC JTable` and `JTree` components.

The container control requires a concrete definition of the business object types displayed in it, along with their attributes and a map to establish the sequence of columns on the screen. This definition is called a viewer. The information provided in the viewer, together with the data provided by maintainers, is used to build the appropriate JFC components.

There is always a notion of a "root object" defined for the container control, and this object is the root of the tree displays. This object should have a maintainer attached to it. The object maintainer attached to any other business object in a container is no different than a maintainer of the same object when viewed inside a form. The "viewer" needs to define the following data items.

- *Viewable Objects*. Description of the business object types to be shown in the rows.
- *Viewable Attributes*. Description of the business object attributes (per business object) to be shown in the columns of the container control.
- *Details View Definition*. Description of the details view, which is an enumeration of column specifications. Each column specification has a column identification, column width, and column header defined.
- *Tree View Definition*. Succinct description of the tree view. This requires defining the root object and identifying the object attribute (per object) used for the tree column.

- *Tree-details View Definition*. Description of the tree-details view definition. This is pretty much the same as the details view, only that the column specification defines the tree-details view.

The properties for the container control are shown in Table 13-19.

Referenced Object Control

This control is used to show a business object referenced by another business object. It contains a text field with the identifier of the referenced object along with an optional text field showing its description. In addition, a select button opening a selection window and an optional edit button (opening this object for editing) are provided. When the user clicks the selection button the GUI framework pops up a selection window showing the collection of all objects of the type represented by the control. When the user chooses an item in the selection window, the list closes and the selected item is set as the current object in the control. When the user clicks the edit button the GUI framework opens the frame for the current referenced object, so that it can be edited. The application must include a selection viewer class for the selection window as well as the subclassed frame, form, and object maintainer for the edit window to work. In order to use this control, it is necessary to subclass a corresponding `UIReferencedMaintainer` component maintainer.

Validity Checks

Typically (this behavior can be modified), when a basic control loses focus to another control in the same frame, the GUI framework immediately validates the data in the control and modifies the data in the business object through the associated object maintainer. The validity checks actually performed depend on the specific control type. If the checks fails (i.e. an error occurs), the control error state is set and the control is colored to reflect that. The parent form maintainer is notified and initiates the display of the appropriate error message. In case of errors, the exception handling mechanism used in the GUI framework can set the error state of a control.

A group of controls can be grouped into a validation group allowing them to be updated all at once when focus is lost to a control outside the validation group.

TABLE 13-19

`UIContainer Control` properties

Property Name	Description
componentName	For use if you want to retrieve this component by its JFC component name in your subclassed maintainer.
helpId	Name of the HTML help file provided for the control as context-sensitive help that the GUI framework should pop up in a help frame, when the control has focus and the user presses the help key.
toolTipTextResource	Text resource for the tool-tip to be displayed when the user positions the mouse over the control.
viewerData	If you are not providing a handwritten viewer class, in the properties editor for this field you need to define five sets of properties shown below.
	`Viewable Objects Properties`
name	Short name for the business object.
objectClassName	Fully qualified class name of the business object.
maintainerClassName	Fully qualified name of the subclassed object maintainer that is to handle the business object specified in the *objectType* setting.
Viewable Attributes Properties:	
name	Short name for the viewable attribute.
attributeId	Integer constant that uniquely identifies the business object attribute within the containing form.
useCheckbox	Flag indicating whether the editor is a text field or a checkbox. Set this flag to `True` for a Boolean business attribute so that a checkbox is used.
enabled, mandatory, readOnly	Boolean fields that specify the graphic and functional style flag settings for the column.
isCollection	Flag that if set to `True` means that the viewable attribute represents a nested node. In this case, the attribute id of the viewable attribute is passed on to the object maintainer, which must return a *UIIterator*, this being used by the container control to iterate over the collection.
formatterClassName	If the editor is a text field, the formatter class to be used.
converterClassName	Name of the converter to be used for converting a data type between that of the business object attribute and that required for display in the column.
	`Tree View Properties`
treeAttribute	Name of the viewable attribute displayed in the tree column within the associated viewable object. The attribute id defined for the viewable attribute is passed to the object maintainer, which must return a String object or any object that has a valid implementation of `toString()`.
root	Marks the tree root (only one object can be the root)
entityForCreate	Flag to indicate which business object is to be created when the user chooses the New menu action. Only one viewable object can be marked as the one used for creation.
	`Details View Properties`
number	Physical column number in the container control. Specifies the sequence of the columns.

TABLE 13-19

(Cont'd)

Property Name	Description
headerResource	Text resource key and bundle for the text to be displayed in the column header of the container control. Specify as `key, bundle`.
width	Initial width of the column in the container control.
viewableAttribute/viewableObject	Business object attribute as shown in the physical column. Lists horizontally all viewable objects defined. In this field, set the viewable attribute (per viewable object) to be displayed in the column specified with the *number* property.
Tree-details view **properties**: *Same As Details View*	

Data Type Converters

The GUI framework provides several data type converters. These converters should be used to translate the values of object attributes into values that can be displayed inside controls (usually Strings). For each control you can specify the converter to be used in the Beans property editor. There are some generic converters and specific SF GUI framework converters. You can provide your own converter by implementing a class that implements the `UIConverter` interface.

You can assign a formatter to a text control (i.e. text field, password field, text area, and the text parts of a referenced object control). You do that by choosing the formatter from the list in the Beans property editor for the control, and specify the format string. Whenever the user enters data the formatter attempts to re-format the string that is currently displayed. Depending on the data type displayed, the string representation may also change when the input focus is gained or lost.

The base class for all formatters in the SF GUI framework is *UIFormatter*. This is an abstract base class for which some methods must be overridden. The concrete formatter classes are the following.

- *UIDateFormatter*. Formats date and time strings.
- *UINumberFormatter*. Abstract base class for all formatters of numeric data.
- *UIDecimalFormatter*. Formats decimal numbers.
- *UIIntFormatter*. Formats integer numbers.

- *UIMoneyFormatter*. Formats strings that represent a monetary value.
- *UITextFormatter*. Formats non-numeric strings, with features for limiting text input to a specified number of characters, and setting characters at a given position to uppercase or lowercase. The format string uses a few special control characters. An asterisk is used to indicate that the character at a given position should be left as is, and "!" to indicate that it should be changed to uppercase, and "?" to indicate that it should be changed to lowercase. A number appended to one of these symbols in the format string limits the field length. Invalid characters in the format string are ignored. If you do not provide a format string, the text formatter does not change strings.

Defining Maintainers

As explained at the beginning of this chapter, maintainers provide the link between forms and the business objects displayed in them. Application-specific maintainers, subclassed from the appropriate maintainers must be provided for application forms. In addition, maintainers should also be provided for each viewable object inside a container control.

As shown in Figure 13-2, maintainers can be derived from `UIObjectMaintainer`, `UICollectionMaintainer`, and `UIReferenced Maintainer`. These maintainers all inherit from `UIForm Maintainer`.

Object Maintainer

An object maintainer (i.e. a maintainer derived from `UIObject Maintainer`) provides the link between controls in a form and business objects displayed in the same form. The maintainer is in charge of initializing the view, and performing any modifications in the business object realm (that is, modifying object attributes, deleting, and creating objects). These maintainer responsibilities are implemented by the various maintainer methods that can be overridden in your subclassed maintainer.

Collection Maintainer

The collection maintainer has similar responsibilities to that of the object maintainer. In addition, it can provide filter criteria. Filter criteria are provided by implementing the `initializeFilterAttributeSequence()` method.

Referenced Maintainer

The referenced object control requires that you provide a subclassed `UIReferencedMaintainer`, in which you implement the methods `getObjectBy()`, `getObjectName()`, and `getObjectDescription()`. These methods provide the framework with the object reference, the object name, and the object description, respectively.

Defining Menu Bars and Toolbars

The SF GUI framework provides several standard menu bars and standard toolbars for use with your application frames. In addition, a popup menu is provided for the main form in a frame.

Action handling for these components is handled by the `actionPerformed()` method in the maintainer for the form. The form maintainer is also responsible for modifying the menubars, toolbars, and popup menus as needed.

A menu bar is built out of menus, which are represented by `UIMenu` objects. Each menu is composed of menu items (of type `UIMenuItem`), checkbox menu items (`UICheckboxMenuItem` objects) or cascaded menus that are `UIMenus` themselves. `UIMenu` is derived from JFC's `JMenu` object.

In order to associate a menu bar with your frame, all you need to do is specify the class name of the menu bar you want to use as the *menuBarClassName* property of the frame (this can be done using a property editor, or hard-coded).

The framework provides several menu bars, which can be used as is, or modified. These are `UIFrameMenuBar`, `UIObjectMenuBar`, `UICollectionMenuBar`, and `UICollectionDirectEditMenuBar`. Each one of these adds more buttons and actions to the previous one.

Similar to a menu, a toolbar consists of one or more toolbar buttons (`UIToolBarButton`), with separators in it. The SF GUI framework derives the toolbar from `JToolBar`. Just like the menu bar, you associate a toolbar with your frame using the *ToolBarClassName* property of the frame.

A toolbar button is a specialized form of `UIButton`. A toolbar button has an action command attached to it. The SF GUI framework uses this action command to determine which action must be carried out in the generic or subclassed main form's maintainer.

The framework provides the following toolbars: `UIFrameToolBar`, `UIObjectToolBar`, `UICollectionToolBar`, and `UICollectionDirectEditToolBar`. Here, too, each toolbar provides more functionality than the previous one.

Defining Helps

The GUI framework has built-in support for both general help and context-sensitive help, through the UIHelpController object. This object manages the display of help panels showing HTML documents. General help is displayed through the help menu on the menu bar. This help can be customized just like any menu bar is customized. Context-sensitive help depends on the specific component that has the input focus, and help for it is shown by pressing the F1 key. Context-sensitive help is sought after using a "chain of responsibility" pattern [GOF]. That is, if a component does not include any help definition, the framework looks for help in the component containing it (e.g. a form or a frame). An error message appears if we go all the way up to the frame and find no help information.

Help in the application can be enabled either through the `UIInitializer` properties (shown in Table 13.1), or by directly using the interfaces of the `UIHelpController`.

When you are defining application components that should have context-sensitive help, you link them to their help file using the *helpId* property. The default help Id setting for a component is null.

Using the helpButton property of `UIButton`, you can set any button to be the frame help button. When the user clicks this button (or presses F1 if the button has the focus), the help controller will bring up the context-sensitive help panel for the frame.

Tool-tip help (i.e. short messages shown when the cursor rests for a certain while on a control) can be defined at the level of the single control, as shown in the property listings of the various controls.

Exception Handling

The GUI framework provides a message dispatcher (this can be either `UISFMessageDispatcher` or `UIMessageDispatcher`) for handling and routing all user messages (`UIMessage`). These user messages can be either general information messages, or exceptions. Exception messages are routed to the frame message area (which is part of the status area) or to a popup message dialog (in the case of severe exceptions). General information messages are usually routed to the frame message area. It is also possible to derive one of these dispatchers to enable your own message dispatcher to implement any specific message routing logic needed.

If you want, you can generate application-specific exception and information messages and provide a subclassed message dispatcher to handle them.

In addition to handling exceptions and routing messages to the application user, the message dispatcher provides other functionality, such as removing messages, and setting or removing control error states.

PART 3

The Foundation Layer

CHAPTER 14

Foundation Layer Services

The Foundation layer is the core layer of SanFrancisco. As the name implies, it provides the most fundamental services. The main roles of this layer are to provide the necessary mechanisms for creating cross-platform distributed object applications. Specifically, providing a consistent application development model in which issues of transparent access, persistency, and security are addressed.

Foundation Layer Roles

The execution of a distributed object-oriented application is quite a complex process which requires coordination. The Foundation layer does exactly that, i.e. it coordinates the activities of different objects. The metaphor commonly used to describe it is a "Control Tower" in an airport. This metaphor is based on the fact that the Foundation Layer takes a variety of requests and handles them, possibly by routing them to the appropriate component.

The SanFrancisco Foundation defines the capabilities and services required for constructing large-scale distributed applications. By providing a well-defined and platform-independent interface for these capabilities and services, the Foundation allows developers to focus on the logic of their applications and not on the technicalities relating to communication, synchronization, persistence, security, and so on. Essentially, the Foundation insulates the developer from the peculiarities of the specific platform, making the code truly portable.

The Foundation layer provides the following services:

- *Naming Services*. Support for "user aliases" and accessing objects by a logical name. This service is described in Chapter 17.
- *Notification Services*. Support a general method for objects to be informed of changes to other objects. This service is described in Chapter 18.
- *Transaction Services*. Support for ACID transactions. This service is described in Chapter 16.
- *Security Services*. Support for user authorization and authentication.
- *Persistence*. Built-in support for Entity persistence is provided.

- *Transparent Distribution*. Supported through access modes.
- *Distributed Synchronization*. Supported through various lock modes.
- *Lifecycle Support*. Support for distributed creation, access, and destruction of objects. Lifecycle facilities are described in Chapter 15.

Environment Initialization

The first use of the Foundation layer made in any SanFrancisco application is for initializing the SanFrancisco environment. Static methods are provided on the `Global` class for initializing and un-initializing your SanFrancisco environment. Their signatures are shown in Figure 14-1.

The `initialize()` method takes care of starting the SanFrancisco execution environment, including server process startup if required. This method should be called exactly once within each application. If it is not called, the Foundation layer automatically invokes it at the time of the first access of the `BaseFactory` object. Using other SanFrancisco objects or services before the `initialize()` is called can produce unexpected results.

The use of `initialize()` and `uninitialize()` is highly recommended, because it is safer and it also makes clear which parts of your application make use of SanFrancisco.

Calling the `uninitialize()` method is also important because it allows the system to release resources, including remote resources that might not even be released when your client application exits. Similar to the `initialize()` method, the `uninitialize()` method is implicitly called once SanFrancisco can determine the client application no longer exists. However, because of implementation considerations, this might not necessarily happen immediately when the client process terminates. Once `uninitialize()` is called, SanFrancisco cannot be used during the execution of the current instance of the application.

Figure 14-1
Initialization and un-initialization methods.

```
public static void initialize() throws GFException;
public static void uninitialize() throws GFException;
```

Access Control

When you request access to an object, you specify which kind of access you need using the `AccessMode` class described in Figure 14-2. In general, programmers do not really need to be aware of all the details of the various access mode possibilities. Instead, the `AccessMode` class provides special static create methods that return access mode objects applicable in the most common situations.

Client programmers would generally use the `createNormal()` method when an object is needed for reading, whereas the `createPlusWrite()` method would be used to get an access mode that allows writing, or to explicitly upgrade an already accessed object from reading to writing. Since methods that update objects will implicitly get an access mode that allows writing, client code is not required to explicitly upgrade, but it is recommended because correct locking by the client code can reduce the chance of deadlock. If you know beforehand that you need to update an Entity, there is some performance advantage to getting update access right away rather than upgrading later. Plus, there is the advantage of knowing that the transaction will not fail later because of inability to get an access mode that allows writing.

Another method (which is rarely in use) is the `createCritical()` method used when access is needed for critical operations that require the highest level of isolation and exclusive access (which obviously must be of short duration). By default, `createCritical()` and `createPlusWrite()` are identical, but you can modify them. For example you can make `createPlusWrite()` use optimistic-local access and `createCritical()` use pessimistic-home access.

The `createNoLock()` method provides NO_LOCK access, which is used if access to the data from an object is desired for use outside of a transaction or across transactions without the ability to make changes to the real object.

While these `create<>()` methods are useful in most cases, the `AccessMode` objects can be tailored to your specific needs. The `create<>()` methods hide the attributes of the access, which are the following.

Figure 14-2
Class
`AccessMode.`

Class com.ibm.sf.gf.AccessMode

public class **AccessMode**
extends Object
implements Externalizable

Name	*Signature*	*Description*
AccessMode	`public AccessMode()`	Constructor
create	`public static AccessMode create( int entityLock, int entityLocation, int entityCompatibility, int elementLock, int elementLocation, int elementCompatibility, long startingElement, int elementsEachAccess, int waitTime) throws GFException`	Create a new instance of an AccessMode. The new instance is initialized according to the parameters. The parameters indicate the type of lock (valid values are defined in LockMode), desired location (valid values defined in AccessLocation), access compatibility (valid values defined in CompatibilityMode), location and compatibility mode for elements of a collection (if the accessed entity if collection), collection starting elements and elements per access (performance hints relevant only if the accessed entity is a collection), a timeout definition which is either a number of one of the special values in TimeOut.
setNoLock	`public static void setNoLock( AccessMode accessMode) throws GFException, SmWorkAreaNotActiveException, SmContextInvalidException`	Set the global behavior of the NoLock Access Mode equal to that of the specified `AccessMode`. `AccessModes` created using the `createNoLock` method subsequent to calling this method will be initialized to a state equal to the state of the specified `AccessMode`.
setNormal	`public static void setNormal( AccessMode accessMode) throws GFException, SmWorkAreaNotActiveException, SmContextInvalidException`	Set the global behavior of the Normal Access Mode equal to that of the specified `AccessMode`. `AccessModes` created using the `createNormal` method subsequent to calling this method will be initialized to a state equal to the state of the specified `AccessMode`.
setPlusWrite	`public static void setPlusWrite( AccessMode accessMode) throws GFException, SmWorkAreaNotActiveException, SmContextInvalidException`	Set the global behavior of the PlusWrite Access Mode equal to that of the specified `AccessMode`. AccessModes created using the `createPlusWrite` method subsequent to calling this method will be initialized to a state equal to the state of the specified AccessMode.
setCritical	`public static void setCritical( AccessMode accessMode) throws GFException, SmWorkAreaNotActiveException, SmContextInvalidException`	Set the global behavior of the Critical Access Mode equal to that of the specified `AccessMode`. `AccessModes` created using the `createCritical` method subsequent to calling this method will be initialized to a state equal to the state of the specified `AccessMode`.

Figure 14-2
(Cont'd)

createNoLock	`public static AccessMode createNoLock() throws GFException, SmWorkAreaNotActiveException, SmContextInvalidException`	Create a new `AccessMode` object, which attributes are according to the Global NoLock defaults. The Global NoLock default values may be changed using the `setNoLock` method. If the latter was not called, the default values are as per Table 14.2
createNormal	`public static AccessMode createNormal() throws GFException, SmWorkAreaNotActiveException, SmContextInvalidException`	Create a new AccessMode object, which attributes are according to the Global Normal defaults. The Global Normal default values may be changed using the setNormal method. If the latter was not called, the default values are as per Table 14.2.
createPlusWrite	`public static AccessMode createPlusWrite() throws GFException, SmWorkAreaNotActiveException, SmContextInvalidException`	Create a new `AccessMode` object, which attributes are according to the Global `PlusWrite` default. The Global `PlusWrite` default values may be changed using the `setPlusWrite` method. If the latter was not called, the default values are as per Table 14.2.
createCritical	`public static AccessMode createCritical() throws GFException, SmWorkAreaNotActiveException, SmContextInvalidException`	Create a new `AccessMode` object, which attributes are according to the Global Critical defaults. The Global Critical default values may be changed using the `setCritical` method. If the latter was not called, the default values are as per Table 14.2.
isIdentical	`public boolean isIdentical(Object object)`	Check if this `AccessMode` object is equal to the one passed as parameters.
equals	`public boolean equals(AccessMode object)`	Check if this `AccessMode` object is equal to the one passed as parameters.
setEqual	`public void setEqual(AccessMode am)`	Assignment method, which sets this `AccessMode` values to be the values in the input `AccessMode`.

Lock Mode

In Chapter 10, we have already mentioned that SanFrancisco supports a variety of locking mechanisms. When you access an entity, you specify the type of lock you want to have, and this way correct concurrency control is achieved. The class `LockMode` defines the types of locks you can specify, as shown in Table 14-1.

A conflict occurs whenever you attempt to gain a write lock when some other transaction is holding a pessimistic read lock, or whenever you attempt to gain any lock when some other transaction already has a pessimistic write lock. In such cases, you cannot obtain the requested lock. Then, the requesting transaction has to wait until the lock is available. The TimeOut attribute of the `AccessMode` defines this timeout.

TABLE 14-1

Summary of access mode attributes

	Mode Field	Meaning
com.ibm.sf.gf.LockMode	NO_LOCK	Access the Entity with no lock.
	OPTIMISTIC	Traditional optimistic lock.
	OPTIMISTIC_CLEAN	Non-traditional optimistic lock.
	READ	Pessimistic read lock.
	WRITE	Pessimistic write lock.
com.ibm.sf.gf.AccessLocation	HOME	Access the Entity in the address space that the entity is configured to persist in.
	LOCAL	Access the Entity in the local address space of the calling process.
com.ibm.sf.gf.CompatibilityMode	CONTAINER	Provides the capability of getting compatibility of location and NO_LOCK access between a contained Entity and a containing Entity.
	NO_CHANGE	Do not allow the LockMode or Location values specified in the AccessMode to be changed.
	SELF	If a lock already exists in the current transaction on the Entity being accessed, upgrade this lock to be compatible with the level of access requested.
com.ibm.sf.gf.Timeout	**DEFAULT_WAIT**	Indicates that the default timeout value should be used during an access.
	NO_WAIT	Indicates that an access should not wait if the desired lock is unavailable.
	WAIT_FOREVER	Indicates that an access call should wait until the lock becomes available.

The simplest and most intuitive types of locks are the pessimistic READ and WRITE locks, which are the defaults. The pessimistic approach is most suitable when the chances of multiple users wanting to modify the same object concurrently are high. Pessimistic locks prevent other transactions from acquiring certain access to the same object. Specifically, if a certain transaction holds a READ lock, this mean that no other transaction will be able to obtain a WRITE lock, and if a WRITE lock is held, other transactions cannot acquire any lock.

In addition to traditional pessimistic READ and WRITE locks, SanFrancisco provides OPTIMISTIC and OPTIMISTIC_CLEAN locks.

As already discussed in Chapter 10, When OPTIMISTIC lock mode is specified for access to most objects (`EntityOwningExtents` are an exception), each requester is granted access to the object and given their own copy of that object. Changes made are private to the user until the changes are committed. At commit time, the system checks to make sure the real business object has not changed since it was copied, a write lock is obtained on the object, and the changes are made. If any modified object was also changed by some other user, or the write lock cannot be obtained, the commit will fail and either a recovery procedure will resolve the conflict and determine what changes to make, or the business task will fail and have to be reinitiated.

Optimistic locking can improve throughput of the system in some cases by reducing contention, and the use of Local access (required with optimistic locking) can improve performance in some cases by providing local copies of the locked object. The copies mean that method calls to the business object execute in the address space of the using process, and do not require remote method calls to other processes or other machines on the network. This can significantly decrease network traffic and improve performance when many operations will be invoked on the same object during a single transaction. However, this benefit comes at the expense of creating the local copies, which can be expensive for collections, so the net effect on performance depends on the application.

The `NO_LOCK` lock mode allows getting local, non-transactional access to an object, usually by providing a copy of the real object. When you combine `NO_LOCK` access to some objects with access to other objects, things become tricky. You must make sure you do not pass `NO_LOCK` copies as parameters to method call to objects accessed with other lock modes, because methods receiving an Entity usually expect a real persistent object. If you do pass `NO_LOCK` objects as parameters, any modifications made by the called method will not be recorded on the real object and will not be affected by transaction commit or rollback. This might have some severe consequences such as data loss or database corruption. Instead of passing the `NO_LOCK` object as parameter, you should use its handle to get a different access to the object and then pass the real object as a parameter.

An exception to the rule stated above (that `NO_LOCK` access provides a copy of the object) is `NO_LOCK` and Local access to `EntityOwningExtent`. In this case, it is not practical to implement access by making a copy of the real object, because these collections are intended for use in cases where the number of elements is large. Maintaining a copy of the whole collection would cause poor performance during runtime. When you request `NO_LOCK` or `LOCAL` access to an `EntityOwningExtent`, you get a special object that delegates some of the operations performed on it to the real extent and the real underlying persistent data. Because locks are not used to ensure consistency of the state of the real extent, the outcome may not be consistent with the state of the extent at any single point in time. Furthermore, you might even get different results if you iterate over the collection more than once. Using a NO_LOCK or Local accessed extent is a little tricky in other respects, too. You cannot create new entities into the copy you have, or remove elements from the collection. Also, any access problems you might have are delayed to the time you actually access a specific element. For example, if a lock timeout exception occurs because of someone else locking the object you need to access, the exception will only be thrown when you access elements of the collection copied, and not when you create the copy.

Location

The location attribute of the `AccessMode` indicates where the methods invoked on the accessed entity should execute. The values for the location are defined in the `AccessLocation` class, and are shown in Table 14-1.

If you specify LOCAL location, a copy of the Entity is made to the process of the accessing client, and any subsequent method calls will be performed on the local copy, in the address space of the caller. This may improve performance by reducing the required network traffic if several method invocations are made of the Entity.

HOME location means that operations on the object are actually made through a proxy object, meaning that method parameters and returned values are transmitted over the network. This location mode is not applicable when using the OPTIMISTIC, OPTIMISTIC_CLEAN, or NO_LOCK lock mode.

Compatibility

The compatibility mode attribute in `AccessMode` objects specifies whether and how the framework may modify the lock and location requests to be compatible with an existing lock on the object or another object that contains it. The `CompatibilityMode` class defines the values for this attribute. The effects of these values are:

- `NO_CHANGE`. The same lock types and location must be provided for all contained objects, or the access request will fail.
- `SELF`. Same as NO_CHANGE, only that if the object is already locked in this transaction, use the lock and location as is, or upgrade as necessary to meet or exceed the semantics required for the requested lock.
- `CONTAINER`. Try to reconcile location and access differences between a contained object and a containing object with regard to NO_LOCK access. If the accessed (contained) object is already locked in this transaction (and the collection object is accessed `NO_LOCK`), this is the same as SELF. If you either request `NO_LOCK` access or the containing object is access `NO_LOCK`, the object is accessed `NO_LOCK`. Otherwise, if the containing object is locked, the location of the containing object is used instead of the location requested (the `lockMode` requested is unchanged). If neither the object nor the containing object is access locked in this transaction, the lock mode and location requested are used (just like in `NO_CHANGE`).

Lock Timeout

A timeout value specifies how long an access method should wait for a lock to become available. The timeout value can be any non-zero positive integer, or one of the special values defined in the Timeout class as shown in Table 14-1.

The DEFAULT_WAIT value is usually set to 30 seconds. However, each server process has its own DEFAULT_WAIT value. You can change this value for a specific server process through the Server Management console, as explained in Chapter 34.

Tailored Access Mode

The different attributes of the `AccessMode`, which were described above, can be set individually. This is done by creating a specific `AccessMode` using the static `create()` method in which you specify each attribute

(Figure 14-2 shows the signature of this method). Note that some parameters relate to the way you access the elements of a collection. These parameters are relevant only when the accessed Entity is indeed a collection; their use is explained below.

In general, you should not use the `create()` method to explicitly create specific access modes. The reason is that, as previously discussed, it is more convenient to use the standard `BaseFactory` `create<>` methods. Furthermore, if you define specific `AccessMode` objects, you might end up with having wrong access semantics in your application. In any case, the resulting code will be difficult, if not impossible to maintain (e.g. if you would like to change your locking mode from pessimistic to optimistic, you would have to make changes in a lot of places throughout your code). Another advantage of the standard access mode creation methods is that they can be used by pieces of code you call (like the query mechanism described in Chapter 19). In other words, code you use can share your access semantics without actually knowing them.

Table 14-2 shows the default configuration of the `AccessMode` objects returned by each of these methods. These characteristics of the standard access mode can be modified, using static `set<>()` methods. The `set<>()` methods can be called to modify the specific values of the access mode objects, which are returned from the static `create<>()` methods and can be modified dynamically at runtime. A modification affects all use within the caller's Distributed Process Context, which is normally per application process (or per Java applet). The `set<>()` methods are shown in Figure 14-2. To use these methods, you first create the access mode object using the `create()` method. This way you can specify the values for each one of the attributes of your access mode. Then, you pass this object to the appropriate `set<>()` method that copies the access mode object so that it can be used later when the corresponding `create<>()` method is called. Note that the `setNoLock()` method ignores

TABLE 14-2

Default configuration of standard `AccessMode` creation methods

Method	Lock	Location	Compatibility	Time
`createNormal()`	READ	HOME	CONTAINER	DEFAULT_TIMEOUT
`createPlusWrite()`	WRITE	HOME	CONTAINER	DEFAULT_TIMEOUT
`createCritical()`	WRITE	HOME	CONTAINER	DEFAULT_TIMEOUT
`createNoLock()`	NO_LOCK	LOCAL	CONTAINER	DEFAULT_TIMEOUT

the LockMode and AccessLocation parts of the passed AccessMode object, and always uses NO_LOCK and LOCAL, respectively, for these attributes.

When you use the set<> methods, you should create a consistent way of accessing objects. For example, the createNormal() and createPlusWrite() should have the same Location attribute. Table 14-3 shows an example of setting the AccessLocation attributes so that createPlusWrite() uses optimistic-local access and createCritical() uses pessimistic-home access. Figure 14-3 shows a code sample illustrating how you modify the standard access modes to achieve these access semantics.

In this case, application functions that want to make a quick change to an object without interference from other transactions could benefit from using the createCritical() access mode. Using the createPlusWrite() would allow the possibility that the commit() may fail with an optimistic lock failure because some other transaction got in and changed the object before this transaction committed. Note, however, that if the Entity you are accessing using createCritical() had already accessed Local-Optimistic in your transaction, the use of CONTAINER compatibility will allow the access to be successful and upgrade from Optimistic to Write, but will remain Local access. If you want the access with createCritical() to fail if it can't get Home access, use NO_CHANGE compatibility.

The way you tailor the access modes for your application heavily depends on the nature of the transactions you make. If transactions are relatively short (and specifically do not wait for any user interaction to take place), then you can use the pessimistic lock types READ or WRITE, and compatibility type CONTAINER. Typically, you would use HOME location access, but you may use LOCAL to improve performance in case you make many operations on the same object during a transaction.

TABLE 14-3

A different configuration of standard AccessMode creation methods

Method	Lock	Location	Compatibility	Timeout
createNormal()	OPTIMISTIC	LOCAL	CONTAINER	DEFAULT_TIMEOUT
createPlusWrite()	OPTIMISTIC	LOCAL	CONTAINER	DEFAULT_TIMEOUT
createCritical()	WRITE	HOME	CONTAINER	DEFAULT_TIMEOUT
createNoLock()	NO_LOCK	LOCAL	CONTAINER	DEFAULT_TIMEOUT

Figure 14-3 Code sample: changing the configuration standard `AccessMode` creation methods.

```
AccessMode normalMode = AccessMode.create(
      LockMode.OPTIMISTIC,
      AccessLocation.LOCAL,
      CompatibilityMode.CONTAINER,
      LockMode.OPTIMISTIC,
      AccessLocation.LOCAL,
      CompatibilityMode.CONTAINER,
      1,
      20,  // same as default, this is ignored anyway
      TimeOut.DEFAULT);

AccessMode.setNormal(normalMode);

// Set settings for PlusWrite are the same
AccessMode.setPlusWrite(normalMode);

AccessMode criticalMode = AccessMode.create(
      LockMode.WRITE,
      AccessLocation.HOME.
      CompatibilityMode.CONTAINER,
      LockMode.WRITE,
      AccessLocation.HOME.
      CompatibilityMode.CONTAINER,
      1,
      20,  // same as default, this is ignored anyway
      TimeOut.DEFAULT);

AccessMode.setCritical(criticalMode);

AccessMode nolockMode = AccessMode.create(
      LockMode.NO_LOCK,
      AccessLocation.LOCAL.
      CompatibilityMode.CONTAINER,
      LockMode.NO_LOCK,
      AccessLocation.LOCAL.
      CompatibilityMode.CONTAINER,
      1,
      20,  // same as default, this is ignored anyway
      TimeOut.DEFAULT);

AccessMode.setNoLock(nolockMode);
```

Transactions that include user interaction must avoid the use of pessimistic locks, because they limit the ability of other transactions to access the object. This way, other transactions are blocked for an indefinite time, waiting for the user. For such transactions, you should use NO_LOCK or optimistic access.

Collection Element Access

As previously mentioned, some of the `AccessMode` attributes apply to accessing entities inside a collection Entity. When accessing a collection two lock types are specified: one for the collection itself and the other for the contained elements. Similarly, two access location types are specified: one for the collection itself and the other for accessing contained elements.

The collection elements access specification is relative to where the code getting access is executed. This make a difference only when using an access mode on a collection that specifies the collection is to be accessed *Home*, and the elements are to be accessed *Local*. In that case, the collection is accessed through a proxy in its Home location. So, when "next" is called on the collection it will be executed on the server and will get Local access there to the next element, which creates a local copy of the element on the server, and then the client ends up getting a proxy to that copy.

The other parameters for collection access, namely, `starting Element` and `elementsEachAccess`, are performance hints indicating how the collection is going to be used. The latter indicates how many elements of the collection are accessed at a time, and the former where you start the access from. These parameters are currently not supported, i.e. the values you specify will have no effect.

More on Locks and Access

The `EntityManagement` interface, described in Chapter 15, provides the `refreshEntity()` method. This method updates the Entity passed as parameter with any changes committed since the current transaction accessed it. If no transaction has committed changes to the Entity since this transaction accessed the Entity, then `refreshEntity()` does not change the current state of the Entity in this transaction. Note that `refreshEntity()` only refreshes the `Entity` it is called on. It does not refresh other Entities that might be owned or used by that `Entity`. If you need to be assured that all objects that might be used by this Entity are also refreshed, you will need to commit the current transaction and begin a new one (if you are using `NO_LOCK` access, you will need to create a new work area).

Note that the behavior of `refreshEntity()` depends on the kind of access mode you currently have. If a pessimistic lock is held, no action takes place. For optimistic locks, no action takes place if the object was not changed on the server. If it was, then the local object is replaced by a new copy. A copy is also made if you have `NO_LOCK` access. In the last two cases, when a copy is made, all changes made to the previous copy are discarded.

The `EntityManagement` interface also provides the `dropEntity()` method, which essentially reverses the action of obtaining access. This method can be called when the referenced object is no longer needed in a transaction. This is meaningful only if you had any lock other than `NO_LOCK` copy, and you did not make any changes to the object. If both conditions are met, the `Entity` is dropped from the transactions and any corresponding locks are released.

Both `refreshEntity()` and `dropAccess()` must be used with special care because they operate only on the specific `Entity` they are called on. They are not automatically applied to other Entities owned or referenced by the specified `Entity`. Therefore, the caller needs to call `refreshEntity()` or `dropAccess()` on each of the Entities whose state they want refreshed. Since the behavior of the target Entity might depend on the use of other Entities that are internal implementation details (specifically, they are not exposed in the public interface), it is often not possible for the application developer to refresh or drop access to those specific hidden Entities. For this reason, you are usually better off using the transaction management features to release locks, as described in Chapter 16 (i.e. use `commit()` or `rollback()`).

Another way around the usual transaction management is the `syncEntity()` method also available through the `EntityManagement` interface and part of the `BaseFactory`. This method makes an update of the object in the underlying data store immediately, without waiting for a `commit()` of the transaction. This allows you to handle any exceptions coming from the data store. For example, if you are using a relational database and some constraint violation occurs, you can handle it immediately. Just like `refreshEntity()` and `dropAccess()`, this method only operates on the `Entity` specified so it should be used only when really needed.

Distributed Processes

SanFrancisco introduces the notion of a distributed process (DP). A distributed process is a natural extension of the notion of a regular process. A DP is composed of several threads actively working under it, only that these threads can be spread over the network beyond the boundaries of a single JVM. Just like a normal process, the DP has a context, or shared information space, that each thread in the distributed process can access and modify. This context is called the distributed process context (DPC). The power of the DP abstraction stems from the fact that changes made to the DPC by one thread are immediately available to the other threads in the same DP.

A *work area* is a data area internal to a thread. A work area may include both transactional and non-transactional data. A thread may be working in just one work area at a time but is allowed to switch work areas if required. When the initial client thread starts (i.e. it calls the `Global.initialize()` method), it immediately has a default work area that all transaction and certain non-transaction work is performed in. Work areas can be transferred between threads. In order to do that, the thread using the work area suspends it, and another thread resumes it. Once a thread resumes the work area, the thread has full access to the data inside the work area.

The work area encapsulates all of the transaction-related data. In addition, it includes security context, transient Entities, and NO_LOCK Entities.

In most cases, threads must be associated with a work area to reliably perform any SanFrancisco operation. If an attempt to perform such an operation is made without having a work area active, the result would be an `SmWorkAreaNotActiveException` thrown. The only things you can do without having a work area are calling methods that can help you start a work area. Namely, these methods are `factory().createWorkArea()`, `factory().resume()`, `Global. initialize()`, and `Global.factory()`.

When client code wants to create a new thread, it should do so using the `SMSFThread` class. This class is derived from Thread, and the main benefit of using it is that the resulting thread immediately has a work area created for it. In addition, it provides faster access to the work area than a regular thread would. The client must be presently in a work area when creating an `SmSFThread`.

If you create a new Java thread, this thread must either create a new work area of its own or resume work on a work area that was suspended in a different thread. Note that such threads do not automatically have any work areas associated with them. A thread must be in a work area to access the distributed process context. Threads running on a server are associated with the work area of the remote thread making the call.

When using `SmSFThread`, you may either derive your own subclasses and override the `run()` method, or create an object of this class and pass it a `Runnable` object in the constructor. Before finishing its `run()` method, your thread must class `BaseFactory.deleteWorkArea()` to explicitly free up any resources associated with your thread in server processes.

The `SmDistributedProcessManagement` methods shown in Figure 14-4, provide interfaces for working with the DPs, DPCs, and managing work areas and getting access to the DPC. The most common ways these methods are used are shown in Figures 14-5–14-8.

Conflict Control

In a single application, or in a group of integrated applications, some actions must not run concurrently, since this might result in wrong or inconsistent results. Such an action usually corresponds to a single Java method. The SanFrancisco Foundation layer provides support for controlling such conflicts. The conflict control utility allows you to define the potential conflicts. A conflict may either exist for an action with itself, meaning that this action must not be initiated more than once, or for one action or group of actions with another action or group of actions. As an example of the first case notice that a certain initialization function such as the initialization of a new warehouse cannot be done while another instance of this operation is being performed.

SanFrancisco provides two utilities for creating and maintaining conflict definitions and for monitoring conflicts at runtime. These are described in Chapter 35.

Figure 14-4 Interface `SmDistributedProcessManagement`

Interface com.ibm.sf.gf.SmDistributedProcessManagement

public interface **SmDistributedProcessManagement**
extends AllowRemote

Name	*Signature*	*Description*
getDP	`public abstract DistributedProcess getDP() throws GFException, SmWorkAreaNotActiveException`	Returns the Distributed Process that this thread is currently working under.
createWorkArea	`public abstract void createWorkArea( DistributedProcess dp) throws GFException, SmWorkAreaAlreadyActiveException`	Creates a new Work Area under the specified Distributed Process and associates it with this thread. This method should be called only when there is no WorkArea which is currently active (e.g. following a suspend()). If the current thread already has an active WorkArea, then a SmWorkAreaAlreadyActiveException is thrown.
deleteWorkArea	`public abstract void deleteWorkArea() throws GFException, SmWorkAreaNotActiveException`	Destroys the threads currently active in the Work Area. Again, this method should be used only when the current thread has an active WorkArea, otherwise an SmWorkAreaNotActiveException is thrown.
suspend	`public abstract Control suspend() throws GFException, SmWorkAreaNotActiveException, SmOperationNotAllowedException`	Suspends all activity in the threads current Work Area and effectively disassociates it from the thread. No further WA activity can occur in this thread until an association with a new WorkArea is done, through either a resume, or a create operation). The Control object that is returned from this operation can be used in a later resume operation to allow further work in this WA.
resume	`public abstract void resume(Control control) throws GFException, SmWorkAreaAlreadyActiveException, SmWorkAreaBusyException, InvalidParameterException`	Associates the current thread with the Work Area of the specified Control object. After this call, the thread can begin working within the Work Area.

```
main() {
   try {
        •
        •
        •

   Global.initialize();
   dp = Global.factory().getDP();

        •
        •
        •

   Control  suspendedWA= Global.factory().suspend();
   Global.factory().createWorkArea(dp);

        •
        •
        •
   // User can suspend this WA and resume an existing WA
   wa2Control = Global.factory().suspend();
   Global.factory().resume(waControl);

        •
        •
        •

   Global.factory().destroyWorkArea();
   Global.uninitialize();
        •
        •
        •

   } catch (GFException sfex) {
        •
        •
        •
   }
}
```

Any application specific initialization would go here

Initialize San Francisco (creates a DP, WA, both associated with the running thread)

Do whatever work is needed. This work is done in the current WA

Now we suspend the current WA and create a new one to work with

Do whatever work is needed. This work is done in the newly created WA

Now we suspend the current WA and resume the previous one

Do whatever work is needed. This work is done in original WA of this thread

Destroy the current WA and uninitialize San Francisco

More application specific cleanup code can go here

Figure 14-5
Primary thread example.

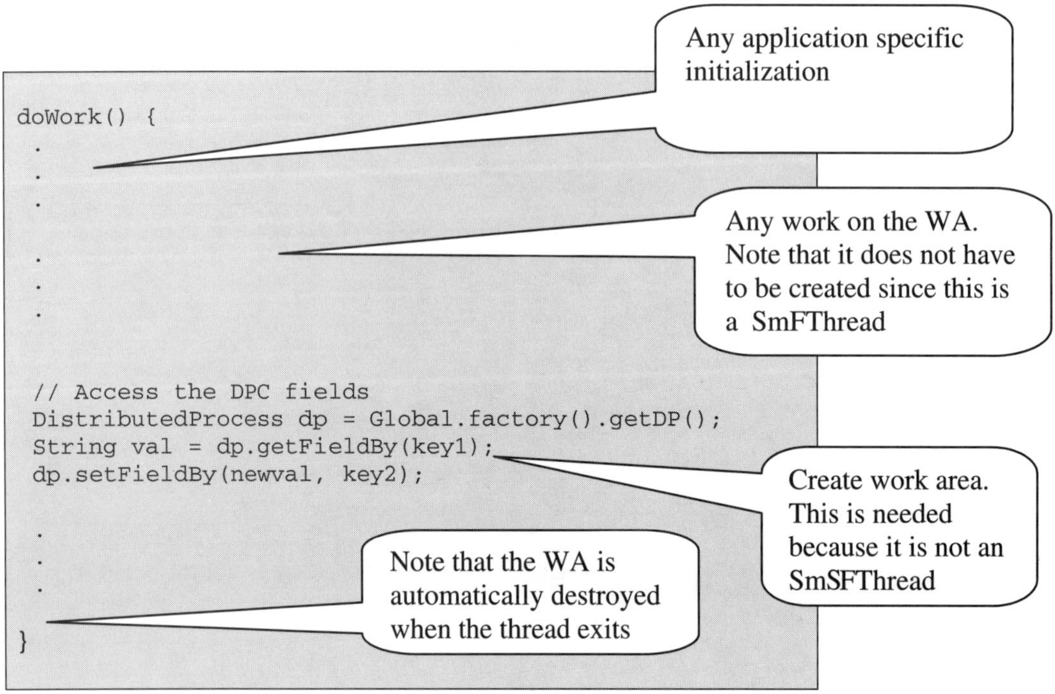

Figure 14-6
`SmSFThread` example.

Defining Conflicts

In order to have conflict control for your application, you must first define conflicts. Once the application is deployed, the administrator at the site can manage these conflicts using the utilities described in Chapter 35.

In order to define conflicts, you need to go through several steps. First, you create a list of actions that might cause conflicts. Each of these actions has a unique id and can also have some descriptive text (which would turn out to be helpful when administering the conflicts). During runtime, you can define action parameters for each action, which specify the conditions under which it exists. In other words, during runtime you actually define what the action is.

Actions can be grouped into categories, and these categories can themselves be grouped into higher-level categories. Once you define a conflict for a certain action, this conflict is propagated down to all subcategories

```
awtCallback() {
  .
  .
  .

 String key, newval;


 // Resume processing in a previously suspended WA
 Global.factory().resume(suspendedWA);
  .
  .
  .


 DistributedProcess dp = Global.factory().getDP();
 String val = dp.getFieldBy(key);
 dp.setFieldBy(newval, key);


 suspendedWA = Global.factory().suspend();

 •
 •
 •

}
```

Application-specific setup code

Application-specific handling

Access DPC fields, to update other threads in the DPC

Suspend the WA when finished

Application specific handling

Figure 14-7
AWT callback thread example.

and contained actions. Categories and actions are essentially organized in a tree-like structure. Figure 14-9 shows an example of such a tree.

In order to provide your action, category, and conflict definitions, you place them in one or more files that are used as input to a batch utility. For each of these definitions you can either place the definitions in one file, or in several. In the latter case, you must provide a file holding the list of individual lines in separate lines. The syntax for the action definition files is quite simple. The file contains a sequence of definitions. Each of these definitions spans several lines, and may contain comments, which are indicated by a line starting with a double hyphen. Figure 14-10 shows the syntax for an action definition, and Figure 14-11 shows a sample action definition file.

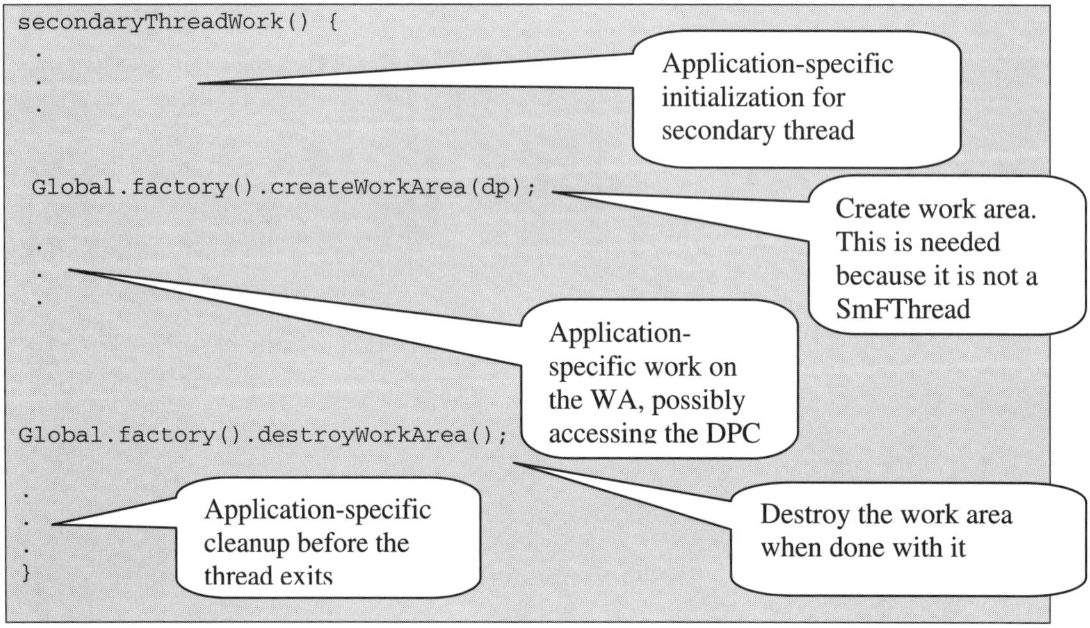

Figure 14-8
Secondary thread example.

Similarly, Figure 14-12 shows the syntax for a category definition, and Figure 14-13 shows a sample category definition file. Figure 14-14 shows the syntax for conflict definitions, and Figure 14-15 shows a sample file.

Once you created all these files, you use the conflict batch utility for creating the action, category and conflict definitions in persistent form. To run the batch utility, you should have the LSFN up and running. If not started already, you need to start it using “Start LSFN” from the “Base Utilities” folder in the SanFrancisco folder. The syntax for using

Figure 14-9
Sample conflict category tree.

```
ActionId:    <action name>
ParentCategoryId: <parent category name>
ActionDescription:  <action description>
```

Optional

Optional, may span several lines (until the next ActionId)

Figure 14-10
Syntax for action definition.

```
------------------------------------------------------------------
--------
-- Sample action definition file
------------------------------------------------------------------
--------
actionId: Action no. 1
actionDescription: This action might cause a conflict
actionId: Action no. 2
actionDescription: This action might cause a conflict
actionId: Action no. 3
parentCategoryId: Category no. 1
actionId: Action no. 4
actionDescription: This action might cause a serious
conflict.
It also has a long description that takes more than one
line.
```

Figure 14-11
Sample action definition file.

```
CategoryId: <action name>
ParentCategoryId: <parent category name>
CategoryDescription:  <category description>
```

Optional, may span several lines (until the next `CategoryId`)

Optional; if you don't specify this, the new category is added to the root category

Figure 14-12
Syntax for category definition.

Figure 14-13 Sample category definition file.

```
-------------------------------------------------------------
--------
-- Sample category definition file
-------------------------------------------------------------
--------
categoryId: Category no. 1
categoryDescription: This category will contain Action no.3
categoryId: Category no. 2
categoryDescription: This category has a long description.
     It will be used later as a parent category
categoryId: Category no. 3
categoryDescription: This category has a parent
parentCategoryId: Category no. 2
```

Figure 14-14 Syntax for conflict definition.

```
firstId:    <action or category name>
secondId: <action or category name>
```

Figure 14-15 Sample conflict definition file.

```
-----------------------------------------------------------------
-- Sample conflict Definition File
-----------------------------------------------------------------

firstId: Action No. 1
secondId: Action No. 2
firstId: Category No. 1
secondId: Category No. 1
```

Action 1 conflict with Action 2

Category 1 conflicts with itself. Without our definitions, this means that Action 3 conflicts with itself

this program is shown in Figure 14-16. You must of course specify the whole command in one line, and make sure the files are in the right order. If you don't need one of the components, you must still provide an empty file.

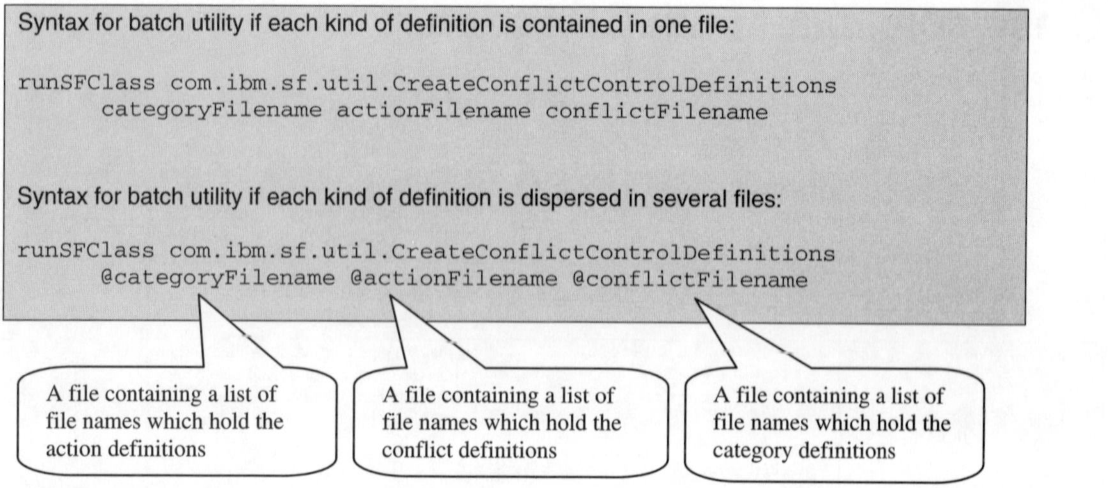

Figure 14-16
Using the conflict batch program.

Performing a Conflict-Controlled Action

Once you have the conflicts in your data store, you can actually perform a conflict-controlled action. To do that, you use the class `CCaction` (this class is described in Figure 14-17). This class provides static `create()` methods, for which you specify either just the action name or the action names along with action parameters. All parameters are String objects. Note that the action you specify here must be already defined.

When the `CCAction` object is created, the Foundation layer contacts a special server (the Conflict Management server) and finds out whether a conflicting action is currently active. If not, your action is immediately recorded as active. You may inquire the status of your action using the `isStartAllowed()` method on the `CCAction` object you created. If the result is false, you may not start the action, since there is a conflict. You can find out the conflicting actions using the `getConflictingActions()` method. The information is represented in objects in `DCCActionInformation`. This class provides you with information about the conflicting actions through access methods described in Figure 14-18. You must not forget to inform the Conflict Management server when you are finished with the action, using the `CCAction` object you have.

Class com.ibm.sf.util.CCAction

public class **CCAction**
extends Object

Name	*Signature*	*Description*
createCCAction	`public static CCAction createCCAction( String actionId) throws NoConflictItemException, ConflictControlException, GFException`	Creates and returns a new conflict controlled action from the given action Id and tests whether or not the action may be performed at this time.
createCCAction	`public static CCAction createCCAction( String actionId,String actionParms) throws NoConflictItemException, InvalidActionParameterStringException, ConflictControlException, GFException`	Creates a new conflict controlled action from the given action Id and parameter string and tests whether or not the action may be performed at this time.
isStartAllowed	`public synchronized boolean isStartAllowed()`	Indicates whether or not this action may be performed at this time, according to the decision made by the ConflictControlManager.
isActionRegistrationDisabled	`public synchronized boolean isActionRegistrationDisabled ()`	Indicates whether action registration is currently disabled by maintenance. Can be used if isStartAllowed() returns false, to find out the reasons.
deregister	`public synchronized boolean deregister()`	Deregisters this action from the ConflictControlManager, if it was registered.
getConflictingActions	`public synchronized DSet getConflictingActions() throws GFException`	Returns a list of action information records, holding all the currently active actions which are in conflict with this action. Can be used if isStartAllowed() returns false, to find out the reasons. Note that null is returned if there are no conflicts.
newParmString	`public static String newParmString (String parmName, String parmValue, String oldParmString)`	Builds and returns a new action parameter string from the provided parameter name and value and the given old parameter string. The given parameter name and value are added to the given old parameter string. The old parameter string may be null. If the given parameter name and/or value is null or empty the old parameter string is returned. This method can be used to incrementally construct the parameter string, by repeatedly calling it, each time using the result of the previous call as the old parameter string.

Figure 14-17
Class `CCAction`.

Interface com.ibm.sf.util.DCCActionInformation

public interface **DCCActionInformation** extends Dependent

Name	*Signature*	*Description*
getActionId	`public abstract String getActionId()`	Returns the action Id.
getActionHandle	`public abstract int getActionHandle()`	Returns the action handle. This handle is the unique identifier of an active action registered with the ConflictControlManager (note that several handles can be associated with one actionid).
getActionParms	`public abstract String getActionParms()`	Returns the string of parameters used for the active action.
getActionRegistrationTime	`public abstract long getActionRegistrationTime()`	Returns the time of registration for the action.
getActionRegistrationTimeAsDate	`public abstract Date getActionRegistrationTimeAsDate()`	Returns the time of registration for the action, as a Date object.
getActionDescription	`public abstract String getActionDescription()`	Returns the action description.
getActionUserId	`public abstract String getActionUserId()`	Returns the user-id of the user who initiated the action.
initialize	`public abstract void initialize (String actionId, String actionDescription, String actionParms, String actionUserId, Long actionRegTime, int actionHandle) throws SFException`	Initializes this action information object from the provided parameters.

Figure 14-18
Interface `DCCAction Information`

When using the second variant of the `create()` method, you need to specify parameters using the format shown in Figure 14-19, along with an example. Note that you may specify as many parameters as you want. You can also use the `newParmString` method of `CCAction` to build the parameter string for you.

It is imperative that you use the parameter names consistently. For this purpose, you might consider having a class with constant definitions of all the parameter names and corresponding strings.

Parameter String Format:

```
[PName: name PValue: value {PName: name PValue: value …}]
```

Examples of Parameter Strings:

```
PName: Company PValue: MyCompany
PName: Company PValue: MyCompany PName: Branch PValue: Arizona
PName: Company PValue: MyCompany PName: Branch PValue: Arizona
      PName: Manager PValue: Joe
```

Figure 14-19
Action parameters format.

Conflict Detection

The Conflict Management server is responsible for detecting conflicts. Whenever a new action request is made, the new action is compared with all the currently active actions. A conflict is generated between two actions if they are defined as conflicting (using the action ids), *and* all their parameters have the same values. The Conflict Management server ignores any parameters appearing in one action only.

Figure 14-20 shows some examples for conflicts.

Action A Parameters	Action B Parameters	Conflict?
PName: Company PValue: MyCompany	PName: Company PValue: MyCompany	
PName: Company PValue: MyCompany	PName: Company PValue: OtherCompany	
PName: Company PValue: MyCompany	PName: Company PValue: MyCompany PName: Branch PValue: Arizona	
PName: Company PValue: MyCompany	PName: Company PValue: MyCompany PName: Branch PValue: Nevada	

Figure 14-20
Example of conflicts.

Security

SanFrancisco addresses the issues of security in two ways:

- *Authentication*. Establishing the identity of the user, who is running an application.
- *Authorization*. Controlling the actions a user is allowed to perform while running an application.

The actual decision regarding the details of the way security is enforced is left to the discretion of the system administrator. The administrator defines a security policy, which is based on the specific requirements of the application and the way it is being used.

The implementation of security in the application is, therefore, a process involving the application developer, the Foundation layer, and the administrator at the installation site. The programmer defines the specifics of the security handling in the application. The administrator can define the security policy for the installation, which defines the particulars of the implementation of the security handling in the application. For example, the administrator can associate specific users with permissions to do specific operations. During runtime, the Foundation dynamically combines the definitions made by the programmer and the administrator, and makes sure security is enforced accordingly.

Detailed descriptions of the utilities that can be used by the system administrator to define security policies are described in Chapter 35.

The security management features of the Foundation layer are accessed through the `SecurityAPI` interface, using the `Global.security()` object. This interface is shown in Figure 14-21.

Authentication

As described in detail in Chapter 25, the administrator of a SanFrancisco installation may choose to specify that the users-ids and passwords are required. This means that each user must be assigned a user-id and password (this too is done using the tools described in Chapter 35), and that when a SanFrancisco application runs, and before it can access any resources on servers, it must identify the user. Such identification is done either using the SanFrancisco Security Controller, or using a simpler solution in the form of `LogonController`. The latter is a ready-made

Figure 14-21 `SecurityAPI` interface.

Interface com.ibm.sf.gf.SecurityAPIs

public interface **SecurityAPIs**

Name	Signature	Description
validateUserid	`public abstract void validateUserid() throws GFException, InvalidUseridException, InvalidPasswordException, InvalidNewPasswordException, SecurityMaxRetriesException`	Checks if the current user information is valid.. The user-id, password and optional new password that have been set will all be sent to the Master Security Controller for validation. A normal return means the authentication succeeded and that the user information provided has been successfully validate. An exception is thrown if one of the elements is not valid. If the user-id and password are good, and only the new password is invalid, authentication succeeds and an exception is thrown.
setUserid	`public abstract void setUserid(String userid) throws GFException`	Sets the user-id identifying end user of the application.
setPassword	`public abstract void setPassword(char password[]) throws GFException`	Sets the password that is to be used to authenticate the user-id. Note the parameter is a character array and not a String.
getUserid	`public abstract String getUserid() throws GFException`	Gets the user-id identifying the user of the application. This will usually be the user-id previously set by a previous call to setUser-id. In case the setUser-id has not been called, it will be the JVM user-id.
isUseridRequired	`public abstract boolean isUseridRequired() throws GFException`	Returns whether the current security policy requires users to specify their user-ids for authentication
isPasswordRequired	`public abstract boolean isPasswordRequired() throws GFException`	Returns whether the current security policy requires users to provide a password for authentication.
setNewPassword	`public abstract void setNewPassword(char password[]) throws GFException, InvalidNewPasswordException`	Sets the new password provided, and replaces the old password for the user. The new password will actually be set only when the user is validated (i.e. after setting the user-id and password using the setUser-id and setPassword methods. The new password provided must conform to the restrictions set as part of the security policy.
beginSecureTask	`public abstract void beginSecureTask(String secureTaskName,String nameServerContext) throws GFException, NotAuthorizedException`	Begins the specified SecureTask. An authorization check will occur to make sure that an AccessRight exists for the SF user for this task. The endSecureTask() method must be used to end the scope of the SecureTask.

Figure 14-21
(Cont'd)

beginSecureTask	`public abstract void beginSecureTask( String secureTaskName,String nameServerContext,Handle resource) throws GFException, NotAuthorizedException, SecureTaskNotFoundException`	Begins the specified SecureTask for specified resource. An authorization check will occur to make sure that an AccessRight exists for the SF user for this task and resource. The endSecureTask() method must be used to end the scope of the SecureTask.
endSecureTask	`public abstract void endSecureTask( String secureTaskName,String nameServerContext) throws GFException`	Indicates the end of a SecureTask scope for current thread. If this SecureTask contains Permissions, the SecureTask and associated Permissions will be removed from the thread SecurityContext.
endSecureTask	`public abstract void endSecureTask( String secureTaskName,String nameServerContext,Handle resource) throws GFException`	Indicates the end of a SecureTask scope for current thread. If this SecureTask contains Permissions, the SecureTask and associated Permissions will be removed from the thread SecurityContext.
checkSecureTaskAccess	`public abstract boolean checkSecureTaskAccess( String secureTaskName,String nameServerContext) throws GFException, SecureTaskNotFoundException`	Checks whether the user is authorized to run the SecureTask, without actually starting a new SecureTask scope. Returns true if a corresponding AccessRight is found.
checkSecureTaskAccess	`public abstract boolean checkSecureTaskAccess( String secureTaskName,String nameServerContext,Handle resource) throws GFException, ecureTaskNotFoundException`	Checks whether the user is authorized to run the specified SecureTask, on the specified resource. True is returned if a corresponding AccessRight is found.
addSecureTask	`public abstract void addSecureTask( SecureTask secureTask,String nameServerContext) throws GFException`	Adds the SecureTask object to the specified name server context.
deleteSecureTask	`public abstract void deleteSecureTask( String secureTaskName,String nameServerContext) throws GFException`	Removes the specified task from the specified name server context.
isUserValidated	`public abstract boolean isUserValidated() throws GFException`	Returns whether the current user-id for this application has been successfully validated.

GUI object that handles the login process of a user. Figure 14-22 shows how this object is used, and Figure 14-23 shows what this looks like to the user.

The advantage of using the `LoginController` is that it takes into consideration the security policy set for the LSFN by the administrator (e.g. if no user-id and passwords are required, the login process is always successful). Also, it provides the user with the capability to change the password (it actually asks her/him to do so if the password has expired).

Figure 14-22
Code sample: using `LogonController`.

```
import com.ibm.sf.gf;

try
{
   // Set the Login window location
   LogonController.setLogonWindowLocation(250,250);

   // Attempt login
   LogonController.processLogon();
}
catch (GFSecurityException e)
{
       // Authentication FAILED
}
```

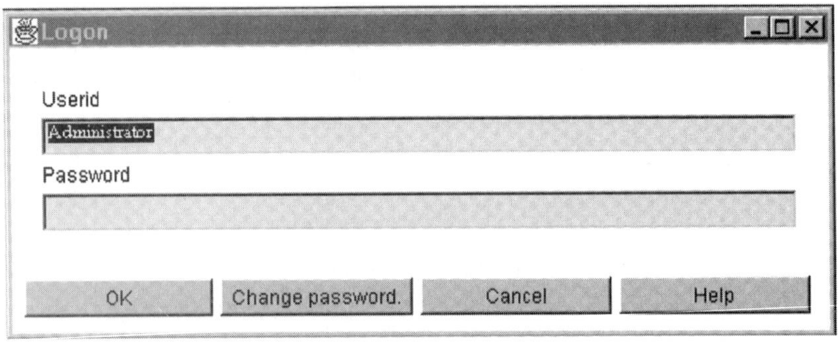

Figure 14-23
User perspective of `LogonController`.

The `processLogon()` method handles login failures according to the security policy for the LSFN, such as the maximal allowed number of retries, and when repeated failures occur it throws the `GFSecurityException`.

The alternative to using the `LoginController` is the Security Controller, which is a singleton object that exists within every SanFrancisco process and is returned by calling the static class method `security()` on the Global class. As mentioned above, it implements the SecurityAPIs methods whose signatures are shown in Figure 14-21. Using the Security Controller is useful in cases when specific tailoring of the login window is needed, or if the application is not interactive and the application wants to provide the user-id and password itself. Figure 14-24 shows an example of using the Security Controller directly without user interaction. Although there is no direct user interaction in this

Figure 14-24
Code sample: directly using `Security Controller`.

```
{
  Global.security().setUserid("Joe");
  char [] password = {'z','u','i','k','a','k', 'o'};
  Global.security().setPassword(password);
  try
  {
     Global.security().validateUserid();
  }
  catch (GFSecurityException e)
  {
     // Authentication failed, exit the program
  }
}
```

example, the effect is very much the same. That is, if the policy requires a user-id and password, the appropriate checks are performed (and an exception thrown if a failure occurs). Otherwise, the call to `validateUser()` does nothing. It is important to note that the `LoginController` also makes direct use of the Security Controller and does not have any additional security-related capabilities.

One important point to note is that unlike most character strings, passwords are maintained as a character array and not using a String object. The reason for this is that a String in Java is immutable and, therefore, it cannot be modified or destroyed after its creation. By using a character array the Security Controller can make sure that once the password is accepted, the object containing it will be cleared from the password string. This cannot be done when using a String object, since you cannot change it and deletion depends on the whims of the garbage collector. This way, the duration the password is "exposed" to anyone hacking the JVM when running the program is minimized.

When an application requires a specifically tailored login window, it might need to know the specific security policy. A schematic example of using these methods is shown in Figure 14-25. Note how in this example special code is required to handle the different login failure exceptions, which are masked away by the `LoginController` when you use it.

The Client Security Controller keeps track of the number of times an authorization has failed because of invalid input by the user, and is also aware of the security policy for retries, so the application does not need to keep track of the number of failures that have accumulated.

There are a few other methods that can be used to obtain information relating to authentication. The `getUserid()` method returns a String containing the currently active user-id. The `isUserValidated()`

```
import com.ibm.sf.gf;

.
.

while (true)
{
  if (Global.security().isUseridRequired())
  {
      if (Global.security().isPasswordRequired())
      {
          // Prompt the user to provide user-id and password
                .
                .
          char[] password = …;
          // Pass the password for verification
          Global.security().setPassword(password);
      }
      else // Prompt the user to provide user-id only
      {
                .
                .
      }

      // Pass the user-id for verification
      Global.security().setUserid(userid);
      try
      {
         Global.security().validateUserid();
      }
      catch (NonRetryableAuthenticationException e)
      {
         // Exit the application - authentication failed
      }
      catch (ExpiredPasswordException e)
      {
         // Give a message indicating the password expired
         // Prompt the user for new password
                .
                .
         Global.security().setNewPassword(newPassword);
         continue;
      }
      catch (RetryableAuthenticationException e)
      {
         // Give a message and prompt the user again for the password
         continue;
      }
      break;    // authentication succeeded
  }
}
```

Figure 14-25
Code sample: inquiring the current security policy.

method checks if a user login process has already successfully completed. This can be useful when multiple applets are running in the same JVM and you don't want each of them to prompt the user for id and password. This method is used by the `LogonController` in order to ensure that it performs the login process only if it wasn't completed successfully before.

Authorization

The management of authorization is made through access rights. Access rights determine who has the permission to do what, to which data items. In SanFrancisco terms, which actor can perform what action on what resources. The actor is identified by a user-id, the resource is identified with a SanFrancisco entity (which currently can be either a Server or a Company), and the action depends on the resource. For servers, the action is just "use"—meaning that the user is allowed to use this server. Server authorization is relatively coarse-grained and is solely under the control of the administrator. If the resource is a Company object then it is possible to specify "secure tasks" that are defined by the programmer.

The security administration tool allows the administrator to aggregate access rights to contain groups of actors or actions.

The concept of a secure task represents a piece of work that needs to be secured for whatever reason. A secure task can be of any length or complexity. It could be a whole application or just the retrieval of a specific attribute in a given object (i.e. executing some `get<>()` method).

In order to define a secure task, you must first create a single persistent instance of the class `SecureTask` shown in Figure 14-26 (this is usually done during installation). This class is defined through the `SecureTask` class `createSecureTask` method and then made persistent in the name server using the `addSecureTask` method. The first method takes, as a parameter, the name and description of the task (the latter is used for display when the administrator manipulates the access rights), and the latter takes the `SecureTask` object returned from the first method along with a relative name for the object. The concatenation of the relative name and the secure task name should form a unique name. The relative name is usually formed as a path name similar to the way Java packages are qualified. Figure 14-27 shows an example illustrating the creation of a secure task for a command and for making it persistent.

Figure 14-26
Class SecureTask

Class com.ibm.sf.gf.SecureTask

public class **SecureTask**
extends Object
implements Serializable

Name	*Signature*	*Description*
ACTOR_USER	`public static final int ACTOR_USER`	Used for setActorType() to indicate that the user must be specifically authorized to this SecureTask.
ACTOR_ANY_USER	`public static final int ACTOR_ANY_USER`	Used for setActorType() to indicate that this SecureTask can be executed for any user. Note: This can only be set for a ServerOnlySecureTask
RESOURCE_COMPANY	`public static final int RESOURCE_COMPANY`	Used for setResourceType() to indicate that this SecureTask requires a Company object to be specified on the beginSecureTask() method and for an AccessRight.
RESOURCE_NONE	`public static final int RESOURCE_NONE`	Used for setResourceType() to indicate that this SecureTask does not require any resource to be specified on the beginSecureTask() method or for an AccessRight.
NAME_SERVER_ PERMISSIONS	`public static final int NAME_SERVER_PERMISSIONS`	
ivActorType	`protected int ivActorType`	The type of Actor that may be authorized to this task. Valid values are ACTOR_USER and ACTOR_NONE.
ivResourceType	`protected int ivResourceType`	The type of resource that may be associated with this task in an AccessRight. Valid values are RESOURCE_COMPANY and RESOURCE_NONE.
ivName	`protected String ivName`	A unique identifier for the task within a naming service context.
ivDescription	`protected String ivDescription`	Detailed description of the task.
ivNameServerPermissions	`protected Vector ivNameServerPermissions`	Vector to hold NameServerPermissions
ivPermissions	`protected UnsynchHashtable ivPermissions[]`	Hashtable to hold Permissions
SecureTask	`public SecureTask()`	Constructor
SecureTask	`public static SecureTask createSecureTask(String name,String description) throws GFException`	Creates a new SecureTask transient object, given its name and description. The Permissions and other optional values may be added to this transient object. After it is completely defined, a persistent object may be created using the addSecureTask() method on the SecurityAPIs interface.
getName	`public String getName() throws GFException`	Returns the name of the secure task. This name is unique within the naming service context in which it exists (or will be created), and is displayed in the list of secure tasks in the security administration utility.

Figure 14-26
(Cont'd)

getDescription	`public String getDescription() throws GFException`	Gets the detailed descriptive information for this task.
setResourceType	`public void setResourceType( int resourceType) throws GFException`	Set the type of resource that may be associated with this task in an AccessRight. The possible values are RESOURCE_COMPANY, indicating the resource must be a Company object, and RESOURCE_NONE indicating no resource is required.
getResourceType	`public int getResourceType() throws GFException`	Gets the type of resource that may be associated with this task in an AccessRight.
getActorType	`public int getActorType() throws GFException`	Gets The type of Actor that may be authorized to this task. In the first release, the only valid values are "User" and "None". The return value is either ACTOR_USER, meaning that the actor must be a User, or ACTOR_ANY_USER, meaning the actor can be any User, who does not have to be explicitely authorized.
toString	`public String toString()`	Generates a string to contain information about this object
setName	`protected void setName(String name) throws GFException`	Set a unique identifier for the task within a naming service context. It may also be displayed on a GUI, in a list format. Therefore, it may be desirable to keep it short. This value is required to be set.
setDescription	`protected void setDescription(String description) throws GFException`	Set detailed descriptive information for this task.

Once the secure task is created, the Access Rights Administration utility can be used to associate it with an actor (i.e. user or user group) and a resource (usually a company), as described in Chapter 35. In your code, whenever a secure task should be performed, the code for the task is surrounded by calls to `beginSecureTask()` and `endSecureTask()`. The first method is called at the beginning of the secure task, and it makes sure that the user has the appropriate access rights. An example showing how this is done is shown in Figure 14-28.

Note that if a new thread is started within the scope of a secure task, the new thread runs under this secure task, regardless of what the original thread does (i.e. it is still considered part of the secure task if the original thread ends the secure task). The task must be explicitly deactivated in both threads in order to be done with.

When creating the `SecureTask`, it is possible to detach this task from any specific resource (e.g. Company). To do that, call the

```
.
.
.
SecureTask mySecureTask = SecureTask.createSecureTask(
        "DoMyCommand",
        "Perform a specific command for demonstration purposes");
Global.security().addSecureTask(
        mySecureTask,
        "COM/MyCompany/MyApplication");
.
.
.
```

Figure 14-27
Code sample: creating a `SecureTask` object.

`setResourceType()` method on the `SecureTask` class and specify `NONE` as the type of `SecureTask`. The default is `COMPANY`.

A special variant of `SecureTask` is `ServerSecureTask`. This means that `beginSecureTask()` can only be called from server code. This is useful when you want to increase the security in your system, and you know that client code is running on machines that cannot be trusted. It also prevents others from activating the secure task by writing a different client program.

The `SecurityAPI` allows you to determine whether a user is authorized to do a secure task without actually activating it. For this purpose you can use the `checkSecureTaskAccess()` method. This can be useful for disabling (or not showing) certain options in menus, based on access permissions.

General Security Guidelines

Cutout 14-1, taken from the SanFrancisco Programmers guide, explains some of the assumptions made for SanFrancisco security along with some guidelines that relate to its use.

```
.
.
.

SecureTask mySecureTask = SecureTask.createSecureTask(
        "DoMyCommand",
        "Perform a specific command for demonstration purposes");
Global.security().addSecureTask(
        mySecureTask,
        "COM/MyCompany/MyApplication");


.
.
.

try {
        MyCommand theCommand;
        Handle theCompany = Global.security().beginSecureTask(
                "DoMyCommand",
                "COM/MyCompany/MyApplication",
                theCompany);

        // Create and initialize the command as needed
          .
          .

        // Run the Command within a transaction. The begin() and
        // commit() are invoked from within the doTransaction() method,

        myCommand.doTransaction();

        Global.security().endSecureTask(
                "DoMyCommand",
                "MyCompany/MyApplication",
                theCompany);
} catch (NotAuthorizedException authex) {
        // Handle the case where the user is not authorized
} catch (SFException sfex) {
        // Handle other exceptions.
}
```

Figure 14-28
Code sample: performing a secure task.

The SanFrancisco authorization is based on the following assumptions:

1. The server is secure. This assumes that the server system security will provide the following support:

- Prevent unauthorized users from using system interfaces (or other non-SanFrancisco interfaces) to access data that make up SanFrancisco and application business objects.
- Prevent unauthorized users from replacing SanFrancisco and application class files.

2. The client is not necessarily secure. If a sophisticated user has a valid SanFrancisco userid, that user can easily write Java code to access a SanFrancisco business object under either of the following conditions:

- There is a `UserAlias` for the object that is generally known.
- A Handle can be obtained to the object through objects that the user is authorized to use.

In order to provide a more secure SanFrancisco application, the following guidelines should be followed:

- Minimize the use of user aliases. This is true not only for objects that contain the data but also for objects containing handles to other objects, such as collections. If a user alias must be used for either of these, do not publish the name. Also, do not make the name so obvious that someone could guess it.
- Use server-only secure tasks (class `ServerOnlySecureTask`) to access the containing collections and possibly the objects themselves. A server-only secure task requires that the `beginSecureTask()` for it be executed on a server. You should also make sure that the corresponding `endSecureTask()` and all of the code between the begin and end secure task methods are executed on the server by default.
- For critical data where access should be limited to a specific set of people, the classes should be defined to allow these objects to be placed in a separate container from other objects so they can be placed in a separate server and server authorization can be used.

Cutout 14-1

General Authorization Guidelines, the IBM SF Programmer's Guide.

CHAPTER 15

SanFrancisco Object Lifecycle

From the moment it is created till the time it is destroyed, a SanFrancisco object goes through several stages (pretty much like any other object in any other system). These stages are related to operations of creation, copying, moving, and deleting objects. We refer to this whole process as "object lifecycle."

Transitions between the stages of the lifecycle of a SanFrancisco object take place through special SanFrancisco mechanisms that ensure that this object will co-exist with the SanFrancisco framework. The class in charge of lifecycle operations, like many other operations, is the `BaseFactory` class, which we have already met before. We will start this chapter by taking a closer look at its lifecycle-related interfaces.

BaseFactory Interface

The `BaseFactory` interface offers several methods for lifecycle support. These methods are provided through the `EntityManagement` and `DependentManagement` interfaces, used for managing the lifecycle of Entities and Dependents, respectively. Figure 15-1 describes the `EntityManagement` interface, and Figure 15-2 describes the `DependentManagement` interface.

The create method calls (such as `createEntity()` and `createDependent()`) within the `BaseFactory` interface use the *classNameToken* to specify which class to create. A *classNameToken* is a symbolic string token that must identify the interface for a concrete Entity, Dependent, or Command class. Usually, this string is the package-qualified interface name. The concrete class associated with the *classNameToken* may change over the time, allowing for class replacement. These tokens are assigned in a special file called *Global.name* or through the configuration utility. They are passed on factory interfaces so that the factory can determine the correct concrete class to use, based on class configuration information. The *classNameToken* can be any string, as long as you provide configuration information for it. Still, the convention of using interface names as *classNameTokens* should be followed, to avoid collisions between class tokens. However, the *classNameToken* can be any arbitrary String if explicit configuration information is provided to map this String to the correct class.

As mentioned in Chapter 13, this approach for allowing class replacement follows the "Abstract Factory" design pattern, which allows exten-

Figure 15-1 Entity Management interface.

Interface com.ibm.sf.gf.EntityManagement

public interface **EntityManagement**
extends AllowR ote

Methods

Name	*Signature*	*Description*
getEntity	`public abstract Entity getEntity( String userAlias, AccessMode accessMode) throws GFException FactoryException, LockingException ConfigurationException, LockUnavailableException`	Gets the Entity associated with the input user alias, using the specified access mode.
getEntity	`public abstract Entity getEntity(Handle handleOfObject, AccessMode accessMode) throws GFException, FactoryException, LockingException, ConfigurationException, LockUnavailableException`	Gets the Entity associated with the input Handle, using the specified access mode. If the provided input Handle is null the factory will a null Entity is returned null Entity.
getArrayOfEntities	`public abstract void getArrayOfEntities( Handle handles[],Object targetArray, AccessMode accessMode) throws GFException, FactoryException, LockingException, ConfigurationException, LockUnavailableException`	Gets an array of Entities referred to by the array of input Handles. The caller must create the array for which the Entity elements to be returned will be assigned into. If the provided input Handle array contains a null element the factory will return a null Entity at the corresponding position in the return targetArray. Other non-null elements will be processed as in the normal case.
deleteEntity	`public abstract void deleteEntity( String userAlias) throws GFException, FactoryException, LockingException, ConfigurationException, ContainerRequestingRollbackException, LockUnavailableException`	Deletes the Entity associated with the specified input user alias.
deleteEntity	`public abstract void deleteEntity( Handle handle) throws GFException, FactoryException, LockingException, ConfigurationException, ContainerRequestingRollbackException, LockUnavailableException`	Deletes the Entity associated with the input Handle. If the passed handle refers to a PersistentEntity then a transaction must be active.

Figure 15-1
(Cont'd)

deleteEntity	`public abstract void deleteEntity( Entity entity) throws GFException, FactoryException, LockingException, ConfigurationException, ContainerRequestingRollbackException, LockUnavailableException`	Deletes the input Entity. A transaction must be active if the handle passed as parameter refers to a PersistEntity.
createEntity	`public abstract Entity createEntity( String classNameToken, AccessMode accessMode, Handle locationHandle, Dependent identifyingKey) throws GFException, ConfigurationException, FactoryException`	Creates and returns a new entity. This method is used for creating entities by class factories for entity. The classNameToken is used to look up the configuration class substitution information. The real class name corresponding to the classNameToken (as defined by Configuration) is instantiated. The returned entity will be accessible in the current transaction as specified in the accessMode argument. If persistent, the entity will in the same container as the entity referenced by the locationHandle. If the locationHandle refers to an ExtentCollection, the new entity is created as an element of that extent. To create an entity in the container specified in the configuration information, rather than in the same container as another object, the locationHandle can be specified as the return value from the getContainer(classNameToken) method on the factory. If locationHandle is null, the entity will be created as a transient object in the local address space of the calling process.
dropAccess	`public abstract void dropAccess( Entity entity) throws GFException`	Drops access to the input Entity in the current transaction. If the specified Entity is not dirty in the current transaction, any locks on it will be released and it will no longer be tracked as accessed in this transaction. If the specified Entity is dirty in the current transaction, the Entities access is not dropped..
changeAccess	`public abstract void changeAccess( Entity entity, AccessMode accessMode) throws GFException`	Attempt to change the accessed lock mode of the input Entity in the current transaction, in order to gain different access mode to the object.
getHandle	`public abstract Handle getHandle( String userAlias) throws GFException`	Gets the Handle of the Entity associated with the input user alias. The userAlias passed must have been previously associated (using addUserAlias) with the entity.

Figure 15-1
(Cont'd)

reinitializeHandle	`public abstract Handle reinitializeHandle( Handle handleNeedingFixup, Handle sourceHandle) throws GFException`	A factory interface to allow an entity to be created with the wrong key in the handle, then fixed up when the right key is known. The sourceHandle is a handle that contains the key value to be copied into the handleNeedingFixup. The handleNeedingFixup is used to identify the entity whose handle needs fixing up. The returned Handle is a copy of the fixed up Handle. This method must only be called within the same transaction that the entity referred to by the handleNeedingFixup is being created. Because this fixup is only done on the entity's own internal handle, and cannot locate any other copies of the handle that may have been made, it is essential that between the time that an entity is created with the "wrong" key and when the handle gets fixed up, the programmer must not propagate or store that handle or copies of that handle, or add the entity to a collection (because that makes a copy of the handle), or call syncEntity on that new entity or commit the transaction the entity was created in (because it would get schema mapped to the wrong row if syncEntity or commit were done).
refreshEntity	`public abstract void refreshEntity( Entity entityToRefresh) throws GFException`	This method is used to replace the current copy with the latest committed changes. The ability for a transaction (different than our own) to make changes while we have access is dependent on our access mode (optimistic vs pessimistic), consequently the results of using refreshEntity also depend on access mode (that is, it is not access-mode neutral)
syncEntity	`public abstract void syncEntity( Entity modifiedEntity) throws GFException`	If the specified entity is marked dirty in this transaction, calling this method during the transaction forces its state to be written to the persistent store, still uncommitted. For entities stored in RDB's this allows referential integrity or other contraints to be checked and exceptions to result now, rather than at commit() time.

Interface com.ibm.sf.gf.DependentManagement

public interface **DependentManagement**
extends AllowRemote

Name	*Signature*	*Description*
createDependent	public abstract Dependent createDependent(Base containingObject, String classNameToken) throws GFException, NamingNameNotFoundException, FactoryParameterRejectedException , FactoryException	Translate the specified classNameToken to a real class, create and return an instance of that class with persistence scoping specified by the containingObject. The containingObject must be a subclass of Entity, Dependent or null. If the containingObject is null, the created Dependent is transient, otherwise the created Dependent has the same scope (persistent or transient) as the containingObject. A NO_LOCK copy of an Entity is considered transient. The containingObject must be local to this JVM.
deleteDependent	public abstract void deleteDependent(Base containingObject, Dependent dependentToDelete) throws GFException, FactoryException, FactoryParameterRejectedException	Delete the specified Dependent object and any subobjects it may contain. If the dependentToDelete is transient or null, no action is performed. If the dependentToDelete is persistent, the destroy() method is called on the dependentToDelete. The containingObject must be a subclass of Entity, Dependent or null, and local to this JVM. If the containingObject is null or transient, the dependentToDelete is considered transient. If the containingObject is persistent, the dependentToDelete is considered persistent.
copyDependent	public abstract Dependent copyDependent(Base containingObject, Dependent dependentToCopy) throws GFException, FactoryParameterRejectedException , FactoryException	Create a copy of the specified Dependent with persistence scoping specified by the containingObject. If the specified Dependent is null, null is returned. The containingObject must be a subclass of Entity, Dependent, or null. If the containingObject is null, a transient copy is returned, otherwise the returned Dependent has the same scope (persistent or transient) as the containingObject. A NO_LOCK copy of an Entity is considered transient. The containingObject must be local to this JVM.

Figure 15-2
`Dependent Management` interface.

sion of the domain business process components by allowing a concrete subclass to be substituted for the default implementation. The client programmer generally does not have to be concerned about these details.

The `BaseFactory` also provides interfaces for String management, through the `StringManagement` interface shown in Figure 15-3. These interfaces are only required for creating persistent Strings that are to be held in Entities. There is no need to use this interface to create String

Interface com.ibm.sf.gf.StringManagement

public interface **StringManagement**
extends AllowRemote

Name	*Signature*	*Description*
deleteString	public abstract void deleteString(Base containingObject, String stringToDelete) throws GFException, FactoryParameterRejectedException	Delete the specified String. If the specified String is transient or null, no action is performed. The containingObject must be a subclass of Entity, Dependent, or null. If the containingObject is null, the specified String is assumed to be transient, otherwise the specified String is assumed to have the same scope (persistent or transient) as the containingObject. A NO_LOCK copy of an Entity is considered transient. The containingObject must be local to this JVM.
copyString	public abstract String copyString(Base containingObject, String stringToCopy) throws GFException, FactoryParameterRejectedException	Create a copy of the specified String at the persistence scope specified by the containingObject. The containingObject must be a subclass of Entity, Dependent, or null. If the containingObject is null, the created String is transient, otherwise the created String has the same scope (persistent or transient) as the containingObject. A NO_LOCK copy of an Entity is considered transient. The containingObject must be local to this JVM.

Figure 15-3
`StringManagement` interface.

objects as transient Strings. Transient Strings can be created by just assigning a String literal to a String variable.

Entity Lifecycle

Entity Creation

Whenever a new business object is created, it should be done using the `BaseFactory` object. The Java `new` operation and class constructors should *never* be explicitly used. Creation is normally done indirectly through a static create method on a class factory associated with the class being instantiated. In all cases, the actual work of creating the business objects is delegated to the `BaseFactory` object. The `BaseFactory` must be involved to locate the right object server process, to register any user alias names, to interact with the correct persistent store, to register the new object in the current transaction, and to perform other functions necessary to the correct operation of the distributed object environment.

The convention in SanFrancisco is that the name of an abstract class factory is the name of the interface to the class being instantiated followed by a "`Factory`" suffix. So, for example, the class factory for `Address` objects is called `AddressFactory`. There are some exceptions in which this convention is not applied, but in these cases too, the `BaseFactory` is being used to actually create the object.

New Entities should be created within a transaction and must be committed before they are guaranteed to exist in a persistent store, and before any other process can access them. Note that a newly created Entity whose transaction failed to commit will disappear once the program terminates.

The static create methods of the class factory delegate the actual creation of an object to the `createEntity()` method of the `BaseFactory`. As mentioned above, the class actually instantiated by the `BaseFactory` might be a subclass of the class whose static `create` method was called, depending on configuration information. As discussed, this allows further modification to the business process components or applications by other developers. However, the programmer using the class is oblivious to this substitution since the substituted class must support all the interface and behavior semantics of the parent class.

The BaseFactory creates Entities using the single method createEntity(). This method is called by the class factory (for example, BusinessPartnerFactory for BusinessPartner objects). The signature of the createEntity() method is shown in Figure 15-1. The first parameter is classNameToken, discussed in the previous section, and it identifies the class. The accessMode parameter specifies the way the new Entity should be accessed; for example, whether access is home or remote (i.e. should methods on the new Entity run locally or remotely). The lock mode portion of the accessMode is irrelevant to the creation methods, as the new object cannot be shared until it has first been committed. In general, client programmers should specify AccessMode.createNormal() when creating a new Entity. The locationHandle argument controls whether the Entity is created as a transient or persistent object. If locationHandle is null, then a transient Entity is created (and in this case, the accessMode parameter is ignored). Otherwise, the new Entity is created in the same persistent store as the one used for the Entity referred to by the locationHandle.

When a persistent Entity is not being created in the same persistent store as another known object, it can be created using a location determined by the global configuration information for the class. A locationHandle for use when calling the createEntity() method can be obtained using the getContainer() and getContainer ByName() methods of the BaseFactory. These are described in Chapter 17.

Entity creation in SanFrancisco also establishes the ownership relationship between objects (the idea of ownership was described in Chapter 10). There are two common variants of Entity ownership: tightly coupled and loosely coupled.

In the tightly coupled case, an Entity subclass and the owning class are designed with knowledge of each other. In this case, the class implementing the owned objects is aware of the method in the owning class that should be used to establish the ownership relationship. The static create<class name>() methods take the owning object as a parameter, and the create method implementation calls the method in the owning class in order to establish the ownership relationship.

The tightly coupled class factory methods are slightly different from the BaseFactory creation method. They include initialization parameters and also simplify specification of locationHandle and location in some cases. There are at least two static creation methods for tightly coupled Entities, and their form is shown in Figure 15-4. In the first method signature, there is no locationHandle specified. The

```
static final <entity subclass name> create<class name>(
   Base owningObject,
   AccessMode access,     // passed to BaseFactory
   <parm1, parm2, ...>)  // initialization values for new entity
   throws SFException;

static final <entity subclass name> create<entity subclass name>(
   Base owningObject,
   AccessMode access,
   Handle locationHandle,
   <parm1, parm2, ...>)
   throws SFException;
```

Figure 15-4
Static creation methods for tightly coupled owned Entities.

`locationHandle` is obtained from the `owningObject`, which is the handle of the `owningObject`. This parameter must be specified; if the `owningObject` is null, an exception occurs. In the second method signature, the `locationHandle` argument is specified, and is passed to the `BaseFactory` `createEntity()` method as it is. If you need to create transient Entities, the second method should be used with a null `locationHandle`.

If the `owningObject` is non-null, both creation methods call the method that establishes ownership. The `locationHandle` and the `owningObject` should be consistent with each other with regard to persistence. In other words, if we are creating a transient object and pass a null `locationHandle`, then the `owningObject` should be transient.

The Room class in the "House of Rooms" sample program is an example of a tightly coupled Entity subclass, which is always owned by a House object.

In the loosely coupled case, an Entity subclass is implemented independently of any specific object that might own its instances. In this case, there is only one static `create` method, as shown in Figure 15-5. Note

```
static final <entity subclass name> create<entity subclass name>(
   AccessMode requestedAccess,
   Handle locationHandle,
   <other parameters>)
   throws SFException;
```

Figure 15-5
Static creation methods for loosely coupled owned Entities.

how this creation method does not have an owningObject argument and, therefore, uses the locationHandle argument to determine where to locate a persistent object. This argument is passed on to the BaseFactory createEntity() method without change. To create a transient Entity, the locationHandle should be set to null. Also, you must explicitly establish ownership using the addOwned<>() or setOwned()<> method on the desired owning object (this also means you should take care of any exceptions thrown from these methods). These methods are used for establishing ownership of objects owning collections and single Entities, respectively. The form of these methods is shown in Figure 15-6, along with the form for the two other methods that can be used for objects owning collections of specific kinds.

Deleting Entity Objects

Similar to object creation, object destruction is performed using the BaseFactory object. You must never use the Java delete operation. You delete owned persistent objects by using methods on the owning object. These methods on the owning objects call a BaseFactory delete...() method to actually destroy the owned object. You delete non-owned Entities by directly calling a deleteEntity() method on the BaseFactory. Deleting a business object deletes any objects owned by that object, and causes the object's destroy() method to be called by the Foundation. If any exceptions are thrown from the destroy() method during deletion of a persistent object, the BaseFactory catches them and marks the transaction as rollbackOnly(). This protects the

```
public void addOwned<Element name>(<element class> elementToAdd) throws
GFException;
   // for sets and lists

public void insertOwned<Element name>At(elementToAdd, Iterator
position) throws GFException;
   // for lists

public void addOwned<Element name>By(elementToAdd, <key class> key)
throws GFException;
   // for maps
```

Figure 15-6
Methods for establishing ownership for loosely coupled owned Entities.

application from committing an inconsistent state, which might result from a destroy operation trying to delete several owned objects where some of the deletes failed. This marking is inapplicable if the `destroy()` method to throw the exception was invoked on a transient object or a NO_LOCK copy, because these are non-transactional.

You delete transient Entities by using the same interfaces as for persistent objects. As already discussed (see Chapter 10), persistent objects must be explicitly deleted, since the garbage collection process does not cover persistent objects. Transient objects are garbage collected when there are no longer any references to them.

Client programmers can delete non-owned Entities by using the `deleteEntity()` methods on the `BaseFactory`. For owned Entities, there is a different treatment. These should be deleted using methods on their owning object. You can either use the `SetOwned<>()` method described above with a null parameter or the `removeOwned<>()` method to delete an owned object. The different forms of `removeOwned<>()` are shown in Figure 15-7.

If you don't want to delete an owned Entity, but just remove it from containment in another object, then you can use the `oprhanOwned...()` method of the containing object, which is of the form shown in Figure 15-8. These methods are not always available in each owning class. The last two methods usually provide better performance than the first two ones because they specify information that can be used for locating the Entity.

Note that there is no automatic mechanism to prevent inappropriate deletion of persistent Entity, even though other persistent objects still contain Handles referring to it. In this respect, programming that

```
public void removeOwned<name>(Entity entityToDelete) throws
GFException;

public void removeOwned<name>At(Iterator positionOfEntityToDelete)
throws GFException;

public void removeOwned<name>By(Object keyOfEntityToDelete) throws
GFException;

public void removeAllOwned<name>s() throws GFException;
```

Figure 15-7
Methods for removing owned Entities.

```
public void orphanOwned<name>() throws GFException;
public void orphanOwned<name>(
   Entity entityToRemove) throws GFException;
public void orphanOwned<name>At(
   Iterator positionOfEntityToRemove) throws GFException;
public void orphanOwned<name>By(
   Object keyOfEntityToRemove) throws GFException;
```

Figure 15-8
Methods for removing ownership for owned Entities.

involves persistent objects is more like C++ than Java. You cannot rely on the garbage collector and forget about proper memory management. Therefore, it is important to always use the proper interfaces for deleting objects. It is up to the class developer to design the class in a manner that rejects a request to delete an object that is in use. Obviously, there are other behaviors that can be implemented in such cases, such as automatic updates to the referencing objects, or referencing objects that are tolerant to having the object deleted.

The `BaseFactory` `deleteEntity()` methods take a single argument that specifies the Entity to be deleted. The Entity is represented by the object itself, the object Handle, or a user alias name. The `BaseFactory` `deleteEntity()` methods signatures are shown in Figure 15-1.

The `deleteEntity()` method using a Handle or alias does not require you to have acquired access to the target Entity, and a deletion of the real object will take place even if you have only a NO_LOCK copy of this Entity. To make things more confusing, a call to `deleteEntity()` method using a *reference* to the NO_LOCK copy deletes just the NO_LOCK copy rather than the real object. To improve performance by freeing up memory, delete should even be called on transient Entity objects when they are no longer needed.

When an object has a different way for creation other than through a class factory, it would have a special deleting method as well. You should remember to use this method when creating objects using a special creation method.

Entity Access

Entities do not exist in the memory address space of the server or any client until they are explicitly required for. To activate persistent Entity objects, client programs must call "get" methods in *each* transaction in which the Entities are needed. Entities may be concurrently used by multiple client programs. For this purpose, the SanFrancisco Foundation introduces locks, which can be used for object access.

The `BaseFactory` is used to access instances of subclasses descended from Entity, including Entity collections. These can be requested either by their unique Handle or by a user alias if they have one. In addition to providing the Handle (or user alias) of the Entity to be located and accessed, the caller passes an `AccessMode` object that determines lock type and other access characteristics. `AccessMode` objects have been already described in the previous chapter.

In some cases, a business object is being accessed through a containing object, without having a specific Handle or user alias. The contained object in this case is part of, or has a relationship to, the containing object. For example, in the "House of rooms" sample problem, a House object contains an Architect object. In this case, as in other similar cases, the containing object supports a `get()` method for accessing the contained object. The `get()` methods takes no arguments, and has a return type of the object being accessed.

Unlike the `BaseFactory` access methods, standard `get<>()` methods that access contained Entities do not take an `AccessMode` argument. Instead, the contained Entities are accessed using `createNormal()` access, which by default uses CONTAINER compatibility mode to ensure that the contained object is accessed in the same location (or with NO_LOCK) as the containing object. In addition to the standard `get<>()` methods, some classes have overloaded `get<>()` methods with an extra parameter for specifying the desired access mode.

You can change the access mode of a persistent `Entity` (within some limits based on your existing access), by calling the `changeAccess()` method on the `BaseFactory`. The most common reason to call `changeAccess()` is that write access is needed and you want to ensure that it is successfully acquired explicitly in advance rather than waiting for the first call to `setDirty()` to implicitly attempt it. Another reason to use `changeAccessMode()` is that frequently the method or routine that needs write access does not know what the current `AccessMode` is.

Updating Entity Objects

In order to modify an Entity, you first have to access it, i.e. obtain a reference to the Entity object. Using this reference you can then call methods that perform the desired modification. If the Entity is persistent and the Entity is not accessed with `NO_LOCK`, then, pretty much like with any Java object, changes made to the Entity are immediately effective for any other Java reference to that Entity in the same transaction. However, other transactions will see these changes only once the changes are committed. If for some reason the transaction is rolled back or the commit fails, the changes are lost.

When accessing an Entity that is contained in another object the `get...()` method returns a Java reference to the contained Entity. Therefore, modifications to that Entity are immediately visible to the containing object and, specifically, there is no need to call a `set...()` method to "put back" the modified object. Actually, you should avoid doing that because a `set<name>(entity)` method is used to initially set an `Entity` that is contained in another object, and you are not really changing the contained `Entity`. If it is not mandatory for the attribute to always be set to a non-null value, `set<name>(null)` can be used to remove an Entity from a containing object without setting a new one. As discussed above, when the containing object owns an Entity, rather than just containing a reference to it, the set method will have the name `setOwned<name>()`.

Note that instance variables of a business object must never be accessed directly by any other object, even another object of the same class. Instead, an accessor `get...()` method must be used. This is essential for the SanFrancisco distributed object model. If you don't follow these rules, some weird things can happen, depending on how objects are distributed.

Entity Update Using Commands

Commands can be used to perform updates on objects in a way that allows for remote execution, logging, or undoing changes.

After the `Command` is properly initialized, the `doAll()` or `doTransaction()` method is called on the `Command`. This causes the `Command` to execute whatever actions it encapsulates. Use `doTransaction()` if the `Command` should execute as an atomic transaction. You should use `doAll()` if the `Command` is part of a larger transaction scope. It is not possible to `undo()` or `redo()` a Command executed with `doTransaction()`, or other commands that represent complex operations. All Commands provide a `supportsUndo()` method that returns true if the `Command` is undoable.

After calling `doAll()` on a `Command` it is in the "DONE" state, and it is not allowed to call `doAll()` on that Command again (unless you reset it).

Using an Entity after Access

When a certain piece of code accesses a persistent Entity, it holds a (transient) Java reference to the object. This reference can be used within the scope of the current transaction. In other words, after the transaction performs either `commit()` or `rollback()`, the reference is invalid, and another `get()` operation must be performed to get a valid Java object reference in a new transaction.

If a method continues processing after a `commit()` or `rollback()` with the invalid Java object reference (Object) variable still in scope (that is, accessible), then these references would be better off being set to "null" before continuing execution, in order to ensure that an exception is thrown if the reference to the unlocked Entity is used. It is recommended to correlate transaction scope to Java block scopes (i.e. surround transaction code with braces), in order to avoid such problems altogether.

As usual, NO_LOCK access is an exception to this rule, and a NO_LOCK copy may be used without any regard to transaction scope.

Dependent Lifecycle

Creating Dependent Objects

Dependent objects exist either as transient objects or as persistent objects that are contained in an Entity. In other words, persistent instances of Dependent subclasses are always part of and owned by some containing Entity, as they are not persistent or sharable by themselves. Because they are usually part of a larger object, Dependent objects are usually passed around by copying rather than by reference, in a manner resembling non-object primitive data types.

Client programmers always work with transient Dependent objects. Only business object developers manipulate contained objects, which are persistent or transient according to the Entity in which they are contained.

Similar to Entity objects, Dependent subclasses usually have a factory class (named `<class-name>Factory`). In some cases there are special create methods that reside in a related business object. Figure 15-9 shows the form of the static method supplied by the class factory associated with any Dependent concrete subclass for creating a transient object.

Note that the static `create<class name>()` method delegates the actual creation of an object to the `createDependent()` `BaseFactory` method. Similar to Entities, class replacement can take place, depending on configuration information.

Copying Dependent Objects

A new Dependent object can also be created by copying an existing object using the `copyDependent` method defined in the `DependentManagement` interface (see Figure 15-2). A "null" object should be passed as the `containingObject` argument, indicating that the Dependent object is not contained and should be transient. The new transient Dependent object can then be used as temporary information. Usually it is later passed on to an Entity to set the value of the corresponding contained Dependent object.

```
static final <class name> create<class name>(
   <parameters>) throws SFException
```

Figure 15-9
Static creation method for dependent objects.

Deleting Dependent Objects

No delete method is required for transient Dependent objects, because they are deleted automatically by the Java garbage collector.

Command Lifecycle

Creating Command Objects

Command objects are also Dependent objects, as Command inherits from Dependent. Like all other Dependents, Commands can be streamed or contained in another Entity or Dependent, and this capability is used by the business process components to facilitate logging of actions and undo/redo of Commands. Client code can create a Command in order to perform an action on a target object and possibly additional objects. The Command accesses the target and any other business objects as necessary to perform the action it represents.

Like most Dependent objects, a Command object is created using a class factory associated with the class being instantiated. This Command class factory, as with other Dependents, delegates the actual creation of the new Command instance to the `BaseFactory createDependent()` method.

Specifying Where a Command Should Run

Static create methods on Command factories allow you to specify where the Command will be executed. This way you can execute the Command where the objects used by the Command object are located, and get better performance. Simply specify an appropriate target object (on which the Command operates) or `locationHandle` when creating the Command. A "null" `locationHandle` (or usage of a create method that does not have a `locationHandle` parameter) causes the Command to be executed in the local address space of the calling thread. When a target is specified by its Handle and no separate `locationHandle` is specified, the target handle is used as the `locationHandle`. This means that the Command executes in the server process of the target, unless the target Entity is already accessed locally (in which case the Command will execute locally). This is usually the most efficient location for executing a Command because the Command is executing in the same location as the target object. Note that if both a target and a `locationHandle` are specified, the `locationHandle` is used to determine where the Command will execute.

The `handleDo()` method is the method that actually performs the operation of the commands, and it is called as a result of calling the `doAll()` or `doTransaction()` method on the Command. This `handleDo()` method is executed at the specified location. In addition, other methods such as `handleUndo()` and `handleRedo()` are also executed at the specified location, if called. If the `returnCommand` argument is "true," then when the remotely executed method finishes, the state of the remote Command is copied back into the local Command object. Normally a client programmer does not specify the `returnCommand` argument, but takes the default supplied by the specific Command subclass.

Client programmers create Commands using the class factory associated with the desired Command subclass. As described above for other Dependents, this class factory class has the same name as the Command interface with "Factory" as a suffix. The static create methods for a Command all take at least one initialization parameter that is the main target object for the Command, which could be either an Entity or a Dependent.

The `create` methods of a class factory for any Command are of the form shown in Figure 15-10.

Reusing Command Objects

Commands that are already executed (using the `doAll()` or `doTransaction()` methods) can usually be used again by first calling the `reset()` method on the command object. This is useful in case you activate several commands having similar attributes, and you wish to avoid creating different instances for each. The `reset()` method has no parameters. The `reset()` method calls `handleReset()`, which the Command class can override to perform other actions when a command is reset, or can even prevent reset of the command by throwing the `SFCommandResetNotAllowed` exception. If `handleReset()` throws this or any other exception, `reset()` just returns that exception without

```
static final <class name> create<class name>(
   Base target, <parm1, ...>) throws SFException;
   // run command locally

and if the target inherits from Dependent:
static final <class name> createContained<class name>(
   Base containingObject, Handle locationHandle, boolean returnCommand,
   Base target, <parm1, ..>) throws SFException;

and if the target inherits from Entity:
static final <class name> create<class name>(
   Handle handleOfTarget, <parm1,...>);
   // run in target server process, no return

static final <class name> createContained<class name>(
   Base containingObject, Handle locationHandle, boolean returnCommand,
   Handle handleOfTarget, <parm1, ..>) throws SFException;
```

Figure 15-10
Static creation methods for command objects.

changing the state of the command. Otherwise, `reset()` changes the state of the command to the NEW state, which is the same state as when a command is first created, except that instance variables such as the target of the command or variables introduced by subclasses are not modified by `reset()`. The default implementation of `handleReset()` does nothing.

The `reset()` method can be called regardless of the current state of the command. If the command is already in the NEW state, `reset()` has no effect, regardless of whether `handleReset()` throws an exception. If the command is in the DONE or UNDONE state, `reset()` makes it possible to call `doAll()` or `doTransaction()` method on the command, but impossible to `undo()` or `redo()` an operation that happened before `reset()` was called.

Once you call `reset()`, you would usually use other methods on the command object to change its target object and/or the instance data before executing the command.

Copying and Deleting Command Objects

Commands are copied and deleted just like any other Dependent object, as previously discussed.

Collection Lifecycle

Creating Collections

SanFrancisco business object collections are implemented as concrete classes. These concrete collections inherit from either `Entity` or `Dependent`. Subclassing is not supported for the concrete collection classes provided with SanFrancisco. The different types of collection interfaces provided in the Foundation Layer are described in Chapter 11.

The static create methods for Entity collections take the `locationHandle` and access arguments in the same way all Entity object creation methods do. Both Entity and Dependent collections also take an additional `elementClassName`, which must be a full name of an interface (i.e. package-qualified) that all the elements in the collection will support. This interface is needed to determine what elements can be added to the collection and, more importantly, what methods can be used when querying elements contained in the collection (this is possible only for `Entity` collections). All collections, except `EntityOwning<>`, are able to hold a mixture of Entities and Dependent, as long as each single element held in the collection conforms to the interface specified during the creation of the collections.

All the elements of a collection must be instances of a subclass of `Base` (from which `Entity`, `Dependents`, and `Command` are all derived). As described in Chapter 11, Dependent wrapper classes are provided for each of the Java primitive types, corresponding to the Java object wrappers, so that these can be used in persistent collections. The static creation methods for Entity containers are of the form shown in Figure 15-11. The class factory methods create empty collections. A new transient collection holding a certain set of elements from a given collection can be generated using the query mechanism, as described in Chapter 19.

The signatures used for the static creation methods of a Dependent collections is shown in Figure 15-12.

```
static final <collection-type> create<collection-type>(Handle
locationHandle, AccessMode access,
   String elementClassName) throws GFException;
```

Figure 15-11
Static creation methods for entity containers.

Deleting Collections

Collections should be deleted in accordance to their type. In other words, depending on whether they are Dependents or Entities. Transient collections are automatically deleted by the Java garbage collector. For this reason and others, transient collections can have persistent Entities as elements, but should not own these elements.

Copying Collections

In order to copy Dependent collections (e.g. `DSet`, `DList`) use the `BaseFactory copyDependent()` method, just like any other collection. An attempt to copy a Dependent collection that owns Entities will cause an exception.

To make a copy of an Entity collection (e.g. `Set`, `EntityOwningSet`) you must first create a new empty collection and then copy the elements. This can be done either by iterating over the collection, adding each of the Entity elements to the new collection, or by using the `addAllElements()` method.

```
static final D<collection-type> createD<collection-type>(String
elementClassName) throws GFException;

static final D<collection-type> createContainedD<collection-type>(Base
containingObject,
   String elementClassName) throws GFException;
```

Figure 15-12
Static creation method for dependent containers.

Special care should be exercised not to copy an owned Entity into an owning collection, since an Entity must not have more than one owner.

Accessing Contained Objects

SanFrancisco collections support accessing elements through an iterator. Furthermore, some of the collections also support accessing an element by an associated key. The iterator element access style supports an iterator that can be incrementally positioned at each consecutive element in the collection. The containing business object supports an operation to create the iterator over the elements in the collection. Using the iterator, the individual elements of the collection can be accessed.

The iterator `getNext<>()` method advances it to the next element and returns that element. In some cases, the containing business object also supports a `getPrevious<>()` method for moving the iterator to the previous element and returning that element. There is also an operation for getting the element at the current iterator position without incrementing the iterator, and a method to see if a collection contains a specific element. By convention, methods that create iterators and access elements are of the form shown in Figure 15-13.

In order to iterate over the elements of the collection, an Iterator object is used. The Iterator interface is shown in Figure 15-14. You can acquire an iterator for a collection using the `createIterator()` method on the collection. There are two ways to use the Iterator to iterate over the collection: passing the Iterator as a parameter to iteration methods sup-

```
public Iterator create<Name>Iterator() throws GFException;

public <element class> getNext<Name>(Iterator position) throws
GFException;

public <element class> get<Name>At(Iterator position) throws
GFException;

public boolean contains<Name>(<element class> element) throws
GFException;
```

Figure 15-13
Static creation methods for iterators.

Interface com.ibm.sf.gf.Iterator

public interface **Iterator**
extends GFRemote

Name	Signature	Description
reset	`public abstract void reset() throws GFException`	Positions the iterator before the first element of the collection. Sets the iterator to a valid state if it is currently not valid.
more	`public abstract boolean more() throws GFException`	A predicate returning true if more elements exist that can be iterated over. That means a subsequent call to "next()" or "nextElement()" will be successful. If this method returns false, then the iteration loop is complete.
next	`public abstract Object next() throws GFException`	Advances the iterator to the element after the current element, then returns the new current element. This method returns null if it failed because the iterator is currently on the last element, and for other failures it throws an exception.
hasMoreElements	`public abstract boolean hasMoreElements() throws GFException`	Same as more().
nextElement	`public abstract Object nextElement() throws GFException`	Same as next().
resetBefore	`public abstract void resetBefore() throws GFException`	Same as reset()
positionOn	`public abstract void positionOn( Object elementToPositionOn) throws GFException`	Positions the iterator to the location of the element passed as parameter.
setAccessMode	`public abstract void setAccessMode( AccessMode am)`	Sets optional user-specified AccessMode used when Entity elements are accessed using this iterator. Normally, the AccessMode used when accessing the Entity elements in a collection is the same one that was used to access the Entity collection (or the Entity owner of a Dependent collection). Specifically, the elementLock, elementLocation, and elementCompatibility fields of the AccessMode used to access the collection are used to determine how the Entity elements of the collecion are accessed. If you wish to use different lock/location/compatibility values, then this "setAccessMode" method may be used. If this method is not used, the Entity elements are accessed based upon the collection's AccessMode, as described above.
current	`public abstract Object current() throws GFException`	Returns the element of the collection at the current iterator position. If this method is called on an Iterator that has just been passed to "removeElementAt" and that Iterator has not yet been moved to a valid position, then an exception will be thrown if current() is called on that Iterator. To avoid that, you need to move the Iterator to a valid position after using it as the parameter by using one of the following methods: Iterator methods: next(), nextElement(), reset(), resetBefore(), positionOn().

Figure 15-14
Iterator interface.

ported by the collection, or calling iteration methods on the Iterator itself. The methods on the Iterator are quite primitive because they are compatible with all the collections types. For specific kinds of collections such as Lists, additional methods such as `getPrevious<>()` are supported. Each individual Collection class supports its own variety of specialized iteration methods. When using Iterator methods with Entity collections, a substantial increase in performance may result. If your code is structured such that you have to call `getEntity()` each time, just to get a reference to the collections, it will perform worse than using the iteration methods on the iterator.

SanFrancisco provides another way to access collection elements, using a unique key for each element. This method is only supported for some of the collections. A key for a `Map` type of collection must be assigned when the element is added to the collection, and this key is fixed and cannot be changed. Keys for `Map` collections can be of type `String` or `Base`. For `Extent` collections, key must be of type `DMethodAccessKey`. Client code creates key objects just like it creates any other object (i.e. Strings are created as usual, and Base objects using the respective class factory).

The `get...()` retrieval methods of Map and Extent collections takes as argument a key value, and returns an element that has the same key (to be exact, equal key) associated with it. As shown in Figure 15-15, keyed collections support methods to check whether a key corresponds to any element in the collection, and to get the key associated with an element. A business object that contains keyed collections of objects provides interfaces to such methods (as users of the objects cannot access its internals). Such methods follow the form shown in Figure 15-16.

```
public <element class> get<Name>By(<key class> key) throws GFException;
// e.g., Address getContractorBy(String key)

public boolean contains<Name>Key(<key class> key) throws GFException;
// e.g., boolean containsContractorKey(String key);

public Object get<Name>KeyAt(Iterator position) throws GFException;

public Object get<Name>Key(Object element) throws GFException;
```

Figure 15-15
Keyed collection interface.

```
public <element class> get<Name>By(<key class> key) throws GFException;

public boolean contains<Name>Key(<key class> key) throws GFException;

public Object get<Name>KeyAt(Iterator position) throws GFException;

public Object get<Name>Key(Object element) throws GFException;
```

Figure 15-16
Methods for keyed collection accesses.

Additional methods are provided for checking if the collection is empty and for determining how many elements are in the collection, as shown in Figure 15-17.

Interface com.ibm.sf.gf.CommonKeyedCollection

public interface **CommonKeyedCollection**
extends AllowRemote

Methods

Name	*Signature*	*Description*
ContainsKey	`public abstract boolean containsKey(Object key) throws GFException`	Indicates whether an element with the specified key is a member of this collection
getElementBy	`public abstract Object getElementBy(Object key) throws GFException`	Returns an element in this collection associated with the key, or null if no element matches this key.
	`public abstract Object getElementBy(Object key, AccessMode am) throws GFException`	Returns an element in this collection associated with the key, using specified AccessMode if element is an Entity, or null if no element matches this key.
getElementKey	`public abstract Object getElementKey(Object element) throws GFException`	Returns Key object for "element", or throws GFException if element not found.
GetKeyAt	`public abstract Object getKeyAt(Iterator position) throws GFException`	Returns the key of object at "position"
getCardinality	`public abstract long getCardinality()`	Returns number of elements in collection.

Figure 15-17
Generic collection interface

CHAPTER 16

The SanFrancisco Transaction Model

Locking and Commit Control

In previous chapters we have outlined the different types of locking mechanism available for persistent SanFrancisco object.

- NO_LOCK. Access the object without any locking
- OPTIMISTIC. Traditional optimistic locking
- OPTIMISTIC_CLEAN. Non-traditional optimistic locking
- READ. Pessimistic read lock
- WRITE. Pessimistic write lock

In a transaction, when you need access to an object, you should consider the benefits and drawbacks of each of the approaches. The Pessimistic approach is the most intuitive, easiest to implement, and best performing. In addition, it allows you to completely ignore the issue of concurrency since there cannot be concurrent writers. On the downside, in this approach you might keep locks on objects for a long time, or if you don't then the object might change during the time your are working on it. The Optimistic approach enables concurrent access (by the locking transaction as well as others) to the object. The system automatically detects whether concurrent writing by other transactions has invalidated your own operations. These nice features of Optimistic locking have disadvantages. The optimistic approach may not be suitable because of the additional overhead of making the copies of objects required, and also because of the performance penalty and other problems with the risk of commit failure (such systems sometimes cause user frustration because an error is raised only after much data entry has been performed—and in some cases the fact that a commit will fail may be known before data entry begins). The NO_LOCK mode really lets you forget about concurrency, and you can access objects without any concerns, but then it does have an extra overhead for making copies. If you want to record any changes you made to the object, then you are in trouble because you would need to obtain a write lock, and the system does not automatically check for changes made by other transactions.

Defining Transaction Scope

Transaction scope is defined by the client code. The scope can be defined implicitly through the use of commands, or explicitly using the transaction management interface of the `BaseFactory`.

Commands can be executed either as independent transactions or as part of a larger transaction. Commands can be designed to execute a series of other commands. When a command is used to define a transaction, it handles calling the individual transaction management commands, such as `begin()` and `commit()`, and also handles any automatic recovery or `rollback()` in the case of failures.

To execute a command atomically, as a complete transaction, use the command's `doTransaction()` method. To execute a command as part of a larger transaction use the command's `doAll()` method. Figure 16-1 shows an example, based on the "House of Rooms" sample program, of how a command is used to define scope transaction.

The `BaseFactory` inherits interfaces for transaction management from `TransactionManagement`, the latter provides several methods that can be used for defining transaction scope independently of commands, as shown in Figure 16-2. These methods should be called on the `BaseFactory` object accessible with the `Global.factory()` call. Client code must initiate a transaction by using the `BaseFactory .begin()` method before accessing any persistent SanFrancisco object; otherwise, inconsistent object state may be read, changes to business objects will be lost, and other nasty side-effects might occur. An exception is that `NO_LOCK` allows object "copies" to be manipulated outside of any transaction scope. When the `BaseFactory.commit()` method is invoked, a traditional commit protocol takes place, and what it does is either update all the objects and their images in the persistent storage or invoke recovery procedures. Note that the interface does not support nesting of `begin()` calls.

At any point in the transaction, `rollback()` can be called to undo all the actions performed by the transactions. Specifically, `rollback()` releases all the locks on the objects accessed so far during the transaction, and for each of these objects it restores its state at the time of the `begin()` call. A `rollback()` ends the current transaction, so any access to business objects must be preceded by yet another call to `begin()`. You should call `rollback()` if any method executed in the transaction raises a SanFrancisco exception for which there is no recovery. Objects that were created in a transaction that is rolled back will not persist, but

```
Global.factory().begin();   // start a transaction
try
{
      RoomSizeAdjustCmd myCommand;

      // get handle for house
      houseHandle = ...

      // get the house object
      House house = (House)Global.factory().getEntity(
            houseHandle, AccessMode.createPlusWrite());

      // create a command that will run in the server process
      // of the house object, and reduce room sizes by 25% each
      RoomSizeAdjustCmd myCommand =
            RoomSizeAdjustCmdFactory.createRoomSizeAdjustCmd(
                  houseHandle, -25);

      // execute the command
      myCommand.doAll();

      Global.factory().commit();  // commit transaction
}
catch (SFException ex)
{
   ...
}
```

Figure 16-1
Example: defining transaction scope using command.

their `destroy()` methods will not be called (instead, they will simply be garbage collected).

The `rollbackOnly()` method marks the transaction as requiring a `rollback()`. If `commit()` is called on the transaction, the commit fails and the transaction is aborted. This is useful when a situation occurs where the current transaction should be rolled-back, and you want to make sure an invalid state is not committed, but your code is not the one initiating the transaction. So, in addition to throwing an exception you can call the `rollbackOnly()` method. This way you give the code initiating the transaction a chance to record information about the changes that took place in this transaction—in case it would like to take a shot at recovering the transaction (that's not too realistic, but still possible).

`BaseFactory` also provides `suspend()` and `resume()` methods that allow the currently active transaction of a thread to be temporarily sus-

Figure 16-2
Interface to `TransactionManagement`

Interface com.ibm.sf.gf.TransactionManagement

public interface **TransactionManagement**
extends AllowRemote

Methods

Name	*Signature*	*Description*
begin	`public abstract void begin() throws SmWorkAreaNotActiveException, GFException`	Begin a new transaction.
commit	`public abstract void commit() throws DataStoreException, TransactionException, GFException`	Commit the current transaction.
rollback	`public abstract void rollback() throws DataStoreException, TransactionException, GFException`	Rollback the current transaction.
rollbackOnly	`public abstract void rollbackOnly() throws TransactionException, GFException`	Mark current transaction as "rollback-only", which means it cannot be committed. If and when `commit()` is called, the transaction is forced to rollback.
getTransactionStatus	`public abstract int getTransactionStatus() throws TransactionException, GFException`	Indicate the status of the current transaction. Return values that represent the transaction status may be used by the application to attempt recovery from failure.

pended. The suspended transaction can be resumed in the same thread or in a different thread. Just like `begin()`, the `resume()` must not be called from within a transaction. The `suspend()` and `resume()` methods are useful in user interface programming where a transaction needs to come to terms with the pace of user interaction. So, the transaction can be suspended while waiting for user input, and later on resume once some user interface event is received. These interfaces are inherited from `SmDistributedProcessManagement`.

The example in Figure 16-3 uses the `BaseFactory` to manage a transaction that includes modifying the owner of a House object, of the kind used in the "House of Rooms" sample program. In the current example, the command is not run as a transaction because some additional modifications to the house are part of the transaction. This example demonstrates proper use of `begin()`, `commit()`, and `rollback()`. Notice how statements within a transaction belong to a single block (i.e. they are surrounded by braces). This allows the system to provide more efficient garbage collection, and business object references are properly invalidated so that they cannot be re-accessed after the `commit()` statement without starting a new transaction. Also notice that the transaction block scope is a try block. This is useful because if a SanFrancisco exception occurs in a transaction, the transaction must be terminated using a `rollback()` operation in order to properly clean up the transaction. If you fail to do that, then the next time you start a new transaction, a `SubtransactionException` will be raised.

```
Global.factory().begin();    // start a transaction
try
{
Handle houseHandle = …

// get the house object
House house = (House)Global.factory().getEntity(
   houseHandle, AccessMode.createPlusWrite());

// change house owner
house.setOwner("Mr. H. Owner");

Global.factory().commit();  // commit transaction
}
catch (SFException sfex)
{
   ...
}
```

Figure 16-3
Example: defining transaction scope using `BaseFactory` methods.

Recovering From Transaction Failures

As shown in Figure 16-2, the `BaseFactory` provides the `getTransactionStatus()` method, which can be used whenever the catch block of a `commit()` or `rollback()` operation needs to check the status of a transaction. This status information, along with the exception data, can be used to determine what recovery (if any) is possible. This decision is highly dependent on the specifics of the transaction.

This method returns an integer with one of the Status enumerated values as follows.

- NO_TRANSACTION. Transaction has completed. A heuristic exception may require the database to be re-synchronized manually. You may need to terminate the application. NO_TRANSACTION means there is no active transaction in the current thread. Once a thread is in a NO_TRANSACTION state, the following transaction operations are allowed: `begin()`, `getTransactionStatus()`, `resume()`.
- ACTIVE. Transaction is still active in the current thread, and you may perform the following transaction operations: `begin()` `commit()` `rollback()`, `rollbackOnly()`. If a lock timeout exception occurred, you may want to wait and retry `commit()`. If an optimistic time stamp conflict exception occurred, it is not possible to recover the current transaction. The only thing you can do in this case is try to save information about changes that you were attempting to make in this transaction before doing rollback() and beginning a new transaction to retry your changes. You may also be able to recover from other exceptions.
- MARKED_ROLLBACK_ONLY. The transaction is still current but is marked as Rollback only. Only the following transaction operations are allowed: `rollback()`, `getTransactionStatus()`. If you try to use `suspend()` operation, then `InActiveException` is raised, and a `commit()` will cause a `rollback()` with a `TransactionRolledBack` exception.
- UNKNOWN. The transaction is in an unknown state. None of the transaction operations are allowed. If this status is returned, the

trace log should be examined. Most likely, the database is not in sync and should be fixed manually.

- There are other Internal statuses, which are not visible to client programmers, but only to the Foundation, so we will just mention their names: PREPARED, PREPARING, COMMITTED, COMITTING, ROLLED_BACK, RESYNCH_IN_PROGRESS.

NO_LOCK Access

When accessing a persistent object using the NO_LOCK mode, you actually can work outside of the SanFrancisco transactional model, and this access mode is an exception to many SanFrancisco rules. This section tries to summarize the consequences of using the NO_LOCK mode.

Once you request access to an object using NO_LOCK, you typically get a copy of the actual persistent object (there are some exceptions, such as `EntityOwningExtent` objects). Any changes on this copy will not be reflected back on the original object, even when using any accessor methods (that is, `get<>()` methods) without being in a transaction. As discussed previously, you will not be synchronized with any updates of the object made by other transactions running concurrently.

Any object that is intended to be accessed in the NO_LOCK mode and contains other entities, must use the CONTAINER compatibility mode and `getObjectFromHandle()` when accessing the contained Entities. In other words, when an Entity is accessed NO_LOCK, if this Entity accesses contained Entities, they are also accessed NO_LOCK. This is true regardless of what lock state was requested or what lock state is currently held on those contained Entities, as long as the access is made through calls to `getObjectFromHandle()` for the contained object and the access mode is such that it specifies CONTAINER compatibility mode.

In contrast, if you have a NO_LOCK copy of an Entity and in the same scope you call `getEntity()` to access an `Entity` using the `Handle` returned from `getHandle()` on a copy you have, the access obtained will be based on the access mode you actually requested. So NO_LOCK access will be also used for the copy you already have if you asked for NO_LOCK access, or you will obtain access to the real object if you made a different request. To summarize, you can use the `Handle` obtained from a NO_LOCK copy of an object using its `getHandle()` method to

```
{

   Handle houseHandle = …

   // get a NO_LOCK copy of a House
   House houseCopy = (House)Global.factory().getEntity(
      houseHandle, AccessMode.createNoLock());

   // let user update the house owner, wait for "OK" to be
pressed
   .
   .
   .
   // user pressed the "OK" button,
   // take modification from the houseCopy commit it
   Global.factory().begin();      // start a transaction
   try
   {
      // get the house object using the handle, with write access
      House house = (Address)Global.factory().getEntity(
         houseHandle, AccessMode.createPlusWrite());

      // copy modified values from houseCopy to actual house
object
      house.setOwner(houseCopy.getOwner());

      Global.factory().commit();    // commit changes made in this
transaction
   }
   catch (SFException ex)
   {
      ...
      }
      throw ex;
   }
}
```

Figure 16-4
Example: using NO_LOCK access mode

access the real persistent object. This might come in handy in user interface programming when NO_LOCK copies are used to hold modifications made by the user. These changes often occur outside of any transaction scope, because it might take the user a long time to decide when entering several attributes of a certain object. In such cases, a useful approach is to wait until the user clicks the OK or "confirm" button, and then start a transaction where the actual persistent object is accessed, and the modifications previously made to the NO_LOCK copy are recorded on the real object. This idea is illustrated in the example shown in Figure 16-4. This example uses NO_LOCK copies during user editing, and then uses the handle in the NO_LOCK copy to access the real persistent object in a subsequent transaction.

CHAPTER 17

The Naming Service

The naming service is responsible for storage and retrieval of objects based on user aliases. This service insulates application code from deployment-level issues such as object location and the kind of persistent data stores used.

The Role of the Naming Service in SanFrancisco

The naming service is used in the following cases.

- Assigment of user aliases
- Retrieval of objects based on user aliases
- Storing objects in the appropriate persistent data store (based on the configuration)
- Performing class replacement

Similar to other Foundation layer services, the interfaces for working with user aliases and other naming service features are provided by the `BaseFactory`. Figure 17-1 shows the interface `NameService Management`, from which `BaseFactory` inherits the naming service interfaces.

User Aliases

When developing client programs, we obviously need to gain access to objects residing on servers (or containers). Giving user aliases to persistent entities provides an easy way to point out a specific object. The Naming Service lets you add a user alias using the `addUserAlias` method, which takes as parameters a handle to an `Entity` and the alias you want to assign to it. Figure 17-2 shows an example of how this method is used. This example is taken from the CheckBook sample program, and the code shown is responsible for initializing a record of a person. It attempts to associate the name of the person with the object, as a user alias.

Figure 17-1
Interface to class `Name Service Management`

Interface com.ibm.sf.gf.NameServiceManagement

public interface **NameServiceManagement**
extends AllowRemote

Methods

Name	*Signature*	*Description*

addUserAlias	`public abstract void`
	`addUserAlias(`
	` String entityUserAlias,`
	` Handle handleOfEntity)`
	`throws GFException`
		Associates (or binds) the given userAlias with the entity referred to by the input handle. Once a userAlias has been added through this interface, applications may then use this alias (in addition to its handle) to access the persistent entity. A single entity may be referred to by mulitple userAliases.

getContainer	`public abstract Handle`
	`getContainer(`
	` String classNameToken)`
	`throws GFException`
		Returns a handle containing the default persistent container location information as specified in the configuration information for the specified class name token (must correspond to an Entity, or a class that extends from Entity). This Handle can then be used as the locationHandle argument in a `createEntity()` call to place the new entity in the container according to the configured default persistent container.

getContainerByName	`public abstract Handle`
	`getContainerByName(`
	` String containerName)`
	`throws GFException`
		Returns a handle containing the default persistent container location information as specified by the container name, as specified in the naming data priming source file. This method provides a bootstrap mechanism for creating top level hierarchical objects (a situation where one cannot specify another object with which the new object should be stored). This Handle can then be used as the locationHandle argument in a `createEntity()` call to place the new entity in the container according to the configured persistent container.

Figure 17-1
(Cont'd)

getSpecialFactory	public abstract Object getSpecialFactory(String classNameToken) throws GFException	Returns an instance of any special factory class configured for the specified class name token. Null is returned when there is no special factory class associated with this class name token and the normal Factory class methods should be used for creation. Special factories are intended to be called from within class factories and provide functions relating to legacy databases.
removeUserAlias	public abstract void removeUserAlias(String entityUserAlias, Handle handleOfEntity) throws GFException	Removes the existing user alias (assumed to have been previously associated) for the Entity referred to by the input `Handle`.
replaceUserAliasEntity	public abstract void replaceUserAliasEntity(String entityUserAlias, Handle handleOfSourceEntity, Handle handleOfTargetEntity) throws GFException	Re-assigns the specified user alias from the source `Entity` referred to by the first handle to the target `Entity` referred to by the second handle.
getRealClassName	public abstract String getRealClassName(String classNameToken) throws GFException	Returns the real class that should be instantiated, given a class name token. In order to do that, the class name token is looked up in the configuration information. If there is a substitute class name mapped to this token, that is used. Otherwise, if there is a substitute interface name with a corresponding <>Impl class, that class is used. Otherwise, if the class name token is an actual class that class is used, and if the class name token is an interface which has a corresponding <>Impl class, then the latter is used. Once exception is that the classNameToken "`String`" is mapped hard-coded to "`java.lang.String`", and no class substitution is allowed for it.

In order to remove the association between the object and the user alias, you can use the `removeUserAlias` method, taking the same parameters. In case you want to change the object referred to by a specific alias, you can use the method `replaceUserAliasEntity`, taking the user alias string, and the handles to the `Entity` currently associated with it, and the `Entity` to which you wish to assign it. Although this result can be achieved by using `removeUserAlias` and then `addUserAlias`, this method is useful because it guarantees that the

```
import com.ibm.sf.gf.*;

public class MyNamedObjectImpl extends EntityImpl
implements MyNamedObject {


  ...

   public void initialize(String name) throws com.ibm.sf.gf.SFException
   {

     ...

     try {
       Global.factory().addUserAlias(name, getHandle());
     } catch (FactoryParameterRejectedException f) {};
   }
  ...

}
```

Figure 17-2
Sample use of `addUserAlias`

user alias exactly names one object throughout the execution of the renaming operation.

Note that extensive use of user aliases is not considered to be good programming practice. While convenient in the development phase, using too many user aliases complicates deployment and administration. In a production application, only a few top-level objects should get a user alias. These top-level objects should contain other objects, and the latter can be retrieved using any of the SanFrancisco container interfaces.

Containers

As we saw in Chapter 15, a new `Entity` object that is required to be persistent, must be associated with a specific container when it is created. This container can either be the container of another object, or it can be retrieved by a logical name using the Naming service.

These persistent containers are a part of the SanFrancisco object persistency service. They exist in a business object process running on a specific host. These containers are an abstraction of a persistent storage mechanism, such as a hierarchical file system or relational database. As already discussed, the persistence of business objects in SanFrancisco is transparent to the application code, so developers do not need to know where persistent business objects reside. Instead, a data administrator with the knowledge of the particular network and underlying data storage, deals with these issues through the SanFrancisco configuration tools.

There are two ways to retrieve a `Handle` to a container. The method `getContainerByName` is usually used for bootstrapping purposes, i.e. when creating new structures from scratch. Figure 17-1 shows the signature of this method, along with the method `getContainer`. This method is used to get the default container for a class given the *class token*. An example of this is shown in Figure 17-3. In this example, the `NaturalCalendar` is created under the current company, but its description (a `descriptiveInformation` object) is placed in the default container for its interface.

Class Replacement

When an application requests the creation of an instance, it uses a *class token* to indicate the SanFrancisco class the instance should belong to. The Naming service dynamically associates this token with a specific class, which might be a different class than the original one intended (e.g. a class that wasn't even coded when the application was implemented). The definition of which class to use is done using the configuration tools. This mechanism ensures that, if you want to globally substitute a class with a different one (typically a subclass—so you won't get into too much trouble), you can do it without modifying the applications. For example, suppose you run an application that uses a `ProductPackage` class. You might want to integrate with your own application that uses a subclass of `ProductPackage`, say `WhiteProductPackage`. Class replacement allows you to instruct the `BaseFactory` to use `WhiteProductPackage` whenever `ProductPackage` is requested.

Using the method `getRealClassName` you can find out which class is associated with a specific class token.

```
import com.ibm.sf.gf.*;
import com.ibm.sf.cf.*;


public class NaturalCalendarCreator
{
  ...


  public void createCalendar() throws Exception
  {


    try {
          Global.factory.begin();

          Company theEnterprise = CompanyContext.getActiveCompany(
                                     AccessMode.createPlusWrite());
          if (theEnterprise == null){
            // Cannot find company
                return;
          }

      // Find natural calendar
      NaturalCalendar theCalendar = (NaturalCalendar)
                   theEnterprise.getPropertyBy("cf.NaturalCalendar");

      if (theCalendar == null) {

       // If non-existent, create it, and add description to container
       DescriptiveInformation description =
           DescriptiveInformationFactory.createDescriptiveInformation
                AccessMode.createNormal(),
                Global.factory()
                        .getContainer("gf.DescriptiveInformation"));
       description.addDefaultDescription(
                 "Demonstration Natural Calendar");


      // Create parameters for calendar
        DTime presentTime =
          DTimeFactory.currentLocalTime((DAmountOfTime)null);
       int presentYear = presentTime.getYear();
       DTimePeriod workingDay = DTimePeriodFactory.createDTimePeriod(
                        DTimeFactory.createDTime(1999,1,1,9,0,0, null),
                        DTimeFactory.createDTime(1999,1,1,17,0,0,
                        null),
                        null);

       DresultDateAdjustmentPolicyDefault
         policy =
            DResultDateAdjustmentPolicyDefaultFactory.
                   createDResultDateAdjustmentPolicyDefault();
```

Figure 17-3
Sample use of `getContainer`

```
        // Create calendar object
         theCalendar = NaturalCalendarFactory.createNaturalCalendar(
                         AccessMode.createPlusWrite(),
                         theEnterprise.getHandle(),
                         presentYear,
                         presentYear,
                         true,
                         true,
                         true,
                         true,
                         true,
                         true,
                         true,
                         true,
                         workingDay,
                         workingDay,
                         workingDay,
                         workingDay,
                         workingDay,
                         workingDay,
                         workingDay,
                         description,
                         DaysOfTheWeekEnum.MONDAY,
                         policy);

         theEnterprise.addDirectlyOwnedPropertyBy(
                         theCalendar,
                         "cf.NaturalCalendar");
         Global.factory().dropAccess(theEnterprise);
        }
      } catch ( Exception ex ) {
        ex.printStackTrace();
      }
      Global.factory.commit();

    }
    ...
  }
```

Figure 17-3
(Cont'd)

CHAPTER 18

Notification Services

This chapter covers another service provided by the SanFrancisco Foundation Layer—the notification service. Objects can generate an event whenever some specific conditions are met (e.g. certain changes in their state occur). Client programmers can exploit this built-in notification in order to keep them up-to-date with any important changes in the objects they are currently accessing.

Observer and Observable

A very common behavioral design pattern is the "observer" pattern, already discussed in Chapter 12. The goal of this pattern is to define a one-to-many dependency between objects so that when one object changes states, all its dependents are notified and updated automatically. This pattern is supported in Java through the class `java.util.Observer`. The SanFrancisco notification service extends this support to SanFrancisco entities.

Let's try to define the basic terms used for notification. An *observer* is the object that is interested in receiving notifications. An *observable* is the object that generates the notifications to all the observers that have registered interest in it.

The SanFrancisco notification service supports two types of observer objects. On the one hand are objects that implement the `java.util.Observer` interface. These objects do not extend the `Entity` interface and, therefore, do not have all the advantages offered by the SanFrancisco Foundation (e.g. persistency). These objects have a lifecycle lasting only for the duration of the process in which they were created. On the other hand are objects that extend the `Entity` interface. These objects have all the same functionality provided by the SanFrancisco Foundation, so they are persistent, transactional, and can be distributed in a transparent manner. In addition, they also have the functionality of objects of type `java.util.Observer` and need not extend this interface.

On the observable object side, things are somewhat different. The notification service will only work with Observable objects of type `Entity`. In other words, every `Entity` can be either an observable or an observer, but non-Entity objects can only be observers.

In order to demonstrate the issues related to notification, we will use a simple example in which we have a warehouse class called `MyWarehouse` representing a warehouse used for temporarily storing packages that arrive from overseas. The events of interest for notification are arrival of a package, removal of a package, and a customs inspection that occurs once in a while. The code extract in Figure 18-1 defines `MyWarehouseEntityObserver` and `MyWarehouseJavaObserver`, extending Entity and `java.util.Observer`, respectively.

Notification Mechanisms

So far, we have seen that any Java object can become an *observer* and is notified when an event belonging to a certain category (referred to as Interest) occurs. Observers can be SanFrancisco Entities or normal Java objects, such as user interface components. Actually, the most common use of the notification mechanism is for graphical interacting with SanFrancisco server-side objects.

A notification is generated when changes are committed on a persistent `Entity`. SanFrancisco defines the following two notification mechanisms:

- *Synchronous*. This mechanism is pretty simple: once the changes on the source object are performed, the observer is notified of these changes. The observer can react to these changes properly as soon as the source object is committed. When this approach is used, the notification service takes care of directly notifying the observers by invoking an `update()` method they need to implement. Figure 18-2 schematically shows how this mechanism works.
- *Asynchronous*. In this mechanism, the changes are stored in a notification mailbox. It is up to the observer to pick up outstanding notification messages. This mechanism is used whenever the observer wishes to exercise some degree of freedom as to when to react to changes that were committed in the observed object. When using this approach, the Foundation posts the event notifications in a mailbox from which the observer can later retrieve them. Figure 18-3 schematically shows how this mechanism works (Note: this mechanism is also known as "On demand").

```
import com.ibm.sf.gf.Entity;

public interface MyWarehouse extends Entity {
        •
        •
        •
}

// Example of an observer of type java.util.Observer
public class MyWarehouseJavaObserver
        implements java.util.Observer
        {
        •
        •
        •
  public update(Observable o, Object arg) {
        •
        •
        •

  }
}


// Example of an observer of type Entity:
public interface MyWareHouseEntityObserver
   extends Entity {
        •
        •
        •

}

public class MyWareHouseEntityObserverImpl
   implements MyWareHouseEntityObserver
   {
        •
        •
        •
  public update(Handle observable, Interest notificationInterest,
                       Serializable notificationData) {
        •
        •
        •
  }
}
```

Figure 18-1
Examples of `observer` definitions.

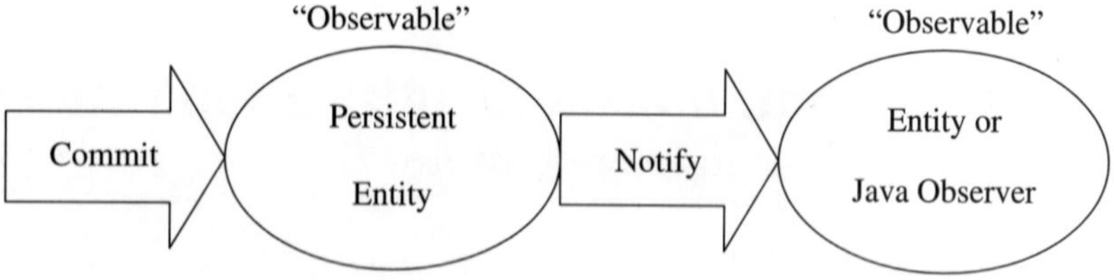

Figure 18-2
Synchronous notification.

Figure 18-3
Asynchronous notification.

Using SanFrancisco Notification Services

Registering for Notification

As with so many other Foundation services, the notification services are accessed via the BaseFactory class. This class extends the `NotificationManagement` interface, which supports the notification services. Figure 18-4 shows the methods of `NotificationManagement.`

Objects that want to become observers and receive notification need to register using the `addObserver` method. The parameters to this method specify which observable object is to be the monitor and what the interest subject is. The `addObserver` method allows registering observers for notification by an observable. As shown in Figure 18-4, this method is provided in three different variants. The first two variants register observers of type `Entity`, whereas the latter is used to register observers of

Figure 18-4 `Notification Management` interface.

Interface com.ibm.sf.gf.NotificationManagement

public interface **NotificationManagement**
extends AllowRemote

Name	*Signature*	*Description*
addObserver	`public abstract void addObserver( Entity observerEntity, Interest notificationInterest,AccessMode access, Handle observable) throws GFException`	Adds an entity observer to the observer list of an observable for the specified Interest. This method can only be invoked from within a transaction. Registration is transactional, so it does not become effective until after commit.
	`public abstract void addObserver( Entity observerEntity, Interest notificationInterest,AccessMode access, Handle observable) throws GFException`	
	`public abstract void addObserver( Handle observerHandle, Interest notificationInterest, AccessMode access,Handle observable) throws GFException`	
deleteObserver	`public abstract void deleteObserver( Observer observer,Interest notificationInterest,Handle observable) throws GFException`	Removes an observer (Java observer in the first form, Entity observer in the other two) from the observer list of an observer for the specified Interest.
	`public abstract void deleteObserver( Entity observerEntity,Interest notificationInterest,Handle observable) throws GFException`	
	`public abstract void deleteObserver( Handle observerHandle, Interest notificationInterest, Handle observable) throws GFException`	

type `java.util.Observer`. The access parameter used is the `AccessMode` that observables use to get the observer and notify it. The `observableHandle` parameter is the `Handle` to the observable `Entity`, as the name implies. Using the notification `Interest`, observers can filter the notifications, and receive only certain kinds of notifications.

The registration notification must be explicitly undone once it is no longer needed. For this purpose, we have the `deleteObserver` method. Similar to `addObserver`, this method is provided in three variants. Again, the first two variants are used for `Entity` observers, and the third for `java.util.Observers`.

An important technical point is that registration and unregistration of observers must be performed from within a transaction, and always in the same `WorkArea`.

Using Notification Interest Objects

As previously mentioned, we use a notification `Interest` object to identify a certain type of notification generated by an observable, in order to filter notifications. In other words, Interests provide a way for observers to register for several different kinds of notifications, and are the means for an observable to indicate the type of notification it dispatches to its observers.

Every observable may have an `Interest` class associated with it. Such an `Interest` class is derived from `Interest` and should define what types of notifications observers can register for with an observable. Figure 18-5 shows the interface for `Interest`.

The convention is that `Interest` classes have several static variables that specify the different interests available for observers. In addition, they implement a `create(int)` method, which creates an `Interest` object, sets the value for the `Interest`, and returns it.

In Figure 18-6 we define `MyWarehouseInterest`, associated with our `MyWarehouse` example. This definition illustrates the use of `create (int)` for `Interest` classes. Using the class `MyWarehouseInterest`, an observer on a `MyWarehouse` object can register for a notification on a specific event. So, for instance, a `MyWarehouseEntityObserver` object could register for notification upon the arrival of a new package, just by passing the static variable `MyWareHouseInterest.PACKAGE_ARRIVED` as the interest parameter in the `addObserver` method.

The notification service supports the use of a null Interest. Passing null as the Interest parameter when registering for a notification by a specific observable is functionally equivalent to registering for every single Interest in this observable.

For example, say a `MyWarehouseEntityObserver` registers with a MyWarehouse object with the Interest specified as null when calling

Figure 18-5 `Interest` interface.

Class com.ibm.sf.gf.Interest

public abstract class **Interest**
extends Object
implements Serializable

Fields

Name	*Signature*	*Description*
ivInterestValue	`protected int ivInterestValue`	A unique value uniquely representing this `Interest` object

Methods

Name	*Signature*	*Description*
Interest	`public Interest()`	Constructor
getInterestValue	`public int getInterestValue()`	Returns the current value of the Interest
setInterestValue	`public void setInterestValue(int interestValue)`	Sets value for the Interest
setEqual	`public void setEqual(Interest interest) throws GFException`	Sets state of this interest equal to state of passed interest parameter

Figure 18-6 Definition of an `Interest` subclass for the `MyWarehouse`

```
public class MyWarehouseInterest extends Interest {

  public MyWarehouseInterest create(int interestValue) {
    MyWarehouseInterest interest = new MyWarehouseInterest ();
    interest.setInterestValue(interestValue);
    return interest;
  }

 // static type variables for filtered notification registration
  public static MyWarehouseInterest PACKAGE_ARRIVED =
     MyWarehouseInterest.create(1);
  public static MyWarehouseInterest PACKAGE_REMOVED =
     MyWarehouseInterest.create(2);
  public static MyWarehouseInterest CUSTOMS_INSPECTION =
     MyWarehouseInterest.create(3);

}
```

addObserver. Whenever an event occurs (i.e. whenever a package arrives, a package is removed or a customs inspection takes place), the `MyWarehouseEntityObserver` receives notification with the Handle of the MyWarehouse object. In addition, the new or removed package is passed along with one the following values, identifying the notification type: `MyWarehouseInterest.PACKAGE_ARRIVED`, or `MyWarehouse Interest.PACKAGE_REMOVED` or `MyWarehouseInterest.CUSTOMS_ INSPECTION`.

If you wish to avoid defining your own `Interest` classes, the Notification Service provides a generic `EntityInterest` class. This class provides a static `EntityInterest.CHANGED` variable of type `EntityInterest`, which clients can use to register observers with any Entity for non-specific change of state notification. The function of the `EntityInterest.CHANGED` interest is to notify registered observers that do not want to receive any special information other than the fact that there has been a state change in the observable. To indicate the change, observables pass observers only the "CHANGED_data" string. So, for example, suppose a `MyWarehouseJavaObserver` registers with a `MyWarehouse` passing to addObserver `EntityInterest.CHANGED` as Interest. Then as in the previous example (when null was passed), when any of the events occur, the `MyWarehouseEntityObserver` is notified, but the only information it receives is the "`CHANGED_data`" `String`, with a `Handle` to MyWarehouse, along with `Entity Interest.Changed` as the corresponding Interest identification.

Receiving Notifications

Up to this point we discussed how we register for receiving notifications, but we didn't really say how the observable Entities notify their registered observers. This is done using a method called `update` in each observer. The observable object can initiate such a call invoking the `notifyObservers()` method. This method should be called from all the methods in the `observable` that are expected to trigger notifications. The `notifyObservers` method takes as parameters the Interest corresponding to the notification being generated and a `Serializable` data argument containing any related data that should be provided to the observers. If `notifyObservers` is not called, but `setDirty()` is, only those observers that have registered with the `EntityInterest`.

Figure 18-7 Sample use of `notify Observers`

```
public class MyWarehouseImpl implements MyWarehouseInterest {
  ...
  private void insertPackage(Package pkg) {
      setDirty();
      ivPackages.append(pkg);
      notifyObservers(MyWarehouseInterest.PACKAGE_ARRIVED, pkg);
    }
  }
  ...
}
```

`CHANGED` Interest are notified. Figure 18-7 shows an example of using `notifyObservers`.

Once the `notifyObservers` method gets activated, all the observers registered for notification will receive the notifications through their update methods. For observers of type `java.util.Observer` the method signature is:

```
update(Observable o, Object arg)
```

What you get as arguments are a null and a `NotificationEvent` object. The `NotificationEvent` object encapsulates the observable `Handle`, `Interest`, and the `Serializable notificationData`. It also offers public methods for observers of type `java.util.Observer` to obtain them. Namely, these are `getObservable()`, `get NotificationData()`, and `getInterest()`. However, since observers of type `java.util.Observer` are notified outside of transactions, they initiate a transaction if they need to access the observable.

For Entity observers, the update method signature is shown in Figure 18-8. All Entities have a default implementation of `update()` that does nothing. It is up to the observer to implement this update method according to its specific needs, overriding the default implementation. In the update method, observers of `type Entity` receive as parameters the handle to the observable from which the notification originated, the related `Interest`, and the `Serializable` notification data.

An observer registering for multiple Interests can use the `Interest` argument to determine the notification type in order to act upon it. This can be accomplished by using the `equals()` method for comparison. Similarly, if the observer registers with multiple observables, it can get the observable that generated the notification if it desires. In order to access a specific method, it might be required to find out the class type using `instanceof`, and then cast it to that class.

Consider a case in which a `MyWarehouseJavaObserver` and a `MyWarehouseEntityObserver` have been registered for notification

Figure 18-8
`Entity` interface.

Interface com.ibm.sf.gf.Entity

public interface **Entity**
extends BusinessObject, GFRemote

Methods

Name	*Signature*	*Description*
getHandle	`public abstract Handle getHandle() throws GFException`	Gives a handle referring to this entity object. The returned handle is allocated as a transient object in the local address space of the caller.
isDirty	`public abstract boolean isDirty()`	Indicates whether the state of this Entity has been changed in the current transaction.
notifyObservers	`public abstract void notifyObservers( Interest notificationInterest, Serializable notificationData) throws GFException`	This methods notifies any observer that is registered for notifications with this object.
update	`public abstract void update( Handle observable, Interest notificationInterest,Serializable notificationData) throws SFException`	Called whenever this entity (as an observer) is notified about a state change in the observable.

with a `MyWarehouse` for all Interests (we do that by passing a null `Interest` to the `addObservers` method). Figure 18-9 shows how the `update` could look in the case of the Entity observer. The `update()` method is overridden, and what it does is just print a message indicating the event. Figure 18-10 shows how the server of type `java.util.Observable` would implement `update()`.

Note that notifications are generated on `commit()` only. Hence, only committed changes are reflected by notifications. For instance, if the list of package in the `MyWarehouse` changes 10 times during a transaction, only the value it has after the last change is committed and, thus, sent as notification to the observers.

```
public MyWarehouseEntityObserverImpl implements
   MyWarehouseEntityObserver {

    public update(Handle observableHandle,
       Interest notificationInterest,
       Serializable notificationData) {

         Entity observableEntity = Global.factory().getEntity(
            observableHandle, AccessMode.createNormal());

         if (notificationInterest.equals(
                MyWarehouseInterest.PACKAGE_ARRIVED)) {
                        System.out.println("A package arrived");
                        break;
         }
         else if (notificationInterest.equals(
                MyWarehouseInterest.PACKAGE_REMOVED)) {
                        System.out.println("A package Removed");
                        break;
          }
          else if (notificationInterest.equals(
                MyWarehouseInterest.CUSTOMS_INSPECTION)) {
                        System.out.println("Custom inspection now...");
                        break;
          }
         else if (notificationInterest.equals(EntityInterest.CHANGED) {
             if (observableEntity instanceof MyWarehouse) {
                 System.out.println("The MyWarehouse state has changed.
                 The notificationData passed is simply the string
                 'CHANGED_data');
             }
         }
    }
}
```

Figure 18-9
Sample implementation of `update` method for Entity observer.

Notification Polling Using a `NotificationMailbox`

Earlier in the chapter we discussed the difference between the synchronous and asynchronous modes of notification. The synchronous notification mode offers an alternative to registering observers for notifications. Clients are able create a `NotificationMailbox` object and register it for notifications with an observable. Creation is done using the

```
public MyWarehouseJavaObserver
   implements java.util.Observer {

  public update(Observable o, Object arg) {

     if (arg instanceof NotificationEvent) {

       // Get the observable
       Global.factory().begin();
          Handle observableEntityHandle = (
             (NotificationEvent)arg).getObservable();
       Entity observableEntity = Global.factory().getEntity(
          observableEntityHandle, AccessMode.createNormal());
       Global.factory().commit();

       // Extract the Interest
       Interest notificationInterest = (
          (NotificationEvent)arg).getInterest();

       if (notificationInterest.equals(
               MyWarehouseInterest.PACKAGE_ARRIVED)) {
               System.out.println("A package arrived");
               break;
        }
        else if (notificationInterest.equals(
               MyWarehouseInterest.PACKAGE_REMOVED)) {
               System.out.println("A package Removed");
               break;
        }
        else if (notificationInterest.equals(
               MyWarehouseInterest.CUSTOMS_INSPECTION)) {
               System.out.println("Custom inspection now...");
               break;
        }
        else if (notificationInterest.equals(EntityInterest.CHANGED) {
             if (observableEntity instanceof MyWarehouse) {
                System.out.println("The MyWarehouse state has changed.
                The notificationData passed is simply the string
                'CHANGED_data'");
             }
         }
     }
  }
}
```

Figure 18-10
Sample implementation of `update` method for Java observer.

`NotificationMailboxFactory.createNotificationMailbox()` method. Note that a `NotificationMailbox` type object is actually an Entity, so it can be registered for notification just like other observers of type `Entity`. In addition, being Entities, `NotificationMailboxes` are also transactional, persistent, and so on. The interface for `NotificationMailBox` is shown in Figure 18-11. The `getNotificationEvent()` method is used to poll notifications, and it returns a `NotificationEvent` type object. An example is shown is Figure 18-12.

Figure 18-11 `NotificationMailBox` interface.

Interface com.ibm.sf.gf.NotificationMailbox

public interface interface **NotificationMailbox**
extends Entity

Methods

Name	*Signature*	*Description*
getNotificationEvent	`public abstract NotificationEvent getNotificationEvent() throws GFException`	Returns the last NotificationEvent stored.

```
public class ClientAImpl extends ClientA {

   private CashRegisterObserverEntity ivCashRegisterObserverEntity;
   private NotificationMailbox ivMailBox;

   public void initialize() {
     ivCashRegisterObserverEntity =

CashRegisterObserverEntityFactory.createCashRegisterObserverEntity(...)
;
     NotificationMailbox ivMailBox =
        NotificationMailboxFactory.createNotificationMailbox(
        AccessMode.createNormal(),
        Global.factory().getContainer( "gf.NotificationMailbox" ),
        (DMethodAccessKey)null );
   }

   public void addNotificationMailbox() {
     Global.factory().begin();
     Global.factory.addObserver(
         ivMailBox, CashRegisterInterest.NAME_CHANGED,
         Global.factory().getHandle("CashRegister"));
     Global.factory().commit();
   }

   public void getNotificationsFromBox() {

     NotificationEvent notificationEvent =
        ivMailBox.getNotificationEvent();

     while (notificationEvent != null) {
         Serializable notificationData =
         notificationEvent.getNotificationData();
        ...

        ivCashRegisterObserverEntity.repaint(notificationData);
        notificationEvent = ivMailBox.getNotificationEvent();
   }
}
```

Figure 18-12
Example of synchronous notification.

CHAPTER 19

Query Mechanisms

SanFrancisco includes, as part of the Foundation Layer, a powerful querying mechanism that allows you to extract a subset of a certain collection given a pretty natural query language. The query language conforms to a subset of SQL92 with some extensions, which allow you to invoke object methods. Using this query mechanism you get the power of database searching and filtering, right in your application.

Querying and Sorting Collections

The Foundation Layer provides special `Command` subclasses that query an `Entity` collection and return a transient result collection of elements that satisfy the query criteria. The collections that have query operators include `Set`, `List`, `Map`, `EntityOwningSet`, `EntityOwningList`, `EntityOwningMap`, and `EntityOwningExtent` collections.

When we perform a query on a collection such as a `Set`, a `List`, or a `Map`, the returned result is a new transient collection that is of the same class. A query on an `EntityOwningSet`, `EntityOwningList`, or `EntityOwingMap` returns a result collection of type `Set`, `List`, or `Map`, respectively. The result collection does not own its `Entity` elements, as they are already owned by the original collection. A query on an `EntityOwningExtent` returns a result collection of type `Set`, where any `Entity` elements are unowned. `EntityOwningExtents` also support an overloaded query method that takes an additional `specificationKeyId` parameter and returns a result collection of type `Map`.

Two types of `Command` classes are used in creating collections by querying existing collections. The concrete `AdhocQueryCmd` class can be used to query using any arbitrary select statement. Subclasses of the `QueryCmd` class are used to query using predefined select statements. These predefined queries are used in business tasks implemented in the business process components and also sometimes may be useful to client programmers. The advantage of a `Command` encapsulating a predefined query is that the implementation of the query inside the `Command` can be optimized to use query support provided by the underlying persistent object data store, for example an SQL relational database query. Generally this optimization is possible only when the collection is an `EntityOwningExtent`.

For best performance, client programmers should use a Command's static `create<class name>()` method that specifies the target by handle, or that explicitly specifies a locationHandle. Specifying the target handle or locationHandle allows the query to run in a server process. Specifying the target by passing the target object is generally slower, both because the collection may be unnecessarily brought to the client, and also because the Command runs locally if no target or location handle is specified.

The query commands take a Boolean accessResults argument. This parameter controls whether the Entities in the resultCollection that were not already accessed when the query was called, should be available in the transaction when the query returns to the caller. If accessResults is false, they should not be accessed (unless they already were before the query was called). If accessResults is true, they are available. Entities that are in the collection that the query operated on, but are not selected into the resulting collection, should be accessed if, and only if, they were accessed before the query ran. Unless the elements in the resultCollection are going to be operated on in this transaction, accessResults should be specified as "false" to minimize unnecessary contention resulting from multiple users.

The static `create` methods of the `AdhocQueryCmdFactory` are shown in Figure 19-1. The `AdhocQueryCmd` has two mandatory (i.e. non-null) arguments: a String holding the select statement, and a String holding a logical name that is used within the select statement to identify the collection that is being queried. The `AdhocQueryCmd` may also need, depending on the specific select statement, a `SelectCompare` object, a `SortCompare` object or both, each with corresponding String objects identifying them in the select statement. Any class can implement the `SelectCompare` or `SortCompare` interface. Both interfaces have a single method, `compare()`, that allows object comparison inside the query select statement.

The `SelectCompare compare()` method takes a single object as an argument, looks at that object, and returns true or false according to whether the object meets the desired selection criteria. The select compare object may be referenced by its `bindName` in the "where" clause of the select statement. The `SortCompare compare()` method takes two objects as arguments, compares them, and returns a negative, zero, or positive value according to whether the second object is less than, equal, or greater than the first argument, respectively. The sort compare object may be referenced by its `bindName` in the "order-by" clause of the select statement.

Figure 19-1 Static create methods of the `AdhocQueryCmdFactory`

```
static final AdhocQueryCmd createAdhocQueryCmd(
   CommonCollectionIteration collectionToQuery,
   String selectStatement,
   String bindNameOfCollection,
   SelectCompare selectCompareObject,
   String bindNameOfSelectCompareObject,
   SortCompare orderbyCompareObject,
   String bindNameOfOrderbyCompareObject,
   boolean accessResults) throws SFException;

static final AdhocQueryCmd createAdhocQueryCmd(
   CommonCollectionIteration collectionToQuery,
   String selectStatement,
   String bindNameOfCollection,
   SelectCompare selectCompareObject,
   String bindNameOfSelectCompareObject,
   SortCompare orderbyCompareObject,
   String bindNameOfOrderbyCompareObject,
   boolean accessResults,
   String specificationKeyId) throws SFException;

static final AdhocQueryCmd createAdhocQueryCmd(
   CommonCollectionIteration collectionToQuery,
   String selectStatement,
   String bindNameOfCollection,
   SelectCompare selectCompareObject,
   String bindNameOfSelectCompareObject,
   SortCompare orderbyCompareObject,
   String bindNameOfOrderbyCompareObject,
   boolean accessResults,
   String[] hostVariableNames,
   Object[] hostVariableValues) throws SFException;

static final AdhocQueryCmd createAdhocQueryCmd(
   CommonCollectionIteration collectionToQuery,
   String selectStatement,
   String bindNameOfCollection,
   SelectCompare selectCompareObject,
   String bindNameOfSelectCompareObject,
   SortCompare orderbyCompareObject,
   String bindNameOfOrderbyCompareObject,
   boolean accessResults,
   String specificationKeyId,
   String[] hostVariableNames,
   Object[] hostVariableValues) throws SFException;

static final AdhocQueryCmd createAdhocQueryCmd(
   Handle handleOfCollectionToQuery,
   String selectStatement,
   String bindNameOfCollection,
   SelectCompare selectCompareObject,
   String bindNameOfSelectCompareObject,
   SortCompare orderbyCompareObject,
   String bindNameOfOrderbyCompareObject,
```

Figure 19-1
(Cont'd)

```
boolean accessResults) throws SFException;

static final AdhocQueryCmd createAdhocQueryCmd(
   Handle handleOfCollectionToQuery,
   String selectStatement,
   String bindNameOfCollection,
   SelectCompare selectCompareObject,
   String bindNameOfSelectCompareObject,
   SortCompare orderbyCompareObject,
   String bindNameOfOrderbyCompareObject,
   boolean accessResults,
   String specificationKeyId) throws SFException;

static final AdhocQueryCmd createAdhocQueryCmd(
   Handle handleOfCollectionToQuery,
   String selectStatement,
   String bindNameOfCollection,
   SelectCompare selectCompareObject,
   String bindNameOfSelectCompareObject,
   SortCompare orderbyCompareObject,
   String bindNameOfOrderbyCompareObject,
   boolean accessResults,
   String[] hostVariableNames,
   Object[] hostVariableValues) throws SFException;
static final AdhocQueryCmd createAdhocQueryCmd(
   Handle handleOfCollectionToQuery,
   String selectStatement,
   String bindNameOfCollection,
   SelectCompare selectCompareObject,
   String bindNameOfSelectCompareObject,
   SortCompare orderbyCompareObject,
   String bindNameOfOrderbyCompareObject,
   boolean accessResults,
   String specificationKeyId,
   String[] hostVariableNames,
   Object[] hostVariableValues) throws SFException;

static final AdhocQueryCmd createAdhocQueryCmd(
   Handle locationHandle,
   boolean returnCommand,
   Handle handleOfCollectionToQuery,
   String selectStatement,
   String bindNameOfCollection,
   SelectCompare selectCompareObject,
   String bindNameOfSelectCompareObject,
   SortCompare orderbyCompareObject,
   String bindNameOfOrderbyCompareObject,
   boolean accessResults) throws SFException;

static final AdhocQueryCmd createAdhocQueryCmd(
   Handle locationHandle,
   boolean returnCommand,
   Handle handleOfCollectionToQuery,
   String selectStatement,
```

Figure 19-1 (Cont'd)

```
String bindNameOfCollection,
    SelectCompare selectCompareObject,
    String bindNameOfSelectCompareObject,
    SortCompare orderbyCompareObject,
    String bindNameOfOrderbyCompareObject,
    boolean accessResults,
    String specificationKeyId) throws SFException;
static final AdhocQueryCmd createAdhocQueryCmd(
    Handle locationHandle,
    boolean returnCommand,
    Handle handleOfCollectionToQuery,
    String selectStatement,
    String bindNameOfCollection,
    SelectCompare selectCompareObject,
    String bindNameOfSelectCompareObject,
    SortCompare orderbyCompareObject,
    String bindNameOfOrderbyCompareObject,
    boolean accessResults,
    String[] hostVariableNames,
    Object[] hostVariableValues) throws SFException;
static final AdhocQueryCmd createAdhocQueryCmd(
    Handle locationHandle,
    boolean returnCommand,
    Handle handleOfCollectionToQuery,
    String selectStatement,
    String bindNameOfCollection,
    SelectCompare selectCompareObject,
    String bindNameOfSelectCompareObject,
    SortCompare orderbyCompareObject,
    String bindNameOfOrderbyCompareObject,
    boolean accessResults,
    String specificationKeyId,
    String[] hostVariableNames,
    Object[] hostVariableValues) throws SFException;
```

`QueryCmd` subclasses that provide predefined queries do not generally need the `selectStatement` or bind names because they are actually hard coded into the subclass implementation. The `QueryCmd` subclasses may support `SelectCompare` or `SortCompare` object arguments, depending on the select statement that is encapsulated in it.

A business object that contains one or more queryable collections may provide methods for executing an `AdhocQueryCmd` on those collections to create a resulting collection containing only the elements that match the query criteria. This might be needed, because client code usually cannot directly access the internal collections. The convention is that the form of these methods is as shown in Figure 19-2.

Figure 19-2 Form of query methods for business objects containing queriable collections.

```
public <query collection class> query<Element name>s(
   String  selectStatement,
   String  nameUsedForCollectionInSelect,
   SelectCompare  selectCompareObject,
   String  bindNameOfSelectCompareObject,
   SortCompare  orderbyCompareObject,
   String  bindNameOfOrderbyCompareObject
   boolean  accessResults) throws SFException;
```

Query Syntax

Let's start with the formalities. The query syntax used by the SanFrancisco query engine is an extension of SQL92 called OOSQL. The idea of this extension is to take regular SQL92 and beef it up with an object query engine that works with objects in their object form. In order to preserve object visibility constraints, the query engine can only access the public methods defined for the object. During a query, the query engine is directed to perform a query against the objects contained in a queryable collection. This includes `Set`, `List`, `Map`, `EntityOwningSet`, `EntityOwningList`, `EntityOwningMap`, and `EntityOwningExtent`.

The query can only use public methods defined on the objects in the collection, and it cannot query any properties associated with these objects. If the collection contains Map objects, it may not use the key object. During the query, the objects to be tested will be accessed by asking the collection/extent to create an iterator, which will be used to step through the collection.

Query Statement

The application programmer never directly accesses the query engine. The only interface is via the `queryElements()` method on the `QueryCollection` interface or perhaps via the `QueryCmd`. In general, all queries will have the form shown in Figure 19-3.

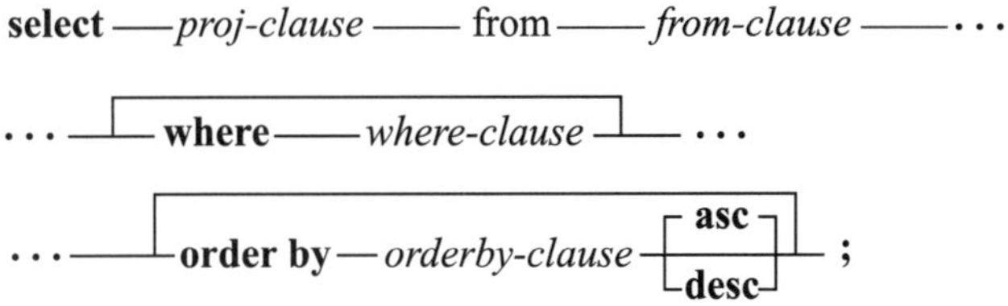

The keywords in the figure above are shown in bold, but the case of the keywords is not significant. The internal representation of the query is in unicode, as the parsing of the query string is done in Java.

Tokens are names that do not refer to keyword or methods. The identifiers must start with a character conforming with the

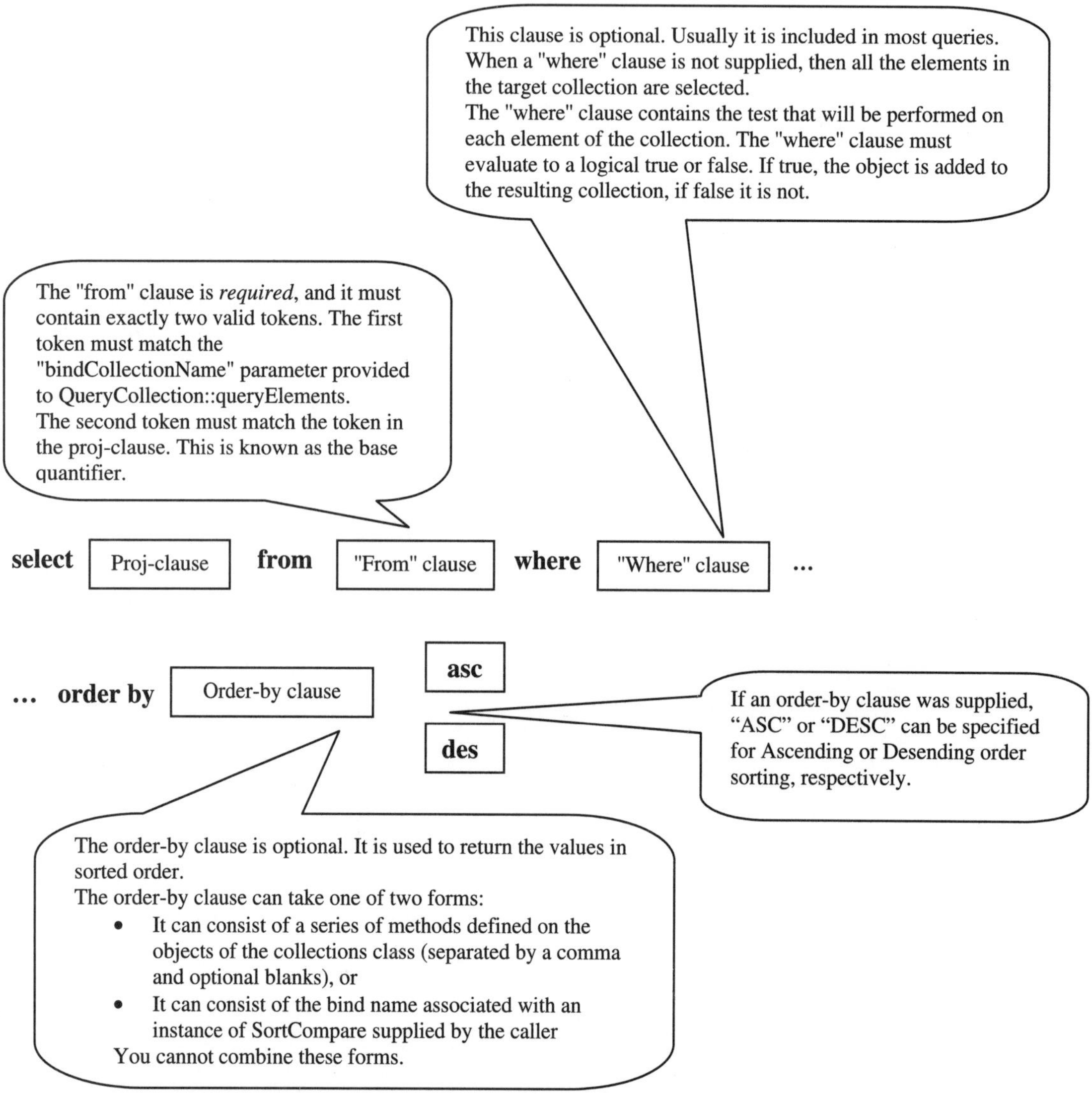

Figure 19-3
The syntax of a query statement.

java.lang.Character.isJavaIdentifierStart validity check, and continue with characters conforming to java.lang.Character.isJavaIdentifierPart. A token identifier that does not comply with this rule will cause an exception to be thrown.

Constants appearing within queries roughly correspond to constant expressions in any programming language such as Java. Table 19-1 lists the different kinds of constants allowed in expressions, along with their internal representation and examples.

The elements of the queried collection are referenced via the proj-clause token, sometimes referred to as the "base quantifier." You can think of it as the reference to the member of the collection currently being tested by the query engine against the query statement.

TABLE 19-1

Constants in Query statements

Constant Kind	Definition	Internal Representation	Examples
Numeric Integer	Sequence of digit with optional sign in front	Java long	11 −13 +9 1984
Decimal	Sequence of digits with optional sign in front, and decimal point somewhere in the sequence	Java.lang.double	11.0 2.5 04.30
Floating Point	Two decimals separated by a capital E, where the second decimal has no decimal point.	Java.lang.double	1.1E1 −1.3E2 3.E-1 +.5E5
Character strings	A sequence of characters starting with and ending with either a single quote (') or a double quote("). The characters used for beginning and ending the string (i.e. single or double quote) should match. Two consecutive single (or double) quotes are combined to represent one single (or double) quote within a character string constant that starts and ends with a single quote (or double quote, respectively). Any other Java "escape sequences" such as \b, \n, \t can be included in the character string constant. The query engine does not modify their value.	Java.lang.String	'green' 'what''s up?'

"Where" Clause

Inside the "where" clause, you can use methods, but you can never use instance variables. The main reason for this is that the SanFrancisco programming model does not support public instance variables. When using a method, the method arguments must be specified if they are required. Just like when writing Java code, the parameters can be either simple value or method calls by themselves. It is important to note that static method calls are not supported, even for public static methods.

The query engine can only use public methods defined on the interface designated as the interfaces for the elements of the queried collections. The name of this interface can be accessed by calling `getElementsClassName()` on the target collection. Obviously, the query engine will not recognize methods defined on subclasses of the collected class, but will be able to use inherited methods.

The method invocation syntax is again quite similar to Java syntax. You specify the base quantifier, followed by a dot, then the name of the method, and the parameters surrounded by parenthesis. Figure 19-4 shows some examples of such method invocations. In case of method overloading, the query engine will use the type information of parameters to determine which variant of the method to use (recall that constants in the query string are internally represented as Java primitive types). The value returned by the method will be used in evaluating the "where" clause.

SQL92 introduces the concept of a host variable and it is a way to avoid hard-coding constant values inside the select statement. When performing a SanFrancisco query, the value that will be associated with the host variable is passed to the query engine at runtime; a non-null value must be passed. Following SQL92 syntax, a host variable is specified by inserting a colon in front of an alphanumeric string starting with a letter (for example "`:x1`", "`:yyy`", "`:AbC`"). Figure 19-5 shows a sample use of host variables in the "where" clause. The only way you can

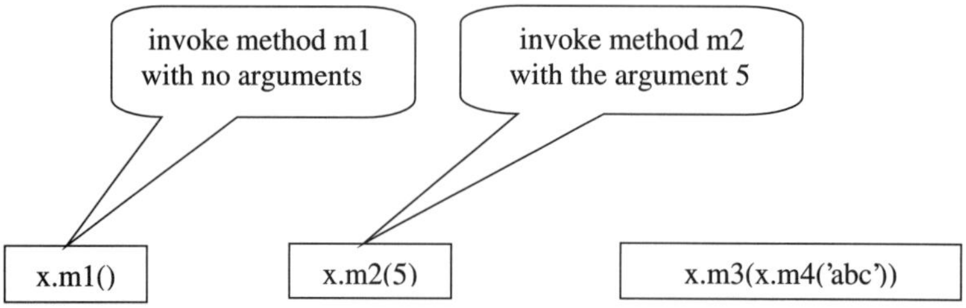

Figure 19-4 Sample method invocations in a "where" clause.

```
select x from coll x where x.getDTime() = :hostVariable;
```

Figure 19-5
Sample use of host variable.

compare Handles is using host variables. Figure 19-8 shows an example of how host variables can be used for comparing Handles (for these, you only use either == or <>).

As we have already seen, the "where" clause must ultimately evaluate to a Boolean (true or false). On the way, you are allowed to use a multitude of logical and mathematical operators. These are shown in Figure 19-6 along with their precedence. Note that for values that are of type Object, the == test is made using the `equals()` method, and that the . and .. operator (method invocation and navigation, respectively) have the highest levels of precedence. The actual order of precedence is based on the levels shown in Figure 19-5, and within a given level, the precedence of operator is based on their order in this level (left to right, i.e. the leftmost operator in a level has the highest precedence). The actual order of operators can always be modified with the use of parentheses. Table 19-2 shows which operators can be used on which types.

Inside the "where" clause, you specify constants as shown in Table 19-1. It is easy to get confused when using this kind of query interface for the first time. The most common mistake you should try to avoid is accessing variables that exist in your code. Values in query strings must be obtained either by a method call, a host variable, or hard coded into the query string. Figure 19-7 shows the wrong and right ways of using the value of a specific variable.

SQL92 supports the notion of type casting, and this is offered in SanFrancisco too, following the same syntax. The cast is specified immediately after the method on which you wish to cast the results. The type specified in the cast must be fully qualified (i.e. contain the package name). Casting is performed by specifying the type name surrounded by "(%" and "%)". If there is a type mismatch, the casting result is "unknown". Figure 19-9 shows an example in which casting is used to select objects of a certain type only. In this example we make use of the fact that an "unknown" value is also treated as null. OOSQL supports a notion of an undefined value, called "unknown." This value can be generated when performing operations when the result is not well-defined, such as adding an `DDecimal` value to a null value. An UNKNOWN value ultimately evaluates to false, so objects for which the conditional turns out to be UNKNOWN are not added to the result correction. An unknown is generated when arithmetic and comparison operators are given a null

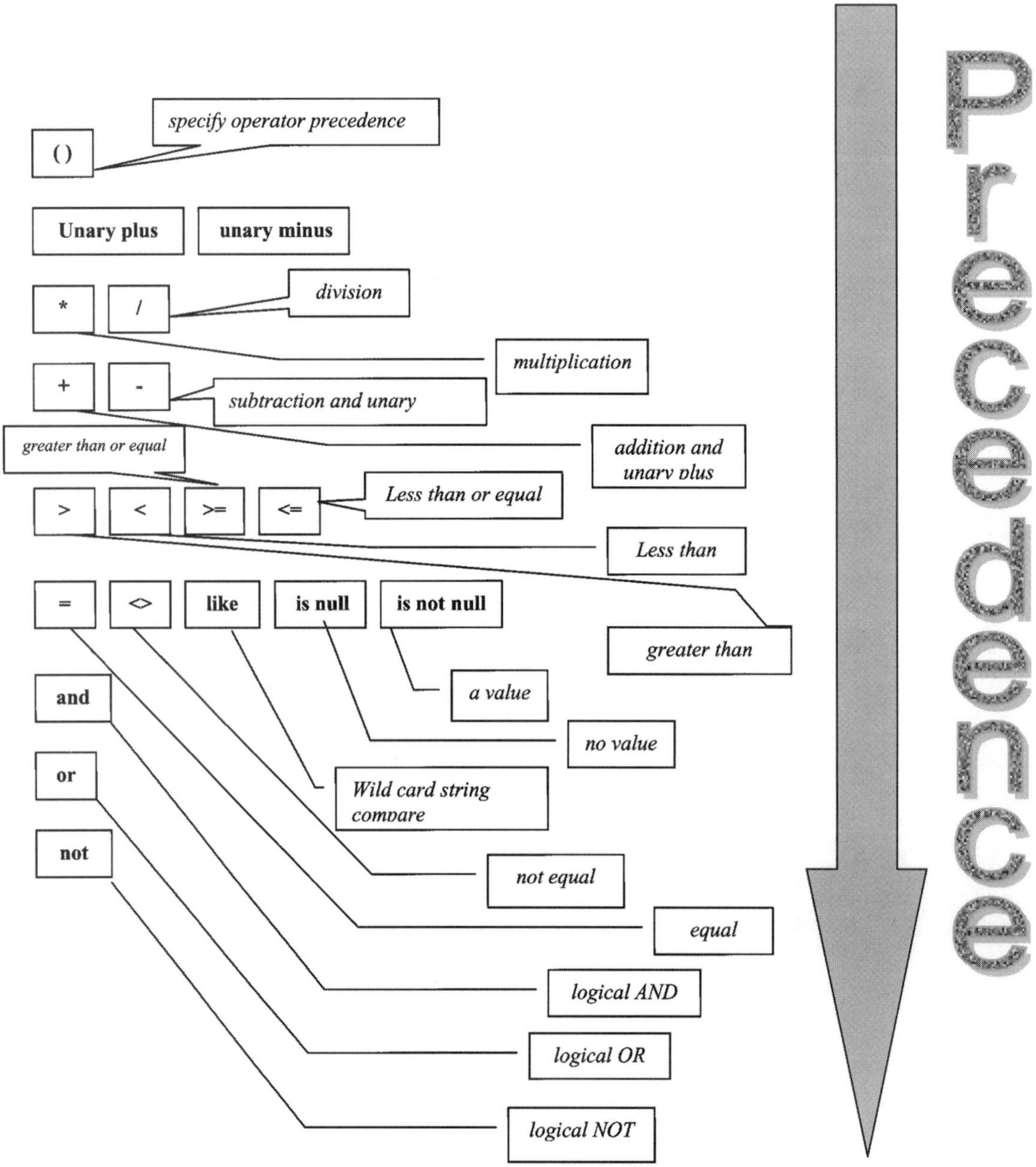

Figure 19-6
Logical and mathematical operators for use in "where" clause.

TABLE 19-2

Allowed operations on different types inside Queries

Java type	Allowed operations
int, short, byte, long, double, float, DInteger, DShort, DLong, DFloat, DDouble, DDecimal	+, –, *, /, =, <>, >, <, >=, <=, - (unary minus), + (unary plus)
String, char, DCharacter	=, <>, >, <, >=, <=, like
DTime	=, <>, >, <, >=, <=
boolean, Object, DBoolean, Handle	=, <>

```
int a = 1;
String queryStr = "select x from
  coll x where x.myMeth() = a;" ;
```

Wrong example of ''where'' clause

```
int a = 1;
String queryStr = "select x from
 coll x  where x.myMeth() = " +
 a + ";" ;
```

Correct example of ''where'' clause

Figure 19-7
Example: how to use a variable value from within a query.

```
String[] hostVarNames = { "hd;" };
Object[] hosrVarValues = { obj.getHandle() };
```

Set up the names and values of host variable

```
String queryStr = "select x from coll x where x.getMyHandle() = :hdl;";
```

Query string comparing the result of a method with a constant Handle:

Figure 19-8
Comparing handles using host variables.

```
select anElement
from myCollection anElement
where anElement.getDependent()(%com.ibm.sf.om.Order%) is null

select anElement
from myCollection anElement
where anElement.getDependent()(%com.ibm.sf.om.Order%)).
getCompleteInvoicing() = true;

select anElement
from myCollection anElement
where anElement(%com.ibm.sf.om.Order%).getCompleteInvoicing() = 0;
```

Figure 19-9
Sample use of casting.

value. The behavior of null in logical operators is summarized in Table 19-3.

Navigation is the chaining together of method calls. Put another way, it is the process of calling a method on the result of a method. Figure 19-10 shows an example of using navigation. In the case of navigation, the first method call might return null. In such a case, the expression would evaluate to null. In other words, if any piece of the navigation chain evaluates to null, the whole chain evaluates to null.

In some cases, you might need to have a complex query that cannot be expressed within the limitations of the query syntax. In these cases you can provide an instance of an object (either an Entity or Dependent) that implements the `SelectCompare` interface. If you do so, this user-supplied object will participate in the query evaluation. The interface for `SelectCompare` is very simple and is shown in

TABLE 19-3

Truth table for logical operators with unknown values

P	Q	P AND Q	P OR Q
True	Unknown	Unknown	True
False	True	False	True
False	False	False	False
False	Unknown	False	Unknown
Unknown	True	Unknown	True
Unknown	False	False	Unknown
Unknown	Unknown	Unknown	Unknown

Assume in the examples below that `anOrderPartner` is of type `com.ibm.sf.om.OrderPartner` and that `aWarehouse` is if type `com.ibm.sf.whs.Warehouse`.

The following lines are examples that use the navigation operator ..

```
aWarehouse.containsSharedPropertyKey()
```

Returns a boolean

```
anOrderPartner.getDefaultOrderWarehouse()
```

Returns a Warehouse object

```
anOrderPartner.getDefaultOrderWarehouse()..containsSharedPropertyKey()
```

Returns a boolean
(`getDefaultOrderWarehouse` returns an object of type `Warehouse`)

```
anOrderPartner.getOrderFinancialPartner()..getDefaultOrderWarehouse()..
containsSharedPropertyKey()
```

Returns a boolean
(`getOrderFinancialPartner` returns an object of type `OrderPartner`)

Figure 19-10
Sample use of navigation.

Figure 19-11. If you pass a `SelectCompare` object to the query engine as part of the query, you must also provide a "bind name" that will be used as a select–compare quantifier. This name will be used by the query engine to identify the `SelectCompare` object within the query string. The select–compare quantifier basically works like the base quantifier, the only difference being that the bind quantifier identifies an object from the collection, and the select–compare quantifier identifies the instance of SelectCompare provided by the caller of the query method.

Figure 19-11 SelectCompare interface.

Interface com.ibm.sf.gf.SelectCompare

public interface interface **SelectCompare**
extends AllowRemote

Name	*Signature*	*Description*
compare	`public abstract boolean compare( Object obj) throws SFException`	This method is used by the query engine to evaluate the query. You can use this interface to implement this method for specific queries. The only argument is the object defined in the query string that will be passed to this object. The implementer of this interface must cast it to the correct value. The value returned by this method is be used for evaluating the query string.

The `compare()` method introduced by `SelectCompare` takes a Java object. This can be supplied as the result of a method call or by referring to the base quantifier. Figure 19-12 shows an example using a `SelectCompare` object for a query.

There are some limitations to keep in mind when using the `SelectCompare`. This object should never by referenced from the "order-by" clause, it is only valid inside the "where" clause. Also, just like for the base-quantifier, you may not invoke any specific methods implemented in your specific `SelectCompare` object (other than the `compare()` method).

There are no restrictions on what can be included in the body of the `compare()` method, other than it should return true or false.

One more operator that the query engine supports is the "like" operator. This operator searches for String values, returned by a method, and looks for matches of a certain pattern. The search pattern is specified by a character string constant in which the percent sign (%) and underscore (_) have special meanings. The "like" operator is applied immediately after the method invocation, and the search pattern appears immediately after the "like" keyword (which must appear in lower-case letters only). Inside the search pattern, underscores represent a single character, and a percentage sign represents a sequence of zero or more characters. Figure 19-13 shows an example of a "where" clause using the "like" operator, along with some strings it will match and other strings it will not match.

Assume in the examples below that we start out with a collection of objects of type `com.ibm.sf.whs.Warehouse`.

Assume also that `aSelectCompareObject` is the object doing the `SelectCompare` on our behalf (i.e. comparing each element of the collection and if the comparison operator is satisfied select the object into the result collection).

```
select x
from aCollectionOfWarehouses x
where aSelectCompareObject.compare(x)=true
```

This invocation traverses the collection and for each element activates the `compare` method on the `SelectCompare` instance to check whether the selection condition is satisfied and if so adds it to the result collection.

You can also mix and match select-compares with navigation and even with method invocations internal to the select-compare instance. For example:

```
select x
from aCollectionOfWarehouses x
where x.getAddress()..toString()..size() > 0
and aSelectCompareObject.compare(x.getAddress())=true
```

In this example the collection is traversed and for each warehouse in the collection we first check if the size of the string generated from the address is larger than zero. If so, then we activate the select-compare instance which uses the address of the warehouse to determine whether the warehouse should be added to the result.

Figure 19-12
Example of using SelectCompare.

"Order-by" Clause

Callers can order the results of the query using methods on the selected objects (defining the sorting criteria). Methods that are specified in the "order-by" clause must be defined in the elements of the collection, and must return a "primitive" datatype that has a natural order (i.e. String, `DDecimal, DTime, int/Dinteger, short/Dshort, long/DLong,`

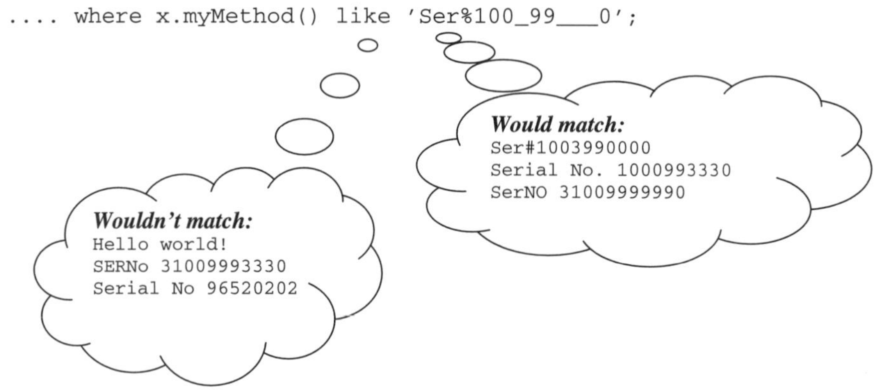

Figure 19-13 Sample use of the like operator.

float/DFloat, double/DDouble, char/DCharacter, boolean/DBoolean [here false <true], byte). Also, these methods cannot be part of a navigation chain. Navigation is not valid in the "order-by" clause. Methods specified in the order by clause must be separated by a comma.

If you need to implement a sophisticated sorting algorithm, the query engine provides you with a construct similar to the SelectCompare described in the previous section. You can specify the bindNameForSortCompareObject as instance of an Entity or Dependent that implements the SortCompare interface. The provided object becomes the sort–compare quantifier that is used to identify the instance of SortCompare in the query string. If this form of "order-by" clause is used, it is used instead of specifying methods in the "order-by" statement. That is, there must not be any methods specified in the "order-by" clause when using a SelectCompare object. The SortCompare interface is shown in Figure 19-14, and it contains only one method, called compare(). This method should return less than zero, zero, or greater than zero, depending on whether the relationship between the two parameter objects is less than, equal to, or greater than. If a SortCompare object is specified in the "order-by" clause, then the sort engine invokes this method on several pairs of objects to determine the correct sorted order of all the objects being returned. As in the SelectCompare object, there are no restrictions on the implementation of the compare() method.

Regardless of which form of "order-by" clause the caller chooses, the caller can also specify a single keyword indicating the ordering to be used. This keyword (as shown in Figure 19-3) can be either ASC (the

Figure 19-14 SortCompare Interface.

Interface com.ibm.sf.gf.SelectCompare

public interface interface **SelectCompare**
extends AllowRemote

Methods

Name	*Signature*	*Description*
compare	`public abstract boolean compare( Object o1, o2) throws SFException`	This method is used by the query engine to order the query results. You can use this interface to implement this method for specific queries. The objects o1 and o2 should be cast to the appropriate type. This method should return one of the following values • if `o1 < o2` return(less than zero) • `if o1 == o2` return(zero) • `if o1 > o2` return(greater than zero)

default) for sorting in ascending order, or DESC for sorting in descending order. The ordering policy used is applied to all the methods specified in the "order-by" clause. Figure 19-15 shows some simple examples of using an "order-by" clause, using the `queryElements()` interface of an `Entity` container.

```
answer = myColl.queryElements(
   "Select x from coll x order by srtComp ASC;",
   "coll", null, null, mySortComp, "srtComp",
   false);
```

Select everything (with empty where clause), then sort it with the `SortCompare` object

```
answer = myColl.queryElements(
   "Select x from coll selComp where selComp(x)=
   false order by srtComp;", "coll",
   mySelectCompObj, "selComp",
   mySortCompObj, "srtComp", false);
```

Select using `SelectCompare` object and then sort using `SortCompare` object

```
answer = myColl.queryElements(
   "Select x from coll x where x.myMeth1() == 1
order by x.myMeth2(), x.myMeth3() DESC;",
"coll", null, null, null, null, false);
```

Select using method `myMeth1` then order using methods `MyMeth2 MyMeth3`.

```
answer = myColl.queryElements(
   "Select x from coll x where x.myMeth1()>0 and
   selComp.compare(x)=true order by
x.myMeth2();",
   "coll", mySelectComp, "selComp", null,  null,
false);
```

Select using method `myMeth1` and `SelectCompare` object then order using method `myMeth2()`

```
answer = myColl.queryElements(
   "Select x from coll x order by x.myMeth1(),
x.myMeth2() ASC;",
"coll", null, null, null, null, false);
```

Select everything (with empty "where" clause) and using the sort methods `myMeth1()` and `myMeth2()`

Figure 19-15
Using an "order-by" clause

CHAPTER 20

International-ization and Localization in SanFrancisco

This chapter reviews the way SanFrancisco frameworks handle the issues of Internationalization and localization. SanFrancisco is built to facilitate the development of complex business applications, and today's business applications are often required to support users which that differ in language and culture.

What is a Locale?

In recent years, there has been an increased awareness in the need for standardized support for culture-specific data-processing. This kind of support is of special importance in countries with mutiple languages and cultures (e.g. Canada and Switzerland), but is also required for applications developed for multinational global corporations and applications developed for export.

Before we proceed to discussing how SanFrancisco supports culture- and language-specific data-processing, let's take a look at some examples of the domains in which we require flexibility for internationalization and localization.

- Language and underlying character set
- Number format: for example, where would you place a comma or a point
- Time format: 12 hours or 24 hours format, presentation format (e.g. 12:45)
- Date format: for example, what does 10/02/11 mean?
- Time zone support

A locale is a specific cultural region, characterized by a location, a certain language and other attributes which that are "locale-specific."

Locale Support in Java

The initial area of deployment for Java was the Internet, which is a domain in which internationalization plays a significant role. For this reason (and probably a couple more), Java goes a long way in supporting multilingual application development.

The first and most significant feature of Java that supports internationalization is the adoption of Unicode characters as the standard for text representation. The Unicode representation of a character is two bytes, and specific ranges of character encodings represent different alphabets and writing systems.

Java also supports the notion of locales in a straightforward manner through the class `java.util.Locale`. At all times, there is a default locale that is part of the operating system settings (for example, in Windows95 you have the "Regional Settings" icon in the Control Panel). It is also possible to create Locale objects for specific places by indicating the desired language and country, for example:

```
MyLocale = new Locale("en", "US").
```

For US–English. The two strings we pass as parameters are the two-letter language and country codes as defined by ISO standards.

Locale Support in SanFrancisco

SanFrancisco also supports the notion of a locale, but in a different way. In SanFrancisco, a locale is an abstraction of a unified set of parameters that are specific to a specific region.

This information is not contained in the locale itself. The locale acts as a proxy for this information. The locale-dependent behavior is encapsulated in a locale-sensitive class. Any business object can have locale-dependent data and implement specific SanFrancisco interfaces for exporting this data.

Locale naming in SanFrancisco is quite similar to that of Java. SanFrancisco represents a locale as a String of the format shown in Figure 20-1. Out of the three components comprising the locale string, only the language code is mandatory. Thus, all of the following are valid locales: en, en_US, en_US_WIN. Note that the first two components are

Figure 20-1 A SanFrancisco locale.

LOCALE = <language code>_<country code>_<variant code>

- <language code> is a lowercase two-letter code as defined by ISO-639; for example, ***en*** for English
- <country code> is an uppercase two-letter code as defined by ISO-3166; for example, ***US*** for the United States
- <variant code> is a vendor and browser-specific code; for example, ***WIN*** for Windows

identical to those that identify a Java locale object. SanFrancisco provides conversion methods that allow you to easily convert between those two representations. The conversion methods are implemented by the `LocaleContext` class, which is described in more detail below.

Working with Locales

Working with Locales in SanFrancisco involves using the `LocaleController`. The LocaleController is a single instance class, meaning that there is one system-wide instance of this class and you are not supposed to create new instances of it. The `LocalController` is responsible for holding the collections of available locales, with one locale identified as the current system default.

When the system-wide instance of LocaleController is created, it is initialized with the list of all Locales supported by the JDK. Later on, it allows you to add or remove locales from the list. All running instances of a single application share a single `LocaleController` instance. That instance has to be accessed through the `LocaleContext` interface, shown in Figure 20-2.

The `LocaleContext` is used to perform locale setting within an application. It allows you to designate and retrieve the *active locale* and the *system default locale*. The active locale is the one that is applied during execution. Note that multiple running instances of the same application can have different active locales. The system default locale is the locale most frequently used and, unlike the active locale, it is shared by all running instances of the application. If the application does not explicitly indicate a locale to be used, the active locale is set to be the system default locale.

So far we have concerned ourselves with how to select the locale to be used in the application. But how does the locale actually come into play? Well, the vast majority of SanFrancisco business objects are locale sensitive, or, in other words, they are somehow affected by the locale. SanFrancisco provides two interfaces for locale-sensitive objects.

The most common interface of the two, which is also simpler is called `Describable`, and is shown in Figure 20-3. As the name implies, this interface is relevant for classes of objects that have locale-dependent (usually language-dependent) text associated with each instance. This text associated with a `Describable` is meant to provide a description

Figure 20-2 Locale Context class.

Class com.ibm.sf.gf.LocaleContext

public abstract class **LocaleContext** extends Object implements Serializable

Methods

Name	*Signature*	*Description*
getActiveLocale	`public static final String getActiveLocale() throws SFException`	Returns the locale that is activated for this client.
setActiveLocale	`public static final void setActiveLocale( String locale) throws SFException`	Set the active locale for the current client. Also sets the JDK default locale to the same value.
SetActiveLocale ToDefault	`public static final void setActiveLocaleToDefault() throws SFException`	Sets the active Locale to be the same as the system default Locale.
getSystemDefaultLocale	`public static final String getSystemDefaultLocale( ) throws SFException`	Returns the locale that is used as system default.
setSystemDefaultLocale	`public static final void setSystemDefaultLocale( String locale) throws SFException`	Establishes the given locale as system-wide default locale. Note that running clients are not affected by this.
getStringFromLocale	`public static final String getStringFromLocale(Locale locale) throws SFException`	Returns the identifying name of the given Locale. The name format is: *languageId_countryId_variantId*, where both variantId and countryId are optional.
getLocaleFromString	`public static final Locale getLocaleFromString( String localeString) throws SFException`	Returns the Locale instance identified by the given localeString parameter. The format for this string is: *languageId_countryId_variantId*, where both variantId and countryId are optional.
GetLocaleResource Controller	`public static final LocaleResourceController getLocaleResourceController() throws SFException`	Return the `LocaleResourceController` instance that is assigned to the current client (locale context). That instance is a transient instance.
setLocaleController	`protected static final void setLocaleController( LocaleController localeController) throws SFException`	Set the Handle to the LocaleController.

Figure 20-3
Describable interface.

Interface com.ibm.sf.gf.Describable

public interface **Describable** extends AllowRemote

Methods

Name	*Signature*	*Description*
getDescription	`public abstract String getDescription() throws SFException`	Returns the description of this Describable as a String in a format/language determined by the locale that is currently active in the environment this call was made in. If no such description exists, it attempts to retrieve a string partially matching the current locale definition. If no such match is found, null is returned.
getDescription	`public abstract String getDescription( String locale) throws SFException`	Returns the description of this Describable in a format/language determined by the given locale. If no such description exists, it attempts to retrieve a string partially matching the given locale definition. If no such match is found, null is returned.
GetDescriptive Information	`public abstract DescriptiveInformation getDescriptiveInformation() throws SFException`	Returns the `DescriptiveInformation` encapsulating the locale sensitive description of this `Describable`.

of the instance. As an example, consider a `Company` object that includes a short description of the company, and is provided in several languages.

The other interface, called `Translatable`, involves having class instances that implement a method returning a locale-dependent representation. This interface is shown in Figure 20-4. As an example for a `Translatable` class, consider `DTime`, which represents a timestamp (date and time). Different time display formats are supported by implementing the `Translatable` interface.

The `Describable` interface allows you to extract a locale-invariant proxy of the description. In other words, you get an object that can provide you with the different descriptions for different locales. This proxy is called `DescriptiveInformation`. `Descriptive Information` itself does not contain any messages; it is merely is an identifier (encapsulates a unique id) that is used to retrieve the corresponding

Figure 20-4
Translatable interface.

Interface com.ibm.sf.gf.Translatable

public interface **Translatable** extends AllowRemote

Methods

Name	*Signature*	*Description*
format	`public abstract String format() throws SFException`	Returns a `String` representation of this object in a format determined by the currently active Locale in the environment that the call was made in.
format	`public abstract String format(String locale) throws SFException`	Returns a `String` representation of this object in a format determined by the given Locale.

locale-dependent messages from the DynamicMessageCatalogs they are actually stored in.

Because most SanFrancisco objects support multiple locales, we have interfaces for `DescribableDependent` and `TranslatableDependent`, which are interfaces for Dependent objects supporting the Describable and Translatable interfaces, respectively. These interfaces are provided to ensure type safety in cases we require `Dependent` objects with one of the two latter interfaces.

In the same way, we have `DescribableDynamicEntity` that is used for `Entity` objects that support multi-lingual descriptions.

Managing Locale-dependent Resources

When developing a complex application that needs to support multiple locales, you usually end up with a large number of resources that have different versions for different locales, or in other words, locale-sensitive resources. SanFrancisco allows you to easily manage the localized resources in your application. A localized resource is an object that represents information in a locale-specific manner.

Locale-dependent resources are divided into three groups, each handled in a different way:.

- Static messages—stored in `StaticMessageCatalogs`
- Dynamic messages—stored in `DynamicMessageCatalogs`
- Objects (of types `Entity`, `Dependent`, `String`)

The `StaticMessageCatalog` is a read-only message repository that is initialized from a file. The `DynamicMessageCatalog` is also a message repository, but it can be updated during runtime. Specifically, you can add new messages, remove messages, or modify messages. The `DynamicMessageCatalog` can (but doesn't have to) be initialized from a file, and it can also write itself to a file. In order to leave room for other kinds of application-specific resources (which are locale-dependent), the frameworks supports generic collections of locale-dependent objects.

All these localized resources are accessed through the class `LocaleResourceController`. The interfaces provided by this class distinguish between the previously mentioned groups of resources. So, for example, it has different accessor methods for different kinds of resources:

- `String getDynamicMessageBy(String locale, String catalogId, String messageId)`
- `DynamicMessageCatalog getDynamicMessageCatalogBy (String locale, String catalogId)`
- `String getStaticMessageBy(String locale, String catalogId, String messageId)`
- `StaticMessageCatalog getStaticMessageCatalogBy (String locale, String catalogId)`
- `Object getObjectBy(String locale, String id)`

Keep in mind that the distinction between accessors to different resources does not have anything to do with the actual Java type of the resource, as both static and dynamic messages are Strings, and both `StaticMessageCatalogs` and `DynamicMessageCatalogs` are Entities. The distinction is related to the mechanism that the `LocaleResourceController` uses to manage and store them. Like the `LocaleController`, the `LocaleResourceController` is retrieved through the `LocaleContext`.

StaticMessageCatalog

Static messages are the simplest kind of locale-specific resource. These are basically text strings which are stored in an external file. In any case it is a good practice to maintain message text strings outside your application code in order to avoid re-compiling every time you need to make changes to the displayed text strings. SanFrancisco implements external text string message files using `StaticMessageCatalog`.

`StaticMessageCatalogs` are used by the framework to manage and store error messages, and can be used by applications to store GUI control labels and other immutable information that can be determined when the application is generated (as opposed to during runtime). One catalog exists per locale, so messages for the same locale are stored together.

The SanFrancisco framework follows a naming convention for static message strings. This convention is described in Figure 20-5.

Figures 20-6 and 20-7 show a portion of the static messages for the GL (General Ledger framework). The first one is in English, and the other in French. As you can see, the file just contains a list of identifiers, each one on a separate line, followed by an equal sign and then the value for the identifier. Lines that start with a number sign (#) are considered to be comments.

DynamicMessageCatalog

In some situations, the need might arise for having locale-specific messages that are created or modified dynamically during runtime. SanFrancisco provides the mechanism for implementing this through `DynamicMessageCatalogs`.

`DynamicMessageCatalogs` are used by the framework itself to manage the description messages associated with a `Describable` object. So actually, every time you store or retrieve a locale-dependent description for a `Describable`, a `DynamicMessageCatalog` is accessed.

Like the static messages, dynamic messages for the same locale are managed together in one catalog.

Form	Usage	Example
TXT_xxx	For all descriptive static text displayed in windows, that is, text to be placed into labels. Also used for informational messages that do not require a message help.	TXT_USER_ID=User Id
MSG_xxx	For warning, and error messages.	MSG_BASE_HANDLE_CREATE=MSG_BaseException_006: Unable to create the Handle because the unique identifier could not be created.
CMD_xxx	For texts describing actions, that is, text displayed on buttons or menus.	CMD_SAVE_AND_CLOSE=Save and close

Figure 20-5
SanFrancisco static message naming convention.

```
##################################################
# Category: GLACOMMON
# Severity: Severe
# {0} = $Class
# {1} = &instance
GLACOMMON001=MSG_GLACOMMON_001: {0}, {1} is of type 'memo account'.
##################################################
# Category: GLACOMMON_
# Severity: Severe
# {0} = $Class
# {1} = &instance
GLACOMMON002=MSG_GLACOMMON_002: {0}, {1} is not of type 'memo account'.
##################################################
# Category: GLACOMMON
# Severity: Severe
# {0} = $Class
# {1} = &instance
GLACOMMON003=MSG_GLACOMMON_003: {0}, {1} is of type 'balance sheet
account'.
```

Figure 20-6
Part of the GL static messages (English).

```
####################################################
# Category: GLACOMMON
# Severity: Severe
# {0} = $Class
# {1} = &instance
GLACOMMON001=MSG_GLACOMMON_001: {0}, {1} est de type \u00b4compte pour
m\u00e9moire\u00b4.
####################################################
# Category: GLACOMMON_
# Severity: Severe
# {0} = $Class
# {1} = &instance
GLACOMMON002=MSG_GLACOMMON_002: {0}, {1} n\u00b4est pas de type \u00b4compte
pour m\u00e9moire\u00b4.
####################################################
# Category: GLACOMMON
# Severity: Severe
# {0} = $Class
# {1} = &instance
GLACOMMON003=MSG_GLACOMMON_003: {0}, {1} est de type \u00b4compte de
bilan\u00b4.
```

Figure 20-7
Part of the GL static messages (French).

Locale-specific Objects

The `LocaleResourceController` allows you to go beyond static and dynamic message texts. It holds an associative array of locale-sensitive objects that you can access using the `getObjectBy` method mentioned previously.

The collection of locale-sensitive objects maintained by the `LocaleResourceController` can contain these kinds of objects.

- Entity
- Dependent
- String

When you add an Entity object, you may specify whether you want it to be owned by the controller or not. Strings and Dependent objects will be owned.

The following methods are used for maintaining the collection of locale-sensitive objects in the controller:

```
■ public abstract void addObjectBy(Object object,
                String locale,
                String id) throws SFException
■ public abstract void addOwnedObjectBy(Entity object,
                  String locale,
                  String id) throws SFException
■ public abstract void removeObjectBy(String locale,
                 String id) throws SFException
■ public abstract void removeOwnedObjectBy(String
  locale,
                   String id) throws SFException
```

The first method adds a new object to the collection, which is either an `Entity` not to be owned by the controller, a `Dependent`, or a `String`. The second method does the same, only that it adds an owned `Entity`. The two other methods do the opposite: they remove an object given its id and the locale.

Timezone Support

A timezone is an identifier for a geographical region in which the same standard time is used. SanFrancisco represents a timezone as a string in the standard format of three upper case letters. Examples of timezones are:

Time Zone	Representation
Central Standard Time	CST
Eastern Standard Time	EST
Central European Time	CET
Greenwich Mean Time	GMT

Needless to say, any application, specifically one that intends to support multiple locales, must facilitate working with multiple time zones. In SanFrancisco it is possible to have several time zones defined. As with locales, one specific time zone is considered to be active (i.e. applied to the application) at a certain time, and there is a notion of a system default timezone that represents the timezone most commonly used. Multiple

Figure 20-8
`DTimeContext` interface

Class com.ibm.sf.gf.DTimeContext

public abstract class **DTimeContext** extends Object implements Serializable

Methods

Name	*Signature*	*Description*
getActiveTimeZone	`public static final String getActiveTimeZone() throws SFException`	Returns a string with the active time zone
setActiveTimeZone	`public static final void setActiveTimeZone(String timeZone) throws SFException`	Sets the active time zone.
SetActiveTimeZone ToSystemDefault	`public static final void setActiveTimeZoneToSystemDefault() throws SFException`	Set the active time zone string to the System default time zone stored in the DPC.
SetSystemDefault TimeZone	`public static final void setSystemDefaultTimeZone(String timeZone) throws SFException`	Sets the default time zone according to the parameter timezone string.
GetSystemDefault TimeZone	`public static final String getSystemDefaultTimeZone() throws SFException`	Returns the system default time zone

running instances of a single application can have different active timezones, whereas the system default timezone is shared by all running instances of an application (again, notice the resemblance to locales). If the application does not explicity designate a timezone, the active timezone automatically adopts the setting of the Java Virtual Machine. If the system default timezone is not explicitly set, it defaults to Greenwich Mean Time (GMT).

Timezone setting are controlled by `DTimeContext`. This class is shown in Figure 20-8. `DTimeContext` allows you to designate and retrieve both the active timezone and the system default timezone.

PART 4

Common Business Objects

CHAPTER 21

Common Business Objects

Common Business Objects (CBOs) are a collection of classes providing functionality commonly needed for business applications. The need for such objects appears in different domains. They are required in more than one of the SanFrancisco frameworks. By placing them in a separate layer and not inside one of the frameworks, a higher level of abstraction and reusability is achieved. This chapter introduces CBOs and goes into the details of a group of CBOs are called "General" CBOs, which actually account for most of the CBOs. The next couple of chapters deal with other kinds of CBOs.

As the CBOs are aimed at solving specific business problems, most of them are quite intuitive and easy to understand. These business problems are expected to recur in different business contexts.

CBOs in SanFrancisco

CBOs are the building blocks for SanFrancisco applications. They introduce many concepts that are reusable across most business domains. In order to illustrate the role of CBOs in SanFrancisco, consider MFC (Microsoft Foundation Classes) as an example of a framework. In this framework, you can actually get complete out-of-the-box skeletal applications using Visual C++ Wizards. In this framework, GUI controls such as a button or a radio box are the building blocks for applications. They are repeatedly used, and sometimes customized by the needs of the application developers. The same applies to CBOs in SanFrancisco. The CBO layer provides you with a handful of useful classes, which can be easily combined together to build a larger application. You may customize them by deriving your own classes from them, and you can place them inside CBPs (Core Business Processes) to create fully functional applications.

When developing a SanFrancisco application, we can use CBOs directly or indirectly (through the Core Business Processes). The decision whether to use them directly or not, depends on how well the application scenario maps to the CBPs, as explained in Chapter 25.

The Common Business Objects categories are divided into three different groups:

- *General Business Objects*. These objects (and their functionality) are common across business domains

- *Financial Business Objects*. These objects are related to financials and are common across business domains
- *Generalized Mechanisms*. Consists of functions used to solve problems common across many different business domains. These CBOs provide functionality that is external to the business domain but comes in handy at times.

The remainder of this chapter deals with General Business Objects. As mentioned before, the two other groups of categories are dealt with in the following chapters. Table 21-1 lists the General Business Object interfaces. In the following sections, we describe each of these interfaces.

It is important to understand that CBOs are not used in the way you would use a class library providing some specialized utilities. Being a framework, the classes of SanFrancisco are bound by various interactions and relationships. So in order to use a specific category or object, you might be required to configure and possibly use other classes. The most common example is the company category, which must be set up in order to work with some of the CBOs, because the notion of a company is in the essence of the CBO layer design. Some CBOs do not exist unless they are owned by a company object.

Another consideration when using the Common Business Objects is how different applications using the CBOs coexist and interact. This is especially true when CBOs are customized using derivation because you would like the different components of SanFrancisco to continue to work correctly with your extension for a certain object. For example, if you define your own extension of the `BusinessPartner` object, you would probably like the Accounts Receivable/Accounts Payable Core Business Process to be able to use this object. In order to accomplish that, you should follow the rules described in Chapter 24 for extending CBOs.

To use the CBOs you usually follow a standard usage pattern. You have a factory to create objects that are then managed using a controller attached to the company. See Chapter 12 for some background on the notion of factories and controllers in SanFrancisco.

Addresses

Addresses are a basic component in virtually any business system. An address record is necessary whenever we need to locate and commun-

TABLE 21-1

SanFrancisco general CBO categories.

Name	Class/Interface Name (all are under com.ibm.sf.cf)
Address	Address
Business Partner	BusinessPartner
	BusinessPartnerCustomerSupplierData
	BusinessPartnerSharedData
	BusinessPartnerFactory
	BusinessPartnerCustomerSupplierDataFactory
	BusinessPartnerSharedDataFactory
Business Partner Balances	BusinessPartnerBalances
	DBusinessPartnerSpecificationKey
	DBusinessPartnerAccessKey
Classification	ClassificationType
	ClassificationTypeController
	ClassificationTypeFactory
Company	Company
	Enterprise
	CompanyController
	CompanyFactory
	EnterpriseFactory
Credit Check	DCreditCheck
	CreditCheckPolicyOrganizer
	CreditCheckPolicyOrganizerController
	DCreditCheckPolicy
Currencies	Currency
	CurrencyController
	DCurrencyValue
	DCurrencyValueFactory
	CurrencyFactory
	ExchangeRateController
	DExchangeRateTypeDateBased
	DExchangeRateTypeDateFixed
	DExchangeRateRetrievalPolicy
	DTransactionValue
	DTransactionValueExtended
Document Location	DocumentLocation
	DocumentLocationController
	DocumentLocationFactory
Fiscal Calendar	FiscalCalendar
	FiscalYear
	FiscalPeriod
Initials	Initials
	InitialsController
	InitialsFactory
	SignatoryAbility
	SignatoryAbilitiesGroup
	SignatoryAbilityFactory
	SignatoryAbilityGroupFactory
	DInitialsExtension

TABLE 21-1

(Contd)

Name	Class/Interface Name (all are under com.ibm.sf.cf)
Natural Calendar	NaturalCalendar NaturalCalendarFactory DResultDateAdjustmentPolicy DNaturalCalendarWorkTimePolicy DWorkperiodManagerPolicy
Number Series	NumberSeries NumberSeriesFactory
Payment Method	PaymentMethod PaymentMethodFactory PaymentMethodController
Payment Terms	PaymentTerms DPaymentTermsDetails PaymentTermsFactoryD PaymentTermsDetailsFactory
Periodized Calendar	PeriodizedCalendar PeriodizedYearCalendarPeriod
Process token	ProcessToken ProcessTokenValue ProcessTokenController
Project	Project ProjectFactory
Specific Information	DSpecificInformation DSpecificInformationFactory
Supplementary Charge	SupplementaryCharge DSupplementaryCharge DSupplementaryChargeFactory DSupplementaryChargeTypeIdOnly DSupplementaryChargeTypeFixedAmount DSupplementaryChargeTypeIdOnlyFactory DSupplementaryChargeTypeFixedAmountFactory SupplementaryChargeController
Unit of Measure	UnitOfMeasure UnitCategoryUnitLink UnitOfMeasureFactory UnitCategoryUnitLinkFactory UnitOfMeasureController DMeasurementValue DMeasurement

icate with different parties such as suppliers, customers, and staff. Specifically, this information is essential for issuing invoices, purchase orders, letters, and, in fact, any kind of document.

The SanFrancisco interface for address record information is called `Address`. In SanFrancisco the same kind of address object is used for all addresses: both the company's addresses and for the addresses of the company's business partners. Addresses contain the basic contact information, a collection of free form address lines and references to a country, and, optionally, a user-defined "*area*." (You can think of *area* as an application-defined notion of a geographical region.)

Figure 21-1 shows the implementation model for the `Address` Business Object in SanFrancisco. Most `Address` attributes are strings, the only exceptions being Country and Area, which are references to persistent objects, and the address lines that are implemented as a collection of strings. SanFrancisco does not impose any required format on the Strings, although `LocaleInformation` should conform to the standard for Java locales (e.g. "en_US"; see Chapter 20 for more details on locales).

At first glance, you might think that the use of a single phone number is a limitation but what actually happens is that in places where addresses are used, an open-ended collection is maintained. Therefore, you can have a separate address object for each phone number per company business partner. This could also be handled by using the generic address line support to add address lines that represent additional phone numbers. As previously mentioned, this address line is a collection in which each line is a string. Each such line has a key, which is defined by the user or the developer. If all you want to do is store values of an address label, you might key your address lines with sequential numbers; if you want more meaningful access to the address information, you might use meaningful keys like "street address", "PO Box", "city", and so on.

Figure 21-2 shows the `Address` interface. In Figure 21-3, you can see a simple example of how we use an address. In this example, we create a new address and then print out the address information given an address object.

Note that contrary to many other persistent Entities in SanFrancisco addresses are not maintained by controllers. Instead, addresses are explicitly associated with the business object whose address it is. Therefore, a company object owns its addresses, and it provides methods to access and maintain addresses. The reason for using explicit containment and not using controllers is that as in the real word, addresses are tightly coupled to whomever they belong to. There is no point in keeping a large pool of shared address objects because usually only one object would be interested in accessing them.

Business objects that have addresses, have a uniform way of providing access to them, through the `getPrimaryAddress ()` and

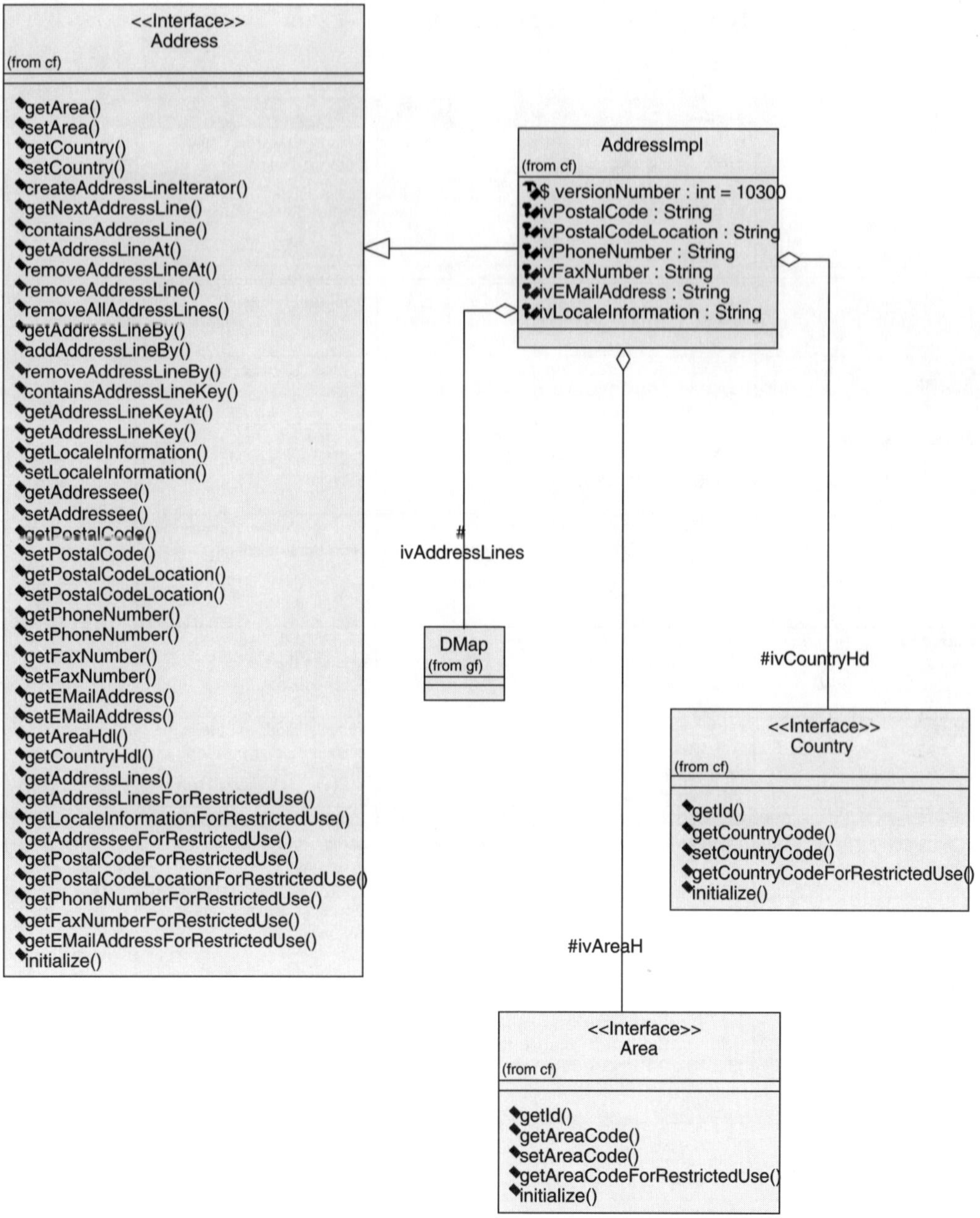

Figure 21-1
Address implementation model.

Interface com.ibm.sf.cf.Address

public interface **Address** extends DynamicEntity

Name	*Signature*	*Description*
GetArea	`public abstract Area getArea() throws SFException`	Returns the Area, copied from the Handle
setArea	`public abstract void setArea(Area newArea) throws SFException`	Set the Handle of the Area
getCountry	`public abstract Country getCountry() throws SFException`	Returns the Country, copied from the Handle
setCountry	`public abstract void setCountry(Country newCountry) throws SFException`	Set the Handle of the Country
createAddressLineIterator	`public abstract Iterator createAddressLineIterator() throws SFException`	Create Iterator for Collection of AddressLines
getNextAddressLine	`public abstract String getNextAddressLine(Iterator position) throws SFException`	Gets the AddressLine at the Next Iterator Position
containsAddressLine	`public abstract boolean containsAddressLine(String addressline) throws SFException`	Checks if the AddressLine exists in the Collection of AddressLines
getAddressLineAt	`public abstract String getAddressLineAt(Iterator position) throws SFException`	Gets the AddressLine at the current iterator position
removeAddressLineAt	`public abstract void removeAddressLineAt(Iterator position) throws SFException`	Removes the AddressLine at the Current Iterator Position
removeAddressLine	`public abstract void removeAddressLine(String addressline) throws SFException`	Removes the specified AddressLine
addAddressLineBy	`public abstract void addAddressLineBy(String addressLine, String key) throws SFException`	Adds a AddressLine to the Collection of AddressLines by the Specified Key

Figure 21-2
Interface `Address`

removeAddressLineBy	`public abstract void removeAddressLineBy(String key) throws SFException`	Removes the AddressLine by the specified key
containsAddressLineKey	`public abstract boolean containsAddressLineKey(String key) throws SFException`	Checks if the AddressLine exists by the specified Key
getAddressLineKeyAt	`public abstract String getAddressLineKeyAt(Iterator position) throws SFException`	Gets the AddressLineKey at the current iterator position
getAddressLineKey	`public abstract String getAddressLineKey(String addressLine) throws SFException`	Gets the AddressLine at the Current Iterator Position
getLocaleInformation	`public abstract String getLocaleInformation() throws SFException`	Gets LocaleInformation
setLocaleInformation	`public abstract void setLocaleInformation(String newLocaleInformation) throws SFException`	Sets LocaleInformation
setAddressee	`public abstract void setAddressee(String newAddressee) throws SFException`	Sets Addressee
getPostalCode	`public abstract String getPostalCode() throws SFException`	Gets PostalCode
setPostalCode	`public abstract void setPostalCode(String newPostalCode) throws SFException`	Sets PostalCode
getPostalCodeLocation	`public abstract String getPostalCodeLocation() throws SFException`	Gets PostalCodeLocation
setPostalCodeLocation	`public abstract void setPostalCodeLocation(String newPostalCodeLocation) throws SFException`	Sets PostalCodeLocation
getPhoneNumber	`public abstract String getPhoneNumber() throws SFException`	Gets PhoneNumber
setPhoneNumber	`public abstract void setPhoneNumber(String newPhoneNumber) throws SFException`	Sets PhoneNumber
getFaxNumber	`public abstract String getFaxNumber() throws SFException`	Gets FaxNumber
setFaxNumber	`public abstract void setFaxNumber(String newFaxNumber) throws SFException`	Sets FaxNumber

Figure 21-2
(Cont'd)

getEMailAddress	`public abstract String getEMailAddress() throws SFException`	Gets EMailAddress
setEMailAddress	`public abstract void setEMailAddress(String newEMailAddress) throws SFException`	Sets EMailAddress
getAreaHdl	`public abstract Handle getAreaHdl() throws SFException`	Returns the Handle to the Area of the area of the Address
getCountryHdl	`public abstract Handle getCountryHdl() throws SFException`	Returns the Handle to the Country of the country of the Address
getAddressLines	`public abstract DMap getAddressLines() throws SFException`	Returns a copy of the Collection of AddressLine, used by framework—NOT FOR CLIENT USE (client code should use iterators).
getAddressLinesForRestrictedUse	`public abstract DMap getAddressLinesForRestrictedUse () throws SFException`	Returns the actual AddressLine, used by framework for SetEqual()—NOT FOR CLIENT USE
initialize	`public abstract void initialize(Country country,String localeInformation) throws SFException`	This method is invoked by the Factory after Construction of an instance of this class to ensure proper initialization

Figure 21-2
(Cont'd)

`setPrimaryAddress()` methods. In addition to the primary address, there is a notion of a general collection of addresses, which also has a uniform interface (refer to `BusinessPartner` below to see how this collection is used).

Business Partner

Any company interacts with other businesses. Hence, it needs to record information about these businesses, namely customers and suppliers. Often these customers and suppliers are the same organization. A business partner may have different information depending on whether you look at it as a supplier or as a customer.

Business partners are often large organizations in a hierarchy. For such organizations, you may have relevant information at any level of

```
public void displayAddress(Address anAddress) throws SFException {

      System.out.println(theAddress.getAddressee());
      System.out.println(theAddress.getAddressLineBy("addr1"));
      String addr2 = theAddress.getAddressLineBy("addr2");
      if (addr2 != null) {
            System.out.println (addr2);
      }
      System.out.println(theAddress.getAddressLineBy("city")
            + ", "
            + theAddress.getAddressLineBy("state")
            + "  "
            + theAddress.getPostalCode());
}
```

Figure 21-3
Code sample: example of using Address.

the organization. A business partner, whether customer or supplier, must have a primary address, which is an Address object. In addition, it can have a list of other addresses that an application needs to track. For example, additional addresses might include overseas offices, or warehouses.

The class `BusinessPartner`, shown in Figure 21-4, holds common information to all kinds of business partners, whereas the `BusinessPartnerCustomerSupplierData` (see Figure 21-5) holds the variable information that is part of the customer or supplier context. In addition, you have `BusinessPartnerSharedData` (Figure 21-6), which holds business partner attributes you might want to share between companies (this is especially relevant for addresses). The latter also holds the hierarchy of business partners.

Interface com.ibm.sf.cf.BusinessPartner

public interface BusinessPartner extends DescribableDynamicEntity, Shared, Distinguishable

Name	*Signature*	*Description*
getLegalName	`public abstract String getLegalName() throws SFException`	Retrieves the legal name for this BusinessPartner.
getPrimaryAddress	`public abstract Address getPrimaryAddress() throws SFException`	Retrieves the primary address for this BusinessPartner.
getRegistrationId	`public abstract String getRegistrationId() throws SFException`	Returns the registrationId for this BusinessPartner.
getShortName	`public abstract String getShortName() throws SFException`	Returns the short name for this BusinessPartner.
setLegalName	`public abstract void setLegalName(String legalName) throws SFException`	Sets the legal name for this object.
setPrimaryAddress	`public abstract void setPrimaryAddress(Address primaryAddress) throws SFException`	Sets the primary address to the passed value
setRegistrationId	`public abstract void setRegistrationId(String registrationId) throws SFException`	Sets the registrationId for this object.
setShortName	`public abstract void setShortName(String shortName) throws SFException`	Sets the short name for this BusinessPartner
getBusinessPartnerSharedData	`public abstract BusinessPartnerSharedData getBusinessPartnerSharedData() throws SFException`	Get the BusinessPartnerSharedData object that this BusinessPartner is associated with.
getDirectlyOwnedAddressBy	`public abstract Address getDirectlyOwnedAddressBy(String key) throws SFException`	Get the specified Address from those Addresses directly owned by this BusinessPartner.
queryDirectlyOwnedAddresses	`public abstract QueryCollection queryDirectlyOwnedAddresses(String select, String collectionBindName, SelectCompare selectCompareObject, String bindNameOfSelectCompareObject, SortCompare orderByCompareObject, String bindNameOfOrderByObject, boolean accessResults) throws SFException`	Select the Addresses satisfying the Query.
removeDirectlyOwnedAddressBy	`public abstract void removeDirectlyOwnedAddressBy(String key) throws SFException`	Removes and deletes the Address with the specified key.

Figure 21-4
Interface `BusinessPartner`

removeAllDirectlyOwnedAddresses	`public abstract void removeAllDirectlyOwnedAddresses() throws SFException`	Removes and deletes all elements from the directly owned collection of Addresses.
isAddressesDirectlyEmpty	`public abstract boolean isAddressesDirectlyEmpty() throws SFException`	Determine if the locally-contained collection is empty.
directlyContainsAddressKey	`public abstract boolean directlyContainsAddressKey(String key) throws SFException`	Checks if the Address exists by the specified key.
getHierarchyDescriptiveInformation	`public abstract DescriptiveInformation getHierarchyDescriptiveInformation() throws SFException`	Get the DescriptiveInformation object for the private BusinessPartner hierarchy within this Company that this BusinessPartner belongs to.
getSharedHierarchyDescriptiveInformation	`public abstract DescriptiveInformation getSharedHierarchyDescriptiveInformation() throws SFException`	Get the DescriptiveInformation object for the shared BusinessPartner hierarchy that this BusinessPartner belongs to.
getSharedDescriptiveInformation	`public abstract DescriptiveInformation getSharedDescriptiveInformation() throws SFException`	Get the shared DescriptiveInformation object for this BusinessPartner.
getHierarchyDescription	`public abstract String getHierarchyDescription() throws SFException`	Get the description for the private BusinessPartner hierarchy within this Company that this BusinessPartner belongs to, formatted to the active locale.
getHierarchyDescription	`public abstract String getHierarchyDescription(String locale) throws SFException`	Get the description for the private BusinessPartner hierarchy within this Company that this BusinessPartner belongs to, formatted to the given locale.

Figure 21-4
(Cont'd)

The `BusinessPartnerCustomerSupplierData` is associated with payment methods, currencies, payment plans, addresses, credit checks, business partner balances, and business partner groups. Most of these are described in other parts of this chapter. These associations are made using "chaining" (basically following the "Chain of Responsibility" pattern [GOF]). The idea is that if for a component such as the address, if the specific business partner customer/supplier data is missing in the component, it looks in its parent for it.

Interface com.ibm.sf.cf.BusinessPartnerCustomer SupplierData

public interface BusinessPartnerCustomerSupplierData extends DynamicEntity

Name	*Signature*	*Description*
getBusinessPartnerGroup	`public abstract BusinessPartnerGroup getBusinessPartnerGroup() throws SFException`	Get the BusinessPartnerGroup for this BusinessPartner if one exists.
getDirectlyContainedBusinessPartnerGroup	`public abstract BusinessPartnerGroup getDirectlyContainedBusinessPartnerGroup() throws SFException`	Get the directly contained BusinessPartnerGroup for this BusinessPartner if one exists.
setDirectlyContainedBusinessPartnerGroup	`public abstract void setDirectlyContainedBusinessPartnerGroup(BusinessPartnerGroup newBusinessPartnerGroup) throws SFException`	Set the directly contained BusinessPartnerGroup
setDirectlyContainedCurrency	`public abstract void setDirectlyContainedCurrency(Currency newCurrency) throws SFException`	Set the directly contained Currency
getDirectlyContainedCurrency	`public abstract Currency getDirectlyContainedCurrency() throws SFException`	Get the directly contained Currency (either supplier or customer) for this BusinessPartner if one exists.
getCurrency	`public abstract Currency getCurrency() throws SFException`	Get the Currency (either supplier or customer) for this BusinessPartner if one exists.
setDirectlyContainedPaymentMethod	`public abstract void setDirectlyContainedPaymentMethod (PaymentMethod newPaymentMethod) throws SFException`	Set the directly contained PaymentMethod
getPaymentMethod	`public abstract PaymentMethod getPaymentMethod() throws SFException`	Get the PaymentMethod (either supplier or customer) for this BusinessPartner if one exists.
getDirectlyContainedPaymentMethod	`public abstract PaymentMethod getDirectlyContainedPaymentMethod () throws SFException`	Get the directly contained PaymentMethod (either supplier or customer) for this BusinessPartner if one exists.
setDirectlyContainedPaymentTerms	`public abstract void setDirectlyContainedPaymentTerms( PaymentTerms newPaymentTerms) throws SFException`	Set the directly contained PaymentTerms
getPaymentTerms	`public abstract PaymentTerms getPaymentTerms() throws SFException`	Get the PaymentTerms (either supplier or customer) for this BusinessPartner if one exists.
getDirectlyContainedPaymentTerms	`public abstract PaymentTerms getDirectlyContainedPaymentTerms( ) throws SFException`	Get the directly contained PaymentTerms (either supplier or customer) for this BusinessPartner if one exists.

Figure 21-5
Interface `BusinessPartnerCustomerSupplierData`

getParent	public abstract BusinessPartnerCustomerSupplierData getParent() throws SFException	Returns the BusinessPartnerCustomerSupplierData object that is the parent of this object if one exists.
performCreditCheck	public abstract boolean performCreditCheck(DTransactionValue amount, ProcessTokenValue processToken, DTime time) throws SFException	This method performs a credit check based on the process token and value passed in and returns whether or not this Business Partner has exceeded their credit limit.
performCreditCheck	public abstract boolean performCreditCheck(DTransactionValue amount, ProcessTokenValue processToken, DTime time, ResultsCollection resultsCollection) throws SFException	This method will perform a credit check based on the process token and value passed in and returns whether or not this Business Partner has exceeded their credit limit along with any informational messages that may have been generated during the credit checking process.
setCreditLimit	public abstract void setCreditLimit(DCurrencyValue creditLimitValue) throws SFException	Establishes the credit limit for a business partner given a credit limit value.
getCreditLimit	public abstract DCurrencyValue getCreditLimit() throws SFException	Retrieves the credit limit for this business partner.
getChainParent	public abstract PropertyContainer getChainParent() throws SFException	Overridden to chain PropertyContainer lookup to parent BusinessPartnerCustomerSupplierData if one exists
getOwner	public abstract BusinessPartner getOwner()throws SFException	Returns the Owner, copied from the Handle
getTypeValue	public abstract BusinessPartnerTypeValue getTypeValue() throws SFException	Returns the TypeValue, copied from the Handle
getCreditCheckPolicyOrganizer	public abstract CreditCheckPolicyOrganizer getCreditCheckPolicyOrganizer() throws SFException	Returns the CreditCheckPolicyOrganizer, copied from the Handle
setCreditCheckPolicyOrganizer	public abstract void setCreditCheckPolicyOrganizer(CreditCheckPolicyOrganizer newCreditCheckPolicyOrganizer) throws SFException	Set the Handle of the CreditCheckPolicyOrganizer
getOwnerHdl	public abstract Handle getOwnerHdl()throws SFException	Returns the Handle to the BusinessPartner of the owner of the BusinessPartnerCustomerSupplierData
getTypeValueHdl	public abstract Handle getTypeValueHdl() throws SFException	Returns the Handle to the BusinessPartnerTypeValue of the typeValue of the BusinessPartnerCustomerSupplierData

Figure 21-5
(Cont'd)

getCreditCheckPolicyOrganizerHdl	`public abstract Handle getCreditCheckPolicyOrganizerHdl() throws SFException`	Returns the Handle to the CreditCheckPolicyOrganizer of the CreditCheckPolicyOrganizer of the BusinessPartnerCustomerSupplierData
initialize	`public abstract void initialize(BusinessPartner businessPartner, Currency currency, BusinessPartnerGroup group, PaymentMethod paymentMethod, PaymentTerms paymentTerms, int usage) throws SFException`	This method is invoked by the Factory after Construction of an instance of this class to ensure proper initialization
getUsage	`public abstract int getUsage() throws SFException Note: getUsage() is deprecated.`	Determine the usage by the BusinessPartner of this object.

Figure 21-5
(Cont'd)

Business Partner Balances

In any sort of business, you would like to record the balance of your business partners. At the very least, you need to know the current amount of money you owe your suppliers, and the current amount of money your customers owe you. In reality, you might need much more than that, depending on the specific business.

SanFrancisco provides the `BusinessPartnerBalance` object, shown in Figure 21-7. This object works together with `BusinessPartner` and `FiscalPeriod` as depicted in Figure 21-8. It contains a `DTransactionAmount` (see the discussion of the `Currency` category below) to represent the current balance. When you actually make a transaction that changes the balance, you should specify a key of type `DBusinessPartnerSpecificationKey` (see Figure 21-9) to identify the kind of transaction. This can be used later on for accessing specific kinds of transactions and to provide a balance for them. In a similar way, there are `DBusinessPartnerAccessKey` (see Figure 21-10) objects, which are used to cache balances. A detailed explanation of how to use these keys and caching balances is deferred until Chapter 23. Access to `BusinessPartnerBalance` objects is always done through the `BusinessPartner` object.

Interface com.ibm.sf.cf.BusinessSharedData

public interface BusinessPartnerSharedData
extends DescribableDynamicEntity, Distinguishable

Main Methods

Name	*Signature*	*Description*
removeFromHierarchy	`public abstract void removeFromHierarchy() throws SFException`	Remove the BusinessPartner from the hierarchy to which it belongs.
addParent	`public abstract void addParent(BusinessPartnerSharedData newParent) throws SFException`	Set the hierarchical parent for this BusinessPartnerSharedData.
getAddressBy	`public abstract Address getAddressBy(String id) throws SFException`	Retrieve an address with the given address Id.
getDirectlyOwnedAddressBy	`public abstract Address getDirectlyOwnedAddressBy(String id) throws SFException`	Get the directly owned Address with the given address id.
isSundry	`public abstract boolean isSundry() throws SFException`	Determine if the BusinessPartner is sundry (i.e. inactive).
setIdUsingPolicy	`public abstract void setIdUsingPolicy(String newId) throws SFException`	Set the Id of the BusinessPartner.
getId	`public abstract String getId() throws SFException`	Get the ID (as Distinguishable object)
getRegistrationId	`public abstract String getRegistrationId() throws SFException`	Gets RegistrationId
setRegistrationId	`public abstract void setRegistrationId(String newRegistrationId) throws SFException`	Sets RegistrationId
getLegalName	`public abstract String getLegalName() throws SFException`	Gets LegalName
setLegalName	`public abstract void setLegalName(String newLegalName) throws SFException`	Sets LegalName
getParent	`public abstract BusinessPartnerSharedData getParent() throws SFException`	Returns the Parent, copied from the Handle
getPrimaryAddress	`public abstract Address getPrimaryAddress() throws SFException`	Returns the PrimaryAddress, copied from the Handle
setOwnedPrimaryAddress	`public abstract void setOwnedPrimaryAddress(Address newPrimaryAddress) throws SFException`	Set the Handle of the PrimaryAddress
createAddressIterator	`public abstract Iterator createAddressIterator() throws SFException`	Create Iterator for Collection of Addresses
getNextAddress	`public abstract Address getNextAddress(Iterator position) throws SFException`	Gets the Address at the Next Iterator Position
setAddresses	`public abstract void setAddresses(EntityOwningMap Addresses) throws SFException`	Sets the collection of Addresses
containsAddress	`public abstract boolean containsAddress(Address address) throws SFException`	Checks if the Address exists in the Collection of Addresses

Figure 21-6
Interface `BusinessPartnerSharedData`

getAddressAt	public abstract Address getAddressAt(Iterator position) throws SFException	Gets the Address at the current iterator position
removeOwnedAddressAt	public abstract void removeOwnedAddressAt(Iterator position) throws SFException	Removes and deletes the Address at the Current Iterator Position
removeOwnedAddress	public abstract void removeOwnedAddress(Address address) throws SFException	Removes and deletes the specified Address
removeAllOwnedAddresses	public abstract void removeAllOwnedAddresses() throws SFException	Removes and deletes all elements from the Collection of Addresses
containsAddressKey	public abstract boolean containsAddressKey(String key) throws SFException	Checks if the Address exists by the specified Key
getAddressKeyAt	public abstract String getAddressKeyAt(Iterator position) throws SFException	Gets the AddressKey at the current iterator position
getAddressKey	public abstract String getAddressKey(Address address) throws SFException	Gets the Address at the Current Iterator Position
removeOwnedAddressBy	public abstract void removeOwnedAddressBy(String key) throws SFException	Removes and deletes the Address by the specified key
orphanOwnedAddressBy	public abstract void orphanOwnedAddressBy(String key) throws SFException	Orphans the Address by the specified key
addOwnedAddressBy	public abstract void addOwnedAddressBy(Address address, String key) throws SFException	Adds a Address to the Collection of Addresses by the Specified Key
isAddressesEmpty	public abstract boolean isAddressesEmpty() throws SFException	Determine if the Address collection is empty.
getShortName	public abstract String getShortName() throws SFException	Gets ShortName
getHierarchyDescriptiveInformation	public abstract DescriptiveInformation getHierarchyDescriptiveInformation() throws SFException	Returns the HierarchyDescriptiveInformation, copied from the Handle
getDirectlyOwnedHierarchyDescriptiveInformation	public abstract DescriptiveInformation getDirectlyOwnedHierarchyDescriptiveInformation() throws SFException	Returns the HierarchyDescriptiveInformation, copied from the Handle
setDirectlyOwnedHierarchyDescriptiveInformation	public abstract void setDirectlyOwnedHierarchyDescriptiveInformation(DescriptiveInformation newHierarchyDescriptiveInformation) throws SFException	Set the Handle of the HierarchyDescriptiveInformation
getParentHdl	public abstract Handle getParentHdl() throws SFException	Returns the Handle to the BusinessPartnerSharedData of the parent of the BusinessPartnerSharedData
getPrimaryAddressHdl	public abstract Handle getPrimaryAddressHdl() throws SFException	Returns the Handle to the Address of the primaryAddress of the BusinessPartnerSharedData
GetHierarchyDescriptiveInformationHdl	public abstract Handle getHierarchyDescriptiveInformationHdl() throws SFException	Returns the Handle to the DescriptiveInformation of the hierarchyDescriptiveInformation of the BusinessPartnerSharedData

Figure 21-6
(Cont'd)

Interface com.ibm.sf.cf.BusinessPartnerBalance

public interface BusinessPartnerBalance extends DynamicEntity

Name	*Signature*	*Description*
updateBalance	`public abstract void updateBalance( DTransactionValuevalue) throws SFException`	Updates the balance with the passed value.
getFiscalPeriod	`public abstract FiscalPeriod getFiscalPeriod() throws SFException`	Returns the FiscalPeriod, copied from the Handle
getJournalDate	`public abstract DTime getJournalDate() throws SFException`	Returns the Journal Date
getDueDate	`public abstract DTime getDueDate() throws SFException`	Returns the Due Date
getBusinessPartnerBalanceValue	`public abstract BusinessPartnerBalanceValue getBusinessPartnerBalanceValue() throws SFException`	Returns the BusinessPartnerBalanceValue, copied from the Handle
getBusinessPartnerTypeValue	`public abstract BusinessPartnerTypeValue getBusinessPartnerTypeValue() throws SFException`	Returns the BusinessPartnerTypeValue, copied from the Handle
getBusinessPartnerBalanceSequenceValue	`public abstract BusinessPartnerBalanceSequenceValue getBusinessPartnerBalanceSequenceValue() throws SFException`	Returns the BusinessPartnerBalanceSequenceValue, copied from the Handle
getBalance	`public abstract DTransactionValue getBalance() throws SFException`	Gets Balance
getFiscalPeriodHdl	`public abstract Handle getFiscalPeriodHdl() throws SFException`	Returns the Handle to the FiscalPeriod of the FiscalPeriod of the BusinessPartnerBalance
getBusinessPartnerBalanceValueHdl	`public abstract Handle getBusinessPartnerBalanceValueHdl() throws SFException`	Returns the Handle to the BusinessPartnerBalanceValue of the businessPartnerBalanceValue of the BusinessPartnerBalance
getBusinessPartnerTypeValueHdl	`public abstract Handle getBusinessPartnerTypeValueHdl() throws SFException`	Returns the Handle to the BusinessPartnerTypeValue.
getBusinessPartnerBalanceSequenceValueHdl	`public abstract Handle getBusinessPartnerBalanceSequenceValueHdl() throws SFException`	Returns the Handle to the BusinessPartnerBalanceSequenceValue.

Figure 21-7
Interface `BusinessPartnerBalance`

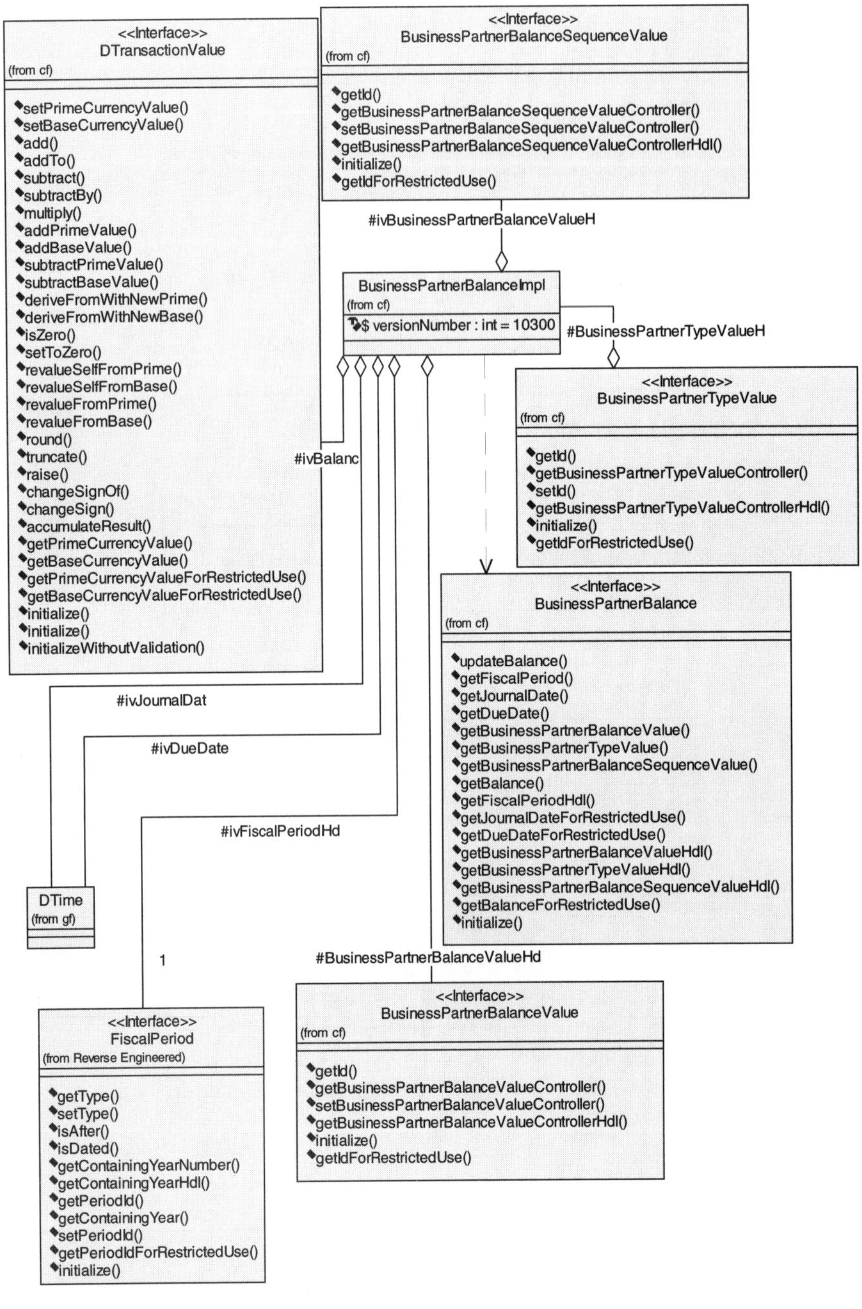

Figure 21-8
`BusinessPartnerBalance` implementation model

Interface com.ibm.sf.cf.BusinessSharedData

public interface BusinessPartnerSharedData
extends DescribableDynamicEntity, Distinguishable

Name	Signature	Description
addBusinessPartnerTypeValue	`public abstract void addBusinessPartnerTypeValue(BusinessPartnerTypeValue businessPartnerTypeValue) throws SFException`	Adds the passed in item to the specification ket. It gets the Keyable from the internal defined position in the key and uses the input to create the appropriate DSpecificValueKayable. This keyable is added to the new keyable of the key and this modified keyable will be set at the internal position in the key again.
addBusinessPartnerTypeValueNotSpecified	`public abstract void addBusinessPartnerTypeValueNotSpecified() throws SFException`	Gets the keyable at the internal defined position in the key and wires-through to the appropriate class on feature CF Keys. Then it sets the modified keyable at the internal position in the key.
allBusinessPartnerTypeValues	`public abstract void allBusinessPartnerTypeValues() throws SFException`	Gets the keyable at the internal defined position in the key and creates the appropriate keyable that represents an DAllValuesKeyable. This keyable is set at the internal internal position in the key.
clearBusinessPartnerTypeValues	`public abstract void clearBusinessPartnerTypeValues() throws SFException`	Creates an appropriate (empty) keyable (which represents a DIgnoredKeyable) for the items position and sets the new keyable at the internal position of the key.
getBusinessPartnerTypeValueSpecification	`public abstract DSet getBusinessPartnerTypeValueSpecification() throws SFException`	Gets the appropriate keyable at the internal position in the key and iterates through the content while building a DSet of DSpecificationKeyables.
isAllBusinessPartnerTypeValues	`public abstract boolean isAllBusinessPartnerTypeValues() throws SFException`	Gets the keyable at the internal defined position in the key and wire-through to equalsDAllValuesKeyable() method of CF keys feature. It returns whatever the method on Cf Keys returns.
isBusinessPartnerTypeValueClear	`public abstract boolean isBusinessPartnerTypeValueClear() throws SFException`	Checks whether the keyable at the defined position in the key is set with a DIgnoredKeyable. Is so TRUE is returned otherwise FALSE.
removeBusinessPartnerTypeValue	`public abstract void removeBusinessPartnerTypeValue(BusinessPartnerTypeValue businessPartnerTypeValue) throws SFException`	Gets the keyable at the internal position in the key, and creates a specific value to build a DSpecificValueKeyable from it. Then it removes the DSpecificValueKeyable from the internal keyable, as far as it exists and sets the modified new keyable at the internal position in the key.
removeBusinessPartnerTypeValueNotSpecified	`public abstract void removeBusinessPartnerTypeValueNotSpecified() throws SFException`	Gets the keyable at the internal position of the key and wires-through to appropriate class on feature CF Keys. It sets the modified keyable at the internal position in the key.

Figure 21-9
Interface `DBusinessPartnerSpecification Key`

addBusinessPartnerBalanceValue	`public abstract void addBusinessPartnerBalanceValue(BusinessPartnerBalanceValue businessPartnerBalanceValue) throws SFException`	Adds the passed in item to the DBusinessPartnerBalanceSpecificationKey It gets the Keyable from the internal defined position in the key and uses the input to create the appropriate DSpecificValueKayable. This keyable is added to the new keyable of the key and this modified keyable will be set at the internal position in the key again.
addBusinessPartnerBalanceValueNotSpecified	`public abstract void addBusinessPartnerBalanceValueNotSpecified() throws SFException`	Gets the keyable at the internal defined position in the key and wires-through to the appropriate class on feature CF Keys. Then it sets the modified keyable at the internal position in the key
allBusinessPartnerBalanceValues	`public abstract void allBusinessPartnerBalanceValues() throws SFException`	Gets the keyable at the internal defined position in the key and creates the appropriate keyable that represents an DAllValuesKeyable. This keyable is set at the internal internal position in the key.
clearBusinessPartnerBalanceValues	`public abstract void clearBusinessPartnerBalanceValues() throws SFException`	Creates an appropriate (empty) keyable (which represents a DIgnoredKeyable) for the items position and sets the new keyable at the internal position of the key.
getBusinessPartnerBalanceValueSpecification	`public abstract DSet getBusinessPartnerBalanceValueSpecification() throws SFException`	Gets the appropriate keyable at the internal position in the key and iterates through the content while building a DSet of DSpecificationKeyables.
isAllBusinessPartnerBalanceValues	`public abstract boolean isAllBusinessPartnerBalanceValues() throws SFException`	Gets the keyable at the internal defined position in the key and wire-through to equalsDAllValuesKeyable() method of CF keys feature. It returns whatever the method on CF Keys returns.
isBusinessPartnerBalanceValueClear	`public abstract boolean isBusinessPartnerBalanceValueClear() throws SFException`	Checks whether the keyable at the defined position in the key is set with a DIgnoredKeyable. Is so TRUE is returned otherwise FALSE.
removeBusinessPartnerBalanceValue	`public abstract void removeBusinessPartnerBalanceValue(BusinessPartnerBalanceValue businessPartnerBalanceValue) throws SFException`	Gets the keyable at the internal position in the key, and creates a specific value to build a DSpecificValueKeyable from it. Then it removes the DSpecificValueKeyable from the internal keyable, as far as it exists and sets the modified new keyable at the internal position in the key.
removeBusinessPartnerBalanceValueNotSpecified	`public abstract void removeBusinessPartnerBalanceValueNotSpecified() throws SFException`	Gets the keyable at the internal position of the key and wires-through to appropriate class on feature CF Keys. It sets the modified keyable at the internal position in the key.
addBusinessPartnerBalanceSequenceValue	`public abstract void addBusinessPartnerBalanceSequenceValue(BusinessPartnerBalanceSequenceValue businessPartnerBalanceSequenceValue) throws SFException`	Adds the passed in item to the DBusinessPartnerBalanceSpecificationKey It gets the Keyable from the internal defined position in the key and uses the input to create the appropriate DSpecificValueKayable. This keyable is added to the new keyable of the key and this modified keyable will be set at the internal position in the key again.

Figure 21-9
(Cont'd)

addBusinessPartnerBalanceSequenceValueNotSpecified	`public abstract void addBusinessPartnerBalanceSequenceValueNotSpecified() throws SFException`	Gets the keyable at the internal defined position in the key and wires-through to the appropriate class on feature CF Keys. Then it sets the modified keyable at the internal position in the key.
allBusinessPartnerBalanceSequenceValues	`public abstract void allBusinessPartnerBalanceSequenceValues() throws SFException`	Gets the keyable at the internal defined position in the key and creates the appropriate keyable that represents an DAllValuesKeyable. This keyable is set at the internal internal position in the key.
clearBusinessPartnerBalanceSequenceValues	`public abstract void clearBusinessPartnerBalanceSequenceValues() throws SFException`	Creates an appropriate (empty) keyable (which represents a DIgnoredKeyable) for the items position and sets the new keyable at the internal position of the key.
getBusinessPartnerBalanceSequenceValueSpecification	`public abstract DSet getBusinessPartnerBalanceSequenceValueSpecification() throws SFException`	Gets the appropriate keyable at the internal position in the key and iterates through the content while building a DSet of DSpecificationKeyables.
isAllBusinessPartnerBalanceSequenceValues	`public abstract boolean isAllBusinessPartnerBalanceSequenceValues() throws SFException`	Gets the keyable at the internal defined position in the key and wire-through to equalsDAllValuesKeyable() method of Cf keys feature. It returns whatever the method on Cf Keys returns.
isBusinessPartnerBalanceSequenceValueClear	`public abstract boolean isBusinessPartnerBalanceSequenceValueClear() throws SFException`	Checks whether the keyable at the defined position in the key is set with a DIgnoredKeyable. Is so TRUE is returned otherwise FALSE.
removeBusinessPartnerBalanceSequenceValue	`public abstract void removeBusinessPartnerBalanceSequenceValue(BusinessPartnerBalanceSequenceValue businessPartnerBalanceSequenceValue) throws SFException`	Gets the keyable at the internal position in the key, and creates a specific value to build a DSpecificValueKeyable from it. Then it removes the DSpecificValueKeyable from the internal keyable, as far as it exists and sets the modified new keyable at the internal position in the key.
removeBusinessPartnerBalanceSequenceValueNotSpecified	`public abstract void removeBusinessPartnerBalanceSequenceValueNotSpecified() throws SFException`	Gets the keyable at the internal position of the key and wires-through to appropriate class on feature CF Keys. It sets the modified keyable at the internal position in the key.
addDueDate	`public abstract void addDueDate(DTime dueDate) throws SFException`	Adds the passed in item to the DBusinessPartnerBalanceSpecificationKey It gets the Keyable from the internal defined position in the key and uses the input to create the appropriate DSpecificValueKayable. This keyable is added to the new keyable of the key and this modified keyable will be set at the internal position in the key again.
addDueDateRange	`public abstract void addDueDateRange(DTime fromDate,DTime toDate) throws SFException`	Gets the keyable at the internal position in the key and uses input items to create two DOrderableKeyables using these keyables to create a DRangeKeyable. Further it add the new range to the internal keyable and replaces the modified new internal keyable with the old keyable at the appropriate position in the key. Whenever a null is passed for either one or both range leafs (the to and from value) means that either one end is considered to be open or in case both were set with null it is interpreted as an all values range. void.

Figure 21-9
(Cont'd)

addDueDateNotSpecified	public abstract void addDueDateNotSpecified() throws SFException	Gets the keyable at the internal defined position in the key and wires-through to the appropriate class on feature CF Keys. Then it sets the modified keyable at the internal position in the key
allDueDates	public abstract void allDueDates() throws SFException	Gets the keyable at the internal defined position in the key and creates the appropriate keyable that represents an DAllValuesKeyable. This keyable is set at the internal internal position in the key.
clearDueDates	public abstract void clearDueDates() throws SFException	Creates an appropriate (empty) keyable (which represents a DIgnoredKeyable) for the items position and sets the new keyable at the internal position of the key.
getDueDateSpecification	public abstract DSet getDueDateSpecification() throws SFException	Gets the appropriate keyable at the internal position in the key and iterates through the content while building a DSet of DSpecificationKeyables.
isAllDueDates	public abstract boolean isAllDueDates() throws SFException	Gets the keyable at the internal defined position in the key and wire-through to equalsDAllValuesKeyable() method of Cf keys feature. It returns whatever the method on Cf Keys returns.
isDueDateClear	public abstract boolean isDueDateClear() throws SFException	Checks whether the keyable at the defined position in the key is set with a DIgnoredKeyable. Is so TRUE is returned otherwise FALSE.
removeDueDate	public abstract void removeDueDate(DTime dueDate) throws SFException	Gets the keyable at the internal position in the key, and creates a specific value to build a DSpecificValueKeyable from it. Then it removes the DSpecificValueKeyable from the internal keyable, as far as it exists and sets the modified new keyable at the internal position in the key.
removeDueDateRange	public abstract void removeDueDateRange(DTime fromDate,DTime toDate) throws SFException	Gets the keyable at the internal defined position in the key and uses input items to create two DSpecificValueKeyables using these keyables to create a DRangeKeyable. Then it removes the DRangeKeyable from the internal keyable, as far as it's existent and sets the modified new keyable at the internal position in the key.
removeDueDateNotSpecified	public abstract void removeDueDateNotSpecified( ) throws SFException	Gets the keyable at the internal position of the key and wires-through to appropriate class on feature CF Keys. It sets the modified keyable at the internal position in the key. void
addJournalDate	public abstract void addJournalDate(DTime journalDate) throws SFException	Gets the keyable at the internal defined position in the key and wires-through to the appropriate class on feature CF Keys. Then it sets the modified keyable at the internal position in the key

Figure 21-9
(Cont'd)

addJournalDateRange	`public abstract void addJournalDateRange(DTime fromDate,DTime toDate) throws SFException`	Gets the keyable at the internal position in the key and uses input items to create two DOrderableKeyables using these keyables to create a DRangeKeyable. Further it add the new range to the internal keyable and replaces the modified new internal keyable with the old keyable at the appropriate position in the key. Whenever a null is passed for either one or both range leafs (the to and from value) means that either one end is considered to be open or in case both were set with null it is interpreted as an all values range.
addJournalDateNotSpecified	`public abstract void addJournalDateNotSpecified() throws SFException`	Gets the keyable at the internal defined position in the key and wires-through to the appropriate class on feature CF Keys, then it sets the modified keyable at the internal position in the key.
allJournalDates	`public abstract void allJournalDates() throws SFException`	Gets the keyable at the internal defined position in the key and creates the appropriate keyable that represents an DAllValuesKeyable. This keyable is set at the internal internal position in the key.
clearJournalDates	`public abstract void clearJournalDates() throws SFException`	Creates an appropriate (empty) keyable (which represents a DIgnoredKeyable) for the items position and sets the new keyable at the internal position of the key.
getJournalDateSpecification	`public abstract DSet getJournalDateSpecification() throws SFException`	Gets the appropriate keyable at the internal position in the key and iterates through the content while building a DSet of DSpecificationKeyables.
isAllJournalDates	`public abstract boolean isAllJournalDates() throws SFException`	Gets the keyable at the internal defined position in the key and wire-through to equalsDAllValuesKeyable() method of CF keys feature. It returns whatever the method on Cf Keys returns.
isJournalDateClear	`public abstract boolean isJournalDateClear() throws SFException`	Checks whether the keyable at the defined position in the key is set with a DIgnoredKeyable. Is so TRUE is returned otherwise FALSE.
removeJournalDate	`public abstract void removeJournalDate(DTime journalDate) throws SFException`	Gets the keyable at the internal position in the key, and creates a specific value to build a DSpecificValueKeyable from it. Then it removes the DSpecificValueKeyable from the internal keyable, as far as it exists and sets the modified new keyable at the internal position in the key.
removeJournalDateRange	`public abstract void removeJournalDateRange(DTime fromDate,DTime toDate) throws SFException`	Gets the keyable at the internal defined position in the key and uses input items to create two DSpecificValueKeyables using these keyables to create a DRangeKeyable. Then it removes the DRangeKeyable from the internal keyable, as far as it's existent and sets the modified new keyable at the internal position in the key.
removeJournalDateNotSpecified	`public abstract void removeJournalDateNotSpecified() throws SFException`	Gets the keyable at the internal position of the key and wires-through to appropriate class on feature CF Keys. It sets the modified keyable at the internal position in the key.

Figure 21-9
(Cont'd)

addFiscalPeriod	public abstract void addFiscalPeriod(FiscalPeriod fiscalPeriod) throws SFException	Gets the keyable at the internal defined position in the key and wires-through to the appropriate class on feature CF Keys. Then it sets the modified keyable at the internal position in the key.
addFiscalPeriodRange	public abstract void addFiscalPeriodRange(FiscalPeriod fromFiscalPeriod,FiscalPeriod toFiscalPeriod) throws SFException	Gets the keyable at the internal position in the key and uses input items to create two DOrderableKeyables using these keyables to create a DRangeKeyable. This method then adds the new range to the internal keyable and replaces the modified new internal keyable with the old keyable at the appropriate position in the key.
addFiscalPeriodNotSpecified	public abstract void addFiscalPeriodNotSpecified() throws SFException	Gets the keyable at the internal defined position in the key and wires-through to the appropriate class on feature CF Keys. Then it sets the modified keyable at the internal position in the key.
allFiscalPeriods	public abstract void allFiscalPeriods() throws SFException	Gets the keyable at the internal defined position in the key and creates the appropriate keyable that represents an DAllValuesKeyable. This keyable is set at the internal internal position in the key.
clearFiscalPeriods	public abstract void clearFiscalPeriods() throws SFException	Creates an appropriate (empty) keyable (which represents a DIgnoredKeyable) for the items position and sets the new keyable at the internal position of the key.
getFiscalPeriodSpecification	public abstract DSet getFiscalPeriodSpecification() throws SFException	Gets the appropriate keyable at the internal position in the key and iterates through the content while building a DSet of DSpecificationKeyables.
isAllFiscalPeriods	public abstract boolean isAllFiscalPeriods() throws SFException	Gets the keyable at the internal defined position in the key and wire-through to equalsDAllValuesKeyable() method of Cf keys feature. It returns whatever the method on Cf Keys returns.
isFiscalPeriodClear	public abstract boolean isFiscalPeriodClear() throws SFException	Checks whether the keyable at the defined position in the key is set with a DIgnoredKeyable. Is so TRUE is returned otherwise FALSE.
removeFiscalPeriod	public abstract void removeFiscalPeriod(FiscalPeriod fiscalPeriod) throws SFException	Gets the keyable at the internal position in the key, and creates a specific value to build a DSpecificValueKeyable from it. Then it removes the DSpecificValueKeyable from the internal keyable, as far as it exists and sets the modified new keyable at the internal position in the key.
removeFiscalPeriodRange	public abstract void removeFiscalPeriodRange(FiscalPeriod fromFiscalPeriod,FiscalPeriod toFiscalPeriod) throws SFException	Gets the keyable at the internal defined position in the key and uses input items to create two DSpecificValueKeyables using these keyables to create a DRangeKeyable. Then it removes the DRangeKeyable from the internal keyable, as far as it's existent and sets the modified new keyable at the internal position in the key.
removeFiscalPeriodNotSpecified	public abstract void removeFiscalPeriodNotSpecified() throws SFException	Gets the keyable at the internal position of the key and wires-through to appropriate class on feature CF Keys. It sets the modified keyable at the internal position in the key.

Figure 21-9
(Cont'd)

compare	public abstract boolean compare(Object elementToCompare) throws SFException	This method is used within the BalancesForBusinessPartnerBalanceSpecificationKey for quering BusinessPartnerBalances. It checks whether a BusinessPartnerBalance is included within this specification key or not. Returns true, if the BusinessPartnerBalance is included within this specification key, otherwise it returns false.
getBusinessPartner	public abstract BusinessPartner getBusinessPartner() throws SFException	Returns the BusinessPartner, copied from the Handle
getBusinessPartnerHdl	public abstract Handle getBusinessPartnerHdl() throws SFException	Returns the Handle to the BusinessPartner of this object.
initialize	public abstract void initialize(boolean completeBalanceDirectory) throws SFException	This method is invoked by the Factory after Construction of an instance of this class to ensure proper initialization

Figure 21-9
(Cont'd)

Company

The `Company` is the most important abstraction in SanFrancisco. It plays a major role in any kind of operation because most of the data is accessed through the company properties (as explained in other parts of this chapter). During the work on business objects you always have a notion of the currently active company.

Companies are organized in a tree-like hierarchical structure that is dynamic. The topmost company is represented by the interface `Enterprise` (see Figure 21-11) while other companies are represented by `Company` objects (see Figure 21-12). Figure 21-13 shows a diagram illustrating the components of the `Company` object. Note that the hierarchical structure of companies implements a "Chain of Responsibilities" pattern [GOF] by which the `PropertyContainer` for a company consults the parent company for properties not defined in it.

Figure 21-14 shows an example of setting up a company hierarchy and Figure 21-15 shows a simple example of using a `Company` object.

Interface com.ibm.sf.cf.DBusinessPartnerBalance AccessKey

public interface DBusinessPartnerBalanceAccessKey extends DAccessKey, SelectCompare

Name	*Signature*	*Description*
getBusinessPartnerTypeValue	`public abstract BusinessPartnerTypeValue getBusinessPartnerTypeValue() throws SFException`	If the Keyable on the internal position fot the BusinessPartnerTypeValue contains a NotSpecifiedKeyable as the specific value, NULL is returned, otherwise it is wired-through to the actual Keyable and the BusinessPartnerTypeValue held by this keyable is returned.
setBusinessPartnerTypeValue	`public abstract void setBusinessPartnerTypeValue (BusinessPartnerTypeValue businessPartnerTypeValue) throws SFException`	A Keyable for the BusinessPartnerTypeValue internal position is created using the BusinessPartnerTypeValue passed.
clearBusinessPartnerTypeValue	`public abstract void clearBusinessPartnerTypeValue() throws SFException`	Replaces Keyable with a DNotSpecifiedKeyable at the internal position of the key for the BusinessPartnerTypeValue.
getBusinessPartnerBalanceValue	`public abstract BusinessPartnerBalanceValue getBusinessPartnerBalanceValue() throws SFException`	If the Keyable on the internal position fot the BusinessPartnerBalanceValue contains a NotSpecifiedKeyable as the specific value, NULL is returned, otherwise it is wired-through to the actual Keyable and the BusinessPartnerBalanceValue held by this keyable is returned.
setBusinessPartnerBalanceValue	`public abstract void setBusinessPartnerBalanceValue(BusinessPartnerBalanceValue businessPartnerBalanceValue) throws SFException`	A Keyable for the BusinessPartnerTypeValue internal position is created using the BusinessPartnerTypeValue passed.
clearBusinessPartnerBalanceValue	`public abstract void clearBusinessPartnerBalanceValue () throws SFException`	Replaces Keyable with a DNotSpecifiedKeyable at the internal position of the key for the BusinessPartnerBalanceValue.
getBusinessPartnerBalanceSequenceValue	`public abstract BusinessPartnerBalanceSequenceValue getBusinessPartnerBalanceSequenceValue() throws SFException`	If the Keyable on the internal position for the BusinessPartnerBalanceSequenceValue contains a NotSpecifiedKeyable as the specific value, NULL is returned, otherwise it is wired-through to the actual Keyable and the BusinessPartnerBalanceSequenceValue held by this keyable is returned.

Figure 21-10
Interface `DBusinessPartnerAccess Key`

setBusinessPartnerBalanceSequenceValue	`public abstract void setBusinessPartnerBalanceSequenceValue(BusinessPartnerBalanceSequenceValue businessPartnerBalanceSequenceValue) throws SFException`	A Keyable for the BusinessPartnerBalanceSequenceValue internal position is created using the BusinessPartnerBalanceSequenceValue passed.
clearBusinessPartnerBalanceSequenceValue	`public abstract void clearBusinessPartnerBalanceSequenceValue() throws SFException`	Replaces Keyable with a DNotSpecifiedKeyable at the internal position of the key for the BusinessPartnerBalanceSequenceValue.
getDueDate	`public abstract DTime getDueDate() throws SFException`	If the Keyable on the internal position fot the dueDate DTime contains a NotSpecifiedKeyable as the specific value, NULL is returned, otherwise it is wired-through to the actual Keyable and the dueDate DTime held by this keyable is returned.
setDueDate	`public abstract void setDueDate(DTime dueDate) throws SFException`	A Keyable for the dueDate DTime internal position is created using the DTime passed.
clearDueDate	`public abstract void clearDueDate() throws SFException`	Replaces Keyable with a DNotSpecifiedKeyable at the internal position of the key for the dueDate DTime.
getJournalDate	`public abstract DTime getJournalDate() throws SFException`	If the Keyable on the internal position fot the journalDate DTime contains a NotSpecifiedKeyable as the specific value, NULL is returned, otherwise it is wired-through to the actual Keyable and the journalDate DTime held by this keyable is returned.
setJournalDate	`public abstract void setJournalDate(DTime journalDate) throws SFException`	A Keyable for the journalDate DTime internal position is created using the DTime passed.
clearJournalDate	`public abstract void clearJournalDate() throws SFException`	Replaces Keyable with a DNotSpecifiedKeyable at the internal position of the key for the journalDate DTime.
getFiscalPeriod	`public abstract FiscalPeriod getFiscalPeriod() throws SFException`	If the Keyable on the internal position for the FiscalPeriod a NotSpecifiedKeyable as the specific value, NULL is returned, otherwise it is wired-through to the actual Keyable and the FiscalPeriod held by this keyable is returned.
setFiscalPeriod	`public abstract void setFiscalPeriod(FiscalPeriod fiscalPeriod) throws SFException`	A Keyable for the FiscalPeriod internal position is created using the FiscalPeriod passed.
clearFiscalPeriod	`public abstract void clearFiscalPeriod() throws SFException`	Replaces Keyable with a DNotSpecifiedKeyable at the internal position of the key for the FiscalPeriod.

Figure 21-10
(Cont'd)

compare	public abstract boolean compare(Object elementToCompare) throws SFException	This method is used within the BalancesForBusinessPartnerBalanceSpecificationKey for querying BusinessPartnerBalances . It checks whether a BusinessPartnerBalance is included within this specification key or not. Returns true, if the BusinessPartnerBalance is included within this specification key, otherwise it returns false.
initialize	public abstract void initialize(BusinessPartnerTypeValue businessPartnerTypeValue, BusinessPartnerBalanceValue businessPartnerBalanceValue, BusinessPartnerBalanceSequenceValue businessPartnerBalanceSequenceValue, FiscalPeriod fiscalPeriod, DTime journalDate, DTime dueDate) throws SFException	This method is invoked by the Factory after Construction of an instance of this class to ensure proper initialization
initialize	public abstract void initialize(BusinessPartnerBalance businessPartnerBalance) throws SFException	This method is invoked by the Factory after Construction of an instance of this class to ensure proper initialization

Figure 21-10
(Cont'd)

Interface com.ibm.sf.cf.Enterprise

public interface Enterprise extends Company

Name	*Signature*	*Description*
setParentCompany	public abstract void setParentCompany(Company newParentCompany) throws SFException	Assigns a new parent company this company. Will remove this Company from the current parent's collection of subcompanies and add it as subcomapny to the new parent.
initialize	public abstract void initialize(CompanyController companyController, String id, String shortName, String legalName, boolean usedAsContext, String locale, DescriptiveInformation scriptiveInformation) throws SFException	This method is invoked by the Factory after Construction of an instance of this class to ensure proper initialization

Figure 21-11
Interface `Enterprise`

Interface com.ibm.sf.cf.Company

public interface **Company** extends DescribableDynamicEntity, Distinguishable

Name	*Signature*	*Description*
getParentCompany	`public abstract Company getParentCompany() throws SFException`	Retrieves the parent of the company in the hierarchy of Companies. In case there is no parent, null is returned.
setParentCompany	`public abstract void setParentCompany(Company newParentCompany) throws SFException`	Assigns a new the parent of the company. Will remove this Company from the current parent's collection of subcompanies and add it as subcomapny to the new parent.
getPrimaryAddress	`public abstract Address getPrimaryAddress() throws SFException`	Get the primary Address of the Company. This is the main address that is used for all general external contacts.
setPrimaryAddress	`public abstract void setPrimaryAddress(Address primaryAddress) throws SFException`	Set the primary Address of the Company. This is the main address that is used for all general external contacts. Get the PropertyContainer for the parent of the company
getChainParent	`public abstract PropertyContainer getChainParent() throws SFException`	
createSubcompanyIterator	`public abstract Iterator createSubcompanyIterator() throws SFException`	Create Iterator for Collection of Subcompanies
getNextSubcompany	`public abstract Company getNextSubcompany(Iterator position) throws SFException`	Gets the Subcompany at the Next Iterator Position
containsSubcompany	`public abstract boolean containsSubcompany(Company subcompany) throws SFException`	Checks if the Subcompany exists in the Collection of Subcompanies
getSubcompanyAt	`public abstract Company getSubcompanyAt(Iterator position) throws SFException`	Gets the Subcompany at the current iterator position
removeSubcompanyAt	`public abstract void removeSubcompanyAt(Iterator position) throws SFException`	Removes the Subcompany at the Current Iterator Position
removeSubcompany	`public abstract void removeSubcompany(Company subcompany) throws SFException`	Removes the specified Subcompany
removeAllSubcompanies	`public abstract void removeAllSubcompanies() throws SFException`	Removes all Subcompany from the Collection of Subcompanies
getSubcompanyBy	`public abstract Company getSubcompanyBy(String key) throws SFException`	Gets the Subcompany associated with the specified key

Figure 21-12
Interface Company

addSubcompanyBy	`public abstract void addSubcompanyBy(Company subcompany,String key) throws SFException`	Adds a Subcompany to the Collection of Subcompanies by the Specified Key
removeSubcompanyBy	`public abstract void removeSubcompanyBy(String key) throws SFException`	Removes the Subcompany by the specified key
containsSubcompanyKey	`public abstract boolean containsSubcompanyKey(String key) throws SFException`	Checks if the Subcompany exists by the specified Key
getSubcompanyKeyAt	`public abstract String getSubcompanyKeyAt(Iterator position) throws SFException`	Gets the SubcompanyKey at the current iterator position
getSubcompanyKey	`public abstract String getSubcompanyKey(Company subcompany) throws SFException`	Gets the Subcompany at the Current Iterator position
getLocale	`public abstract String getLocale() throws SFException`	Gets this as the default locale for the company. If the locale is not set, the default locale of the enterprise is taken.
setLocale	`public abstract void setLocale(String newLocale) throws SFException`	Set this as the default locale for the company. If the locale is not set, the default locale of the enterprise is taken.
createAddressIterator	`public abstract Iterator createAddressIterator() throws SFException`	Create Iterator for Collection of Addresses
getNextAddress	`public abstract Address getNextAddress(Iterator position) throws SFException`	Gets the Address at the Next Iterator position
containsAddress	`public abstract boolean containsAddress(Address address) throws SFException`	Checks if the Address exists in the Collection of Addresses
getAddressAt	`public abstract Address getAddressAt(Iterator position) throws SFException`	Gets the Address at the Current Iterator position
removeOwnedAddressAt	`public abstract void removeOwnedAddressAt(Iterator position) throws SFException`	Removes and deletes the Address at the Current Iterator Position
removeOwnedAddress	`public abstract void removeOwnedAddress(Address address) throws SFException`	Removes and deletes the parameter Address
removeAllOwnedAddresses	`public abstract void removeAllOwnedAddresses() throws SFException`	Removes and deletes all elements from the Collection of Addresses
getAddressBy	`public abstract Address getAddressBy(String key) throws SFException`	Gets the Address associated with the specified key

Figure 21-12
(Cont'd)

containsAddressKey	public abstract boolean containsAddressKey(String key) throws SFException	Checks if the Address exists by the specified Key
getAddressKeyAt	public abstract String getAddressKeyAt(Iterator position) throws SFException	Gets the AddressKey at the current iterator position
getAddressKey	public abstract String getAddressKey(Address address) throws SFException	Gets the Address at the Current Iterator position
removeOwnedAddressBy	public abstract void removeOwnedAddressBy(String key) throws SFException	Removes and deletes the Address by the specified key
orphanOwnedAddressBy	public abstract void orphanOwnedAddressBy(String key) throws SFException	Orphans the Address by the specified key
addOwnedAddressBy	public abstract void addOwnedAddressBy(Address address,String key) throws SFException	Adds a Address to the Collection of Addresses by the Specified Key
isUseableAsContextCompany	public abstract boolean isUseableAsContextCompany() throws SFException	Returns flag indicating if a Company can be used as active Company or not.
setUseableAsContextCompany	public abstract void setUseableAsContextCompany(boolean newUseableAsContextCompany) throws SFException	Returns flag indicating if a Company can be used as active Company or not.
getId	public abstract String getId() throws SFException	Gets identifier for the companywhich is used as a key to retrieve it from the GlobalCompanyController.
getLegalName	public abstract String getLegalName() throws SFException	Gets legalName describing the official complete name.
setLegalName	public abstract void setLegalName(String newLegalName) throws SFException	Set legalName describing the official complete name.
getShortName	public abstract String getShortName() throws SFException	Gets shortName is short version or marketing name
setShortName	public abstract void setShortName(String newShortName) throws SFException	Set shortName is short version or marketing name
getOfficialRegistrationId	public abstract String getOfficialRegistrationId() throws SFException	Gets official Registration for the Company
setOfficialRegistrationId	public abstract void setOfficialRegistrationId(String newOfficialRegistrationId) throws SFException	Set official Registration for the Company

Figure 21-12
(Cont'd)

getParentCompanyHdl	`public abstract Handle getParentCompanyHdl() throws SFException`	Returns the Handle to the Company of the parentCompany of the Company
initialize	`public abstract void initialize(CompanyController companyController, String id,String shortName,String legalName,boolean usedAsContext, Company parentCompany,String locale,DescriptiveInformation descriptiveInformation) throws SFException`	This method is invoked by the Factory after Construction of an instance of this class to ensure proper initialization

Figure 21-12
(Cont'd)

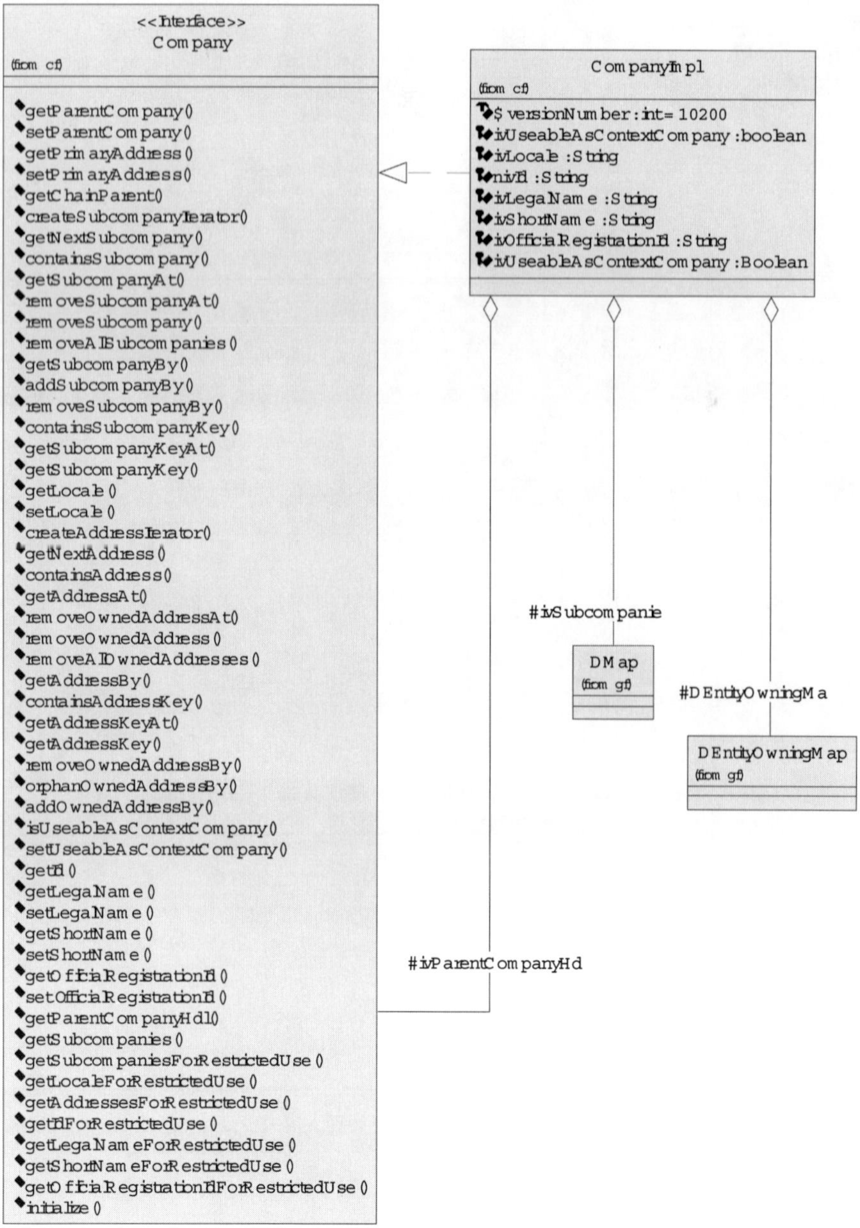

Figure 21-13 `Company` implementation model.

Figure 21-14 Code sample: setting up a `company` hierarchy.

```
.
.
.
DescriptiveInformation description = null;
AccessMode modeCPW = AccessMode.createPlusWrite();

// Get the company controller
CompanyController companyController  =
                       CompanyContext.getCompanyController();

// Create the Enterprise
description = DescriptiveInformationFactory.
                 CreateDescriptiveInformation(
                       AccessMode.createPlusWrite(),
                       companyController.getHandle());

description.addDefaultDescription("Our Enterprise");

Enterprise thEnterprise = EnterpriseFactory.createEnterprise
                                  (companyController,
                                    modeCPW,
                                    "ENT",
                                    "Enterprise",
                                    "Enterprise Inc.",
                                    true,
                                    "en_US",
                                    description);

description = DescriptiveInformationFactory.
                 CreateDescriptiveInformation(
                       modeCPW,
                       companyController.getHandle());

description.addDefaultDescription("RTS");
CompanyFactory.createCompany(companyController,
                            modeCPW,
                            "RTS",
                            "RTS",
                            "RTS Ltd.",
                            true,
                            theEnterprise,
                            "en_US",
                            description);

description = DescriptiveInformationFactory.
                 CreateDescriptiveInformation(
                       modeCPW,
                       companyController.getHandle());

description.addDefaultDescription("RTL");
CompanyFactory.createCompany(companyController,
                            modeCPW,
                            "RTL",
                            "RTL",
                            "RTL Ltd.",
                            true,
                            theEnterprise,
                            "en_US",
                            description);
```

Figure 21-15
Code sample: using a `Company` object.

```
.
.
.

Company theCompany = ...

// Print the name and full name of a company
// and its parent company
System.out.println("Company: " + company.getId()
+ " (Full Name:"
+ company.getLegalName()+ ")";
Company parentCompany = company.getParentCompany();
System.out.println("Parent Company: "
+ parentCompany.getId()
+ " (Full Name:"
+ parentCompany.getLegalName() + ")";
```

Credit Check

Credit checking is required whenever an order is made on credit. The process of credit checking might be arbitrarily complex. Sometimes it might be very simple, just involving a simple check to see if the credit for the customer exceeds a certain fixed limit. In some cases, it might involve some other considerations such as credit history for this customer, value and importance of the sale, and risk associated with extending the credit for this customer.

It is quite natural that different organizations treat the issue of credit checking differently. Furthermore, the same organization might exercise different credit checking policies at different times or for different customers. SanFrancisco addresses this need for flexibility in the definitions of credit checking by allowing you to build your own policies and procedures for credit checking. These can be embedded into the system and then used when you need to do credit checking. Credit checking policies are associated with specific business partners since these are the objects affecting how credit checking occurs.

The policies for a company can be organized in different ways. First of all, if the enterprise is divided into several companies, each of these can have its own different policies for business partners. For each business partner, you can either have a uniform policy, or you may have a different policy when treated as customer or as supplier. You might even have a different policy depending on the business process in which you do the credit check. This way you can use a certain policy when placing and order, and another policy, which is more strict, during actual shipping.

Credit checks are performed on `BusinessPartnerCustomer SupplierData`. This interface provides two variants of the `performedCreditCheck()` methods, which differ in the amount of additional information they provide in case of failure. The method signatures are shown in Figure 21-5. The only mandatory parameter is the `ProcessTokenValue` parameter, which indicates the transaction that requires approval. The time and amount parameters are optional, but might be needed, based on the specific policy used.

The process token, combined with the specific `BusinessPartner CustomerSupplierData`, determines the policy to be used. Once the right policy is determined control is passed to this object and the specific logic implemented in this policy is used.

The selection of a policy for a specific business partner is done using the `CreditCheckPolicyOrganizer`. Each such organizer implements a certain selection criteria, so the same organizer can be shared by all business partners using this criteria. The policies selected by the organizer depend, of course, on the process token. Policies are associated with companies through a controller of the company. When you create a customer-supplier object the policy organizer for it is automatically set to the default organizer in the controller and you can later change it. This is done using the method `setCreditCheckPolicyOrganizer(Credit CheckPolicyOrganizer newCreditCheckPolicyOrganizer)`.

In order to obtain the controller object you use the `PropertyContainer` interface of the company (see Chapter 23 for a full description of this interface). The controller property is called `cf.CreditCheckPolicyOrganizer`. You can create organizers into the controller using the `CreditCheckPolicyOrganizerFactory`, which provides a static create method for organizers. The policies themselves are created with an appropriate factory for your policy objects. When you create an organizer you must supply a default credit check for this organizer (this is required so that the organizer can make credit checks immediately). You can add additional credit check policies to it using the `addCreditCheckPolicyBy` method, which takes as parameter the credit check policy along with the associated process token.

To provide specific credit-checking policies you must implement the `DCreditCheckPolicy` interface whose main method is the `performCreditCheck` method. This method takes the information related to the credit check, which is the customer-supplier data, transaction amount, process token, time, and results collection. The amount and time are optional, whereas the rest are mandatory. The returned value indicates the success of the check, where true means success and false means failure. Inside the `performCreditCheck` method, you can use the `BusinessPartnerCustomerData` to inquire specific attributes of the business partner that might be relevant, such as the credit limit for the business partner, which is accessed using the `getCreditLimit()` method.

Cutout 21-1, taken from the SanFrancisco CBO Guide, defines some conventions to follow when creating a credit checking policy. These conventions are implemented in the default credit checking policy of SanFrancisco.

Currencies

In today's business environment, many companies have business transactions in multiple currencies. Therefore, there is a need to have inherent support for working with multiple currencies and supporting the notion of exchange rates that fluctuate along time and might be different for different purposes (e.g. you might have a different rate used for internal accounting as opposed to charging customers).

In SanFrancisco, the class `Currency` represents a single currency. The interface for this class is shown in Figure 21-16. This class allows

The default credit check policy in SanFrancisco, together with the documentation, suggests some further conventions to follow when you create a credit checking policy.

- If the policy is called without an amount, treat it as a zero amount.
- If the partner has a null credit limit treat the partner as if they have not had a proper limit set. Return false and supply the informational message "CFCRDCHK700".
- If the partner has a zero credit limit, treat the partner as if they had unlimited credit. Return true and supply the informational message "CFCRDCHK701".
- If the credit check fails because the partner's credit limit is exceeded supply the informational message "CFCRDCHK702".
- The error messages that have been predefined for credit checking can be reviewed in the SanFrancisco documentation.

Cutout 21-1

SanFrancisco CBO guide: conventions for creating a credit checking policy.

Interface com.ibm.sf.cf.Currency

public interface Currency extends DescribableDynamicEntity, Distinguishable

Name	*Signature*	*Description*
getCurrencyScaleFactor	`public abstract int getCurrencyScaleFactor() throws SFException`	Return the scale factor defined for currency values associated with this currency. The figure is derived from the ratioOfFractionsToCurrency and the smallestUnit settings on this instance
getCurrencyCode	`public abstract String getCurrencyCode() throws SFException`	Gets preferably the three-letter internationally standardized code for the currency. The codes are defined in the ISO 4217 Standard.
getCurrencyName	`public abstract String getCurrencyName() throws SFException`	Gets the commonly used name of the currency the object represents
setCurrencyName	`public abstract void setCurrencyName(String newCurrencyName) throws SFException`	Set the commonly used name of the currency the object represents
getFractionName	`public abstract String getFractionName() throws SFException`	Gets the name of this currency's fraction, i.e cent if the object represents US dollars or pfennig if the the currency is Deutsche Mark.
setFractionName	`public abstract void setFractionName(String newFractionName) throws SFException`	Set the name of this currency's fraction, i.e cent if the object represents US dollars or pfennig if the the currency is Deutsche Mark.
getRatioOfFractionToCurrency	`public abstract DDecimal getRatioOfFractionToCurrency () throws SFException`	Gets defines the number of fractional pieces making up one unit in this currency; i.e. how many cents make a dollar. The number can be given as a whole number (i.e. 100) or as a fractional number (i.e. 0 .01). In both cases the numbering has to match the scheme used for the 'SmallestUnit' attribute
setRatioOfFractionToCurrency	`public abstract void setRatioOfFractionToCurrency (DDecimal newRatioOfFractionToCurrency ) throws SFException`	Set defines the number of fractional pieces making up one unit in this currency; i.e. how many cents make a dollar. The number can be given as a whole number (i.e. 100) or as a fractional number (i.e. 0 .01). In both cases the numbering has to match the scheme used for the 'SmallestUnit' attribute
getSmallestUnit	`public abstract DDecimal getSmallestUnit() throws SFException`	Gets the smallest fraction of a currency value commonly used in daily (business) life, i.e. it is common practice in Sweden to deal with amounts not less than 25 oere. Thus the smallest fraction for any mounts in Swedish krona is 0.25 or 25 depending on the numbering scheme chosen

Figure 21-16
Interface `Currency`

setSmallestUnit	`public abstract void setSmallestUnit(DDecimal newSmallestUnit) throws SFException`	Set the smallest fraction of a currency value commonly used in daily (business) life, i.e. it is common practice in Sweden to deal with amounts not less than 25 oere. Thus the smallest fraction for any amounts in Swedish krona is 0.25 or 25 depending on the numbering scheme chosen (see documentation for 'RatioOfFractionToBase' attribute).
showDecimalsOnExternalOutput	`public abstract boolean showDecimalsOnExternalOutput () throws SFException`	Gets a flag which determines whether amounts of this currency will be displayed with or without fractions.
setShowDecimalsOnExternalOutput	`public abstract void setShowDecimalsOnExternalOutput(boolean newShowDecimalsOnExternalOutput) throws SFException`	Set a flag which determines whether amounts of this currency will be displayed with or without fractions.
showDecimalsOnInternalOutput	`public abstract boolean showDecimalsOnInternalOutput () throws SFException`	Gets a flag which determines whether amounts of this currency will be displayed internally with or without fractions.
setShowDecimalsOnInternalOutput	`Public abstract void setShowDecimalsOnInternalOutput(boolean newShowDecimalsOnInternalOutput) throws SFException`	Set a flag which determines whether amounts of this currency will be displayed internally with or without fractions.
isExternalOutputShowingFractions	`public abstract boolean isExternalOutputShowingFractions() throws SFException`	This method is identical to showDecimalsOnExternalOutput() and exists for the sole purpose of GUI framework compatibility (beans)
isInternalOutputShowingFractions	`public abstract boolean isInternalOutputShowingFractions() throws SFException`	This method is identical to showDecimalsOnInternalOutput() and exists for the sole purpose of GUI framework compatibility (beans)
setExternalOutputShowingFractions	`public abstract void setExternalOutputShowingFractions(boolean showingFractions) throws SFException`	This method is identical to setShowDecimalsOnExternalOutput() and exists for the sole purpose of GUI framework compatibility (beans)
setInternalOutputShowingFractions	`public abstract void setInternalOutputShowingFractions(boolean showingFractions) throws SFException`	This method is identical to setShowDecimalsOnInternalOutput() and exists for the sole purpose of GUI framework compatibility (beans)

Figure 21-16
(Cont'd)

initialize	`public abstract void initialize(CurrencyController owningObject, String currencyCode, String currencyName, String fractionName, DDecimal ratioOfFractionToCurrency, Decimal smallestUnit, boolean showDecimalsOnExternalOutput, boolean showDecimalsOnInternalOutput, DescriptiveInformation description) throws SFException`	This method is invoked by the Factory after Construction of an instance of this class to ensure proper initialization

Figure 21-16
(Cont'd)

you to find out the name of a currency, its three-letter ISO code, the name of the fractional part of the currency, the ratio of the fractional to the currency (e.g. 1/100 in the case of Cents to US Dollar), and the smallest unit of currency used.

The `CurrencyController` holds the currencies in use by the `Company`. It provides methods for getting the base currency and other currencies by three letter codes. The base currency is the currency in which the company does its bookkeeping and reports. `Currency` objects are creates using the static `create()` method in the `CurrencyFactory` class.

Once we know how to describe a currency, a sum of money is not represented by a number, but instead by a pairing of a number and a currency. The class `DCurrencyValue` holds such a pair, and its methods are shown in Figure 21-17. A `DCurrencyValue` object is created using the `DCurrencyValueFactory`, given the base currency and the amount. As shown in Figure 21-17, it provides various arithmetic operations each of which comes in various flavors. The different flavors of the same operation differ in where the result is stored (that is, is it returned or stored in the object on which the operation is performed), and how the result is rounded. There are also rounding methods, that allow you to round up sums, either according to a given parameter, or according to the smallest unit (an attribute of the currency). Other methods allow comparison of currency values and also printing (i.e. providing a locale-dependent string holding the currency value). `DCurrencyValue` also provides a conversion method, which takes a new currency with a fixed conversion rate and returns a new currency value (in the given currency).

Interface com.ibm.sf.cf.DCurrencyValue

public interface DCurrencyValue extends Dependent, TranslatableDependent, CumulativeResult

Name	*Signature*	*Description*
add	`public abstract DCurrencyValue add(DcurrencyValue anotherCurrencyValue) throws SFException`	Add the value of this DCurrencyValue and the value of the passed-in parameter and return the result in a new DcurrencyValue object
addTo	`public abstract void addTo(DcurrencyValue anotherCurrencyValue) throws SFException`	Add anotherCurrencyValue to the internal value of this object
addToAndRound	`Public abstract void addToAndRound(DCurrencyValue currencyValue) throws SFException`	Sums up the passed argument to the value currently stored in this object and the result is stored in the object. The scale factor of this object will not change.The computation is carried out using the higher scale factor of both operands by expanding the scale factor of the operand with the lower setting before calculating. The result is then rounded if required
addToAndTruncate	`Public abstract void addToAndTruncate (DCurrencyValue aValue) throws SFException`	Sums up the passed argument to the value currently stored in this object and the result is stored in the object. The scale factor of this object will not change. The computation will be carried out using the higher scale factor of both operands, thus expanding the scale factor of the operand with the lower setting before calculating. The result is then truncated if required
addToAndRaise	`public abstract void addToAndRaise(DCurrencyValue aValue) throws SFException`	Sums up the passed argument to the value currently stored in this object and the result is stored in the object. The scale factor of this object will not change. The computation will be carried out using the higher scale factor of both operands, thus expanding the scale factor of the operand with the lower setting before calculating. The result is then raised if required
subtract	`public abstract DCurrencyValue subtract(DCurrencyValue amount) throws SFException`	Subtracts the passed amount from this object and returns the difference of both numbers in a new DCurrencyValue object. The scale factor setting of the operand with the lower setting is expanded to the higher setting of both for the computation. The result, therefore, always has the larger scale factor
subtractBy	`public abstract void subtractBy(DCurrencyValue amount) throws SFException`	Subtract the passed argument from this object making the difference the new value this instance represents. Adjust scale factor if required. The computation is carried out using the higher scale factor of both operands by expanding the scale factor of the operand with the lower setting before calculating. The result, therefore, always has the higher scale factor
subtractByAndRound	`public abstract void subtractByAndRound(DCurrencyValue amount) throws SFException`	Subtract the passed argument from this object making the difference the new value this instance represents. The scale factor of this object will not change. The computation will be carried out using the higher scale factor of both operands, thus expanding the scale factor of the operand with the lower setting before calculating. The result is then rounded if required

Figure 21-17
Interface `DCurrencyValue`

subtractByAndTruncate	`public abstract void subtractByAndTruncate(DCurrencyValue amount) throws SFException`	Subtract the passed argument from this object making the difference the new value this instance represents. The scale factor of this object will not change. The computation will be carried out using the higher scale factor of both operands, thus expanding the scale factor of the operand with the lower setting before calculating. The result is then truncated if required
subtractByAndRaise	`public abstract void subtractByAndRaise(DCurrencyValue subtrahend) throws SFException`	Subtract the passed argument from this object making the difference the new value this instance represents. The scale factor of this object will not change.The computation will be carried out using the higher scale factor of both operands, thus expanding the scale factor of the operand with the lower setting before calculating. The result is then raised if required
multiply	`public abstract DCurrencyValue multiply(DDecimal multiplier) throws SFException`	Multiply this object by the passed argument and return the product of both numbers in a new DCurrencyValue object. The computation is performed using a scale factor equal to the sum of both operands' scale factor settings [this.scaleFactor()+aDecimal.scaleFactor()]. The result is returned in a new DCurrencyValue object
multiplyAndRound	`public abstract DCurrencyValue multiplyAndRound(DDecimal factor) throws SFException`	Multiply this object by the value of the passed argument and return the product of both numbers in a new DCurrencyValue object. The computation is performed using a scale factor equal to the greater scale factor of the two operands. The result is rounded to the scale factor employed in the calculation and then used to construct the returned DCurrencyValue from.
multiplyAndTruncate	`public abstract DCurrencyValue multiplyAndTruncate(DDecimal factor) throws SFException`	Multiply the value of this object by the value of the passed argument and return the product of both numbers in a new DCurrencyValue object. The computation is performed using a scale factor equal to the greater scale factor of the two operands. The result is being truncated to the scale factor used in the calculation (the higher of both operands). The scale factor of the returned object is determined by the one employed in the computation.
multiplyAndRaise	`public abstract DCurrencyValue multiplyAndRaise(DDecimal factor) throws SFException`	Multiply the value of this object by the value of the passed argument and return the product of both numbers in a new DCurrencyValue object. The computation is performed using a scale factor equal to the greater scale factor of the two operands. The result is being rounded-up (raised) to the scale factor used in the calculation (the higher of both decimals). If the value of the most significant truncated (extra) digit is > 0, the last shown digit is rounded to the next higher value. The scale factor of the returned object is determined by that one employed in the computation.
multiplyBy	`public abstract void multiplyBy(DDecimal muliplier) throws SFException`	Multiply this object by the passed argument and make the product of both the new value. The computation is performed using a scale factor equal to the sum of both operands' scale factor settings [this.scaleFactor()+aDecimal.scaleFactor()]. The result is assigned to the internal value of this object
multiplyByAndRound	`public abstract void multiplyByAndRound(Ddecimal factor) throws SFException`	Multiply the value of this object by the value of the passed decimal and make the product of both the new value. The original scale factor of this object will be preserved by the multiplication. The result is rounded following standard rounding rules meaning that digits > 4 will lead to an increment of the next higher fraction (decimal position).

Figure 21-17
(Cont'd)

multiplyByAndTruncate	`public abstract void multiplyByAndTruncate(Ddecimal factor) throws SFException`	Multiply the value of this object by the value of the passed decimal and make the product of both the new value. The original scale factor of this object will be preserved by the operation and the result is being truncated to that scale factor if required.
multiplyByAndRaise	`public abstract void multiplyByAndRaise(DDecimal factor) throws SFException`	Multiply the value of this object by the value of the passed decimal and make the product of both the new value. The original scale factor of this object will be preserved by the operation. The result is being rounded-up (raised) to that scale factor: if the value of the most significant truncated (extra) digit is > 0, the last shown digit is rounded to the next higher value
divide	`public abstract DCurrencyValue divide(DDecimal denominator) throws SFException`	Divide this object by the value of the passed argument and return the quotient of both numbers in a new DCurrencyValue object.Adjust scale factor if required. The limit for the number of fractional digits of the result is determined by the setting of the 'maximumDecimalScaleFactor' system constant
divideAndRound	`public abstract DCurrencyValue divideAndRound(DDecimal aDecimal) throws SFException`	Divide the value of this object by the value of the passed argument and return the quotient of both numbers in a new DCurrencyValue object. The computation is performed using the larger scale factor from the two operands involved. The result is rounded to the scale factor employed in the calculation and then used to construct the returned DCurrencyValue from
divideAndTruncate	`public abstract DCurrencyValue divideAndTruncate(DDecimal aDecimal) throws SFException`	Divide the value of this object by the value of the passed argument and return the quotient of both numbers in a new DCurrencyValue object. The computation is performed using a scale factor equal to the greater scale factor of the two operands. The result is being truncated to the scale factor used in the calculation (the higher one of both). The scale factor of the returned object is determined by that one employed in the computation.
divideAndRaise	`public abstract DCurrencyValue divideAndRaise(DDecimal aDecimal) throws SFException`	Divide the value of this object by the value of the passed argument and return the quotient of both numbers in a new DCurrencyValue object. The computation is performed using a scale factor equal to the greater scale factor of the two operands. The result is being rounded-up (raised) to the scale factor used in the calculation (the higher one of both). If the value of the most significant truncated (extra) digit is > 0, the last shown digit is rounded to the next higher value. The scale factor of the returned object is determined by that one employed in the computation.
divideBy	`public abstract void divideBy(DDecimal aDecimal) throws SFException`	Devide this object by the passed decimal and make the quotient of both the new value of this. Adjust scale factor if required. The limit for the number of fractional digits of the result is determined by the setting of the 'maximumDecimalScaleFactor' system constant
divideByAndRound	`public abstract void divideByAndRound(DDecimal aDecimal) throws SFException`	Divide the value of this object by the value of the passed decimal and make the quotient of both the new value of this. The original scale factor of this object will be preserved by the division. The result is rounded following standard rounding rules meaning that digits > 4 will lead to an increment of the next higher decimal position.
divideByAndTruncate	`public abstract void divideByAndTruncate(DDecimal aDecimal) throws SFException`	Divide the value of this object by the value of the passed decimal and make the quotient of both the new value of this. The original scale factor of this object will be preserved by the operation and the result is being truncated to that scale factor if required.

Figure 21-17
(Cont'd)

divideByAndRaise	`public abstract void divideByAndRaise(DDecimal denominator) throws SFException`	Divide the value of this object by the value of the passed decimal and make the quotient of both the new value of this. The original scale factor of this object will be preserved by the operation. The result is being rounded-up (raised) to that scale factor: if the value of the most significant truncated (extra) digit is > 0, the last shown digit is rounded to the next higher value
convert	`public abstract DCurrencyValue convert(Currency currencyToConvertTo, DDecimal conversionRate) throws SFException`	Convert the value of this CurrencyValue to the equivalent amount in the currency passed as first parameter applying the conversion rate given. The scale factor of the converted currency value will match the setting of this object.
convert	`public abstract DCurrencyValue convert(Currency currencyToConvertTo, DDecimal divident, DDecimal divisor) throws SFException`	Convert the value of this CurrencyValue to the equivalent amount in the currency passed as first parameter applying a conversion rate which is derived from the passed divident and divisor.
changeSign	`public abstract DCurrencyValue changeSign() throws SFException`	Create a copy of this CurrencyValue with reversed sign
changeSignOf	`public abstract void changeSignOf() throws SFException`	Reverse the sign of this object to the opposite of the original setting
greater	`public abstract boolean greater(DCurrencyValue anotherCurrencyValue) throws SFException`	Compare the value of anotherCurrencyValue to the internal value of this object
greaterEqual	`public abstract boolean greaterEqual(DCurrencyValue anotherCurrencyValue) throws SFException`	Compare the value of anotherCurrencyValue to the internal value of this object
greaterThanZero	`public abstract boolean greaterThanZero() throws SFException`	Test whether the internal value of this object is greater than zero
less	`public abstract boolean less(DCurrencyValue anotherCurrencyValue) throws SFException`	Compare the value of anotherCurrencyValue to the internal value of this object
lessEqual	`Public abstract boolean lessEqual(DCurrencyValue anotherCurrencyValue) throws SFException`	Compare the value of the passed object to the internal value of this object
lessThanZero	`Public abstract boolean lessThanZero() throws SFException`	Test whether the internal value of this object is less than zero
isZero	`public abstract boolean isZero() throws SFException`	Test the internal value of this object for equality to zero
setToZero	`public abstract void setToZero() throws SFException`	Reset internal value of the DCurrencyValue to '0'
round	`public abstract void round(int newScaleFactor) throws SFException`	Re-sets the number of decimal digits past the decimal point the amount or value of this object is set to. If the internal value has more decimals than the passed argument suggests, the internal value will be adjusted to the new precision following standard rounding rules as described in the general section above.
truncate	`public abstract void truncate(int newScaleFactor) throws SFException`	Re-sets the number of decimal digits past the decimal point the amount or value of this object is set to. If the internal value has more decimals than the passed argument suggests, all digits past the newScaleFactor will be dropped.

Figure 21-17
(Cont'd)

raise	`public abstract void raise(int newScaleFactor) throws SFException`	Re-sets the number of decimal digits past the decimal point the amount or value of this object is set to. If the internal value has more decimals than the passed argument suggests, the internal value will be adjusted to the new precision following the raising procedure as described in the general section above.
isOfSameCurrency	`public abstract boolean isOfSameCurrency(DCurrencyValue anotherCurrencyValue) throws SFException`	Compare currency codes of both currencyValues for equivalence
roundToSmallestUnit	`public abstract void roundToSmallestUnit() throws SFException`	Rounds the value of this object to the smallest unit defined on the associated Currency
truncateToSmallestUnit	`public abstract void truncateToSmallestUnit() throws SFException`	Truncates the value of this object to the smallest unit defined on the associated Currency
raiseToSmallestUnit	`public abstract void raiseToSmallestUnit() throws SFException`	Raises the value of this object to the smallest unit defined on the associated Currency
format	`public abstract String format() throws SFException`	Returns the state of this object in a Java string. This textual representation will be formatted according to the formatting information found in the active locale of the system. The three letter ISO code of the associated currency preceedes the amount.
format	`public abstract String format(String locale) throws SFException`	Returns the state of this object in a Java string. This textual representation is formatted according to the format information found in the passed argument. The three letter ISO code of the associated currency preceedes the amount.
accumulateResult	`public abstract void accumulateResult(CumulativeResult cumulativeResultObject) throws SFException`	Adds the passed CumulativeResult, which must be an instance of DCurrencyValue, to this DCurrencyValue.
getCurrency	`public abstract Currency getCurrency() throws SFException`	Returns the Currency, copied from the Handle
setCurrency	`public abstract void setCurrency(Currency newCurrency) throws SFException`	Set the Handle of the Currency
getValue	`public abstract DDecimal getValue() throws SFException`	Gets the amount this instance represents
setValue	`public abstract void setValue(DDecimal newValue) throws SFException`	Set the amount this instance represents
getCurrencyHdl	`public abstract Handle getCurrencyHdl() throws SFException`	Returns the Handle to the Currency of the currency of the DCurrencyValue
getValueForRestrictedUse	`public abstract DDecimal getValueForRestrictedUse() throws SFException`	Returns the actual Value, used by framework for SetEqual()
initialize	`public abstract void initialize(Currency aCurrency, DDecimal amount) throws SFException`	This method is invoked by the Factory after Construction of an instance of this class to ensure proper initialization

Figure 21-17
(Cont'd)

For a few decades now, currency exchange rates have fluctuated around the clock based on the movements in international markets. For this reason, the fixed conversion rate method is not enough and currency conversion should be addressed in a more flexible way. The situation is usually a little more complicated because, as mentioned at the beginning of this section, companies need to support several exchange rates. So `CurrencyContoller` also has a conversion method that takes more parameters. Namly, it uses the target currency, rate-type, date, fiscal period, default conversion factor, and exchange rate retrieval policies. All these factors, apart from the target currency, are optional. The `ExchangeRateController` holds the currency exchange rates used, and the conversion is actually delegated to it.

The currency exchange rate controller maintains a list of exchange rate types assigned to it, each with a key string associated with it. The exchange rate types in SanFrancisco are the following:

- `DExchangeRateTypePeriodBased`—period-based exchange rates
- `DExchangeRateTypeDateBased`—date-based exchange rates
- `DExchangeRateTypeDateBasedFixed`—fixed exchange rates

Each of these exchange rate types holds a set of concrete exchange rates along with the associated dates or periods. These sets can be accessed and modified. Usually these access method are not needed for application developers because the exchange rate controller provides means for working with exchange rates (e.g. the method `removeExchangeRate`).

The conversion method also takes as parameter a conversion policy. This policy determines how to use the data in the exchange rate controller. The default policy, which is `DExchangeRateRetrievalPolicyDefault`, looks for an explicit conversion rate. Specific applications might need more than that. For example, you might consider having a mechanism for automatically figuring out cross-rates. One example is finding the DEM/JPY rate (the German Marks to Japanese Yens rate) by dividing the USD/JPY (i.e. the US Dollars to Japanese Yens rate) by the USD/DEM rate (the US Dollar to German Marks rate). Another option is using reverse rates. For example, the rate for British Pounds might be stored as US Dollars per Pound so to convert a sum in Dollars you would need the reciprocal of the rate.

In order to set up the currencies and the exchange rates for a company or enterprise you should use a `Command` object. An example of such an object is provided in SanFrancisco—the CFCurrenciesSetupCmd. If you design your own such Command, note you have some flexibility in where to place controllers. As with other controllers, you can use only one controller for the whole enterprise or place specific controllers in different companies.

In order to represent transactions in multiple currencies SanFrancisco uses the DTransactionValue. Such a transaction value involves two different currencies: the "prime" currency, and the base currency. The former is the currency in which the transaction took place, whereas the latter is the base currency used for bookkeeping in the company. Figure 21-18 shows the interface for using transaction values. As you can see, these transaction values support various operations of conversion and arithmetic. Of course, the currencies need to match for this to work (e.g. if you add one transaction value to another the prime currencies and base currencies must both match).

SanFrancisco also has a notion of TransactionValueExtended, which is similar to TransactionValue, but provides support for having a base currency different from the reporting currency. This is needed for companies that are part of the European Monetary Union (EMU) which introduced a unified currency in the beginning of January 1999. The transition to this currency is gradual, hence the need for keeping records in two currencies (one is the native one, such as French francs in France, or German marks in Germany, and the other is the Euro, which is the new single currency).

Document Location

The concept of Document Location in SanFrancisco is aimed at providing a uniform way for describing where documents are placed. This replaces the common practice of having a non-structured way of describing locations, such as adding a free-text description field for each document record, which indicates its location.

DocumentLocation objects are shared persistent objects, which means all objects with the same location share the same DocumentLocation object. This is useful when any of the details relating to the location changes (e.g. the person in charge of managing a certain archive) in which case all documents in this location readily have the updated information. The interface for DocumentLocation is

Interface com.ibm.sf.cf.DTransactionValue

public interface DTransactionValue extends Dependent, CumulativeResult

Name	*Signature*	*Description*
setPrimeCurrencyValue	`public abstract void setPrimeCurrencyValue(DCurrencyValue newPrimeValue) throws SFException`	Replace current prime currencyValue by the passed argument and recalculate the base currency value to match the new prime value. The computation of the new base value is done by applying the quotient of the original prime / original base value
setBaseCurrencyValue	`public abstract void setBaseCurrencyValue(DCurrencyValue newBaseValue) throws SFException`	Replace current base currencyValue by the passed argument and recalculate the prime currency value to match the new base value. The computation of the new base value is done by applying the quotient of the original base / original prime values
add	`public abstract DTransactionValue add(DTransactionValue aTransactionValue) throws SFException`	Add this DTransactionValue to the passed argument and return the result in a new DTransactionValue object.
addTo	`public abstract void addTo(DTransactionValue transactionValueToAdd) throws SFException`	Add the passed argument to this object making the sum the new value this instance represents. Adjust precision if required. The precision setting of the lower precision operand is expanded to the higher setting of both for the computation. The result therefore always has the higher precision. This is being handled on an individual base for prime and base value respectively, i.e. if the prime value of this object has a value of 3.07 (precision set to 2) and the passed argument's prime value has a value of 1.234, the result of the computation is 4.304. The new prime value of this object is then 4.304 and the precision setting is modified to 3.
subtract	`public abstract DTransactionValue subtract(DTransactionValue aTransactionValue) throws SFException`	Subtract the passed argument from this and return the result of the operation in a new DTransactionValue object
subtractBy	`public abstract void subtractBy(DTransactionValue valueToSubtract) throws SFException`	Subtract the passed argument from this object making the difference the new value this instance represents. Adjust precision if required. The precision setting of the lower precision operand is expanded to the higher setting of both for the computation. The result therefore always has the higher precision. This is being handled on an individual base for prime and base value respectively, i.e. if the prime value of this object has a value of 3.07 (precision set to 2) and the passed argument's prime value has a value of 1.234, the result of the computation is 1.846. The new prime value of this object is then 1.846 and the precision setting is modified to 3. Note: In case the operation's result exceeds the system's precision limit the resulting number will be automatically rounded to that limit (no exception !).

Figure 21-18
Interface `DTransactionValue`

multiply	`public abstract DTransactionValue multiply(DDecimal multiplier) throws SFException`	Multiply this object by the passed argument and return the result of the operation in a new DTransactionValue object. The computation is performed individually for prime and base values. On each computation a precision equal to the sum of both operands' precision settings is used prime/baseValue.precision()+multiplier.precision()]. The result is returned in a new DtransactionValue, i.e. if this object has a primValue of 2.12 (precision set to 2) and the passed argument has a value of 3.123, the result of the computation is 6.62076. The new value of this object's primeValue is then 6.62076 and the precision setting is set to 5. Note: In case the operation's result exceeds the system's precision limit the resulting number will be automatically rounded to that limit (no exception !).
addPrimeValue	`public abstract DTransactionValue addPrimeValue(DCurrencyValue primeValueToAdd) throws SFException`	Add the passed argument to the prime currencyValue and recalculate a new base currency value from the sum of the prime values. The computation of the new base value is done by applying the quotient of the original prime / original base value. From the new prime and base values a new DTransactionValue is created and returned
addBaseValue	`public abstract DTransactionValue addBaseValue(DCurrencyValue baseValueToAdd) throws SFException`	Add the passed argument to the base currencyValue and recalculate a new prime currency value from the sum of the base values. The computation of the new prime value is done by applying the quotient of the original prime / original base value. From the new prime and base values a new DTransactionValue is created and returned
subtractPrimeValue	`public abstract DTransactionValue subtractPrimeValue(DCurrencyValue primeValueToSubtract) throws SFException`	Subtract the passed argument from the prime currencyValueand recalculate a new base currency value from the difference of the prime values. The computation of the new base value is done by applying the quotient of the original prime / original base value. From the new prime and base values a new DTransactionValue is created and returned
subtractBaseValue	`public abstract DTransactionValue subtractBaseValue(DCurrencyValue baseValueToSubtract) throws SFException`	Subtract the passed argument from the base currencyValue and recalculate a new prime currency value from the difference of the base values. The computation of the new prime value is done by applying the quotient of the original prime / original base value. From the new prime and base values a new DTransactionValue is created and returned
deriveFromWithNewPrime	`public abstract DTransactionValue deriveFromWithNewPrime(DCurrencyValue newPrimeValue) throws SFException`	Create a new DTransactionValue from the passed argument making it the new primeCurrencyValue. The base currency value of the new object is calculated using the quotient of the prime / base values of this.
deriveFromWithNewBase	`public abstract DTransactionValue deriveFromWithNewBase(DCurrencyValue newBaseValue) throws SFException`	Create a new DTransactionValue from the passed argument making it the new baseCurrencyValue. The prime currency value of the new object is calculated using the quotient of the base/prime values of this.

Figure 21-18
(Cont'd)

isZero	`public abstract boolean isZero() throws SFException`	Test the internal value of this object for equality to zero
setToZero	`public abstract void setToZero() throws SFException`	Reset internally held prime value and base value of this DTransactionValue to '0'
revalueSelfFromPrime	`public abstract void revalueSelfFromPrime(DDecimal revaluationFactor) throws SFException`	Revalue this object using its prime currency value by applying the passed factor. A new base currency value is being calculated and the current value is replaced by the result. Precision is adjusted to the original setting of base currency value if necessary.
revalueSelfFromBase	`public abstract void revalueSelfFromBase(DDecimal revaluationFactor) throws SFException`	Revalue this object using its base currency value by applying the passed factor. A new prime currency value is being calculated and the current value is replaced by the result. Precision is adjusted to the original setting of prime currency value if necessary.
revalueFromPrime	`public abstract DTransactionValue revalueFromPrime(DDecimal revaluationFactor) throws SFException`	Create a new and revalued DTransactionValue by copying the prime currency value of this object to the new prime value and applying the passed factor to calculate the new base currency value . Precision is adjusted to match the setting of base currency value of this—if necessary.
revalueFromBase	`public abstract DTransactionValue revalueFromBase(DDecimal revaluationFactor) throws SFException`	Create a new and revalued DTransactionValue by copying the base currency value of this object to the new base value and applying the passed factor to calculate the new prime currency value . Precision is adjusted to match the setting of prime currency value of this—if necessary.
round	`public abstract void round(int newPrecision) throws SFException`	Re-sets the number of decimal digits past the decimal point of the contained prime and base currency values. See also corresponding method on DCurrenyValue.
truncate	`public abstract void truncate(int newPrecision) throws SFException`	Re-sets the number of decimal digits past the decimal point of the contained prime and base currency values. See also corresponding method on DCurrenyValue.
raise	`public abstract void raise(int newPrecision) throws SFException`	Re-sets the number of decimal digits past the decimal point the amount or value of this object is set to. If the internal value has more decimals than the passed argument suggests, the internal value will be adjusted to the new precision re-sets the number of decimal digits past the decimal point of the contained prime and base currency values. See also corresponding method on DCurrenyValue.
changeSignOf	`public abstract void changeSignOf() throws SFException`	Reverse the sign of this object to the opposite of the original setting
changeSign	`public abstract DTransactionValue changeSign() throws SFException`	Create a copy of this DTransactionValue object with reversed sign
accumulateResult	`public abstract void accumulateResult(CumulativeResult cumulativeResultObject) throws SFException`	Adds the passed CumulativeResult, which must be an instance of DTransactionValue, to this DTransactionValue. Assumptions: Passed CumulativeResult is an instance of DTransactionValue.
getPrimeCurrencyValue	`public abstract DCurrencyValue getPrimeCurrencyValue() throws SFException`	Gets PrimeCurrencyValue

Figure 21-18
(Cont'd)

getBaseCurrencyValue	`public abstract DCurrencyValue getBaseCurrencyValue() throws SFException`	Gets BaseCurrencyValue
initialize	`public abstract void initialize(DCurrencyValue primeValue, DCurrencyValue baseValue) throws SFException`	This method is invoked by the Factory after Construction of an instance of this class to ensure proper initialization
initialize	`public abstract void initialize(DCurrencyValue primeValue, String dictionaryToken, DTime date) throws SFException`	This method is invoked by the Factory after Construction of an instance of this class to ensure proper initialization
initializeWithoutValidation	`public abstract void initializeWithoutValidation(DCurrencyValue primeValue, DCurrencyValue baseValue) throws SFException`	This method is invoked by the Factory after Construction of an instance of this class to ensure proper initialization without Validation

Figure 21-18
(Cont'd)

shown in Figure 21-19. `DocumentLocation` uses dynamic identifiers, using the `PropertyContainer` interface. Dynamic identifiers are used in other CBOs (e.g. classifications, process tokens). The idea of a dynamic identifier is to associate a certain value with a certain type, using the `PropertyContainer` interface. The value has an id and a description.

Interface com.ibm.sf.cf.DocumentLocation

public interface **DocumentLocation** extends DescribableDynamicEntity, Distinguishable

Name	*Signature*	*Description*
setId	`public abstract void setId(String id) throws SFException`	The attribute set by this method is used by the framework as primary key in a collection. This method should be used with extreme caution
getId	`public abstract String getId() throws SFException`	Get the id of the Distinguishable object
initialize	`public abstract void initialize(DocumentLocationController owner, String id, DescriptiveInformation locationDescription) throws SFException`	This method is invoked by the Factory after Construction of an instance of this class to ensure proper initialization

Figure 21-19
Interface `DocumentLocation`

DocumentLocation objects are owned by a DocumentLocationController, which is kept in the "cf.DocumentLocationController" property of a company. This controller provides interfaces for finding an object given a location or performing queries on the owned locations.

Classification

Classifications are required to categorize groups of products, employees, customers, or other entities in the business realm. SanFrancisco provides support for the notion of classification through ClassificationTypeValue objects (interface shown in Figure 21-20), which are dynamic identifiers. These are created using the respective

Interface com.ibm.sf.cf.ClassificationTypeValue

public interface ClassificationTypeValue extends DescribableDynamicEntity, Distinguishable

Name	*Signature*	*Description*
getId	`public abstract String getId() throws SFException`	Get the id of the Distinguishable object
getContainingClassificationTypeController	`public abstract ClassificationTypeController getContainingClassificationTypeController() throws SFException`	Returns the ContainingClassificationTypeController, copied from the Handle
setId	`public abstract void setId(String newId) throws SFException`	Sets Id
GetContainingClassificationTypeControllerHdl	`public abstract Handle getContainingClassificationTypeControllerHdl() throws SFException`	Returns the Handle to the ClassificationTypeController of the containingClassificationTypeController of the ClassificationTypeValue
Initialize	`public abstract void initialize(ClassificationTypeController owningController, String id, DescriptiveInformation description) throws SFException`	This method is invoked by the Factory after Construction of an instance of this class to ensure proper initialization

Figure 21-20
Interface ClassificationTypeValue

factory and owned by the respective controller. The way dynamic identifiers are manipulated was covered previously.

Fiscal Calendar

Financial transactions must be reported to tax authorities and to company shareholders for the fiscal period (usually a quarter or a year) they occur in. Whenever a specific transaction occurs, e.g. a customer pays for some goods, the revenues must be booked in the correct fiscal period.

SanFrancisco provides a `FiscalCalendar` object that answers the need for maintaining fiscal periods. Usually, the `FiscalCalendar` is created and modified during configuration of the system. A fiscal calendar defines the fiscal year, and divides them further into smaller periods. A fiscal period can be of any length, depending on the needs of your application or company. A fiscal period could be, for example, a quarter or a single month.

The interface to `FiscalCalendar` is shown in Figure 21-21. Usually, a `FiscalCalendar` object is associated with the enterprise (through the property "`cf.FiscalCalendar`"). A company within the enterprise might have its own version (for example, if it is an offshore subsidiary that works with different fiscal periods).

The interfaces `FiscalYear` and `FiscalPeriod`, shown in Figures 21-22 and 21-23 respectively, and also the `FiscalCalendar` interface, provide methods for getting the boundary dates (i.e. the beginning and ending dates), checking for containment, iterating over calendar components, and so on.

SanFrancisco supports the notion of undated fiscal periods, which can be one of the following types.

- *OPENING*. Always the first period of the year. It should contain tasks and transactions associated with opening the new year.
- *CLOSING*. The last period of the year, containing transactions for closing the year.
- *ADJUSTMENT*. Period placed anywhere in the year, used for special adjustment transactions.

One more type marks the regular, dated, fiscal periods, and that is **NORMAL**.

Interface com.ibm.sf.cf.FiscalCalendar

public interface FiscalCalendar extends DescribableDynamicEntity

Name	*Signature*	*Description*
appendFiscalYear	`public abstract void appendFiscalYear(DTime endDate) throws SFException`	Appends a FiscalYear to the calendar. The new year ends at the given end date and begins the day after the last year of the calendar ends
prependFiscalYear	`public abstract void prependFiscalYear(DTime startDate) throws SFException`	Prepends a FiscalYear to the calendar. The new year begins with the given start date and ends the day before the first year of the calendar begins.
deleteStartingYear	`public abstract void deleteStartingYear() throws SFException`	Removes the FIRST year from the calendar, provided it is NOT the only remaining year in the calendar.
deleteEndingYear	`public abstract void deleteEndingYear() throws SFException`	Removes the LAST year from the calendar, provided it is NOT the only remaining year in the calendar
getFiscalYearBy	`public abstract FiscalYear getFiscalYearBy(int yearNumber) throws SFException`	Returns the FiscalYear associated with the given year number. If no matching FiscalYear has been found, null is returned.
getFirstFiscalYear	`public abstract FiscalYear getFirstFiscalYear() throws SFException`	Returns the FIRST year of the calendar (in chronological order)
getNextFiscalYear	`public abstract FiscalYear getNextFiscalYear(FiscalYear currentYear) throws SFException`	Returns the year which falls chronologically after the given year, i.e. where nextYear.getYearNumber() == currentYear.getYearNumber() + 1. If the specified year is the LAST in the calendar, null is returned.
getPreviousFiscalYear	`public abstract FiscalYear getPreviousFiscalYear(FiscalYear currentYear) throws SFException`	Returns the year which chronologically precedes the specified year, i.e. where nextYear.getYearNumber() == currentYear.getYearNumber() - 1. If the specified year is the FIRST in the calendar, null is returned.
getLastFiscalYear	`public abstract FiscalYear getLastFiscalYear() throws SFException`	Returns the LAST year of the calendar (in chronological order)
isComplete	`public abstract boolean isComplete() throws SFException`	Determine whether all years in the calendar are complete, i.e. the entire date range for each year in the calendar is partitioned into [mutually exclusive] periods. Typically, only calendars which are complete would be used by clients.
containsYear	`public abstract boolean containsYear(int yearNumber) throws SFException`	Determines whether the calendar contains a year matching the given year number
getPeriodBy	`public abstract FiscalPeriod getPeriodBy(DTime containedDate) throws SFException`	Returns the period the given date falls in or null if the given date is not contained within any period in the calendar
getPeriodBy	`public abstract FiscalPeriod getPeriodBy(int yearNumber, String periodId) throws SFException`	Returns the period with matching identifier for the given year or null if no match found
getPeriodBy	`public abstract FiscalPeriod getPeriodBy(String periodId) throws SFException`	Returns the FIRST period with matching identifier within the calendar or null if no match found

Figure 21-21
Interface `FiscalCalendar`

	throws SFException	
containsYear	public abstract boolean containsYear(FiscalYear year) throws SFException	Determines whether the calendar contains the given year
getContainingCompany	public abstract Company getContainingCompany() throws SFException	Returns the ContainingCompany, copied from the Handle
getStartDate	public abstract DTime getStartDate() throws SFException	Gets the date the calendar starts with
getEndDate	public abstract DTime getEndDate() throws SFException	Gets the date the calendar ends with
getFirstYearNumber	public abstract int getFirstYearNumber() throws SFException	Gets the number of the first year in the calendar
setFirstYearNumber	public abstract void setFirstYearNumber(int newFirstYearNumber) throws SFException	Set the number of the first year in the calendar
getLastYearNumber	public abstract int getLastYearNumber() throws SFException	Gets the number of the last year in the calendar
setLastYearNumber	public abstract void setLastYearNumber(int newLastYearNumber) throws SFException	Set the number of the last year in the calendar
getContainingCompanyHdl	public abstract Handle getContainingCompanyHdl() throws SFException	Returns the Handle to the Company of the containingCompany of the FiscalCalendar
getYearsHdl	public abstract Handle getYearsHdl() throws SFException	Get handle to Years,used by framework
getStartDateForRestrictedUse	public abstract DTime getStartDateForRestrictedUse() throws SFException	Returns the actual StartDate, used by framework for SetEqual()
getEndDateForRestrictedUse	public abstract DTime getEndDateForRestrictedUse() throws SFException	Returns the actual EndDate, used by framework for SetEqual()
initialize	public abstract void initialize(Company containingCompany, DTime initialStartDate, DTime initialEndDate, int initialYearNumber, DescriptiveInformation description) throws SFException	Initializes the calendar with the given initial start and end dates and the year number, used to identify individual years. The year number is a sequential number the calendar computes each time a year is appended/ prepended. It starts with the given initialYearNumber which is then incremented/ decremented when a year is appended/ prepended. For convenience, this method associates the Calendar with a provided Company.
initialize	public abstract void initialize(DTime initialStartDate, DTime initialEndDate, int initialYearNumber, DescriptiveInformation description) throws SFException	Initializes the calendar with the given initial start and end dates and the year number, used to identify individual years. The year number is a sequential number the calendar computes each time a year is appended/ prepended. It starts with The given initialYearNumber which is then incremented/ decremented when a year is appended/ prepended. This method does not associate the Calendar with any other entity.

Figure 21-21
(Cont'd)

Interface com.ibm.sf.cf.FiscalYear

public interface FiscalYear extends DescribableDynamicEntity

Name	*Signature*	*Description*
appendDatedPeriod	`public abstract void appendDatedPeriod(String periodId, DTime endDate) throws SFException`	Creates and appends a new dated period which will become the last period within the FiscalYear. The start date of the new period is implicitly defined as the day after the end date of the last dated period within the year. The given end date should neither exceed this year's end date nor should it precede the implicitly defined start date.
insertDatedPeriodBefore	`public abstract void insertDatedPeriodBefore(String newPeriodId, DTime itsEndDate, String insertBeforePeriodWithId) throws SFException`	Creates and inserts a dated fiscal period before the period identified by the specified id. If the contained period which the new period is to precede is dated, split the contained period to create the new period. Thus, the start date of the new period becomes the start date of the contained period, whose start date we move forward to the day after the end date specified for the new period. Hence, the end date for the new period must fall after the start date of the contained period but not after its end date. If the contained period is undated:- the contained period may not be the 'opening' period of the year (where 'opening' refers to the type of the fiscal period) the next dated period in the year would be used or if no dated period exists after this undated period, within the year and the year is not complete, append the new period to the FiscalYear which would extend the date range covered by the periods within the year. Hence, initialize the start date for the new period to the day after the end date of the last dated period of the year. The given end date should neither precede the implicit start date for the new period nor exceed the end date of the year.
insertDatedPeriodAfter	`public abstract void insertDatedPeriodAfter(String newPeriodId, DTime itsStartDate, String insertAfterPeriodWithId) throws SFException`	Creates and inserts a dated fiscal period after the period identified by the specified id. If the period after which the new period is to be inserted is dated, split the contained period to create the new period. Thus, the end date of the new period becomes the end date of the contained period, whose end date we move back to the day before the start date specified for the new period. Hence, the start date for the new period must fall on or after that of the contained period but before its end date. If the contained period is undated, it may not be the 'closing' period of the year (where 'closing' refers to the type of the fiscal period). The last dated period which precedes the contained period would then be used. Thus, if the contained period is undated, there must exist some dated period within the year which precedes that period within the year.

Figure 21-22
Interface `FiscalYear`

appendUndatedPeriod	`public abstract void appendUndatedPeriod(String periodId, int type) throws SFException`	Creates and appends an UndatedFiscalPeriod to the FiscalYear
insertUndatedPeriodBefore	`public abstract void insertUndatedPeriodBefore(String newPeriodId, String insertBeforePeriodWithId, int type) throws SFException`	Creates and inserts an undated fiscal period before the period identified by the specified id
insertUndatedPeriodAfter	`public abstract void insertUndatedPeriodAfter(String newPeriodId, String insertAfterPeriodWithId, int type) throws SFException`	Creates and inserts an undated fiscal period after the period identified by the specified id.
changePeriodEndDate	`public abstract void changePeriodEndDate(String periodId, DTime newEndDate) throws SFException`	Changes the end date of a [dated] fiscal period, adjusting the start date of the next dated period to compensate (it moves the boundary between two adjacent dated periods), if one exists.
replacePeriodId	`public abstract void replacePeriodId(String periodId, String newPeriodId) throws SFException`	Replaces the identifier for the period with the given id Note: If the new id is the same as the existing id, nothing is done
replacePeriodId	`public abstract void replacePeriodId(FiscalPeriod period, String newPeriodId) throws SFException`	Replaces the identifier for the given period Note: If the new id is the same as the existing id, nothing is done
removeOwnedPeriodBy	`public abstract void removeOwnedPeriodBy(String periodId, boolean absorbWithPreviousDatedPeriod) throws SFException`	Removes a period from the year. If the period to remove is dated, either the end date of the preceding dated period or the start date of the next dated period is adjusted to incorporate the vacated days, unless the period is the last dated period of the year and the request is not to incorporate the vacated days into the previous period. If the period is undated, adjustments, of any kind, will not be required.
isComplete	`public abstract boolean isComplete() throws SFException`	Determine whether the entire date range for the year is covered by periods, i.e. If the year's end date is the same as the end date of the last dated period within the year.
getPeriodBy	`public abstract FiscalPeriod getPeriodBy(DTime containedDate) throws SFException`	Returns the period the given date falls in or null if the date is not contained within any period in the year.
getPeriodBy	`public abstract FiscalPeriod getPeriodBy(String periodId) throws SFException`	Returns the period with matching identifier or null if no match found.
createPeriodIterator	`public abstract Iterator createPeriodIterator() throws SFException`	Creates an iterator which provides the ability to step through the collection of periods in chronological sequence
getNextPeriod	`public abstract FiscalPeriod getNextPeriod(Iterator position) throws SFException`	Gets the next period, in chronological sequence, from the current iterator position
getPreviousPeriod	`public abstract FiscalPeriod getPreviousPeriod(Iterator position) throws SFException`	Gets the previous period, in chronological sequence, from the current iterator position
getPeriodAt	`public abstract FiscalPeriod getPeriodAt(Iterator position) throws SFException`	Gets the period at the current iterator position
containsPeriod	`public abstract boolean containsPeriod(FiscalPeriod period) throws SFException`	Checks if the period is in this year

Figure 21-22
(Cont'd)

containsPeriod	`public abstract boolean containsPeriod(String periodId) throws SFException`	Checks if a period exists with the specified id in this year
getStartDate	`public abstract DTime getStartDate() throws SFException`	Gets the date the year starts with
getEndDate	`public abstract DTime getEndDate() throws SFException`	Gets the date the year ends with
getEndDateOfLastDatedPeriod	`public abstract DTime getEndDateOfLastDatedPeriod() throws SFException`	Gets the end date of the last dated period of the year. If this date is equal to the date the year ends with, the year is said to be 'complete' Note: NULL may be returned since ivEndDateOfLastDatedPeriod is an optional attribute
getYearNumber	`public abstract int getYearNumber() throws SFException`	Gets the year number, e.g. 1996, which identifies a year
setYearNumber	`public abstract void setYearNumber(int newYearNumber) throws SFException`	Set the year number, e.g. 1996, which identifies a year
getPeriodsHdl	`public abstract Handle getPeriodsHdl() throws SFException`	Get handle to Periods,used by framework Note: NULL may be returned since ivPeriodsHdl is an optional attribute
getStartDateForRestrictedUse	`public abstract Dtime getStartDateForRestrictedUse() throws SFException`	Returns the actual StartDate, used by framework for SetEqual()
getEndDateForRestrictedUse	`public abstract Dtime getEndDateForRestrictedUse() throws SFException`	Returns the actual EndDate, used by framework for SetEqual()
getEndDateOfLastDatedPeriodForRestrictedUse	`public abstract Dtime getEndDateOfLastDatedPeriodForRestrictedUse() throws SFException`	Returns the actual EndDateOfLastDatedPeriod, used by framework for SetEqual() Note: NULL may be returned since ivEndDateOfLastDatedPeriod is an optional attribute
getChronologicalPeriodOrderHdl	`public abstract Handle getChronologicalPeriodOrderHdl() throws SFException`	Get handle to ChronologicalPeriodOrder,used by framework Note: NULL may be returned since ivChronologicalPeriodOrderHdl is an optional attribute
getContainingCalendarHdl	`public abstract Handle getContainingCalendarHdl() throws SFException`	Returns the Handle to the FiscalCalendar of the containingCalendar of the FiscalYear

Figure 21-22
(Cont'd)

Interface com.ibm.sf.cf.FiscalPeriod

public interface FiscalPeriod extends DescribableDynamicEntity

Name	*Signature*	*Description*
getType	`public abstract int getType() throws SFException`	Returns the type of the fiscal period
setType	`public abstract void setType(int newType) throws SFException`	Sets the type for the fiscal period
isAfter	`public abstract boolean isAfter(FiscalPeriod comparand) throws SFException`	Determines whether this FiscalPeriod exists after the given period within the calendar. The FiscalPeriods need not necessarily belong to the same year within the calendar
isDated	`public abstract boolean isDated() throws SFException`	Returns true if a fiscal period is of the Dated variety.
getContainingYearNumber	`public abstract int getContainingYearNumber() throws SFException`	Returns the year number identifying they year which contains this FiscalPeriod
getContainingYearHdl	`public abstract Handle getContainingYearHdl() throws SFException`	Returns the Handle to the FiscalYear of the containingYear of the FiscalPeriod
getPeriodId	`public abstract String getPeriodId() throws SFException`	Gets used to uniqely identify a FiscalPeriod within a containing year

Figure 21-23
Interface `FiscalPeriod`

Initials

A common need across all business applications is to identify employees and to associate their identification with specific actions they do. Furthermore, usually each employee has authorization to perform certain actions only (e.g. sign a check of up to $10,000, or authorize a refund on a product).

SanFrancisco provides the `Initials` object to represent an employee (usually by her/his full name), and the `SignatoryAbility` object that can be attached to the initials object. The signatory ability object indicates the actions the employee is authorized to do. `SignatoryAbility` objects can be grouped into `SignatoryAbilityGroup` objects. Note that authorization here has nothing to do with authorization done as part of SanFrancisco (or the operating system level) security layer.

The interface for Initials object is pretty straightforward, and is shown in Figure 21-25; its implementation model is shown in Figure 21-24. Initials are stored in an InitialsController object for a company. Note that this object supports the abstraction of a dictionary by which you associate different keys with an initials object (for example, you might associate the key "CEO" with the Initials object corresponding to the company CEO). The controller is associated with the company using the attribute "cf.InitialsController". To create new initials objects you use the InitialsFactory class.

Signatory abilities are represented using the SignatoryAbility object whose interface is shown in Figure 21-26. The interface for signatory ability groups is shown in Figure 21-27. Note that you can dynamically add and remove SignatoryAbility objects from a SignatoryAbilityGroup.

To associate a signatory ability group with an initials object you use an object of type DInitialsExtension (see Figure 21-28), which is essentially a wrapper for the group. This is an abstract class so you actually need to provide your own implementation of such an extension. The way Initials objects handle these extensions is actually an instance of a more generalized mechanism, which is the ExtensibleItem. This is described in Chapter 23.

Natural Calendar

The NaturalCalendar object is used to maintain the list of working days in the year. These working days vary between different countries based on local customs and religion. This in turn has a significant impact on businesses. Certain dates cannot be considered "value dates" for transactions and, therefore, deadlines for submitting documents or shipping products must be offset to represent the last working day before the deadline.

The NaturalCalendar is created and modified during configuration of the system. It provides various methods for initializing and adding specific dates that are holidays. In addition, it provides methods for manipulating dates in relation to working dates. This includes working

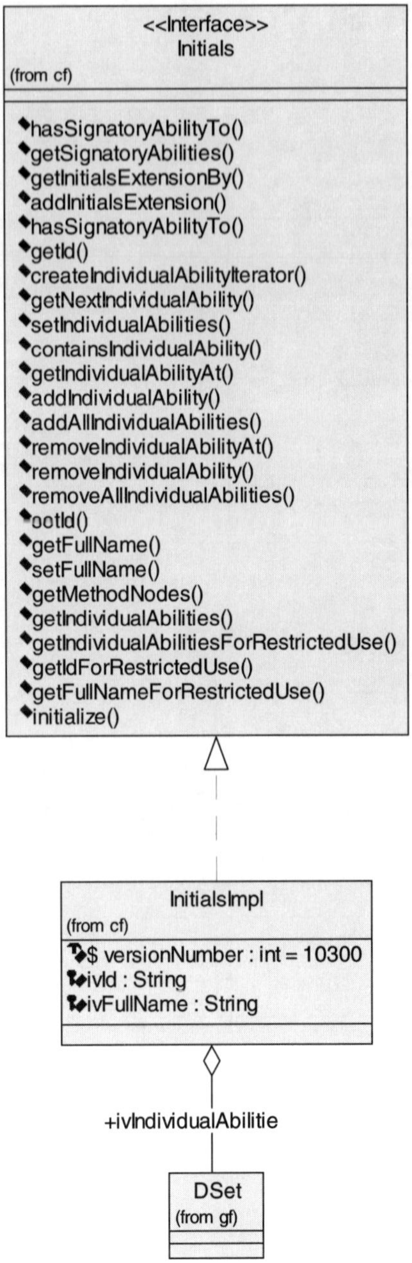

Figure 21-24 `Initials` implementation model.

Interface com.ibm.sf.cf.Initials

public interface **Initials** extends ExtensibleItem, Distinguishable

Name	*Signature*	*Description*
hasSignatoryAbilityTo	`public abstract boolean hasSignatoryAbilityTo(String abilityId) throws SFException`	Determine whether the e.g.signer.hasSignatoryAbilityTo("confirmPurchaseOrder")
getSignatoryAbilities	`public abstract DMap getSignatoryAbilities() throws SFException`	Get a collection of all SignatoryAbilities associated directly or through SignatoryAbilityGroups for this Initials object.
getInitialsExtensionBy	`Public abstract DInitialsExtension getInitialsExtensionBy(String key) throws SFException`	Returns an initials extension by key
addInitialsExtension	`public abstract void addInitialsExtension(DInitialsExtension initialsExtension) throws SFException`	Returns an initials extension by key
hasSignatoryAbilityTo	`public abstract boolean hasSignatoryAbilityTo(SignatoryAbility signatoryAbility) throws SFException`	Determine whether the initials object has the specified ability.
getId	`public abstract String getId() throws SFException`	Get the id of the Distinguishable object
createIndividualAbilityIterator	`Public abstract Iterator createIndividualAbilityIterator() throws SFException`	Create Iterator for collection of IndividualAbilities
getNextIndividualAbility	`Public abstract SignatoryAbility getNextIndividualAbility(Iterator position) throws SFException`	Gets the IndividualAbility at the Next Iterator Position
setIndividualAbilities	`Public abstract void setIndividualAbilities(DSet individualAbilities) throws SFException`	Sets the collection of IndividualAbility
containsIndividualAbility	`public abstract boolean containsIndividualAbility(SignatoryAbility individualAbility) throws SFException`	Checks if the IndividualAbility exists in the collection of IndividualAbilities
getIndividualAbilityAt	`public abstract SignatoryAbility getIndividualAbilityAt(Iterator position) throws SFException`	Gets the IndividualAbility at the current iterator position

Figure 21-25
Interface `Initials`

addIndividualAbility	`public abstract void addIndividualAbility(SignatoryAbility individualAbilityToAdd) throws SFException`	Adds a IndividualAbility to the collection of IndividualAbilities
addAllIndividualAbilities	`public abstract void addAllIndividualAbilities(DSet individualAbilitiesToAdd) throws SFException`	Adds all SignatoryAbilities from the collection of individualAbilitiesToAdd to the collection of IndividualAbilities maintained by this Initials
removeIndividualAbilityAt	`public abstract void removeIndividualAbilityAt(Iterator position) throws SFException`	Removes the IndividualAbility at the Current Iterator Position
removeIndividualAbility	`public abstract void removeIndividualAbility(SignatoryAbility individualAbility) throws SFException`	Removes the specified IndividualAbility
removeAllIndividualAbilities	`public abstract void removeAllIndividualAbilities() throws SFException`	Removes all IndividualAbility from the collection of IndividualAbilities
setId	`public abstract void setId(String newId) throws SFException`	Set unique identifier of the Initials
getFullName	`public abstract String getFullName() throws SFException`	Gets the full name of the person or group represented by this Initials
setFullName	`public abstract void setFullName(String newFullName) throws SFException`	Set the full name of the person or group represented by this Initials
getMethodNodes	`public abstract DMap getMethodNodes() throws SFException`	Used during object initialization to retrieve the set of MethodNodes for this Blockable. Must be overridden by subclasses to create the correct set for the supported methods of the subclass. This method is invoked by Extensible Item and is not for general client use.
initialize	`public abstract void initialize(InitialsController initialsController, DInitialsExtension initialExtension, String id, String fullName) throws SFException`	This method is invoked by the Factory after Construction of an instance of this class to ensure proper initialization

Figure 21-25
(Cont'd)

Interface com.ibm.sf.cf.SignatoryAbility

public interface SignatoryAbility extends DescribableDynamicEntity, Distinguishable

Name	*Signature*	*Description*
getId	`public abstract String getId() throws SFException`	Description: get the id of the Distinguishable object
setId	`public abstract void setId(String newId) throws SFException`	Set the unique id of the signatory ability
initialize	`public abstract void initialize(SignatoryAbilityController signatoryAbilityController, String id, DescriptiveInformation description) throws SFException`	This method is invoked by the Factory after Construction of an instance of this class to ensure proper initialization

Figure 21-26
Interface `Signatory Ability`

days and arithmetic, i.e. calculating a given date by going a certain amount of working days forward or backwords.

The `NaturalCalendar` object is attached to the company through the "`cf.NaturalCalendar`" property. You may have more such objects attached to different companies or any other entities (either using the `DynamicEntity` properties or as contained instance variables). Figure 21-29 shows the interface to this class.

The `NaturalCalendar` also supports policies for defining certain behaviors. You have the `DResultDateAdjustmentPolicy` used to make certain adjustments to dates to reflect the realities of your business environment (Figure 21-30). For example, if a delivery date is calculated based on certain scheduling rules and turns out to be a Friday evening, you would probably want to change it to the following Monday morning. Other policies are:

- `DNaturalCalendarWorkTimePolicy`
- `DWorkperiodManagerPolicy`

Interface com.ibm.sf.cf.SignatoryAbilityGroup

public interface SignatoryAbilityGroup extends DescribableDynamicEntity, Distinguishable

Name	*Signature*	*Description*
containsAbilityKey	`public abstract boolean containsAbilityKey(String key) throws SFException`	This method checks if the group contains a SignatoryAbility with the specified key.
getId	`public abstract String getId() throws SFException`	Get the Id of the Distinguishable object
createAbilityIterator	`public abstract Iterator createAbilityIterator() throws SFException`	Create Iterator for Collection of Abilities
getNextAbility	`public abstract SignatoryAbility getNextAbility(Iterator position) throws SFException`	Gets the Ability at the Next Iterator Position
setAbilities	`public abstract void setAbilities(DSet newAbilities) throws SFException`	Sets the Collection of Abilities
containsAbility	`public abstract boolean containsAbility(SignatoryAbility ability) throws SFException`	Checks if the Ability exists in the Collection of Abilities
getAbilityAt	`public abstract SignatoryAbility getAbilityAt(Iterator position) throws SFException`	Gets the Ability at the current iterator position
addAbility	`public abstract void addAbility(SignatoryAbility abilityToAdd) throws SFException`	Adds a Ability to the Collection of Abilities
addAllAbilities	`public abstract void addAllAbilities(DSet signatoryAbilitiesToAdd) throws SFException`	Adds all Abilities from the Collection of signatoryAbilitiesToAdd to the Collection of Abilities maintained by this SignatoryAbilityGroup
removeAbilityAt	`public abstract void removeAbilityAt(Iterator position) throws SFException`	Removes the Ability at the Current Iterator Position
removeAbility	`public abstract void removeAbility(SignatoryAbility ability) throws SFException`	Removes the specified Ability
removeAllAbilities	`public abstract void removeAllAbilities() throws SFException`	Removes all Ability from the Collection of Abilities
setId	`public abstract void setId(String newId) throws SFException`	Set unique id of this Signatory Ability Group
initialize	`public abstract void initialize(SignatoryAbilityGroupController signatoryAbilityGroupController, String id, DescriptiveInformation description) throws SFException`	This method is invoked by the Factory after Construction of an instance of this class to ensure proper initialization

Figure 21-27
Interface `SignatoryAbilityGroup`

Number Series

The NumberSeries object allows you to implement logic related to the generation of serial numbers. Such serial numbers might be used to denote specific instances of a product. Another example is the number of an order form or an invoice.

To create number series, you can use the create methods in the respective factory. This factory provides methods for both the creation of a "loosely coupled" (usually temporary) number series, and for a number series object tightly coupled to a controller.

The interface to the NumberSeries object is shown in Figure 21-31. The main method for this class is getNextValue(), which generates the next element in a series. If you want to create a serial number based on your own input, it is possible to do so using the createValidatedValue method. This method checks the input using the rules allowing allocation of values; the rules are passed as a parameter to the creation of the series. The possible rules are defined in the class NumberSeries UserAllocatedEnum, and Table 21-2 shows the values and their meaning.

Payment Method

Most businesses take payment in one of various forms including cash, credit card, money transfer, letter of credit, and so on. The PaymentMethod object is used to identify specific payment methods. The PaymentMethod is a DynamicEntity. This means it implements a PropertyContainer interface. Payment methods are held in the respective controller, which is attached to a company through the "cf.PaymentMethodController" property. The PaymentMethod interface is shown in Figure 21-32.

Interface com.ibm.sf.cf.DInitialsExtension

public interface DInitialsExtension extends DExtension

Name	*Signature*	*Description*
hasSignatoryAbilityTo	`public abstract boolean hasSignatoryAbilityTo(String signatoryAbilityId) throws SFException`	Determines whether the DInitialsExtension object has the specified ability. e.g. signer.hasSignatoryAbilityTo("confirmPurchaseOrder"). This method supports the implementation of the hasSignatoryAbilityTo method on the associated Initials object.
hasSignatoryAbilityTo	`public abstract boolean hasSignatoryAbilityTo(SignatoryAbility signatoryAbility) throws SFException`	Determines whether the DInitialsExtension object has the specified ability. This method supports the implementation of the hasSignatoryAbilityTo method on the associated Initials object.
getSignatoryAbilityGroup	`public abstract SignatoryAbilityGroup getSignatoryAbilityGroup() throws SFException`	Returns the SignatoryAbilityGroup, copied from the Handle
setSignatoryAbilityGroup	`public abstract void setSignatoryAbilityGroup(SignatoryAbilityGroup newSignatoryAbilityGroup) throws SFException`	Set the Handle of the SignatoryAbilityGroup
createAbilityIterator	`public abstract Iterator createAbilityIterator() throws SFException`	Create Iterator for Collection of Abilities
getNextAbility	`public abstract SignatoryAbility getNextAbility(Iterator position) throws SFException`	Gets the Ability at the Next Iterator Position
getSignatoryAbilityGroupHdl	`public abstract Handle getSignatoryAbilityGroupHdl() throws SFException`	Returns the Handle to the SignatoryAbilityGroup of the SignatoryAbilityGroup of the InitialsExtension
initialize	`public abstract void initialize(SignatoryAbilityGroup signatoryAbilityGroup) throws SFException`	This method is invoked by the Factory after Construction of an instance of this class to ensure proper initialization

Figure 21-28
Interface `DInitialsExtension`

Interface com.ibm.sf.cf.NaturalCalendar

public interface **NaturalCalendar** extends DescribableDynamicEntity

Name	*Signature*	*Description*
appendYear	`public abstract void appendYear() throws SFException`	Appends a new year to this calendar, immediately after the current year.
prependYear	`public abstract void prependYear() throws SFException`	Prepends a year to this calendar, and places it before the current year.
deleteStartingYear	`public abstract void deleteStartingYear() throws SFException`	Removes the earliest year in the calendar.
isWorkingDay	`public abstract boolean isWorkingDay(DTime date) throws SFException`	Returns true in case the given date is a working day.
differenceInWorkingDays	`public abstract int differenceInWorkingDays(DTime startDate, DTime endDate) throws SFException`	Calculates the number of working days within the date range defined by startDate and endDate (neither including startDate nor endDate)
offsetDateByWorkingDays	`public abstract DTime offsetDateByWorkingDays(DTime startDate, int numberOfWorkingDays) throws SFException`	Returns the date that lies numberOfWorkingDays after the given startDate, i.e. offsets the given startDate by numberOfWorkingDays. In case the offset date exceeds the date range covered by this calendar an exception is raised.
getNextWorkingDay	`public abstract DTime getNextWorkingDay(DTime currentDate) throws SFException`	Returns the next date that is a working day. In case the resulting date exceeds the date range covered by this calendar, an exception is raised.
getPreviousWorkingDay	`public abstract DTime getPreviousWorkingDay(DTime currentDate) throws SFException`	Returns the previous date that is a working day. In case the resulting date exceeds the date range covered by this calendar, an exception is raised.
containsDate	`public abstract boolean containsDate(DTime date) throws SFException`	Determine if a date is contained in the scope of the calendar.
setDateWorkingDayIndicator	`public abstract void setDateWorkingDayIndicator(DTime date, boolean newWorkingDayIndicator, DTimePeriod workperiod, DescriptiveInformation descriptiveInformation) throws SFException`	Defines the working day status of the designated calendar day: If the parameter newWorkingDayIndicator == true, the given date is defined to be a working day. If the parameter newWorkingDayIndicator == false, the given date is defined to be a non-working day. Working day numbers of subsequent dates will be adjusted.
deleteEndingYear	`public abstract void deleteEndingYear() throws SFException`	Removes the latest year in the calendar.

Figure 21-29
Interface `NaturalCalendar`

setDefaultDayWorkingDayIndicator	`public abstract void setDefaultDayWorkingDayIndicator(int dayOfWeek, boolean newWorkingDayIndicator, DTimePeriod workperiod, DescriptiveInformation escriptiveInformation) throws SFException`	Defines the working day status of the designated default day: If the parameter newWorkingDayIndicator == true, the given default day is defined to be a working day. If the parameter newWorkingDayIndicator == false, the given default day is defined to be a non-working day. Working day numbers of the entire natural calendar will be adjusted.
getTimestamp	`public abstract DTime getTimestamp(DTime baseTime, DAmountOfTime duration) throws SFException`	Returns the timestamp using working hours only.
getFutureTimestamp	`public abstract DTime getFutureTimestamp(DTime baseTime, DAmountOfTime duration) throws SFException`	Returns the future timestamp adjusted to working hours.
getPreviousTimestamp	`public abstract DTime getPreviousTimestamp(DTime baseTime, DAmountOfTime duration) throws SFException`	Returns the previous timestamp adjusted to working hours.
getWorkingTime	`public abstract DAmountOfTime getWorkingTime(DTime startTime, DTime endTime) throws SFException`	Returns the time worked given a start date and an end date.
addDefaultDayWorkperiod	`public abstract void addDefaultDayWorkperiod(int dayOfWeek, DTimePeriod workperiod) throws SFException`	Add a workperiod to the collection of workperiods for a default day of the week that is a workday.
removeDefaultDayWorkperiod	`public abstract void removeDefaultDayWorkperiod(int dayOfWeek, DTimePeriod workperiod) throws SFException`	Remove a workperiod from the collection of workperiods for a default day of the week that is a workday.
getDefaultDayWorkperiod	`public abstract DList getDefaultDayWorkperiod(int dayOfWeek) throws SFException`	Gets the workperiod from the collection of workperiods for a default day of the week that is a workday.
addDateWorkperiod	`public abstract void addDateWorkperiod(DTime date, DTimePeriod workperiod) throws SFException`	Add a workperiod to the collection of workperiods for the date that is a workday.
removeDateWorkperiod	`public abstract void removeDateWorkperiod(DTime date, DTimePeriod workperiod) throws SFException`	Remove a workperiod from the collection of workperiods for a date that is a workday.
getDateWorkperiod	`public abstract DList getDateWorkperiod(DTime date) throws SFException`	Gets the workperiod from the collection of workperiods for a date that is a workday.
copyDefaultDayPropertyMap	`public abstract Map copyDefaultDayPropertyMap(int dayOfWeek) throws SFException`	Returns a new transient entity Map collection holding all properties contained within the default day.
copyDatePropertyMap	`public abstract Map copyDatePropertyMap(DTime date) throws SFException`	Returns a new transient entity Map collection holding all properties contained within the date.

Figure 21-29
(Cont'd)

addContainedDefaultDayPropertyBy	`public abstract void addContainedDefaultDayPropertyBy(int dayOfWeek, Object property, String propertyKey) throws SFException`	Adds an unowned Entity, owned Dependent, or owned String property to the default day of the week.
addContainedDatePropertyBy	`public abstract void addContainedDatePropertyBy(DTime date, Object property, String propertyKey) throws SFException`	Adds an unowned Entity, owned Dependent, or owned String property to a given date.
addOwnedDefaultDayPropertyBy	`public abstract void addOwnedDefaultDayPropertyBy(int dayOfWeek, Object property, String propertyKey) throws SFException`	Adds an owned Entity property to the default day of the week.
addOwnedDatePropertyBy	`public abstract void addOwnedDatePropertyBy(DTime date, Object property, String propertyKey) throws SFException`	Adds an owned Entity property to a given date.
removeContainedDefaultDayPropertyBy	`public abstract void removeContainedDefaultDayPropertyBy(int dayOfWeek, String propertyKey) throws SFException`	Removes either the non-owned Entity, owned Dependent or owned String property associated with the given propertyKey from the default day.
removeContainedDatePropertyBy	`public abstract void removeContainedDatePropertyBy(DTime date, String propertyKey) throws SFException`	Removes either the non-owned Entity, owned Dependent or owned String property associated with the given propertyKey from the specified date.
orphanOwnedDefaultDayPropertyBy	`public abstract void orphanOwnedDefaultDayPropertyBy(int dayOfWeek, String propertyKey) throws SFException`	Removes the owned Entity associated with the given propertyKey from the default day—but does not delete it..
orphanOwnedDatePropertyBy	`public abstract void orphanOwnedDatePropertyBy(DTime date, String propertyKey) throws SFException`	Removes the owned Entity associated with the given propertyKey from the specified date—but does not delete it.
removeOwnedDefaultDayPropertyBy	`public abstract void removeOwnedDefaultDayPropertyBy(int dayOfWeek, String propertyKey) throws SFException`	Removes the owned Entity associated with the given propertyKey from the default day and also deletes it..
removeOwnedDatePropertyBy	`public abstract void removeOwnedDatePropertyBy(DTime date, String propertyKey) throws SFException`	Removes the owned Entity associated with the given propertyKey from the specified date and also deletes it.
containsDefaultDayPropertyKey	`public abstract boolean containsDefaultDayPropertyKey(int dayOfWeek, String propertyKey) throws SFException`	Checks if the default day contains a property identified by the key parameter.
containsDatePropertyKey	`public abstract boolean containsDatePropertyKey(DTime date, String propertyKey) throws SFException`	Checks if the date contains a property identified by the key parameter.
getDefaultDayPropertyBy	`public abstract Object getDefaultDayPropertyBy(int dayOfWeek, String propertyKey) throws SFException`	Returns the property by key of the default day.
getDatePropertyBy	`public abstract Object getDatePropertyBy(DTime date, String propertyKey) throws SFException`	Returns the property by key of the desired date. If the date doesn't contain such a property, the default day associated with the date will be searched for the property.

Figure 21-29
(Cont'd)

IsDefaultDayWorkingDay	`public abstract boolean isDefaultDayWorkingDay(int dayOfWeek) throws SFException`	Returns true in case the given day of the week is a working day.
getDayOfWeek	`public abstract int getDayOfWeek(DTime date) throws SFException`	Returns the day of the week for the date (date portion of DTime) passed as input in relation to the starting day of the week specified on Natural Calendar creation. The days of the week start at 1 and go through 7.
isWorkTime	`public abstract boolean isWorkTime(DTime time) throws SFException`	Returns true in case the given time is on a working day, and within the working time of that day.
GetNextWorkTime	`public abstract DTime getNextWorkTime(DTime startTime) throws SFException`	Returns the next working time found in the Natural Calendar based on the precision of the provided start time. In case the date portion of resulting time exceeds the date range covered by this calendar, an exception is raised.
getPreviousWorkTime	`public abstract DTime getPreviousWorkTime(DTime startTime) throws SFException`	Returns the previous working time found in the Natural Calendar based on the precision of the provided start time. In case the date portion of resulting time exceeds the date range covered by this calendar, an exception is raised.
adjustDate	`public abstract DTime adjustDate(DTime preliminaryDate, DResultDateAdjustmentPolicy resultDateAdjustmentPolicy) throws SFException`	Adjust a result date based on an input preliminary date. This operation uses a DResultDateAdjustmentPolicy to determine the actual adjusted date. **Note:** This operation is just a wire-through to the DResultDateAdjustmentPolicy.
containsCalendarDate	`public abstract boolean containsCalendarDate(DCalendarDate calendardate) throws SFException`	Checks if the CalendarDate exists in the Collection of CalendarDates
queryCalendarDates	`public abstract Map queryCalendarDates(String selectStatement, String bindCollectionName, SelectCompare selectCompareObject, String bindNameOfSelectCompareObject, SortCompare orderByCompareObject, String bindNameOfOrderByObject, boolean accessResults) throws SFException`	Query the CalendarDate from the Collection
queryCalendarDates	`public abstract Map queryCalendarDates(String selectStatement, String bindCollectionName, SelectCompare selectCompareObject, String bindNameOfSelectCompareObject, SortCompare orderByCompareObject, String bindNameOfOrderByObject, boolean String hostVariableNames[],Object hostVariableValues[]) throws SFException`	Query the CalendarDate from the Collection
removeCalendarDate	`public abstract void removeCalendarDate(DCalendarDate calendardate) throws SFException`	Removes the specified CalendarDate

Figure 21-29
(Cont'd)

removeAllCalendarDates	public abstract void removeAllCalendarDates() throws SFException	Removes all CalendarDate from the Collection of CalendarDates
addCalendarDateBy	public abstract void addCalendarDateBy(DCalendarDate calendarDate, DTime key) throws SFException	Adds a CalendarDate to the Collection of CalendarDates by the Specified Key
removeCalendarDateBy	public abstract void removeCalendarDateBy(DTime key) throws SFException	Removes the CalendarDate by the specified key
containsCalendarDateKey	public abstract boolean containsCalendarDateKey(DTime key) throws SFException	Checks if the CalendarDate exists by the specified Key
getCalendarDateKey	public abstract DTime getCalendarDateKey(DCalendarDate calendarDate) throws SFException	Gets the CalendarDate at the Current Iterator Position
containsDefaultDay	public abstract boolean containsDefaultDay(Day defaultday) throws SFException	Checks if the DefaultDay exists in the Collection of DefaultDays
removeOwnedDefaultDay	public abstract void removeOwnedDefaultDay(Day defaultday) throws SFException	Removes and deletes the specified DefaultDay
removeAllOwnedDefaultDays	public abstract void removeAllOwnedDefaultDays() throws SFException	Removes and deletes all elements from the Collection of DefaultDays
containsDefaultDayKey	public abstract boolean containsDefaultDayKey(int key) throws SFException	Checks if the DefaultDay exists by the specified Key
getDefaultDayKey	public abstract DaysOfTheWeekEnum getDefaultDayKey(Day defaultDay) throws SFException	Gets the DefaultDay at the Current Iterator Position
removeOwnedDefaultDayBy	public abstract void removeOwnedDefaultDayBy(int key) throws SFException	Removes and deletes the DefaultDay by the specified key
orphanOwnedDefaultDayBy	public abstract void orphanOwnedDefaultDayBy(int key) throws SFException	Orphans the DefaultDay by the specified key
addOwnedDefaultDayBy	public abstract void addOwnedDefaultDayBy(Day defaultDay, int key) throws SFException	Adds a DefaultDay to the Collection of DefaultDays by the Specified Key
getResultDateAdjustmentPolicy	public abstract DResultDateAdjustmentPolicy getResultDateAdjustmentPolicy() throws SFException	Gets ResultDateAdjustmentPolicy
getWorkTimePolicy	public abstract DNaturalCalendarWorkTimePolicyDefault getWorkTimePolicy() throws SFException Gets	Gets Application wide default policy that controls the work time operations of the Natural Calendar (isWorkingTime, getNextWorkingTime, getPreviousWorkingTime).
getStartYear	public abstract int getStartYear() throws SFException	Gets the year the calendar starts with (e.g. 1997)
getEndYear	public abstract int getEndYear() throws SFException	Gets the year the calendar ends with (e.g. 1997).

Figure 21-29
(Cont'd)

getUseWorkperiodFlag	`public abstract boolean getUseWorkperiodFlag() throws SFException`	Gets Tells whether or not to use workperiods per workday.
getDaysOfTheWeekAt	`public abstract int getDaysOfTheWeekAt(int index) throws SFException`	Gets the DaysOfTheWeek at the index position
getDaysOfTheWeekArray	`public abstract int[] getDaysOfTheWeekArray() throws SFException`	Gets a copy of the DaysOfTheWeek array
initialize	`public abstract void initialize(int startYear, int endYear, boolean useWorkperiodFlag, boolean defaultSundayWorkingDayIndicator, boolean defaultMondayWorkingDayIndicator, boolean defaultTuesdayWorkingDayIndicator, boolean defaultWednesdayWorkingDayIndicator, boolean defaultThursdayWorkingDayIndicator, boolean defaultFridayWorkingDayIndicator, boolean defaultSaturdayWorkingDayIndicator, DTimePeriod sundayWorkperiod, DTimePeriod mondayWorkperiod, DTimePeriod tuesdayWorkperiod, DTimePeriod wednesdayWorkperiod, DTimePeriod thursdayWorkperiod, DTimePeriod fridayWorkperiod, DTimePeriod saturdayWorkperiod, DescriptiveInformation descriptiveInformation, int beginningDayOfWeek, DResultDateAdjustmentPolicy resultDateAdjustmentPolicy) throws SFException`	This method is invoked by the Factory after Construction of an instance of this class to ensure proper initialization

Figure 21-29
(Cont'd)

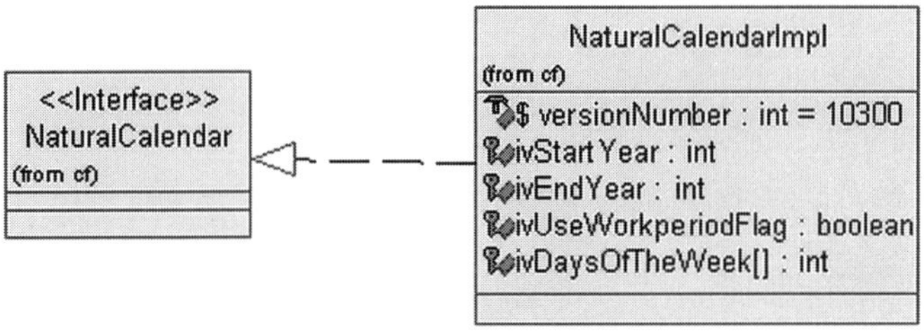

Figure 21-30
`NaturalCalendar` implementation model.

Interface com.ibm.sf.cf.NumberSeries

public interface **NumberSeries** extends DescribableDynamicEntity, Distinguishable

Name	*Signature*	*Description*
getNextValue	`public abstract DNumberSeriesValue getNextValue(String subSeriesKey) throws SFException`	Get the next value in the specified sub-series. If the specified sub-series does not exist yet, it will be created and the returned value will be the minimumValue for this numberSeries. If the mask for this NumberSeries contains a "%k", the given subSeriesKey will be inserted into the formatted value in the indicated position.
reset	`public abstract void reset(String subSeriesKey) throws SFException`	Reset the specified sub-series so that its next value equals minVal (is current value will be undefined). If a sub-series with the specified key does not exist, it will be created and placed in a reset state.
resetAll	`public abstract void resetAll() throws SFException`	Reset all existing sub-series so that their next values equal minVal (their current values will be undefined).
validateValue	`public abstract DResultsCollection validateValue(String value) throws SFException`	Determine if the given formatted value is a valida user allocated value for this NumberSeries. Validation Criteria: getAllowedUserAllocatedValues() != NO_VALUES_ALLOWED value must be in a format that could have been generated from the mask associated with this NumberSeries. Additionally, if getAllowedUserAllocatedValues() == ALLOWED_INSIDE_SERIES the numerical value part of the value string must be a number that is contained in the range defined for this number series if getAllowedUserAllocatedValues() == ALLOWED_OUTSIDE_SERIES the numerical value part of the value string must be a number that is not contained in the range defined for this number series (it must be either less than minimumValue or greater than maximumValue)
getNextValue	`public abstract DNumberSeriesValue getNextValue(String subSeriesKey, String formattedKeyString) throws SFException`	Get the next value in the specified sub-series. If the specified sub-series does not exist yet, it will be created and the returned value will be the minimumValue for this numberSeries. If the mask for this NumberSeries contains a "%k", the given formattedKeyString will be inserted into the formatted value in the indicated position.
getHighestUsedValue	`public abstract DNumberSeriesValue getHighestUsedValue(String subSeriesKey) throws SFException`	Get the highest used value in the specified sub-series. If the specified sub-series does not exist yet or if it has just been reset, null will be returned. If the mask for this NumberSeries contains a "%k", the given subSeriesKey will be inserted into the formatted value in the indicated position.

Figure 21-31
Interface `NumberSeries`

getHighestUsedValue	`public abstract DNumberSeriesValue getHighestUsedValue(String subSeriesKey, String formattedKeyString) throws SFException`	Get the highest used value in the specified sub-series. If the specified sub-series does not exist yet or if it has just been reset, null will be returned. If the mask for this NumberSeries contains a "%k", the given formattedKeyString will be inserted into the formatted value in the indicated position
getHighestUsedNumericValue	`public abstract long getHighestUsedNumericValue(String subSeriesKey) throws SFException`	Get the highest used numeric value of the given sub-series. If the specified sub-series does not exist yet or if it has just been reset, -1 will be returned.
setHighestUsedValue	`public abstract void setHighestUsedValue(String subSeriesKey, long newHighestUsedValue) throws SFException`	Set the specified sub-series so that its highest used value equals newHighestUsedValue. If a sub-series with the specified key does not exist, it will be created and its highest used value set to the given highest used value.
setAllHighestUsedValues	`public abstract void setAllHighestUsedValues(long newHighestUsedValue) throws SFException`	Set all existing sub-series so that their highest used values equal newHighestUsedValue.
validateNumericValue	`public abstract DResultsCollection validateNumericValue(long value) throws SFException`	Determine whether the given numeric value is valid for this NumberSeries. Validation Criteria: getAllowedUserAllocatedValues() != NO_VALUES_ALLOWED if getAllowedUserAllocatedValues() = ALLOWED_INSIDE_SERIES value must be a number that is contained in the range defined for this number series. if getAllowedUserAllocatedValues = ALLOWED_OUTSIDE_SERIES value must be a number that is either less than minimumValue or greater than maximumValue.
validateValue	`public abstract DResultsCollection validateValue(String value, String formattedKeyStringInValue) throws SFException`	Determine if the given formatted value with the given formatted key String is a valid value for this NumberSeries. Validation Criteria: getAllowedUserAllocatedValues() != NO_VALUES_ALLOWED value must be in a format that could have been generated from the mask associated with this NumberSeries. Additionally, if getAllowedUserAllocatedValues() == ALLOWED_INSIDE_SERIES the numerical value part of the value string must be a number that is contained in the range defined for this number series. if getAllowedUserAllocatedValues = ALLOWED_OUTSIDE_SERIES the numerical value part of the value string must be a number that is either less than minimumValue or greater than maximumValue.
createValidatedValue	`public abstract DNumberSeriesValue createValidatedValue(long userAllocatedNumericValue, String subSeriesKey) throws SFException`	If the given user allocated value is valid (see validateNumericValue method) a properly formated DNumberSeriesValue for the given value will be returned. if getAllowedUserAllocatedValues() is ALLOWED_INSIDE_SERIES and the given value is higher than the highest used value for the given sub-series, the highest used value for the given sub-series will be set to the given user-allocated value.

Figure 21-31
(Cont'd)

deleteSubSeries	`public abstract void deleteSubSeries(String subSeriesKey) throws SFException`	Delete the given sub-series from the NumberSeries.
createValidatedValue	`public abstract DNumberSeriesValue createValidatedValue(String userAllocatedValue, String subSeriesKey) throws SFException`	If the given user allocated value is valid (see validateValue method) a DNumberSeriesValue for the given value will be returned. if getAllowedUserAllocatedValues() is ALLOWED_INSIDE_SERIES and the given value is higher than the highest used value for the given sub-series, the highest used value for the given sub-series will be set to the given user-allocated value.
createValidatedValue	`public abstract DNumberSeriesValue createValidatedValue(long userAllocatedNumericValue, String subSeriesKey, String formattedKeyStringInValue) throws SFException`	If the given user allocated value is valid (see validateNumericValue method) a properly formated DNumberSeriesValue for the given value will be returned. if getAllowedUserAllocatedValues() is ALLOWED_INSIDE_SERIES and the given value is higher than the highest used value for the given sub-series, the highest used value for the given sub-series will be set to the given user-allocated value. If the mask for this NumberSeries contains a "%k", the given formattedKeyStringInValue will be inserted into the formatted value in the indicated position.
createValidatedValue	`public abstract DNumberSeriesValue createValidatedValue(String userAllocatedValue, String subSeriesKey, String formattedKeyStringInValue) throws SFException`	If the given user allocated value is valid (see validateValue method) a DNumberSeriesValue for the given value will be returned. if getAllowedUserAllocatedValues() is ALLOWED_INSIDE_SERIES and the given value is higher than the highest used value for the given sub-series, the highest used value for the given sub-series will be set to the given user-allocated value.
setMask	`public abstract void setMask(String newMask) throws SFException`	Change the format mask for this NumberSeries. significant digits in the generated value is less than the number of "%v"s in the mask, the value will be placed right-justified into the "%v" positions with the unused "%v" to the left of the value replaced with "0"s. It is mandatory to include at least one "%v" in the given mask. Optionally, one (and only one) "%k" can be placed in the mask to indicate that the subSeriesKey (or supplied string) should be inserted in place of the %k in the generated string. If formatMask is null a default mask of "%v"s matching the number of digits in maximumValue will be used (e.g. if formatMask is null, minimumValue = 1, maximumValue = 999, values will be in the format "001","002", etc.) Examples: formatMask = "%v" value = 3 -> "3" formatMask = "%v%v" value = 3 -> "03" if expandNumberField == true: formatMask = "%v" value = 123 -> "123" formatMask = "x%vy%vz" value = 123 -> "x12y3z" if specified key string == "May" formatMask = "%k%v" value = 3 -> "May3" formatMask = "pre%kxyz%vabc%vsuf" value = 1 -> "preMayxyz0abc1suf"

Figure 21-31
(Cont'd)

setMinimumValue	`public abstract void setMinimumValue(long newMinimumValue) throws SFException`	Change the minimum value for this NumberSeries.
setMaximumValue	`public abstract void setMaximumValue(long newMaximumValue) throws SFException`	Change the maximum value for this NumberSeries.
getHighestUsedNumericValue	`public abstract long getHighestUsedNumericValue() throws SFException`	Get the highest used numeric value of all sub-series within the NumberSeries.
setIncrementValue	`public abstract void setIncrementValue(long newIncrementValue) throws SFException`	Change the increment value for this NumberSeries.
getDefinedSubSeries	`public abstract DMap getDefinedSubSeries() throws SFException`	Returns a DMap of the existing sub-series for this NumberSeries. key = sub-series keys value = currentValue for sub-series (if a sub-series has just been reset its current value will be -1)
getAllowedUserAllocatedValues	`public abstract int getAllowedUserAllocatedValues() throws SFException`	Gets this enum determines the type of user allocated values that will be accepted.
setAllowedUserAllocatedValues	`public abstract void setAllowedUserAllocatedValues(int newAllowedUserAllocatedValues) throws SFException`	Set this enum determines the type of user allocated values that will be accepted.
getMask	`public abstract String getMask() throws SFException`	Gets formatting mask for produced values.
getMinimumValue	`public abstract long getMinimumValue() throws SFException`	Gets minimum value of all subSeries
getMaximumValue	`public abstract long getMaximumValue() throws SFException`	Gets maximum value of all subSeries
getIncrementValue	`public abstract long getIncrementValue() throws SFException`	Gets amount to increment current value by to produce next value for all subSeries.
isAllowedToWrap	`public abstract boolean isAllowedToWrap() throws SFException`	Gets destermines if subSeries are allowed to wrap.
setAllowedToWrap	`public abstract void setAllowedToWrap(boolean newAllowedToWrap) throws SFException`	Set destermines if subSeries are allowed to wrap.
isAllowedToExpandNumberField	`public abstract boolean isAllowedToExpandNumberField() throws SFException`	Gets determine if the formatted values produced are allowed to expand to hold larger numbers.
setExpandNumberFieldAllowed	`public abstract void setExpandNumberFieldAllowed(boolean newExpandNumberFieldAllowed) throws SFException`	Set determine if the formatted values produced are allowed to expand to hold larger numbers.
getId	`public abstract String getId() throws SFException`	Gets Id

Figure 21-31
(Cont'd)

setId	public abstract void setId(String newId) throws SFException	Sets Id
initialize	public abstract void initialize(String formatMask, long minimumValue, long maximumValuelong incrementAmount, boolean allowedToWrap, boolean expandNumberFieldAllowed, int allowedUserAllocatedValues, DescriptiveInformation description) throws SFException	This method is invoked by the Factory after Construction of an instance of this class to ensure proper initialization
initialize	public abstract void initialize(String formatMask, long minimumValue, long maximumValue, boolean allowedToWrap, boolean expandNumberFieldAllowed, int allowedUserAllocatedValues, DescriptiveInformation description) throws SFException	This method is invoked by the Factory after Construction of an instance of this class to ensure proper initialization
initialize	public abstract void initialize(NumberSeriesController owningControllerString formatMask, long minimumValue, long maximumValue, boolean allowedToWrap, boolean expandNumberFieldAllowed, int allowedUserAllocatedValues, DescriptiveInformation description, String id) throws SFException	This method is invoked by the Factory after Construction of an instance of this class to ensure proper initialization
initialize	public abstract void initialize(NumberSeriesController owningControllerString long minimumValue, long maximumValue, long incrementAmount, boolean allowedToWrap, boolean expandNumberFieldAllowed, int allowedUserAllocatedValues, DescriptiveInformation description, String id) throws SFException	This method is invoked by the Factory after Construction of an instance of this class to ensure proper initialization

Figure 21-31
(Cont'd)

Payment Terms

When doing business it is common to provide payment terms other than immediate payment. These terms might be monthly installments, or just delayed payments. SanFrancisco supports payment plans using the `PaymentTerms` class. This class is described in Figure 21-33. The actual

TABLE 21-2

User allocation rules for `NumberSeries`

Value	Meaning
ALLOWED_INSIDE_SERIES	Only user allocated values within the range of the NumberSeries allowed (in other words, values lying between minimumValue and maximum value)
ALLOWED_OUTSIDE_SERIES	Only user allocated values outside of the range of the NumberSeries allowed (either less than minimumValue or greater than maximum value)
ALL_VALUES_ALLOWED	All values allowed, without restrictions
NO_VALUES_ALLOWED	No user allocated values are allowed.

Interface com.ibm.sf.cf.PaymentMethod

public interface PaymentMethod extends DescribableDynamicEntity, Distinguishable

Name	*Signature*	*Description*
getId	`public abstract String getId() throws SFException`	Description: get the id of the Distinguishable object
isNegativePaymentsAllowed	`public abstract boolean isNegativePaymentsAllowed() throws SFException`	Gets NegativePaymentsAllowed
setNegativePaymentsAllowed	`public abstract void setNegativePaymentsAllowed(boolean newNegativePaymentsAllowed) throws SFException`	Sets NegativePaymentsAllowed
initialize	`public abstract void initialize(PaymentMethodController paymentMethodController, String id, boolean negativePaymentsAllowed, DescriptiveInformation description) throws SFException`	This method is invoked by the Factory after Construction of an instance of this class to ensure proper initialization

Figure 21-32
Interface `Payment Method`

Interface com.ibm.sf.cf.PaymentTerms

public interface PaymentTerms extends DescribableDynamicEntity, Distinguishable

Name	Signature	Description
generateSnapShot	`public abstract DPaymentTerms generateSnapShot() throws SFException`	Generates a copy of the DPaymentTerms and all of its contained classes to be used as a snap shot of this PaymentTerms. Post-conditions: object not modified
validatePaymentTerms	`public abstract DResultsCollection validatePaymentTerms(PaymentMethod paymentMethod, DTransactionValue transactionValue, DTime documentDate) throws SFException`	A PaymentTerms is validated for use with a specific item (based on the input). The due dates and amounts due are compared to the date and total value of the item, and negative payments are checked against the payment method to be used.
calculateInstallmentValues	`public abstract DList calculateInstallmentValues(DTransactionValue transactionValue, DTime baseDate, NaturalCalendar naturalCalendar, DResultDateAdjustmentPolicy resultDateAdjustmentPolicy) throws SFException`	Get collection of DPaymentTermsDetails with corresponding due dates and amounts due for each installment of a payment. Results will be be returned in a collection of DInstallmentValueCalculationResult objects representing the information for each detail of the PaymentTerms.
addPaymentTermsDetail	`public abstract void addPaymentTermsDetail(DPaymentTermsDetail paymentTermsDetail) throws SFException`	A PaymentTermsDetail is added to the collection of PaymentTermsDetails.
setRemainingAmount	`public abstract void setRemainingAmount(DPaymentTermsDetail paymentTermsDetail) throws SFException`	A PaymentTermsDetail that represents the remaining amount is added to this PaymentTerms.
getBusinessPartnerBalanceValue	`public abstract BusinessPartnerBalanceValue getBusinessPartnerBalanceValue() throws SFException`	Returns the BusinessPartnerBalanceValue, copied from the Handle
getRemainingAmount	`public abstract DPaymentTermsDetail getRemainingAmount() throws SFException`	Gets RemainingAmount
createPaymentTermsDetailIterator	`public abstract Iterator createPaymentTermsDetailIterator() throws SFException`	Create Iterator for Collection of PaymentTermsDetails
getNextPaymentTermsDetail	`public abstract DPaymentTermsDetail getNextPaymentTermsDetail(Iterator position) throws SFException`	Gets the PaymentTermsDetail at the Next Iterator Position
getPreviousPaymentTermsDetail	`public abstract DPaymentTermsDetail getPreviousPaymentTermsDetail(Iterator position) throws SFException`	Gets the PaymentTermsDetail at the Previous Iterator Position
containsPaymentTermsDetail	`public abstract boolean containsPaymentTermsDetail(DPaymentTermsDetail paymenttermsdetail) throws SFException`	Checks if the PaymentTermsDetail exists in the Collection of PaymentTermsDetails

Figure 21-33
Interface `PaymentTerms`

getPaymentTermsDetailAt	`public abstract DPaymentTermsDetail getPaymentTermsDetailAt(Iterator position) throws SFException`	Gets the PaymentTermsDetail at the current iterator position
addAllPaymentTermsDetails	`public abstract void addAllPaymentTermsDetails(DList newDPaymentTermsDetails) throws SFException`	Adds all PaymentTermsDetails to the Collection of PaymentTermsDetails
removePaymentTermsDetailAt	`public abstract void removePaymentTermsDetailAt(Iterator position) throws SFException`	Removes the PaymentTermsDetail at the Current Iterator Position
removePaymentTermsDetail	`public abstract void removePaymentTermsDetail(DPaymentTermsDetail paymenttermsdetail) throws SFException`	Removes the specified PaymentTermsDetail
removeAllPaymentTermsDetails	`public abstract void removeAllPaymentTermsDetails() throws SFException`	Removes all PaymentTermsDetail from the Collection of PaymentTermsDetails
insertPaymentTermsDetailAt	`public abstract void insertPaymentTermsDetailAt(DPaymentTermsDetail paymentTermsDetailToInsert, Iterator position) throws SFException`	Inserts the PaymentTermsDetail at the Current Iterator Position
getBusinessPartnerBalanceValueHdl	`public abstract Handle getBusinessPartnerBalanceValueHdl() throws SFException`	Returns the Handle to the BusinessPartnerBalanceValue of the DPaymentTerms
getId	`public abstract String getId() throws SFException`	Description: get the id of the Distinguishable object
initialize	`public abstract void initialize(PaymentTermsController paymentTermsController, String id, DPaymentTermsDetail remainingAmount, BusinessPartnerBalanceValue businessPartnerBalanceValue, DescriptiveInformation descriptiveInformation) throws SFException`	This method is invoked by the Factory after Construction of an instance of this class to ensure proper initialization

Figure 21-33
(Cont'd)

payments are represented by `DPaymentTermsDetail`, an interface shown in Figure 21-34; Figure 21-35 shows the interface to a base class from which it is derived. When creating a new `PaymentTerms` object you must specify the last (possibly only) payment, after which you can add on other payments. Once you have the payment plan configured, you can use it to find out specific details about the plan.

Note that SanFrancisco supports the common practice of giving discounts for payments done immediately or within a few days through the `DSettlementDiscount` class. Such objects are defined and manipulated just like DPaymentTermDetails (actually, both are derived from a common base), and they support the flexibility given to the payer.

Periodized Calendar

The PeriodizedCalendar object provides similar functionality to that of the FiscalCalendar. Figure 21-36 shows the interface to this class. Figures 21-37 and 21-38 show the interfaces to PeriodizedYear and CalendarPeriod providing similar capabilities to those provided by FiscalYear and FiscalPeriod for the FiscalCalendar.

PeriodizedCalendar objects can be used to define and use calendars that are not related to finances. For example, a university might need to define the academic year including semester breaks and the specific start and end dates.

Process Token

In order to keep track of where you are within a certain business process SanFrancisco introduces the notion of a process token. Such a token is useful when you want to have a behavior that depends on which step of a process you are in.

Process tokens are implemented as dynamic identifiers. There is a ProcessTokenController on the Enterprise and it contains ProcessTokenValues (see Figure 21-39). This controller manages a list of valid process tokens. The ProcessTokenValues are the dynamic identifier values for that type. In the case of the process token controller, there is only a root controller on the enterprise, and no controllers on the companies below it. The reason is that the processes are usually not different in different companies in the enterprise (and even if they are, you do not want to have the same token describe different things within the same enterprise).

Interface com.ibm.sf.cf.DPaymentTermsDetail

public interface DPaymentTermsDetail extends DPaymentTermsDetailAndSettlementDiscountCommonBase

Name	*Signature*	*Description*
addSettlementDiscount	`public abstract void addSettlementDiscount(DSettlementDiscount settlementDiscount) throws SFException`	A SettlementDiscount is added to the collection of SettlementDiscounts.
validateDPaymentTermsDetail	`public abstract DCurrencyValue validateDPaymentTermsDetail(PaymentMethod paymentMethod, DTransactionValue transactionValue, DTime documentDate) throws SFException`	A DPaymentTermsDetail is validated for use with a specific item (based on the input). The due dates and amounts due are compared to the date and total value of the item, and negative payments are checked against the PaymentMethod to be used.
changeSign	`public abstract void changeSign() throws SFException`	For this DPaymentTermsDetail and each associated DSettlementDiscount, that has a Currency Value, the sign is changed. The base class's changeSign method is called for each individiual DPaymentTermsDetail & DSettlementDiscount.
getPaymentMethod	`public abstract PaymentMethod getPaymentMethod() throws SFException`	Returns the PaymentMethod, copied from the Handle
createSettlementDiscountIterator	`public abstract Iterator createSettlementDiscountIterator() throws SFException`	Create Iterator for Collection of SettlementDiscounts
getNextSettlementDiscount	`public abstract DSettlementDiscount getNextSettlementDiscount(Iterator position) throws SFException`	Gets the SettlementDiscount at the Next Iterator Position
containsSettlementDiscount	`public abstract boolean containsSettlementDiscount(DSettlementDiscount settlementdiscount) throws SFException`	Checks if the SettlementDiscount exists in the Collection of SettlementDiscounts
getSettlementDiscountAt	`public abstract DSettlementDiscount getSettlementDiscountAt(Iterator position) throws SFException`	Gets the SettlementDiscount at the current iterator position
addAllSettlementDiscounts	`public abstract void addAllSettlementDiscounts(DList newDSettlementDiscounts) throws SFException`	Adds all SettlementDiscounts to the Collection of SettlementDiscounts

Figure 21-34
Interface `DPaymentTermsDetails`

removeSettlementDiscountAt	`public abstract void removeSettlementDiscountAt(Iterator position) throws SFException`	Removes the SettlementDiscount at the Current Iterator Position
removeSettlementDiscount	`public abstract void removeSettlementDiscount(DSettlementDiscount settlementdiscount) throws SFException`	Removes the specified SettlementDiscount
removeAllSettlementDiscounts	`public abstract void removeAllSettlementDiscounts() throws SFException`	Removes all SettlementDiscount from the Collection of SettlementDiscounts
insertSettlementDiscountAt	`public abstract void insertSettlementDiscountAt(DSettlementDiscount settlementDiscountToInsert, Iterator position) throws SFException`	Inserts the SettlementDiscount at the Current Iterator Position
getPreviousSettlementDiscount	`public abstract DSettlementDiscount getPreviousSettlementDiscount(Iterator position) throws SFException`	Gets the SettlementDiscount at the Previous Iterator Position
getPaymentTerms	`public abstract PaymentTerms getPaymentTerms() throws SFException`	Returns the PaymentTerms, copied from the Handle
getPaymentTermsHdl	`public abstract Handle getPaymentTermsHdl() throws SFException`	Returns the Handle to the PaymentTerms of the DPaymentTermsDetail
initialize	`public abstract void initialize(DInteger days, DInteger months, DInteger fixedMonthday, DTime specificDate, DInteger baseWeekday, DInteger baseMonthday, DDecimal percentage, DCurrencyValue currencyValue, PaymentMethod paymentMethod) throws SFException`	This method is invoked by the Factory after Construction of an instance of this class to ensure proper initialization

Figure 21-34
(Cont'd)

Interface com.ibm.sf.cf.DPaymentTermsDetailAndSettlementDiscountCommonBase

public interface DPaymentTermsDetailAndSettlementDiscountCommonBase extends Dependent

Name	*Signature*	*Description*
calculateDate	`public abstract DTime calculateDate(DTime baseDate, NaturalCalendar naturalCalendar, DResultDateAdjustmentPolicy resultDateAdjustmentPolicy) throws SFException`	Calculates a date that could be interpreted as either a due date (when used with a DPaymentTermsDetail) or a expiration date (when used with a DSettlementDiscount).
calculateAmount	`public abstract DTransactionValue calculateAmount(DTransactionValue transactionValue) throws SFException`	Calculates an amount that could be interpreted as either a amount due (when used with a DPaymentTermsDetail) or a discount amount (when used with a DSettlementDiscount).
calculateValue	`public abstract DAmountAndDateResult calculateValue(DTransactionValue transactionValue, DTime baseDate, NaturalCalendar naturalCalendar, DResultDateAdjustmentPolicy resultDateAdjustmentPolicy) throws SFException`	Gets a date (depending on context, could be either a due date for a DPaymentTermsDetail, or a expiration date for a DSettlementDiscount) and an amount (could be either an amount due for a DPaymentTermsDetail, or discount amount for a DSettlementDiscount). Results will be returned in a DPaymentValueResult object containing the date and amount information.
getMonths	`public abstract DInteger getMonths() throws SFException`	Gets Months.
getDays	`public abstract DInteger getDays() throws SFException`	Gets Days.
getBaseMonthday	`public abstract DInteger getBaseMonthday() throws SFException`	Gets BaseMonthday.
getFixedMonthday	`public abstract DInteger getFixedMonthday() throws SFException`	Gets fixed day of the month from which the due date will be calculated.
getBaseWeekday	`public abstract DInteger getBaseWeekday() throws SFException`	Gets BaseWeekday.
getSpecificDate	`public abstract DTime getSpecificDate() throws SFException`	Gets SpecificDate.
getCurrencyValue	`public abstract DCurrencyValue getCurrencyValue() throws SFException`	Gets CurrencyValue.

Figure 21-35
Interface DpaymentTermins DetailAndSettlement DiscountCommonBase

getPercentage	`public abstract DDecimal getPercentage() throws SFException`	Gets Percentage.
getMonthsForRestrictedUse	`public abstract DInteger getMonthsForRestrictedUse() throws SFException`	Returns the actual Months, used by framework for SetEqual().
getDaysForRestrictedUse	`public abstract DInteger getDaysForRestrictedUse() throws SFException`	Returns the actual Days, used by framework for SetEqual().
getBaseMonthdayForRestrictedUse	`public abstract DInteger getBaseMonthdayForRestrictedUse() throws SFException`	Returns the actual BaseMonthday, used by framework for SetEqual().
getFixedMonthdayForRestrictedUse	`public abstract DInteger getFixedMonthdayForRestrictedUse() throws SFException`	Returns the actual FixedMonthday, used by framework for SetEqual().
getBaseWeekdayForRestrictedUse	`public abstract DInteger getBaseWeekdayForRestrictedUse() throws SFException`	Returns the actual BaseWeekday, used by framework for SetEqual().
getSpecificDateForRestrictedUse	`public abstract DTime getSpecificDateForRestrictedUse() throws SFException`	Returns the actual SpecificDate, used by framework for SetEqual().
getCurrencyValueForRestrictedUse	`public abstract DCurrencyValue getCurrencyValueForRestrictedUse() throws SFException`	Returns the actual CurrencyValue, used by framework for SetEqual().
getPercentageForRestrictedUse	`public abstract DDecimal getPercentageForRestrictedUse() throws SFException`	Returns the actual Percentage, used by framework for SetEqual().
initialize	`public abstract void initialize(DInteger days, DInteger months, DInteger fixedMonthday, DTime specificDate, DInteger baseWeekday, DInteger baseMonthday, DDecimal percentage, DCurrencyValue currencyValue) throws SFException`	This method is invoked by the Factory after Construction of an instance of this class to ensure proper initialization

Figure 21-35
(Cont'd)

Project

The notion of a project is widely used to represent a grouping of various activities and personnel, along with scheduling constraints, all tied together to achieve a certain objective. SanFrancisco allows you to define projects as object.

Basically, these objects are similar to `DocumentLocation` objects. These, too, are `DynamicIdentifier` objects, and are managed by a controller on the company. The project itself is a `DynamicEntity`, so you can add properties to it. Figure 21-40 shows an example of creating a project and setting some properties of it.

Interface com.ibm.sf.cf.PeriodizedCalendar

public interface **PeriodizedCalendar** extends PeriodizedCalendarBase

Name	*Signature*	*Description*
appendPeriodizedYear	`public abstract void appendPeriodizedYear(DTime endDate) throws SFException`	Appends a PeriodizedYear to the calendar. The new year ends at the given end date and begins the day after the last year of the calendar ends
prependPeriodizedYear	`public abstract void prependPeriodizedYear(DTime startDate) throws SFException`	Prepends a PeriodizedYear to the calendar. The new year begins with the given startDate and ends the day before the first year of the calendar begins
deleteStartingYear	`public abstract void deleteStartingYear() throws SFException`	Removes the FIRST year from the calendar, provided it is NOT the only remaining year in the calendar
deleteEndingYear	`public abstract void deleteEndingYear() throws SFException`	Removes the LAST year from the calendar, provided it is NOT the only remaining year in the calendar
getPeriodizedYearBy	`public abstract PeriodizedYear getPeriodizedYearBy(int yearNumber) throws SFException`	Returns the PeriodizedYear associated with the given year number. If no matching PeriodizedYear has been found, null is returned.
getFirstPeriodizedYear	`public abstract PeriodizedYear getFirstPeriodizedYear() throws SFException`	Returns the FIRST year of the calendar (in chronological order)
getNextPeriodizedYear	`public abstract PeriodizedYear getNextPeriodizedYear(PeriodizedYear currentYear) throws SFException`	(Provides iteration in chronological sequence) Returns the year which falls chronologically after the given year, i.e. nextYear.getYearNumber() == currentYear.getYearNumber() + 1. If the specified year is the LAST in the calendar, null is returned. Assumptions: containsYear(currentYear) == true
getPreviousPeriodizedYear	`public abstract PeriodizedYear getPreviousPeriodizedYear (PeriodizedYear currentYear) throws SFException`	(Provides iteration in chronological sequence) Returns the year which chronologically precedes the specified year, i.e. nextYear.getYearNumber() == currentYear.getYearNumber() - 1. If the specified year is the FIRST in the calendar, null is returned. Assumptions: containsYear(currentYear) == true
getLastPeriodizedYear	`public abstract PeriodizedYear getLastPeriodizedYear() throws SFException`	Returns the LAST year of the calendar (in chronological order)
initialize	`public abstract void initialize(DTime initialStartDate, DTime initialEndDate, int initialYearNumber, DescriptiveInformation description) throws SFException`	This method is invoked by the Factory after Construction of an instance of this class to ensure proper initialization

Figure 21-36
Interface `Periodized Calendar`

Interface com.ibm.sf.cf.PeriodizedYear

public interface PeriodizedYear extends PeriodizedYearBase

Name	*Signature*	*Description*
appendDatedPeriod	`public abstract void appendDatedPeriod(String periodId, DTime endDate) throws SFException`	Creates and appends a new dated period which will become the last period within this Periodized Year. The start date of the new period is implicitly defined as the day after the end date of the last dated period within the year. The given end date should neither exceed this year's end date nor should it precede the implicitly defined start date.
insertDatedPeriodBefore	`public abstract void insertDatedPeriodBefore(String newPeriodId, DTime itsEndDate, String insertBeforePeriodWithId) throws SFException`	Creates and inserts a dated period into the Periodized Year before the given period. If the contained period which the new period is to precede is dated, split the contained period to create the new period. Thus, the start date of the new period becomes the start date of the contained period, whose start date we move forward to the day after the end date specified for the new period. Hence, the end date for the new period must fall after the start date of the contained period but not after its end date. If the contained period is undated:- the next dated period in the year would be used or if no dated period exists after this undated period within the year and the year is incomplete, append the new period to the PeriodizedYear which would extend the date range covered by the periods within the year. Hence, initialize the start date for the new period to the day after the end date of the last dated period of the year. The given end date should neither precede the implicit start date for the new period nor exceed the end date of the year.
insertDatedPeriodAfter	`public abstract void insertDatedPeriodAfter(String newPeriodId, DTime itsStartDate, String insertAfterPeriodWithId) throws SFException`	Creates and inserts a dated period into the year after the specified period. If the period after which the new period is to be inserted is dated, split the contained period to create the new period. Thus, the end date of the new period becomes the end date of the contained period, whose end date we move back to the day before the start date specified for the new period. Hence, the start date for the new period must fall on or after that of the contained period but before its end date. If the contained period is undated, the last dated period which precedes the contained period would be used. Thus, if the contained period is undated, there must exist a dated period which precedes that period within the year.
appendUndatedPeriod	`public abstract void appendUndatedPeriod(String periodId) throws SFException`	Creates and appends a new undated period to the Periodized Year

Figure 21-37
Interface Periodized Year

insertUndatedPeriodBefore	`public abstract void insertUndatedPeriodBefore (String newPeriodId, String insertBeforePeriodWithId) throws SFException`	Creates and inserts a undated period before the period identified by the specified id
insertUndatedPeriodAfter	`public abstract void insertUndatedPeriodAfter( String newPeriodId, String insertAfterPeriodWithId) throws SFException`	Creates and inserts an undated period after the period identified by the specified id.
changePeriodEndDate	`public abstract void changePeriodEndDate(String periodId, DTime newEndDate) throws SFException`	Changes the end date of a given [dated] period, adjusting the start date of the next dated period to compensate (it effectively moves the boundary between two adjacent dated periods), if one exists.
replacePeriodId	`public abstract void replacePeriodId(String periodId, String newPeriodId) throws SFException`	Replaces the identifier for the period with the given id
replacePeriodId	`public abstract void replacePeriodId(CalendarPeriod period, String newPeriodId) throws SFException`	Replaces the identifier for the given period
removeOwnedPeriodBy	`public abstract void removeOwnedPeriodBy(String periodId, boolean absorbWithPreviousDatedPeriod) throws SFException`	Removes a period from the year. If the period to remove is dated, either the end date of the preceding dated period or the start date of the next dated period is adjusted to incorporate the vacated days, unless the period is the last dated period of the year and the request is not to incorporate the vacated days into the previous period. If the period is undated, adjustments of any kind will not be required.
initialize	`public abstract void initialize(PeriodizedCalendar containingCalendar, DTime startDate, DTime endDate, int yearNumber, DescriptiveInformation description) throws SFException`	This method is invoked by the Factory after Construction of an instance of this class to ensure proper initialization

Figure 21-37
(Cont'd)

Interface com.ibm.sf.cf.CalendarPeriod

public interface CalendarPeriod extends DescribableDynamicEntity

Name	Signature	Description
isAfter	`public abstract boolean isAfter(CalendarPeriod comparand) throws SFException`	Determines whether this CalendarPeriod exists after the given period within the calendar. The CalendarPeriods need not necessarily belong to the same year within the calendar Assumptions: Both CalendarPeriods belong to the same calendar
isDated	`public abstract boolean isDated() throws SFException`	Returns true if a calendar period covers a specific date range within a given year. A period which returns true implements the DateRangeMixin interface
getContainingYearNumber	`public abstract int getContainingYearNumber() throws SFException`	Returns the year number identifying they year which contains this CalendarPeriod
getPeriodId	`public abstract String getPeriodId() throws SFException`	Gets Used to uniqely identify a CalendarPeriod within a containing year
getContainingYearHdl	`public abstract Handle getContainingYearHdl() throws SFException`	Returns the Handle to the PeriodizedYearBase of the containingYear of the CalendarPeriod
initialize	`public abstract void initialize(PeriodizedYearBase containingYear, String periodId, DescriptiveInformation description) throws SFException`	This method is invoked by the Factory after Construction of an instance of this class to ensure proper initialization

Figure 21-38
Interface `CalendarPeriod`

Interface com.ibm.sf.cf.ProcessTokenValue

public interface ProcessTokenValue extends DynamicEntity, Distinguishable

Name	Signature	Description
getId	`public abstract String getId() throws SFException`	Gets id
initialize	`public abstract void initialize(ProcessTokenController processTokenController, String aProcessTokenId) throws SFException`	This method is invoked by the Factory after Construction of an instance of this class to ensure proper initialization

Figure 21-39
Interface `ProcessTokenValue`

```
// Get the ProjectController from the active company
Company company  = CompanyContext.getActiveCompany();
projectController = (ProjectController)
                    company.getPropertyBy("cf.ProjectController");


// Generate project description
DescriptiveInformation description =
      DescriptiveInformationFactory.createDescriptiveInformation
           (accessCPW,
            projectController.getHandle());
            di.addDefaultDescription("Project SF3");

// Create the project
Project theProject = ProjectFactory.createProject
            (projectController,            the project
             accessCPW,
             projectController.getHandle(),
             "Prj123",
             description);


// Retrieve manager
Initials theManager = ...;

p.addDirectlyContainedPropertyBy(theManager,
                          "com.Mycompany.sfbased.Manager");
```

Figure 21-40
Code sample: creating a project and setting some properties.

Specific Information

The `SpecificInformation` interface is used to represent generic pieces of information that are attached to objects. This interface is shown in Figure 21-41. `SpecificInformation` objects in SanFrancisco are used in conjunction with process tokens. This way, they have some inherent structure to them, which separates them from free-text strings attached to objects. The `SpecificInformation` interface provides methods for adding or removing process tokens associated with a specific note.

Interface com.ibm.sf.cf.SpecificInformation

public interface interface SpecificInformation extends AllowRemote

Name	*Signature*	*Description*
createProcessTokenValueIterator	public abstract Iterator createProcessTokenValueIterator () throws SFException	Create Iterator for Collection of ProcessTokenValues
getNextProcessTokenValue	public abstract ProcessTokenValue getNextProcessTokenValue(Iterator position) throws SFException	Gets the ProcessTokenValue at the Next Iterator Position
setProcessTokenValues	public abstract void setProcessTokenValues(DSet ProcessTokenValues) throws SFException	Sets the collection of ProcessTokenValues
containsProcessTokenValue	public abstract boolean containsProcessTokenValue(ProcessTokenValue processtokenvalue) throws SFException	Checks if the ProcessTokenValue exists in the Collection of ProcessTokenValues
getProcessTokenValueAt	public abstract ProcessTokenValue getProcessTokenValueAt(Iterator position) throws SFException	Gets the ProcessTokenValue at the current iterator position
addProcessTokenValue	public abstract void addProcessTokenValue(ProcessTokenValue processTokenValueToAdd) throws SFException	Adds a ProcessTokenValue to the Collection of ProcessTokenValues
addAllProcessTokenValues	public abstract void addAllProcessTokenValues(DSet newProcessTokenValues) throws SFException	Adds all ProcessTokenValues to the Collection of ProcessTokenValues
removeProcessTokenValueAt	public abstract void removeProcessTokenValueAt(Iterator position) throws SFException	Removes the ProcessTokenValue at the Current Iterator Position
removeProcessTokenValue	public abstract void removeProcessTokenValue(ProcessTokenValue processtokenvalue) throws SFException	Removes the specified ProcessTokenValue
removeAllProcessTokenValues	public abstract void removeAllProcessTokenValues() throws SFException	Removes all ProcessTokenValue from the Collection of ProcessTokenValues
setText	public abstract void setText(String newText) throws SFException	Sets Text
getText	public abstract String getText() throws SFException	Gets Text

Figure 21-41
Interface `SpecificInformation`

Note that you can extend the notion of specific information according to your own needs. So, if your organization has specific fields that are associated with every such "note" you attach to an object, you can create your own class implementing this interface and use it. You would need to provide a factory for it as explained in Chapter 24.

Supplementary Charge

In some businesses, you have charges that are independent of the specific products or services ordered. Such charges might be a fixed handling fee, or a shipping charge depending on the value of the order. SanFrancisco provides the `DSupplementaryCharge` interface for this purpose. This is only an interface and the `DSupplementaryChargeCommon` class provides a basic implementation of this interface. You can provide your own implementations according to your needs.

The creation methods for supplementary charges are provided in the appropriate factory. These creation methods take a `DSupplementaryChargeType` parameter that indicates the type of charge being made. SanFrancisco provides two kinds of supplementary charge types. `DSupplementaryChargeTypeIdOnly` holds an id tag for the charge. In contrast, `DSupplementaryChargeTypeFixedAmount` holds a charge id but also a fixed amount associated with it. Supplementary charge types are managed through their respective controllers. Such a controller can be placed on the company to hold to charges associated with it. Just like other controllers, you may implement a "chain of responsibility" by which each company can have its own charges, but also share some enterprise-wide charges.

Unit of Measure

Business applications often need to describe and record various measurable quantities. This might be used for describing products (e.g. the dimensions of a book) or to represent pricing of raw material (e.g. the price of a gold nugget would be based on how many ounces it weighs).

SanFrancisco addresses this issue by providing built-in support for both recording and manipulating measurable quantities. This is obviously a significant improvement over using plain numbers to represent these quantities in which the unit of measurement is lost. Using plain numbers obviously makes the software more difficult to understand and use because users and developers might both have some uncertainty as to what was the original intent of the unit of measure. In fact, the whole issue of the Y2K bug is in many ways caused by loss of the unit of measurement.

```
UnitOfMeasure meters = aUnitController.getUnitOfMeasureBy("meters");
UnitCategory length = aUnitController.getUnitCategoryBy("length");
UnitCategory width = aUnitController.getUnitCategoryBy("width");
DQuantityUnit len = DQuantityUnitFactory(5, meters, length);
DQuantityUnit wid = DQuantityUnitFactory(5, meters, width);
DDecimal mult = w.getQuantity().multiply(l.getQuantity());
DQuantityUnit area = DQuantityUnitFactory (mult, meters,null);
```

Figure 21-42 Code sample: using units of measurement in SanFrancisco.

SanFrancisco defines quantity classes as unit of measure-qualified amounts. Quantit

ies in SanFrancisco have units, and an optional unit category. The unit category represents what exactly is being measured, such as length, height, weight, etc.

Quantities are represented by `QuantityUnit` objects. These objects provide various methods for arithmetic, rounding, comparison, and printing, similar to currencies. The analogy to currencies goes a long way, because currency values too are basically numbers paired with a "unit" that is the name of a currency.

Units of measurement are implemented as `UnitOfMeasure` objects. Units of measure are associated with unit categories through `UnitCategoryUnitLink` objects, which specify conversion factors between measurement units in the same category.

Standard measurements of physical objects are represented by `DMeasurement` and `DMeasurementValue`. The latter is just an object that contains two `DQuantityUnit` values, gross and net. The `DMeasurement` interface encapsulates all the standard measures of an object, namely the length, width, height, volume, and weight.

To summarize, Figure 21-42 shows how to use units of measurement to calculate the volume of a box.

CHAPTER 22

Financial Business Objects

All business revolves around money. Because the domain of business applications is business (as implied by the name), finance and money play an important role in these applications. Financial objects are used to represent money, bank accounts, and so on.

SanFrancisco includes a rich collection of classes responsible for representing financial objects—these will be described in this chapter. To be accurate, the classes described are responsible for integrating the financial aspect into the General CBOs from the previous chapter and the Core Business Processes. More financial objects appear in the Core Business Processes and also in the General CBOs (e.g. `Currency`). The financial integration objects are grouped together in the CFFI package. Table 22-1 shows the categories of Financial Business Objects and the major interfaces and classes composing them.

Note that some of the categories below make use of the "Generalized Mechanisms" CBOs that are described in the next chapter. Most of the categories here make use of the `PropertyContainer` interface of Company and some of the other General CBO layer objects. Table 22-2 summarizes all such properties used by this layer (the CFFI package) on these objects.

Interface to General Ledger

This category provides well-defined interfaces to the General Ledger. Most businesses need to record the effect of activities on the financial status. So, applications must be able to notify the General Ledger of changes in financial status. This category provides the interface for doing that easily. This interface is provided as part of the CBOs since it is required even if the General Ledger is not used (other parts of the CFFI need the GL interface). These interfaces are provided in a way that does not require users of the GL to know its details or even to know if it is actually present.

The main abstraction in this category is the `GenericPostingCombination`, which is also used to model the GL's own `PostingCombination` object (see Chapter 26). The posting combination is the equivalent of an account. The `GenericPostingCombination` interface (see Figure 22-1) provides methods that indicate if the account is a balance sheet account or a profit and loss account, return the currency used for this account, and so on. The account is divided into pieces

TABLE 22-1

CFFI package categories

Category	Components
Bank Accounts	InternalBankAccountController ExternalBankAccountController InternalBankAccount ExternalBankAccount DAccountDetails DBankAccountPCombUsageValidationPolicy
Currency Gain/Loss Accounts	CurrencyGainLossAccountsController DCurrencyGainLossAccountsValidationPolicy DUnrealizedGainLossPCombUsageValidationPolicy DUnrealizedContraPCombUsageValidationPolicy DRealizedGainLossPCombUsageValidationPolicy
Financial Batches	FinancialBatchController DFinancialBatchValidationPolicy DFinancialBatchIdGenerationPolicy FinancialSubbatch DFinancialBatchHandlingPolicyDefault FinancialBatchHandlingPolicy BatchableDomainEntity BatchableDomainEntitySubbatch DFinancialSubbatchHandlingPolicy FinancialBatch
Financial Calendar	FinancialCalendarSetupCmd
Financial Integration	GenericDissectionGLCreateCmd AnalysisCodeMap DomainGenericDissectionType DIntegrationKey DomainGLTransactionIntegrator DMaintenanceIntegrationKey DLookupIntegrationKey DAccountControlType DomainGLTransactionIntegratorSharedData FinancialIntegrationCommandQueue DGenericGLDissectionPostSet DGenericGLDissectionSelectionPolicy DomainGLTransactionIntegratorRoot DomainGLTransactionIntegratorAggregating DUsedAccountControlTypes DAnalysisCodeMapping DUnusedAccountControlTypeValues DBusinessPartnerAccountControlType DInitialsAccountControlType DSupplementaryChargeTypeAccountControlType
Interface to Banks	Bank BankController
Interface to Accounts Receivable/Accounts Payable	GenericLogItem GenericLedgerItem GenericLogLedgerItemController GenericLEAccount

TABLE 22-1

(Contd)

Category	Components
Interface to General Ledger	GenericPostingCombination GenericAnalysisGroup GenericAnalysisCode GenericDissection GenericGLJournal
Invoicing	InvoiceDetail InvoiceableDetail InvoicingDetail InvoicingTypeValue InvoiceTypeController

TABLE 22-2

Properties used by the CFFI package on CF objects

Property on	Property type	Name
Company	DomainGLTransactionIntegrator	cffi.DomainGLTransactionIntegrator.
	TransactionTypeController	cffi.TransactionTypeController
	FinancialTransactionSourceController	cffi.FinancialTransactionSourceController
	GenericJournalController	Cffi.GenericJournalController
	GenericChartOfAccounts	Cffi.GenericChartOfAccounts
	GenericGLFiscalCalendar	Cffi.GenericGLFiscalCalendar
	CurrencyGainLossAccountsController	Cffi.CurrencyGainLossAccountsController
	DCurrencyGainLossAccounts ValidationPolicy	Cffi.DCurrencyGainLossAccounts ValidationPolicy
	D_DFinancialBatchHandling PolicyDefault	cffi.DFinancialBatchHandling Policy.Default
	InvoicingTypeController	cffi.InvoicingTypeController
	InvoiceDocumentTypeController	cffi.InvoiceDocumentTypeController
	DissectionTypeValueController	cffi.DissectionTypeValueController
	DInteger	cffi.InvoiceDetailIncrement
	NumberSeries	cffi.NumberSeriesForInvoice
	NumberSeries	cffi.NumberSeriesForCreditInvoice
	InvoiceController	cffi.InvoiceController
	GenericLogLedgerItemController	cffi.GenericLogLedgerItemController
	DBoolean	cffi.DBoolean.LedgerUpdatesGLTransactions
	BankMovementParameters	cffi.BankMovementParameters
	GenericBankTransactionController	cffi.GenericBankTransactionController
	BankMovementController	cffi.BankMovementController
	InternalBankAccountController	cffi.InternalBankAccountController
	ExternalBankAccountController	cffi.ExternalBankAccountController
	BankController	cffi.BankController
	FinancialBatchController	cffi.FinancialBatchController
Fiscal Calendar	FinancialCalendar	cffi.FinancialCalendar.
Business Partner-Customer Supplier Data	GenericLEAccount	cffi.BankMovementParameters

Interface com.ibm.sf.cffi. GenericPostingCombination

public interface interface **GenericPostingCombination**
extends DescribableDynamicEntity

Main Methods

Name	*Signature*	*Description*
genericValidate	`public abstract DResultsCollection genericValidate(int creationCode) throws SFException`	Validate this posting combination. A results collection or NULL is returned from this operation. It can be tested for any result messages detected during validation, as well as indicating success or failure of operation. If NULL is returned, then no messages are reported. Throws an exception if GL is not installed.
isGenericMemoAccount	`public abstract boolean isGenericMemoAccount() throws SFException`	Checks if this is a memo Account.
isGenericAnalysisAccount	`public abstract boolean isGenericAnalysisAccount( ) throws SFException`	Checks if this is an analysis Account.
isGenericProfitAndLossAccount	`public abstract boolean isGenericProfitAndLossAccount() throws SFException`	Checks if this is a profit and loss Account.
isGenericBalanceSheetAccount	`public abstract boolean isGenericBalanceSheetAccount() throws SFException`	Checks if this is a balance sheet Account.
isGenericControlAccount	`public abstract boolean isGenericControlAccount() throws SFException`	Checks if this GenericPostingCombination has been designated a control account.
genericUsageValidate	`public abstract DResultsCollection genericUsageValidate(DGenericPCombUsageValidationPolicy genericPCombUsageValidationPolicy) throws SFException`	Validate this posting combination. A results collection or NULL is returned from this operation. It can be tested for any result messages detected during validation, as well as indicating success or failure of operation. If NULL is returned, then no messages are reported.
getGenericDesignatedCurrency	`public abstract Currency getGenericDesignatedCurrency() throws SFException`	Returns the designated currency of the ChartOfAccountAttributes associated with this PostingCombination
getGenericUseBaseCurrencyOnly	`public abstract boolean getGenericUseBaseCurrencyOnly() throws SFException`	Checks if the associated ChartOfAccountAttributes is to use Base Currency Only

Figure 22-1
Interface `GenericPostingCombination`

getGenericInstanceId	`public abstract String getGenericInstanceId() throws SFException`	Returns the id for this Generic Posting Combination
genericUsageValidate	`public abstract DResultsCollection genericUsageValidate(DGenericPCombUsageValidationPolicy genericPCombUsageValidationPolicy) throws SFException`	Validate this posting combination. A results collection or NULL is returned from this operation. It can be tested for any result messages detected during validation, as well as indicating success or failure of operation. If NULL is returned, then no messages are reported.
getGenericDesignatedCurrency	`public abstract Currency getGenericDesignatedCurrency() throws SFException`	Returns the designated currency of the ChartOfAccountAttributes associated with this PostingCombination
genericInitialize	`public abstract void genericInitialize(GenericChartOfAccounts owner, DGenericAnalysisCodeSet analysisCodeSet) throws SFException`	This method is invoked by the Factory after Construction of an instance of this class to ensure proper initialization
genericInitialize	`public abstract void genericInitialize(DGenericAnalysisCodeSet analysisCodeSet) throws SFException`	This method is invoked by the Factory after Construction of an instance of this class to ensure proper initialization

Figure 22-1
(Cont'd)

implemented as `GenericAnalysisGroup` objects. These objects use application-specific `GenericAnalysisCode` objects.

Similar to the posting combination, other abstractions are common with the GL. The `GenericGLDissection` represents a dissection, which is an amount associated with an account (i.e. a posting combination) and several of these make up a journal. `GenericGLJournal` represents a GL journal, which represents a single transaction.

In this category, we have the following controllers.

- `FinancialTransactionSourceController`. Manages Transaction Source objects that identify the source for journal and dissection creation.
- `TransactionTypeValueController`. Manages the different transaction types.
- `DissectionTypeValueController`. Manages the dissection types. The DissectionTypeValue controls the use of a posting combination for a specific type of dissection, through the `GenericPCombUsageValidationPolicy` object. This object has one method that is used to validate a given `GenericPostingCombination`.

Interface to Accounts Receivable/ Accounts Payable

Similar to the previous category, this category provides interfaces to the Accounts Receivable/Accounts Payable (AR/AP) Core Business Process. Many applications need to be able to easily record information in either the Accounts Receivable or Accounts Payable records. These interfaces are provided as a part of CBOs because they need to be available even when AR/AP is not available. These interfaces do not require their user to have any knowledge about AR/AP in order to function properly.

The main abstractions here are the `GenericLedgerItem`, and `GenericLogItem`, which represent AR/AP items approved by the company and those that are pending approval, respectively. An AR/AP account is represented by the abstract interface `GenericLEAccount`.

Interface to Banks

This category provides interfaces for working with bank transactions. Note that full support for working with banks, such as supporting bank statements, is part of the General Ledger Core Business Process.

This category includes the `Bank` interface, shown in Figure 22-2. The Bank object includes some details relating to the bank, such as its name, code number, country, and address. A `BankController` object placed in the company (through the "`cffi.BankController`" attribute) owns the banks relevant for a specific company.

Bank Accounts

This category treats issues related to banks and bank accounts. Banks (like in the real world) are financial institutions the company interacts with, and which manage accounts. This category distinguishes between internal bank accounts that are the company's bank account and external bank accounts that belong to other parties (usually its business partners).

Interface com.ibm.sf.cffi.Bank

public interface interface **Bank** extends DescribableDynamicEntity

Name	*Signature*	*Description*
setBankDetails	`public abstract void setBankDetails( String bankCode, Country country, String bankName, Address address, String swiftCode) t hrows SFException`	Set the bank attributes
destroy	`public abstract void destroy() throws SFException`	Destroy method
getAddress	`public abstract Address getAddress() throws SFException`	Returns the Address, copied from the Handle
setOwnedAddress	`public abstract void setOwnedAddress( Address newAddress) throws SFException`	Set the Handle of the Address
getCountry	`public abstract Country getCountry() throws SFException`	Returns the Country, copied from the Handle
setCountry	`public abstract void setCountry(Country newCountry) throws SFException`	Set the Handle of the Country
setSwiftCode	`public abstract void setSwiftCode(String newSwiftCode) throws SFException`	Sets SwiftCode
setBankName	`public abstract void setBankName(String newBankName) throws SFException`	Sets BankName
setBankCode	`public abstract void setBankCode(String newBankCode) throws SFException`	Set The bankCode of the bank. This attribute is used by the framework as part of a primary key in a collection..
getAddressHdl	`public abstract Handle getAddressHdl() throws SFException`	Returns the Handle to the Address of the address of the Bank
getCountryHdl	`public abstract Handle getCountryHdl() throws SFException`	Returns the Handle to the Country of the country of the Bank
getSwiftCode	`public abstract String getSwiftCode() throws SFException`	Gets SwiftCode
getBankName	`public abstract String getBankName() throws SFException`	Gets BankName
getBankCode	`public abstract String getBankCode() throws SFException`	Returns the bankCode of the bank.

Figure 22-2
Bank interface.

The common details for both internal and external bank accounts are recorded in `DAccountDetails` objects. Such details are the account name, account number at the bank, and a Handle to the bank involved. The `DAccountDetails` interface is shown in Figure 22-3.

Internal bank accounts are represented by `InternalBankAccount` objects, which have the interface shown in Figure 22-4. These objects are owned by the respective controller placed in the company. `InternalBankAccount` objects are created using the respective factory with parameters including the owning controller, the access mode, the account details (i.e. a `DAccountDetails` object), and possibly a location handle.

Similarly, `ExternalBankAccount` objects (see Figure 22-5) are used to represent bank accounts of business partners, and are managed by the respective controller. The factory method for `ExternalBankAccount` objects takes similar parameters to the one for internal bank accounts. Both controllers mentioned are placed on the company and accessed using the properties "`cffi.InternalBankAccountController`" and "`cffi.ExternalBankAccountController`", respectively.

Currency Gain/Loss Accounts

This category is responsible for taking care of currency gain and losses resulting from currency revaluations. To be exact, this category provides support for determining what General Ledger account to use for currency gains and losses.

As an example of how a currency gain occurs, consider a US-based company that runs a business in US-dollars. Say this company has a foreign currency bank account holding a sum of one million Japanese yens. If there is a sudden fluctuation in the US$/JPY (i.e. yen per US-dollar) rate the company might make or lose a lot of yens (if the account held a more significant sum, that would also amount to a lot of dollars).

This category supports accounts for both realized and unrealized gains and losses. The currency gain and loss accounts are represented by `CurrencyGainLossAccounts`. This interface is shown in Figure 22-6. The respective controller is placed on a company using the `cffi.CurrencyGainLossAccountsController` property. For these accounts, there is the notion of a validation policy, which checks the account. The interface to such policies is shown in Figure 22-7, and is

Interface com.ibm.sf.cffi.DAccountDetails

public interface interface **DAccountDetails**
extends Dependent .

Name	*Signature*	*Description*
getBank	`public abstract Bank getBank() throws SFException`	Returns the Bank, copied from the Handle
SetBank	`public abstract void setBank(Bank newBank) throws SFException`	Set the Handle of the Bank
getBankAccountNumber	`public abstract String getBankAccountNumber() throws SFException`	Gets account number at bank
setBankAccountNumber	`public abstract void setBankAccountNumber(String newBankAccountNumber) throws SFException`	Set account number at bank
getBankAccountName	`public abstract String getBankAccountName() throws SFException`	Gets BankAccountName
setBankAccountName	`public abstract void setBankAccountName(String newBankAccountName) throws SFException`	Sets BankAccountName
getBankAccountType	`public abstract String getBankAccountType() throws SFException`	Gets type of the bank account, for example: Current, Deposit, ...
setBankAccountType	`public abstract void setBankAccountType(String newBankAccountType) throws SFException`	Set type of the bank account, for example: Current, Deposit, ...
getChequeFormLayout	`public abstract String getChequeFormLayout() throws SFException`	Gets ChequeFormLayout
setChequeFormLayout	`public abstract void setChequeFormLayout(String newChequeFormLayout) throws SFException`	Sets ChequeFormLayout
getBankHdl	`public abstract Handle getBankHdl() throws SFException`	Returns the Handle to the Bank of the bank of the DAccountDetails
initialize	`public abstract void initialize(Bank bank, String bankAccountNumber, String bankAccountName, String bankAccountType, String chequeFormLayout) throws SFException`	Initialization method invoked from factory.

Figure 22-3
`Daccount Details` interface.

Interface com.ibm.sf.cffi.InternalBankAccount

public interface interface **InternalBankAccount**
extends DescribableDynamicEntity, Distinguishable

Methods

Name	*Signature*	*Description*
getInternalBankAccountId	`public abstract String getInternalBankAccountId() throws SFException`	Returns the unique Id of the internal bank account. This Id is the same as the one returned in the getId method.
setInternalBankAccountId	`public abstract void setInternalBankAccountId (StringnewInternalBankAccountId) throws SFException`	Set The unique identifier for the internal bank account. This attribute is used by the framework as a primary key in a collection. The attribute's set method should be used with extreme caution.
destroy	`public abstract void destroy() throws SFException`	destroy method
setBankAccount	`public abstract void setBankAccount( GenericPostingCombination bankAccount) throws SFException`	Set the Generic Posting Combination for Bank Account
setBankCharges	`public abstract void setBankCharges(GenericPostingCombination bankCharges) throws SFException`	Set the Generic Posting Combination for Bank Charges
setBankSuspense	`public abstract void setBankSuspense(boolean autoSuspendFlag, GenericPostingCombination bankSuspense) throws SFException`	Set the Generic Posting Combination for Bank Suspense
getId	`public abstract String getId() throws SFException`	Return id
getAccountDetails	`public abstract DAccountDetails getAccountDetails() throws SFException`	Gets AccountDetails
setAccountDetails	`public abstract void setAccountDetails(DAccountDetails newAccountDetails) throws SFException`	Sets AccountDetails
getCurrency	`public abstract Currency getCurrency() throws SFException`	Returns the Currency, copied from the Handle
getBankAccount	`public abstract GenericPostingCombination getBankAccount() throws SFException`	Returns the BankAccount, copied from the Handle

Figure 22-4
Interface `InternalBankAccount`

getBankCharges	public abstract GenericPostingCombination getBankCharges() throws SFException	Returns the BankCharges, copied from the Handle
getBankSuspense	public abstract GenericPostingCombination getBankSuspense() throws SFException	Returns the BankSuspense, copied from the Handle
isPostInhibited	public abstract boolean isPostInhibited() throws SFException	Gets flag to prevent or allow the usage of the internal bank account in financial transactions.
setPostInhibited	public abstract void setPostInhibited(boolean newPostInhibited) throws SFException	Set flag to prevent or allow the usage of the internal bank account in financial transactions.
isAutoSuspended	public abstract boolean isAutoSuspended() throws SFException	Gets AutoSuspended
getAccountDetailsForRestrictedUse	public abstract DAccountDetails getAccountDetailsForRestrictedUse() throws SFException	Returns the actual AccountDetails, used by framework for SetEqual()
getCurrencyHdl	public abstract Handle getCurrencyHdl() throws SFException	Returns the Handle to the Currency of the currency of the InternalBankAccount
getBankAccountHdl	public abstract Handle getBankAccountHdl() throws SFException	Returns the Handle to the GenericPostingCombination of the bankAccount of the InternalBankAccount
getBankChargesHdl	public abstract Handle getBankChargesHdl() throws SFException	Returns the Handle to the GenericPostingCombination of the bankCharges of the InternalBankAccount
getBankSuspenseHdl	public abstract Handle getBankSuspenseHdl() throws SFException	Returns the Handle to the GenericPostingCombination of the bankSuspense of the InternalBankAccount
initialize	public abstract void initialize(InternalBankAccountController internalBankAccountController, String internalBankAccountId, DAccountDetails accountDetails, Currency currency, boolean postInhibitFlag, boolean autoSuspendFlag, GenericPostingCombination genericPCombForBankAccount , GenericPostingCombination genericPCombForBankCharges , GenericPostingCombination genericPCombForSuspenseAccount) throws SFException	Initialization method invoked from factory.

Figure 22-4
(Cont'd)

Interface com.ibm.sf.cffi.ExternalBankAccount

public interface interface **ExternalBankAccount**
extends DescribableDynamicEntity

Methods

Name	*Signature*	*Description*
setAccountDetails	`public abstract void setAccountDetails (DAccountDetails accountDetails) throws SFException`	Set the account details.
getAccountDetails	`public abstract DAccountDetailsgetAccountDetails() throws SFException`	Gets AccountDetails
getBank	`public abstract Bank getBank() throws SFException`	Returns the Bank, copied from the Handle
getBankAccountNumber	`public abstract String getBankAccountNumber() throws SFException`	Gets a copy of the bankAccountNumber of the account details. It is needed to use this as part of the key for this item.
GetAccountDetailsForRestrictedUse	`public abstract DAccountDetails getAccountDetailsForRestrictedUse() throws SFException`	Returns the actual AccountDetails, used by framework for SetEqual(), not intended for normal client use.
getBankHdl	`public abstract Handle getBankHdl() throws SFException`	Returns the Handle to the Bank of the bank of the ExternalBankAccount
initialize	`public abstract void initialize(ExternalBankAccountController theExternalBankAccountController, DAccountDetails accountDetails) throws SFException`	This method is invoked by the Factory after Construction of an instance of this class to ensure proper initialization

Figure 22-5
Interface `ExternalBankAccount`

Interface com.ibm.sf.cffi.CurrencyGainLossAccounts

public interface interface **CurrencyGainLossAccounts**
extends DescribableDynamicEntity, Distinguishable

Name	*Signature*	*Description*
setUnrealized	`public abstract void setUnrealized(GenericPostingCombination unrealizedGain, GenericPostingCombination unrealizedLoss, GenericPostingCombination unrealizedContra) throws SFException`	This method sets the three unrealized Posting Combinations
setRealized	`public abstract void setRealized(GenericPostingCombination realizedGain, GenericPostingCombination realizedLoss) throws SFException`	This method sets the two realized Posting Combinations.
setRealizedGain	`public abstract void setRealizedGain(GenericPostingCombination realizedGain) throws SFException`	This method sets the realized gain Posting Combination.
setRealizedLoss	`public abstract void setRealizedLoss(GenericPostingCombination realizedLoss) throws SFException`	This method sets the realized loss Posting Combination.
setUnrealizedGain	`public abstract void setUnrealizedGain(GenericPostingCombination unrealizedGain) throws SFException`	This method sets the unrealized gain Posting Combination.
setUnrealizedLoss	`public abstract void setUnrealizedLoss(GenericPostingCombination unrealizedLoss) throws SFException`	This method sets the unrealized loss Posting Combination.
setUnrealizedContra	`public abstract void setUnrealizedContra(GenericPostingCombination unrealizedContra) throws SFException`	This method sets the unrealized contra Posting Combination.

Figure 22-6
Interface `CurrencyGainLossAccounts`

getRealizedGain	public abstract GenericPostingCombination getRealizedGain() throws SFException	Returns the RealizedGain, copied from the Handle
getRealizedLoss	public abstract GenericPostingCombination getRealizedLoss() throws SFException	Returns the RealizedLoss, copied from the Handle
getUnrealizedGain	public abstract GenericPostingCombination getUnrealizedGain() throws SFException	Returns the UnrealizedGain, copied from the Handle
getUnrealizedLoss	public abstract GenericPostingCombination getUnrealizedLoss() throws SFException	Returns the UnrealizedLoss, copied from the Handle
getUnrealizedContra	public abstract GenericPostingCombination getUnrealizedContra() throws SFException	Returns the UnrealizedContra, copied from the Handle
getIdentifier	public abstract String getIdentifier() throws SFException	Gets Identifier
getRealizedGainHdl	public abstract Handle getRealizedGainHdl() throws SFException	Returns the Handle to the GenericPostingCombination of the realizedGain of the CurrencyGainLossAccounts
getRealizedLossHdl	public abstract Handle getRealizedLossHdl() throws SFException	Returns the Handle to the GenericPostingCombination of the realizedLoss of the CurrencyGainLossAccounts
getUnrealizedGainHdl	public abstract Handle getUnrealizedGainHdl() throws SFException	Returns the Handle to the GenericPostingCombination of the unrealizedGain of the CurrencyGainLossAccounts
GetUnrealizedLossHdl	public abstract Handle getUnrealizedLossHdl() throws SFException	Returns the Handle to the GenericPostingCombination of the unrealizedLoss of the CurrencyGainLossAccounts
getUnrealizedContraHdl	public abstract Handle getUnrealizedContraHdl() throws SFException	Returns the Handle to the GenericPostingCombination of the unrealizedContra of the CurrencyGainLossAccounts
initialize	public abstract void initialize(CurrencyGainLossAccountsController currencyGainLossAccountsController, String identifier, GenericPostingCombination realizedGain, GenericPostingCombination realizedLoss, GenericPostingCombination unrealizedGain, GenericPostingCombination unrealizedLoss, GenericPostingCombination unrealizedContra, DescriptiveInformation descriptiveInformation) throws SFException	This method is invoked by the Factory after Construction of an instance of this class to ensure proper initialization

Figure 22-6
(Cont'd)

Interface com.ibm.sf.cffi.DCurrencyGainLossAccountsValidationPolicy

public interface interface **DCurrencyGainLossAccountsValidationPolicy**
extends DescribableDependent

Name	*Signature*	*Description*
validateRealizedPostingCombinations	`public abstract DResultsCollection validateRealizedPostingCombinations( GenericPostingCombination realizedGain, GenericPostingCombination realizedLoss) throws SFException`	The realized gain and realized loss Posting Combinations will be validated.
validateUnrealizedPostingCombinations	`public abstract DResultsCollection validateUnrealizedPostingCombinations( GenericPostingCombination unrealizedGain, GenericPostingCombination unrealizedLoss, GenericPostingCombination unrealizedContra) throws SFException`	The unrealized gain, unrealized loss, and unrealized contra Posting Combinations will be validated.

Figure 22-7
Interface `DCurrencyGainLoss AcountsValidation Policy`

composed of two methods: one for unrealized gains/losses and one for realized gains/losses. The default policy, provided in the `DCurrencyGainLossAccountsValidationPolicyDefault` object, only makes the most basic checks. That includes checking that the respective gain and loss Posting Combinations passed as parameter are compatible (i.e. either both are Balance Sheet accounts, or both are Profit and Loss accounts).

Financial Batches

This category provides the ability to process a group of financial data items together in a "batch." The exact composition of such a group is dynamic, and of course, is application-dependent. For example, a financial batch can be used to concentrate all the work relating to a specific business partner.

Financial batches are managed by a controller with an interface of `FinancialBatchController`. This controller is placed on the unit via the "`cffi.FinancialBatchController`" attribute. The `FinancialBatch` objects are created using the `FinancialBatchFactory` create method and their interface is shown in Figure 22-8. `FinancialBatch` objects hold collections of application-defined subbatches (implementing the `FinancialSubbatch` interface, which is just an open-ended interface).

When actually executing the batch, some errors might occur—the policy by which to handle them is defined by objects of type `DFinancialBatchHandlingPolicy`. This policy can also be in charge of initiating some additional processing under certain conditions, thereby providing more flexibility. The policy here actually contains a collection of policies for subbatches (each derived from `DFinancialSubbatchHandlingPolicy`). The default policy for batch handling will report all errors detected in subbatches.

Another policy associated with batches determines the ids of batches that should be unique, at least within the scope of their controller. This is handled by `DFinancialBatchIdGenerationPolicy`. The default policy here uses a `NumberSeries` object (see Chapter 21) to generate ids of the form "batch #xx". The class `FinancialBatchStateEnum` defines the different states in which a `FinancialBatch` object can be. Namely, these are: INCOMPLETE, SUSPENDED, READY_FOR_POSTING, POSTED, LOCKED..

Financial Calendar

This category handles the financial calendar. Financial applications require some specific calendar-related concepts, such as the current period or a period status. Like the Natural Calendar in the General

Interface com.ibm.sf.cffi.FinancialBatch

public interface **FinancialBatch**
extends DescribableDynamicEntity, Distinguishable

Main Methods

Name	*Signature*	*Description*
setIdUsingPolicy	`public abstract void setIdUsingPolicy(String newId) throws SFException`	Passes the id provided on to the id generation policy which then determines and updates, as necessary, the id for this FinancialBatch.
isAllowedToBeChanged	`public abstract boolean isAllowedToBeChanged() throws SFException`	Returns true if the contents of the FinancialBatch is open to modification, i.e. whether new batchable items be may be added or exiting ones modified or removed, etc.
prepareForPosting	`public abstract void prepareForPosting() throws SFException`	Delegates the processing of the individual subbatches and any additional validation to the default batch handling policy (which is held on the Company as the property cffi.DFinancialBatchHandlingPolicy) and prepares the FinancialBatch for posting. The policy would determine how errors are handled and collated.
prepareForPosting	`public abstract void prepareForPosting(DFinancialBatchHandlingPolicy validationPolicy) throws SFException`	Delegates the processing of the individual subbatches and any additional validation to the given batch handling policy and prepares the FinancialBatch for posting. The policy determines how errors are handled and collated.
suspend	`public abstract void suspend() throws SFException`	Suspends the FinancialBatch
restart	`public abstract void restart() throws SFException`	Restarts the FinancialBatch
post	`public abstract void post() throws SFException`	Posts each subbatch within the FinancialBatch
getId	`public abstract String getId() throws SFException`	get the Id of the Distinguishable object
getBatchDate	`public abstract DTime getBatchDate() throws SFException`	Gets The date the batch was created
setBatchDate	`public abstract void setBatchDate(DTime newBatchDate) throws SFException`	Set The date the batch was created
getState	`public abstract int getState() throws SFException`	Gets The Financial Batch state
getBatchOwner	`public abstract String getBatchOwner() throws SFException`	Gets BatchOwner
setBatchOwner	`public abstract void setBatchOwner(String newBatchOwner) throws SFException`	Sets BatchOwner

Figure 22-8
Interface `FinancialBatch`

Business Objects, policies are used to implement different functions such as changing the current period or closing a period. The use of policies allows you to extend these functionality to provide a tailored set of rules for period-related activities.

The `FinancialCalendar` object (see interface specification in Figure 22-9) allows one to manage an association between items from the CFFI domain to `FiscalPeriod` objects, while maintaining the current accounting period. It maintains policies for validity checks on closing a fiscal period or changing the current fiscal period. The Financial Calendar has certain policies that can be associated with it. All of these are implementation specific.

- `DFinancialCalendarCurrentPeriodChange Policy`. Defines particular conditions to be checked and processing to be made when the period is changed.
- `DFinancialCalendarPeriodClosePolicy`. Defines particular conditions to be checked and processing to be made when a period is closed.
- `DFinancialCalendarYearEndClosingPolicy`. Defines particular conditions to be checked and processing to be made when a year is closed
- `DFinancialCalendarYearEndValidationPolicy`. Defines particular conditions to be checked and processing to be made on a specific year when the `FinancialCalendar` is closed. This policy has one method: `validateYearEnd(FinancialCalendar, FiscalYear)`.

Financial Integration

This category provides support for integrating a specific business domain with the General Ledger (GL). In other words, these components let you define how your business uses the General Ledger framework. In most business, almost any activity has a financial effect and hence needs to be registered in the General Ledger. Since you cannot expect an arbitrary application to work with a model that immediately maps into the General Ledger domain, an integration layer that acts as a mediator, is required. The abstractions used in this category are similar to the ones used for the

Interface com.ibm.sf.cffi.FinancialCalendar

public interface **FinancialCalendar**
extends DescribableDynamicEntity

Main Methods

Name	*Signature*	*Description*
containsPeriod	`public abstract boolean containsPeriod(FiscalPeriod financialPeriod) throws SFException`	Determines whether the Financial Calendar contains the given fiscal period
isPeriodOpen	`public abstract boolean isPeriodOpen(FiscalPeriod financialPeriod) throws SFException`	Returns the status of the fiscal period which indicates whether items from features using CFFI may be associated with a certain FiscalPeriod (this includes adjustment periods which have no date range but may have transactions posted against them). For example, the status returned could indicate whether GL Journals and LE Ledger Items can be posted or LE Log Items logged against a given fiscal period.
getCurrentPeriod	`public abstract FiscalPeriod getCurrentPeriod() throws SFException`	Returns the current fiscal period for the Financial Calendar
getPeriodBy	`public abstract FiscalPeriod getPeriodBy(DTime containedDate) throws SFException`	Returns the fiscal period the given date falls in or null if the given date is not contained within any period in the calendar (or is not initialized for the Financial Calendar)
setFinancialPeriodStatus	`public abstract void setFinancialPeriodStatus(FiscalPeriod financialPeriod, boolean status) throws SFException`	Changes the status of the fiscal period to OPEN or CLOSED, which indicates whether or not items from features using CFFI may be associated with a certain FiscalPeriod (this includes adjustment periods which have no date range but may have transactions posted against them). For example, this could include items such as GL Journals or LE Ledger Items.
setCurrentPeriod	`public abstract void setCurrentPeriod(FiscalPeriod newCurrentPeriod) throws SFException`	Sets the current accounting period for the FinancialCalendar
moveCurrentPeriodToNextPeriod	`public abstract void moveCurrentPeriodToNextPeriod() throws SFException`	Sets the current accounting period to the next fiscal period which falls chronologically after the existing current period and which has a type that is valid for a current accounting period

Figure 22-9
Interface `FinancialCalendar`

closeFinancialYear	public abstract void closeFinancialYear(FiscalYear financialYear) throws SFException	Closes a fiscal year to enable various consistency checks to be made and perform additional year end processing, which are detailed in the appropriate YearEndClosingPolicy to be used. There is no default handling if the YearEndClosingPolicy does not exist.
extendFinancialCalendar	public abstract void extendFinancialCalendar(FiscalPeriod breakPeriod, boolean openPeriodsPreBreak, boolean openPeriodsBreakAndBeyond) throws SFException	Extends the Financial Calendar to be consistent with the CF Fiscal Calendar This method should be invoked whenever additional periods are created within the CF Fiscal Calendar associated with this calendar. Failure to do so would mean that the two calendars would not be consistent, which could result in unexpected circumstances during later processing.
setValidCurrentPeriodTypes	public abstract void setValidCurrentPeriodTypes(int validCurrentPeriodTypes) throws SFException	Defines the period types which are valid for the current accounting period. This is a composite of the possible types which can be assigned to a fiscal period (see the FiscalPeriodTypeEnum enumeration class in the CF Fiscal Calendar category for a complete definition of the types which are available), where any combination of these types is valid, e.g. NORMAL ADJUSTMENT.
getContainingFiscalCalendar	public abstract FiscalCalendar getContainingFiscalCalendar() throws SFException	Returns the ContainingFiscalCalendar, copied from the Handle
getPeriodClosePolicy	public abstract DFinancialCalendarPeriodClosePolicy getPeriodClosePolicy() throws SFException	Gets PeriodClosePolicy.
setPeriodClosePolicy	public abstract void setPeriodClosePolicy(DFinancialCalendarPeriodClosePolicy newPeriodClosePolicy) throws SFException	Sets PeriodClosePolicy.
getYearEndClosingPolicy	public abstract DFinancialCalendarYearEndClosingPolicy getYearEndClosingPolicy() throws SFException	Gets YearEndClosingPolicy.
setYearEndClosingPolicy	public abstract void setYearEndClosingPolicy(DFinancialCalendarYearEndClosingPolicy newYearEndClosingPolicy) throws SFException	Sets YearEndClosingPolicy.
getCurrentPeriodChangePolicy	public abstract DFinancialCalendarCurrentPeriodChangePolicy getCurrentPeriodChangePolicy() throws SFException	Gets CurrentPeriodChangePolicy.

Figure 22-9
(Cont'd)

setCurrentPeriodChangePolicy	`public abstract void setCurrentPeriodChangePolicy(DFinancialCalendarCurrentPeriodChangePolicy newCurrentPeriodChangePolicy) throws SFException`	Sets CurrentPeriodChangePolicy
getYearEndValidationPolicy	`public abstract DFinancialCalendarYearEndValidationPolicy getYearEndValidationPolicy() throws SFException`	Gets YearEndValidationPolicy
setYearEndValidationPolicy	`public abstract void setYearEndValidationPolicy(DFinancialCalendarYearEndValidationPolicy newYearEndValidationPolicy) throws SFException`	Sets YearEndValidationPolicy
getValidCurrentPeriodTypes	`public abstract int getValidCurrentPeriodTypes() throws SFException`	Gets Purpose: Represents the types which could be assigned to be the current period Description: A fiscal period holds type information which specifies whether the period is a normal posting, adjustment, opening or closing period. Possible values are NORMAL, ADJUSTMENT, OPENING and CLOSING Note: The value assigned to each enumerator/identifier enables these to be used as masks in bitwise operations, eg. int filter = FiscalPeriodTypeEnum.NORMAL FiscalPeriodTypeEnum.ADJUSTMENT; ... FiscalPeriodTypeEnum type = fiscalPeriod.getType(); if (type.getId() & filter) // do something interesting...
GetContainingFiscalCalendarHdl	`public abstract Handle getContainingFiscalCalendarHdl() throws SFException`	Returns the Handle to the FiscalCalendar of the containingFiscalCalendar of the FinancialCalendar
getCurrentPeriodHdl	`public abstract Handle getCurrentPeriodHdl() throws SFException`	Returns the Handle to the FiscalPeriod of the currentPeriod of the FinancialCalendar

Figure 22-9
(Cont'd)

GL. The basic abstractions here are a "Journal" that records transactions, a "Posting Combination", and a "Dissection," which is a pairing between a "Posting Combination" and an amount. See Chapter 26 for a complete discussion of these abstractions.

If a GL is installed in the system, then a `GenericGLController` will exist in the respective companies (i.e. at least in the current active company), and it will be used for recording transactions.

The main idea of this category is to provide means for doing the mapping between the application-specific domain to the GL. This is facilitated through the use of various keys. The focus of this category is the

GenericGLDissectionCreateCmd objects, which are processed to create a dissection in the GL. Different mappings are used to determine account types, analysis codes, and so on.

Invoicing

As implied by its name, this category is in charge of representing invoices. This category supports having different kinds of invoices, such as credit notes, sales orders, and so on. The invoices can be selected for processing manually, on review, or automatically by company-defined criteria. The selected invoices can be processed individually or grouped together and processed off-line.

The focus of this category is the Invoice interface. This interface is used to hold together a set of one or more InvoiceDetail objects that are to be invoiced to a specific financial partner. The Invoice object holds all the information required to invoice a specific Business Partner, and some information to generate the associated financial transactions.

The InvoiceDetail object can be used to hold a collection of InvoicingDetails (in most cases only one invoicing detail is used, but this flexibility can be used for some applications). The InvoicingDetail holds all the concrete data for the invoice.

The InvoiceController maintains the collection of invoices and is the entry point for generating new invoice objects. It includes a policy for determining new unique ids for invoices whose interface is DInvoiceIdGenerationPolicy. The controller also has an invoice generation policy, DInvoiceGenerationPolicy, which generates a set of invoices given the controller, a list of invoicing details, invoice date, and fiscal period (the latter two are optional).

TABLE 22-3

Different states of a FinancialBatch object

State	Meaning
INCOMPLETE	The FinancialBatch is incomplete
SUSPENDED	The FinancialBatch has been suspended
READY_FOR_POSTING	The FinancialBatch is ready for posting
POSTED	The FinancialBatch has been posted
LOCKED	The FinancialBatch has been locked

Having different types of invoices is supported through the `InvoicingTypeValue` object. The `InvoicingTypeController` object manages the set of invoicing types available.

CHAPTER 23

Generalized Mechanisms

In this chapter we look at a group of CBOs providing generalized mechanisms. These mechanisms are not directly related to business-related problems, but can help in solving them. The various CBOs described in this chapter are used throughout SanFrancisco for providing ease of use, ease of extension and, in the case of Cached Balances, also efficiency. Table 23-1 summarizes the list of categories in this layer, along with the major components in each of the categories. Note that Generalized Mechanisms CBOs are part of the CF package.

Keys

More often than not, applications need to manipulate information stored within an object based on specific characteristics. The identification of these characteristics can be either direct (like in the case of object attributes), or indirect, using some link or association.

TABLE 23-1

Summary of generalized mechanisms categories and their composition

Category	Major Components
Keys	DAccessKey DAccessKeyable DSpecificValueKeyable DSpecificationKey DSpecificationKeyable DKeyable
Caches Balances	DCachedBalance CachedBalanceSetD CachedBalanceSetCollection
Validation Results	DResultMessage DResultsCollectionD ReplacementText ValidationLevelEnum
Extensible Item	ExtensibleItem DExtension DExtensibleItemAdapter HierarchialExtensibleItem
Life Cycle	LifeCycle LifeCycleManagedItem LifeCycleController ConditionSetKeyedLifeCycle DLifeCycleManagedItemExtension DLifeCycleContionDefinition DLifeCycleConditionChangeResult

The idea of this category is to support the notion of a key in a manner that is independent from the way it is used. This is useful because while the logic of an application (i.e. how the data is used) is quite stable, the particular characteristics are usually more flexible, and the developer and the end-user might need to customize these according to changing needs.

A key encapsulates a particular set of characteristics and allows the key to be used without knowledge of the actual characteristics. The individual characteristics in the key are encapsulated in "*keyables*," allowing the key to work with the characteristics in an abstract way. This category includes two types of keys. The first, called an access key, is used to encapsulate a set of specific characteristics, and corresponds to the intuitive notion of a key. The other, called a specification key, is used to encapsulate a set of grouped access keys. The interfaces for these keys are shown in Figures 23-1 and 23-2.

Interface com.ibm.sf.cf.DAccessKey

public interface **DAccessKey** extends Dependent, DGenericAccessKey

Name	*Signature*	*Description*
getKeyableAt	`public abstract DAccessKeyable getKeyableAt(int position) throws SFException`	Gets a keyable; the positions for the Keyables start at 0.
getNumberOfKeyables	`public abstract int getNumberOfKeyables() throws SFException`	Returns the number of Keyables in the AccessKey.
setKeyableAt	`public abstract void setKeyableAt(DAccessKeyable keyable, int position) throws SFException`	Sets a keyable; the positions for the Keyables start at 0.
isCondensibleTo	`public abstract boolean isCondensibleTo(DGenericAccessKey key) throws SFException`	An AccessKey isCondensible to another AccessKey when the keyables in the same position are equal OR the target's keyable is a SpecificValueKeyable and the input is a NoValueNeededKeyable.
getKeyableArray	`public abstract DAccessKeyable[] getKeyableArray() throws SFException`	Gets a copy of the Keyable array
getKeyableArrayForRestrictedUse	`public abstract DAccessKeyable[] getKeyableArrayForRestrictedUse() throws SFException`	Returns the actual Keyable array

Figure 23-1
Interface DAccessKey

Interface com.ibm.sf.cf.DSpecificationKey

public interface **DSpecificationKey** extends Dependent, DGenericSpecificationKey

Name	*Signature*	*Description*
GetKeyableAt	`public abstract DSpecificationKeyable getKeyableAt(int position) throws SFException`	The positions for the Keyables start at 0.
getPositionsForKeyablesThatAreNotASubsetOf	`public abstract DSet getPositionsForKeyablesThatAreNotASubsetOf(DGenericSpecificationKey key) throws SFException`	This method returns a DSet that contains the positions of those Keyables in the target SpecificationKey that are not a subset of the corresponding Keyables in the passed-in SpecificationKey. If the SpecificationKey is a subset of the passed-in SpecificationKey, NULL is returned. For a detailed description of isSubsetOf see that method.
isComplete	`public abstract boolean isComplete() throws SFException`	Returns the Boolean flag complete, which indicates if this GenericSpecificationKey is complete. 'Complete' means that any collection mapped by AccessKeys associated with the SpecificationKey will contain all possible inputs.
getNumberOfKeyables	`public abstract int getNumberOfKeyables() throws SFException`	Returns the number of Keyables in the SpecificationKey.
setKeyableAt	`public abstract void setKeyableAt(DSpecificationKeyable keyable, int position) throws SFExceptionSets`	A keyable; the positions for the Keyables start at 0.
includesAccessKey	`public abstract int includesAccessKey(DGenericAccessKey key) throws SFException`	Determine if the AccessKey is included in the set of AccessKeys defined by the SpecificationKey, either exactly or as a set of more specific AccessKeys.
convertAccessKey	`public abstract DGenericAccessKey convertAccessKey(DGenericAccessKey key) throws SFException`	Converts the AccessKey into an AccessKey that can be used with this SpecificationKey. If it cannot be converted, NULL is returned.
isSubsetOf	`public abstract boolean isSubsetOf(DGenericSpecificationKey key) throws SFException`	Compares the two SpecificationKeys by simply calling isSubsetOf on all SpecificationKeyables in the same positions.
getKeyableArray	`public abstract DSpecificationKeyable[] getKeyableArray() throws SFException`	Gets a copy of the Keyable array
getKeyableArrayForRestrictedUse	`public abstract DSpecificationKeyable[] getKeyableArrayForRestrictedUse() throws SFException`	Returns the actual Keyable array, not intended for client use usually.
initialize	`public abstract void initialize(int numberOfKeyables, boolean complete, DSpecificationKeyable initialKeyable) throws SFException`	This method is invoked by the Factory after Construction of an instance of this class to ensure proper initialization

Figure 23-2
Interface `DSpecification Key`

Specification keys are used in the frameworks together with controllers and policies to build a highly flexible and extensible mechanism for retrieving attribute values. This category of keys supports a large variety of keyables, such as `DAnyEntityKeyable`, `DAnyDependentKeyable`, `DRangeKeyable`, etc.

An example for a use of this category is in the way mappings are built between different domains, such as from the Warehouse Management framework to General Ledger Analysis Groups and Analysis Codes (see Chapter 26 for more details on these notions).

Cached Balances

When using a business application, the need to repeatedly calculate values that involve collecting data from multiple objects is quite common. Such calculations often need to be performed quite frequently, and the results are required rapidly because these calculations are made in the context of an interactive session, i.e. a user is sitting across a screen waiting for the result. This category provides the means for caching some of the calculations and thus avoiding the need to perform tedious calculations from scratch.

The information to cache is kept in objects of type `DCachedBalance` (the interface for this class is shown in Figure 23-3); this is obviously application-specific. These objects are grouped together in `CachedBalanceSet` objects. Each of the `DCachedBalance` objects in the `CachedBalanceSet` is associated with a `GenericAccessKey` used for its retrieval. The interface for `CachedBalancedSet` is shown in Figure 23-4.

`CachedBalanceSet` objects are grouped together into `DCached BalancedSetCollection` objects (see Figure 23-5). This collection can retrieve a cached balance, or a `CachedBalanceSet` based on the key.

Validation Results

In many cases the different frameworks need to provide a way for validation logic to be implemented. Such validation logic is usually supposed to approve a certain set of items, and report back success or failure. This

Interface com.ibm.sf.cf.DCachedBalance

public interface **DCachedBalance** extends Dependent, CumulativeResult

Name	*Signature*	*Description*
addTo	`public abstract void addTo(DCachedBalance balanceToAdd) throws SFException`	Adds the parameter DCachedBalance to the current one.
isInitialValue	`public abstract boolean isInitialValue() throws SFException`	Returns TRUE if the DCachedBalance has the same value it would have if it was constructed with no parameters, otherwise FALSE is returned.

Figure 23-3
Interface `DCachedBalance`

category provides support for reporting back results of validation logic. Specifically, it provides the ability to collect validation failures together so that they can be returned all at the same time. This mechanism is used throughout the CBOs and Core Business Processes layers.

An individual result message from a validation check is represented by `DResultMessage`, which includes an error description, possibly along with some context that might help clarify the cause of the problem (this context can include Dependent objects, Strings, or Handles). These results are grouped together into `DResultsCollection` objects. In order to provide multilingual support for error messages, `DReplacementText` objects are used.

The class `ValidationLevelEnum` contains values that are used to indicate the level of validation to perform on a specific method call. Possible values are:

- NO_VALIDATION. No validation logic is to be performed
- SEVERE_ERRORS. Only validation logic relating to severe errors is to be performed
- ALL. Full validation logic (including warnings) is to be performed

Extensible Item

The Extensible Item category provides support for dynamic changes in the attributes and/or the behavior of an object. Ways are provided to

Interface com.ibm.sf.cf.CachedBalanceSet

public interface **CachedBalanceSet** extends DescribableDynamicEntity

Main Methods

Name	Signature	*Description*
updateCachedBalanceBy	`public abstract void updateCachedBalanceBy(DCachedBalance balanceToUpdateWith, DGenericAccessKey key) throws SFException`	This method is used to update a DCachedBalance in the CachedBalanceSet. The DGenericAccessKey key specifies what item is supposed to be updated and the DCachedBalance (balanceToUpdateWith) represents the value(s) to update with. The passed in balanceToUpdateWith value is added to the current one, if exists and will be replaced in the Map. If the DCachedBalance is the initialValue even after the balanceToUpdateWith was added, the DCachedBalance doesn't get added to the CachedBalanceSet, since initialValues aren't kept within the collection.
generateCachedBalanceFor	`public abstract DCachedBalance generateCachedBalanceFor(DGenericAccessKey key) throws SFException`	Return DCachedBalance for a converted DGenericAccessKey Assumptions: Convertion of the DGenericAccessKey must have been done before passing it in to this method.
removeCachedBalanceBy	`public abstract void removeCachedBalanceBy(DGenericAccessKey key) throws SFException`	Removes the DCachedBalance associated with the passed in DGenericAccessKey from the Map.
generateCondensedCachedBalanceFor	`public abstract DCachedBalance generateCondensedCachedBalanceFor(DGenericAccessKey key) throws SFException`	Create the DCachedBalance for the DGenericAccessKey by condensing the DCachedBalances for the DGenericAccessKeys which can be condensed to make the requested DCachedBalance.
generateCondensedCachedBalanceSetFor	`public abstract CachedBalanceSet generateCondensedCachedBalanceSetFor(DGenericSpecificationKey key) throws SFException`	Creates a new CachedBalanceSet from an already existing CachedBalanceSet by condensing the existing superset CachedBalanceSet into the new CachedBalanceSet. This means the requested CachedBalanceSet, has to be a subset of the related DGenericSpecificationKey of this CachedBalanceSet. When there isn't a superset available in the Map, an empty CachedBalanceSet is returned.
total	`public abstract DCachedBalance total() throws SFException`	This method simply adds all DCachedBalance Values of the CachedBalanceSet together and returns the result.
copy	`public abstract CachedBalanceSet copy(AccessMode accessMode, Handle location) throws SFException`	This method will return a new CachedBalanceSet that is a copy of the current CachedBalanceSet. It does three things: Copy the Map of cachedBalances item for item into a new Map; Copy the specificationKey; Copy the defaultCachedBalance

Figure 23-4
Interface `CachedBalanceSet`

createCachedBalanceIterator	`public abstract Iterator createCachedBalanceIterator() throws SFException`	Create Iterator for Collection of CachedBalances
getNextCachedBalance	`public abstract DCachedBalance getNextCachedBalance(Iterator position) throws SFException`	Gets the CachedBalance at the Next Iterator Position
containsCachedBalance	`public abstract boolean containsCachedBalance(DCachedBalance cachedbalance) throws SFException`	Checks if the CachedBalance exists in the Collection of CachedBalances
getCachedBalanceAt	`public abstract DCachedBalance getCachedBalanceAt(Iterator position) throws SFException`	Gets the CachedBalance at the current iterator position
queryCachedBalances	`public abstract Map queryCachedBalances(String selectStatement, String bindCollectionName, SelectCompare selectCompareObject, String bindNameOfSelectCompareObject, SortCompare orderByCompareObject, String bindNameOfOrderByObject, boolean accessResults) throws SFException`	Query the CachedBalance from the Collection
removeCachedBalanceAt	`public abstract void removeCachedBalanceAt(Iterator position) throws SFException`	Removes the CachedBalance at the Current Iterator Position
removeCachedBalance	`public abstract void removeCachedBalance(DCachedBalance cachedbalance) throws SFException`	Removes the specified CachedBalance
removeAllCachedBalances	`public abstract void removeAllCachedBalances() throws SFException`	Removes all CachedBalance from the Collection of CachedBalances
getCachedBalanceBy	`public abstract DCachedBalance getCachedBalanceBy(DGenericAccessKey key) throws SFException`	Returns the CachedBalance associated with the specified key
containsCachedBalanceKey	`public abstract boolean containsCachedBalanceKey(DGenericAccessKey key) throws SFException`	
getCachedBalanceKeyAt	`public abstract DGenericAccessKey getCachedBalanceKeyAt(Iterator position) throws SFException`	Returns the CachedBalanceKey at the current iterator position
getCachedBalanceKey	`public abstract DGenericAccessKey getCachedBalanceKey(DCachedBalance cachedBalance) throws SFException`	Returns the CachedBalance at the Current Iterator Position
getSpecificationKey	`public abstract DGenericSpecificationKey getSpecificationKey() throws SFException`	Returns SpecificationKey
getDefaultCachedBalance	`public abstract DCachedBalance getDefaultCachedBalance() throws SFException`	Returns DefaultCachedBalance

Figure 23-4
(Cont'd)

Interface com.ibm.sf.cf.DCachedBalanceSetCollection

public interface **DCachedBalanceSetCollection** extends Dependent

Name	*Signature*	*Description*
getCachedBalanceSetBy	`public abstract CachedBalanceSet getCachedBalanceSetBy(DGenericSpecificationKey theSpecificationKey) throws SFException`	This is a standard method returning the cached balance set given the key.
generateCachedBalanceSetFor	`public abstract CachedBalanceSet generateCachedBalanceSetFor(DGenericSpecificationKey theSpecificationKey) throws SFException`	Retrieve a CachedBalanceSet from the DCachedBalanceSetCollection. This may involve simply passing a copy of one CachedBalanceSet held by the CachedBalanceSetCollection, or condensing from a Superset of an already cached CachedBalanceSet, if possible. If it is impossible to condense the requested CachedBalanseSet from one of the existing CachedBalanceSets in the Map a NULL is returned.
updateCachedBalanceSetsBy	`public abstract void updateCachedBalanceSetsBy(DCachedBalance balanceToUpdateWith, DGenericAccessKey key) throws SFException`	Iterates over all elements in the contained CachedBalanceSets and calls updateCachedBalanceBy on each CachedBalanceSet.
generateCachedBalanceFor	`public abstract DCachedBalance generateCachedBalanceFor(DGenericAccessKey key) throws SFException`	Get a balance for a particular DGenericAccessKey by either retrieving it from a CachedBalanceSet that contains it or by condensing it from a CachedBalanceSet that is a superset of it. If the balance cannot be retrieved an exception is thrown.
createCachedBalanceSetIterator	`public abstract Iterator createCachedBalanceSetIterator() throws SFException`	This is a standard iterator creation method.
isEmpty	`public abstract boolean isEmpty() throws SFException`	This is a standard method, indicating if the collection is empty.
getNextCachedBalanceSet	`public abstract CachedBalanceSet getNextCachedBalanceSet(Iterator position) throws SFException`	This is a standard iteration method, returning the next element.
containsCachedBalanceSet	`public abstract boolean containsCachedBalanceSet(CachedBalanceSet cachedBalanceSet) throws SFException`	This method checks containment of a cached balance set.
getCachedBalanceSetAt	`public abstract CachedBalanceSet getCachedBalanceSetAt(Iterator position) throws SFException`	This is a standard retrieval method using an iterator.
removeOwnedCachedBalanceSetAt	`public abstract void removeOwnedCachedBalanceSetAt(Iterator position) throws SFException`	This is a standard removal method using an iterator.

Figure 23-5
Interface `DCachedBalancedSetCollection`

removeOwnedCachedBalanceSet	public abstract void removeOwnedCachedBalanceSet(CachedBalanceSet cachedBalanceSet) throws SFException	This is a standard removal method
removeAllOwnedCachedBalanceSets	public abstract void removeAllOwnedCachedBalanceSets() throws SFException	This is a standard removal method.
containsCachedBalanceSetKey	public abstract boolean containsCachedBalanceSetKey(DGenericSpecificationKey key) throws SFException	This is a standard containment testing method.
getCachedBalanceSetKeyAt	public abstract DGenericSpecificationKey getCachedBalanceSetKeyAt(Iterator position) throws SFException	This is a standard retrieval method.
getCachedBalanceSetKey	public abstract DGenericSpecificationKey getCachedBalanceSetKey(CachedBalanceSet cachedBalanceSet) throws SFException	This is a standard retrieval method for collections,
removeOwnedCachedBalanceSetBy	public abstract void removeOwnedCachedBalanceSetBy(DGenericSpecificationKey key) throws SFException	This is a standard removal method.
orphanOwnedCachedBalanceSetBy	public abstract void orphanOwnedCachedBalanceSetBy(DGenericSpecificationKey key) throws SFException	This is a standard set method for collections.
addOwnedCachedBalanceSet	public abstract void addOwnedCachedBalanceSet(CachedBalanceSet cachedBalanceSet) throws SFException	Retrieves the DGenericSpecificationKey from the passed in CachedBalanceSet and adds it to the Map.
getSpecificationKeyMap	public abstract DEntityOwningGenericSpecificationKeyMap getSpecificationKeyMap() throws SFException	Gets SpecificationKeyMap
getSpecificationKeyMapForRestrictedUse	public abstract DEntityOwningGenericSpecificationKeyMap getSpecificationKeyMapForRestrictedUse() throws SFException	Returns the actual SpecificationKeyMap. Not intended for client use, but rather for the framework to implement SetEqual().
initialize	public abstract void initialize(DEntityOwningGenericSpecificationKeyMap theSpecificationKeyMap) throws SFException	This method is invoked by the Factory after Construction of an instance of this class to ensure proper initialization

Figure 23-5
(Cont'd)

dynamically add, remove, or modify methods and/or attributes of a particular object. It is also possible to temporarily override a method. This is implemented by keeping a stack of the different versions of the method (with the same name) allowing only the top one to be used until it is removed, and the previous version gets back to be the one used.

The interface to ExtensibleItem is shown in Figure 23-6. Single operations and attributes added to the ExtensibleItem are represented by DExtension objects. Concrete instances of this type provide specific methods or operations. DExtension objects are associated with a DExtensibleItemAdapter object that is used for interfacing with the ExtensibleItem.

The best way to think of an ExtensibleItem is as an application-level implementation of a C++ or Java object with attributes and with methods. The methods are managed and invoked in a way that resembles virtual function tables.

A special variant of ExtensibleItem is provided in the form of HierarchialExtensibleItem. This variant supports placing extensible items in a tree-like hierarchy and then uses this tree to look for method implementations inside other items. The search for a method can be done either going up the tree (i.e. to ancestor nodes) or down the tree (to all the child objects).

Lifecycle

This category provides "lifecycle" support for objects in the application level. Certain entities in the business domain, such as orders, go through a set of states during their existence. The transition from one state to another is usually triggered by some external event, for example, someone confirming an order. The states through which an entity may go through and the events that cause these state changes can vary according to the specific application. In some cases these states and events can even vary from instance to instance. In abstract terms, the lifecycle of an entity is composed of a graph whose nodes are states and edges are acceptable state transitions, along with the events that trigger each state traversal.

The approach used in this category allows for flexibility in the definition and maintenance of the lifecycle of a business object. This is done by placing the lifecycle behavior into a separate, dynamically configurable object. Changes to lifecycle can be made independently of the object itself.

In the Core Business Processes, business entities with lifecycles are represented as LifeCycleManagedItem objects. Each LifeCycle ManagedItem (see Figure 23-7) is associated with a LifeCycle (see Figure 23-8) object that encapsulates the lifecycle of the associated

Interface com.ibm.sf.cf.ExtensibleItem

public interface **ExtensibleItem** extends DescribableDynamicEntity, Blockable

Main Methods

Name	*Signature*	*Description*
removeExtensionBy	`public abstract void removeExtensionBy(String id) throws SFException`	Deletes the DExtension with the passed id from the Extensible Item and remove its DMethodNodeBlockings from the DVFT. If the DExtension was at the beginning of the collection the primaryExtension will be set to the DExtension that is now at the beginning of the collection.
invokeMethod	`public abstract Object invokeMethod(String methodName, Object parameterList[]) throws SFException`	This function allows clients to request various methods to be processed by the Extensible Item. The Array paramterlist argument is ordered. Each Object (one for each argument for each method) must be added in the same order as the arguments for the signature of the method that will be called.
checkIfMethodSupported	`public abstract boolean checkIfMethodSupported(String methodName) throws SFException`	Returns TRUE if the method specified as a parameter is supported by the Extensible Item or one of its Extensions, otherwise FALSE.
getSupportedMethods	`public abstract DSet getSupportedMethods() throws SFException`	This method iterates through the DMap of MethodNodes, building a DSet of all the keys in the DMap to return to the client.
update	`public abstract boolean update(DExtension extensionDoingTheUpdate, Object updateObject) throws SFException`	Called to update the Extensions contained by this ExtensibleItem. If this method was called by an DExtension contained by the ExtensibleItem, that DExtension is passed as a parameter. If this method was called by the ExtensibleItem itself or by another client, the DExtension parameter is then passed as null. All Extensions other than the calling DExtension will be updated by the ExtensibleItem. Returns true if one or more Extensions used the passed update object, otherwise returns false. It is the responsibility of each DExtension to cast the updateObject to the expected class before use.
castTo	`public abstract Object castTo(String className) throws SFException`	Attempts to create an Adapter for the ExtensibleItem that can be used polymorphically as the specified class or interface. For the Adapter creation to succeed, at least one DExtension must implement or extend the given class or interface. If no DExtension supports the given class or interface, null is returned.
getPrimaryExtension	`public abstract DExtension getPrimaryExtension() throws SFException`	Returns a copy of the primary extension (possibly NULL).
getPrimaryExtension ForRestrictedUse	`public abstract DExtension getPrimaryExtensionForRestrictedUse() throws SFException`	Returns a reference to the actual contained primary extension

Figure 23-6
Interface `ExtensibleItem`

getPrimaryExtensionId	`public abstract String getPrimaryExtensionId() throws SFException`	Gets PrimaryExtensionId
getAdapters	`public abstract DList getAdapters() throws SFException`	Get a collection of all DExtensibleItemAdapters supported by this ExtensibleItem. Returns: DList of DExtensibleItemAdapter objects
getProcessOperationAdapters	`public abstract DList getProcessOperationAdapters() throws SFException`	Get a collection of all DProcessOperationAdapters supported by this ExtensibleItem. Returns: DList of DProcessOperationAdapter objects
containsExtensionKey	`public abstract boolean containsExtensionKey(String key) throws SFException`	Checks if the Extension exists by the specified Key
getMethodNodes	`public abstract DMap getMethodNodes() throws SFException`	Used during object initialization to retrieve the set of MethodNodes for this Blockable. Must be overridden by subclasses to create the correct set for the supported methods of the subclass. This method is invoked by Extensible Item and is not for general client use.

Figure 23-6
(Cont'd)

`LifeCycleManagedItem` objects. The Lifecycle managed item is an extensible item, with the state-transitions being supported by the lifecycle affecting the extensions on the Lifecycle managed item, which are of type `DLifeCycleManagedItemExtension`. The conditions for lifecycle state-transitions are maintained as `DLifeCycleDefinition` objects. When a change takes place, the effects are represented by a `DLifeCycleConditionChangedResult`. Lifecycle objects are managed using a `LifeCycleController` placed on the company.

Interface com.ibm.sf.cf.LifeCycleManagedItem

public interface **LifeCycleManagedItem** extends HierarchicalExtensibleItem

Main Methods

Name	*Signature*	*Description*
addConditionById	`public abstract void addConditionById(String conditionId) throws SFException`	Notify the associated LifeCycle of the adding of a conditionID. If the conditionId does not exist in the LCMI's (LifeCycle Management Item) associated LifeCycle's ConditionDefinition map, no action will be performed on the LCMI. If the conditionId is successfully mapped to a DLifeCycleConditionDefinition object, the handleConditionChange method on that object (see DLifeCycleConditionDefinition and subclass documentation) will be called passing this LCMI object.
getHighestAggregateState	`public abstract DLifeCycleManagedItemState getHighestAggregateState() throws SFException`	Return a DLifeCycleManagedItemState object representing highest weighted existing state of the aggregate LCMI tree consisting of this LCMI and all its child LCMIs.
getLowestAggregateState	`public abstract DLifeCycleManagedItemState getLowestAggregateState() throws SFException`	Return a DLifeCycleManagedItemState object representing lowest weighted existing state of the aggregate LCMI tree consisting of this LCMI and all its child LCMIs.
addExtension	`public abstract void addExtension(DLifeCycleManagedItemExtension extension) throws SFException`	Override of method from ExtensibleItem that makes sure that only DLifeCycleManagedItemExtensions may be added to an LCMI
externalAddConditionById	`public abstract void externalAddConditionById(String conditionId) throws SFException`	Method for clients of the LCMI to add a condition to the LCMI. Calls processConditionChange on the LifeCycle if applicable.
addConditionByIdUsingDrillUp	`public abstract void addConditionByIdUsingDrillUp(String conditionId) throws SFException`	A drillUp version of addConditionById that calls addConditionById on this LCMI and each ancestor LCMI. See addConditionById for additional information on adding conditions by Id to an LCMI.
setCurrentState	`public abstract void setCurrentState(DLifeCycleManagedItemState newState) throws SFException`	Set the current state of the LCMI. ConditionIds: cf.LifeCycleManagedItem.setCurrentState
externalAddConditionByIdUsingDrillUp	`public abstract void externalAddConditionByIdUsingDrillUp(String conditionId) throws SFException`	Method for clients of the LCMI to add a condition to the LCMI using drillUp. Calls processConditionChange on the LifeCycle if applicable.
invokeMethod	`public abstract Object invokeMethod(String methodName, Object parameterList[]) throws SFException`	Overridden to check for condition set changes after the specified method is completed and call processConditionChange on the associated LifeCycle if necessary.

Figure 23-7
Interface `LifeCycleManagedItem`.

connectToLifeCycle	`public abstract void connectToLifeCycle() throws SFException`	Method to connect this object to its LifeCycle. This method can only be called once on an LCMI and that LCMI must have been created as disconnected. This method triggers the initial processConditionChange to be called
updateUsingDrillUp	`public abstract boolean updateUsingDrillUp(DExtension extensionDoingTheUpdate, Object updateObject) throws SFException`	Overridden to internally use externalUpdateUsingDrillUp.
getLifeCycle	`public abstract LifeCycle getLifeCycle() throws SFException`	Returns the LifeCycle, copied from the Handle
getCurrentState	`public abstract DLifeCycleManagedItemState getCurrentState() throws SFException`	Gets CurrentState
getConditionsChanged	`public abstract boolean getConditionsChanged() throws SFException`	Gets working variable used by DConditionDefinition objects to indicate an actual change in the LCMI's condition set. ConditionsChanged is set to false at the beginning of the invokeMethod and update methods, then checked on completion of the methods to determine if a processConditionChange on the LifeCycle needs to be called.
setConditionsChanged	`public abstract void setConditionsChanged(boolean newConditionsChanged) throws SFException`	Set working variable used by DConditionDefinition objects to indicate an actual change in the LCMI's condition set. ConditionsChanged is set to false at the beginning of the invokeMethod and update methods, then checked on completion of the methods to determine if a processConditionChange on the LifeCycle needs to be called.
isConnected	`public abstract boolean isConnected() throws SFException`	Returns flag indicating whether the LCMI has been connected to a LifeCycle yet.
getLifeCycleHdl	`public abstract Handle getLifeCycleHdl() throws SFException`	Returns the Handle to the LifeCycle of the LifeCycle of the LifeCycleManagedItem

Figure 23-7
(Cont'd)

Interface com.ibm.sf.cf.LifeCycle

public interface **LifeCycle** extends DescribableDynamicEntity, Distinguishable

Main Methods

Name	Signature	Description
processConditionChange	`public abstract void processConditionChange(LifeCycleManagedItem theManagedItem) throws SFException`	This function is used by the LifeCycleManagedItem to notify the LifeCycle that a change in the LCMI's condition set has occurred. Upon invocation, this function uses the LifeCycleManagedItem's current list of Conditions as well as any other LCMI state that may be of interest to a specific LifeCycle subclass to select the appropriate LifeCycleConditionChangeResult to apply to the passed LCMI object. If a LifeCycleConditionChangeResult does not exist for the LCMI's current state, no change will be applied. This method is also used by the LifeCycleManagedItem during its initialize method to retrieve its initial set of Extensions and/or the initial method which is to be automatically invoked.
getId	`public abstract String getId() throws SFException`	Returns identifier for LifeCycle.
setId	`public abstract void setId(String newId) throws SFException`	Sets identifier for LifeCycle.
createLifeCycleConditionDefinitionIterator	`public abstract Iterator createLifeCycleConditionDefinitionIterator() throws SFException`	Create Iterator for Collection of LifeCycleConditionDefinitions
getNextLifeCycleConditionDefinition	`public abstract DLifeCycleConditionDefinition getNextLifeCycleConditionDefinition(Iterator position) throws SFException`	Gets the LifeCycleConditionDefinition at the Next Iterator Position
containsLifeCycleConditionDefinition	`public abstract boolean containsLifeCycleConditionDefinition(DLifeCycleConditionDefinition lifecycleconditiondefinition) throws SFException`	Checks if the LifeCycleConditionDefinition exists in the Collection of LifeCycleConditionDefinitions
getLifeCycleConditionDefinitionAt	`public abstract DLifeCycleConditionDefinition getLifeCycleConditionDefinitionAt(Iterator position) throws SFException`	Gets the LifeCycleConditionDefinition at the current iterator position
removeLifeCycleConditionDefinitionAt	`public abstract void removeLifeCycleConditionDefinitionAt(Iterator position) throws SFException`	Removes the LifeCycleConditionDefinition at the Current Iterator Position
removeLifeCycleConditionDefinition	`public abstract void removeLifeCycleConditionDefinition(DLifeCycleConditionDefinition lifecycleconditiondefinition) throws SFException`	Removes the specified LifeCycleConditionDefinition

Figure 23-8
Interface `LifeCycle`

removeAllLifeCycleConditionDefinitions	`public abstract void removeAllLifeCycleConditionDefinitions() throws SFException`	Removes all LifeCycleConditionDefinition from the Collection of LifeCycleConditionDefinitions
getLifeCycleConditionDefinitionBy	`public abstract DLifeCycleConditionDefinition getLifeCycleConditionDefinitionBy(String key) throws SFException`	Gets the LifeCycleConditionDefinition associated with the specified key
addLifeCycleConditionDefinitionBy	`public abstract void addLifeCycleConditionDefinitionBy(DLifeCycleConditionDefinition lifeCycleConditionDefinition, String key) throws SFException`	Add a DLifeCycleConditionDefinition to the LifeCycle keyed by the given id.
removeLifeCycleConditionDefinitionBy	`public abstract void removeLifeCycleConditionDefinitionBy(String key) throws SFException`	Removes the LifeCycleConditionDefinition by the specified key
containsLifeCycleConditionDefinitionKey	`public abstract boolean containsLifeCycleConditionDefinitionKey(String key) throws SFException`	Checks if the LifeCycleConditionDefinition exists by the specified key
getLifeCycleConditionDefinitionKeyAt	`public abstract String getLifeCycleConditionDefinitionKeyAt(Iterator position) throws SFException`	Gets the LifeCycleConditionDefinitionKey at the current iterator position
getLifeCycleConditionDefinitionKey	`public abstract String getLifeCycleConditionDefinitionKey(DLifeCycleConditionDefinition lifeCycleConditionDefinition) throws SFException`	Gets the LifeCycleConditionDefinition at the Current Iterator Position
containsCondition	`public abstract boolean containsCondition(String condition) throws SFException`	Check if a condition is defined in the LifeCycleConditionDefinition map of this lifecycle.

Figure 23-8
(Cont'd)

CHAPTER 24

Derivation in SanFrancisco

Even though the intention of SanFrancisco is to provide you with out-of-the box solutions for business applications, at times, some specific customization and tailoring is required. Such tailoring might be needed for specific user interfaces, country- and industry-specific requirements, business rules, competitive differentiators and any other specific application functions. The mechanism used to do that is derivation, or in other words exercising inheritance.

This chapter focuses on how to derive new domain classes from the SanFrancisco base classes. The first section describes other extension mechanisms that can be used instead of derivation.

Other Extension Mechanisms

Inheritance is the most common paradigm for extension in Java or any object-oriented programming language. SanFrancisco provides an arsenal of versatile extension methods that might allow you to avoid subclassing. These are provided in order to allow you to easily extend the various abstractions available in SanFrancisco as easily as possible. When subclassing, you have to put in some effort that does not directly serve the purpose of your code (e.g. defining the interface and then the implementation, or overriding specific base class methods), but rather, are formalities required by the language or the framework. Using the other extensions might prove to be easier.

Dynamic Properties

Many of the SanFrancisco CBOs are derived from `DynamicEntity` (e.g. `NaturalCalendar, Company`). `DynamicEntity` extends the `PropertyContainer` interface shown in Figure 24-1. Using this interface you are able to hold within each object a repository of properties that are not implemented as class variables, but rather as a generic collection of attributes managed at runtime. The advantage of this approach is that it is extremely flexible. For example, suppose that in a business you develop, applications for each company must have a legal advisor. You may implement this relationship using properties. In such a case, in order to retrieve the legal advisor, you use `getPropertBy()`.

Interface com.ibm.sf.gf.PropertyContainer

public interface **PropertyContainer**
extends AllowRemote

Name	*Signature*	*Description*
directlyContainsPropertyKey	`public abstract boolean directlyContainsPropertyKey(String propertyKey) throws SFException`	Predicate indicating if `propertyKey` is contained directly within this `PropertyContainer`. If this `PropertyContainer` is part of a chain of responsibility, the chain will not be searched.
getPropertyBy	`public abstract Object getPropertyBy(String propertyId) throws SFException`	Returns the first property found in the chain of responsibility with id matching `propertyId`.
getPropertyBy	`public abstract Object getPropertyBy(String propertyId, AccessMode am) throws SFException`	Returns the first property found in the chain of responsibility with id matching `propertyId`. If the property is an Entity the `AccessMode` provided is used, otherwise the `AccessMode` parameter is ignored.
getDirectlyContainedPropertyBy	`public abstract Object getDirectlyContainedPropertyBy(String propertyId) throws SFException`	Retrieve the first property found directly within this `PropertyContainer` with id matching `propertyId`. In case this `PropertyContainer` is part of a chain of responsibility, the chain will not be searched.
getDirectlyContainedPropertyBy	`public abstract Object getDirectlyContainedPropertyBy(String propertyId, AccessMode am) throws SFException`	Retrieve the property found directly within this `PropertyContainer` with id matching `propertyId`. If this `PropertyContainer` is part of a chain of responsibility the chain will not be searched. If the property is an `Entity`, the `AccessMode` provided, and otherwise the `AccessMode` parameter is ignored.
getPropertyHdlBy	`public abstract Handle getPropertyHdlBy(String propertyId) throws SFException`	Retrieve the first property found in the chain of responsibility with id matching `propertyId`. If it is an Entity property, return a copy of its Handle, otherwise throw a CollectionException.

Figure 24-1
`PropertyContainer` interface.

getDirectlyContainedPropertyHdlBy	`public abstract Handle getDirectlyContainedPropertyHdlBy(String propertyId) throws SFException`	Retrieve the first property found in this `PropertyContainer` with id matching `propertyId`. If it is an `Entity` property, a copy of a handle is returned. If not an `Entity`, a `CollectionException` is thrown. This method does no search a chain or responsibility if applicable.
getChainParent	`public abstract PropertyContainer getChainParent() throws SFException`	Retrieve the chain of responsibility parent for this `PropertyContainer`. If this object is a root of a chain, or if no chain exists, `null` is returned. The default implementation of this method is to return `null` (no parent), the method should be overriden by derived objects within a chain.

Figure 24-1
(Cont'd)

Usually property names are qualified to indicate their type. In our example if the legal advisor is represented by a law firm, you could call it "`cf.Company.Legaladvisor`". When this advisor needs to be accessed (e.g. you need to get its address in order to send a letter), then you would use code similar to that shown in Figure 24-2.

Note that property containers can implement the chain of responsibility pattern. This means that if the property container can't find a certain property it looks for it in a "parent" property container to which it is chained. This allows you to store company data in a hierarchical manner that implements "inheritance" of properties in your hierarchy.

Property containers can also be used for objects contained in other objects. For example, you may use properties of `Day` objects inside `NaturalCalendar` in order to record specific events (e.g. appointments) relating to this day.

```
Company myCompany = …
Company myLawAdvisor = (Company)
                myCompany.getPropertyBy("cf.Company.LegalAdvisor")
```

Figure 24-2
Example: using company properties.

Using ExtensibleItem

The `ExtensibleItem` object, described in the previous chapter, allows you to add extensions to an object each of which has dynamic methods attached to it, in addition to properties. This can be used to implement different behaviors of different instances without actually changing their Java type. It can also be used to create an extension used for different Business Objects without actually making their code depending on the extension.

For example, `Initials` is an `ExtensibleItem`, so you might have an extension of it for maintaining a salary attached to the Initials object. Then, using the `addInitialsExtension()` method of the `Initials` interface we can add such an extension to the object. So, to set the salary, we could use code similar to that shown in Figure 24-3. This kind of extension can provide more capabilities. For example, you might add a method "`GetNetSalary()`", which calculates the tax deductions and indicates the actual salary for payment. This method might use properties of the extension in order to determine applicable taxation rules. You can later change this object if the employee is deployed overseas and different taxation rules apply to him/her.

Using Policy Objects

Policy objects are used to implement the Strategy pattern mentioned in Chapter 12. Using these objects you can extend the functionality of a given class without actually changing it. This can be demonstrated with a simple example. Again, consider the `NaturalCalendar` described in Chapter 21. This CBO has a "date adjustment" policy giving you the capability to use only "working days." That is, given a date you can

```
Initials theInitials = •••
String args[] = { "100000" };
theInitials.invokeMethod("setSalary", args);
```

Figure 24-3
Using an initials extension.

"adjust," you either leave it as is if it refers to a working day, or change it to the first working day following it if it is not a working day. This is the default adjustment policy. You may wish to define your own adjustment policy. For example, say you have monthly reports you submit to some authority in your company, and the date for these reports varies (i.e. you submit the report on a different day each month). Consider a case where you want to take invoice dates and figure out in which the invoices are listed. Instead of implementing special time calculations, you can readily use the `NaturalCalendar`, and supply it with a new "date adjustment policy," which is derived from `DResultDate AdjustmentPolicy`.

Extension by Containment

One of the drawbacks of extension by derivation is the issue of maintaining compatibility. You need to making sure the subclass you design can be used by users of the original class without noticing the difference. If you just want to extend a class in order to gain some functionality it provides then you are actually better off using delegation (i.e. using containment of the class you want to use, and not subclassing it). The reason is that subclassing can slightly violate the encapsulation of the object you are extending. In general, using inheritance to model roles is considered to be bad design, or even an "Anti Pattern" (see for example, [Grand]). A common example of modeling roles that appear when using SanFrancisco is extending `BusinessPartners`. Say you want to implement a `GovernmentCustomer` with `BusinessPartner` functionality. Then, you can implement the `BusinessPartner` as an instance variable of `GovernmentCustomer`, and provide proper access to it through `get<>()` and `set<>()` methods.

Extension by Class Replacement

You can extend SanFrancisco classes simply by replacing them. This is not an extension in the classic sense, but sometimes it may prove useful. For example, if you have a working application in which a certain component is implemented in one way (e.g. `Employees`), and now you need to implement an identical system where the only difference relates to the `Employee` internal structure, you might consider class replacement.

Using class replacement for extending SanFrancisco Business Objects or Core Business Processes would usually prove to be a bad choice because you have to make a lot of effort to ensure compatibility; however, you may extend your own classes using this technique.

The Use of Derivation

This section explains how to use derivation in SanFrancisco.

Choosing the Right Base Class

The first dilemma you encounter when coming to design a new domain class, is what SanFrancisco base class to derive the class from. Basically, there are three major alternatives, all of which have been discussed at length in previous chapters.

- `Entity`. Used for Business Objects for which you need to have persistence, distribution, and so on.
- `Dependent`. For lightweight abstractions that are either non-persistent or contained in other Entity objects.
- `Command`. Encapsulations of algorithms or operations.

A new domain class should be derived from Entity in case one or more of the following conditions are met.

- The object has to be shared by more than one other object.
- The object must have a unique application-wide identity, or you need to be able to access this specific instance by its identity.
- The object must be able to persist independently of the existence of any other object.
- The object is very large.

The first three conditions are pretty straightforward and the motivation for including them is quite obvious based on the characteristics of `Entity`. In these cases, one would like to benefit from the services provided by the Foundation layer. The motivation for including the last condition is performance. `Dependents` tend to get copied relatively often (for example, when being passed as a parameter on a remote method call or when being stored in a persistent object), and repeatedly creating copies of very large objects is quite wasteful.

You derive a class from `Command` if you intend to use it to encapsulate the functionality of a business-related task or procedure. `Command` subclasses can be persistent, but usually are not.

What do you Need to Implement?

In order to implement a subclass of any kind of SanFrancisco business object requires the creation of the following components.

- Java interface source file
- Java class implementation source file
- Abstract Java class for the factory

Client programmers use the interfaces of business objects and the class factory. As previously discussed, the implementation class and the class factory have the same name as the interface with "`Impl`" and "`Factory`" suffixes, respectively.

The interface definition for the new subclass should extend the appropriate Foundation Layer interface: `Command`, `Dependent`, or `Entity`. The class definition for the new subclass must extend the appropriate Foundation Layer implementation class, corresponding to the interface used: `CommandImpl`, `DependentImpl`, or `EntityImpl`.

In order to illustrate the ideas of interface and class derivation, Figure 24-4 shows some of the inheritance relationships for the "House of Rooms" sample program.

Programming Model Considerations

When implementing a new business object, it is important to correctly implement it in accordance with the SanFrancisco object model.

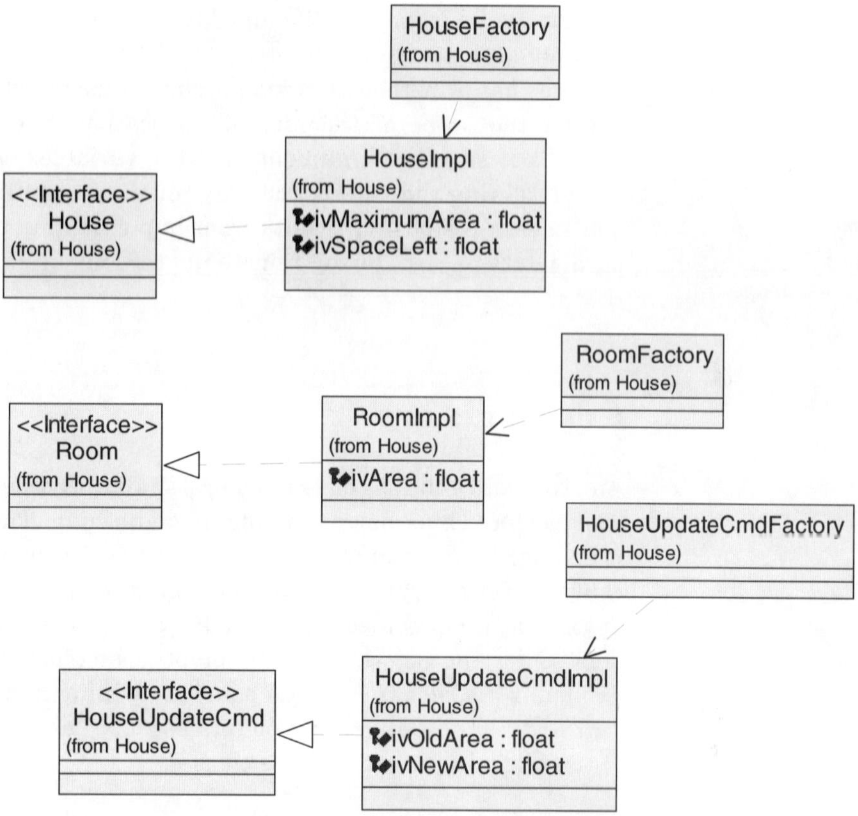

Figure 24-4 House of Rooms inheritance diagram.

Parameter Passing

Methods that are distributable, i.e. can be remotely invoked, must have all object argument treated as "`const`" or read-only input arguments. This is essential in order to facilitate transparency in remote access. In other words, Java objects passed by reference in calls to the method cannot be modified. Furthermore, if an object passed is a `Dependent`, no changes to the state of the objects should be made. If a modification of a `Dependent` argument is necessary, a copy of the object should be made inside the called method. Modifications to `Entity` object arguments are allowed, but the object reference itself cannot be changed.

These restrictions relating to parameter passing do not apply to private methods in an object because these methods are only called by an object on itself, meaning that there is no risk of remote invocation.

Private methods may modify any Java object reference arguments or the parameter object itself.

Note that a method receiving a parameter should not store an object beyond the scope of the method invocation. Specifically, the method should not save the argument in static variables or instance variables. If maintaining the value of the argument is essential, a copy should be made. This restriction results from implementation considerations (i.e. parameters passed during remote invocations are temporary in nature).

Constructors

Any concrete subclass of `Entity` or `Dependent` should contain an empty constructor. This constructor should do nothing. This empty constructor is invoked by the SanFrancisco Foundation during object creation, before calling `initialize()`. If no such constructor is explicitly defined, it is automatically provided by Java. However, if any other constructor is defined for the object, then the empty constructor has to be explicitly defined. Note that there is no point in defining non-default constructors for `Entity` and `Dependent` objects because "`new`" should never be used for creating instances of these classes.

Visibility Restrictions

All the methods included in the interface to a business object must be public. As you can imagine, it must include any method that may be called by another object. Even methods intended for use by subclasses have to be public and in the interface if method invocations that cross object boundaries are to take place. In the class implementation of a business object you may place as many `public`, `protected`, `private` or `package` methods as you need, as long as you remember to implement all the methods of the interface. Needless to say, the implementation also contains any necessary instance variables.

Attributes must not be declared `public`, because public access would allow bypassing proper locking and security support and would subject the object to the risk of becoming corrupted. Any visibility specification other than public is allowed for instance variables.

Limitations on Static Data and Methods

Although Java interfaces can include static data, SanFrancisco business objects cannot persist or distribute static data. Therefore, business objects usually do not contain any static state unless it is declared `final static`. If non-final static state is used in business object classes, some implementation difficulties can arise and you would be better off avoiding this.

Unlike static data, static methods cannot appear in Java interfaces. This means that static methods can appear in the realm of business objects only in the context of business object `Impl` classes, and then only for private implementation purposes. Static methods can be used on public, non-distributed objects. An example of such an object in the Foundation layer is `Global`.

Persistency Limitations

You should never store a transient object (i.e. `Handle`, `Dependent`, array, or `String`) inside a persistent Entity. Actually, this could only happen if the provided interfaces for creating contained `Handles`, `Dependent` and `Strings` are bypassed somehow, and will never happen if the provided interfaces are used for creating contained `Handles`, `Dependents`, and `Strings` (because a copy that has the same persistence as the containing object is stored).

Specifically, you must never use business object instance variables to store or cache data that is transient in nature. So for example, you should not store a Handle to a transient entity inside a persistent object.

Dependent and Entity subclasses can only contain data members (instance variables) that are primitive types, `Strings`, `Handles`, arrays, `Dependents`, or `Dependent` subclasses. In other words, plain Java object types (e.g. `Vector`) are not allowed as instance variables of `Dependents` or `Entities`. However, such objects can still be used as local variables or parameters in methods. The only restriction is that for objects passed as parameter to a remote method invocation, the `java.io.Serializable` interface should be supported.

A business object attribute can also be a single-dimensional array of `Handles`, `Dependents`, `Strings`, or primitive types. Mixing these types within the same array is not allowed.

Other Considerations

Refrain from using the Java `synchronized` keyword and capability on any `Dependent` or `Entity` subclass or method. The use of synchronized will interfere with the SanFrancisco locking and transaction support.

The `final` modifier should be used in situations where it is important to prevent subclassing, or overriding of methods. You should avoid using it for the purpose of gaining a performance boost because that isn't necessarily the case. A serious drawback of using the `final` modifier is that it might require recompilation of existing application code that uses it in cases where the implementation is changed. One of the most important differences between SanFrancisco client programming and Business Object development is the issue of object lifecycle management. Inside business objects, you need to create and delete `Dependent` objects and `Strings` contained in persistent objects. In client programming, such objects are always considered to be transient, hence they are easier to handle. Contained String and Dependent objects can be created during object initialization, and updated or re-created using `set<>()` methods. The `BaseFactory` provides an interface for creating persistent String objects, owned by the containing objects. This interface is provided through the `StringManagement` interface, described in Figure 24-5. Similarly, Dependent objects contained in the Entity should be created, copied, and deleted using the respective lifecycle methods (these are shown in Figure 15.2). Creation should not be done directly through the `BaseFactory`, but rather through a class factory that delegates this action to the `BaseFactory`.

Using Exceptions

SanFrancisco provides a hierarchy of exception objects. At the top of the SanFrancisco exception hierarchy is `SFException.` `SFException` supports the stack printout facilities provided with SanFrancisco through linkage methods and constructors that allow chaining exceptions (when re-throwing).

The SFException class resides in the `com.ibm.sf` package. Several exception subclasses are derived from it, such as `GFException` (from which all the exceptions defined by the base `gf` package are derived). Of course `GFException` has further subclasses for different logical

Interface com.ibm.sf.gf.StringManagement

public interface **StringManagement** extends AllowRemote
ClassName: StringManagement Factory interface for creating and deleting String objects.

Name	*Signature*	*Description*
deleteString	`public abstract void deleteString(Base containingObject, String stringToDelete) throws GFException, FactoryParameterRejectedException`	Delete the provided `String`; if it is transient or null, nothing is done. The `containingObject` must be a subclass of `Entity`, `Dependent` or null. If the containing `Object` is null, the specified String is assumed to be transient, otherwise the specified `String` is assumed to have the same scope (persistent or transient) as the `containingObject`. A NO_LOCK copy of an `Entity` is considered transient. The `containingObject` must be a local object this JVM
copyString	`public abstract String copyString(Base containingObject, String stringToCopy) throws GFException, FactoryParameterRejectedException`	Create a copy of the specified `String`, in the persistence scope specified by the `containingObject`. The `containingObject` must be a subclass of `Entity`, `Dependent` or `null`. If the `containingObject` is null, the created `String` is transient, otherwise the created `String` has the same scope (persistent or transient) as the `containingObject`. A NO_LOCK copy of an `Entity` is considered transient. The `containingObject` must be a local object in this JVM.

Figure 24-5
`StringManagement` interface.

groupings of exceptions, finally ending with the concrete exceptions that actually get thrown. All remote method calls could result in `SFRemoteException` being thrown. Runtime exceptions from remote method calls turn into `SFRemoteException`, but the original stack trace is lost. `SFException`, on the other hand, preserves the stack trace.

If you need to implement new exceptions, you should attempt to derive them from the existing ones. This way, you increase the chances of other pieces of SanFrancisco code being able to catch your exceptions.

Subclassing Entity

Previously, we indicated what elements should be defined in order to properly derive a SanFrancisco subclass. One of these components is the class factory. Every concrete subclass of Entity must provide an abstract factory class with create methods that have the signature shown in Figure 24-6. This figure shows create methods that are both loosely coupled and tightly coupled (see Chapter 15 for explanation relating to these create methods and the meaning of coupling). A new `Entity` subclass can implement either of these, or both, depending on its intended usage. The static create methods use the `BaseFactory` to create an uninitialized object, and then call the `initialize()` method on the new object. These static class methods replace constructors because constructors are never used for Entity objects. When creating an Entity subclass that might be used as a substitute for the parent class, the respective class factory must inherit from the class factory of the parent class.

In addition to abstract factories, sometimes you implement a concrete factory called a special factory that implements non-static create methods. A special factory is dynamically accessed at runtime using

```
public static final create<classname>(accessMode,
                    locationHdl, initParms...);
public abstract create(accessMode,
                     locationHdl, key, initParms...)
```

Loosely Coupled Create Methods

```
public static final create<classname>(owner,
                          accessMode, initParms...)
public static final create<classname>(owner,
                          accessMode, locationHdl, initParms...)
public abstract create(owner, access, locationHdl, key,
                          initParms...)
```

Tightly Coupled Create Methods

Figure 24-6
Static create method signatures for Entity subclasses.

the BaseFactory getSpecialFactory() method, and it allows you to dynamically bind your object creation method to the class token. Examples where this might be used include providing the correct key for putting an Entity in a legacy database and dynamically determining what locationHandle value to specify on the BaseFactory createEntity().

The class factories for Entities support the ability for a subclass to provide a special factory. If a special factory is configured for a class, this factory is used for creating the object.

When implementing your Entity subclass, you should provide its users get<>() and set<>() methods for accessing the object attributes (the latter should be omitted for read-only attributes). For primitive data types, Dependents and String objects, these are implemented in a straightforward manner—you only need to keep in mind that the latter two kinds of attributes are stored persistently in your Entity object, so you should create your own copies of the objects passed as parameter. For Entity attributes, you might need to implement get<>() and set<>() methods in a different variant indicating the ownership approach used—as described in Chapter 15 (e.g. getOwned<>()). Figure 24-7 shows the signatures for these variants.

If your object contains a collection, you should provide access methods to it, as shown in Figures 15-15 and 15-16 in Chapter 15. Similarly, if it contains an array, you should provide methods to access it, as shown in Figure 24.8.

If you want to hold a very large collection inside an Entity, then an EntityOwningExtent collection should be used. The interface to this kind of collection is shown in Figure 24-9. EntityOwningExtent collections support map-like semantics and are optimized for maintaining very large numbers of elements. This optimization is achieved by mapping the collection to a relational database, and also by having elements in such a collection created right into the extent (using a tightly coupled creation model). This implies that extent collections do not support any add, replace, or orphan methods. When creating an object into the EntityOwningExtent, the creation method calls the register Owned<> method of the collection and this method must be supported by each EntityOwningExtent (typically it does nothing, but it might do some validation checks).

EntityOwningExtents can be configured so that the rows of an existing database table are implicitly elements of the EntityOwningExtent. With all other collection types the only elements that are part of the collection are those objects that have been explicitly added to the

```
public <class > get<EntityName>() throws SFException;

public void set<EntityName>(<class> <entityName>)
   throws SFException

public void setOwned<EntityName>(<class> <entityName>)
   throws SFException;
public void orphanOwned<EntityName>(<class> <entityName>)
   throws SFException;

public Handle get<EntityName>Hdl()  throws SFException;
```

Getter Method

Setter for contained unowned Entity

Setter for contained owned Entity

Setter for contained owned Entity, if supported

Handle get method, usually not for client use

Figure 24-7
Getters and setters signatures for different ownership paradigms.

```
public <element class> get<Element name>At(int index) throws SFException;

public void set<Element name>At(<element class> element, int index) throws SFException;

public <element class or Handle>[] get<Element name>Array() throws SFException;
```

Figure 24-8
Signature of Access methods to a contained array.

Interface com.ibm.sf.gf.EntityOwningExtent

public interface **EntityOwningExtent** extends BaseExtent, EntityOwningRemoveCollectionIteration

Name	*Signature*	*Description*
removeOwnedElementBy	`public abstract void removeOwnedElementBy (DMethodAccessKey keyOfEntityToDelete) throws GFException`	Removes (and deletes) the first element identified by the key. An exception will be thrown if the `DMethodAccessKey` provided was not created with a `DMethodSpecificationKey` that has been added to this extent.
initialize	`public abstract void initialize (String elementClassName, Base containingObject) throws SFException`	Used only by static 'create' methods, initializes the object.
getSpecKeys	`public abstract DMap getSpecKeys() throws GFException`	Get a copy of the specification keys. This method is not intended for client use; instead, query and iterator should be used.

Figure 24-9
`EntityOwningExtent` interface.

collection. In such cases, all objects in the database table must use the same schema mapping definition (see Chapters 30–32 for discussion of schema mapping).

When searching an extent collection, the key used must be a `DMethodAccessKey` whose value is determined from method calls on the element as determined by the corresponding `DMethodSpecificationKey`. Arbitrary keys whose values do not come from the element cannot be used.

Furthermore, the extent collection must be told what keys will be used to access its elements. This is done by calling the `addSpecificationKey()` method on the extent collection. Key specifications can be removed using the `removeSpecificationKeyBy()` method on the extent collection. A `DMethodAccessKey` object is created from the same factory as the corresponding `DMethodSpecificationKey`. The `DMethodAccessKey` can be initialized with the values that match the element needed, and this key can then be used to get the element from the collection with the `get<...>By()` method. Keys for use with extent collections are implemented as a single class that supports both the `DMethodAccessKey` and `DMethodSpecificationKey` interfaces. Any concrete key used in an extent collection will have a single class factory that supports both `createDMethodAccessKey()` and `createDMethodSpecificationKey()` methods.

To summarize, Figure 24-10 shows the method signatures for methods of an extent collection subclass.

The EntityManagement interface, described in detail in Chapter 15, provides the `setDirty()` method. This method should be called by the developer on an Entity class before making any modifications to its state (including any contained Dependents). This method implicitly takes care of having a proper access (i.e. upgrading it if needed) of the Entity being modified. Although it is tempting to use this feature in order to bypass the need for explicit lock upgrades, you are strongly discouraged from doing so. Explicit requests makes your code easier to maintain and understand but, more importantly, minimizes the risk of running into deadlock.

When you call `setDirty()`, if the current access is NO_LOCK, OPTIMISTIC, or OPTIMISTIC_CLEAN, or if the object is transient, the object is marked dirty, but no access changes are made. Only if the object is not already marked dirty and the current access is exactly READ, with the `setDirty()` method attempt to upgrade the lock to a WRITE lock. If this cannot be done, an exception is thrown.

Note that if the object is not already marked dirty, but has no current access and is not a transient Entity, then it must be the case of mistakenly using a left-over reference to an Entity accessed in a previous transaction, and `setDirty()` will throw an exception. The `setDirty()` method is unaffected by what lock might be held on a containing object, or by what the static AccessMode methods like createPlusWrite() are set to.

There are some reasons why you should not rely on `setDirty()` implicitly upgrading from read to write access for you.

- If you know before you access an Entity that you need to update it, there is some performance advantage to getting write access right away rather than upgrading later, and avoiding the implicit upgrade reduces the chance of deadlock.
- You find out earlier and at a point under your control whether the lock you need is available (rather than not finding out until

Methods for Keyed Access

```
public <element class> get<Element name>By( DMethodAccessKey key)
throws SFException;

public <Class> get<Element name>By (DMethodAccessKey, AccessMode)
throws SFException;

public Iterator get<Element name>sBy (DMethodAccessKey) throws
SFException;

public Iterator get<Element name>sBy (DMethodAccessKey, AccessMode)
throws SFException;

public void registerOwned<Element name>(
               <element class> elementToRegister) throws SFException;

public void removeOwned<Element name>By(DMethodAccessKey key)
                                throws SFException;

public boolean contains<Element name>Key(DMethodAccessKey key)
                               throws SFException;
         public DMethodAccessKey get<Element name>Key(    <element
         class> element, String specificationId)    throws SFException;
```

Iterator access

```
public Iterator create<Element name>Iterator() throws SFException;

public <element class> getNext<Element name>(Iterator position) throws
SFException;

public void removeAllOwned<Element name>s() throws SFException;

public boolean contains<Element name>(<element class>
                      elementToFind) throws SFException;

public List query<Element name>s(
             String selectStatement,
             String bindCollectionName,
             SelectCompare selectCompareObject,
             String bindNameOfSelectCompareObject,
             SortCompare orderByCompareObject,
             String bindNameOfOrderByObject,
             boolean accessResults) throws SFException;

public abstract QueryCollection query<Element name>s(
             String selectStatement,
             String bindCollectionName,
             SelectCompare selectCompareObject,
             String bindNameOfSelectCompareObject,
             SortCompare orderByCompareObject,
             String bindNameOfOrderByObject,
             boolean accessResults,
             String hostVariableNames[],
             Object hostVariableValues[]) throws SFException;
```

Figure 24-10
Method signatures for `EntityOwningExtent` subclasses.

```
public abstract QueryCollection query<Element name>s(
             String selectStatement,
             String bindCollectionName,
             SelectCompare selectCompareObject,
             String bindNameOfSelectCompareObject,
             SortCompare orderByCompareObject,
             String bindNameOfOrderByObject,
             boolean accessResults,
             String specificationKeyId,
             String hostVariableNames[],
             Object hostVariableValues[]) throws SFException;
```

Optional Methods for Keyed Access

```
public void add<Element name>SpecificationKey(DMethodSpecificationKey
key) throws SFException;

public void remove<Element name>SpecificationKeyBy(String key) throws
SFException;
```

Methods for Iterator AccessIterator access

```
public <element class> get<Element name>At(
            Iterator position) throws SFException;

public DMethodAccessKey get<Element name>At(
            Iterator position, String specificationId) throws
        SFException;

public void removeOwned<Element name>(<element class>
            elementToRemove) throws SFException;

public void removeOwned<Element name>At(Iterator position)
   throws SFException
```

Figure 24-10
(Cont'd)

later in whichever code first calls `setDirty()` that the lock is not available).

- When you need write access to more than one object, you can use explicit locking of the objects in a particular order to reduce or eliminate the chance for deadlock (rather than having the order of the lock acquiring depend on the order of calling update methods on the objects).

Subclassing Dependent

As explained in Chapter 11, `Dependent` objects are used for implementing lightweight persistent objects that do not need to be shared by other objects. Specifically, `Dependent` objects can only be accessed or locked through the Entity containing them.

For each concrete subclass of `Dependent` you implement, you must provide an abstract class factory with static create methods as shown in Figure 24-11. For `Dependent` classes there are no special factories, hence all create methods must be static.

Similar to `Entity` objects, each subclass of dependent should provide an interface and also an implementation class. You usually override or define the methods shown in Figure 24-12.

Subclassing Command

As previously described in Chapter 11, `Commands` are used to encapsulate actions that are not considered an inherent part of any existing persistent object. Most `Commands` can be categorized either as commands that are used for user editing of object data (i.e. commands that are undoable) and commands that represent a business task. `Commands` are derived from `Dependent`, but are usually not persistent.

`Commands` can encapsulate a whole transaction, and they can also encapsulate other commands executing subtasks. Note that commands are not intended to generate any user interaction but rather to perform a task involving several Business Objects.

```
static final create<class name>(initParms...)

static final createContained<classname>(
        containingObject, initParms...)
```

Figure 24-11
Static create methods signature for Dependent class factory.

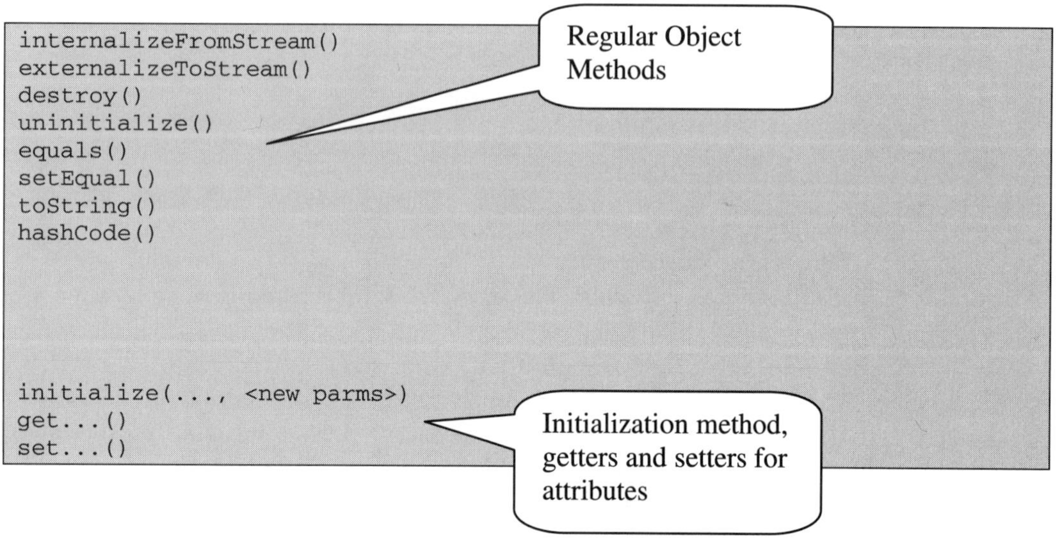

Figure 24-12
`Dependent` subclass methods.

New commands in SanFrancisco can be derived from the `Command` class. `Command` subclass names should follow the form `<noun><action verb>Cmd`, where the noun indicates the main target of the `Command` and the action verb describes its basic task. As `Commands` inherit from `Dependent`, they generally follow the same rules for those inherited methods. The factory class interface is a little different and is shown in Figure 24-13.

Every subclass of `Command`, whether concrete or abstract, has an interface and implementation class, similar to other SanFrancisco objects. Figure 24-14 shows the methods which can be overridden, and which methods should be added.

Don't Forget a Towel

The seemingly most appropriate way to conclude this chapter is to provide a checklist of common pitfalls in SanFrancisco object programming. This list is taken from the SanFrancisco Programmer's manual, and is shown in Cutout 24-1.

```
// Command Factory Creation Method signature
static final create<class name>(targetObject, initParms...)

// This additional method should implemented if the target is an Entity
static final create<class name>(targetHandle, initParms...)

static final createContained<class name>(containingObject,
   locationHdl, returnCommand, targetHandle, initParms)

// This additional method should be implemented if the target is a
Dependent
static final createContained<class name>(containingObject,
   locationHdl, returnCommand, targetObject, initParms)
```

Figure 24-13
Command class factory method signatures.

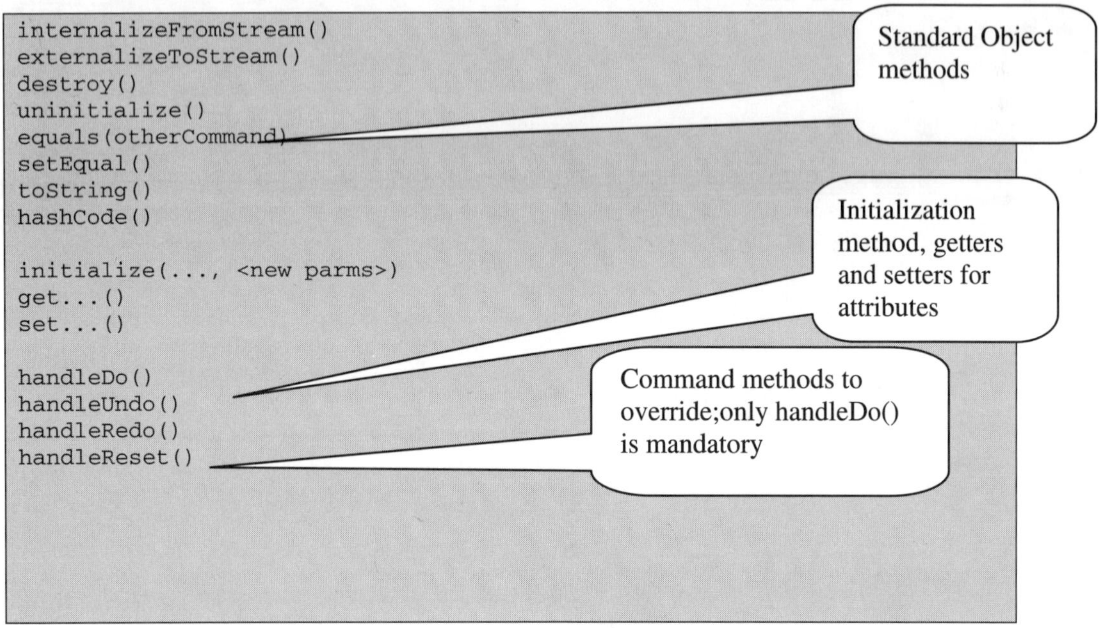

Figure 24-14
Command subclass methods.

Programming rules easy to overlook: If you fail to follow SanFrancisco programming rules, in many cases you will quickly get either a compile-time or runtime error that makes it easy to locate and correct the problem. However, some of the programming rules could be inadvertently violated without any immediate consequence, and in some cases might appear not to cause any immediate problem. However, your code may fail in a different environment (such as using a different kind of persistent storage, or when used with different code) or in the future (such as in a future release of SanFrancisco), or might cause a problem that is hard to detect or debug. There is no guarantee of what will happen if you fail to follow all of the programming rules. Here is a summary of such rules that may affect programmers who are creating new classes:

1. The code must not reference any persistent objects outside the scope of a transaction. This includes persistent Strings, Entities, Dependents, Handles, and arrays. References to persistent Entities and Strings are very common, since that is what is normally returned by get<>() methods. References to persistent Dependents and arrays are returned by get<>ForRestrictedUse() methods. References to persistent Handles are returned by get<>Hdl() methods. References to persistent Strings, Dependents, Handles, and arrays are also common as instance variables.
2. The code must not modify any object returned by any get<>ForRestrictedUse() or get<>Hdl() method.
3. The code must not store transient Handles (such as that returned by the getHandle() method) or any other transient object into an attribute of a persistent object. For example, you must not directly store what's returned from a get<>() method into your persistent attribute. Attempting this could cause the attribute to be persistent in some cases, or transient in others, or to cause an exception. Likewise, you must not use an instance variable as a cache for temporary results during method execution (use variables local to the method implementation instead).
4. The code must not use the transient modifier on business object attributes (transient attributes of a persistent object are not supported). Attempting this could cause the attribute to be persistent in some cases, or transient in others, or to cause an exception.
5. The code must not attempt to make an attribute of a business object transient by simply not externalizing or internalizing it (transient attributes of a persistent object are not supported). Attempting this could cause the attribute to be persistent in some cases, or transient in others, or to cause an exception.
6. The code must not store any object as a business object attribute which was not created through a factory or helper method call (directly or indirectly). In order to create a persistent object, you must supply a persistent containing object in the Factory or Helper method call. The Factory and Helper methods only support creating Handles, Strings, arrays, or instances of subclasses of Entity or Dependent. Therefore, you cannot store a non-SanFrancisco Java object (such as a Hashtable or Vector) as an attribute in a business object. Attempting this could cause the attribute to be persistent in some cases, or transient in others, or to cause an exception or other unpredictable behavior.
7. The code must specify the correct containing object. Many of the Factory and Helper methods take a containingObject parameter. The containing object is typically used to create a contained object in the same container as the containing object. Failure to do this could cause the object to be transient instead of persistent, or to have its persistent storage allocated incorrectly, or to cause an exception, or to cause container compatibility locking to work incorrectly.
8. When you are deleting a contained object (Handle, Dependent, String, or array), the referencing instance variable must be set to null unless the whole containing object is also being deleted. Failure to do so could cause the contained object to not get deleted.
9. The internalizeFromStream() and externalizeToStream() overrides must avoid directly or indirectly invoking any Factory or Helper methods. The internalizeFromStream() method must also avoid calling methods that validate attributes, because of cases where an object has been deleted so the

Cutout 24-1
Programming Rules Easy to Overlook, taken from the *IBM SanFrancisco Programmer's Manual*.

read<>() method returns a null or default value. Failure to do so may cause an exception or incorrect results.

10. The code must not use an Entity as an instance variable. To refer to another Entity, the instance variable must be a Handle, not the Entity itself. Failure to do so may cause loss of data, or an exception, or other unpredictable behavior.
11. Make sure that each Dependent subclass has an appropriate implemenation of hashCode().

Cutout 24-1
(Cont'd)

PART 5

Core Business Processes

CHAPTER 25

Using Core Business Processes

This chapter introduces the Core Business Process layer of SanFrancisco, and describes the role that the Core Business Processes play in SanFrancisco application development. In this chapter we only introduce the general concept of Core Business Processes and how they are used; the following chapters relate to specific instances of these processes.

What are Core Business Processes?

Core business processes are abstractions aimed at extracting useful building blocks that are common for a variety of business applications. SanFrancisco includes built-in support for several core business processes. More importantly, it is open to extension, i.e. allows developers to add their own business processes (either completely new or derived from existing ones) that may use SanFrancisco Common Business Objects.

In order to be useful, the Core Business Processes have to include some substance (i.e. code that actually does something), while being flexible. Flexibility is important in areas where different developers will have different needs because of the specifics of the business domain, local legislation and tax system, or just customer requirements.

As already discussed previously, the SanFrancisco Core Business processes are designed as object-oriented frameworks. A framework is a set of interacting and related classes that provide the basic architecture, design, and functions of a business domain. These functions can be extended to meet the specific requirements of an application. The Core Business Processes build upon the Common Business Objects layer (described in Chapters 21–23). Each Core Business Process adds new classes that are needed by the specific domain of this process.

How to Use Core Business Processes

So far, we have explained that the Core Business Processes are the topmost layer of SanFrancisco and that they are used to develop applications in a specific domain. The Core Business Processes provide domain-specific functionality in the form of an object-oriented framework. Using the Core Business Processes consists of determining what your application will do, mapping this function to what is provided by the Core Business Processes, and then determining where there are gaps that you have to fill with your own externsions to the Core Business Processes. Once you pinpoint these gaps, you can decide how to fill them.

Like in many other situations, when mapping a specific problem to the Core Business Processes, there are three possible outcomes: the good, the bad, and the frequent one (which is neither that good nor that bad).

- *One of the Core Business Process matches the functionality required for your application.* In this case, you can just go ahead and use what is implemented in the Core Business Process.
- *None of the Core Business Process have the functionality needed by your application.* Too bad! In this case, your application will have to be implemented by using the Common Business Objects, and the Foundation layer, possibly combining it with your own classes. You may still use some of the classes that are part of the Common Business Processes.
- *The Core Business Process gives you what you want, but you don't have a perfect fit.* In this case, you need to look for extension points in the Core Business Process. Extensions points are places where the architecture for the Core Business Processes has been made easy to change. For example, places where volatile logic was put into a separate object so that it is easy to replace.

Core Business Processes Lineup

The following Core Business Processes are part of SanFrancisco, and they are described in the following chapters:

- *General Ledger*. Deals with issues of cashflow (money) in the enterprise
- *Accounts Receivable/Accounts Payable*. Deals with representing the level of indebtness between the enterprise and its business partners.

- *Warehouse Management*. Deals with tracking stocks of goods stored in warehouses.
- *Order Management*. Deals with issues of order-processing.

CHAPTER 26

The General Ledger Framework

In this chapter we will explore the details of the General Ledger (GL) framework. The main purpose of the General Ledger is to keep record of the flow of money in a company. The General Ledger offers a standard approach for performing accounting.

General Ledger Business Objects

This section describes the Business Objects introduced by the GL framework for representing accounting information. Such information is organized into accounts that are grouped together into a chart of accounts: a single account group together with a set of related transactions (business transactions, not transactions internal to your applications). You can customize the chart of accounts according to the specifics of the business for which your application is designed for, specially tailoring the kind of information that should be recorded in accounts. The specifics of the chart of account vary between companies and are heavily dependent on local regulations and tax laws. Thus, the framework focuses on providing the correct structures that will allow any such composition to be built as opposed to trying to provide a very specific solution.

In order to be able to provide a useful abstraction that can support all these different needs the GL introduces the concept of a Posting Combination. The Posting Combination represents various ways to relate transactions. Mostly you can think of it as an account because it usually defines the internal organization of an account. In a typical application, a Posting Combination is indeed used to represent an account. Internally, this account can be broken down into smaller pieces—for example based on department and process. Similarly, the Posting Combination is divided into Analysis Groups. An Analysis Group names a particular piece of the Posting Combination and controls the valid values (e.g. expense, project, department), called Analysis Codes, which can go into that piece. The Analysis Codes used are specific to the application. Using the notion of application-specific Analysis Codes, you can customize the framework to your own needs.

The SanFrancisco General Ledger framework provides a flexible way of managing different kinds of accounts like P&L (profit and loss) accounts (recording revenues and expenses that should be part of the P&L statement) and balance accounts (recording assets vs liabilities).

General Ledger Processes

Day-to-Day Activities

One category of processes is routine day-to-day activities related to transactions. A transaction, in GL terms, consists of a number of pairings of an account (i.e. Posting Combination) with an amount for a particular time period. Under normal circumstances, the transaction will balance. For example, when you pay some supplier for goods, you would record a debit in your "Acquisition" account (or a similar account) and a credit in your Bank account. The General Ledger provides the abstraction called `Dissection`, which represents the pairing of a Posting Combination with an amount. Several Dissections together are called a `Journal`. The `Journal` corresponds to the intuitive notion of a business transaction. The fact that the GL provides abstractions for each of these concepts and the relationships between them allows for many differing implementations to be provided.

The `Dissection` keeps the amount using the `TransactionValue`. The `TransactionValue` captures both the prime value (the value denominated in the currency in which the transaction is carried out) and the base value (the value in the currency in which the whole General Ledger is kept) of the transaction amount. For example, if a US-based company buys something in France, the prime value is denominated in French francs (or maybe in Euros) and the base value in US dollars. You can make things a little more complicated by assigning your `Dissection` objects with quantities. This is done by associating `DQuantityDissections` with it.

In a specific application you would have rules that distinguish a valid Journal from an invalid one. For example, you might require certain types of Dissections to have amounts or certain restrictions on the how the group of Dissections looks like. The framework allows you to customize this notion of what constitutes a valid Journal using specific policy objects.

In the same way, you have policies that define when a Journal can be classified as final. Again, this is quite application-specific because in some countries you would want to be able to modify the `Journal` information until you actually report it to the government tax authorities.

In summary, what happens in day-to-day activities is that Journals are created; during their lifetime, `Dissections` and `DQuantity Dissections` are added to, and removed from them, until they are valid. Finally, the Journal is posted and becomes final.

Periodic Activities

Another category of processes that take place in the GL are periodical activities. These activities usually correspond to fiscal periods. The most common periodical activity is report generation. Once a period is closed, or the fiscal year is over, you need to perform certain activities that typically include:

- Closing certain accounts
- Reconciliation
- Adjustments to correct mismatches in balancing accounts
- Dealing with currency revaluation

These tasks are again quite specific to the accounting practices used in a company (usually influenced by tax legislation). Hence, the GL provides a basic definition of these processes designed in an extensible manner so that you tailor the way they are executed and the times they are executed at, to the needs of your application. Another issue is the generation of reports required for reviewing the corporate performance by its owners (or shareholders), managers, and the tax authorities. The two main kinds of reports are:

- P&L (profit and loss) statement, showing income versus expenses
- Balance sheet, showing assets and liabilities.

Although these report types are common and exist across different domains, hardly any two companies produce the same form of reports. For this reason the GL framework provides you with a flexible way of retrieving information needed for producing reports. However, it does not include any default reports because reports are so specific to the company; this is an example in which divergence is so common that it doesn't even make sense to create a default implementation.

General Ledger Framework Categories

Similar to the different CBO groups, the General Ledger is divided into several categories. Each category groups together a certain set of processes and the interfaces and classes implementing them. Following is a short description of each category. The list of major components included in each category is shown in Table 26-1.

Most of the categories below have a specific "setup command" (e.g. `GLJournalsSetupCmd` for the "Journal" category). These commands are responsible for performing the setup operations for the appropriate category. This includes creating the necessary controllers and policies. In most applications the commands are replaced by specific commands, which perform application-specific setup.

Most of the categories have various "adapter" objects included (e.g. the `GenericAnalysisCodeAdapter` in the Posting Combinations category). These adapters form the glue connecting the GL classes (`AnalysisCode` in this case) and the Generic classes provided in the CFFI package (`GenericAnalysisCode` in this case). The CFFI package, described in Chapter 22, provides an interface (or "developer contract" if you will) that is used to hide the details of the GL. The various adapters do the work of bi-directional translation between the "Generic" terms and types to the actual GL terms and types.

Posting Combinations

This category implements the process for defining and working with the chart of accounts. It includes the account definition and specification of validation criteria. The main abstractions in this category are `PostingCombination` (see Figure 26-1), `AnalysisCode` (see Figure 26-2), and `AnalysisGroup` (see Figure 26-3). These abstractions and the way they are used are described earlier. The validation criteria for the various components of the chart of accounts are provided through policy objects.

Journal

This category defines and implements the concept of a transaction. It takes care of the whole lifecycle of a `Journal` object, including creation, maintenance, and finalization. `Dissection` objects (interface shown in Figure 26-4) are used to build a `Journal` object. As discussed above, this category includes support for both value and quantity through the `DQuantityDissection`. Also, it is possible to conduct transactions in

TABLE 26-1
Summary of General Ledger Categories and their composition

Category	Component
Posting Combinations	PostingCombination
	AnalysisCode
	AnalysisCodeSpecifier
	AnalysisCodeSubset
	AnalysisGroupAnalysisGroupCodeController
	AccountTypeValue
	ChartOfAccountAttributes
	ChartOfAccountAttributesUpdateCmd
	ChartOfAccountAttributesValidationAttributes
	ChartOfAccounts
	DAnalysisCodeSet
	DAnalysisCodeSpecifierSet
	GenericAnalysisCodeAdapter
	GenericAnalysisGroupAdapter
	GenericChartOfAccountsAdapter
	GenericPostingCombinationAdapter
	DChartOfAccountAttributesValidationPolicy
	DGenericAnalysisCodeSetAdapter
	DAnalysisGroupCodeAccessKeyable
	DAnalysisGroupCodeSpecificationKeyable
	DAnalysisSuspensePCombUsageValidationPolicy
	DPostingCombinationUsageValidationPolicy
	DPostingCombinationValidationPolicy
Journal	GLJournal
	GLJournalAddToBatchCmd
	GLJournalDissectionController
	GLJournalQueryCmd
	GLJournalRemoveFromBatchCmd
	GLJournalSpreadCmd
	GLJournalSubbatch
	Dissection
	DQuantityDissection
	DissectionSpreadInformation
	DissectionsForBalanceAccessKeyQueryCmd
	DissectionsForBalanceDirectoryQueryCmd
	DissectionsForBalanceSpecificationKeyQueryCmd
	GenericGLJournalAdapter
	GenericGLJournalAddToBatchCmdAdapter
	GenericDissectionAdapter
	GenericQuantityDissectionAdapter
	GenericGLJournalControllerAdapter
	GenericGLJournalQueryCmdAdapter
	GenericGLJournalRemoveFromBatchCmdAdapter
	DDissectionBalanceValueUpdate
	DDissectionConsolidationKey
	DDissectionConsolidationPolicy
	DDissectionConsolidationPolicyDefault

TABLE 26-1
(cont'd)

Category	Component
	DDissectionMethodKeyJournalAndDissectionId
	DDissectionSpreadInformationDetail
	DDissectionSpreadInformationValidationPolicy
	DDissectionValidationPolicy
	DGLJournalBookingPolicy
	DGLJournalIdGenerationPolicy
	DGLJournalSubbatchHandlingPolicy
	DGLJournalValidationPolicy
	DGLSpreadJournalAnalysisParameters
	DGLSpreadJournalFiscalParameters
	DGLSpreadJournalMemoParameters
	DGLSpreadJournalParameters
Banks	BankStatement
	BankStatementController
	BankToBankTransfer
	BankTransaction
	BankTransactionController
	DBankStatementIdGenerationPolicy
	DBankStatementValidationPolicy
	DBankToBankTransferIdGenerationPolicy
	DBankTransactionIdGenerationPolicy
	StatementLineReconciliationEvent
	ReconciliationEventController
	GenericBankTransactionAdapter
	GenericBankTransactionControllerAdapter
Closing	GLClosingCmd
	GLClosingParameters
Balances	DBalanceValues
	DBalanceValuesForDissections
	BalanceDirectory
	BalanceType
	DBaseOnlyBalances
	DPrimeAndBaseBalances
	DPrimeOnlyBalances
	DBalanceValuesForQuantityDissections
	DQuantityBalances
	DGLBalanceAccessKey
	DGLCachedBalancesBookingPolicy
	GLBalanceTypeController
	GLCachedBalances
GL Financial Calendar	GLFiscalCalendarSetupCmd
Budgets	BudgetProfile
	BudgetProfileController
Revaluation	DCurrencyRevaluation
	DRevaluationInformation

Interface com.ibm.sf.gl.PostingCombination

public interface **PostingCombination** extends GenericPostingCombinationAdapter

Main Methods

Name	*Signature*	*Description*
isAnalysisCodeUsed	`public abstract boolean isAnalysisCodeUsed(AnalysisCode analysisCode) throws SFException`	Checks if the specified AnalysisCode is contained in the PostingCombination's DAnalysisCodeSet.
isUnitOfMeasureLegal	`public abstract boolean isUnitOfMeasureLegal(UnitOfMeasure unitOfMeasure) throws SFException`	Determine if the specified UnitOfMeasure is legal for this PostingCombination.
isPostInhibited	`public abstract boolean isPostInhibited(int creationCode) throws SFException`	Determines if the PostingCombination's associated ChartOfAccountAttributes is post-inhibited with regard to the GenericCreationCodeEnum. If it is AUTOMATIC, then check for System-post inhibited. If it is MANUAL, then check for Manual-post inhibitted.
isMemoAccount	`public abstract boolean isMemoAccount() throws SFException`	Checks if the associated ChartOfAccountAttributes is a memo Account
getDesignatedCurrency	`public abstract Currency getDesignatedCurrency() throws SFException`	Returns the designated currency of the ChartOfAccountAttributes associated with this PostingCombination

	`public abstract PostingCombination instantiate(AccessMode accessMode, int creationCode) throws SFException`
	
	`public abstract PostingCombination instantiate(AccessMode accessMode, int creationCode, DPostingCombinationValidationPolicy postingCombinationValidationPolicy) throws SFException`
	
	`public abstract PostingCombination instantiate(AccessMode accessMode, int creationCode, Handle locationHandle) throws SFException`
	
	`public abstract PostingCombination instantiate(AccessMode accessMode, int creationCode,`
		Create a posting combination use at the active company, using the set of AnalysisCodes from the specified PostingCombination. This instantiate method should be used when a PostingCombination defined at one Company level is to be used in a different Company, e.g. Cross Company Journals or PostingCombinations setup for a Designated Purpose. If a PostingCombination already exists with the set of AnalysisCodes of the specified PostingCombination, it will be returned, otherwise a new PostingCombination is created and associated with a ChartOfAccountAttributes. The validate method will be called on the new PostingCombination using the default validation policy. If validation fails, the PostingCombination will not be created and an exception will be thrown.

Figure 26-1
Interface `PostingCombination`

	DPostingCombinationValidationPolicy postingCombinationValidationPolicy, Handle locationHandle) throws SFException	
isAnalysisAccount	public abstract boolean isAnalysisAccount() throws SFException	Checks if the associated ChartOfAccountAttributes is an analysis Account
isProfitAndLossAccount	public abstract boolean isProfitAndLossAccount() throws SFException	Checks if the associated ChartOfAccountAttributes is a profit and loss Account
isBalanceSheetAccount	public abstract boolean isBalanceSheetAccount() throws SFException	Checks if the associated ChartOfAccountAttributes is a balance sheet Account
isIncludedInCurrencyRevaluation	public abstract boolean isIncludedInCurrencyRevaluation() throws SFException	Checks if the associated ChartOfAccountAttributes is included in currency revaluation
getBalanceSheetProfitAndLossEnum	public abstract int getBalanceSheetProfitAndLossEnum() throws SFException	Returns the value of the balance sheet profit and loss of the associated ChartOfAccountAttributes
isAllowedToBeConsolidated	public abstract boolean isAllowedToBeConsolidated() throws SFException	Checks if the associated ChartOfAccountAttributes is allowed to be consolidated
getAccountTypeValue	public abstract AccountTypeValue getAccountTypeValue() throws SFException	Returns the AccountTypeValue of the ChartOfAccountAttributes associated with this PostingCombination
isFiscalAccount	public abstract boolean isFiscalAccount() throws SFException	Checks if the associated ChartOfAccountAttributes is a fiscal Account. It is deemed to be a fiscal account if it is not a memo account and not an Analysis Type
validate	public abstract DResultsCollection validate(int creationCode) throws SFException	Validate this PostingCombination. The default DPostingCombinationValidationPolicy will be used
validate	public abstract DResultsCollection validate(int creationCode, DPostingCombinationValidationPolicy validationPolicy) throws SFException	Validate this PostingCombination. The specified DPostingCombinationValidationPolicy will be used.
usageValidate	public abstract DResultsCollection usageValidate(DPostingCombinationUsageValidationPolicy validationPolicy) throws SFException	Validate this PostingCombination for its designated usage. The specified DPostingCombinationUsageValidationPolicy will be used.
getInstanceId	public abstract String getInstanceId() throws SFException	Returns the instance Id of the PostingCombination to be used in ResultMessages
isControlAccount	public abstract boolean isControlAccount() throws SFException	Checks if the PostingCombination is a Control Account
isUseBaseCurrencyOnly	public abstract boolean isUseBaseCurrencyOnly() throws SFException	Checks if the associated ChartOfAccountAttributes is to use Base Currency Only
getAnalysisCodeBy	public abstract AnalysisCode getAnalysisCodeBy(AnalysisGroup analysisGroup) throws SFException	Gets the AnalysisCode of the specified AnalysisGroup within this PostingCombination.

Figure 26-1
(Cont'd)

getChartOfAccountAttributes	`public abstract ChartOfAccountAttributes getChartOfAccountAttributes() throws SFException`	Returns the ChartOfAccountAttributes, copied from the Handle
getAnalysisCodeSet	`public abstract DAnalysisCodeSet getAnalysisCodeSet() throws SFException`	Gets AnalysisCodeSet
getCompany	`public abstract Company getCompany() throws SFException`	Returns the Company, copied from the Handle
getChartOfAccountAttributesHdl	`public abstract Handle getChartOfAccountAttributesHdl() throws SFException`	Returns the Handle to the ChartOfAccountAttributes of the ChartOfAccountAttributes of the PostingCombination
getCompanyHdl	`public abstract Handle getCompanyHdl() throws SFException`	Returns the Handle to the Company of the Company of the PostingCombination

Figure 26-1
(Cont'd)

a currency different from the base currency in the General Ledger. Using policy objects, it is possible to refine the notions of a valid transaction and a final transaction.

Balances

This category takes care of managing balances. Balances are implemented using the `CachedBalances` mechanism (explained in Chapter 23), which is part of the CBO layer. The facilities provided by this category are used for creating balance inquiries and reports. It is possible to define category criteria according to which balances are created and maintained. Such criteria could be a specific currency, type of account, or fiscal period. Cached values are represented by `DBalanceValue` objects. Two flavors of this type are provided—one for Dissections and one for `QuantityDissections`. Caching is managed by a `GLCachedBalances` object held as a property of the GL `JournalDissectionController`.

Interface com.ibm.sf.gl.AnalysisGroup

public interface **AnalysisGroup** extends GenericAnalysisGroupAdapter

Name	*Signature*	*Description*
compareSequence	`public abstract int compareSequence(AnalysisGroup analysisGroup) throws SFException`	Compare the specified AnalysisGroup with this one.
getAnalysisCodeSubsetBy	`public abstract AnalysisCodeSubset getAnalysisCodeSubsetBy(String key) throws SFException`	Gets the AnalysisCodeSubset. Warning: The current active company must be the same as that in effect when the AnalysisGroup (and its corresponding ChartOfAccounts) was retrieved. Otherwise, unpredicatable results may occur.
containsAnalysisCodeSubsetKey	`public abstract boolean containsAnalysisCodeSubsetKey (String key) throws SFException`	Checks if the AnalysisCodeSubset exists by the specified Key. Warning: The current active company must be the same as that in effect when the AnalysisGroup (and its corresponding ChartOfAccounts) was retrieved. Otherwise, unpredicatable results may occur.
queryOwnedAnalysisCodeSubsets	`public abstract QueryCollection queryOwnedAnalysisCodeSubsets (String selectStatement, String bindCollectionName, SelectCompare selectCompareObject, String bindNameOfSelectCompareObject , SortCompare orderByCompareObject, String bindNameOfOrderByObject, boolean accessResults) throws SFException`	Select the AnalysisCodeSubsets Satisfying the Query. Warning: The current active company must be the same as that in effect when the AnalysisGroup (and its corresponding ChartOfAccounts) was retrieved. Otherwise, unpredicatable results may occur.
getOwnedAnalysisCodeSubsets	`public abstract QueryCollection getOwnedAnalysisCodeSubsets() throws SFException`	Retrieves a logical copy of the collection of all object instances held by this controller. Warning: The current active company must be the same as that in effect when the AnalysisGroup (and its corresponding ChartOfAccounts) was retrieved. Otherwise, unpredicatable results may occur.
getDirectlyOwnedAnalysisCodeSubsetBy	`public abstract AnalysisCodeSubset getDirectlyOwnedAnalysisCodeSubsetBy(String key) throws SFException`	Returns the AnalysisCodeSubset in this AnalysisGroup. Warning: The current active company must be the same as that in effect when the AnalysisGroup (and its corresponding ChartOfAccounts) was retrieved. Otherwise, unpredicatable results may occur.
queryDirectlyOwnedAnalysisCodeSubsets	`public abstract QueryCollection queryDirectlyOwnedAnalysisCodeSubsets(String selectStatement, String bindCollectionName, SelectCompare selectCompareObject, String bindNameOfSelectCompareObject , SortCompare orderByCompareObject, String bindNameOfOrderByObject, boolean accessResults) throws SFException`	Select the AnalysisCodeSubsets Satisfying the Query. Note that the current active company must be the same as that in effect when the AnalysisGroup (and its corresponding ChartOfAccounts) was retrieved. Otherwise, unpredicatable results may occur.

Figure 26-2
Interface `AnalysisGroup`

getDirectlyOwnedAnalysisCodeSubsets	`public abstract QueryCollection getDirectlyOwnedAnalysisCodeSubsets() throws SFException`	Retrieves a copy of the collection of all object instances directly held by this controller.
removeDirectlyOwnedAnalysisCodeSubsetBy	`public abstract void removeDirectlyOwnedAnalysisCodeSubsetBy(String key) throws SFException`	Removes and deletes the AnalysisCodeSubset by the specified key.
removeAllDirectlyOwnedAnalysisCodeSubsets	`public abstract void removeAllDirectlyOwnedAnalysisCodeSubsets() throws SFException`	Removes and deletes all elements from the Collection of AnalysisCodeSubsets in this AnalysisGroup.
isAnalysisCodeSubsetsDirectlyEmpty	`public abstract boolean isAnalysisCodeSubsetsDirectlyEmpty() throws SFException`	Determine if the locally-contained collection is Empty
directlyContainsAnalysisCodeSubsetKey	`public abstract boolean directlyContainsAnalysisCodeSubsetKey(String key) throws SFException`	Checks if the AnalysisCodeSubset exists by the specified Key.
getAnalysisCodeBy	`public abstract AnalysisCode getAnalysisCodeBy(String key) throws SFException`	Returns the AnalysisCode by the specified key.
containsAnalysisCodeKey	`public abstract boolean containsAnalysisCodeKey(String key) throws SFException`	Checks if the AnalysisCode exists by the specified Key.
queryOwnedAnalysisCodes	`public abstract QueryCollection queryOwnedAnalysisCodes(String selectStatement, String bindCollectionName, SelectCompare selectCompareObject, String bindNameOfSelectCompareObject, SortCompare orderByCompareObject, String bindNameOfOrderByObject, boolean accessResults) throws SFException`	Select the AnalysisCodes Satisfying the Query.
getOwnedAnalysisCodes	`public abstract QueryCollection getOwnedAnalysisCodes() throws SFException`	Retrieves a logical copy of the collection of all object instances held by this controller.
getDirectlyOwnedAnalysisCodeBy	`public abstract AnalysisCode getDirectlyOwnedAnalysisCodeBy(String key) throws SFException`	Returns the AnalysisCode by the specified key.
queryDirectlyOwnedAnalysisCodes	`public abstract QueryCollection queryDirectlyOwnedAnalysisCodes(String selectStatement, String bindCollectionName, SelectCompare selectCompareObject, String bindNameOfSelectCompareObject, SortCompare orderByCompareObject, String bindNameOfOrderByObject, boolean accessResults) throws SFException`	Select the AnalysisCodes Satisfying the Query

Figure 26-2
(Cont'd)

getDirectlyOwnedAnalysisCodes	`public abstract QueryCollection getDirectlyOwnedAnalysisCodes () throws SFException`	Retrieves a copy of the collection of all object instances directly held by this controller.
removeDirectlyOwnedAnalysisCodeBy	`public abstract void removeDirectlyOwnedAnalysisCodeBy(String key) throws SFException`	Removes and deletes the AnalysisCode by the specified key
removeAllDirectlyOwnedAnalysisCodes	`public abstract void removeAllDirectlyOwnedAnalysisCodes() throws SFException`	Removes and deletes all elements from the Collection of AnalysisCodes
isAnalysisCodesDirectlyEmpty	`public abstract boolean isAnalysisCodesDirectlyEmpty( ) throws SFException`	Determine if the locally-contained collection is empty
directlyContainsAnalysisCodeKey	`public abstract boolean directlyContainsAnalysisCodeKey(String key) throws SFException`	Checks if the AnalysisCode exists by the specified Key
containsAnalysisCodeDictionaryEntryKey	`public abstract boolean containsAnalysisCodeDictionaryEntryKey(String dictionaryKey) throws SFException`	Indicates if dictionary entry is contained by this controller or any of its parent controllers
getAnalysisCodeDictionaryEntryBy	`public abstract AnalysisCode getAnalysisCodeDictionaryEntryBy(String dictionaryKey) throws SFException`	Gets the AnalysisCode Dictionary Entry associated with the specified key
directlyContainsAnalysisCodeDictionaryEntryKey	`public abstract boolean directlyContainsAnalysisCodeDictionaryEntryKey(String dictionaryKey) throws SFException`	Checks if the AnalysisCode Dictionary Entry exists by the specified Key
getDirectlyContainedAnalysisCodeDictionaryEntryBy	`public abstract AnalysisCode getDirectlyContainedAnalysisCodeDictionaryEntryBy(String dictionaryKey) throws SFException`	Return AnalysisCode associated with the specified dictionary key at this controller
setDirectlyContainedAnalysisCodeDictionaryEntry	`public abstract void setDirectlyContainedAnalysisCodeDictionaryEntry(String entityId, String dictionaryKey) throws SFException`	Associate AnalysisCode identified by passed-in id with passed-in dictionary key at this controller (if id is null, remove dictionary entry)
getId	`public abstract String getId() throws SFException`	Get the id of the Distinguishable object
setId	`public abstract void setId(String newId) throws SFException`	Set the id of this Analysis Group. This attribute is used by the framework as a primary key in a collection. The set method should be used with extreme caution.
getSequenceNumber	`public abstract int getSequenceNumber() throws SFException`	Gets
registerDirectlyOwnedAnalysisCode	`public abstract void registerDirectlyOwnedAnalysisCode(AnalysisCode analysisCodeToRegister) throws SFException`	Registers the AnalysisCode

Figure 26-2
(Cont'd)

getAnalysisCodesHdl	`public abstract Handle getAnalysisCodesHdl() throws SFException`	Returns the Handle to the Collection of AnalysisCodes in the corresponding AnalysisGroupCodeController for this AnalaysisGroup. The AnalysisGroupCodeControllers are maintained by the ChartOfAccounts. If one does not exist, an aggregating controller is created.
registerDirectlyOwnedAnalysisCodeSubset	`public abstract void registerDirectlyOwnedAnalysisCodeSubset(AnalysisCodeSubset analysisCodeSubsetToRegister) throws SFException`	Registers the AnalysisCodeSubset
getAnalysisCodeSubsetsHdl	`public abstract Handle getAnalysisCodeSubsetsHdl() throws SFException`	Returns the Handle to the Collection of AnalysisCodeSubsets in the corresponding AnalysisGroupCodeController for this AnalysisGroup. The AnalysisGroupCodeControllers are maintained by the ChartOfAccounts. If one does not exist, an aggregating controller is created.

Figure 26-2
(Cont'd)

GL Financial Calendar

This category uses the Financial Calendar from the CBO layer (see Chapter 22) to add GL-specific information. It does not include any new objects, just a `Command` to setup the required information.

Closing

This category deals with closing a fiscal period, typically a fiscal year. This category includes only a very simple notion of closing because it varies between businesses. Company-level parameters relating to closing are held in a `GLClosingParameters` object that contains three `PostingCombination` objects (for net-profit, retained loss, and retained profit). The actual closing process is performed by `GLClosingCmd`. What this command does is calculate the overall balance for P&L accounts for the year, and then add dissections to a final profit and loss journal. For a real application, a more sophisticated Command object is needed to implement the specific actions required at year-end.

Interface com.ibm.sf.gl.AnalysisCode

public interface **AnalysisCode** extends GenericAnalysisCodeAdapter, AnalysisCodeSpecifier

Main Methods

Name	*Signature*	*Description*
isUnitOfMeasureLegal	`public abstract boolean isUnitOfMeasureLegal(UnitOfMeasure unitOfMeasure) throws SFException`	Determine if the given UnitOfMeasure is legal for this AnalysisCode
isPostInhibited	`public abstract boolean isPostInhibited(int genericCreationCodeEnum) throws SFException`	Determines if this AnalysisCode is post-inhibited for the specified GenericCreationCodeEnum.
getId	`public abstract String getId() throws SFException`	get the id of the Distinguishable object
getAnalysisGroup	`public abstract AnalysisGroup getAnalysisGroup() throws SFException`	Returns the AnalysisGroup of the AnalysisCodes specified by this AnalysisCodeSpecifier.
createUnitOfMeasureIterator	`public abstract Iterator createUnitOfMeasureIterator() throws SFException`	Create Iterator for Collection of UnitOfMeasures
getNextUnitOfMeasure	`public abstract UnitOfMeasure getNextUnitOfMeasure(Iterator position) throws SFException`	Gets the UnitOfMeasure at the Next Iterator Position
setUnitOfMeasures	`public abstract void setUnitOfMeasures(DSet UnitOfMeasures) throws SFException`	Sets the collection of UnitOfMeasures
containsUnitOfMeasure	`public abstract boolean containsUnitOfMeasure(UnitOfMeasure unitofmeasure) throws SFException`	Checks if the UnitOfMeasure exists in the Collection of UnitOfMeasures
getUnitOfMeasureAt	`public abstract UnitOfMeasure getUnitOfMeasureAt(Iterator position) throws SFException`	Gets the UnitOfMeasure at the current iterator position
addUnitOfMeasure	`public abstract void addUnitOfMeasure(UnitOfMeasure unitOfMeasureToAdd) throws SFException`	Adds a UnitOfMeasure to the Collection of UnitOfMeasures
addAllUnitOfMeasures	`public abstract void addAllUnitOfMeasures(DSet newUnitOfMeasures) throws SFException`	Adds all UnitOfMeasures to the Collection of UnitOfMeasures
removeUnitOfMeasureAt	`public abstract void removeUnitOfMeasureAt(Iterator position) throws SFException`	Removes the UnitOfMeasure at the Current Iterator Position
removeUnitOfMeasure	`public abstract void removeUnitOfMeasure(UnitOfMeasure unitofmeasure) throws SFException`	Removes the specified UnitOfMeasure

Figure 26-3
Interface `AnalysisCode`

removeAllUnitOfMeasures	`public abstract void removeAllUnitOfMeasures() throws SFException`	Removes all UnitOfMeasure from the Collection of UnitOfMeasures
setId	`public abstract void setId(String newId) throws SFException`	Set the id of the Analysis Code. This attribute is used by the framework as a primary key in a collection. The set method should be used with extreme caution.
isManualPostInhibited	`public abstract boolean isManualPostInhibited() throws SFException`	Gets the manual post-inhibit flag. When set dissections may not be posted to posting combinations that include this analysis code when the dissections are generated by the user. This would normally indicate that the analysis code is used as part of posting combinations that represent another entity, e.g. Business partner, control account, bank account.
setManualPostInhibited	`public abstract void setManualPostInhibited(boolean newManualPostInhibited) throws SFException`	Set the manual post-inhibit flag. When set dissections may not be posted to posting combinations that include this analysis code when the dissections are generated by the user. This would normally indicate that the analysis code is used as part of posting combinations that represent another entity, e.g. Business partner, control account, bank account.
isSystemPostInhibited	`public abstract boolean isSystemPostInhibited() throws SFException`	Gets the system post-inhibit flag. When set dissections may not be posted to posting combinations that include this analysis code when the dissections are generated by the system (e.g. to a bank account).
setSystemPostInhibited	`public abstract void setSystemPostInhibited(boolean newSystemPostInhibited) throws SFException`	Set the system post-inhibit flag. When set dissections may not be posted to posting combinations that include this analysis code when the dissections are generated by the system (e.g. to a bank account).
getAnalysisGroupHdl	`public abstract Handle getAnalysisGroupHdl() throws SFException`	

Figure 26-3
(Cont'd)

Banks

This category deals with the Banks and the processes related to them. This includes tracking transactions in bank accounts, managing bank statements, and reconciling the bank statement with transactions in case that it is required. Bank statements are represented by `BankStatement` objects that contain `StatementLine` objects. `BankStatement` objects keep record of whether they are reconciled. Bank transactions are represented by `BankTransaction` objects, each composed of a set of `BankMovement` objects. A `ReconciliationEvent` object represents the association between `BankTransaction` objects and `StatementLine` objects that were reconciled against each other.

Interface com.ibm.sf.gl.Dissection

public interface **Dissection** GenericDissectionAdapter

Main Methods

Name	*Signature*	*Description*
getBaseCurrencyValue	`public abstract DCurrencyValue getBaseCurrencyValue() throws SFException`	Retrieves the BaseCurrencyValue from the DTransactionValue.
removeQuantityDissectionAt	`public abstract void removeQuantityDissectionAt(Iterator position) throws SFException`	Removes the QuantityDissection at the Current Iterator Position
removeQuantityDissection	`public abstract void removeQuantityDissection(DQuantityDissection quantityDissection) throws SFException`	Removes the first QuantityDissection matching the specified QuantityDissection.
insertQuantityDissectionAt	`public abstract void insertQuantityDissectionAt(DQuantityDissection quantityDissection, Iterator position) throws SFException`	Inserts the QuantityDissection at the Current Iterator Position
replaceQuantityDissectionAt	`public abstract void replaceQuantityDissectionAt(DQuantityDissection quantityDissection, Iterator position) throws SFException`	Replaces the QuantityDissection at the specified Iterator Position with the passed QuantityDissection
removeAllQuantityDissections	`public abstract void removeAllQuantityDissections() throws SFException`	Removes all QuantityDissections from the collection of QuantityDissections
setDebitCreditBalanceReverseIndicator	`public abstract void setDebitCreditBalanceReverseIndicator(boolean newDebitCreditBalanceReverseIndicator) throws SFException`	Sets the new DebitCreditBalanceReverseIndicator.
getBaseCurrency	`public abstract Currency getBaseCurrency() throws SFException`	Returns the Base currency retrieved from the DTransactionValue
getPrimeCurrency	`public abstract Currency getPrimeCurrency() throws SFException`	Returns the Prime currency retrieved from the DTransactionValue
getPrimeCurrencyValue	`public abstract DCurrencyValue getPrimeCurrencyValue() throws SFException`	Retrieves the PrimeCurrencyValue from the DTransactionValue.
consolidateQuantityDissections	`public abstract void consolidateQuantityDissections(DDissectionConsolidationPolicy dissectionConsolidationPolicy) throws SFException`	Consolidates all quantity dissections according to consolidation policy parameter.
consolidateQuantityDissections	`public abstract void consolidateQuantityDissections() throws SFException`	This method retrieves the default Consolidation Policy. It consolidates all quantity dissections according to this default Policy.

Figure 26-4
Interface `Dissection`

consolidateQuantityDissections	`public abstract void consolidateQuantityDissections(ResultsCollection results) throws SFException`	This method retrieves the default Consolidation Policy. It consolidates all quantity dissections according to this default Policy.
consolidateQuantityDissections	`public abstract void consolidateQuantityDissections(ResultsCollection results, DDissectionConsolidationPolicy dissectionConsolidationPolicy) throws SFException`	Consolidates all quantity dissections according to the passed in consolidation policy.
baseLessThanZero	`public abstract boolean baseLessThanZero() throws SFException`	Boolean,TRUE if Base Value is less than 0, FALSE otherwise.
baseGreaterThanZero	`public abstract boolean baseGreaterThanZero() throws SFException`	Boolean,TRUE if Base Value is greater than 0, FALSE otherwise.
baseIsZero	`public abstract boolean baseIsZero() throws SFException`	Boolean,TRUE if Base Value is 0, FALSE otherwise.
validate	`public abstract DResultsCollection validate() throws SFException`	The default validation policy for the company is retrieved and used by this method. The dissection is validated according to the steps detailed in the default dissection validation policy. A results collection is returned from this operation. It can be tested for any result messages detected during validation, as well as indicating success or failure of operation.
validate	`public abstract DResultsCollection validate(DDissectionValidationPolicy validationPolicy) throws SFException`	The dissection is validated according to the steps detailed in the passed dissection validation policy. A results collection is returned from this operation. It can be tested for any result messages detected during validation, as well as indicating success or failure of operation.
isEmpty	`public abstract boolean isEmpty() throws SFException`	True: no base currency value specified in dissection, and no quantity dissections either. False: it has a base currency value and/or quantity dissections
isDebit	`public abstract boolean isDebit() throws SFException`	Returns TRUE if the actual journal is 'debit' . Otherwise, FALSE is returned.
isCredit	`public abstract boolean isCredit() throws SFException`	Returns TRUE if the actual journal is 'credit' . Otherwise, FALSE is returned.
isBudget	`public abstract boolean isBudget() throws SFException`	Returns TRUE if the actual journal is 'Budget'. Otherwise, FALSE is returned.
addQuantityDissection	`public abstract void addQuantityDissection(DQuantityDissection quantityDissection) throws SFException`	Adds a QuantityDissection to the Collection of QuantityDissections
getPostingCombination	`public abstract PostingCombination getPostingCombination() throws SFException`	Return PostingCombination for this Dissection
getGLJournal	`public abstract GLJournal getGLJournal() throws SFException`	Return GLJournal for this Dissection

Figure 26-4
(Cont'd)

setGLJournal	public abstract void setGLJournal(GLJournal newGLJournal) throws SFException	Set the Handle of the GLJournal
getTransactionValue	public abstract DTransactionValue getTransactionValue() throws SFException	Return TransactionValue for this Dissection
copy	public abstract Dissection copy(GLJournal owner, AccessMode access, FinancialTransactionSource transactionSource, boolean changeDebitCreditBalanceReverseIndicator, boolean reverseDissection) throws SFException	A new dissection that is a copy of this dissection is created and added to the specified journal.
setPostingCombination	public abstract void setPostingCombination(PostingCombination postingCombination) throws SFException	Sets the Handle of the PostingCombination.
setTransactionValue	public abstract void setTransactionValue(DTransactionValue transactionValue) throws SFException	Sets the TransactionValue.
isMemo	public abstract boolean isMemo() throws SFException	Simply wire-through to Posting Combination. Returns True if posting combination has associated Chart of Account Attributes and is a memo account. Otherwise, FALSE is returned
isAnalysis	public abstract boolean isAnalysis() throws SFException	Simply wires through to Posting Combination. Returns True if posting combination has associated Chart of Account Attributes and is an analysis account. Otherwise, FALSE is returned
getDebitCreditBalanceReverseIndicator	public abstract boolean getDebitCreditBalanceReverseIndicator() throws SFException	Return the indicator.
isAllowedToBeConsolidated	public abstract boolean isAllowedToBeConsolidated() throws SFException	Returns true if the associated Posting Combination is allowed to be consolidated. otherwise false.
createQuantityDissectionIterator	public abstract Iterator createQuantityDissectionIterator() throws SFException	Create Iterator for Collection of QuantityDissections
getNextQuantityDissection	public abstract DQuantityDissection getNextQuantityDissection(Iterator position) throws SFException	Gets the QuantityDissection at the Next Iterator Position
containsQuantityDissection	public abstract boolean containsQuantityDissection(DQuantityDissection quantitydissection) throws SFException	Checks if the QuantityDissection exists in the Collection of QuantityDissections
getQuantityDissectionAt	public abstract DQuantityDissection getQuantityDissectionAt(Iterator position) throws SFException	Gets the QuantityDissection at the current iterator position

Figure 26-4
(Cont'd)

getPreviousQuantityDissection	`public abstract DQuantityDissection getPreviousQuantityDissection(Iterator position) throws SFException`	Gets the QuantityDissection at the Previous Iterator Position
getCreationCode	`public abstract int getCreationCode() throws SFException`	Gets CreationCode
getFinancialTransactionSource	`public abstract FinancialTransactionSource getFinancialTransactionSource() throws SFException`	Returns the FinancialTransactionSource, copied from the Handle
getDissectionTypeValue	`public abstract DissectionTypeValue getDissectionTypeValue() throws SFException`	Returns the DissectionTypeValue, copied from the Handle
getDissectionId	`public abstract int getDissectionId() throws SFException`	Gets is used internally to guarantee uniqueness.
getPostingCombinationHdl	`public abstract Handle getPostingCombinationHdl() throws SFException`	Returns the Handle to the PostingCombination of the PostingCombination of the Dissection
getGLJournalHdl	`public abstract Handle getGLJournalHdl() throws SFException`	Returns the Handle to the GLJournal of the GLJournal of the Dissection
getFinancialTransactionSourceHdl	`public abstract Handle getFinancialTransactionSourceHdl() throws SFException`	Returns the Handle to the FinancialTransactionSource of the FinancialTransactionSource of the Dissection
getDissectionTypeValueHdl	`public abstract Handle getDissectionTypeValueHdl() throws SFException`	Returns the Handle to the DissectionTypeValue of the DissectionTypeValue of the Dissection

Figure 26-4
(Cont'd)

Budgets

This category provides the ability to manage budgets in the General Ledger. Budgets can be associated with several posting combinations and GL Journals. Budgets are represented by `BudgetProfile` interfaces, managed by the respective controller placed on a company.

Revaluation

This category supports updating GL records following revaluation of currencies. Transactions recorded in the GL might be susceptible to changes relative to values of currencies because of foreign exchange rate fluctuations. When such fluctuations occur, the original value in the base currency may no longer reflect the correct value, so a revaluation is done using an updated exchange rate. This category supports both realized and unrealized gains and losses, based on the currency gain/loss category in the CBO layer (see Chapter 22).

GL Sample Extensions

SanFrancisco includes sample extensions of the GL framework, as mentioned in Chapter 8, and as described by the SanFrancisco release documentation. Three samples are provided. Each of them is GUI-driven, and is based in the SanFrancisco GUI framework, described in Chapter 13. The three samples put together make up a mini-application. Throughout these samples, GUIs are used to create and maintain various GL objects, such as dissections and journals.

The samples are:

- *GL Posting*. An example of extending the chart of account, batches, and journals. It uses a fixed set of analysis groups: Main account, Cost center and Cost carrier.
- *GL Balance Inquiry*. An example of creating inquiries using the GL balances category. It is possible to inquire about a specific Main account for a given year. It is also possible to provide a Cost center and/or a Cost carrier, or a currency. If no currency is specified, the default currency will be used. The result of such an inquiry includes the balances for all periods of the selected year. The dissections included are shown if the balance is selected. Furthermore, selecting a specific dissection shows the information connected with it.
- *GL Hierarchies*. This example provides completely new functionality on top of the GL. It provides the capability to group main accounts into hierarchies for the purpose of reporting. The reporting provides year-to-date values and period values.

CHAPTER 27

The Warehouse Management Framework

In most conventional businesses, there is a notion of stocks of goods being held, either during manufacturing or in the distribution process. In this chapter we look at the warehouse management framework designed to support the development of applications that deal with this domain.

The Warehouse Management (WM) framework defines and implements the core business objects and processes needed for dealing with inventory management. It allows the application developer to define products and warehouses and, based on these definitions, provides support to numerous useful functions such as inventory tracking and stock transactions. The core processes are provided as incomplete implementations that are to be extended by the application developer.

Warehouse Management Business Objects

Product

Product is the most fundamental abstraction of the Warehouse Management Core Business Process. It facilitates product definition and inclusion of descriptive information but, more importantly, it also includes built-in inventory handling capabilities. For example, it supports balance update and retrieval, costing, serial number handling, availability checking, and lead-time calculation. These capabilities are part of the `Product` interface but are typically delegated to other objects that are easily extendable and replaceable. Specific products can be specified as lot-controlled or serial number-controlled, making those respective attributes mandatory for all handling of inventory that is related to that product. Many product-costing approaches are supported, both transaction-based (last in, first out, or first in, first out) and non-transaction based (average, standard, latest inbound). The application end-user can specify a specific costing approach, but later on he/she can select other costing approaches to explore "what-if" scenarios.

Products utilize the unit conversion capability provided in the CBO layer and customize it with product-specific behavior. Each product defines a base unit plus other units in which it can be stocked. It is possible to define a generic set of units and conversion factors (for example, single items, boxes, and containers) but selectively enable only some of those units for a particular product.

Warehouse Management also supports single level kit definitions (a product can be a kit, a kit component, or neither) on a single-unit basis. The framework does not support multi-level kits at this time.

Warehouse

For Warehouse objects, there is a notion of location; using it enforces all inventories to be associated with a specific location. In other words, if a warehouse is location-controlled, any inventory associated with that warehouse must have a location specified for it.

The notion of stock zones introduces an additional (and again, optional) level of organization within a warehouse. Zones can distinguish between different areas of the warehouse based on the facilities in these areas (e.g. a frozen goods section in a food warehouse, or dust-controlled areas where chips are held). Stock locations can contain measurement information. These measurements can be used along with other location information for finding locations for new products or retrieving needed products. The algorithms for storing and retrieving goods are implemented in a way that makes them easily extendible or even replaceable.

Inventory

The Inventory business object is used to represent goods that are held in stock. The level of granularity used to track stock is variable and depends on the specific product and warehouse. For example, for a product that is lot-controlled, lots are required for inventory tracking. The inventory business object also provides means for differentiating different instances of the same product (e.g. based on quality control results).

The Cached Balances mechanism provided by the CBO layer can be used to provide inventory balance summaries in varying levels of granularity, possibly taking into account future receptions and reservations of products. This kind of information can be useful when calculating product availability.

Stock Transactions

All changes to inventory stock are made using stock transactions. Whenever a stock transaction is created the framework makes the full roundtrip, updating the product balances, updating cost information, and creating the necessary financial dissections to record the stock increase or decrease in the General Ledger. For some specific processes, specialized stock transactions are needed. For example, such a specialized stock transaction is provided for manual stock transactions (i.e. transactions that must be manually keyed into the system because they are not associated with any business process supported by the application). Stock transaction objects can be used to perform various forms of analysis that can be used for decision making and for monitoring the activities in warehouses.

Warehouse Business Processes

The Warehouse Management framework introduces a long list of business processes aimed at covering all aspects of warehouse management, even those required for applications that relate to distribution and manufacturing (these are not considered to be warehouse management applications). These processes are left open-ended so that they can be customized and extended to serve specific requirements.

Planning, Re-planning, Reception, Quality Control, Picking, Shipment, Backorder Handling, Replenishment, and Stock Take provide the set of basic processes that need to be extended by the application. Each of these processes will be discussed in more detail as part of the category description in the next section. Note that the Order Management framework, described in Chapter 28, actually extends this framework by extending some of its processes (this framework of course introduces some processes of its own).

Warehouse Management Categories

Similar to other SanFrancisco layers, the Warehouse Management framework consists of a set of classes grouped together into categories. These categories are described below. Most of these categories correspond to a specific process in the framework. Table 27-1 summarizes the composition of each of the categories. The various categories here make extensive use of the `PropertyContainer` interface of companies and other business objects. This use is summarized in Table 27-2. As with other parts of the framework, different controllers and policies are placed on the `Company` object.

Accounting Transactions

This category works with the CFFI financial integration package (see Chapter 22). It captures all the Warehouse Management specific information needed to create financial dissections. This way, all the other components of the Warehouse Management framework remain unaware of financial terms such as dissection.

This category defines the account control types for Warehouse Management (such as `DStockControllerAccountControlType`). It also defines Command objects (which don't have a target) in order to create dissections in different cases. These commands are:

- `StockValueDissectionCreateCmd`. Used to create a dissection for a logistic stock value financial transaction.
- `CostChangeDissectionCreateCmd`. Used to create a dissection for logistic cost change financial transaction
- `ManualCostChangeDissectionCreateCmd`. Used to create a dissection for a logistics manual cost change.
- `StockAdjustmentDissectionCreateCmd`. Used to create a dissection for logistic stock adjustment transaction.
- `CostForReceivedGoodsDissectionCreateCmd`. Used to create a dissection for logistics cost for received goods transaction.

TABLE 27-1

Summary of Warehouse Management Categories and their composition

Category	Components
Backorder Handling	DBackorderHandlingPolicy BackorderableDetail DBackorderHandlingSelectionPolicy
Replenishment	ReplenishmentSuggestion ReplenishmentSuggestionDetails ReplenishmentSource DReplenishmentSourceChooserPolicy DReplenishmentCalculationPolicy DReplenishmentCalculationSelectionPolicy DReplenishmentSuggestionGenerationPolicy ReplenishmentSuggestionController
Picking	PickableDetail PickingDetails PickingStockTransaction PickList PickListDetail PickListController PickConfirmableDetail PickCommitableDetail DPickingDetailCommon DPickingDeliveryShortagePolicy DPickingDetailCreatorPolicy DPickingDeliveryShortageSelectionPolicy DPickConfirmationPolicy DPickConfirmationSelectionPolicy DPickCommitPolicy DPickListGenerationPolicy DPickListGenerationSelectionPolicy DPickListIdGenerationPolicy DPickListConformationPolicy DPickListDetailMethodKeyDetailNumber
Reception	ReceivingDetail ReceivableDetail ReceptionCommitableDetail ReceptionConfirmableDetail ReceptionNote ReceptionNoteDetails DReceptionNoteController ReceptionStockTransaction DReceivingDetailsCreatePolicyUsingOverrides DReceivingDetailCommon DReceptionCommitPolicy DReceivingDetailCreatorPolicy DReceptionCommitSelectionPolicy DReceptionConfirmationPolicy DReceptionNoteGenerationSelectionPolicy DReceptionNoteConfirmationPolicy DReceptionNoteDetailsMethodKeyMethodNumber

TABLE 27-1

(Contd)

Category	Components
Accounting Transactions	DLogisticsIntegrationKey DProductAccountControlType DCostTypeValueAccountControlType DProductGroupAccountControlType DStockControlledAccountControlType DFictitiousProductAccountControlType StockValueDissectionCreateCmd CostChangeDissectionCreateCmd ManualCostChangeDissectionCreateCmd StockAdjustmentDissectionCreateCmd CostForReceivedGoodsDissectionCreateCmd CostForDeliveredGoodsDissectionCreateCmd ReceptionCostDissectionCreateCmd
Transport Information	TermsOfDelivery MannerOfTransport TransportZone TermsOfDeliveryController MannerOfTransportController TransportZoneController DTransportTimeKey
Product	Product Warehouse StockTypeValue ProductWarehouselink StockControlledWarehouse StockControlledProductWarehouseLink NonStockControlledWarehouse NonStockControlledProductWarehouseLink ProductUnitLink ProductGroup SharedProductAttributes SharedWarehouseAttributes StockTransaction StockTransactionTypeValue CostWorkFlowCodeEnum StockTransactionTypeController StockTransactionCreateCmd Cost CostTransaction DCostPriceRetrievalPolicy DCostTypeValue DCostPriceUpdatePolicy DCostTypeController CostingLevel DCostingPolicy DCostingPolicyNonTransactionBased DCostingPolicyTransactionBased DCostingPolicyAverage DCostingPolicyFIFO DProductAvailabilityCheckerPolicy

TABLE 27-1

(Contd)

Category	Components
Product	DShipmentTimeCalculatorPolicy
	DLeadTimeDefinition
	DLeadTimeKey
	DLeadTimeDefinitionKey
	DLeadTimeChooserPolicy
	DLeadTimeDefinitionDController
	Lot
	DLotValidationPolicy
	DLotValidationSelectionPolicy
	DLotChooserPolicy
	DLotChooserSelectionPolicy
	SerialNumber
	DSerialNumberChooserPolicy
	DSerialNumberChooserResult
	DSerialNumberValidationPolicy
	DSerialNumberValidationSelectionPolicy
	DProductTransactionQuantity
	DProductQuantityUnit
	StockLocation
	StockZone
	DStockLocationAssignerPolicy
	DStockLocationChooserPolicy
	DStockLocationValidationPolicy
	DSlockLocationAssignerSelectionPolicy
	DStockLocationChooserSelectionPolicy
	DAssignStockLocationResult
	DChooseStockLocationResult
Balances and Reservations	Inventory
	ProductReservation
	FutureReception
	ProductBalances
	DProductCachedBalance
	ReservationTypeValue
	FutureReceptionTypeValue

- `CostForDeliveredGoodsDissectionCreateCmd`. Used to create a dissection for logistics cost for delivered goods transaction.
- `ReceptionCostDissectionCreateCmd`. Used to create a dissection for a reception cost transaction.

TABLE 27-2

Summary of Warehouse Management Framework properties

Property On	Property Type	Property Name
Company	DCostPriceRetrievalPolicy	whs.CostPriceRetrievalPolicy
	DCostPriceUpdatePolicy	whs.DCostPriceUpdatePolicy
	ReservationTypeController	whs.ReservationTypeController
	FutureReceptionTypeController	whs.FutureReceptionTypeController
	StockTransactionTypeController	whs.StockTransactionTypeController
	ProductPolicyFactoryController	whs.ProductPolicyFactoryController
	String	whs.SEPARATOR STRING
	DSerialNumberChooserPolicy	whs.DSerialNumberChooserPolicy
	DSerialNumberValidationPolicy	whs.DSerialNumberValidationPolicy
	DLotValidationPolicy	whs.DLotValidationPolicy
	DLotChooserPolicy	whs.DLotChooserPolicy
	ProductController	whs.ProductController
	DShipmentTimeCalculatorPolicy	whs.DShipmentTimeCalculatorPolicy
	CostTypeController	whs.CostTypeController
	MannerOfTransportController	whs.MannerOfTransportController
	CostingLevelController	whs.CostingLevelController
	CostingPolicyDController	whs.CostingPolicyDController
	DTransportTimeChooserPolicy	whs.DTransportTimeSearchPolicy
	DPickingDeliveryShortagePolicy	whs.DPickingDeliveryShortagePolicy
	SharedProductAttributesController	whs.SharedProductAttributesController
	ProductGroupController	whs.ProductGroupController
	ABCClassificationController	whs.ABCClassificationController
	StockTypeController	whs.StockTypeController
	WarehouseController	whs.WarehouseController
	SharedWarehouseAttributesController	whs.SharedWarehouseAttributesController
	DStockLocationAssignerPolicy	whs.DStockLocationAssignerPolicy
	DStockLocationValidationPolicy	whs.DStockLocationValidationPolicy
	DStockLocationChooserPolicy	whs.DStockLocationChooserPolicy
	TermsOfDeliveryController	whs.TermsOfDeliveryController
	ER DTimePrecisionPolicy	whs.ER DTimePrecisionPolicy
	LeadTimeDefinitionDController	whs.LeadTimeDefinitionDController
	ReplenishmentSuggestionController	whs.ReplenishmentSuggestionController
	DBackorderHandlingPolicy	whs.DBackorderHandlingPolicy
	PickListController	whs.PickListController
	DPickListConfirmationPolicy	whs.DPickListConfirmationPolicy
	DPickListGenerationPolicy	whs.DPickListGenerationPolicy
	DReservationAndFutureReception UpdatePolicy	whs.DReservationAndFutureReception UpdatePolicy
Address	TransportZone	whs.TransportZone

Transport Information

This category allows the end user to calculate transport times. This category builds upon the *key / keyable* mechanism described in Chapter 23. It defines an extensible set of keys, which include addresses, transport zones, and way of transport. The following basic abstractions are defined:

- `MannerOfTransport`. The way transport is done (e.g. by air).
- `TransportZone`. A location from which or to which goods are transported.
- `TermsOfDelivery`. Defines a notion of terms of delivery (e.g. Deliver to customer premises).

These abstractions do not introduce a lot of functionality but are intended for the describing process of transport times. Each of these objects has a respective controller (e.g. `MannerOfTransport Controller`).

The missing link from what we have described thus far is obviously how time comes into play. A `DTransportTimeDefinition` object represents the time it takes to do a specific transport task. These objects are maintained by a controller in the company object. It is possible that several of these objects will be included for transportation from a certain point A to a certain point B, and specific policies can be included to encapsulate this logic (using `DTransportTimeChooserPolicy`). Actual calculation of shipping and delivery times is made by the `DShipmentTimeCalculatorPolicy` (see Figure 27-1 for interface).

Product

This category includes all of the core business objects of Warehouse Management along with low-level business processes that are used as building blocks for the framework. The functions that are provided by this category include the following.

- Product and warehouse definition
- Kit definition
- Costing
- Unit handling
- Availability checking

Interface com.ibm.sf.whs.DShipmentTimeCalculatorPolicy

public interface **DShipmentTimeCalculatorPolicy** extends DescribableDependent

Name	*Signature*	*Description*
getEarliestShippingTime	`public abstract DTime getEarliestShippingTime(Product product, Warehouse warehouse, DProductTransactionQuantity productTransactionQuantity, ProcessTokenValue processToken, StockTypeValue stockTypeValue, Lot lot, StockLocation stockLocation, SerialNumber serialNumber, DTime timeToStartCalculation, BusinessPartner businessPartner, MannerOfTransport mannerOfTransport) throws SFException`	Returns the earliest shipping time for the product based on the requested quantity and any passed optional arguments for passed warehouse.
getEarliestShippingTime	`public abstract DTime getEarliestShippingTime(Product product, DProductTransactionQuantity productTransactionQuantity, ProcessTokenValue processToken, StockTypeValue stockTypeValue, Lot lot, SerialNumber serialNumber, DTime timeToStartCalculation, BusinessPartner businessPartner, MannerOfTransport mannerOfTransport) throws SFException`	Returns the earliest shipping time for the product based on the requested quantity and any passed optional arguments. All warehouses are inspected to get the earliest shipment time.
calculateShipmentTime	`public abstract DTime calculateShipmentTime(DAmountOfTime transportTime, DTime deliveryTime, Product product, NaturalCalendar calendar, Warehouse warehouse, DAmountOfTime timeAccuracy, BusinessPartner businessPartner) throws SFException`	Returns the shipment time for the passed in product.
calculateDeliveryTime	`public abstract DTime calculateDeliveryTime(DAmountOfTime transportTime, Product product, DTime shipmentTime, NaturalCalendar calendar, Warehouse warehouse, DAmountOfTime timeAccuracy, BusinessPartner businessPartner) throws SFException`	Returns the delivery time for the passed in product.

Figure 27-1
Interface `DShipmentTimeCalculator Policy`

- Lead time retrieval
- Inventory and stock transactions management

The main abstraction in this category is Product, shown in Figure 27-2. This object defines a product in the system, and holds all the information related to it. Products can be grouped using the ProductGroup object. For example, you could make a group of all fragile goods.

In order to define which kinds of units of measurement are relevant for a certain product, a ProductUnitLink object is used in conjunction with the unit of measurement category in the CBO layer.

The association of products with warehouses is done using the ProductWareHouseLink, which comes in two flavors: one for stock-controlled products and one for non stock-controlled products.

Warehouses are represented by Warehouse objects (see Figure 27-3). A warehouse that is divided into specific storage locations is represented by a LocationControlledWarehouse.

Product attributes and warehouse attributes are stored in objects of type SharedProductAttributes and SharedWarehouseAttributes, respectively. This further modularization is performed in order to allow sharing them between companies.

Stock transactions are represented by StockTransaction objects. The different kinds of such transactions (e.g. manual stock transactions) can be defined through StockTransactionType. The Stock Transaction object encapsulates all relevant information including costing. The class CostWorkFlowCodeEnumA supports a multitude of ways to do costing for a stock transaction.

A Cost object holds the standard notion of cost for a certain product or a certain product/warehouse combination. This price might be the average price, or a list price. The actual costs used might be different and these are defined by CostTypeValue. Specific costing policies can be derived from DCostingPolicy. The framework provides several of these (e.g. average, FIFO). The DCostPriceRetrievalPolicy selects the right costing policy in a given case. The actual association between the product quantity and a DTransactionValue object is made using DCostValue.

Availability checking is performed using policy objects of type DProductAvailabilityCheckPolicy. The logic encapsulated in such objects allows them to figure out the available quantity of a given product, quantity and time; possibly in relation to a warehouse, lot, business partner, and other parameters. Similarly, the logic for calculating shipping time is in DShipmentTimeCalculatorPolicy.

Interface com.ibm.sf.whs.Product

public interface **Product** extends DescribableDynamicEntity, Distinguishable, Shared

Main Methods

Name	*Signature*	*Description*
addFutureReception	`public abstract void addFutureReception(FutureReception futureReception) throws SFException`	Adds the passed future reception for a product warehouse relation, the received balances are updated.
addProductReservation	`public abstract void addProductReservation(ProductReservation productReservation) throws SFException`	Adds the reservation for a product warehouse link and updates the cached balances, if any.
addCost	`public abstract void addCost(Cost cost, Warehouse warehouse, Lot lot, UnitOfMeasure unitOfMeasure) throws SFException`	Adds the passed Cost to the appropriate internal collection of Costs held by the corresponding ProductWarehouseLink. Ownership is transferred to the ProductWarehouseLink.
assignStockLocation	`public abstract DSet assignStockLocation(Warehouse warehouse, StockTypeValue stockTypeValue, UnitOfMeasure unitOfMeasure, StockZone stockZone, Lot lot, DMeasurement measurement, DProductTransactionQuantity quantity, DStockLocationValidationSelectionPolicy stockLocationValidationSelectionPolicy, DStockLocationAssignerSelectionPolicy stockLocationAssignerSelectionPolicy) throws SFException`	Assigns a valid StockLocation for a product in a warehouse that is location controlled.
chooseStockLocation	`public abstract DSet chooseStockLocation(Warehouse warehouse, DProductTransactionQuantity productTransactionQuantity, StockTypeValue stockTypeValue, DTime time, Lot lot, DStockLocationChooserSelectionPolicy stockLocationChooserSelectionPolicy) throws SFException`	Returns a set of ChooseStockLocationResult objects.
chooseLot	`public abstract Set chooseLot(DProductTransactionQuantity quantityToCover, Warehouse warehouse, StockTypeValue stockType, DTime time, DTime deliveryTime, DTime shippingTime, DLotChooserSelectionPolicy lotChooserSelectionPolicy, DLotValidationSelectionPolicy lotValidationSelectionPolicy) throws SFException`	Returns a set of DLotChooserResult instances. If lotChooserPolicy is not passed, the chain of responsibility is used to get it.

Figure 27-2
Interface `Product`

chooseSerialNumbers	public abstract Set chooseSerialNumbers(Warehouse warehouse, DProductTransactionQuantity productTransactionQuantity, StockTypeValue stockTypeValue, DTime time, Lot lot, StockLocation stockLocation, DSerialNumberChooserSelectionPolicy serialNumberChooserSelectionPolicy, DSerialNumberValidationSelectionPolicy serialNumberValidationSelectionPolicy) throws SFException	Interface to the SerialNumberChooserPolicy. The Set returned contains 0..n DSerialNumberChooserResults. These objects contain the relevant SerialNumber, Lot and StockLocation.
createCachedBalancesSet	public abstract void createCachedBalancesSet(DProductBalanceSpecificationKey productBalanceSpecificationKey) throws SFException	Adds a CachedBalanceSet for the passed Specification key to the appropriate DCachedBalanceSetCollection. The new CachedBalancesSet is created by condensing the existing superset DCachedBalance into to a new CachedBalancesSet, if possible.
createCosts	public abstract void createCosts(Warehouse warehouse, Lot lot, UnitOfMeasure unitOfMeasure) throws SFException	Create costs for defined cost types. Costs are held by Product and ProductWarehouseLink.
deleteCachedBalanceSet	public abstract void deleteCachedBalanceSet(DProductBalanceSpecificationKey aProductBalanceSpecificationKey) throws SFException	Removes a CachedBalanceSet for the passed DProductSpecificationKey from the appropriate DCachedBalanceSetCollection.
deleteCost	public abstract void deleteCost(Cost cost, Warehouse warehouse, Lot lot, UnitOfMeasure unitOfMeasure) throws SFException	Removes a cost from the set of costs for this product and the specified warehouse.
getCostValueForStockDecrease	public abstract DCostValueReference getCostValueForStockDecrease(CostTypeValue costTypeValue, DCostValueReference costValueReference, Warehouse warehouse, Lot lot) throws SFException	Gets the cost value according to the system costing policy and level. This method is invoked only when stock is decreased. Assumptions: The DCurrencyValue on DCostValue on passed CostValueReference should never be negative, but the DProductQuantityUnit should. Non-stock controlled Products gets Standard cost if this is the system costing policy, but latestInbound cost for all other system costing policies. Fictitious products are always non-stock controlled.
getCostValueForProductBalance	public abstract DCostValueReference getCostValueForProductBalance(Warehouse warehouse, DCostingPolicy costingPolicy, CostingLevel costingLevel, CostTypeValue costTypeValue, Lot lot, UnitOfMeasure unitOfMeasure) throws SFException	Returns the stock value for a specific product and cost type value according to the given costing poliicy.

Figure 27-2
(Cont'd)

getAvailableQuantity	`public abstract DProductTransactionQuantity getAvailableQuantity(DProductTransactionQuantity quantity, ProcessTokenValue processToken, Warehouse warehouse, StockTypeValue stockType, Lot lot, StockLocation location, SerialNumber serialNumber, DTime requestedTime, BusinessPartner businessPartner, MannerOfTransport mannerOfTransport) throws SFExceptionCalculates`	Available quantity of the product based on input arguments.
getBalance	`public abstract DProductQuantityUnit getBalance(DProductBalanceAccessKey productBalanceAccessKey) throws SFException`	Returns available balance for this product based on passsed access key. If the key does not contain a unit, the base unit is used. The Cost Type is converted into a list of associated StockTypes and the balance for each StockType accumulated. Uses the associated Product Balances class.
getBaseUnitOfMeasure	`public abstract UnitOfMeasure getBaseUnitOfMeasure() throws SFException`	This method retrieves the base unit of measure for the product.
getCost	`public abstract Cost getCost(CostTypeValue costTypeValue, Warehouse warehouse, Lot lot, UnitOfMeasure unitOfMeasure) throws SFException`	Returns a Cost for the passed CostTypeValue object from Product if warehouse is null or from ProductWarehouseLink if a warehouse is specified.
getCostPrice	`public abstract DCurrencyValue getCostPrice(DCostingPolicyNonTransactionBased costingPolicyNonTransactionBased, CostTypeValue costTypeValue, Warehouse warehouse, UnitOfMeasure unitOfMeasure, Lot lot) throws SFException`	Returns the cost price for the passed in costingPolicy.
getEarliestShippingTime	`public abstract DTime getEarliestShippingTime(DProductTransactionQuantity requestedQuantity, ProcessTokenValue processToken, Warehouse warehouse, StockTypeValue stockType, StockLocation stockLocation, Lot selectedLot, SerialNumber serialNumber, DTime requestedTime, BusinessPartner businessPartner, MannerOfTransport mannerOfTransport) throws SFException`	Returns the earliest shipping time for the product based on the requested quantity and optional arguments.
getProductGroup	`public abstract ProductGroup getProductGroup() throws SFException`	Returns the ProductGroup for the current Product

Figure 27-2
(Cont'd)

getUnitCategory	`public abstract UnitCategory getUnitCategory() throws SFException`	Returns the contained unit category.
getUnitCategoryUnitLink	`public abstract UnitCategoryUnitLink getUnitCategoryUnitLink(String unitId) throws SFException`	Retrieves the Unit category unit link from the Unit Category for the passed Id
getWarehouses	`public abstract DSet getWarehouses() throws SFException`	Returns the set of warehouses for this product. Iterates throuh the collection of ProductWarehouseLinks for this product and adds the warehouse for each link to the set that is to be returned.
isLocationControlled	`public abstract boolean isLocationControlled(Warehouse warehouse) throws SFException`	Returns true if this product is location controlled in the passed in warehouse
isRelatedToUnitOfMeasure	`public abstract boolean isRelatedToUnitOfMeasure(UnitOfMeasure unitOfMeasure) throws SFException`	Checks whether the product is related to the passed in unit of measure
isRelatedToWarehouse	`public abstract boolean isRelatedToWarehouse(Warehouse warehouse) throws SFException`	Checks whether this product is related to the specified warehouse.
isStockControlled	`public abstract boolean isStockControlled(Warehouse warehouse) throws SFException`	Returns true if this product is stock controlled in the passed in warehouse
isStockControlledInAnyWarehouse	`public abstract boolean isStockControlledInAnyWarehouse() throws SFException`	Returns true if this product is stock controlled in any warehouse related to the product
lotIsValid	`public abstract boolean lotIsValid(Lot lot, Warehouse warehouse, DTime deliveryTime, DTime shippingTime, DLotValidationSelectionPolicy lotValidationSelectionPolicy) throws SFException`	Determines if the passed Lot is valid. Delivery time, shipping time and lotValidationPolicy are passed for future use when validating the lot. Users of the framework may validate dates such as expiration date and maturity date.
manualUpdateCostPrice	`public abstract void manualUpdateCostPrice(DCostingPolicyNonTransactionBased costingPolicyNonTransactionBased, DCurrencyValue newCostPrice, CostTypeValue costTypeValue, Warehouse warehouse, UnitOfMeasure unitOfMeasure, Lot lot, DTime time, FiscalPeriod fiscalPeriod) throws SFException`	Manually update of cost price.
removeFutureReception	`public abstract void removeFutureReception(FutureReception futureReception) throws SFException`	Removes a future reception from a product warehouse relation and updates the cached balances.
removeProductReservation	`public abstract void removeProductReservation(ProductReservation productReservation) throws SFException`	Removes a reservation from a product warehouse relation and updates the cached balances.

Figure 27-2
(Cont'd)

serialNumberExists	`public abstract boolean serialNumberExists(String serialNumberId) throws SFException`	Returns true if the SerialNumberId in the passed string can be mapped to a SerialNumber in the collections of SerialNumbers held by the Product.
serialNumberIsValid	`public abstract boolean serialNumberIsValid(SerialNumber serialNumber, DSerialNumberValidationSelection Policy serialNumberValidationSelectionP olicy) throws SFException`	Validate the passed SerialNumber for the Product.
setLotParameters	`public abstract void setLotParameters(boolean lotControlled, DLotChooserSelectionPolicy lotChooserSelectionPolicy, DLotValidationSelectionPolicy lotValidationSelectionPolicy) throws SFException`	Validates and sets the passed in paramter dealing with lot on product.
setProductGroup	`public abstract void setProductGroup(ProductGroup productGroup) throws SFException`	Sets the product group for this product.
setSerialNumberParamete rs	`public abstract void setSerialNumberParameters(boolea n serialNumberControlled, DSerialNumberChooserSelectionPol icy serialNumberChooserSelectionPoli cy, DSerialNumberValidationSelection Policy serialNumberValidationSelectionP olicy) throws SFException`	Validates and sets the passed in parameter dealing with lot on product.
setUnitCategory	`public abstract void setUnitCategory(UnitCategory unitCategory) throws SFException`	Sets the passed in unit category for this product.
updateBalance	`public abstract void updateBalance(DInventoryBalanceA ccessKey inventoryBalanceAccessKey, DProductTransactionQuantity newBalance) throws SFException`	Updates balance for this product based on passed parms. Uses the associated ProductBalances class. See ProductBalances and its subclass ProductBalancesDefault for a more detailed description.
getProductBalancesForRe adAccess	`public abstract ProductBalances getProductBalancesForReadAccess( ) throws SFException`	Retrieves the contained ProductBalance entity with AccessMode Normal where the compatibility mode has been set to 'SELF'
getProductBalancesForWr iteAccess	`public abstract ProductBalances getProductBalancesForWriteAccess () throws SFException`	Retrieves the contained ProductBalance entity with AccessMode PlusWrite where the compatibility mode has been set to 'SELF'
getEndOfLeadTime	`public abstract DTime getEndOfLeadTime(BusinessPartner businessPartner, Warehouse warehouse, DLeadTimeChooserSelectionPolicy leadTimeDefinitionSearchPolicy) throws SFException`	Returns the lead time for the product based on the passed arguments. leadtime as DTime object
removeSharedContainedP ropertyBy	`public abstract void removeSharedContainedPropertyBy( String propertyName) throws SFException`	Removes the non-owned Entity, owned Dependent, or owned String from the shared PropertyContainer for this object but does not delete the Entity.
getAbcClassification	`public abstract ABCClassification getAbcClassification() throws SFException`	Returns the AbcClassification, copied from the Handle

Figure 27-2
(Cont'd)

setAbcClassification	`public abstract void setAbcClassification(ABCClassification newAbcClassification) throws SFException`	Set the Handle of the AbcClassification
containsProductWarehouseLink	`public abstract boolean containsProductWarehouseLink(ProductWarehouseLink productwarehouselink) throws SFException`	Checks if the ProductWarehouseLink exists in the Collection of ProductWarehouseLinks
getProductResponsibleInitials	`public abstract Initials getProductResponsibleInitials() throws SFException`	Returns the ProductResponsibleInitials, copied from the Handle
setProductResponsibleInitials	`public abstract void setProductResponsibleInitials(Initials newProductResponsibleInitials) throws SFException`	Set the Handle of the ProductResponsibleInitials

Figure 27-2
(Cont'd)

Lead-time definitions are kept in `DLeadTimeDefinition` objects, which hold a time amount optionally associated with a product, warehouse and/or business partner. A "chain of responsibility" is used to find the right lead-time definition when needed. This is implemented in the `DLeadTimeChooserPolicy` class.

Lots are represented by `Lot` objects and various policies are provided for choosing a lot and validating it for a given product. Serial numbers for products are represented by `SerialNumber` objects. As you can expect, several policies allow you to control the specifics of serial number allocation. The resulting number is given in a `DSerialNumberChooserResult` object.

Unit handling is done using `DProductTransactionQuantity` and `DProductQuantityUnit`. The first type of object provides a link between a `DTransactionQuantity` object and a specific product. The other one provides a link between `DQuantityUnit` and a product.

If a warehouse is location-controlled it contains several `StockZone` objects each possibly composed of `StockLocation` objects. Policy objects are provided for selecting the appropriate storage location for a given product.

Interface com.ibm.sf.whs.Warehouse

public interface **Warehouse** extends DescribableDynamicEntity, Distinguishable, Shared

Main Methods

Name	*Signature*	*Description*
getAddress	`public abstract Address getAddress() throws SFException`	Method used to get the Address from the shared attributes.
setAddress	`public abstract void setAddress(Address anAddress) throws SFException`	Method used to set the Address of the Warehouse
getSharedMethods	`public abstract DSet getSharedMethods() throws SFException`	Returns the list of methods used to support shared attributes for this class.
addSharedOwnedPropertyBy	`public abstract void addSharedOwnedPropertyBy(Entity propertyToAddAsOwned, String propertyName) throws SFException`	Adds an owned Entity to the shared property container for this object, keyed by the given propertyName. The Entity property will be destroyed when this PropertyContainer is destroyed.
containsSharedPropertyKey	`public abstract boolean containsSharedPropertyKey(String propertyName) throws SFException`	Determines if propertyName is contained within the shared PropertyContainer for this object.
copySharedPropertyMap	`public abstract Map copySharedPropertyMap() throws SFException`	Returns a new transient Map holding all shared properties contained by this object.
getSharedPropertyBy	`public abstract Object getSharedPropertyBy(String propertyName) throws SFException`	Retrieves the shared property with a name matching the passed-in propertyName
getSharedPropertyBy	`public abstract Object getSharedPropertyBy(String propertyName, AccessMode am) throws SFException`	Retrieves the shared property with a name matching the passed-in propertyName. If the property is an Entity the AccessMode provided is used, otherwise the AccessMode parameter is ignored.
getSharedPropertyHdlBy	`public abstract Handle getSharedPropertyHdlBy(String propertyName) throws SFException`	Retrieves the shared property with a name matching the passed-in propertyName. If it is an Entity property, return a copy of its Handle, otherwise a CollectionException is thrown.
removeSharedContainedPropertyBy	`public abstract void removeSharedContainedPropertyBy(String propertyName) throws SFException`	Removes the non-owned Entity, owned Dependent, or owned String from the shared PropertyContainer for this object but does not delete the Entity.
removeSharedOwnedPropertyBy	`public abstract void removeSharedOwnedPropertyBy(String propertyName) throws SFException`	Removes the owned Entity from the shared PropertyContainer for this object and deletes the Entity.
createProductWarehouseLinkIterator	`public abstract Iterator createProductWarehouseLinkIterator() throws SFException`	Create Iterator for Collection of ProductWarehouseLinks
getNextProductWarehouseLink	`public abstract ProductWarehouseLink getNextProductWarehouseLink(Iterator position) throws SFException`	Gets the ProductWarehouseLink at the Next Iterator Position

Figure 27-3
Interface `Warehouse`

containsProductWarehouseLink	`public abstract boolean containsProductWarehouseLink(ProductWarehouseLink productwarehouselink) throws SFException`	Checks if the ProductWarehouseLink exists in the Collection of ProductWarehouseLinks
getProductWarehouseLinkAt	`public abstract ProductWarehouseLink getProductWarehouseLinkAt(Iterator position) throws SFException`	Gets the ProductWarehouseLink at the current iterator position
queryProductWarehouseLinks	`public abstract Set queryProductWarehouseLinks(String selectStatement, String bindCollectionName, SelectCompare selectCompareObject, String bindNameOfSelectCompareObject, SortCompare orderByCompareObject, String bindNameOfOrderByObject, boolean accessResults) throws SFException`	Query the ProductWarehouseLink from the Collection
addProductWarehouseLink	`public abstract void addProductWarehouseLink(ProductWarehouseLink productWarehouseLinkToAdd) throws SFException`	Adds a ProductWarehouseLink to the Collection of ProductWarehouseLinks
addAllProductWarehouseLinks	`public abstract void addAllProductWarehouseLinks(Set newProductWarehouseLinks) throws SFException`	Adds all ProductWarehouseLinks to the Collection of ProductWarehouseLinks
removeProductWarehouseLinkAt	`public abstract void removeProductWarehouseLinkAt(Iterator position) throws SFException`	Removes the ProductWarehouseLink at the Current Iterator Position
removeProductWarehouseLink	`public abstract void removeProductWarehouseLink(ProductWarehouseLink productwarehouselink) throws SFException`	Removes the specified ProductWarehouseLink
removeAllProductWarehouseLinks	`public abstract void removeAllProductWarehouseLinks() throws SFException`	Removes all ProductWarehouseLink from the Collection of ProductWarehouseLinks
getId	`public abstract String getId() throws SFException`	Gets id
getWeightUnit	`public abstract UnitOfMeasure getWeightUnit() throws SFException`	Returns the WeightUnit, copied from the Handle
setWeightUnit	`public abstract void setWeightUnit(UnitOfMeasure newWeightUnit) throws SFException`	Set the Handle of the WeightUnit
getLengthHeightWidthUnit	`public abstract UnitOfMeasure getLengthHeightWidthUnit() throws SFException`	Returns the LengthHeightWidthUnit, copied from the Handle

Figure 27-3
(Cont'd)

setLengthHeightWidthUnit	`public abstract void setLengthHeightWidthUnit(UnitOfMeasure newLengthHeightWidthUnit) throws SFException`	Set the Handle of the LengthHeightWidthUnit
getMainWarehouse	`public abstract boolean getMainWarehouse() throws SFException`	Gets MainWarehouse
getPhysicalWarehouse	`public abstract boolean getPhysicalWarehouse() throws SFException`	Gets PhysicalWarehouse
getInternalReplenishment	`public abstract boolean getInternalReplenishment() throws SFException`	Gets InternalReplenishment
getWeightUnitHdl	`public abstract Handle getWeightUnitHdl() throws SFException`	Returns the Handle to the UnitOfMeasure of the weightUnit of the Warehouse
getVolumeUnitHdl	`public abstract Handle getVolumeUnitHdl() throws SFException`	Returns the Handle to the UnitOfMeasure of the volumeUnit of the Warehouse
getSharedAttributesHdl	`public abstract Handle getSharedAttributesHdl() throws SFException`	Returns the Handle to the SharedWarehouseAttributes of the sharedAttributes of the Warehouse
getSupplyingWarehouseHdl	`public abstract Handle getSupplyingWarehouseHdl() throws SFException`	Returns the Handle to the Warehouse of the supplyingWarehouse of the Warehouse
getLengthHeightWidthUnitHdl	`public abstract Handle getLengthHeightWidthUnitHdl() throws SFException`	Returns the Handle to the UnitOfMeasure of the lengthHeightWidthUnit of the Warehouse

Figure 27-3
(Cont'd)

Replenishment

This category is in charge of evaluating inventory. Its goal is to make recommendations for orders from the supplier or another warehouse. The specific sources for replenishment (i.e. specific warehouses, either internal or belonging to suppliers) can be set on a per-product or per-warehouse combination. The main abstraction here is the `ReplenishmentSuggestion`, which includes a collection of `ReplenishmentSuggestionDetail` (see Figure 27-4) objects. Once established, this collection can be transformed into stock movements or purchase orders. The actual selection of the source and the need for replenishment calculation are all encapsulated by policy objects.

Interface com.ibm.sf.whs.ReplenishmentSuggestion Detail

public interface **ReplenishmentSuggestionDetail** extends DynamicEntity, ProductReservation, FutureReception

Main Methods:

Name	*Signature*	*Description*
setShippingTime	`public abstract void setShippingTime(DTime newShippingTime) throws SFException`	Sets the shipping time.
setDeliveryTime	`public abstract void setDeliveryTime(DTime newDeliveryTime) throws SFException`	Sets the delivery time.
getShippingTime	`public abstract DTime getShippingTime() throws SFException`	Gets ShippingTime
getDeliveryTime	`public abstract DTime getDeliveryTime() throws SFException`	Gets DeliveryTime
getReplenishmentSuggestionQuantity	`public abstract DProductTransactionQuantity getReplenishmentSuggestionQuantity() throws SFException`	Gets ReplenishmentSuggestionQuantity
setReplenishmentSuggestionQuantity	`public abstract void setReplenishmentSuggestionQuantity(DProductTransactionQuantity newReplenishmentSuggestionQuantity) throws SFException`	Sets ReplenishmentSuggestionQuantity
getAvailableQuantity	`public abstract DProductQuantityUnit getAvailableQuantity() throws SFException`	Gets AvailableQuantity
getROP	`public abstract DProductQuantityUnit getROP() throws SFException`	Gets ROP
setROP	`public abstract void setROP(DProductQuantityUnit newROP) throws SFException`	Sets ROP
setReplenishmentSource	`public abstract void setReplenishmentSource(ReplenishmentSource newReplenishmentSource) throws SFException`	Set the Handle of the ReplenishmentSource
getProductWarehouseLink	`public abstract ProductWarehouseLink getProductWarehouseLink() throws SFException`	Returns the ProductWarehouseLink, copied from the Handle
setId	`public abstract void setId(String newId) throws SFException`	Sets id

Figure 27-4
Interface `ReplenishmentSuggestion Detail`

setIsReservationUpdateable	`public abstract void setIsReservationUpdateable(boolean newIsReservationUpdateable) throws SFException`	Sets IsReservationUpdateable
setIsFutureReceptionUpdateable	`public abstract void setIsFutureReceptionUpdateable(boolean newIsFutureReceptionUpdateable) throws SFException`	Sets IsFutureReceptionUpdateable
getFromStockTypeHdl	`public abstract Handle getFromStockTypeHdl() throws SFException`	Returns the Handle to the StockTypeValue of the fromStockType of the ReplenishmentSuggestionDetail
getToStockTypeHdl	`public abstract Handle getToStockTypeHdl() throws SFException`	Returns the Handle to the StockTypeValue of the toStockType of the ReplenishmentSuggestionDetail
getReservationTypeValueHdl	`public abstract Handle getReservationTypeValueHdl() throws SFException`	Returns the Handle to the ReservationTypeValue of the ReservationTypeValue of the ReplenishmentSuggestionDetail
getFutureReceptionTypeValueHdl	`public abstract Handle getFutureReceptionTypeValueHdl() throws SFException`	Returns the Handle to the FutureReceptionTypeValue of the FutureReceptionTypeValue of the ReplenishmentSuggestionDetail
getUnitOfMeasureHdl	`public abstract Handle getUnitOfMeasureHdl() throws SFException`	Returns the Handle to the UnitOfMeasure of the UnitOfMeasure of the ReplenishmentSuggestionDetail
getReplenishmentSourceHdl	`public abstract Handle getReplenishmentSourceHdl() throws SFException`	Returns the Handle to the ReplenishmentSource of the ReplenishmentSource of the ReplenishmentSuggestionDetail
getProductWarehouseLinkHdl	`public abstract Handle getProductWarehouseLinkHdl() throws SFException`	Returns the Handle to the ProductWarehouseLink of the ProductWarehouseLink of the ReplenishmentSuggestionDetail
getId	`public abstract String getId() throws SFException`	Gets id

Figure 27-4
(Cont'd)

Balances and Reservations

This category maintains balances of inventories. The balance of one object is held in an object of type Inventory. Product reservations and future receptions are represented by objects of types `Product Reservation` and `FutureReception`. Both contain the associated product along with optional location information. Different types of product reservations and future receptions are supported via `ReservationType Value` and `FutureReservationTypeValue` objects.

Product balance retrieval is performed using the `ProductBalances` object using the caching mechanisms of the CBO layer (see Chapter 23). Various keys are provided for accessing inventories.

Picking

This category is in charge of the picking process covering picking products from stock. The picking process can be customized to specific business and finance policies. The picking process usually selects the appropriate locations, lots, or serial numbers for picking products from stock. It also updates inventory to reflect the changes and at the same time creates the necessary financial (i.e. GL) transactions.

`PickingStockTransactions` represent stock transactions caused by picking. Another abstraction in this category is the `PickList`. Its details are stored in a `PickListDetails`, which includes among other things a list of `PickingDetail` objects representing a single "picking". The framework provides `DPickingDetailCommon` as the core implementation of `PickingDetail`. Various policies are provided to determine how to construct and validate the picking list.

Reception

This category manages the reception process covering reception of product into the warehouse. This reception process can be customized to specific business and finance policies. The reception process updates inventory to reflect the correct amount and also creates the necessary financial (i.e. GL) transactions.

`ReceptionStockTransaction` represents stock transactions related to reception. A `ReceivingDetail` is related to a single reception and the framework provides a core implementation for it in `DReceivingDetailCommon`. For each reception made, a `ReceptionNote` object can be created for auditing purposes. Various policies determine the way reception notes are generated, the way the reception is confirmed, and so on.

Planning and Replanning

This category facilitates planning and re-planning of the allocation of stock between warehouses. Specific domain planning policies are implemented using `DPlanningPolicy`. This interface contains one method, called `plan()` which generates a full "planning details" given a "*plannable detail*" and a "*planning details*" containing the specification of the product. Essentially, it looks at a "*plannable details*" (represented by

PlannableDetail) and decides on the planning i.e. which warehouse, quantity, and unit of measure to use, when to do shipping or receiving, and then generates a PlanningDetail to encapsulate the plan.

Backorder Handling

This category supports the ability to optionally incorporate backordering support into the other processes, such as picking. Backordering is needed when there is shortage of some item. The BackorderableDetail interface is used to represent backordering. The DBackorderHandlingPolicy actually implements backordering logic. You can have several of these and then a DBackOrderingHandlingSelectionPolicy can contain logic for selecting the appropriate one.

CHAPTER 28

The Order Management Framework

The Order Management framework provides the infrastructure for developing order processing and management applications. The main abstraction in this framework is an order, and the framework supports an unlimited number of order types. It does, however, include specific examples of common types of orders. These specific examples can be used as are or customized for the specific needs of an application.

The Order Management framework introduces its own specific business objects, which usually extend the capabilities of business objects included in the CBO layer and in the Warehouse Management framework. Some new business objects are also introduced.

Order Management Business Objects

`OrderProduct`

The Product abstraction introduced in the Warehouse Management framework is extended to `OrderProduct` in the Order Management framework. This extension is made using aggregation, i.e. by containment, and essentially supports different "views" of a Product.

`OrderProduct` allows up to three different "views" of a single Product to be active during order processing. A product can be viewed as a purchase product meaning that it is purchased from a supplier. It can also be viewed as a sales product sold by the company to customers. The final way a product can be viewed is as an internal product, meaning that it is transferred internally between company warehouses. Note that a product can share several views, e.g. the same product can be a purchased product and a sales product at the same time.

`OrderProduct` also provides a means for limiting the use of a product to specific units of measurement. For example, it is possible to set up a purchase `OrderProduct` in which the unit of measure is by containers holding 100 pieces of the product and, for the same product, it defines a sales `OrderProduct` in which the unit of measure is a single piece. The Product itself, as provided in the Warehouse Management framework, allows work with different units and defines the conversions between them.

OrderPartner

The BusinessPartner abstraction from the CBO layer is extended to OrderPartner in the Order Management framework. Similar to OrderProduct, this extension is made using aggregation, i.e. by containment. Just like OrderProduct, the OrdnerPartner abstraction allows three different "views."

Corresponding to the views described in the previous section, OrderPartners can be viewed as customers, suppliers, and warehouses. The latter is actually the internal "customer" for internal stock movements. Building upon BusinessPartner, order partners have support for building tree-like hierarchies of partners. This way, the organization of a customer or supplier can be reflected in an application when needed.

Prices and Discounts

When selling products an important and complex task is to properly determine prices. Prices can differ between customers based on different criteria (which might depend on the specific product) and the discount policy of the selling party can vary according to various reasons (e.g. the time of year). Sometimes more than one discount can apply to a particular situation. For example, discounts based on volume, customer, or specific product. The application is required to decide which discounts should be used and if those discounts are multiplicative or additive. The number of potential combinations could be overwhelming and the risk of errors can turn out to be high.

The Order Management framework provides a flexible solution that helps implement a pricing policy in a way that keeps all the pricing information accessible. The Order Management pricing and discounting is built around a single object called the price and discount requester. This object retrieves a price and any applicable discounts given a specific order situation (including, among other things, the customer and order quantities). This requester is policy-based in order to allow for maximum flexibility in customizing it to the needs of a specific application. Prices and discounts are defined using specialized keys based on The Generalized Mechanisms CBO (see Chapter 23). These keys allow you to associate specific price and discount values with different business objects (e.g. an OrderPartner or OrderProduct).

In addition, the framework includes retrieval policies for both prices and discounts. These policies can be implemented in an application-specific way so that various combinations of retrieval attributes are used for retrieval until a match is found.

Order Impacts

In some cases business processes related to ordering have some mutual dependencies. Order impacts provide the structure that allows application developers using the Order Management to make the correct links between the different processes. Most processes that can be associated with an order type have an order impact class defined for them.

Essentially, these "order impact" objects hold information relating to the different stages in processing an order and these stages are maintained in objects that are used for all specific orders. Order impacts are charged with defining and managing four different kinds of information.

- The next processing step allowed for a given order type (this is the "impact"), based on the current step (e.g. in a full sales order, once "picking" is done, the next step is always "shipping"). This in many ways defines the workflow in the organization.
- The LifeCycle to be used for creating order detail instances for a specific order type. These LifeCycle objects control the order flow for the specific order type. In other words, a LifeCycle object determines the valid processing steps that are allowed for the order-details that are associated with it.
- The shared order attributes to which all instances of a particular type make reference.
- The definition of shared business rules that all instances of a particular type used during processing.

A specific set of order detail impacts, related to each other by the "next process steps" relation, makes up an order type.

Order Types

Order Management provides several built-in order types. These order types are actually samples, and it is possible to extend the set of order types as needed. Application developers can either add new types of their own or customize the existing types to the needs of a specific application or customer. The framework defines the following order types.

- *Full Purchase*. Standard purchase order (including planning and receiving)
- *Full Sales*. Standard sales order (includes planning, picking, shipping, and invoicing)
- *Direct Sales*. Sales order that goes directly from order entry to invoicing
- *Credit Sales*. Sales order that is used to handle returned goods
- *Quotation*. Represents a bid and not a sale. An order of this type can be converted to a standard order if the bid is accepted
- *Stock Movement*. Represents internal stock movements between warehouses
- *Direct Back-to-Back Sales*. Automatically creates an associated purchase order to be created. This order type provides for goods to be shipped from the supplier directly to the customer

Order Management Business Processes

The Order Management processes are built upon the processes introduced in the Warehouse Management framework described in the previous chapter. Some new processes are introduced that are specific to the order-processing realm. These processes are built on top of the CBO layer, either directly or using the objects described in the previous section. In many respects therefore, the OM framework is not only built on top of the CBO layer but on parts of CBPs, i.e. the Warehouse Management framework.

All the processes in this framework are designed so that the coupling between the various processes can be managed in a very flexible way. One of the means to achieve this, is that this framework uses the lifecycle mechanisms provided by the Generalized Mechanism CBOs described in Chapter 23. The following new processes are introduced by Order Management.

- *Order*. Entering customer and supplier details (also known as "order header")
- *OrderPriceDetail*. Entering product and price information
- *OrderRequestedDetail*. Determining the quantity, delivery time, and delivery address information (combined with `OrderPriceDetail`, this is known as the order line)
- *OrderAcknowledgment*. Acknowledgment of the order.
- *Invoicing*. This process, based on the Invoicing category in the CFFI package, is used to record the billing information related to an order.
- *Supplementary Charges*. This process, based on the respective CBO layer category, is used to record charges on an order that are not directly related to products. This might be fixed administrative charge, invoicing fees, etc.

The first three processes listed above comprise the order entry mechanism for an order management application. These processes have different views just like `OrderPartner`. In other words, the same design technique is used to support sales, purchase, and internal orders.

Order Management Framework Categories

`OrderProduct` and `OrderPartner`

Following the design of the other SanFrancisco framework, the Order Management framework consists of a set of classes grouped together into categories. These categories are described below. Table 28.1 summarizes the composition of each of the categories. As with the other frameworks, various categories here make extensive use of the `PropertyContainer` interface of companies and other business objects. This use is summarized in Table 28.2.

This category represents the order management framework "views" of the `Product` and `BusinessPartner` classes, as just discussed. This category defines `OrderProduct` (see Figure 28-1), which links an `OrderPartner` and Product. `OrderProduct` objects can be used to

TABLE 28-1

Summary of Order Management Categories and their composition.

Category	Major Components
Order	DOrderCommon DOrderPriceDetailCommon FullSalesOrder FullSalesOrderCreateable FullPurchaseOrder FullSalesOrderPriceDetail FullPurchaseOrderPriceDetail FullSalesOrderPriceDetailCreateable FullPurchaseOrderPriceDetailCreateable FullSalesOrderRequestedDetail FullPurchaseOrderRequestedDetail Order OrderPriceDetail OrderRequestedDetail DOrderExtension DOrderPriceDetailExtension DOrderRequestedDetailExtension DFullSalesOrderCreateableAdapter DFullSalesOrderCreateableExtension DOrderRequestedDetailCommon DBuildFullOrderPolicy DBuildFullOrderPolicyDefault DFullSalesOrderAdapter DFullSalesOrderExtension DFullSalesOrderPriceDetailCreateableAdapter DFullSalesOrderPriceDetailCreateableExtension DBuildFullOrderPriceDetailPolicy DBuildFullOrderPriceDetailPolicyDefault DFullSalesOrderPriceDetailAdapter DFullSalesOrderPriceDetailExtension DFullSalesOrderRequestedDetailAdapter DFullSalesOrderRequestedDetailExtension DFullSalesOrderRequestedDetailCreateableAdapter DFullSalesOrderRequestedDetailCreateableExtension DBuildFullOrderRequestedDetailPolicy DBuildFullOrderRequestedDetailPolicyDefault OrderPriceDetailCreateable OrderCreateable OrderRequestedDetailCreateable DFullPurchaseOrderAdapter DFullPurchaseOrderExtension FullPurchaseOrderCreateable DFullPurchaseOrderCreateableAdapter DFullPurchaseOrderCreateableExtension DFullPurchaseOrderPriceDetailCreateableExtension DFullPurchaseOrderPriceDetailAdapter DFullPurchaseOrderPriceDetailExtension DFullPurchaseOrderRequestedDetailCreateableAdapter DFullPurOrderRequestedDetailCreateableExtension

TABLE 28-1

(Cont'd)

Category	Major Components
	DFullPurchaseOrderRequestedDetailAdapter DFullPurchaseOrderRequestedDetailExtension DOrderDiscountDetail DOrderPriceAndDiscount DPriceAndDiscountChooserPolicy DPriceAndDiscountChooserPolicyDefault OrderPriceAndDiscountRetrievalView DOrderPriceAndDiscountRetrievalViewAdapter DOrderPriceAndDiscountRetrievalView ERDOrderPriceAndDiscountCalculationPolicy OrderRequestedDetailImpact OrderPriceDetailImpact OrderImpact DDeliveryTimeHandlingPolicy DCreditHandlingPolicy DStockTypeHandlingPolicy DBackToBackHandlingPolicy DExchangeRateHandlingPolicy ExchangeRateCalculationView DExchangeRateCalculationViewAdapter DInventoryValidationPolicySalesDebit DInventoryValidationPolicyDirectSalesDebit DInventoryValidationPolicyPurchaseDebit DInventoryValidationPolicySalesCredit OrderValueCalculationView DOrderPriceDetailValueCalculationViewAdapter DOrderRequestedDetailValueCalculationViewAdapter DExchangeRateCalculationView OrderPriceDetailController OrderRequestedDetailController OrderController OrderPlanningDetailController OrderPickingDetailController OrderPricingDetail OrderInvoicingDetailProductController OrderInvoicingDetailChargeController OrderSupplementaryChargeController OrderInvoiceGroup OrderDeliveryGroup OrderDeliveryGroupDetail OrderDeliveryTimeHandling OrderIngCommon
Supplementary Charge	DOrderSupplementaryChargeExtension DOrderSupplementaryChargeAdapter OrderSupplementaryChargeImpact DOrderSupplementaryChargeableAdapter OrderSupplementaryChargeable DOrderSupplementaryChargeableExtension OrderSupplementaryCharge DOrderSupplementaryChargeHandlingPolicy

TABLE 28-1

(Cont'd)

Category	Major Components
Information	DQuantityAndValueLimit DQuantityAndValueLimitEntry OrderPartnerPriceGroupController OrderProductPriceGroupController PriceCategoryController PriceCategory OrderProductPriceGroup OrderPartnerPriceGroup OrderControllerTypeController OrderControllerType OrderPartnerDiscountGroup OrderProductDiscountGroup DiscountCategory OrderPartnerDiscountGroupController OrderProductDiscountGroupController DiscountCategoryController
Accounting Transactions	DCreditOrderAccountControlType DFreeOfChargeAccountControlType DDiscountCategoryAccountControlType DOrderIntegrationKeyInvoicedAssetDissectionCreateCmd InvoicedCoinAdjustmentDissectionCreateCmd InvoicedGrossValueDissectionCreateCmd InvoicedDiscountDissectionCreateCmd InvoiceCostDissectionCreateCmd CostOfInvoicedGoodsDissectionCreateCmd InvoicedSupplementaryChargeDissectionCreateCmd OrderAccountControlTypesAddCmd OrderDomainGenericDissectionTypesAddCmd OrderFinancialTransactionSourcesAddCmd
Pricing and Discounts	DPriceDefinition DPriceDefinitionChooserSelectionPolicy DPriceDefinitionChooserPolicy PriceDefinitionDController DPriceDefinitionKey DPriceKey DDiscountDefinition DDiscountDefinitionKey DDiscountKey DiscountDefinitionDController DDiscountDefinitionChooserSelectionPolicy DDiscountDefinitionChooserPolicy
Reception	OrderReceivableDetail OrderReceivingDetail DOrderReceivingDetailCommon DOrderReceivingDetailDeletePreparationPolicy DOrderReceptionCommitableDetailAdapter

TABLE 28-1
(Cont'd)

Category	Major Components
	DOrderReceptionCommitableDetailExtension OrderReceivingDetailImpact DOrderReceptionConfirmableDetailAdapter DOrderReceptionConfirmableDetailExtension DOrderReceivableDetailAdapter DOrderReceivableDetailExtension DOrderReceivingDetailAdapter DOrderReceivingDetailExtension
Picking	OrderPickableDetail DOrderPickableDetailAdapter DOrderPickableDetailExtension DOrderPickingDetailAdapter DOrderPickingDetailExtension OrderPickingDetail DOrderPickingDetailCommon OrderPickingDetailImpact DOrderPickingDetailDeletePreparationPolicy DOrderPickConfirmableDetailAdapter DOrderPickConfirmableDetailExtension DOrderPickCommitableDetailAdapter DOrderPickCommitableDetailExtension DOrderPickCommitPolicyDefault
Backorder Handling	OrderBackorderableDetail DOrderBackorderableDetailAdapter DOrderBackorderableDetailExtension DOrderIsBackorderExtension DOrderBackorderHandlingPolicyUpdatePicking DOrderBackorderHandlingPolicyUpdatePlanning DOrderBackorderHandlingPolicy DOrderBackorderHandlingConditionChangeResult
Replenishment	ReplenishmentSourceSupplier ReplenishmentSourceWarehouse
Planning	OrderPlanningPolicy DOrderPlanningDetailExtension DOrderPlannableDetailExtension DOrderPlannableDetailAdapter DOrderPlanningDetailAdapter OrderPlannableDetail OrderPlanningDetail DOrderPlanningDetailCreatorPolicyBackToBack DOrderPlanningDetailCommonOrderPlanningDetailImpact DOrderPlanningDetailDeletePreparationPolicy

TABLE 28-1

(Cont'd)

Category	Major Components
Product and Partner	OrderPartner OrderPartnerController OrderProduct OrderProductOrderPartnerLink OrderProductWarehouseLink OrderProductUnitLink DAlternativeOrderProductUnitDefinition OrderProductController DSubstituteOrderProductUnitValidationPolicy DSubstituteOrderProductUnitChooserPolicy DReplacingOrderProductUnitValidationPolicy DReplacingOrderProductUnitChooserPolicy DAlternativeOrderProductUnitDefinitionKey DAlternativeOrderProductUnitKey
Invoicing	OrderInvoiceableDetail OrderInvoicingDetailProduct OrderInvoicingDetailCharge OrderInvoicingDetail DOrderInvoiceableDetailExtension DOrderInvoicingDetailAdapter DOrderInvoicingDetailProductAdapter DOrderInvoicingDetailChargeAdapter DOrderInvoiceableDetailAdapter DOrderInvoicingDetailCommon DOrderInvoicingDetailExtension DOrderInvoiceableDetailProductAdapter DOrderInvoiceableDetailChargeAdapter OrderInvoiceableDetailProduct OrderInvoiceableDetailCharge OrderInvoicingDetailImpact DOrderInvoiceableDetailProductExtension DOrderInvoiceableDetailChargeExtension DOrderInvoicingDetailProductExtension DOrderInvoicingDetailChargeExtension DOrderInvoicingDetailProductCommon DOrderInvoicingDetailChargeCommon DOrderInvoicingDetailDeletePreparationPolicy DOrderInvoiceableDetailValueCalculationViewAdapter

represent Products as purchase, internal or sales products in order management processes. The other important abstraction in this category is the `OrderPartner`—a business partner extended with order-specific information. A `BusinessPartner` may be represented as one or more of the following `OrderPartner` types: customer, supplier, or internal. The `OrderPartner` interface is shown in Figure 28-2.

TABLE 28-2

Summary of Order Management Framework Properties.

Property On	Property Type	Property Name
Company	OrderProductController	om.OrderProductController.OM_SALES
	OrderPartnerController	om.OrderPartnerController.OM_SUPPLIER
	DPriceDefinitionChooserPolicy	om.DPriceDefinitionChooserPolicy
	PriceDefinitionDController	om.PriceDefinitionController.OM_PURCHASE
	OrderPartnerPriceGroupController	om.OrderPartnerPriceGroupController.OM_INTERNAL
	OrderProductPriceGroupController	om.OrderProductPriceGroupController.OM_INTERNAL
	PriceCategoryController	om.PriceCategoryController.OM_PURCHASE
	OrderControllerTypeController	om.OrderControllerTypeController
	DReplacingOrderProductUnitChooserPolicy	om.DReplacingOrderProductUnitChooserPolicy
	DReplacingOrderProductUnitValidationPolicy	om.DReplacingOrderProductUnitValidationPolicy
	DSubstituteOrderProductUnitChooserPolicy	om.DSubstituteOrderProductUnitChooserPolicy
	DSubstituteOrderProductUnitValidationPolicy	om.DSubstituteOrderProductUnitValidationPolicy
	DiscountCategoryController	om.DiscountCategoryController.OM_PURCHASE
	OrderProductDiscountGroupController	om.OrderProductDiscountGroupController.OM_SALES
	OrderPartnerDiscountGroupController	om.OrderPartnerDiscountGroupController.OM_SALES
	OrderPartnerController	om.OrderPartnerController.OM_CUSTOMER
	OrderPartnerController	om.OrderPartnerController.OM_WAREHOUSE
	PriceDefinitionDController	om.PriceDefinitionController.OM_INTERNAL
	PriceDefinitionDController	om.PriceDefinitionController.OM_SALES
	OrderPartnerPriceGroupController	om.OrderPartnerPriceGroupController.OM_SALES
	OrderPartnerPriceGroupController	om.OrderPartnerPriceGroupController.OM_PURCHASE
	OrderProductPriceGroupController	om.OrderProductPriceGroupController.OM_SALES
	OrderProductPriceGroupController	om.OrderProductPriceGroupController.OM_PURCHASE
	PriceCategoryController	om.PriceCategoryController.OM_SALES
	PriceCategoryController	om.PriceCategoryController.OM_INTERNAL
	OrderProductDiscountGroupController	om.OrderProductDiscountGroupController.OM_INTERNAL
	OrderProductDiscountGroupController	om.OrderProductDiscountGroupController.OM_PURCHASE
	OrderPartnerDiscountGroupController	om.OrderPartnerDiscountGroupController.OM_INTERNAL
	OrderPartnerDiscountGroupController	om.OrderPartnerDiscountGroupController.OM_PURCHASE
	OrderProductController	om.OrderProductController.OM_INTERNAL
	OrderProductController	om.OrderProductController.OM_PURCHASE
	DiscountCategoryController	om.DiscountCategoryController.OM_SALES
	DiscountCategoryController	om.DiscountCategoryController.OM_INTERNAL
	OrderPriceDetailController	om.FullSalesOrderPriceDetailController
	OrderRequestedDetailController	om.FullSalesOrderRequestedDetailController
	OrderController	om.FullSalesOrderController
	OrderPlanningDetailController	om.OrderPlanningDetailController
	OrderPickingDetailController	om.OrderPickingDetailController
	OrderInvoicingDetailProductController	om.OrderInvoicingDetailProductController
	OrderInvoicingDetailChargeController	om.OrderInvoicingDetailChargeController
	OrderSupplementaryChargeController	om.OrderSupplementaryChargeController
	OrderController	om.FullPurchaseOrderController
	OrderPriceDetailController	om.FullPurchaseOrderPriceDetailController
	OrderRequestedDetailController	om.FullPurchaseOrderRequestedDetailController
	DInvoiceDissectionCreatorPolicy	om.DInvoiceDissectionCreatorPolicy
	DInteger	om.InvoicingDetailIncrement
	NumberSeries	om.NumberSeriesForInvoice
	NumberSeries	om.NumberSeriesForCreditInvoice
	DDiscountDefinitionChooserPolicy	om.DDiscountDefinitionChooserPolicy
	DPriceAndDiscountChooserPolicy	om.DPriceAndDiscountChooserPolicy

TABLE 28-2

(Cont'd)

Property On	Property Type	Property Name
BusinessPartner Customer SupplierData	OrderPartner	om.OrderPartner
BusinessPartner	OrderPartner	om.OrderFinancialPartner.OM_CUSTOMER
SharedData	NumberSeries	om.NumberSeriesForCreditInvoice

Pricing and Discounts

As already discussed previously, the Order Management framework allows you to set up and manage sales, purchase and internal pricing information in a flexible manner. This category provides support for defining prices within the framework. The main abstraction here is `DPriceDefinition` (see Figure 28-3). Prices can be defined based on a wide range of consideration, including time ranges. Retrieval of prices is done through a policy-based algorithm.

Similarly, this category provides support for defining discounts through the `DDiscountDefinition` interface. Discounts can also be defined based on a wide range of attributes, and their retrieval of discounts is managed through a policy-based algorithm.

Replenishment

This category defines relationships between the classes used to perform replenishment. It allows `OrderPartners` to be treated as `ReplenishmentSources` in the Warehouse Management Replenishment category. Order Management introduces two specific types of replenishment sources: `ReplenishmentSourceSupplier` representing external suppliers, and `ReplenishmentSourceWarehouse` representing internal warehouses.

Interface com.ibm.sf.om.OrderPartner

public interface interface **OrderPartner**
extends DynamicEntity, Shared, Distinguishable, Describable

Main Method:

Name	*Signature*	*Description*
getWarehouse	`public abstract Warehouse getWarehouse() throws SFException`	Get the Warehouse attribute for this object
getTermsOfDelivery	`public abstract TermsOfDelivery getTermsOfDelivery() throws SFException`	This attribute may reside in the current OrderPartner or any OrderPartner of the same OrderControllerType in the BusinessPartner hierarchy.
getOrderPartnerPriceGroup	`public abstract OrderPartnerPriceGroup getOrderPartnerPriceGroup() throws SFException`	This attribute may reside in the current OrderPartner or any OrderPartner of the same OrderControllerType in the BusinessPartner hierarchy.
getOrderPartnerDiscountGroup	`public abstract OrderPartnerDiscountGroup getOrderPartnerDiscountGroup() throws SFException`	This attribute may reside in the current OrderPartner or any OrderPartner of the same OrderControllerType in the BusinessPartner hierarchy
getMannerOfTransport	`public abstract MannerOfTransport getMannerOfTransport() throws SFException`	This attribute may reside in the current OrderPartner or any OrderPartner of the same OrderControllerType in the BusinessPartner hierarchy.
getOrderFinancialPartner	`public abstract OrderPartner getOrderFinancialPartner() throws SFException`	The getOrderFinancialPartner method is implemented on OrderPartner for the convenience of the client.
getDefaultOrderWarehouse	`public abstract Warehouse getDefaultOrderWarehouse() throws SFException`	This attribute may reside in the current OrderPartner or any OrderPartner of the same OrderControllerType in the BusinessPartner hierarchy.
getDirectlyContainedDefaultOrderWarehouse	`public abstract Warehouse getDirectlyContainedDefaultOrderWarehouse() throws SFException`	This returns the defaultOrderWarehouse in the current OrderPartner and does not traverse the business partner hierarchy
getDirectlyContainedTermsOfDelivery	`public abstract TermsOfDelivery getDirectlyContainedTermsOfDelivery() throws SFException`	This returns the termsOfDelivery in the current OrderPartner and does not traverse the business partner hierarchy
getDirectlyContainedOrderPartnerDiscountGroup	`public abstract OrderPartnerDiscountGroup getDirectlyContainedOrderPartnerDiscountGroup() throws SFException`	This returns the orderPartnerDiscountGroup in the current OrderPartner and does not traverse the business partner hierarchy.
getDirectlyContainedOrderPartnerPriceGroup	`public abstract OrderPartnerPriceGroup getDirectlyContainedOrderPartnerPriceGroup() throws SFException`	This returns the orderPartnerPriceGroup in the current OrderPartner and does not traverse the business partner hierarchy.
getDirectlyContainedMannerOfTransport	`public abstract MannerOfTransport getDirectlyContainedMannerOfTransport() throws SFException`	This returns the mannerOfTransport in the current OrderPartner and does not traverse the business partner hierarchy

Figure 28-1
Interface `OrderProduct`

getDirectlyContainedOrderFinancialPartner	`public abstract OrderPartner getDirectlyContainedOrderFinancialPartner() throws SFException`	The getOrderFinancialPartner method is implemented on OrderPartner for the convenience of the client.
setDirectlyContainedOrderFinancialPartner	`public abstract void setDirectlyContainedOrderFinancialPartner(OrderPartner newOrderFinancialPartner) throws SFException`	Set the OrderFinancialPartner
getSharedMethods	`public abstract DSet getSharedMethods() throws SFException`	Returns the list of methods used to support shared attributes for this class.
addSharedContainedPropertyBy	`public abstract void addSharedContainedPropertyBy(Object propertyToAdd, String propertyName) throws SFException`	Adds either an unowned Entity, owned Dependent, or owned String property to the shared property container for this object, keyed by the given propertyName. An Entity property will not be destroyed when this PropertyContainer is destroyed. A Dependent or String property is a copy of the passed in parameter so is owned by this PropertyContainer and therefore deleted when this PropertyContainer is destroyed.
addSharedOwnedPropertyBy	`public abstract void addSharedOwnedPropertyBy(Entity propertyToAddAsOwned, String propertyName) throws SFException`	Adds an owned Entity to the shared property container for this object, keyed by the given propertyName. The Entity property will be destroyed when this PropertyContainer is destroyed.
getSharedPropertyBy	`public abstract Object getSharedPropertyBy(String propertyName) throws SFException`	Retrieves the shared property with a name matching the passed-in propertyName.
getSharedPropertyBy	`public abstract Object getSharedPropertyBy(String propertyName, AccessMode am) throws SFException`	Retrieves the shared property with a name matching the passed-in propertyName. If the property is an Entity the AccessMode provided is used, otherwise the AccessMode parameter is ignored.
getSharedPropertyHdlBy	`public abstract Handle getSharedPropertyHdlBy(String propertyName) throws SFException`	Retrieves the shared property with a name matching the passed-in propertyName. If it is an Entity property, return a copy of its Handle, otherwise a CollectionException is thrown.
getDescription	`public abstract String getDescription() throws SFException`	Retrieves the description of this object as a String in a format/language determined by the locale that is currently active in the environment this call was made in.
getDescriptiveInformation	`public abstract DescriptiveInformation getDescriptiveInformation() throws SFException`	Retrieves the DescriptiveInformation object encapsulating the locale sensitive description of this object.
setYourReference	`public abstract void setYourReference(String newYourReference) throws SFException`	Sets YourReference
setOurReference	`public abstract void setOurReference(String newOurReference) throws SFException`	Sets OurReference

Figure 28-1
(Cont'd)

CreateOrderProductOrderPartnerLinkIterator	`public abstract Iterator createOrderProductOrderPartnerLinkIterator() throws SFException`	Create Iterator for Collection of OrderProductOrderPartnerLinks
GetNextOrderProductOrderPartnerLink	`public abstract OrderProductOrderPartnerLink getNextOrderProductOrderPartnerLink(Iterator position) throws SFException`	Gets the OrderProductOrderPartnerLink at the Next Iterator Position
ContainsOrderProductOrderPartnerLink	`public abstract boolean containsOrderProductOrderPartnerLink(OrderProductOrderPartnerLink orderproductorderpartnerlink) throws SFException`	Checks if the OrderProductOrderPartnerLink exists in the Collection of OrderProductOrderPartnerLinks
GetOrderProductOrderPartnerLinkAt	`public abstract OrderProductOrderPartnerLink getOrderProductOrderPartnerLinkAt(Iterator position) throws SFException`	Gets the OrderProductOrderPartnerLink at the current iterator position
AddOrderProductOrderPartnerLink	`public abstract void addOrderProductOrderPartnerLink(OrderProductOrderPartnerLink orderProductOrderPartnerLinkToAdd) throws SFException`	Adds a OrderProductOrderPartnerLink to the Collection of OrderProductOrderPartnerLinks
AddAllOrderProductOrderPartnerLinks	`public abstract void addAllOrderProductOrderPartnerLinks(Set newOrderProductOrderPartnerLinks) throws SFException`	Adds all OrderProductOrderPartnerLinks to the Collection of OrderProductOrderPartnerLinks
removeOrderProductOrderPartnerLinkAt	`public abstract void removeOrderProductOrderPartnerLinkAt(Iterator position) throws SFException`	Removes the OrderProductOrderPartnerLink at the Current Iterator Position
removeOrderProductOrderPartnerLink	`public abstract void removeOrderProductOrderPartnerLink(OrderProductOrderPartnerLink orderproductorderpartnerlink) throws SFException`	Removes the specified OrderProductOrderPartnerLink
removeAllOrderProductOrderPartnerLinks	`public abstract void removeAllOrderProductOrderPartnerLinks() throws SFException`	Removes all OrderProductOrderPartnerLink from the Collection of OrderProductOrderPartnerLinks
getBusinessPartner	`public abstract BusinessPartner getBusinessPartner() throws SFException`	Returns the BusinessPartner, copied from the Handle
setDirectlyContainedDefaultOrderWarehouse	`public abstract void setDirectlyContainedDefaultOrderWarehouse(Warehouse newDefaultOrderWarehouse) throws SFException`	Set the Handle of the DefaultOrderWarehouse
getOrderControllerType	`public abstract OrderControllerType getOrderControllerType() throws SFException`	Returns the OrderControllerType, copied from the Handle
getBusinessPartnerSharedData	`public abstract BusinessPartnerSharedData getBusinessPartnerSharedData() throws SFException`	Returns the BusinessPartnerSharedData, copied from the Handle

Figure 28-1
(Cont'd)

getBusinessPartnerCustomerSupplierData	`public abstract BusinessPartnerCustomerSupplierData getBusinessPartnerCustomerSupplierData() throws SFException`	Returns the BusinessPartnerCustomerSupplierData, copied from the Handle
isOrderAllowed	`public abstract boolean isOrderAllowed() throws SFException`	Gets OrderAllowed
setOrderAllowed	`public abstract void setOrderAllowed(boolean newOrderAllowed) throws SFException`	Sets OrderAllowed
isBackOrderAllowed	`public abstract boolean isBackOrderAllowed() throws SFException`	Gets BackOrderAllowed
setBackOrderAllowed	`public abstract void setBackOrderAllowed(boolean newBackOrderAllowed) throws SFException`	Sets BackOrderAllowed
isCompleteDelivery	`public abstract boolean isCompleteDelivery() throws SFException`	Gets CompleteDelivery
setCompleteDelivery	`public abstract void setCompleteDelivery(boolean newCompleteDelivery) throws SFException`	Sets CompleteDelivery
isCompleteInvoicing	`public abstract boolean isCompleteInvoicing() throws SFException`	Gets CompleteInvoicing
setCompleteInvoicing	`public abstract void setCompleteInvoicing(boolean newCompleteInvoicing) throws SFException`	Sets CompleteInvoicing
isQualityControlOnReception	`public abstract boolean isQualityControlOnReception() throws SFException`	Gets QualityControlOnReception
setQualityControlOnReception	`public abstract void setQualityControlOnReception(boolean newQualityControlOnReception) throws SFException`	Sets QualityControlOnReception
getYourReference	`public abstract String getYourReference() throws SFException`	Gets YourReference
getOurReference	`public abstract String getOurReference() throws SFException`	Gets OurReference
getMannerOfTransportHdl	`public abstract Handle getMannerOfTransportHdl() throws SFException`	Returns the Handle to the MannerOfTransport of the MannerOfTransport of the OrderPartner
getTermsOfDeliveryHdl	`public abstract Handle getTermsOfDeliveryHdl() throws SFException`	Returns the Handle to the TermsOfDelivery of the TermsOfDelivery of the OrderPartner
getOrderPartnerPriceGroupHdl	`public abstract Handle getOrderPartnerPriceGroupHdl() throws SFException`	Returns the Handle to the OrderPartnerPriceGroup of the OrderPartnerPriceGroup of the OrderPartner

Figure 28-1
(Cont'd)

getOrderPartnerDiscountGroupHdl	`public abstract Handle getOrderPartnerDiscountGroupHdl() throws SFException`	Returns the Handle to the OrderPartnerDiscountGroup of the OrderPartnerDiscountGroup of the OrderPartner
getOrderProductOrderPartnerLinksHdl	`public abstract Handle getOrderProductOrderPartnerLinksHdl() throws SFException`	Get handle to OrderProductOrderPartnerLinks,used by framework
getBusinessPartnerHdl	`public abstract Handle getBusinessPartnerHdl() throws SFException`	Returns the Handle to the BusinessPartner of the BusinessPartner of the OrderPartner
getDefaultOrderWarehouseHdl	`public abstract Handle getDefaultOrderWarehouseHdl() throws SFException`	Returns the Handle to the Warehouse of the defaultOrderWarehouse of the OrderPartner
getOrderControllerTypeHdl	`public abstract Handle getOrderControllerTypeHdl() throws SFException`	Returns the Handle to the OrderControllerType of the OrderControllerType of the OrderPartner
getBusinessPartnerSharedDataHdl	`public abstract Handle getBusinessPartnerSharedDataHdl() throws SFException`	Returns the Handle to the BusinessPartnerSharedData of the BusinessPartnerSharedData of the OrderPartner
getWarehouseHdl	`public abstract Handle getWarehouseHdl() throws SFException`	Returns the Handle to the Warehouse of the warehouse of the OrderPartner
getBusinessPartnerCustomerSupplierDataHdl	`public abstract Handle getBusinessPartnerCustomerSupplierDataHdl() throws SFException`	Returns the Handle to the BusinessPartnerCustomerSupplierData of the BusinessPartnerCustomerSupplierData of the OrderPartner
getId	`public abstract String getId() throws SFException`	Gets id

Figure 28-1
(Cont'd)

Accounting Transactions

Similar to the category of the same name in the Warehouse Management framework, this category works with the CFFI financial integration package (see Chapter 22) to hide away all the details of the CFFI package from the rest of the framework. It captures all the Order Management specific information needed to create financial dissections. This category defines the account control types for Order Management, which are: `DCreditOrderAccountControlType`, `DFreeOfChargeAccountControlType`, `DDiscountCategoryAccountControlType`. As in the respective Warehouse Management category, it also defines Command objects (with no target) in order to create dissections in different cases.

Interface com.ibm.sf.om.OrderProduct

public interface **OrderProduct** extends DynamicEntity, Distinguishable, Shared, Describable

Name	*Signature*	*Description*
isRelatedToUnitOfMeasure	`public abstract boolean isRelatedToUnitOfMeasure (UnitOfMeasure unitOfMeasure) throws SFException`	Checks whether the OrderProduct is related to the passed in UnitOfMeasure.
isRelatedToWarehouse	`public abstract boolean isRelatedToWarehouse(Warehouse warehouse) throws SFException`	Checks whether this OrderProduct is related to the specified Warehouse.
isRelatedToOrderPartner	`public abstract boolean isRelatedToOrderPartner (OrderPartner orderPartner) throws SFException`	Checks whether this OrderProduct is related to the specified OrderPartner.
chooseSubstituteOrderProductUnits	`public abstract Set chooseSubstituteOrderProductUnits( UnitOfMeasure unitOfMeasure, DTime time, ProcessTokenValue orderProcessId) throws SFException`	Interface to the DSubstituteOrderProductUnitChooserPolicy. The Set returned contains 0..n OrderProductUnitLinks.
chooseReplacingOrderProductUnits	`public abstract Set chooseReplacingOrderProductUnits(UnitOfMeasure unitOfMeasure, DTime time, ProcessTokenValue orderProcessId) throws SFException`	Interface to the DReplacingOrderProductUnitChooserPolicy. The Set returned contains 0..n OrderProductUnitLinks.
isOrderAllowed	`public abstract boolean isOrderAllowed(OrderPartner orderPartner) throws SFException`	Check if order of this OrderProduct is allowed for the passed OrderPartner.
isBackOrderAllowed	`public abstract boolean isBackOrderAllowed(OrderPartner orderPartner) throws SFException`	Check if back order of this OrderProduct is allowed for the passed OrderPartner.
hasQualityControlOnReception	`public abstract boolean hasQualityControlOnReception (OrderPartner orderPartner) throws SFException`	Check if this OrderProduct has quality control on reception for the passed OrderPartner.
setOrderProductPriceGroup	`public abstract void setOrderProductPriceGroup (OrderProductPriceGroup orderProductPriceGroup) throws SFException`	Sets the attribute to the passed OrderProductPriceGroup for this OrderProduct. May be passed as null in order to remove an OrderProductPriceGroup.
setOrderProductDiscountGroup	`public abstract void setOrderProductDiscountGroup (OrderProductDiscountGroup orderProductDiscountGroup) throws SFException`	Sets the attribute to the passed OrderProductDiscountGroup for this OrderProduct. May be passed as null in order to remove an OrderProductDiscountGroup.
getSharedMethods	`public abstract DSet getSharedMethods() throws SFException`	Returns the list of methods used to support shared attributes for this class.

Figure 28-2
Interface `OrderPartner`

addSharedContainedPropertyBy	`public abstract void addSharedContainedPropertyBy(Object propertyToAdd, String propertyName) throws SFException`	Adds either an unowned Entity, owned Dependent, or owned String property to the shared property container for this object, keyed by the given propertyName. An Entity property will not be destroyed when this PropertyContainer is destroyed. A Dependent or String property is a copy of the passed in parameter so is owned by this PropertyContainer and therefore deleted when this PropertyContainer is destroyed.
addSharedOwnedPropertyBy	`public abstract void addSharedOwnedPropertyBy(Entity propertyToAddAsOwned, String propertyName) throws SFException`	Adds an owned Entity to the shared property container for this object, keyed by the given propertyName. The Entity property will be destroyed when this PropertyContainer is destroyed.
getSharedPropertyBy	`public abstract Object getSharedPropertyBy(String propertyName) throws SFException`	Retrieves the shared property with a name matching the passed-in propertyName.
getSharedPropertyByForRestrictedUse	`public abstract Object getSharedPropertyByForRestrictedUse(String propertyName) throws SFException`	Retrieves the shared property with a name matching the passed-in propertyName.
getSharedPropertyBy	`public abstract Object getSharedPropertyBy(String propertyName, AccessMode am) throws SFException`	Retrieves the shared property with a name matching the passed-in propertyName. If the property is an Entity the AccessMode provided is used, otherwise the AccessMode parameter is ignored.
removeAllOwnedValidUnits	`public abstract void removeAllOwnedValidUnits() throws SFException`	Removes and deletes all elements from the Collection of ValidUnits
getValidUnitBy	`public abstract OrderProductUnitLink getValidUnitBy(DMethodAccessKey key) throws SFException`	Gets the ValidUnit associated with the specified key
getValidUnitBy	`public abstract OrderProductUnitLink getValidUnitBy(DMethodAccessKey key, AccessMode accessMode) throws SFException`	Gets the ValidUnit associated with the specified key using the access mode provided
getValidUnitsBy	`public abstract Iterator getValidUnitsBy(DMethodAccessKey key) throws SFException`	Returns all objects matching the specified key
getValidUnitsBy	`public abstract Iterator getValidUnitsBy(DMethodAccessKey key, AccessMode accessMode) throws SFException`	Returns all objects matching the specified key using the access mode provided
containsValidUnitKey	`public abstract boolean containsValidUnitKey(DMethodAccessKey key) throws SFException`	Checks if the ValidUnit exists by the specified Key
registerOwnedValidUnit	`public abstract void registerOwnedValidUnit(OrderProductUnitLink validUnitToRegister) throws SFException`	Registers newly created ValidUnit
getDefaultUnitHdl	`public abstract Handle getDefaultUnitHdl() throws SFException`	Get handle to default unit
getSharedPropertyHdlBy	`public abstract Handle getSharedPropertyHdlBy(String propertyName) throws SFException`	Retrieves the shared property with a name matching the passed-in propertyName. If it is an Entity property, return a copy of its Handle, otherwise a CollectionException is thrown.

Figure 28-2
(Cont'd)

orphanSharedOwnedPropertyBy	`public abstract void orphanSharedOwnedPropertyBy(String propertyName) throws SFException`	Removes the owned Entity from the shared PropertyContainer for this object but does not delete the Entity.
removeSharedContainedPropertyBy	`public abstract void removeSharedContainedPropertyBy(String propertyName) throws SFException`	Removes the non-owned Entity, owned Dependent, or owned String from the shared PropertyContainer for this object but does not delete the Entity.
removeSharedOwnedPropertyBy	`public abstract void removeSharedOwnedPropertyBy(String propertyName) throws SFException`	Removes the owned Entity from the shared PropertyContainer for this object and deletes the Entity.
getDescription	`public abstract String getDescription() throws SFException`	Retrieves the description of this object as a String in a format/language determined by the locale that is currently active in the environment this call was made in.
getDescription	`public abstract String getDescription(String locale) throws SFException`	Retrieves the description of this object as a String in a format/language determined by the given Locale.
getDescriptiveInformation	`public abstract DescriptiveInformation getDescriptiveInformation() throws SFException`	Retrieves the DescriptiveInformation object encapsulating the locale sensitive description of this object.
createOrderProductOrderPartnerLinkIterator	`public abstract Iterator createOrderProductOrderPartnerLinkIterator() throws SFException`	Create Iterator for Collection of OrderProductOrderPartnerLinks
getNextOrderProductOrderPartnerLink	`public abstract OrderProductOrderPartnerLink getNextOrderProductOrderPartnerLink(Iterator position) throws SFException`	Gets the OrderProductOrderPartnerLink at the Next Iterator Position
containsOrderProductOrderPartnerLink	`public abstract boolean containsOrderProductOrderPartnerLink(OrderProductOrderPartnerLink orderproductorderpartnerlink) throws SFException`	Checks if the OrderProductOrderPartnerLink exists in the Collection of OrderProductOrderPartnerLinks
removeOwnedOrderProductOrderPartnerLinkAt	`public abstract void removeOwnedOrderProductOrderPartnerLinkAt(Iterator position) throws SFException`	Removes and deletes the OrderProductOrderPartnerLink at the Current Iterator Position
removeOwnedOrderProductOrderPartnerLink	`public abstract void removeOwnedOrderProductOrderPartnerLink(OrderProductOrderPartnerLink orderproductorderpartnerlink) throws SFException`	Removes and deletes the specified OrderProductOrderPartnerLink
removeAllOwnedOrderProductOrderPartnerLinks	`public abstract void removeAllOwnedOrderProductOrderPartnerLinks() throws SFException`	Removes and deletes all elements from the Collection of OrderProductOrderPartnerLinks
getOrderProductOrderPartnerLinkBy	`public abstract OrderProductOrderPartnerLink getOrderProductOrderPartnerLinkBy(DMethodAccessKey key) throws SFException`	Gets the OrderProductOrderPartnerLink associated with the specified key
getOrderProductOrderPartnerLinkBy	`public abstract OrderProductOrderPartnerLink getOrderProductOrderPartnerLinkBy(DMethodAccessKey key, AccessMode accessMode) throws SFException`	Gets the OrderProductOrderPartnerLink associated with the specified key using the access mode provided

Figure 28-2
(Cont'd)

getOrderProductOrderPartnerLinksBy	`public abstract Iterator getOrderProductOrderPartnerLinksBy (DMethodAccessKey key) throws SFException`	Returns all objects matching the specified key
getOrderProductOrderPartnerLinksBy	`public abstract Iterator getOrderProductOrderPartnerLinksBy (DMethodAccessKey key, AccessMode accessMode) throws SFException`	Returns all objects matching the specified key using the access mode provided
containsOrderProductOrderPartnerLinkKey	`public abstract boolean containsOrderProductOrderPartnerLinkKey(DMethodAccessKey key) throws SFException`	Checks if the OrderProductOrderPartnerLink exists by the specified Key
getOrderProductOrderPartnerLinkKeyAt	`public abstract DMethodAccessKey getOrderProductOrderPartnerLinkKeyAt(Iterator position, String specificationKeyId) throws SFException`	Gets the OrderProductOrderPartnerLinkKey
getOrderProductOrderPartnerLinkKey	`public abstract DMethodAccessKey getOrderProductOrderPartnerLinkKey (OrderProductOrderPartnerLink orderProductOrderPartnerLink, String specificationKeyId) throws SFException`	Gets the OrderProductOrderPartnerLink Key
removeOwnedOrderProductOrderPartnerLinkBy	`public abstract void removeOwnedOrderProductOrderPartnerLinkBy(DMethodAccessKey key) throws SFException`	Removes and deletes the OrderProductOrderPartnerLink by the specified key
addOrderProductOrderPartnerLinkSpecificationKey	`public abstract void addOrderProductOrderPartnerLinkSpecificationKey(DMethodSpecificationKey specificationKey) throws SFException`	Adds a Specification Key
removeOrderProductOrderPartnerLinkSpecificationKeyBy	`public abstract void removeOrderProductOrderPartnerLinkSpecificationKeyBy(String specificationKeyId) throws SFException`	Removes the Specification Key
createOrderProductWarehouseLinkIterator	`public abstract Iterator createOrderProductWarehouseLinkIterator() throws SFException`	Create Iterator for Collection of OrderProductWarehouseLinks
getNextOrderProductWarehouseLink	`public abstract OrderProductWarehouseLink getNextOrderProductWarehouseLink(Iterator position) throws SFException`	Gets the OrderProductWarehouseLink at the Next Iterator Position
containsOrderProductWarehouseLink	`public abstract boolean containsOrderProductWarehouseLink(OrderProductWarehouseLink orderproductwarehouselink) throws SFException`	Checks if the OrderProductWarehouseLink exists in the Collection of OrderProductWarehouseLinks
removeOwnedOrderProductWarehouseLinkAt	`public abstract void removeOwnedOrderProductWarehouseLinkAt(Iterator position) throws SFException`	Removes and deletes the OrderProductWarehouseLink at the Current Iterator Position
removeOwnedOrderProductWarehouseLink	`public abstract void removeOwnedOrderProductWarehouseLink(OrderProductWarehouseLink orderproductwarehouselink) throws SFException`	Removes and deletes the specified OrderProductWarehouseLink

Figure 28-2
(Cont'd)

removeAllOwnedOrderProductWarehouseLinks	`public abstract void removeAllOwnedOrderProductWarehouseLinks() throws SFException`	Removes and deletes all elements from the Collection of OrderProductWarehouseLinks
getOrderProductWarehouseLinkBy	`public abstract OrderProductWarehouseLink getOrderProductWarehouseLinkBy(DMethodAccessKey key) throws SFException`	Gets the OrderProductWarehouseLink associated with the specified key
getOrderProductWarehouseLinkBy	`public abstract OrderProductWarehouseLink getOrderProductWarehouseLinkBy(DMethodAccessKey key, AccessMode accessMode) throws SFException`	Gets the OrderProductWarehouseLink associated with the specified key using the access mode provided
getOrderProductWarehouseLinksBy	`public abstract Iterator getOrderProductWarehouseLinksBy(DMethodAccessKey key) throws SFException`	Returns all objects matching the specified key
getOrderProductWarehouseLinksBy	`public abstract Iterator getOrderProductWarehouseLinksBy(DMethodAccessKey key, AccessMode accessMode) throws SFException`	Returns all objects matching the specified key using the access mode provided
containsOrderProductWarehouseLinkKey	`public abstract boolean containsOrderProductWarehouseLinkKey(DMethodAccessKey key) throws SFException`	Checks if the OrderProductWarehouseLink exists by the specified Key
getOrderProductWarehouseLinkKey	`public abstract DMethodAccessKey getOrderProductWarehouseLinkKey(OrderProductWarehouseLink orderProductWarehouseLink, String specificationKeyId) throws SFException`	Gets the OrderProductWarehouseLink Key
removeOwnedOrderProductWarehouseLinkBy	`public abstract void removeOwnedOrderProductWarehouseLinkBy(DMethodAccessKey key) throws SFException`	Removes and deletes the OrderProductWarehouseLink by the specified key
addOrderProductWarehouseLinkSpecificationKey	`public abstract void addOrderProductWarehouseLinkSpecificationKey(DMethodSpecificationKey specificationKey) throws SFException`	Adds a Specification Key
removeOrderProductWarehouseLinkSpecificationKeyBy	`public abstract void removeOrderProductWarehouseLinkSpecificationKeyBy(String specificationKeyId) throws SFException`	Removes the Specification Key
getProduct	`public abstract Product getProduct() throws SFException`	Returns the Product, copied from the Handle
createValidUnitIterator	`public abstract Iterator createValidUnitIterator() throws SFException`	Create Iterator for Collection of ValidUnits
getNextValidUnit	`public abstract OrderProductUnitLink getNextValidUnit(Iterator position) throws SFException`	Gets the ValidUnit at the Next Iterator Position
containsValidUnit	`public abstract boolean containsValidUnit(OrderProductUnitLink validunit) throws SFException`	Checks if the ValidUnit exists in the Collection of ValidUnits

Figure 28-2
(Cont'd)

removeOwnedValidUnit	public abstract void removeOwnedValidUnit(OrderProductUnitLink validunit) throws SFException	Removes and deletes the specified ValidUnit
getValidUnitKey	public abstract DMethodAccessKey getValidUnitKey(OrderProductUnitLink validUnit, String specificationKeyId) throws SFException	Gets the ValidUnit Key
removeOwnedValidUnitBy	public abstract void removeOwnedValidUnitBy(DMethodAccessKey key) throws SFException	Removes and deletes the ValidUnit by the specified key
addValidUnitSpecificationKey	public abstract void addValidUnitSpecificationKey(DMethodSpecificationKey specificationKey) throws SFException	Adds a Specification Key
removeValidUnitSpecificationKeyBy	public abstract void removeValidUnitSpecificationKeyBy(String specificationKeyId) throws SFException	Removes the Specification Key
getDefaultUnit	public abstract OrderProductUnitLink getDefaultUnit() throws SFException	Returns the DefaultUnit, copied from the Handle
getOrderProductPriceGroup	public abstract OrderProductPriceGroup getOrderProductPriceGroup() throws SFException	Returns the OrderProductPriceGroup, copied from the Handle
getOrderProductDiscountGroup	public abstract OrderProductDiscountGroup getOrderProductDiscountGroup() throws SFException	Returns the OrderProductDiscountGroup, copied from the Handle
getOrderControllerType	public abstract OrderControllerType getOrderControllerType() throws SFException	Returns the OrderControllerType, copied from the Handle
getOrderProductOrderPartnerLinks	public abstract EntityOwningExtent getOrderProductOrderPartnerLinks() throws SFException	Returns a copy of the Collection of OrderProductOrderPartnerLink, used by framework—NOT FOR CLIENT USE
getOrderProductOrderPartnerLinksHdl	public abstract Handle getOrderProductOrderPartnerLinksHdl() throws SFException	Get handle to OrderProductOrderPartnerLinks,used by framework—NOT FOR CLIENT USE
registerOwnedOrderProductOrderPartnerLink	public abstract void registerOwnedOrderProductOrderPartnerLink(OrderProductOrderPartnerLink orderProductOrderPartnerLinkToRegister) throws SFException	Registers newly created OrderProductOrderPartnerLink
getOrderProductWarehouseLinks	public abstract EntityOwningExtent getOrderProductWarehouseLinks() throws SFException	Returns a copy of the Collection of OrderProductWarehouseLink, used by framework—NOT FOR CLIENT USE

Figure 28-2
(Cont'd)

getOrderProductWarehouseLinksHdl	`public abstract Handle getOrderProductWarehouseLinksHdl() throws SFException`	Get handle to OrderProductWarehouseLinks,used by framework—NOT FOR CLIENT USE
registerOwnedOrderProductWarehouseLink	`public abstract void registerOwnedOrderProductWarehouseLink(OrderProductWarehouseLink orderProductWarehouseLinkToRegister) throws SFException`	Registers newly created OrderProductWarehouseLink
getProductHdl	`public abstract Handle getProductHdl() throws SFException`	Returns the Handle to the Product of the Product of the OrderProduct
getValidUnits	`public abstract EntityOwningExtent getValidUnits() throws SFException`	Returns a copy of the Collection of ValidUnit, used by framework—NOT FOR CLIENT USE
getOrderProductPriceGroupHdl	`public abstract Handle getOrderProductPriceGroupHdl() throws SFException`	Returns the Handle to the OrderProductPriceGroup of the OrderProduct
getOrderProductDiscountGroupHdl	`public abstract Handle getOrderProductDiscountGroupHdl() throws SFException`	Returns the Handle to the OrderProductDiscountGroup of the OrderProductDiscountGroup of the OrderProduct
getOrderControllerTypeHdl	`public abstract Handle getOrderControllerTypeHdl() throws SFException`	Returns the Handle to the OrderControllerType of the OrderProduct
getId	`public abstract String getId() throws SFException`	Gets id

Figure 28-2
(Cont'd)

Management of Orders

This category is responsible for creating complete orders that include both the associated detail information and the application-specific logic (in the form of policies) that ensure order integrity. This category includes the sample order types mentioned previously. In this category the Order Management framework defines the top three detail levels of the order structure. Namely these are `Order` (shown in Figure 28-4), `OrderPriceDetail` (see Figure 28-5), and `OrderRequested Detail` (shown in Figure 28-6). These three levels represent external information provided as input to the application. The source of such information could be computerized databases or manual feeding of data by a salesperson. The order details are designed using the lifecycle mechanism that comes from the foundation layer.

Another part of this category defines the previously mentioned impact classes for the aforementioned top three levels of the order object

Interface com.ibm.sf.om.DPriceDefinition

public interface **DPriceDefinition** extends Dependent

Main Methods

Name	*Signature*	*Description*
commonValidateForInitialize	public abstract DResultsCollection commonValidateForInitialize(OrderControllerType forOrderControllerType, PriceDefinitionDController priceDefinitionDController, Currency currency, DDecimal price, OrderPartner orderPartner, OrderProduct orderProduct, OrderPartnerPriceGroup orderPartnerPriceGroup, OrderProductPriceGroup orderProductPriceGroup, PriceCategory priceCategory, UnitOfMeasure unitOfMeasure, DTime fromTime, DTime toTime, DDecimal retailPrice, DQuantityAndValueLimit quantityLimit, DInteger scaleFactor) throws SFException	Common validation for methods initializeForSales, initializeForPurchase, and initializeForInternal.
getRetailPrice	public abstract DDecimal getRetailPrice() throws SFException	Gets RetailPrice
getPrice	public abstract DDecimal getPrice() throws SFException	Gets Price
getQuantityAndValueLimit	public abstract DQuantityAndValueLimit getQuantityAndValueLimit() throws SFException	Gets QuantityAndValueLimit
getUnitOfMeasure	public abstract UnitOfMeasure getUnitOfMeasure() throws SFException	Returns the UnitOfMeasure, copied from the Handle
getOrderPartner	public abstract OrderPartner getOrderPartner() throws SFException	Returns the OrderPartner, copied from the Handle
getOrderPartnerPriceGroup	public abstract OrderPartnerPriceGroup getOrderPartnerPriceGroup() throws SFException	Returns the OrderPartnerPriceGroup, copied from the Handle
getOrderProduct	public abstract OrderProduct getOrderProduct() throws SFException	Returns the OrderProduct, copied from the Handle
getOrderProductPriceGroup	public abstract OrderProductPriceGroup getOrderProductPriceGroup() throws SFException	Returns the OrderProductPriceGroup, copied from the Handle
getPriceCategory	public abstract PriceCategory getPriceCategory() throws SFException	Returns the PriceCategory, copied from the Handle

Figure 28-3
Interface `DPriceDefinition`

getCurrency	`public abstract Currency getCurrency() throws SFException`	Returns the Currency, copied from the Handle
getToTime	`public abstract DTime getToTime() throws SFException`	Gets ToTime
getFromTime	`public abstract DTime getFromTime() throws SFException`	Gets FromTime
getOrderControllerType	`public abstract OrderControllerType getOrderControllerType() throws SFException`	Returns the OrderControllerType, copied from the Handle
setOrderControllerType	`public abstract void setOrderControllerType(OrderControllerType newOrderControllerType) throws SFException`	Set the Handle of the OrderControllerType
getScaleFactor	`public abstract DInteger getScaleFactor() throws SFException`	Gets ScaleFactor
getUnitOfMeasureHdl	`public abstract Handle getUnitOfMeasureHdl() throws SFException`	Returns the Handle to the UnitOfMeasure of the UnitOfMeasure of the DPriceDefinition
getOrderPartnerHdl	`public abstract Handle getOrderPartnerHdl() throws SFException`	Returns the Handle to the OrderPartner of the OrderPartner of the DPriceDefinition
getOrderPartnerPriceGroupHdl	`public abstract Handle getOrderPartnerPriceGroupHdl() throws SFException`	Returns the Handle to the OrderPartnerPriceGroup of the DPriceDefinition
getOrderProductHdl	`public abstract Handle getOrderProductHdl() throws SFException`	Returns the Handle to the OrderProduct of the OrderProduct of the DPriceDefinition
getOrderProductPriceGroupHdl	`public abstract Handle getOrderProductPriceGroupHdl() throws SFException`	Returns the Handle to the OrderProductPriceGroup of the DPriceDefinition
getPriceCategoryHdl	`public abstract Handle getPriceCategoryHdl() throws SFException`	Returns the Handle to the PriceCategory of the PriceCategory of the DPriceDefinition
getCurrencyHdl	`public abstract Handle getCurrencyHdl() throws SFException`	Returns the Handle to the Currency of the Currency of the DPriceDefinition
getOrderControllerTypeHdl	`public abstract Handle getOrderControllerTypeHdl() throws SFException`	Returns the Handle to the OrderControllerType of the DPriceDefinition

Figure 28-3
(Cont'd)

Interface com.ibm.sf.om.Order

public interface **Order** extends AllowRemote

Name	*Signature*	*Description*
getInvoiceAddress	`public abstract Address getInvoiceAddress() throws SFException`	Returns the invoice address
getOrderAddress	`public abstract Address getOrderAddress() throws SFException`	Returns the Order address
getProject	`public abstract Project getProject() throws SFException`	Returns the Project or null.
getOrderHandler	`public abstract Initials getOrderHandler() throws SFException`	Returns the OrderHandler or null
getOrderPartner	`public abstract OrderPartner getOrderPartner() throws SFException`	Returns the OrderPartner
getOrderFinancialPartner	`public abstract OrderPartner getOrderFinancialPartner() throws SFException`	Returns the OrderFinancialPartner
getOrderNumber	`public abstract DNumberSeriesValue getOrderNumber() throws SFException`	Returns the OrderNumber
getExchangeRateFactor	`public abstract DDecimal getExchangeRateFactor() throws SFException`	Returns the ExchangeRateFactor or null.
getCurrency	`public abstract Currency getCurrency() throws SFException`	Returns the Currency
getWarehouse	`public abstract Warehouse getWarehouse() throws SFException`	Returns the Warehouse
getOrderTime	`public abstract DTime getOrderTime() throws SFException`	Returns the OrderTime
isBackOrderAllowed	`public abstract boolean isBackOrderAllowed() throws SFException`	Returns true if BackOrder is allowed
getYourReference	`public abstract String getYourReference() throws SFException`	Returns the YourReference or null.
getCompleteInvoicing	`public abstract boolean getCompleteInvoicing() throws SFException`	Returns the CompleteInvoicing
getPaymentTerms	`public abstract PaymentTerms getPaymentTerms() throws SFException`	Returns the PaymentTerms
getInvoiceTime	`public abstract DTime getInvoiceTime() throws SFException`	Returns the InvoiceTime or null
getInvoiceReference	`public abstract String getInvoiceReference() throws SFException`	Returns the InvoiceReference or null
getInvoicePeriod	`public abstract FiscalPeriod getInvoicePeriod() throws SFException`	Returns the InvoicePeriod or null.
getPaymentMethod	`public abstract PaymentMethod getPaymentMethod() throws SFException`	Returns the PaymentMethod
getExchangeRateType	`public abstract ExchangeRateType getExchangeRateType() throws SFException`	Returns the ExchangeRateType or null.

Figure 28-4
Order

setOrderHandler	`public abstract void setOrderHandler(Initials orderHandler) throws SFException`	Sets the Order handler
changeOrderTime	`public abstract void changeOrderTime(DTime orderTime) throws SFException`	Change the OrderTime on this Order.
changeOrderFinancialPartner	`public abstract void changeOrderFinancialPartner(OrderPartner orderFinancialPartner) throws SFException`	Change the OrderFinancialPartner on this Order.
isBackOrder	`public abstract boolean isBackOrder() throws SFException`	Determine if Order is backordered
getCalculatedExchangeRateFactor	`public abstract DDecimal getCalculatedExchangeRateFactor() throws SFException`	This method is used to retrieve the exchange rate factor.
checkCredit	`public abstract DResultsCollection checkCredit(OrderPartner financialPartner, ProcessTokenValue processToken, DTime time, DTransactionValue transactionValue) throws SFException`	Performs credit checking according to passed parameters. DResultsCollection or null.
calculateDeliveryTime	`public abstract DTime calculateDeliveryTime(MannerOfTransport mannerOfTransport, Address fromAddress, Address toAddress, TransportZone fromZone, TransportZone toZone, DTransportTimeChooserPolicy transportTimeDefinitionSearchPolicy, OrderProduct product, Warehouse warehouse, OrderPartner partner, NaturalCalendar calendar, DAmountOfTime timePrecision, DTime fromTime) throws SFException`	Calculates the delivery time from the passed parameters. The calculated delivery time.
getCalculatedExchangeRateType	`public abstract ExchangeRateType getCalculatedExchangeRateType() throws SFException`	This method is used to retrieve the exchange rate type.
getInvoiceCurrency	`public abstract Currency getInvoiceCurrency() throws SFException`	Returns the Currency
getInvoiceExchangeRateType	`public abstract ExchangeRateType getInvoiceExchangeRateType() throws SFException`	Returns the ExchangeRateType or default.
getInvoiceExchangeRateFactor	`public abstract DDecimal getInvoiceExchangeRateFactor() throws SFException`	Returns the ExchangeRateFactor or default.
validateDeliveryTime	`public abstract DResultsCollection validateDeliveryTime(DTime deliveryTime, DTime orderTime, MannerOfTransport mannerOfTransport, Address fromAddress, Address toAddress, TransportZone fromZone, TransportZone toZone, DTransportTimeChooserPolicy transportTimeDefinitionSearchPolicy, OrderProduct product, Warehouse warehouse, OrderPartner partner, NaturalCalendar calendar, DAmountOfTime timePrecision) throws SFException`	Validates the delivery time according to the passed parameters. N/A

Figure 28-4
(Cont'd)

isHoldOrder	`public abstract boolean isHoldOrder() throws SFException`	
associateWithOrderDeliveryGroup	`public abstract OrderDeliveryGroup associateWithOrderDeliveryGroup(OrderPlannableDetail orderPlannableDetail) throws SFException`	This method should be run on the OrderDeliveryGroupPolicy. The method tries to find a OrderDeliveryGroup matching the OrderPlannableDetail. If no one found, a new ORderDeliveryGroup will be created
associateWithOrderInvoiceGroup	`public abstract OrderInvoiceGroup associateWithOrderInvoiceGroup(OrderInvoiceableDetail orderInvoiceableDetail) throws SFException`	This method should be run on the OrderInvoiceGroupPolicy. The method tries to find a OrderInvoiceGroup matching the OrderInvoiceableDetail. If no one found a new OrderInvoiceGroup will be created
validatePlannedDeliveryTime	`public abstract DResultsCollection validatePlannedDeliveryTime(OrderPlannableDetail orderPlannableDetail, DTime deliveryTime) throws SFException`	This method should be run on the OrderDeliveryGroupPolicy. Validates the specified delivery time against the planned delivery time of the Order Delivery Group PreCondition: N/A Postcondition: Object's state unmodified
updatePlannedDeliveryTime	`public abstract void updatePlannedDeliveryTime(OrderPlannableDetail orderPlannableDetail, DTime plannedDeliveryTime) throws SFException`	This method should be run on the OrderDeliveryGroupPolicy. Updates the Planned Delivery Time for the specified OrderPlannableDetail's OrderPlanningDetails when a complete delivery is required.
isCreditCheckToBePerformed	`public abstract boolean isCreditCheckToBePerformed() throws SFException`	Returns true if credit checking is to be performed for this HierarchyLevelInformation object, false otherwise
setInvoiceAddress	`public abstract void setInvoiceAddress(Address invoiceAddress) throws SFException`	Set the default invoice Address for this Order.
setOrderAddress	`public abstract void setOrderAddress(Address orderAddress) throws SFException`	Set the order Address for this Order.
setProject	`public abstract void setProject(Project project) throws SFException`	Set the default Project for this Order.
setExchangeRateFactor	`public abstract void setExchangeRateFactor(DDecimal exchangeRateFactor) throws SFException`	Set the default ExchangeRateFactor for this Order.
setExchangeRateType	`public abstract void setExchangeRateType(ExchangeRateType exchangeRateType) throws SFException`	Set the default ExchangeRateType for this Order.
setCurrency	`public abstract void setCurrency(Currency currency) throws SFException`	Set the defacult Currency for this Order.
setBackOrderAllowed	`public abstract void setBackOrderAllowed(boolean backOrderAllowed) throws SFException`	Set the default BackOrderAllowed flag for this Order.
setYourReference	`public abstract void setYourReference(String yourReference) throws SFException`	Set "your" (second party's) reference for this Order.
setOurReference	`public abstract void setOurReference(String ourReference) throws SFException`	Set "our" reference for this Order.

Figure 28-4
(Cont'd)

setHoldOrder	`public abstract void setHoldOrder(boolean holdOrder) throws SFException`	Set the HoldOrder flag for this Order.
setCompleteInvoicing	`public abstract void setCompleteInvoicing(boolean completeInvoicing) throws SFException`	Set the defaultInvoicing flag for this Order.
setInvoiceReference	`public abstract void setInvoiceReference(String invoiceReference) throws SFException`	Set the default invoice reference for this Order.
changePaymentTerms	`public abstract void changePaymentTerms(PaymentTerms paymentTerms, PaymentMethod paymentMethod) throws SFException`	Change the Default PaymentTerms and PaymentMethod for this Order. If no PaymentMethod is passed, PaymentMethod from PaymentTerms will be used.
changeInvoiceTime	`public abstract void changeInvoiceTime(DTime invoiceTime, FiscalPeriod invoicePeriod) throws SFException`	Change the default Invoice time and period for this Order.
getOrderControllerType	`public abstract OrderControllerType getOrderControllerType() throws SFException`	Get the OrderControllerType for this Order.
getOurReference	`public abstract String getOurReference() throws SFException`	Get "our" reference for this Order.

Figure 28-4
(Cont'd)

hierarchy. Along with those impact classes it also defines various policies used in conjunction with them. Impact class instances are used to define the behavior of a given order type. As mentioned previously, these impact classes hold:

- the lifecycle behavior for the order type;
- other algorithms representing the behavior of the order type;
- a set of valid child order details (i.e. "next step of processing" details, and "static" (in the meaning relevant to Java and C++ objects); and
- data that is the same for all order detail instances associated with this impact.

The "Price and Discount Requester" is also implemented in this category. It incorporates policy-based algorithms used to calculate order prices and discounts. This category also includes some other order-related classes, such as `OrderDeliveryGroup` and `OrderInvoiceGroup` used to group together multiple order details into one delivery or invoice. Finally, this category includes the support for creating the definition of the lifecycle of an order.

Interface com.ibm.sf.om.OrderPriceDetail

public interface **OrderPriceDetail**

Main Methods

Name	*Signature*	*Description*
getInvoiceAddress	`public abstract Address getInvoiceAddress() throws SFException`	Returns the invoice address
getRequestedTotalQuantity	`public abstract DProductTransactionQuantity getRequestedTotalQuantity() throws SFException`	Returns the RequestedTotalQuantity
getOrderProduct	`public abstract OrderProduct getOrderProduct() throws SFException`	Returns the OrderProduct
getOrderPriceDetailNumber	`public abstract int getOrderPriceDetailNumber() throws SFException`	Returns the OrderPriceDetailNumber
getProject	`public abstract Project getProject() throws SFException`	Returns the Project or null.
getExchangeRateFactor	`public abstract DDecimal getExchangeRateFactor() throws SFException`	Returns the ExchangeRateFactor or null.
getCurrency	`public abstract Currency getCurrency() throws SFException`	Returns the Currency
getWarehouse	`public abstract Warehouse getWarehouse() throws SFException`	Returns the Warehouse
getOrderTime	`public abstract DTime getOrderTime() throws SFException`	Returns the OrderTime
isBackOrderAllowed	`public abstract boolean isBackOrderAllowed() throws SFException`	Returns true if BackOrder is allowed
getCompleteInvoicing	`public abstract boolean getCompleteInvoicing() throws SFException`	Returns the CompleteInvoicing
getPaymentTerms	`public abstract PaymentTerms getPaymentTerms() throws SFException`	Returns the PaymentTerms
getInvoiceTime	`public abstract DTime getInvoiceTime() throws SFException`	Returns the InvoiceTime or null
getInvoiceReference	`public abstract String getInvoiceReference() throws SFException`	Returns the InvoiceReference or null
getInvoicePeriod	`public abstract FiscalPeriod getInvoicePeriod() throws SFException`	Returns the InvoicePeriod or null.
getPaymentMethod	`public abstract PaymentMethod getPaymentMethod() throws SFException`	Returns the PaymentMethod
getExchangeRateType	`public abstract ExchangeRateType getExchangeRateType() throws SFException`	Returns the ExchangeRateType or null.
changeOrderTime	`public abstract void changeOrderTime(DTime orderTime) throws SFException`	Change the OrderTime for this Order Price Detail.

Figure 28-5
OrderPriceDetail

getLot	public abstract Lot getLot() throws SFException	Returns the Lot
getProductDescription	public abstract DescriptiveInformation getProductDescription() throws SFException	Returns the ProductDescription
isBackOrder	public abstract boolean isBackOrder() throws SFException	Returns true associated order is a back order false otherwise.
changePriceAndDiscount	public abstract void changePriceAndDiscount(DOrderPriceAndDiscount orderPriceAndDiscount, Currency currency, DDecimal exchangeRateFactor, ExchangeRateType exchangeRateType) throws SFException	Change the OrderPriceAndDiscount on this Order Price Detail.
changeLot	public abstract void changeLot(Lot lot) throws SFException	Change the Lot on this Order Price Detail.
changeRequestedTotalQuantity	public abstract void changeRequestedTotalQuantity(DProductTransactionQuantity totalRequestedQuantity) throws SFException	Change the RequestedTotalQuantity on this Order Price Detail.
validateRequestedTotalQuantity	public abstract DResultsCollection validateRequestedTotalQuantity(DProductTransactionQuantity totalRequestedQuantity) throws SFException	Validates the RequestedTotalQuantity on this Order Price Detail.
chooseReplacingOrderProductUnits	public abstract Set chooseReplacingOrderProductUnits(OrderProductUnitLink orderProductUnitLink, DTime time, ProcessTokenValue processToken) throws SFException	Returns a collection of valid replacing OrderProductUnitLinks for the passed parameters.
checkCredit	public abstract DResultsCollection checkCredit(OrderPartner financialPartner, ProcessTokenValue processToken, DTime time, DTransactionValue transactionValue) throws SFException	Performs credit checking according to passed parameters. DResultsCollection or null.
getCalculatedExchangeRateFactor	public abstract DDecimal getCalculatedExchangeRateFactor() throws SFException	This method is used to retrieve the exchange rate factor.
getOrderPriceAndDiscount	public abstract DOrderPriceAndDiscount getOrderPriceAndDiscount() throws SFException	Get Order Price And Discount.
getCalculatedExchangeRateType	public abstract ExchangeRateType getCalculatedExchangeRateType() throws SFException	This method is used to retrieve the exchange rate type.
getInvoiceCurrency	public abstract Currency getInvoiceCurrency() throws SFException	Returns the Currency
getInvoiceExchangeRateType	public abstract ExchangeRateType getInvoiceExchangeRateType() throws SFException	Returns the ExchangeRateType or default.
getInvoiceExchangeRateFactor	public abstract DDecimal getInvoiceExchangeRateFactor() throws SFException	Returns the ExchangeRateFactor or default.
isCreditCheckToBePerformed	public abstract boolean isCreditCheckToBePerformed() throws SFException	Returns true if credit checking is to be performed for this HierarchyLevelInformation object, false otherwise.

Figure 28-5
(Cont'd)

setInvoiceAddress	`public abstract void setInvoiceAddress(Address invoiceAddress) throws SFException`	Set the default invoice Address for this OrderPriceDetail.
setProject	`public abstract void setProject(Project project) throws SFException`	Set the default Project for this OrderPriceDetail.
setBackOrderAllowed	`public abstract void setBackOrderAllowed(boolean backOrderAllowed) throws SFException`	Set the default BackOrderAllowed flag for this OrderPriceDetail.
setCompleteInvoicing	`public abstract void setCompleteInvoicing(boolean completeInvoicing) throws SFException`	Set the defaultInvoicing flag for this OrderPriceDetail.
setInvoiceReference	`public abstract void setInvoiceReference(String invoiceReference) throws SFException`	Set the default invoice reference for this OrderPriceDetail.
setProductDescription	`public abstract void setProductDescription(DescriptiveInformation productDescription) throws SFException`	Set the optional product description for this Order.
changePaymentTerms	`public abstract void changePaymentTerms(PaymentTerms paymentTerms, PaymentMethod paymentMethod) throws SFException`	Change the Default PaymentTerms and PaymentMethod for this OrderPriceDetail. If no PaymentMethod is passed, PaymentMethod from PaymentTerms will be used.
changeInvoiceTime	`public abstract void changeInvoiceTime(DTime invoiceTime, FiscalPeriod invoicePeriod) throws SFException`	Change the default Invoice time and period for this OrderPriceDetail.
getPricePolicy	`public abstract DPriceDefinitionChooserSelectionPolicy getPricePolicy() throws SFException`	Get the price definition chooser selection policy for this OrderPriceDetail.
getDiscountPolicy	`public abstract DDiscountDefinitionChooserSelectionPolicy getDiscountPolicy() throws SFException`	Get the discount definition chooser selection policy for this OrderPriceDetail.
getOrderControllerType	`public abstract OrderControllerType getOrderControllerType() throws SFException`	Get the OrderControllerType for this OrderPriceDetail.
getOrderDetailNetAmount	`public abstract DTransactionValue getOrderDetailNetAmount() throws SFException`	Get the OrderDetailNetAmount for this OrderPriceDetail.
getOrderDetailGrossAmount	`public abstract DTransactionValue getOrderDetailGrossAmount() throws SFException`	Get the OrderDetailGrossAmount for this OrderPriceDetail.
getTotalOrderDetailGrossAmount	`public abstract DTransactionValue getTotalOrderDetailGrossAmount() throws SFException`	Get the TotalOrderDetailGrossAmount for this OrderPriceDetail.
getTotalOrderDetailNetAmount	`public abstract DTransactionValue getTotalOrderDetailNetAmount() throws SFException`	Get the TotalOrderDetailNetAmount for this OrderPriceDetail.

Figure 28-5
(Cont'd)

Interface com.ibm.sf.om.OrderRequestedDetail

public interface **OrderRequestedDetail** extends FutureReception, ProductReservation

Main Methods:

Name	*Signature*	*Description*
getInvoiceAddress	`public abstract Address getInvoiceAddress() throws SFException`	Returns the invoice address
getRequestedQuantity	`public abstract DProductTransactionQuantity getRequestedQuantity() throws SFException`	Returns the RequestedQuantity
getOrderRequestedDetail Number	`public abstract int getOrderRequestedDetailNumber() throws SFException`	Returns the OrderRequestedDetailNumber
getProject	`public abstract Project getProject() throws SFException`	Returns the Project or null.
getWarehouse	`public abstract Warehouse getWarehouse() throws SFException`	Returns the Warehouse
isBackOrderAllowed	`public abstract boolean isBackOrderAllowed() throws SFException`	Indicated if BackOrder is allowed
getCompleteInvoicing	`public abstract boolean getCompleteInvoicing() throws SFException`	Returns the value of the CompleteInvoicing flag
getPaymentTerms	`public abstract PaymentTerms getPaymentTerms() throws SFException`	Returns the PaymentTerms
getInvoiceTime	`public abstract DTime getInvoiceTime() throws SFException`	Returns the InvoiceTime or null
getInvoiceReference	`public abstract String getInvoiceReference() throws SFException`	Returns the InvoiceReference or null
getInvoicePeriod	`public abstract FiscalPeriod getInvoicePeriod() throws SFException`	Returns the InvoicePeriod or null.
getPaymentMethod	`public abstract PaymentMethod getPaymentMethod() throws SFException`	Returns the PaymentMethod
getLot	`public abstract Lot getLot() throws SFException`	Returns the Lot
isBackOrder	`public abstract boolean isBackOrder() throws SFException`	Returns true if associated order is a Backorder, false otherwise
getStockTypeValue	`public abstract StockTypeValue getStockTypeValue() throws SFException`	Returns the StockTypeValue
getNextStockTypeValue	`public abstract StockTypeValue getNextStockTypeValue() throws SFException`	Returns the StockTypeValue
getCostValueReference	`public abstract DCostValueReference getCostValueReference() throws SFException`	Returns the CostValueReference
getFutureReceptionTypeV alue	`public abstract FutureReceptionTypeValue getFutureReceptionTypeValue() throws SFException`	Returns the FutureReceptionTypeValue
getReservationTypeValue	`public abstract ReservationTypeValue getReservationTypeValue() throws SFException`	Returns the ReservationTypeValue
getShippingTime	`public abstract DTime getShippingTime() throws SFException`	Returns the ShippingTime

Figure 28-6
`OrderRequestedDetail`

chooseSubstituteOrderProductUnits	`public abstract Set chooseSubstituteOrderProductUnits(OrderProductUnitLink orderProductUnitLink, DTime time, ProcessTokenValue processToken) throws SFException`	Returns a collection of valid substitute OrderProductUnitLinks for the passed parameters.
chooseReplacingOrderProductUnits	`public abstract Set chooseReplacingOrderProductUnits(OrderProductUnitLink orderProductUnitLink, DTime time, ProcessTokenValue processToken) throws SFException`	Returns a collection of valid replacing OrderProductUnitLinks for the passed parameters.
checkCredit	`public abstract DResultsCollection checkCredit(OrderPartner financialPartner, ProcessTokenValue processToken, DTime time, DTransactionValue transactionValue) throws SFException`	Performs credit checking according to passed parameters. DResultsCollection or null.
isAvailabilityCheckToBePerformed	`public abstract boolean isAvailabilityCheckToBePerformed() throws SFException`	Returns true if availibitiy checking is to be performed for this HierarchyLevelInformation object, false otherwise.
isCreditCheckToBePerformed	`public abstract boolean isCreditCheckToBePerformed() throws SFException`	Returns true if credit checking is to be performed for this HierarchyLevelInformation object, false otherwise.
calculateDeliveryTime	`public abstract DTime calculateDeliveryTime(MannerOfTransport mannerOfTransport, Address fromAddress, Address toAddress, TransportZone fromZone, TransportZone toZone, DTransportTimeChooserPolicy transportTimeDefinitionSearchPolicy, OrderProduct product, Warehouse warehouse, OrderPartner partner, NaturalCalendar calendar, DAmountOfTime timePrecision, DTime fromTime) throws SFException`	Calculates the delivery time from the passed parameters. The calculated delivery time.
getInvoiceQuantity	`public abstract DProductTransactionQuantity getInvoiceQuantity() throws SFException`	Returns the RequestedQuantity
validateDeliveryTime	`public abstract DResultsCollection validateDeliveryTime(DTime deliveryTime, DTime orderTime, MannerOfTransport mannerOfTransport, Address fromAddress, Address toAddress, TransportZone fromZone, TransportZone toZone, DTransportTimeChooserPolicy transportTimeDefinitionSearchPolicy, OrderProduct product, Warehouse warehouse, OrderPartner partner, NaturalCalendar calendar, DAmountOfTime timePrecision) throws SFException`	Validates the delivery time according to the passed parameters. N/A
validateBackToBackType	`public abstract DResultsCollection validateBackToBackType(OrderControllerType orderType, StockTypeValue stockTypeValue, OrderImpact impact) throws SFException`	Validates passed StockTypeValue and requestedDetailImpact object for backToBack handling. DResultsCollection or null.
validateStockTypeValue	`public abstract DResultsCollection validateStockTypeValue(StockTypeValue stockTypeValue) throws SFException`	Validates the passed StockTypeValue. DResultsCollection or null.

Figure 28-6
(Cont'd)

getInvoicingTypeValue	`public abstract InvoicingTypeValue getInvoicingTypeValue() throws SFException`	Returns the Invoicing TypeValue for this requested detail.
getSerialNumber	`public abstract SerialNumber getSerialNumber() throws SFException`	Get the serial number for this requested detail.
getStockLocation	`public abstract StockLocation getStockLocation() throws SFException`	Get the stock location for this requested detail.
setInvoiceAddress	`public abstract void setInvoiceAddress(Address invoiceAddress) throws SFException`	Set the default invoice Address for this OrderRequestedDetail.
setProject	`public abstract void setProject(Project project) throws SFException`	Set the default Project for this OrderRequestedDetail.
setBackOrderAllowed	`public abstract void setBackOrderAllowed(boolean backOrderAllowed) throws SFException`	Set the default BackOrderAllowed flag for this OrderRequestedDetail.
setCompleteInvoicing	`public abstract void setCompleteInvoicing(boolean completeInvoicing) throws SFException`	Set the defaultInvoicing flag for this OrderRequestedDetail.
setInvoiceReference	`public abstract void setInvoiceReference(String invoiceReference) throws SFException`	Set the default invoice reference for this OrderRequestedDetail.
changePaymentTerms	`public abstract void changePaymentTerms(PaymentTerms paymentTerms, PaymentMethod paymentMethod) throws SFException`	Change the Default PaymentTerms and PaymentMethod for this OrderRequestedDetail. If no PaymentMethod is passed, PaymentMethod from PaymentTerms will be used.
changeInvoiceTime	`public abstract void changeInvoiceTime(DTime invoiceTime, FiscalPeriod invoicePeriod) throws SFException`	Change the default Invoice time and period for this OrderRequestedDetail.
getOrderControllerType	`public abstract OrderControllerType getOrderControllerType() throws SFException`	Get the OrderControllerType for this OrderRequestedDetail.
getOrderDetailGrossAmount	`public abstract DTransactionValue getOrderDetailGrossAmount() throws SFException`	Get the OrderDetailGrossAmount for this OrderPriceDetail.
getOrderDetailNetAmount	`public abstract DTransactionValue getOrderDetailNetAmount() throws SFException`	Get the OrderDetailNetAmount for this OrderPriceDetail.
getTotalOrderDetailGrossAmount	`public abstract DTransactionValue getTotalOrderDetailGrossAmount() throws SFException`	Get the TotalOrderDetailGrossAmount for this OrderPriceDetail.
getTotalOrderDetailNetAmount	`public abstract DTransactionValue getTotalOrderDetailNetAmount() throws SFException`	Get the TotalOrderDetailNetAmount for this OrderPriceDetail.
getProduct	`public abstract Product getProduct() throws SFException`	Returns the Product associated with this OrderPriceDetail
getReservedQuantity	`public abstract DProductTransactionQuantity getReservedQuantity() throws SFException`	Returns getRequestedQuantity
getReservedStockTypeValue	`public abstract StockTypeValue getReservedStockTypeValue() throws SFException`	Returns getStockTypeValue
getReservedWarehouse	`public abstract Warehouse getReservedWarehouse() throws SFException`	Returns getWarehouse
getReservedLot	`public abstract Lot getReservedLot() throws SFException`	Returns getLot
getReservedSerialNumber	`public abstract SerialNumber getReservedSerialNumber() throws SFException`	Returns getSerialNumber
getReservedStockLocation	`public abstract StockLocation getReservedStockLocation() throws SFException`	Returns getStockLocation
getFutureReceptionQuantity	`public abstract DProductTransactionQuantity getFutureReceptionQuantity() throws SFException`	Returns getRequestedQuantity

Figure 28-6
(Cont'd)

getFutureReceptionStockTypeValue	`public abstract StockTypeValue getFutureReceptionStockTypeValue() throws SFException`	Returns getStockTypeValue
getFutureReceptionWarehouse	`public abstract Warehouse getFutureReceptionWarehouse() throws SFException`	Returns getWarehouse
getFutureReceptionLot	`public abstract Lot getFutureReceptionLot() throws SFException`	Returns getLot
getFutureReceptionSerialNumber	`public abstract SerialNumber getFutureReceptionSerialNumber() throws SFException`	Returns getSerialNumber
getFutureReceptionStockLocation	`public abstract StockLocation getFutureReceptionStockLocation() throws SFException`	Returns getStockLocation
createSpecificInformationIterator	`public abstract Iterator createSpecificInformationIterator() throws SFException`	Create Iterator for Collection of SpecificInformation
getNextSpecificInformation	`public abstract SpecificInformation getNextSpecificInformation(Iterator position) throws SFException`	Gets the SpecificInformation at the Next Iterator Position
getPreviousSpecificInformation	`public abstract SpecificInformation getPreviousSpecificInformation(Iterator position) throws SFException`	Gets the SpecificInformation at the Previous Iterator Position
containsSpecificInformation	`public abstract boolean containsSpecificInformation(SpecificInformation specificinformation) throws SFException`	Checks if the SpecificInformation exists in the Collection of SpecificInformation
getSpecificInformationAt	`public abstract SpecificInformation getSpecificInformationAt(Iterator position) throws SFException`	Gets the SpecificInformation at the current iterator position
addSpecificInformation	`public abstract void addSpecificInformation(SpecificInformation specificInformationToAdd) throws SFException`	Adds a SpecificInformation to the Collection of SpecificInformation
addAllSpecificInformation	`public abstract void addAllSpecificInformation(DList newSpecificInformations) throws SFException`	Adds all SpecificInformation to the Collection of SpecificInformation
removeSpecificInformationAt	`public abstract void removeSpecificInformationAt(Iterator position) throws SFException`	Removes the SpecificInformation at the Current Iterator Position
removeSpecificInformation	`public abstract void removeSpecificInformation(SpecificInformation specificinformation) throws SFException`	Removes the specified SpecificInformation
removeAllSpecificInformation	`public abstract void removeAllSpecificInformation() throws SFException`	Removes all SpecificInformation from the Collection of SpecificInformation
insertSpecificInformationAt	`public abstract void insertSpecificInformationAt(SpecificInformation specificInformationToInsert, Iterator position) throws SFException`	Inserts the SpecificInformation at the Current Iterator Position
getSpecificInformationForRestrictedUse	`public abstract DList getSpecificInformationForRestrictedUse() throws SFException`	Returns the actual SpecificInformation, used by framework for SetEqual()
commit	`public abstract void commit() throws SFException`	Commit this OrderRequestedDetail.
getDeliveryOrderPartner	`public abstract OrderPartner getDeliveryOrderPartner() throws SFException`	Returns the DeliveryOrderPartner

Figure 28-6
(Cont'd)

Planning and Replanning

This category implements the planning process for orders. It builds upon the basic planning interfaces provided by the Warehouse Management framework and provides special adapters to make it compatible to the lifecycle based order structure used in this framework. This category establishes the relation between an order detail and the warehouse to which (or from which) it is to be shipped, following the process that is defined in Warehouse Management. It also extends the information available for planning and re-planning defined by Warehouse Management with order-specific information. For example, `Order PlanningDetail` is the respective extension of `PlanningDetails` from the Warehouse Management framework.

Picking

This category implements the picking process for orders. Just like the planning category, it builds upon the basic picking interfaces provided by the Warehouse Management framework and provides special adapters to make it compatible to the lifecycle based order structure used in this framework. The information about each stock pick is associated with the respective order detail. This category maintains product reservations against the specific location, lot, or serial number used for the pick.

Reception

This category also integrates the needs of the Order Management framework with the reception process defined in Warehouse Management. This category is responsible for managing the reception of products into inventory. This category provides the linking between order details and receptions into stock.

Backorder Handling

Order Management extends the backorder handling process that is introduced by Warehouse Management so that it can be incorporated into various order types. Specific business policy examples for backorder handling are supplied as part of the framework.

Order Invoicing

The invoicing process determines how to invoice products and charges. In this category, just like in the CBO layer, an invoiceable detail represents a product or charge that potentially can be invoiced, while an invoicing detail represents a product or charge that is ready to be invoiced. The invoicing process creates the invoicing detail based on the corresponding invoiceable detail. One or more invoicing details are merged into an invoice according to application-specific logic as implemented in the invoice generation policy. Invoicing is typically the last step in the order-processing cycle, and will create and add financial dissections to the GL.

Order Supplementary Charges

This category provides the supplementary charge process for orders. It is based upon the basic supplementary charge category in the CBO layer. Adaptors are provided to make the basic supplementary charge interfaces compatible to the lifecycle-based order management. Supplementary charge can be introduced in any stage in the lifetime of an order.

Information

This category provides some auxiliary classes that are used by other categories within in this framework. Specifically, it provides a group of dynamic identifiers to be used in order processing and provides structures for quantity and value limits that are used in pricing and discounting.

CHAPTER 29

The Ledger Framework (Accounts Payable and Accounts Receivable)

Accounts Receivable/Accounts Payable (AR/AP) is used to record the level of indebtedness between a company and its customers and suppliers. Each transaction (referred to as an item in this framework) that occurs between a company and its business partners is recorded. Accounts Receivable/Accounts Payable has been designed in a flexible manner so that it is not limited to just customers and suppliers, but can be used to keep track of any type of accounts that contain open items. For this purpose, the framework introduces the concept of an account, which is general, and is not restricted to being either a customer or supplier. Having different kinds of accounts is supported by having application-defined ledger types.

AR/AP Business Objects

AR/AP items can be either ledger items or log items. Ledger items are items that have been approved and accepted by the company. Log items are the unapproved items that the company has knowledge of, which are still pending approval. For example, an invoice from a supplier might be approved by the appropriate manager before accepting it into the ledger. In such cases, the relevant item may be recorded on the log as a record of receipt. After a log item has been approved it can be transferred to the ledger, and then it becomes a ledger item. Ledger items are always associated with generic dissections in the General Ledger for the income or expense, respectively, and to the relevant control account. A log item can also have generic dissections in the General Ledger but this is optional and depends on the practices in the specific business. The whole notion of log items is optional; all items can be recorded as ledger items immediately.

The following data must be set up for the operation of AR/AP and is done by appropriate use of Command objects.

- *Ledger Partners.* These objects contain information about the customers and suppliers that a company deals with. The notion of Legal Partner extends the `BusinessPartner` (part of the CBO layer) to contain extra information needed for AR/AP processing.
- *Bank Accounts.* Details of bank accounts used for AR/AP processing.

- *Payment Methods.* Objects containing details on payment methods used in AR/AP (these objects extend the `PaymentMethod` in the CBO layer).
- *Collection Documents.* If collection documents are used to collect payment from ledger partners then the parameters of these documents should be set-up.

AR/AP Business Processes

Day-to-Day Activities

Ledger items and log items can be created and posted for items like invoices, credit notes, and payments. The creation and posting of other types of items is also possible. These items have one or more installments associated with them. An installment contains a sum of money and a date when its payment is due. A number of possible settlement discount values and discount dates can also be associated with an installment. The composition of payments depends on the application, but typically, a payment will have only one installment. Posting of ledger and log items is not performed automatically by the framework. Rather, the application must decide when to do posting.

When applicable, collection documents used to collect payments from customers or suppliers can be used. The framework provides infrastructure for the creation and maintenance of documents, sending them to the bank, and rejecting documents when needed.

Allocations can be performed as necessary between installments. Allocations normally occur when payments are either received or made. However, allocations can occur in other situations. It is possible to post adjustments due to discounts or write-offs during allocation. Realized currency gains or losses are calculated and posted during allocation when there is a difference in exchange rates between the items being allocated. It is also possible to cancel an allocation that was previously created.

Payments to ledger partners can be made in payment runs or on a single payment basis. Items are created for these payments and are allocated with the installments that are being paid. Collection documents can be used to collect payments from customers or suppliers. The Core

Business Processes provide processing for the creation and maintenance of documents, sending or selling them to the bank, and maturity or rejection of the documents. The processing of both ledger items and log items can be performed in batch processing.

Periodic Activities

These processes are generally run before a period is closed or at the end of the fiscal year. These processes include items such as currency revaluation, producing "debt chasing" letters, and reconciliation to the General Ledger.

Currency revaluation calculates the unrealized gains or losses on items in the ledger that are not in the base currency of the company. Currency revaluation also optionally post these gains or losses to the General Ledger. Currency revaluation can either be performed as part of the period end processing or on an as-needed basis.

"Debt chasing" letters and period end reports, such as for reconciliation to the General Ledger and Aged Debtors or Aged Creditors reports, are not provided by the Core Business Process. This is because there are many different ways to report this information. Because AR/AP does not provide a report generator, reporting will vary dramatically from application to application. Applications can differentiate themselves from each other simply by their associated reports. AR/AP provides a flexible method of getting the information necessary to produce any report. As in the General Ledger, AR/AP has a set of criteria that can be used to produce account balances. A mechanism for maintaining and retrieving the balances is provided, but the definition of what balances should be maintained is left to the application.

AR/AP Categories

Similar to other components of SanFrancisco, this framework consists of several categories. Each category is composed of interfaces and classes. Table 29-1 summarizes the main components in each of the categories in the AR/AP framework.

TABLE 29-1
Summary for AR/AP ledger categories and their major components

Category	Major Components
Collection Documents	LECollDocParameters LECollDocConsolidationEnum LECollDocParametersController DProfitAndLossAccountUsageValidationPolicy DBalanceSheetAccountUsageValidationPolicy
Payment Method	LEPaymentMethod LEPaymentMethodController LEPaymentMethodSetupCmd DUnassignedCashUsageValidationPolicy
LedgerType	LedgerType LedgerTypeController
Ledger Partner	LedgerPartner LedgerPartnerController
Ledger Item	LedgerItemSubbatch LedgerItem LedgerItemStateEnum DLedgerItemValidationPolicy DLedgerItemValidationPolicyDefault DLedgerItemBalanceUpdatePolicy DGenericLELedgerItemAdapter
Log Item	LogItemSubbatch DLogItemValidationPolicy LogItemStateEnum LogItem DLoggedLogItemResetPolicy DLoggedLogItemResetPolicyDefault DLogItemBalanceUpdatePolicy LogLedgerItemController LECommonDebtItem GenericLELogItemAdapter DLoggedLogItemDeletePolicy DLogItemTransferPolicy GenericLogLedgerItemControllerAdapter
Debt Management	DebtManagementItem DebtManagementItemController DDebtManagementItemIdGenerationPolicy DControlAccountMovementCollection DControlAccountUsageValidationPolicy Installment InstallmentController DInstallmentMethodKey AllocationEvent AllocationDetail DAdjustmentDetail DAllocationEventEnum DAllocationValidationPolicy LEAllocationEventController DAllocationValidationPolicyDefault LEAccount

Collection Documents

A Collection Document represents a document exchanged with a business partner when making a payment or receiving one. This category is in charge of managing Collection Documents and their association with other objects in the framework. Collection documents involve various parameters, which are treated by this category. During the lifecycle of Collection Documents, postings to the General Ledger framework are generated as required. The main abstraction in this category is the `LECollDocParameters`, shown in Figure 29-1. This class maintains all the parameters of a Collection Document.

Payment Method

This category is responsible for maintaining `LEPaymentMethod` objects that are an extension of `PaymentMethod` from the CF package. `LEPaymentMethod` holds information that is used during processing in the LE framework, such as payment and collection document processing. The Interface for `LEPaymentMethod` is shown in Figure 29-2.

Ledger Type

This category is responsible for maintaining ledger types. Ledger types are used for classifying LE Accounts and holding default information relating to a type, such as the related bank account. Usually, there are ledgers of types "AP" (Accounts Payable) and "AR" (Accounts Receivable). The different types are managed by respective controllers in the unit. The interface for `LedgrTypeValue` representing ledger types is shown in Figure 29-3.

Ledger Partner

This category deals with ledger partners. A ledger partner is an implementation of the generic `LEAccount` interface shown in Figure 29-4. `LedgerPartner` holds information about a business partner that is specific to a certain ledger type. The interface for `LedgerPartner` is shown

Interface com.ibm.sf.le.LECollDocParameters

public interface **LECollDocParameters** extends DescribableDynamicEntity, Distinguishable

Main Methods

Name	*Signature*	*Description*
addWriteOffLimit	`public abstract void addWriteOffLimit(DCurrencyValue writeOffLimit) throws SFException`	Adds a write-off Limit to the LECollDocParameters for the given currency.
setConsolidationMethod	`public abstract void setConsolidationMethod(int consolidationMethod) throws SFException`	Set the consolidationMethod used.
removeDaysBeforeDueDate	`public abstract void removeDaysBeforeDueDate() throws SFException`	Removes the daysBeforeDueDate from LECollDocParameters.
addWriteOffLimitBy	`public abstract void addWriteOffLimitBy(DDecimal writeOffLimit, Currency key) throws SFException`	Adds a writeOffLimit to the LECollDocParameters by the given currency
setAutoCreatable	`public abstract void setAutoCreatable(boolean autoCreatable) throws SFException`	Set autoCreatable in LECollDocParameters
createWriteOffLimitIterator	`public abstract Iterator createWriteOffLimitIterator( ) throws SFException`	Create Iterator for Collection of WriteOffLimits
getNextWriteOffLimit	`public abstract DDecimal getNextWriteOffLimit(Iterator position) throws SFException`	Gets the WriteOffLimit at the Next Iterator Position
setWriteOffLimits	`public abstract void setWriteOffLimits(DMap WriteOffLimits) throws SFException`	Sets the collection of WriteOffLimits
containsWriteOffLimit	`public abstract boolean containsWriteOffLimit(DDecimal writeofflimit) throws SFException`	Checks if the WriteOffLimit exists in the Collection of WriteOffLimits
getWriteOffLimitAt	`public abstract DDecimal getWriteOffLimitAt(Iterator position) throws SFException`	Gets the WriteOffLimit at the current iterator position
removeWriteOffLimitAt	`public abstract void removeWriteOffLimitAt(Iterator position) throws SFException`	Removes the WriteOffLimit at the Current Iterator Position
removeWriteOffLimit	`public abstract void removeWriteOffLimit(DDecimal writeofflimit) throws SFException`	Removes the specified WriteOffLimit

Figure 29-1
Interface `LECollDocuments Parameters`

removeAllWriteOffLimits	`public abstract void removeAllWriteOffLimits() throws SFException`	Removes all WriteOffLimit from the Collection of WriteOffLimits
getWriteOffLimitBy	`public abstract DDecimal getWriteOffLimitBy(Currency key) throws SFException`	Gets the WriteOffLimit associated with the specified key
removeWriteOffLimitBy	`public abstract void removeWriteOffLimitBy(Currency key) throws SFException`	Removes the WriteOffLimit by the specified key
containsWriteOffLimitKey	`public abstract boolean containsWriteOffLimitKey(Currency key) throws SFException`	Checks if the WriteOffLimit exists by the specified Key
getWriteOffLimitKeyAt	`public abstract Currency getWriteOffLimitKeyAt(Iterator position) throws SFException`	Gets the WriteOffLimitKey at the current iterator position
getWriteOffLimitKey	`public abstract Currency getWriteOffLimitKey(DDecimal writeOffLimit) throws SFException`	Gets the WriteOffLimit at the Current Iterator Position
getDaysBeforeDueDate	`public abstract DInteger getDaysBeforeDueDate() throws SFException`	Gets the number of days before its due date that an installment should be included in a Collection Document during automatic creation.
setDaysBeforeDueDate	`public abstract void setDaysBeforeDueDate(DInteger newDaysBeforeDueDate) throws SFException`	Set the number of days before its due date that an installment should be included in a Collection Document during automatic creation.
getDaysAfterMaturity	`public abstract DInteger getDaysAfterMaturity() throws SFException`	Return the number of days after maturity during which it is still possible that a collection document will be returned as unpaid
setDaysAfterMaturity	`public abstract void setDaysAfterMaturity(DInteger newDaysAfterMaturity) throws SFException`	Set the number of days after maturity during which it is still possible that a collection document will be returned as unpaid
getDaysAfterConfirmation	`public abstract DInteger getDaysAfterConfirmation() throws SFException`	Return the number of days after confirmation after which we assume that the collection document will not be returned as unpaid.
setDaysAfterConfirmation	`public abstract void setDaysAfterConfirmation(DInteger newDaysAfterConfirmation) throws SFException`	Set the number of days after confirmation after which we assume that the collection document will not be returned as unpaid.
getDaysBeforeMaturity	`public abstract DInteger getDaysBeforeMaturity() throws SFException`	Gets the number of days before maturity date that collection documents should be sent (or sold) to the Bank.
setDaysBeforeMaturity	`public abstract void setDaysBeforeMaturity(DInteger newDaysBeforeMaturity) throws SFException`	Set the number of days before maturity date that collection documents should be sent (or sold) to the Bank.
getAcceptance	`public abstract TransactionTypeValue getAcceptance() throws SFException`	Returns the Acceptance, copied from the Handle

Figure 29-1
(Cont'd)

setAcceptance	`public abstract void setAcceptance(TransactionTypeValue newAcceptance) throws SFException`	Set the Handle of the Acceptance
getMaturity	`public abstract TransactionTypeValue getMaturity() throws SFException`	Returns the Maturity, copied from the Handle
setMaturity	`public abstract void setMaturity(TransactionTypeValue newMaturity) throws SFException`	Set the Handle of the Maturity
getConsolidationMethod	`public abstract int getConsolidationMethod() throws SFException`	Gets the method of consolidation for a collection document created during autocreation.
isAutoAcceptable	`public abstract boolean isAutoAcceptable() throws SFException`	Gets specifies if the collection document can be automatically accepted
setAutoAcceptable	`public abstract void setAutoAcceptable(boolean newAutoAcceptable) throws SFException`	Sets the flag specifying if the collection document can be automatically accepted
isSaleAllowed	`public abstract boolean isSaleAllowed() throws SFException`	Gets the flag specifying if the collection document can be sold to the bank
setSaleAllowed	`public abstract void setSaleAllowed(boolean newSaleAllowed) throws SFException`	Set the flag specifying if the collection document can be sold to the bank
isAutoCreatable	`public abstract boolean isAutoCreatable() throws SFException`	Gets the flag specifying if the collection document can be created automatically
getAcceptanceHdl	`public abstract Handle getAcceptanceHdl() throws SFException`	Returns a Handle to the TransactionTypeValue of the acceptance of the LECollDocParameters
getMaturityHdl	`public abstract Handle getMaturityHdl() throws SFException`	Returns a Handle to the TransactionTypeValue of the maturity of the LECollDocParameters
getId	`public abstract String getId() throws SFException`	Gets id

Figure 29-1
(Cont'd)

in Figure 29-5. `LedgerPartner` objects are maintained by the respective controller in a company.

Debt Management

This category contains most of the Combined Ledger managing debt information (e.g. invoices and payments). This category is responsible

Interface com.ibm.sf.le.LEPaymentMethod

public interface **LEPaymentMethod** extends DescribableDynamicEntity, Distinguishable

Main Methods

Name	*Signature*	*Description*
addMinimumValue	`public abstract void addMinimumValue(DCurrencyValue currencyMinimum) throws SFException`	Adds the minimumValue (included in the currencyValue) to the minimumValue Collection, using the currency as a key.
addMaximumValue	`public abstract void addMaximumValue(DCurrencyValue currencyMaximum) throws SFException`	Adds the maximumValue (included in the currencyValue) to the maximumValue Collection, using the currency as a key.
addMinimumValueBy	`public abstract void addMinimumValueBy(DDecimal minimumValue, Currency key) throws SFException`	Adds the minimumValue to the minimumValue Collection, using the currency as a key.
addMaximumValueBy	`public abstract void addMaximumValueBy(DDecimal maximumValue, Currency key) throws SFException`	Adds the minimumValue to the manimumValue Collection, using the currency as a key.
getUnassigndCashGenericPostingCombination	`public abstract GenericPostingCombination getUnassigndCashGenericPostingCombination() throws SFException`	Provides the Unassigned Cash Generic Posting Combination for the LE Payment Method, or if that does not exist provides the generic posting combination from the Company.
getId	`public abstract String getId() throws SFException`	get the id of the Distinguishable object
createMaximumValueIterator	`public abstract Iterator createMaximumValueIterator() throws SFException`	Create Iterator for Collection of MaximumValues
getNextMaximumValue	`Public abstract DDecimal getNextMaximumValue(Iterator position) throws SFException`	Returns the MaximumValue at the Next Iterator Position
setMaximumValues	`Public abstract void setMaximumValues(DMap MaximumValues) throws SFException`	Sets the collection of MaximumValues
containsMaximumValue	`Public abstract boolean containsMaximumValue(DDecimal maximumvalue) throws SFException`	Checks if the MaximumValue exists in the Collection of MaximumValues
getMaximumValueAt	`public abstract DDecimal getMaximumValueAt(Iterator position) throws SFException`	Returns the MaximumValue at the current iterator position
removeMaximumValueAt	`public abstract void removeMaximumValueAt(Iterator position) throws SFException`	Removes the MaximumValue at the Current Iterator Position

Figure 29-2
Interface `LEPayment Method`

removeMaximumValue	public abstract void removeMaximumValue(DDecimal maximumvalue) throws SFException	Removes the specified MaximumValue
getMaximumValueBy	public abstract DDecimal getMaximumValueBy(Currency key) throws SFException	Gets the MaximumValue associated with the specified key
removeMaximumValueBy	public abstract void removeMaximumValueBy(Currency key) throws SFException	Removes the MaximumValue by the specified key
containsMaximumValueKey	public abstract boolean containsMaximumValueKey(Currency key) throws SFException	Checks if the MaximumValue exists by the specified Key
getMaximumValueKeyAt	public abstract Currency getMaximumValueKeyAt(Iterator position) throws SFException	Gets the MaximumValueKey at the current iterator position
getMaximumValueKey	public abstract Currency getMaximumValueKey(DDecimal maximumValue) throws SFException	Gets the MaximumValue at the Current Iterator Position
getLECollDocParameters	public abstract LECollDocParameters getLECollDocParameters() throws SFException	Returns the LECollDocParameters, copied from the Handle
setLECollDocParameters	public abstract void setLECollDocParameters(LECollDocParameters newLECollDocParameters) throws SFException	Set the Handle of the LECollDocParameters
createMinimumValueIterator	public abstract Iterator createMinimumValueIterator() throws SFException	Create Iterator for Collection of MinimumValues
getNextMinimumValue	public abstract DDecimal getNextMinimumValue(Iterator position) throws SFException	Gets the MinimumValue at the Next Iterator Position
setMinimumValues	public abstract void setMinimumValues(DMap MinimumValues) throws SFException	Sets the collection of MinimumValues
containsMinimumValue	public abstract boolean containsMinimumValue(DDecimal minimumvalue) throws SFException	Checks if the MinimumValue exists in the Collection of MinimumValues
getMinimumValueAt	public abstract DDecimal getMinimumValueAt(Iterator position) throws SFException	Gets the MinimumValue at the current iterator position
removeMinimumValueAt	public abstract void removeMinimumValueAt(Iterator position) throws SFException	Removes the MinimumValue at the Current Iterator Position
removeMinimumValue	public abstract void removeMinimumValue(DDecimal minimumvalue) throws SFException	Removes the specified MinimumValue

Figure 29-2
(Cont'd)

getMinimumValueBy	`public abstract DDecimal getMinimumValueBy(Currency key) throws SFException`	Gets the MinimumValue associated with the specified key
removeMinimumValueBy	`public abstract void removeMinimumValueBy(Currency key) throws SFException`	Removes the MinimumValue by the specified key
containsMinimumValueKey	`public abstract boolean containsMinimumValueKey(Currency key) throws SFException`	Checks if the MinimumValue exists by the specified Key
getMinimumValueKeyAt	`public abstract Currency getMinimumValueKeyAt(Iterator position) throws SFException`	Gets the MinimumValueKey at the current iterator position
getMinimumValueKey	`public abstract Currency getMinimumValueKey(DDecimal minimumValue) throws SFException`	Gets the MinimumValue at the Current Iterator Position
getCFPaymentMethod	`public abstract PaymentMethod getCFPaymentMethod() throws SFException`	Returns the CFPaymentMethod, copied from the Handle
setCFPaymentMethod	`public abstract void setCFPaymentMethod(PaymentMethod newCFPaymentMethod) throws SFException`	Set the Handle of the CFPaymentMethod

Figure 29-2
(Cont'd)

for the internal management of the common part of the `Log` and `LedgerItems` represented by `DebtManagementItem` objects (see Figure 29-6).

This category also provides the support for the settlement of `DebtManagementItem` objects through installments. The interface to `Installment` is shown in Figure 29-7. Installments are managed by the respective controller placed in the company.

Another role of this category is creating allocation between Log items and/or Ledger items for a `LEAccount`. Such an allocation in its simplest form is a matching between a payment and an outstanding invoice on a ledger partners account. The matching can be done in either one of the prime currency or the base currencies. An `AllocationEvent` (see Figure 29-8) is composed of `AllocationDetail` objects (see interface in Figure 29-9). An `AllocationEvent` handles adjustments that occur and are represented by `DAdjustmentDetail` (see Figure 29-10). Such adjustments might occur because of discounts or rounding. If the allocation is done in prime currency it also calculates currency gain or loss.

Interface com.ibm.sf.le.LedgerType

public interface **LedgerType** extends DescribableDynamicEntity, Distinguishable

Main Methods

Name	*Signature*	*Description*
getPropertyNameForFinancialCalendar	`public abstract String getPropertyNameForFinancialCalendar() throws SFException`	Returns the property name of the FinancialCalendar for this LedgerType on any CFCompany.
getPropertyNameForLedgerPartnerController	`public abstract String getPropertyNameForLedgerPartnerController() throws SFException`	Returns the property name of the LedgerPartnerController for this LedgerType on any Company.
getId	`public abstract String getId() throws SFException`	Get the Id of the Distinguishable object
getDefaultInternalBankAccount	`public abstract InternalBankAccount getDefaultInternalBankAccount() throws SFException`	Returns the DefaultInternalBankAccount, copied from the Handle
setDefaultInternalBankAccount	`public abstract void setDefaultInternalBankAccount(InternalBankAccount newDefaultInternalBankAccount) throws SFException`	Set the Handle of the DefaultInternalBankAccount
getCollDocParameters	`public abstract LECollDocParameters getCollDocParameters() throws SFException`	Returns the CollDocParameters, copied from the Handle.
setCollDocParameters	`public abstract void setCollDocParameters(LECollDocParameters newCollDocParameters) throws SFException`	Set the Handle of the CollDocParameters
getLedgerTypeController	`public abstract LedgerTypeController getLedgerTypeController() throws SFException`	Returns the LedgerTypeController, copied from the Handle.
getPaymentMethod	`public abstract PaymentMethod getPaymentMethod() throws SFException`	Returns the PaymentMethod, copied from the Handle
setPaymentMethod	`public abstract void setPaymentMethod(PaymentMethod newPaymentMethod) throws SFException`	Set the Handle of the PaymentMethod used.
createTransactionTypeValueIterator	`public abstract Iterator createTransactionTypeValueIterator() throws SFException`	Create Iterator for Collection of TransactionTypeValues
getNextTransactionTypeValue	`public abstract TransactionTypeValue getNextTransactionTypeValue(Iterator position) throws SFException`	Gets the TransactionTypeValue at the Next Iterator Position
setTransactionTypeValues	`public abstract void setTransactionTypeValues(DMap TransactionTypeValues) throws SFException`	Sets the collection of TransactionTypeValues

Figure 29-3
Interface `LedgerType Value`

containsTransactionTypeValue	`public abstract boolean containsTransactionTypeValue(TransactionTypeValue transactiontypevalue) throws SFException`	Checks if the TransactionTypeValue exists in the Collection of TransactionTypeValues
getTransactionTypeValueAt	`public abstract TransactionTypeValue getTransactionTypeValueAt(Iterator position) throws SFException`	Returns the TransactionTypeValue at the current iterator position
removeTransactionTypeValueAt	`public abstract void removeTransactionTypeValueAt(Iterator position) throws SFException`	Removes the TransactionTypeValue at the Current Iterator Position
removeTransactionTypeValue	`public abstract void removeTransactionTypeValue(TransactionTypeValue transactiontypevalue) throws SFException`	Removes the specified TransactionTypeValue
removeAllTransactionTypeValues	`public abstract void removeAllTransactionTypeValues() throws SFException`	Removes all TransactionTypeValue from the Collection of TransactionTypeValues
getTransactionTypeValueBy	`public abstract TransactionTypeValue getTransactionTypeValueBy(FinancialTransactionSource key) throws SFException`	Gets the TransactionTypeValue associated with the specified key
addTransactionTypeValueBy	`public abstract void addTransactionTypeValueBy(TransactionTypeValue transactionTypeValue, FinancialTransactionSource key) throws SFExceptionAdds`	a TransactionTypeValue to the Collection of TransactionTypeValues by the Specified Key
removeTransactionTypeValueBy	`public abstract void removeTransactionTypeValueBy(FinancialTransactionSource key) throws SFException`	Removes the TransactionTypeValue by the specified key
containsTransactionTypeValueKey	`public abstract boolean containsTransactionTypeValueKey (FinancialTransactionSource key) throws SFException`	Checks if the TransactionTypeValue exists by the specified Key
getTransactionTypeValueKeyAt	`public abstract FinancialTransactionSource getTransactionTypeValueKeyAt(Iterator position) throws SFException`	Gets the TransactionTypeValueKey at the current iterator position
getTransactionTypeValueKey	`public abstract FinancialTransactionSource getTransactionTypeValueKey(TransactionTypeValue transactionTypeValue) throws SFException`	Gets the TransactionTypeValue at the Current Iterator Position
getDefaultInternalBankAccountHdl	`public abstract Handle getDefaultInternalBankAccountHdl() throws SFException`	Returns the Handle to the InternalBankAccount of the defaultInternalBankAccount of the LedgerType

Figure 29-3
(Cont'd)

getCollDocParametersHdl	`public abstract Handle getCollDocParametersHdl() throws SFException`	Returns the Handle to the LECollDocParameters of the collDocParameters of the LedgerType
getLedgerTypeControllerHdl	`public abstract Handle getLedgerTypeControllerHdl() throws SFException`	Returns the Handle to the LedgerTypeController of the LedgerTypeController of the LedgerType
getPaymentMethodHdl	`public abstract Handle getPaymentMethodHdl() throws SFException`	Returns the Handle to the PaymentMethod of the paymentMethod of the LedgerType

Figure 29-3
(Cont'd)

Ledger Item

This category provides a concrete application of managing and collecting data that are reflected in the GL. It records domain-specific data (e.g. payments, invoices) and, in addition, prepares and validates the data before it is passed on to the GL. The interface to `LedgerItem` is shown in Figure 29-11. A `LedgerItem` can be in one of several states enumerated in `LedgerItemStateEnum`. These states are: `INCOMPLETE`, `SUSPENDED`, `READY_FOR_LEDGER`, and `POSTED`. Policies can be provided for `LedgerItem` validation.

Log Item

This category represents a concrete application of managing and collecting items such as invoices and payment. It is responsible for recording real-world data and then preparing and validating it for further processing in the GL. The main abstraction here is the `LogItem` shown in Figure 29-12. Similar to `LedgerItem` it has several states defined in `LogItemStateEnum`. These are `INCOMPLETE`, `SUSPENDED`, `READY_FOR_LOG`, `LOGGED`, and `TRANSFERRED` (to GL). Here too, policies can be provided for validation.

Interface com.ibm.sf.le.LEAccount

public interface **LEAccount** extends DescribableDynamicEntity, GenericLEAccount

Name	*Signature*	*Description*
getAllocationValidationPolicy	`public abstract DAllocationValidationPolicy getAllocationValidationPolicy() throws SFException`	Returns the allocation validation policy. If not defined on this LEAccount, the allocation validation policy is retrieved from the company.
getDefaultInternalBankAccount	`public abstract InternalBankAccount getDefaultInternalBankAccount() throws SFException`	Returns the default internal bank account.
getDirectlyContainedDefaultInternalBankAccount	`public abstract InternalBankAccount getDirectlyContainedDefaultInternalBankAccount() throws SFException`	Returns the default internal bank account.
getDirectlyContainedExchangeRateTypeBy	`public abstract ExchangeRateType getDirectlyContainedExchangeRateTypeBy(String key) throws SFException`	Returns the exchange rate type for the given key.
getDirectlyContainedExternalBankAccountBy	`public abstract ExternalBankAccount getDirectlyContainedExternalBankAccountBy(String key) throws SFException`	Returns the external bank account for the given key.
getDirectlyContainedPaymentMethod	`public abstract PaymentMethod getDirectlyContainedPaymentMethod() throws SFException`	Returns the payment method.
getDirectlyContainedPaymentTerms	`public abstract PaymentTerms getDirectlyContainedPaymentTerms() throws SFException`	Returns the payment terms.
getDirectlyOwnedInterestRate	`public abstract DDecimal getDirectlyOwnedInterestRate() throws SFException`	Returns the interest rate.
getExchangeRateTypeBy	`public abstract ExchangeRateType getExchangeRateTypeBy(String key) throws SFException`	Returns the exchange rate type for the given key.
getExternalBankAccountBy	`public abstract ExternalBankAccount getExternalBankAccountBy(String key) throws SFException`	Returns the external bank account for the given key.
getGenericPostingCombinationBy	`public abstract GenericPostingCombination getGenericPostingCombinationBy(DissectionTypeValue dissectionTypeValue) throws SFException`	Returns the GenericPostingCombination for the given DissectionTypeValue.
getInterestRate	`public abstract DDecimal getInterestRate() throws SFException`	Returns the interest rate.

Figure 29-4
Interface `LEAccount`

getLedgerType	`public abstract LedgerType getLedgerType() throws SFException`	Returns the ledger type.
getPaymentMethod	`public abstract PaymentMethod getPaymentMethod() throws SFException`	Returns the payment method.
getPaymentTerms	`public abstract PaymentTerms getPaymentTerms() throws SFException`	Returns the payment terms.
isActive	`public abstract boolean isActive() throws SFException`	Get flag which indicates if the ledger account is active.
isExcludedFromChaseLetter	`public abstract boolean isExcludedFromChaseLetter() throws SFException`	Get flag which indicates if the ledger account is to be excluded from chase letters.
isExcludedFromInterestCalculation	`public abstract boolean isExcludedFromInterestCalculation() throws SFException`	Get Boolean which indicates if the ledger account is to be excluded from interest calculation.
isPaymentHeld	`public abstract boolean isPaymentHeld() throws SFException`	Get flag which indicates if payments are to be held for the ledger account.

Figure 29-4
(Cont'd)

Interface com.ibm.sf.le.LedgerPartner

public interface **LedgerPartner** extends LEAccount, Distinguishable, Shared

Main Methods

Name	*Signature*	*Description*
addDirectlyContainedExternalBankAccountBy	`public abstract void addDirectlyContainedExternalBankAccountBy(ExternalBankAccount externalBankAccount, String key) throws SFException`	Adds an external bank account for the given key.
removeDirectlyContainedExternalBankAccountBy	`public abstract void removeDirectlyContainedExternalBankAccountBy(String key) throws SFException`	Removes the external bank account for the given key.
getBusinessPartnerCustomerSupplierData	`public abstract BusinessPartnerCustomerSupplierData getBusinessPartnerCustomerSupplierData() throws SFException`	Returns the customer/supplier data for this ledger partner.
getDefaultInternalBankAccount	`public abstract InternalBankAccount getDefaultInternalBankAccount() throws SFException`	Returns the default internal bank account. If not defined on this ledger partner, the default internal bank account is retrieved from the parent ledger partner. If not found, the default internal bank account is retrieved from the ledger type.
getDirectlyContainedDefaultInternalBankAccount	`public abstract InternalBankAccount getDirectlyContainedDefaultInternalBankAccount() throws SFException`	Returns the default internal bank account defined for this ledger partner.
getDirectlyContainedExchangeRateTypeBy	`public abstract ExchangeRateType getDirectlyContainedExchangeRateTypeBy(String key) throws SFException`	Returns the exchange rate type for the given key from the business partner's customer/supplier data.
getDirectlyContainedExternalBankAccountBy	`public abstract ExternalBankAccount getDirectlyContainedExternalBankAccountBy(String key) throws SFException`	Returns the external bank account for the given key.
getDirectlyContainedPaymentMethod	`public abstract PaymentMethod getDirectlyContainedPaymentMethod() throws SFException`	Returns the payment method by retrieving it from the business partner's customer/supplier data.
getDirectlyContainedPaymentTerms	`public abstract PaymentTerms getDirectlyContainedPaymentTerms() throws SFException`	Returns the payment terms from the business partner's customer/supplier data.
getDirectlyOwnedInterestRate	`public abstract DDecimal getDirectlyOwnedInterestRate() throws SFException`	Returns the interest rate.

Figure 29-5
Interface `LedgerPartner`

getExchangeRateTypeBy	`public abstract ExchangeRateType getExchangeRateTypeBy(String key) throws SFException`	Returns the exchange rate type for the given key from the business partner's customer/supplier data. If not defined on this business partner, the exchange rate type is retrieved from the parent business partner's customer/supplier data, if one exists.
getExternalBankAccountBy	`public abstract ExternalBankAccount getExternalBankAccountBy(String key) throws SFException`	Returns the external bank account for the given key. If not defined on this ledger partner, the external bank account is retrieved from the parent ledger partner, if one exists.
getGenericPostingCombinationBy	`public abstract GenericPostingCombination getGenericPostingCombinationBy(DissectionTypeValue dissectionTypeValue) throws SFException`	Returns the GenericPostingCombination for the given DissectionTypeValue. If not defined on this ledger partner, the generic posting combination is retrieved from the parent ledger partner, if one exists. If not found, the GenericPostingCombination is retrieved from the ledger type, if one exists.
getInterestRate	`public abstract DDecimal getInterestRate() throws SFException`	Returns the interest rate. If not defined on this ledger partner, the interest rate is retrieved from the parent ledger partner, if one exists.
getLedgerType	`public abstract LedgerType getLedgerType() throws SFException`	Returns the ledger type.
getPaymentMethod	`public abstract PaymentMethod getPaymentMethod() throws SFException`	Returns the payment method by retrieving it from the business partner's customer/supplier data. If not defined on this business partner, the payment method is retrieved from the parent business partner, if one exists. If not found, the payment method is retrieved from the ledger type.
getPaymentTerms	`public abstract PaymentTerms getPaymentTerms() throws SFException`	Returns the payment terms from the business partner's customer/supplier data. If not defined on this business partner, the payment terms are retrieved from the parent business partner's customer/supplier data, if one exists.
getId	`public abstract String getId() throws SFException`	Get the id of the Distinguishable object.
getSharedMethods	`public abstract DSet getSharedMethods() throws SFException`	Returns the list of methods used to support shared attributes for this class.
addSharedContainedPropertyBy	`public abstract void addSharedContainedPropertyBy(Object propertyToAdd, String propertyName) throws SFException`	Adds either an unowned Entity, owned Dependent, or owned String property to the shared property container for this object, keyed by the given propertyName. An Entity property will not be destroyed when this PropertyContainer is destroyed. A Dependent or String property is a copy of the passed in parameter so is owned by this PropertyContainer and therefore deleted when this PropertyContainer is destroyed.

Figure 29-5
(Cont'd)

addSharedOwnedPropertyBy	public abstract void addSharedOwnedPropertyBy(Entity propertyToAddAsOwned, String propertyName) throws SFException	Adds an owned Entity to the shared property container for this object, keyed by the given propertyName. The Entity property will be destroyed when this PropertyContainer is destroyed.
removeSharedOwnedPropertyBy	public abstract void removeSharedOwnedPropertyBy(String propertyName) throws SFException	Removes the owned Entity from the shared PropertyContainer for this object and deletes the Entity.
getSharedPropertyHdlBy	public abstract Handle getSharedPropertyHdlBy(String propertyName) throws SFException	Retrieves the shared property with a name matching the passed-in propertyName. If it is an Entity property, return a copy of its Handle, otherwise a CollectionException is thrown.
getChainParent	public abstract PropertyContainer getChainParent() throws SFException	Returns the parent ledger partner. Used for getting aggregating behavior for properties along the business partner hierarchy.
setDirectlyContainedDefaultInternalBankAccount	public abstract void setDirectlyContainedDefaultInternalBankAccount(InternalBankAccount newDirectlyContainedDefaultInternalBankAccount) throws SFException	Set the Handle of the DirectlyContainedDefaultInternalBankAccount
getBusinessPartner	public abstract BusinessPartner getBusinessPartner() throws SFException	Returns the BusinessPartner, copied from the Handle
setDirectlyOwnedInterestRate	public abstract void setDirectlyOwnedInterestRate(DDecimal newDirectlyOwnedInterestRate) throws SFException	Sets DirectlyOwnedInterestRate
isExcludedFromChaseLetter	public abstract boolean isExcludedFromChaseLetter() throws SFException	Returns flag which indicates if the ledger partner is to be excluded from chase letters. True indicates excluded from chase letters, false indicates not excluded from chase letters.
setExcludedFromChaseLetter	public abstract void setExcludedFromChaseLetter(boolean newExcludedFromChaseLetter) throws SFException	Set Boolean which indicates if the ledger partner is to be excluded from chase letters. True indicates excluded from chase letters, false indicates not excluded from chase letters.
isExcludedFromInterestCalculation	public abstract boolean isExcludedFromInterestCalculation() throws SFException	Returns flag which indicates if the ledger partner is to be excluded from interest charge calculation. For a ledger partner of type AR, it indicates if the customer is excluded from interest charge. For ledger partner of type AP, it indicates if the supplier is charging interest. True indicates excluded from interest calculation, false indicates not excluded from interest calculation.

Figure 29-5
(Cont'd)

setExcludedFromInterestCalculation	`public abstract void setExcludedFromInterestCalculation(boolean newExcludedFromInterestCalculation) throws SFException`	Set flag which indicates if the ledger partner is to be excluded from interest charge calculation. For a ledger partner of type AR, it indicates if the customer is excluded from interest charge. For ledger partner of type AP, it indicates if the supplier is charging interest. True indicates excluded from interest calculation, false indicates not excluded from interest calculation.
isPaymentHeld	`public abstract boolean isPaymentHeld() throws SFException`	Gets flag which indicates if payments are to be held for the ledger partner. True indicates that payments are to be held, false indicates that payments are not to be held.
setPaymentHeld	`public abstract void setPaymentHeld(boolean newPaymentHeld) throws SFException`	Set flag which indicates if payments are to be held for the ledger partner. True indicates that payments are to be held, false indicates that payments are not to be held.
isActive	`public abstract boolean isActive() throws SFException`	Gets flag which indicates if the ledger partner is active. True indicates active, false indicates inactive.
setActive	`public abstract void setActive(boolean newActive) throws SFException`	Set Boolean which indicates if the ledger partner is active. True indicates active, false indicates inactive.
getBusinessPartnerHdl	`public abstract Handle getBusinessPartnerHdl() throws SFException`	Returns the Handle to the BusinessPartner of the businessPartner of the LedgerPartner
getLedgerTypeHdl	`public abstract Handle getLedgerTypeHdl() throws SFException`	Returns the Handle to the LedgerType of the ledgerType of the LedgerPartner

Figure 29-5
(Cont'd)

Interface com.ibm.sf.le.DebtManagementItem

public interface **DebtManagementItem** extends DescribableDynamicEntity, Distinguishable

Main Methods

Name	*Signature*	*Description*
getLEAccountHdl	`public abstract Handle getLEAccountHdl() throws SFException`	Returns the Handle to the LEAccount of the LEAccount of the DebtManagementItem
getCurrentLogControlAccountDissectionHdl	`public abstract Handle getCurrentLogControlAccountDissectionHdl() throws SFException`	Returns the Handle to the GenericDissection of the currentLogControlAccountDissection of the DebtManagementItem
getLedgerControlAccountDissectionHdl	`public abstract Handle getLedgerControlAccountDissectionHdl() throws SFException`	Returns the Handle to the GenericDissection of the ledgerControlAccountDissection of the DebtManagementItem
getDebtManagementItemControllerHdl	`public abstract Handle getDebtManagementItemControllerHdl() throws SFException`	Returns the Handle to the DebtManagementItemController of the DebtManagementItem
getBusinessPartnerBalanceValueHdl	`public abstract Handle getBusinessPartnerBalanceValueHdl() throws SFException`	Returns the Handle to the BusinessPartnerBalanceValue of the DebtManagementItem
getDocumentLocationHdl	`public abstract Handle getDocumentLocationHdl() throws SFException`	Returns the Handle to the DocumentLocation of the DebtManagementItem
getCommonDebtItemHdl	`public abstract Handle getCommonDebtItemHdl() throws SFException`	Returns the Handle to the LECommonDebtItem of the commonDebtItem of the DebtManagementItem

Figure 29-6
Interface `DebtManagement Item`

Interface com.ibm.sf.le.Installment

public interface **Installment** extends DescribableDynamicEntity

Main Methods

Name	*Signature*	*Description*
calculatePendingAllocationValue	`public abstract DTransactionValue calculatePendingAllocationValue() throws SFException`	Return the pending allocation TransactionValue for this Installment aggregating the value of all pending Allocation Details. The total will include adjustment values.
calculateAllocatableValue	`public abstract DTransactionValue calculateAllocatableValue() throws SFException`	Gets the allocatable TransactionValue for the Installment as Total Installment Value minus Committed Value and minus Pending Value.
calculateCommittedAllocationValue	`public abstract DTransactionValue calculateCommittedAllocationValue() throws SFException`	Gets the allocated TransactionValue for each committed and deallocated Allocation Detail (that is, its Allocation Event has committed or deallocated status) and adds them up to give the total committed allocated TransactionValue for this Installment.
calculateUnallocatedValue	`public abstract DTransactionValue calculateUnallocatedValue() throws SFException`	Gets the TransactionValue for each committed and deallocated Allocation Details (that is, its Allocation Event has committed or deallocated status), aggregate them and then subtract this aggregated Transaction Value from the Installment Transaction Value to give the Unallocated TransactionValue for this Installment.
changeDueDate	`public abstract void changeDueDate(DTime newDueDate, NaturalCalendar naturalCalendar, DResultDateAdjustmentPolicy policy) throws SFException`	Sets the new Due Date and updates the balances if this Installment is included in the Ledger Account Balances.
getLedgerControlAccountPostingCombination	`public abstract GenericPostingCombination getLedgerControlAccountPostingCombination() throws SFException`	Returns the associated Generic GL Posting Combination for Control Account or null. If the Posting Combination for Ledger Control is not retrieved from Installment, this method gets the Ledger Control Account Dissection from the Debt Management Item and if it is not null, then the Generic GL Posting Combination is retrieved from the Generic GL Dissection.
setPaymentMethod	`public abstract void setPaymentMethod(PaymentMethod newPaymentMethod) throws SFException`	Sets the new Payment Method.

Figure 29-7
Interface `Installment`.

isExcludedFromInterestCalculation	`public abstract boolean isExcludedFromInterestCalculation() throws SFException`	Returns the associated ExcludedFromInterestCalculation Indicator. Returns TRUE if Installment is excluded from Interest Calculations, otherwise FALSE.
isExcludedFromChaseLetter	`public abstract boolean isExcludedFromChaseLetter() throws SFException`	Returns the associated ExcludedFromChaseLetter Indicator. Returns TRUE if Installment is excluded from Chase Letters, otherwise FALSE.
isPaymentHeld	`public abstract boolean isPaymentHeld() throws SFException`	Returns the associated PaymentHeld Indicator. Returns TRUE if Payment is held, otherwise FALSE.
hasAllocations	`public abstract boolean hasAllocations() throws SFException`	Test whether the Installment has associated Allocations. TRUE if Installment has associated Allocations, otherwise FALSE.
getCurrentControlAccount	`public abstract GenericPostingCombination getCurrentControlAccount() throws SFException`	Returns the CurrentControlAccount, copied from the Handle
setCurrentControlAccount	`public abstract void setCurrentControlAccount(GenericPostingCombination newCurrentControlAccount) throws SFException`	Set the Handle of the CurrentControlAccount
getDebtManagementItem	`public abstract DebtManagementItem getDebtManagementItem() throws SFException`	Returns the DebtManagementItem, copied from the Handle
setDebtManagementItem	`public abstract void setDebtManagementItem(DebtManagementItem newDebtManagementItem) throws SFException`	Set the Handle of the DebtManagementItem
getDueDate	`public abstract DTime getDueDate() throws SFException`	Gets date by which payment of the installment should be made/received
setDueDate	`public abstract void setDueDate(DTime newDueDate) throws SFException`	Set date by which payment of the installment should be made/received.
getInstallmentValue	`public abstract DTransactionValue getInstallmentValue() throws SFException`	Gets It's for the total installment value (allocated and unallocated).
setInstallmentValue	`public abstract void setInstallmentValue(DTransactionValue newInstallmentValue) throws SFException`	Set It's the total installment value (allocated and unallocated).
getPaymentTermsDetail	`public abstract DPaymentTermsDetail getPaymentTermsDetail() throws SFException`	Gets base Date by which Installment and Settlement Details are created.
setPaymentTermsDetail	`public abstract void setPaymentTermsDetail(DPaymentTermsDetail newPaymentTermsDetail) throws SFException`	Set base Date by which Installment and Settlement Details are created.

Figure 29-7
(Cont'd)

getRevaluedValue	`public abstract DTransactionValue getRevaluedValue() throws SFException`	Gets If when the installment has been revalued, it represents the revalued value of unallocated installment value.
setRevaluedValue	`public abstract void setRevaluedValue(DTransactionValue newRevaluedValue) throws SFException`	Set If when the installment has been revalued, it represents the revalued value of unallocated installment value.
getUnrealizedGainLossAccount	`public abstract GenericPostingCombination getUnrealizedGainLossAccount() throws SFException`	Returns the UnrealizedGainLossAccount, copied from the Handle
setUnrealizedGainLossAccount	`public abstract void setUnrealizedGainLossAccount(GenericPostingCombination newUnrealizedGainLossAccount) throws SFException`	Set the Handle of the UnrealizedGainLossAccount
getUnrealizedGainLossContraAccount	`public abstract GenericPostingCombination getUnrealizedGainLossContraAccount() throws SFException`	Returns the UnrealizedGainLossContraAccount, copied from the Handle
setUnrealizedGainLossContraAccount	`public abstract void setUnrealizedGainLossContraAccount(GenericPostingCombination newUnrealizedGainLossContraAccount) throws SFException`	Set the Handle of the UnrealizedGainLossContraAccount
createAllocationDetailIterator	`public abstract Iterator createAllocationDetailIterator() throws SFException`	Create Iterator for Collection of AllocationDetails
getNextAllocationDetail	`public abstract AllocationDetail getNextAllocationDetail(Iterator position) throws SFException`	Gets the AllocationDetail at the Next Iterator Position
setAllocationDetails	`public abstract void setAllocationDetails(DSet AllocationDetails) throws SFException`	Sets the collection of AllocationDetails
containsAllocationDetail	`public abstract boolean containsAllocationDetail(AllocationDetail allocationdetail) throws SFException`	Checks if the AllocationDetail exists in the Collection of AllocationDetails
getAllocationDetailAt	`public abstract AllocationDetail getAllocationDetailAt(Iterator position) throws SFException`	Gets the AllocationDetail at the current iterator position
addAllocationDetail	`public abstract void addAllocationDetail(AllocationDetail allocationDetailToAdd) throws SFException`	Adds a AllocationDetail to the Collection of AllocationDetails

Figure 29-7
(Cont'd)

addAllAllocationDetails	`public abstract void addAllAllocationDetails(DSet newAllocationDetails) throws SFException`	Adds all AllocationDetails to the Collection of AllocationDetails
removeAllocationDetailAt	`public abstract void removeAllocationDetailAt(Iterator position) throws SFException`	Removes the AllocationDetail at the Current Iterator Position
removeAllocationDetail	`public abstract void removeAllocationDetail(AllocationDetail allocationdetail) throws SFException`	Removes the specified AllocationDetail
removeAllAllocationDetails	`public abstract void removeAllAllocationDetails() throws SFException`	Removes all AllocationDetail from the Collection of AllocationDetails
getPaymentMethod	`public abstract PaymentMethod getPaymentMethod() throws SFException`	Returns the PaymentMethod, copied from the Handle
getAccessKey	`public abstract DAccessKey getAccessKey() throws SFException`	Gets AccessKey
getUnrealizedGainLossContraAccountDissectionTypeValue	`public abstract DissectionTypeValue getUnrealizedGainLossContraAccountDissectionTypeValue() throws SFException`	Returns the UnrealizedGainLossContraAccountDissectionTypeValue, copied from the Handle
setUnrealizedGainLossContraAccountDissectionTypeValue	`public abstract void setUnrealizedGainLossContraAccountDissectionTypeValue(DissectionTypeValue newUnrealizedGainLossContraAccountDissectionTypeValue) throws SFException`	Set the Handle of the UnrealizedGainLossContraAccountDissectionTypeValue
getUnrealizedGainLossAccountDissectionTypeValue	`public abstract DissectionTypeValue getUnrealizedGainLossAccountDissectionTypeValue() throws SFException`	Returns the UnrealizedGainLossAccountDissectionTypeValue, copied from the Handle
setUnrealizedGainLossAccountDissectionTypeValue	`public abstract void setUnrealizedGainLossAccountDissectionTypeValue(DissectionTypeValue newUnrealizedGainLossAccountDissectionTypeValue) throws SFException`	Set the Handle of the UnrealizedGainLossAccountDissectionTypeValue
getCurrentControlAccountDissectionTypeValue	`public abstract DissectionTypeValue getCurrentControlAccountDissectionTypeValue() throws SFException`	Returns the CurrentControlAccountDissectionTypeValue, copied from the Handle.
setCurrentControlAccountDissectionTypeValue	`public abstract void setCurrentControlAccountDissectionTypeValue(DissectionTypeValue newCurrentControlAccountDissectionTypeValue) throws SFException`	Set the Handle of the CurrentControlAccountDissectionTypeValue

Figure 29-7
(Cont'd)

setExcludedFromInterestCalculation	`public abstract void setExcludedFromInterestCalculation(boolean newExcludedFromInterestCalculation) throws SFException`	Sets ExcludedFromInterestCalculation
setExcludedFromChaseLetter	`public abstract void setExcludedFromChaseLetter (boolean newExcludedFromChaseLetter ) throws SFException`	Sets ExcludedFromChaseLetter
setPaymentHeld	`public abstract void setPaymentHeld(boolean newPaymentHeld) throws SFException`	Sets PaymentHeld
getId	`public abstract int getId() throws SFException`	Gets id
getCurrentControlAccountHdl	`public abstract Handle getCurrentControlAccountHdl() throws SFException`	Returns the Handle to the GenericPostingCombination of the currentControlAccount of the Installment
getDebtManagementItemHdl	`public abstract Handle getDebtManagementItemHdl() throws SFException`	Returns the Handle to the DebtManagementItem of the DebtManagementItem of the Installment
getUnrealizedGainLossAccountHdl	`public abstract Handle getUnrealizedGainLossAccountHdl() throws SFException`	Returns the Handle to the GenericPostingCombination of the unrealizedGainLossAccount of the Installment
getUnrealizedGainLossContraAccountHdl	`public abstract Handle getUnrealizedGainLossContraAccountHdl() throws SFException`	Returns the Handle to the GenericPostingCombination of the unrealizedGainLossContraAccount of the Installment
getPaymentMethodHdl	`public abstract Handle getPaymentMethodHdl() throws SFException`	Returns the Handle to the PaymentMethod of the paymentMethod of the Installment
getAccessKeyForRestrictedUse	`public abstract DAccessKey getAccessKeyForRestrictedUse() throws SFException`	Returns the actual AccessKey, used by framework for SetEqual()
getUnrealizedGainLossContraAccountDissectionTypeValueHdl	`public abstract Handle getUnrealizedGainLossContraAccountDissectionTypeValueHdl() throws SFException`	Returns the Handle to the DissectionTypeValue of the unrealizedGainLossContraAccountDissectionTypeValue of the Installment
getUnrealizedGainLossAccountDissectionTypeValueHdl	`public abstract Handle getUnrealizedGainLossAccountDissectionTypeValueHdl() throws SFException`	Returns the Handle to the DissectionTypeValue of the unrealizedGainLossAccountDissectionTypeValue of the Installment
getCurrentControlAccountDissectionTypeValueHdl	`public abstract Handle getCurrentControlAccountDissectionTypeValueHdl() throws SFException`	Returns the Handle to the DissectionTypeValue of the currentControlAccountDissectionTypeValue of the Installment

Figure 29-7
(Cont'd)

Interface com.ibm.sf.le.AllocationEvent

public interface interface **AllocationEvent**
extends DescribableDynamicEntity, Distinguishable

Main Methods

Name	*Signature*	*Description*
deallocateAllocationEvent	`public abstract void deallocateAllocationEvent(GenericGLJournal genericGLJournal, DBoolean changeBalanceUpdateIndicator, FiscalPeriod accountingPeriod) throws SFException`	Deallocates the AllocationEvents with status COMMIT. All Objects, that belong to this AllocationEvent (including this AllocationEvent) are copied and reversed. For those Dissections and LedgerItems, which have been created during commiting the original AllocationEvent, the copied dissections and ledgerItems are posted. The original AllocationEvent status is set to DEALLOCATED, the new one is set to COMMIT.
commitAllocation	`public abstract void commitAllocation(DescriptiveInformation reversingDescription, GenericGLJournal genericGLJournal, LEAccount gainLossAccount, GenericPostingCombination gainLossGenericPostingCombination, DescriptiveInformation ledgerItemDescription, DescriptiveInformation dissectionDescription, FiscalPeriod accountingPeriod) throws SFException`	Performs commit for the allocation and sets the status of the AllocationEvent to COMMITED. The commit action is done in PrimeCurrency or BaseCurrency based on the PrimeCurrencyAllocation flag. A Generic Dissection will be created for every component Installment and for any currency gain or lost, and a Ledger Item for every Adjustment Detail and for any currency gain or lost.
containsGenericDissection	`public abstract boolean containsGenericDissection(GenericDissection genericDissection) throws SFException`	Checks if the GenericDissection exists in the Collection of GenericDissections. Return: true, if the GenericDissection is included in the collection, false, if not.
createGenericDissectionIterator	`public abstract Iterator createGenericDissectionIterator() throws SFException`	Create an Iterator over GenericDissections.

Figure 29-8
Interface `Allocation Event`.

getGenericDissectionAt	public abstract GenericDissection getGenericDissectionAt(Iterator position) throws SFException	Get the GenericDissection at the current iterator position.
getGenericDissections	public abstract DSet getGenericDissections() throws SFException	Retrieves all GenericDissections from the collection.
getNextGenericDissection	public abstract GenericDissection getNextGenericDissection(Iterator position) throws SFException	Gets the GenericDissections at the Next Iterator Position.
containsAllocationDetail	public abstract boolean containsAllocationDetail(AllocationDetail allocationDetail) throws SFException	Checks if the AllocationDetail exists in the Collection of AllocationDetails. Return true, if the AllocationDetail is included in the collection, false, if not.
createAllocationDetailIterator	public abstract Iterator createAllocationDetailIterator() throws SFException	Creates the Iterator for the collection of AllocationDetails.
getAllocationDetailAt	public abstract AllocationDetail getAllocationDetailAt(Iterator position) throws SFException	Get the AllocationDetail at the current iterator position.
getNextAllocationDetail	public abstract AllocationDetail getNextAllocationDetail(Iterator position) throws SFException	Gets the AllocationDetail at the Next Iterator Position.
removeOwnedAllocationDetail	public abstract void removeOwnedAllocationDetail(AllocationDetail allocationDetail) throws SFException	Deletes an AllocationDetail from the AllocationEvent
containsLedgerItem	public abstract boolean containsLedgerItem(LedgerItem ledgerItem) throws SFException	Checks if the LedgerItem exists in the Collection of LedgerItems.
createLedgerItemIterator	public abstract Iterator createLedgerItemIterator() throws SFException	Creates the Iterator for the collection of LedgerItems.
getLedgerItemAt	public abstract LedgerItem getLedgerItemAt(Iterator position) throws SFException	Get the LedgerItem at the current iterator position.
getLedgerItems	public abstract DSet getLedgerItems() throws SFException	Retrieves all LedgerItems from the collection.
getNextLedgerItem	public abstract LedgerItem getNextLedgerItem(Iterator position) throws SFException	Gets the LedgerItem at the Next Iterator Position.
orphanOwnedAllocationDetailAt	public abstract void orphanOwnedAllocationDetailAt(Iterator position) throws SFException	Orphans the AllocationDetail at the Current Iterator Position
getAllocationDate	public abstract DTime getAllocationDate() throws SFException	Gets allocationDate Specifies the date, when the AllocationEvent is created
setAllocationDate	public abstract void setAllocationDate(DTime newAllocationDate) throws SFException	Set allocationDate. Specifies the date, when the AllocationEvent is created

Figure 29-8
(Cont'd)

getAllocationEventStatus	public abstract int getAllocationEventStatus() throws SFException	Gets status of the AllocationEvent.
addAllGenericDissections	public abstract void addAllGenericDissections(DSet newGenericDissections) throws SFException	Adds all GenericDissections to the Collection of GenericDissections
removeGenericDissectionAt	public abstract void removeGenericDissectionAt(Iterator position) throws SFException	Removes the GenericDissection at the Current Iterator Position
removeGenericDissection	public abstract void removeGenericDissection(GenericDissection genericdissection) throws SFException	Removes the specified GenericDissection
getAllocationEventBalance	public abstract DDecimal getAllocationEventBalance() throws SFException	Gets allocationEventBalance. The allocationEventBalance indicates the balance of the positive and negative allocationDetail Values. It is created, when the first AllocationDetail is added.
getCommitDate	public abstract DTime getCommitDate() throws SFException	Gets commitDate. This date specifies the date when the allocationEvent was commited. Each Object created during commit gets this date as document Date.
addAllLedgerItems	public abstract void addAllLedgerItems(DSet newLedgerItems) throws SFException	Adds all LedgerItems to the Collection of LedgerItems
removeLedgerItemAt	public abstract void removeLedgerItemAt(Iterator position) throws SFException	Removes the LedgerItem at the Current Iterator Position
removeLedgerItem	public abstract void removeLedgerItem(LedgerItem ledgeritem) throws SFException	Removes the specified LedgerItem
getAccountingPeriod	public abstract FiscalPeriod getAccountingPeriod() throws SFException	Returns the AccountingPeriod, copied from the Handle
setId	public abstract void setId(String newId) throws SFException	Sets id
getPrimeCurrencyAllocation	public abstract boolean getPrimeCurrencyAllocation() throws SFException	Gets primeCurrencyAllocation and defines if this AllocationEvent will be allocated in prime or base currency. If primeCurrencyAllocation is TRUE, allocation is done in prime currency. If it is FALSE the allocation is done in base currency.
getAccountingPeriodHdl	public abstract Handle getAccountingPeriodHdl() throws SFException	Returns the Handle to the FiscalPeriod of the accountingPeriod of the AllocationEvent
getId	public abstract String getId() throws SFException	Gets id

Figure 29-8
(Cont'd)

Interface com.ibm.sf.le.AllocationDetail

public interface **AllocationDetail** extends DynamicEntity

Name	*Signature*	*Description*
getAllocationEventStatus	`public abstract int getAllocationEventStatus() throws SFException`	Returns the status of allocationEvent, this AllocationDetail belongs to. Result : The status of the AllocationEvent
validate	`. public abstract DResultsCollection validate() throws SFException`	Purpose: vallidates the AllocationDetail with the DAllocationValidationPolicy. Gets the ValidationPolicy from LEAccount, and validates the AllocationDetail. Return: the result collection of the ValidationPolicy
removeAdjustmentDetail	`public abstract void removeAdjustmentDetail(DAdjus tmentDetail adjustmentDetail) throws SFException`	Deletes an AdjustmentDetail from the allocationDetail
getInstallment	`public abstract Installment getInstallment() throws SFException`	Returns the Installment, copied from the Handle
setInstallment	`public abstract void setInstallment(Installment newInstallment) throws SFException`	Set the Handle of the Installment
createAdjustmentDetailItera tor	`public abstract Iterator createAdjustmentDetailIterato r() throws SFException`	Create Iterator for Collection of AdjustmentDetails
getNextAdjustmentDetail	`public abstract DAdjustmentDetail getNextAdjustmentDetail(Itera tor position) throws SFException`	Gets the AdjustmentDetail at the Next Iterator Position
setAdjustmentDetails	`public abstract void setAdjustmentDetails(DSet AdjustmentDetails) throws SFException`	Sets the collection of AdjustmentDetails
containsAdjustmentDetail	`public abstract boolean containsAdjustmentDetail(DAdj ustmentDetail adjustmentdetail) throws SFException`	Checks if the AdjustmentDetail exists in the Collection of AdjustmentDetails
getAdjustmentDetailAt	`public abstract DAdjustmentDetail getAdjustmentDetailAt(Iterato r position) throws SFException`	Gets the AdjustmentDetail at the current iterator position
addAllAdjustmentDetails	`public abstract void addAllAdjustmentDetails(DSet newDAdjustmentDetails) throws SFException`	Adds all AdjustmentDetails to the Collection of AdjustmentDetails

Figure 29-9
Interface `AllocationDetail`

removeAdjustmentDetailAt	public abstract void removeAdjustmentDetailAt(Iterator position) throws SFException	Removes the AdjustmentDetail at the Current Iterator Position
removeAllAdjustmentDetails	public abstract void removeAllAdjustmentDetails() throws SFException	Removes all AdjustmentDetail from the Collection of AdjustmentDetails
getAllocationEvent	public abstract AllocationEvent getAllocationEvent() throws SFException	Returns the AllocationEvent, copied from the Handle
setAllocationEvent	public abstract void setAllocationEvent(AllocationEvent newAllocationEvent) throws SFException	Returns the Handle of the AllocationEvent
getAllocationValue	public abstract DCurrencyValue getAllocationValue() throws SFException	Returns the DCurrencyValue Specifies the Value for this AllocationDetail.
setAllocationValue	public abstract void setAllocationValue(DCurrencyValue newAllocationValue) throws SFException	Set DCurrencyValue Specifies the Value for this AllocationDetail.
getAllocatedValue	public abstract DTransactionValue getAllocatedValue() throws SFException	Returns AllocatedValue
setAllocatedValue	public abstract void setAllocatedValue(DTransactionValue newAllocatedValue) throws SFException	Sets AllocatedValue
getInstallmentHdl	public abstract Handle getInstallmentHdl() throws SFException	Returns the Handle to the Installment of the installment of the AllocationDetail
getAllocationEventHdl	public abstract Handle getAllocationEventHdl() throws SFException	Returns the Handle to the AllocationEvent of the allocationEvent of the AllocationDetail
initialize	public abstract void initialize(AllocationEvent owner, Installment installment, DCurrencyValue allocationValue) throws SFException	This method is invoked by the Factory after Construction of an instance of this class to ensure proper initialization

Figure 29-9
(Cont'd)

Interface com.ibm.sf.le.DAdjustmentDetail

public interface **DAdjustmentDetail** extends Dependent

Name	*Signature*	*Description*
getDissectionTypeValue	`public abstract DissectionTypeValue getDissectionTypeValue() throws SFException`	Returns the DissectionTypeValue, copied from the Handle
getAdjustmentTransactionTypeValue	`public abstract TransactionTypeValue getAdjustmentTransactionTypeValue() throws SFException`	Returns the AdjustmentTransactionTypeValue, copied from the Handle
getExpenseOrIncome	`public abstract GenericPostingCombination getExpenseOrIncome() throws SFException`	Returns the ExpenseOrIncome, copied from the Handle
getDescriptiveInformationForLedgerItem	`public abstract DescriptiveInformation getDescriptiveInformationForLedgerItem() throws SFException`	Returns the DescriptiveInformationForLedgerItem, copied from the Handle
getDescriptiveInformationForGenericDissection	`public abstract DescriptiveInformation getDescriptiveInformationForGenericDissection() throws SFException`	Returns the DescriptiveInformationForGenericDissection, copied from the Handle.
getAllocationEvent	`public abstract AllocationEvent getAllocationEvent() throws SFException`	Returns the AllocationEvent, copied from the Handle
setAllocationEvent	`public abstract void setAllocationEvent(AllocationEvent newAllocationEvent) throws SFException`	Set the Handle of the AllocationEvent.
getAdjustmentValue	`public abstract DCurrencyValue getAdjustmentValue() throws SFException`	Gets AdjustmentValue
setIdForLedgerItem	`public abstract void setIdForLedgerItem(String newIdForLedgerItem) throws SFException`	Sets IdForLedgerItem.
getDissectionTypeValueHdl	`public abstract Handle getDissectionTypeValueHdl() throws SFException`	Returns the Handle to the DissectionTypeValue of the dissectionTypeValue of the DAdjustmentDetail
getAdjustmentTransactionTypeValueHdl	`public abstract Handle getAdjustmentTransactionTypeValueHdl() throws SFException`	Returns the Handle to the TransactionTypeValue of the adjustmentTransactionTypeValue of the DAdjustmentDetail
getExpenseOrIncomeHdl	`public abstract Handle getExpenseOrIncomeHdl() throws SFException`	Returns the Handle to the GenericPostingCombination of the expenseOrIncome of the DAdjustmentDetail

Figure 29-10
Interface `DAdjustment Detail`

getDescriptiveInformationForLedgerItemHdl	`public abstract Handle getDescriptiveInformationForLedgerItemHdl() throws SFException`	Returns the Handle to the DescriptiveInformation of the descriptiveInformationForLedgerItem of the DAdjustmentDetail
getDescriptiveInformationForGenericDissectionHdl	`public abstract Handle getDescriptiveInformationForGenericDissectionHdl() throws SFException`	Returns the Handle to the DescriptiveInformation of the descriptiveInformationForGenericDissection of the DAdjustmentDetail
getAllocationEventHdl	`public abstract Handle getAllocationEventHdl() throws SFException`	Returns the Handle to the AllocationEvent of the AllocationEvent of the DAdjustmentDetail
getAdjustmentValueForRestrictedUse	`public abstract DCurrencyValue getAdjustmentValueForRestrictedUse() throws SFException`	Returns the actual AdjustmentValue, used by framework for SetEqual()
getIdForLedgerItem	`public abstract String getIdForLedgerItem() throws SFException`	Gets IdForLedgerItem
initialize	`public abstract void initialize(DissectionTypeValue dissectionTypeValue, DCurrencyValue adjustmentValue, TransactionTypeValue adjustmentTransactionTypeValue, String ledgerItemId, DescriptiveInformation ledgerItemDescriptiveInformation, DescriptiveInformation genericDissectionDescriptiveInformation, GenericPostingCombination genericPostingCombination, AllocationDetail owningAllocationDetail) throws SFException`	This method is invoked by the Factory after Construction of an instance of this class to ensure proper initialization

Figure 29-10
(Cont'd)

Interface com.ibm.sf.le.LedgerItem

public interface **LedgerItem** extends GenericLELedgerItemAdapter, Distinguishable, LECommonDebtItem

Main Methods

Name	*Signature*	*Description*
suspend	`public abstract void suspend() throws SFException`	This operation suspends this Ledger Item.
restart	`public abstract void restart() throws SFException`	This operation restarts this Ledger Item.
prepareForPosting	`public abstract void prepareForPosting() throws SFException`	This method validates the Ledger Item to determine if it is ready for posting. The default validation policy for its company is used. The specific validation steps are specified on the default validation policy. If the validation is successful, the Ledger Item state will be marked "ready for posting." If any check of the Ledger Item validation fails, the error messages will be bundled into a combined error message.
prepareForPosting	`public abstract void prepareForPosting (DledgerItemValidationPolicy validationPolicy) throws SFException`	This method validates the Ledger Item to determine if it is ready for posting. The specific validation steps are specified on the validation policy provided. If the validation is successful, the Ledger Item state will be marked "ready for posting." If any check of the Ledger Item validation fails, the error messages will be bundled into a combined error message. The prepare for posting of the Ledger Item will not be performed if the status of the Ledger Item is already "ready for posting."
validate	`public abstract DResultsCollection validate() throws SFException`	The default validation policy from the Company keyed by a Ledger Type is retrieved and used to validate. The Ledger Item is validated according to the steps detailed in the concrete Ledger Item validation policy. This typically includes checking the FiscalPeriod, the associated Ledger control accounts and the TransactionValue. If any check of the Ledger Item validation fails, the error messages will be bundled into a combined error message.
validate	`public abstract DResultsCollection validate (DLedgerItemValidationPolicy validationPolicy) throws SFException`	The Ledger Item is validated using the validation policy provided. The Ledger Item is validated according to the steps detailed in the concrete Ledger Item validation policy. This typically includes checking the FiscalPeriod, the associated ledger control accounts and the TransactionValue. If any check of the Ledger Item validation fails, the error messages will be bundled into a combined error message.

Figure 29-11
Interface `LedgerItem`

post	`public abstract void post() throws SFException`	This method posts this Ledger Item.
unpost	`public abstract void unpost() throws SFException`	This method is based on the unpost function of the General Ledger Journals. It is not possible to unpost a Ledger Item if the General Ledger installed does not support this. The status of the Ledger Item is set to an amendable state
isLedgerItemLocked	`public abstract boolean isLedgerItemLocked() throws SFException`	In some countries, the final closing of postings is based on the processing of a periodical post-registration Journal-book. Until this Journal-book is processed, posted Items may be unposted and changed. This kind of Locking is not included in the framework. This method supports an easy implementation of a locking function. If the locking function is not installed/used, posted Items cannot be unposted. Consequently, the method will return true for an Item with the status posted.
changeLEAccount	`public abstract void changeLEAccount(LEAccount ledgerAccount, GenericPostingCombination ledgerControlAccountPostingCombination, DescriptiveInformation ledgerControlAccountDescription) throws SFException`	This method sets the Ledger Account on the associated Debt Management Item. The Posting Combination on the associated Control Account Dissections may also be changed. If the associated Debt Management Item is reflected in the Ledger Account Balances, the value for each Installment is transferred from the previous to the new Ledger Account. If a Generic GL Disscetion for Ledger control account was not provided, the default Generic Posting Combination for LE_LEDGER_ITEM on the Ledger Account is used instead.
changeTransactionValue	`public abstract void changeTransactionValue( DtransactionValue aTransactionValue, DPaymentTerms paymentTermsSnapShot, NaturalCalendar naturalCalendar, DResultDateAdjustmentPolicy policy) throws SFException`	This method sets the TransactionValue on the associated Debt Management Item and the current ControlAccountDissection for the LogJournal and on the ControlAccountDissection for the LedgerJournal, if existing. In addition: 1. If this DebtManagementItem is for a Payment, then the new Value is set on the single Installment. 2. Otherwise if a PaymentTermsSnapShot is provided, any existing Installments are deleted and new Installments are created using the passed-in PaymentTermsSnapShot. 3. If a new PaymentTermsSnapShot is not provided, the TransactionValues for the existing Installments are updated. The LE Account balances may be updated.
setAccountingPeriod	`public abstract void setAccountingPeriod(FiscalPeriod newAccountingPeriod) throws SFException`	This method sets the Accounting Period on the associated Debt Management Item. The LE Account balances may be updated.

Figure 29-11
(Cont'd)

changeCurrentControlAccountOnInstallment	public abstract void changeCurrentControlAccountOnInstallment(Installment installment, GenericGLJournal journalToPostTo, DissectionTypeValue dissectionTypeValue, FinancialTransactionSource financialTransactionSource, boolean debitCreditBalanceReverseIndicator, GenericPostingCombination account, DescriptiveInformation dissectionDescription) throws SFException	The change of the Generic Posting Combination for the current Ledger Control Account is typically done when the debt is transferred from the normal Ledger Control Account to the Control Account for doubtful debts. (Company policy/legislation often requires this when payment is over-due for a certain amount of time.) Changing the Control Account triggers the creation of two generic GL Dissections.
resetControlAccountOnInstallment	public abstract void resetControlAccountOnInstallment(Installment installment, GenericGLJournal journalToPostTo, FinancialTransactionSource financialTransactionSource, boolean debitCreditBalanceReverseIndicator, DescriptiveInformation dissectionDescription) throws SFException	The Generic Posting Combination for the current Ledger control account is removed from the Installment. This is typically done when the debt is retransferred from the control account for doubtful debts to the normal Ledger control account. Changing the Control Account triggers the creation of two generic GL Dissections.
changePostingCombinationOnControlAccountDissection	Public abstract void changePostingCombinationOnControlAccountDissection(GenericPostingCombination ledgerControlAccountPostingCombination, DescriptiveInformation ledgerControlAccountDissectionDescription) throws SFException	This method changes the Generic PostingCombination on the current Log/Ledger control account Dissection based on the input provided.
getLedgerJournal	Public abstract GenericGLJournal getLedgerJournal() throws SFException	Returns the last GenericGLJournal in the collection of LedgerJournals.
getCommittedAllocationValue	Public abstract DTransactionValue getCommittedAllocationValue() throws SFException	Gets the committed allocated TransactionValue for each Installment and adds them up to give the total committed allocated TransactionValue for this DebtManagementItem.
getPendingAllocationValue	public abstract DTransactionValue getPendingAllocationValue() throws SFException	Gets the pending allocated TransactionValue for each Installment and adds them up to give the total pending allocated TransactionValue for this DebtManagementItem.
getAllocatableValue	public abstract DTransactionValue getAllocatableValue() throws SFException	Gets the allocatable TransactionValue for each Installment and adds them up to give the total allocatable TransactionValue for this DebtManagementItem. Whereby the Allocatable Value = Total Installment Value – Committed Value – Pending Value.
getUnallocatedValue	public abstract DTransactionValue getUnallocatedValue() throws SFException	Gets the unallocated TransactionValue for each Installment and adds them up to give the total unallocated TransactionValue for this DebtManagementItem. Whereby the Unallocated Value = Total Installment Value – Committed Value.

Figure 29-11
(Cont'd)

getLEAccount	`public abstract LEAccount getLEAccount() throws SFException`	Returns the associated LEAccount.
getTransactionValue	`public abstract DTransactionValue getTransactionValue() throws SFException`	Returns the associated TransactionValue
getBaseDate	`public abstract DTime getBaseDate() throws SFException`	Returns the associated Base Date for the PaymentTermsSnapShot.
changeBaseDate	`public abstract void changeBaseDate(DTime newBaseDate, NaturalCalendar naturalCalendar, DResultDateAdjustmentPolicy policy) throws SFException`	Sets a new Base Date for the PaymentTerms and for each Installment a new Due Date is calculated and set.
isPayment	`public abstract boolean isPayment() throws SFException`	Returns the associated Payment Indicator. TRUE—this DebtManagementItem is for a Payment, otherwise FALSE.
changePaymentIndicator	`public abstract void changePaymentIndicator(boolean payment, BusinessPartnerBalanceValue businessPartnerBalanceValue, PaymentMethod paymentMethod, DTime dueDate, NaturalCalendar naturalCalendar, DResultDateAdjustmentPolicy policy) throws SFException`	Sets the Payment Indicator provided. True indicates that this is a Payment, false indicates that this is not a Payment. If it is changed from false to true, existing Installments will be deleted, one new Installment is created and the BusinessPartnerBalanceValue is set (either provided or retrieved default value). An existing PaymentTermsSnapShot will be removed. If it is changed from true to false, then, if provided, the PaymentMethod, the BusinessPartnerBalanceValue and the Due Date are set.
isPaymentHeld	`public abstract boolean isPaymentHeld() throws SFException`	Returns the associated PaymentHeld Indicator.
setPaymentHeld	`public abstract void setPaymentHeld(boolean paymentHeld) throws SFException`	Sets the PaymentHeld Indicator provided. True indicates that this Payment is held, false indicates that this Payment is not held.
getDocumentDate	`public abstract DTime getDocumentDate() throws SFException`	Returns the document date.
changeDocumentDate	`public abstract void changeDocumentDate(DTime newDocumentDate, DTime newBaseDateForPaymentTerms, NaturalCalendar naturalCalendar, DResultDateAdjustmentPolicy policy) throws SFException`	Sets the new Document Date and, if a Base Date for PaymentTerms is provided, this Base Date will be set and new Due Dates will be calculated for each Installment
getExternalReference	`public abstract String getExternalReference() throws SFException`	Returns the ExternalReference associated with the DebtManagementItem or null.
isExcludedFromChaseLetter	`public abstract boolean isExcludedFromChaseLetter() throws SFException`	Returns the associated ExcludedFromChaseLetter Indicator. Returns TRUE if DebtManagementItem is excluded from Chase Letters, otherwise FALSE.

Figure 29-11
(Cont'd)

setExcludedFromChaseLetter	`public abstract void setExcludedFromChaseLetter(boolean excludedFromChaseLetter) throws SFException`	Sets the ExcludedFromChaseLetter Indicator provided. TRUE indicates the DebtManagementItem is excluded from Chase Letters, FALSE, it is not excluded.
isExcludedFromInterestCalculation	`public abstract boolean isExcludedFromInterestCalculation() throws SFException`	Returns the associated ExcludedFromInterestCalculation Indicator. Returns TRUE if DebtManagementItem is excluded from Interest Calculations, otherwise FALSE.
setExcludedFromInterestCalculation	`public abstract void setExcludedFromInterestCalculation(boolean excludedFromInterestCalculation) throws SFException`	Sets the ExcludedFromInterestCalculation Indicator provided. TRUE indicates, the DebtManagementItem is excluded from Interest Calculations, FALSE it is not excluded.
getPaymentTermsSnapShot	`public abstract DPaymentTerms getPaymentTermsSnapShot() throws SFException`	Returns the associated PaymentTermsSnapShot or null.
changePaymentTermsSnapShot	`public abstract void changePaymentTermsSnapShot(DpaymentTerms newPaymentTermsSnapShot, NaturalCalendar naturalCalendar, DResultDateAdjustmentPolicy policy) throws SFException`	Sets the new PaymentTermsSnapShot. Any existing Installments (see Note) will be deleted and new Installments are created. An existing BusinessPartnerBalanceValue, if applicable, will be removed. If applicable, the Balances for the LEAccount will be updated.
getCurrentLogControlAccountDissection	`public abstract GenericDissection getCurrentLogControlAccountDissection() throws SFException`	Returns the associated current ControlAccountDissection for the LogJournal, or null.
getLedgerControlAccountDissection	`public abstract GenericDissection getLedgerControlAccountDissection() throws SFException`	Returns the associated ControlAccountDissection for the LedgerJournal, or null.
getDocumentLocation	`public abstract DocumentLocation getDocumentLocation() throws SFException`	Returns the associated DocumentLocation or null.
setDocumentLocation	`public abstract void setDocumentLocation(DocumentLocation newDocumentLocation) throws SFException`	Sets the new DocumentLocation.
getBusinessPartnerBalanceValue	`public abstract BusinessPartnerBalanceValue getBusinessPartnerBalanceValue() throws SFException`	Returns the BusinessPartnerBalanceValue, either retrieved from the DebtManagementItem or from the PaymentTermSnapShot, associated with the DebtManagementItem.
setBusinessPartnerBalanceValue	`public abstract void setBusinessPartnerBalanceValue(BusinessPartnerBalanceValue newBusinessPartnerBalanceValue) throws SFException`	Sets the new BusinessPartnerBalanceValue for the DebtManagementItem.
getControlAccountMovementCollection	`public abstract DControlAccountMovementCollection getControlAccountMovementCollection() throws SFException`	Returns the associated ControlAccountMovementCollection or null.

Figure 29-11
(Cont'd)

isIncludedInLEAccountBalances	`public abstract boolean isIncludedInLEAccountBalances() throws SFException`	Returns the associated 'IncludeInLEAccountBalances' Indicator. Returns TRUE if DebtManagementItem is included in Balances for this LEAccount, otherwise FALSE.
generateAndAddInstallment	`public abstract void generateAndAddInstallment(DpaymentTermsDetail paymentTermsDetail, Installment installmentForBalancing, DBoolean debitCreditBalanceReverseIndicator, GenericGLJournal journal, DescriptiveInformation descriptionForDissections, NaturalCalendar naturalCalendar, DResultDateAdjustmentPolicy policy) throws SFException`	Creates a new Installment, and changes the value of the balancing Installment, possibly creating Generic Dissections.
removeAndDeleteInstallment	`public abstract void removeAndDeleteInstallment(Installment installmentToBeDeleted, Installment installmentForBalancing, Dboolean debitCreditBalanceReverseIndicator, GenericGLJournal journal, DescriptiveInformation descriptionForDissections) throws SFException`	Creates a new Installment, and changes the value of the balancing Installment, possibly creating Generic Dissections.
changeValueOnInstallments	`public abstract void changeValueOnInstallments(Installment initialInstallment, DCurrencyValue primeCurrency, Installment installmentForBalancing, DBoolean debitCreditBalanceReverseIndicator, GenericGLJournal journal, DescriptiveInformation descriptionForDissections) throws SFException`	When changing the value on one Installment, the value on a balancing Installment must be changed accordingly, in order to ensure that the total value of the Installments equals the value of the DebtManagementItem. This may result in the creation of Generic Dissections. If the Installments had been revalued, the revalued value will be changed on the Installments and Generic Dissections will be created for the original unrealized Currency Gain/Loss and the Contra account. If the two Installments are associated with different Control Account PostingCombinations, two new Generic Dissections will be created.
createInstallmentIterator	`public abstract Iterator createInstallmentIterator() throws SFException`	Create Iterator for Collection of Installments
getNextInstallment	`public abstract Installment getNextInstallment(Iterator position) throws SFException`	Gets the Installment at the Next Iterator Position
containsInstallment	`public abstract boolean containsInstallment(Installment installment) throws SFException`	Checks if the Installment exists in the Collection of Installments
getInstallmentAt	`public abstract Installment getInstallmentAt(Iterator position) throws SFException`	Gets the Installment at the Current Iterator Position

Figure 29-11
(Cont'd)

getId	public abstract String getId() throws SFException	get the id of the Distinguishable object
getState	public abstract int getState() throws SFException	It returns int value of the LedgerItemStateEnum corresponding to the current state of the Ledger Item.
getAccountingPeriod	public abstract FiscalPeriod getAccountingPeriod() throws SFException	It returns the accounting period (FiscalPeriod) of this the Ledger Item.
getTransactionTypeValue	public abstract TransactionTypeValue getTransactionTypeValue() throws SFException	It returns the Transaction Type Value of this the Ledger Item.
createLedgerJournalIterator	public abstract Iterator createLedgerJournalIterator() throws SFException	Create Iterator for Collection of LedgerJournals
getNextLedgerJournal	public abstract GenericGLJournal getNextLedgerJournal(Iterator position) throws SFException	Gets the LedgerJournal at the Next Iterator Position
containsLedgerJournal	public abstract boolean containsLedgerJournal(GenericGLJournal ledgerjournal) throws SFException	Checks if the LedgerJournal exists in the Collection of LedgerJournals
getLedgerJournalAt	public abstract GenericGLJournal getLedgerJournalAt(Iterator position) throws SFException	Gets the LedgerJournal at the current iterator position
setTransactionTypeValue	public abstract void setTransactionTypeValue(TransactionTypeValue newTransactionTypeValue) throws SFException	Set the Handle of the TransactionTypeValue
getOriginalLogItem	public abstract LogItem getOriginalLogItem() throws SFException	Returns the OriginalLogItem, copied from the Handle
getDebtManagementItemHdl	public abstract Handle getDebtManagementItemHdl() throws SFException	Returns the Handle to the DebtManagementItem of the DebtManagementItem of the LedgerItem
getLedgerJournalsForRestrictedUse	public abstract DSet getLedgerJournalsForRestrictedUse() throws SFException	Returns the actual LedgerJournal, used by framework for SetEqual()
getTransactionTypeValueHdl	public abstract Handle getTransactionTypeValueHdl() throws SFException	Returns the Handle to the TransactionTypeValue of the TransactionTypeValue of the LedgerItem
getOriginalLogItemHdl	public abstract Handle getOriginalLogItemHdl() throws SFException	Returns the Handle to the LogItem of the originalLogItem of the LedgerItem
getAccountingPeriodHdl	public abstract Handle getAccountingPeriodHdl() throws SFException	Returns the Handle to the FiscalPeriod of the accountingPeriod of the LedgerItem
getBusinessPartnerBalanceSequenceValueHdl	public abstract Handle getBusinessPartnerBalanceSequenceValueHdl() throws SFException	Returns the Handle to the BusinessPartnerBalanceSequenceValue of the LedgerItem

Figure 29-11
(Cont'd)

Interface com.ibm.sf.le.LogItem

public interface **LogItem** extends GenericLELogItemAdapter, LECommonDebtItem, Distinguishable

Main Methods

Name	*Signature*	*Description*
suspend	`public abstract void suspend() throws SFException`	This method suspends this Log Item.
restart	`public abstract void restart() throws SFException`	This method restarts this Log Item. Assumption: The application should ensure that the associated Log and Ledger Journals are also restarted.
prepareForLog	`public abstract void prepareForLog() throws SFException`	This method validates the Log Item to determine if it is ready for logging. The default validation policy from Ledger Type is used. The specific validation steps are specified on the default validation policy. If the validation is successful, the Log Item state will be marked 'ready for log.' If any check of the Log Item validation fails, the error messages will be bundled into a combined error message. The prepare for log of the Log Item will not be performed if the status of the Log Item is already 'ready for log.'
prepareForLog	`public abstract void prepareForLog(DLogItemValidationPolicy validationPolicy) throws SFException`	This method validates the Log Item to determine if it is ready for logging. The specific validation steps are specified on the validation policy provided. If the validation is successful, the Log Item state will be marked 'ready for log.' If any check of the Log Item validation fails, the error messages will be bundled into a combined error message. The prepare for log of the Log Item will not be performed if the status of the Log Item is already 'ready for log.'
validate	`public abstract DResultsCollection validate() throws SFException`	The default validation policy from the Company keyed by a Ledger Type is retrieved and used to validate. The Log Item is validated according to the steps detailed in the concrete Log Item validation policy. This typically includes checking the FiscalPeriod, the associated log control and Ledger control accounts and the TransactionValue. If any check of the Log Item validation fails, the error messages will be bundled into a combined error message.

Figure 29-12
Interface `LogItem`.

validate	`public abstract DResultsCollection validate(DLogItemValidationPolicy validationPolicy) throws SFException`	The Log Item is validated using the validation policy provided.
log	`public abstract void log() throws SFException`	The method logs this Log Item. The log of the Log Item will not be performed if the status of the Log Item is already 'logged.'
attachCurrentLogJournal	`public abstract void attachCurrentLogJournal(DBoolean debitCreditReverseIndicator, GenericGLJournal logJournal, GenericDissection logControlAccountDissection, GenericPostingCombination logControlAccountPostingCombination, DescriptiveInformation description) throws SFException`	This method sets a Generic GL Journal as the current Log Journal on the Log Item. A Log control account Dissection is associated with the Debt Management Item. If the Log Item already has a current Log Journal, this one cannot be replaced by new one. It has to be detached first and the new one has to be attached again.
detachCurrentLogJournal	`public abstract GenericGLJournal detachCurrentLogJournal() throws SFException`	This method removes the current Generic GL Log Journal of the Log Item. The associated Log control account Dissection will be removed from the Debt Management Item and from its collection of Dissections.
attachLedgerJournal	`public abstract void attachLedgerJournal(DBoolean debitCreditReverseIndicator, GenericGLJournal aLedgerJournal, GenericDissection ledgerControlAccountDissection, GenericPostingCombination ledgerControlAccountPostingCombination, DescriptiveInformation description) throws SFException`	This method sets a Generic GL Journal as the Ledger Journal on the Log Item. A Ledger control account Dissection is associated with the Debt Management Item. If the Log Item already has a Ledger Journal associated, an additional one may not be attached. If the Log Item already has a Ledger Journal, this one cannot be replaced by new one. It has to be detached first and the new one has to be attached again
changeTransactionValue	`public abstract void changeTransactionValue(DTransactionValue aTransactionValue, DPaymentTerms paymentTermsSnapShot, NaturalCalendar naturalCalendar, DResultDateAdjustmentPolicy policy) throws SFException`	This method sets the TransactionValue on the associated Debt Management Item and the current ControlAccountDissection for the LogJournal and on the ControlAccountDissection for the LedgerJournal, if existing. In addition: 1. If this DebtManagementItem is for a Payment, then the new Value is set on the single Installment. 2. Otherwise if a PaymentTermsSnapShot is provided, any existing Installments are deleted and new Installments are created using the passed-in PaymentTermsSnapShot. 3. If a new PaymentTermsSnapShot is not provided, the TransactionValues for the existing Installments are updated. The LE Account balances may be updated.
setAccountingPeriod	`public abstract void setAccountingPeriod(FiscalPeriod anAccountingPeriod) throws SFException`	This method sets the AccountingPeriod on the associated Debt Management Item. The LE Account balances may be updated.

Figure 29-12
(Cont'd)

setTransactionTypeValue	`public abstract void setTransactionTypeValue(TransactionTypeValue transactionTypeValue) throws SFException`	Sets the new TransactionTypeValue.
setDescriptiveInformation	`public abstract void setDescriptiveInformation(DescriptiveInformation descriptiveInformation) throws SFException`	Sets the new DescriptiveInformation.
getCommittedAllocationValue	`public abstract DTransactionValue getCommittedAllocationValue() throws SFException`	Gets the committed allocated TransactionValue for each Installment and adds them up to give the total committed allocated TransactionValue for this DebtManagementItem.
getPendingAllocationValue	`public abstract DTransactionValue getPendingAllocationValue() throws SFException`	Gets the pending allocated TransactionValue for each Installment and adds them up to give the total pending allocated TransactionValue for this DebtManagementItem.
getAllocatableValue	`public abstract DTransactionValue getAllocatableValue() throws SFException`	Gets the allocatable TransactionValue for each Installment and adds them up to give the total allocatable TransactionValue for this DebtManagementItem. Whereby the Allocatable Value = Total Installment Value – Committed Value – Pending Value.
getUnallocatedValue	`public abstract DTransactionValue getUnallocatedValue() throws SFException`	Gets the unallocated TransactionValue for each Installment and adds them up to give the total unallocated TransactionValue for this DebtManagementItem. Whereby the Unallocated Value = Total Installment Value – Committed Value.
getLEAccount	`public abstract LEAccount getLEAccount() throws SFException`	Returns the associated LEAccount.
getTransactionValue	`public abstract DTransactionValue getTransactionValue() throws SFException`	Returns the associated TransactionValue
getBaseDate	`public abstract DTime getBaseDate() throws SFException`	Returns the associated Base Date for the PaymentTermsSnapShot.
changeBaseDate	`public abstract void changeBaseDate(DTime newBaseDate, NaturalCalendar naturalCalendar, DResultDateAdjustmentPolicy policy) throws SFExceptionSets a new Base.`	Date for the PaymentTerms and for each Installment a new Due Date is calculated and set
isPayment	`public abstract boolean isPayment() throws SFException`	Returns the associated Payment Indicator. Returns TRUE if this DebtManagementItem is for a Payment, otherwise FALSE.
changePaymentIndicator	`public abstract void changePaymentIndicator(boolean payment, BusinessPartnerBalanceValue businessPartnerBalanceValue, PaymentMethod paymentMethod, DTime dueDate, NaturalCalendar naturalCalendar, DResultDateAdjustmentPolicy policy) throws SFException`	Sets the Payment Indicator provided. True indicates that this is a Payment, false indicates that this is not a Payment. If it is changed from false to true, existing Installments (see Note) will be deleted, one new Installment is created and the BusinessPartnerBalanceValue is set (either provided or retrieved default value). An existing PaymentTermsSnapShot will be removed. If it is changed from true to false, then, if provided, the PaymentMethod, the BusinessPartnerBalanceValue and the Due Date are set.

Figure 29-12
(Cont'd)

isPaymentHeld	`public abstract boolean isPaymentHeld() throws SFException`	Returns the associated PaymentHeld Indicator. Returns TRUE if Payment is held, otherwise FALSE.
setPaymentHeld	`public abstract void setPaymentHeld(boolean paymentHeld) throws SFException`	Sets the PaymentHeld Indicator provided. True indicates that this Payment is held, false indicates that this Payment is not held.
getDocumentDate	`public abstract DTime getDocumentDate() throws SFException`	Returns the associated Document Date.
changeDocumentDate	`public abstract void changeDocumentDate(DTime newDocumentDate, DTime newBaseDateForPaymentTerms, NaturalCalendar naturalCalendar, DResultDateAdjustmentPolicy policy) throws SFException`	Sets the new Document Date and, if a Base Date for PaymentTerms is provided, this Base Date will be set and new Due Dates will be calculated for each Installment.
getExternalReference	`public abstract String getExternalReference() throws SFException`	Returns the ExternalReference associated with the DebtManagementItem or null.
setExternalReference	`public abstract void setExternalReference(String externalReference) throws SFException`	Sets the new ExternalReference.
isExcludedFromChaseLetter	`public abstract boolean isExcludedFromChaseLetter() throws SFException`	Returns the associated ExcludedFromChaseLetter Indicator. Returns TRUE if DebtManagementItem is excluded from Chase Letters, otherwise FALSE.
setExcludedFromChaseLetter	`public abstract void setExcludedFromChaseLetter(boolean excludedFromChaseLetter) throws SFException`	Sets the ExcludedFromChaseLetter Indicator provided. TRUE indicates, the DebtManagementItem is excluded from Chase Letters, FALSE, it is not excluded
isExcludedFromInterestCalculation	`public abstract boolean isExcludedFromInterestCalculation() throws SFException`	Returns the associated ExcludedFromInterestCalculation Indicator. Returns TRUE if DebtManagementItem is excluded from Interest Calculations, otherwise FALSE.
setExcludedFromInterestCalculation	`public abstract void setExcludedFromInterestCalculation(boolean excludedFromInterestCalculation) throws SFException`	Sets the ExcludedFromInterestCalculation Indicator provided. TRUE indicates, the DebtManagementItem is excluded from Interest Calculations, FALSE it is not excluded.
getPaymentTermsSnapShot	`public abstract DPaymentTerms getPaymentTermsSnapShot() throws SFException`	Returns the associated PaymentTermsSnapShot or null.
changePaymentTermsSnapShot	`public abstract void changePaymentTermsSnapShot(DPaymentTerms newPaymentTermsSnapShot, NaturalCalendar naturalCalendar, DResultDateAdjustmentPolicy policy) throws SFException`	Sets the new PaymentTermsSnapShot. Any existing Installments (see Note) will be deleted and new Installments are created. An existing BusinessPartnerBalanceValue, if applicable, will be removed. If applicable, the Balances for the LEAccount will be updated.
getCurrentLogControlAccountDissection	`public abstract GenericDissection getCurrentLogControlAccountDissection() throws SFException`	Returns the associated current ControlAccountDissection for the LogJournal, or null.
getLedgerControlAccountDissection	`public abstract GenericDissection getLedgerControlAccountDissection() throws SFException`	Returns the associated ControlAccountDissection for the LedgerJournal, or null.

Figure 29-12
(Cont'd)

getDocumentLocation	`public abstract DocumentLocation getDocumentLocation() throws SFException`	Returns the associated DocumentLocation or null.
setDocumentLocation	`public abstract void setDocumentLocation(DocumentLocation newDocumentLocation) throws SFException`	Sets the new DocumentLocation.
getBusinessPartnerBalanceValue	`public abstract BusinessPartnerBalanceValue getBusinessPartnerBalanceValue() throws SFException`	Returns the BusinessPartnerBalanceValue, either retrieved from the DebtManagementItem or from the PaymentTermSnapShot, associated with the DebtManagementItem.
setBusinessPartnerBalanceValue	`public abstract void setBusinessPartnerBalanceValue(BusinessPartnerBalanceValue newBusinessPartnerBalanceValue) throws SFException`	Sets the new BusinessPartnerBalanceValue for the DebtManagementItem.
getControlAccountMovementCollection	`public abstract DControlAccountMovementCollection getControlAccountMovementCollection() throws SFException`	Returns the associated ControlAccountMovementCollection or null.
isIncludedInLEAccountBalances	`public abstract boolean isIncludedInLEAccountBalances() throws SFException`	Returns the associated 'IncludeInLEAccountBalances' Indicator. TRUE—DebtManagementItem is included in Balances for this LEAccount, otherwise FALSE.
createInstallmentIterator	`public abstract Iterator createInstallmentIterator() throws SFException`	Create Iterator for Collection of Installments
getNextInstallment	`public abstract Installment getNextInstallment(Iterator position) throws SFException`	Gets the Installment at the Next Iterator Position
containsInstallment	`public abstract boolean containsInstallment(Installment installment) throws SFException`	Checks if the Installment exists in the Collection of Installments
getInstallmentAt	`public abstract Installment getInstallmentAt(Iterator position) throws SFException`	Gets the Installment at the Current Iterator Position
getId	`public abstract String getId() throws SFException`	Get the id of the Distinguishable object
getState	`public abstract int getState() throws SFException`	It returns int value of the LogItemStateEnum corresponding to the current state of the Log Item.
getAccountingPeriod	`public abstract FiscalPeriod getAccountingPeriod() throws SFException`	It returns the accounting period (FiscalPeriod) of this the Log Item.
getTransactionTypeValue	`public abstract TransactionTypeValue getTransactionTypeValue() throws SFException`	It returns the Transaction Type Value of this the Log Item.
createLogJournalIterator	`public abstract Iterator createLogJournalIterator() throws SFException`	Create Iterator for Collection of LogJournals
getNextLogJournal	`public abstract GenericGLJournal getNextLogJournal(Iterator position) throws SFException`	Gets the LogJournal at the Next Iterator Position

Figure 29-12
(Cont'd)

containsLogJournal	`public abstract boolean containsLogJournal(GenericGLJournal logjournal) throws SFException`	Checks if the LogJournal exists in the Collection of LogJournals
getLogJournalAt	`public abstract GenericGLJournal getLogJournalAt(Iterator position) throws SFException`	Gets the LogJournal at the current iterator position
getCurrentLogJournal	`public abstract GenericGLJournal getCurrentLogJournal() throws SFException`	Returns the CurrentLogJournal, copied from the Handle
getOriginalLogItemHdl	`public abstract Handle getOriginalLogItemHdl() throws SFException`	Returns the Handle to the LogItem of the originalLogItem of the LogItem
getReversingLogItemCopyHdl	`public abstract Handle getReversingLogItemCopyHdl() throws SFException`	Returns the Handle to the LogItem of the reversingLogItemCopy of the LogItem
getBusinessPartnerBalanceSequenceValueHdl	`public abstract Handle getBusinessPartnerBalanceSequenceValueHdl() throws SFException`	Returns the Handle to the BusinessPartnerBalanceSequenceValue of the LogItem

Figure 29-12
(Cont)

PART 6

RDB Persistence

CHAPTER 30

The Schema Mapping Language and the Schema Mapping Tool

This chapter describes the tools provided by SanFrancisco for dealing with RDB persistency. RDB persistency is the main mechanism for providing persistency in SanFrancisco, as the drawbacks of the POSIX persistency prevent it from becoming a serious alternative for real-world applications.

Schema Mapping

Relational Databases are the most common tool for storing large amounts of business-related data. Using a relational database in the context of an object-oriented programming language raises some fundamental problems, sometimes referred to as impedance mismatch problems. Essentially, the source of this problem is that relational databases are designed to store information as tables composed of rows, whereas objects are more complex entities. It is not always possible to easily map an object to a row in a table.

In order to use a relational database as the persistent store for SanFrancisco business objects, mapping between the object model and the relational model is required. This mapping is referred to as the "Schema Mapping," as it maps an object schema to a relational schema. Namely, it maps SanFrancisco classes, objects, and attributes to the tables, rows and columns of the relational model, as illustrated in Figure 30-1.

The Java environment provides means for accessing relational databases through the use of JDBC. Using the SanFrancisco Schema Mapping Tools makes the process of maintaining objects in relational database completely transparent to the programmer, hence reducing the amount of application codes to be programmed.

Schema Mapping Tool

The Schema Mapping tools allows you to establish mappings between objects and relational databases. SanFrancisco provides two different schema mappers:

- Default Schema Mapper (DSM)
- Extended Schema Mapper (ESM)

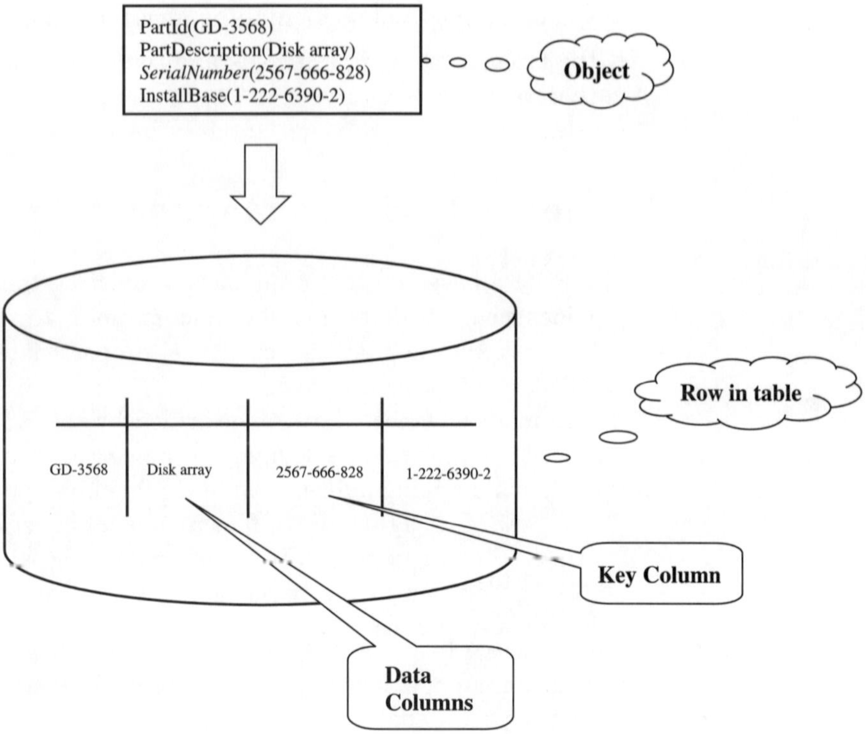

Figure 30-1
Schema mapping.

Default Schema Mapper (DSM)

The DSM provides automatic mapping from a single class to a single database table. This is done by mapping the class members to columns. The DSM automatically creates an `ObjectID` column, which is the primary key column for the new table. It also creates a `PartitionID` column, which is used to identify which entities belong to a specific `EntityOwningExtent`.

The DSM provides a simple way to persist data to relational tables, and hence is easy to use for prototyping. It automatically maps a class to a new table that it defines at runtime, without direct input from the user. Using a general set of rules, the DSM creates the table layout by parsing the class definition at runtime. Using the DSM offers the following advantages.

- no fuss—new tables are created automatically;

- you don't need to know anything about schema mapping; and
- the schema mapping internals and configuration are managed by themselves.

Extended Schema Mapper (ESM)

The ESM allows you to map a class to existing tables or new tables. It provides means to determine the exact mapping to a particular table. The only constraint is that the database support data conversion on the particular data type involved.

The more advanced features provided by the ESM are necessary for real-world application deployment. Using ESM, you can define and save the schema mapping information in a Schema Mapping Language (SML) file. The ESM uses these SML files instead of generating the mapping at runtime, which can result in a performance boost (compared with the DSM). In addition to the performance edge, using the ESM offers the following advantages.

- You can support legacy tables, i.e. map class attributes to an existing table that already contains data.
- You can perform fine-tuning of the record sizes (i.e customize the object datatype length to match column datatype), which can substantially decrease the required space for disk storage, by avoiding fragmentation.
- Allows more extensive use of query pushdown.
- Supports for mapping of joins, handles, null attributes, subclasses, and user-defined partitions.

The next section discusses SML files. As mentioned above, the output from the Schema Mapping Tool is an SML file that contains the mapping between the class and the table. This file is used at runtime by the Schema Mapper.

Schema Mapping Language (SML) Files

A single SML file contains the definition of a specific schema map for a class, including embedded objects and subclasses. SML files extend the usefulness of a schema map through their reuse and modification.

Grouping SML files into common directories provides structure and consistency for their use.

When the SMT creates a new SML file, it uses data mapping preferences as the base values for the Java data types. You can use either the SanFrancisco default preferences or a preference file that you create. Keep a record of the preference file name if you plan to reuse it to create additional SML files. Once an SML file is created, however, you cannot associate a new preference file with it, you can only modify the existing mappings individually.

Using an SML file requires first configuring the file to the appropriate Java class (object) and then connecting the data source to the appropriate container. It is important to remember that a class may be configured to only one SML file.

SanFrancisco loads the configured SML file at runtime to generate the code that is needed for accessing the database. Interpreting the generated SML file results in less overhead than interpreting a .class file.

The Schema Mapping Utilities

The Schema Mapping utilities are used in conjunction with Extended Schema Mapping (ESM). These utilities offer powerful capabilities to users who are interested in going into the details of schema mapping.

These utilities include:

- *Graphical user interface*. The GUI for the ESM provides users with the ability to easily define mappings of classes, objects and attributes in the object schema to one or more relational tables. This GUI can be used to manipulate the output of the SML File Generator utility, customizing the mapping generated. This interface is shown in Figure 30-2.
- *SML File Generator utility*. This is a Java command-line utility that generates an SML file from a user-specified class file. Using command line parameters, the user may customize the following items:
  - the RDB table name;
  - a definition (through a preferences file) of the default Java datatype-to-RDB column mappings; and

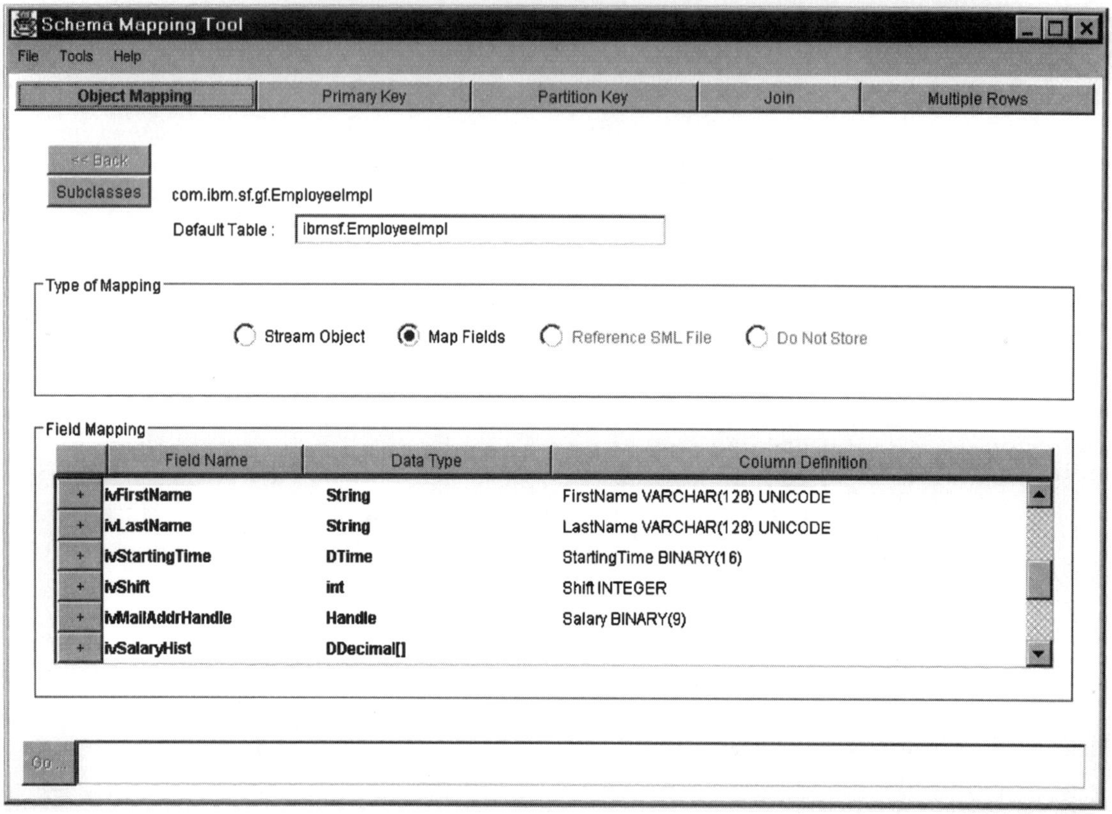

Figure 30-2
Schema mapping GUI.

- a list of subclasses to be be added to the SML.

- *Table Assistant utility*. This is a Java command-line utility that generates table statement source from a user-specified, pre-existing SML file. By using command-line parameters, the user may customize the created table by specifying the following information:
  - the DBMS (or container) for which the statements are generated; and
  - output file name, and whether to use append or truncate mode when writing to it.

CHAPTER 31

Mapping Simple Object Structures

This chapter continues the treatment of relational database (RDB) persistency started in the previous chapter. In this chapter, we address mapping of simple objects that do not contain embedded objects. Mapping such objects is a relatively simple affair. In the next chapter we consider mapping more complex objects, and also other advanced mapping issues. In general, schema mapping can turn out to be quite complex because of the degree of freedom you have in mapping different Java types.

Using the Default Schema Mapper (DSM)

The Default Schema Mapper (DSM) provides automatic mapping from one class to one table by mapping the various attributes of the class to default columns. A generic set of rules helps define and create the table at runtime using Java Reflection support for class inspection. As already mentioned in Chapter 30, an automatically generated `ObjectID` column becomes the primary key column for the new table. In addition, the DSM automatically generates a system-defined partition key column for the new table. The partition key is used to indicate which Entities belong to a specific `EntityOwningExtent` collection. This collection is extensively used when mapping objects to RDB, and was discussed in Chapter 12.

Using the DSM is quite easy as it does not require any input. The whole mapping process is automatic. The only thing you have to take care of is the database management side and, possibly, the access rights. The DSM automatically creates the table with a default name which is `IBMSF.<class name>`.

Using the Schema Mapping Tool

As discussed in the previous chapter, the Schema Mapping Tool is used to integrated SanFrancisco Business Objects with RDB. You can use this tool for working with either new or legacy data. When using ESM, the Schema Mapping Tool user interface is used to define the mapping, as discussed in the previous chapter.

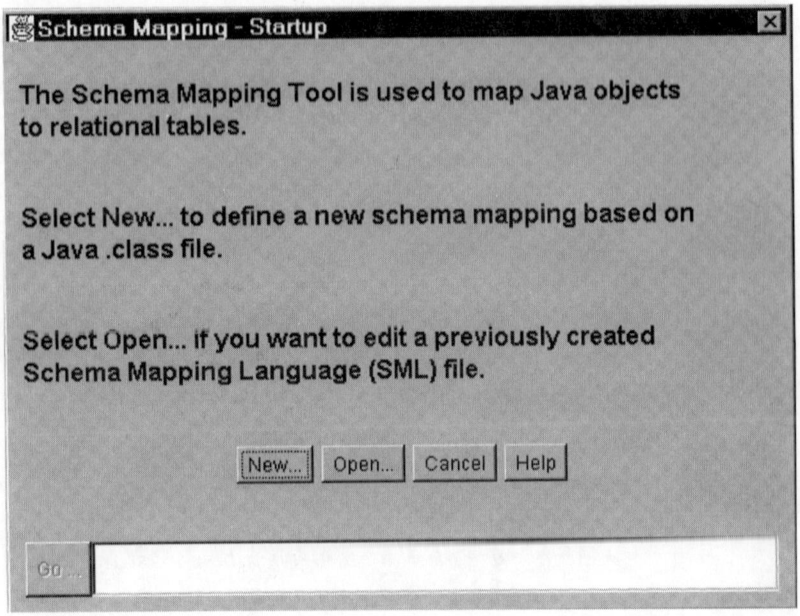

Figure 31-1 Schema mapping tool: startup window.

Another tool that is used is related to SML files. These files contain the details of a specific schema map for a class, including any embedded objects. SML files allow you to modify and reuse schema maps generated by the Schema Mapping tool user interface.

In order to start the Schema Mapping Tool, double-click its icon, which resides in the Base Utilities folder under the SanFrancisco folder. Once this tool starts, you see its startup dialog, as shown in Figure 31-1, which can be used to create a new schema to map or open an existing one. The main window of the Schema Mapping tool is shown in Figure 30-1 of the previous chapter. This main window has a menu bar, and four buttons placed above the remainder of the window, which holds the work area for this application. The menu bar includes three items, namely "File," "Tools," and "Help."

The main interface of the SMT GUI has a menu bar that includes three items: "File," "Tools," and "Help." The "File" menu is pretty standard, as it contains entries for "New," "Open," "Save," "Save as . . .," which all relate to SML files (which are essentially the files you are editing when working with this tool). In addition it contains a "Preferences" entry used to create or select an existing preferences file, and an "Exit" entry for quitting this application. The "Tools" menu is used to get to the "Create Table Assistant" tool, and the

"Help" menu provides help in the dialog and button level, plus lets you access the Schema Mapping Tool documentation.

Using Extended Schema Mapping involves associating database column with the attributes of an object. To do that, you must have a Java .class file corresponding to the object to be mapped, and also the database schema for the tables to be used.

Creating a new schema map for an object with the ESM requires that you go through the following phases.

- *Define the class to be mapped.*
- *Define user preferences.* This phase is optional.
- *Establish the schema map, and save it to an SML file.*
- *Configure the SML file to the class, then connect the database to the appropriate container.* Chapter 34 explains how this is accomplished.
- *Make sure all the required tables exist in the database.* This is accomplished using the create table assistant, as described in the next chapter.

Creating a New Schema Map and Editing Preferences

To create a new schema map, select "New" from either the "File" menu or the startup dialog. A dialog window appears, as shown in Figure 31-2. In this window you should enter the full name of the class you wish to map. You may use the "Browse" button in order to avoid any mistakes in keying in the class name. Remember to select a concrete class and not the interface because the actual attributes are of course placed in the former.

Each mapping has preferences associated with it. The options available to you are to use the default preferences, create a new preferences file, or use an existing one. The dialog window shown in Figure 31-2 allows you to either select an existing preferences file, or use the default one. If you wish to either create a new file, or edit an existing file, click the preferences button in the dialog window. This opens a new dialog titled "Select Preferences," as shown in Figure 31-3. In this dialog you may either create a new preferences file or select an existing one. In both cases, you get to the "Mapping Preferences" dialog shown in Figure 31-4.

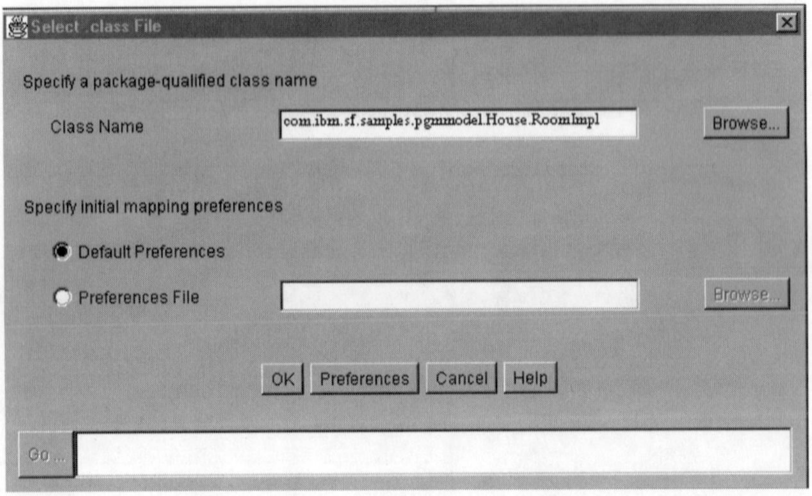

Figure 31-2
Schema mapping tool: new class entry dialog.

Once you set your preferences, click OK to continue with the previous dialog. Clicking again confirms the values in this dialog, and brings you to the "Object Mapping" window. Note that once you associate a certain Schema Mapping (i.e. an SML file) with a given preferences files, these cannot be changed (instead, you have to manually change datatype mappings).

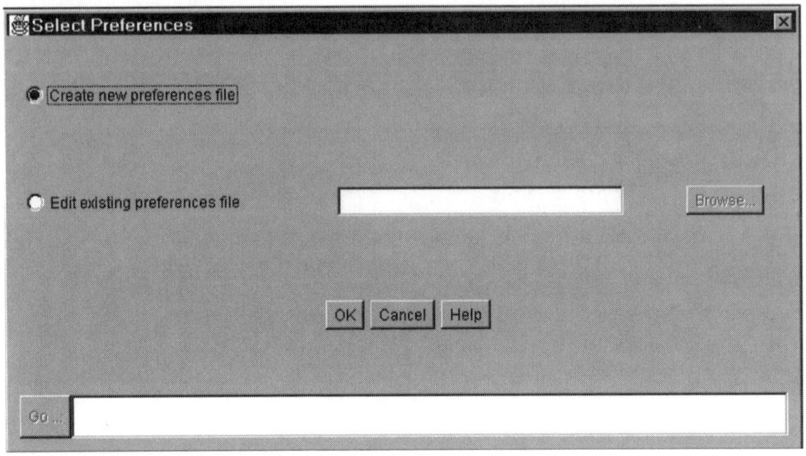

Figure 31-3
Schema mapping tool: select preferences dialog.

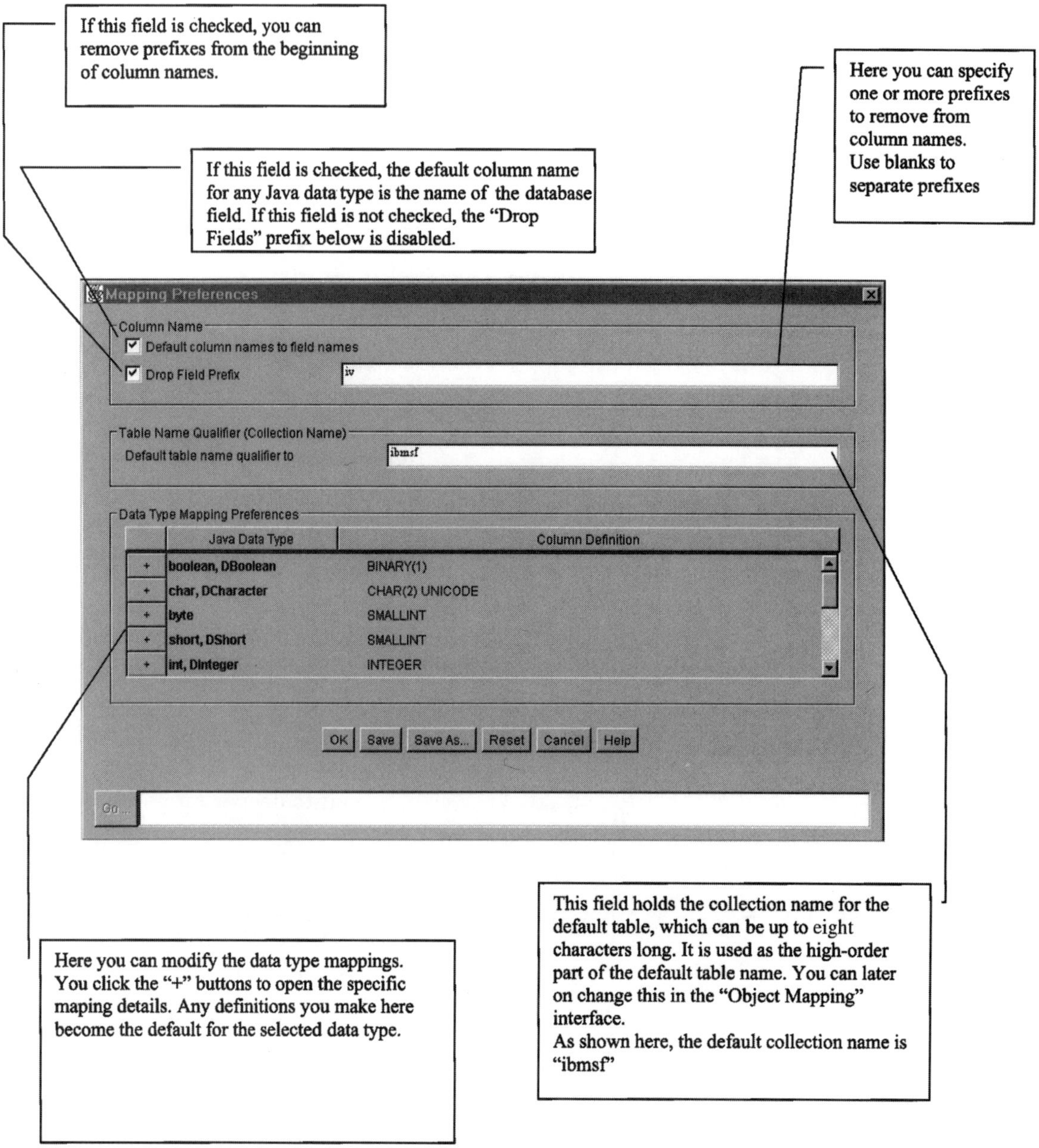

Figure 31-4
Schema mapping tool: mapping preferences dialog.

Establishing the Mapping

In order to establish object schema mapping, follow these steps:

- First, enter the "Object Mapping" interface by clicking the "Object Mapping" button in the main window of the Schema Mapping tool. This interface starts at the class level, which is the top level of mapping. As you start mapping fields, embedded objects, and subclasses, you enter lower (or deeper) levels of mapping. At any time, you can use the "<<Back" button to return to the previous level of mapping.
- Edit the name of the "Default Table" according to your needs. The default value is the class name, qualified with the default table name qualifier supplied in your preferences file.
- You may also select the "Type of Mapping." For now, leave it as "Map fields," which means you may individually map (or not map) each attribute of the object to a column of your choice in a database table. The other options are covered later in Chapter 32.
- Now you can go to each field and perform an individual mapping for it. To view or edit a mapping, click "+" on the button that is left of the Java object (or data type).

The way the mapping is edited depends on the field types. As mentioned above, for embedded objects you go into deeper mapping levels. In order to establish a simple mapping, bypassing the issues of embedded object mapping, you can select "Do not store" in the "Type of Mapping" radio-box group for any embedded objects. This is usually not realistic for real-world applications, but in the context of this chapter, it would suffice.

For example, if you are trying to map the `RoomImpl` class from the "House of Rooms" sample, program, you can select "Do not store" for the `ivProperties` field, as shown in Figure 31-5. Note that before you actually get to this dialog, you are prompted to indicate whether or not to use the corresponding `Impl` class, as shown in Figure 31-6. If you opt not to do so, you cannot map fields later on because the interface itself (`DHashTable` for this specific field) has no attributes.

In contrast to embedded objects, primitive data types are simpler. Instead of going into deeper levels of the mapping, you get a simple dialog box in which you can make your selections as shown in Figure 31-7. The Schema Mapping tool treats a field as a schema that maps a primitive

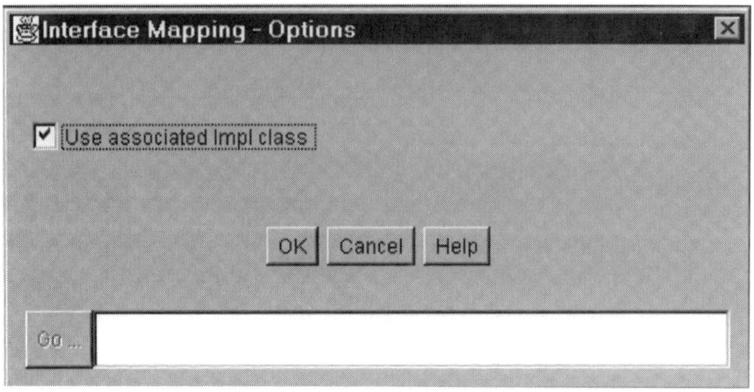

Figure 31-5 Schema mapping sample: `ivProperties` in `RoomImpl` class.

type when it is possible to map it to a database-compatible datatype. The following types of fields are schema that map primitive data types.

- Java primitives (e.g. `int`, `double`)
- `String`
- SanFrancisco Dependent wrappers for Java Primitives (e.g. `DInteger`, `DDouble`)
- `DDecimal`
- `DTime`

Table 31-1 shows the default database types used for each of these types. You may modify these for each of your fields. Note that these defaults are the ones applied when using DSM.

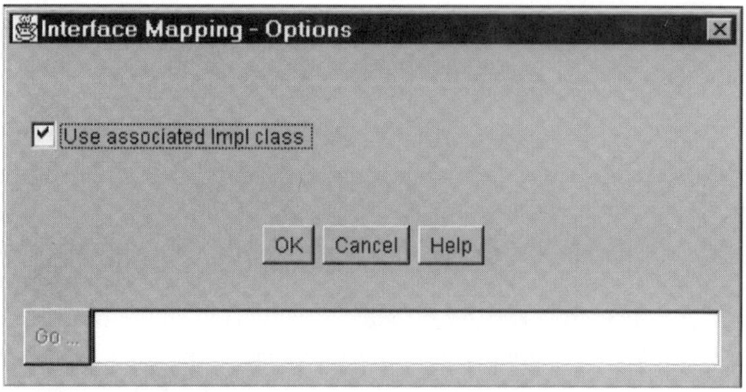

Figure 31-6 Schema mapping tool: use of `Impl` class dialog.

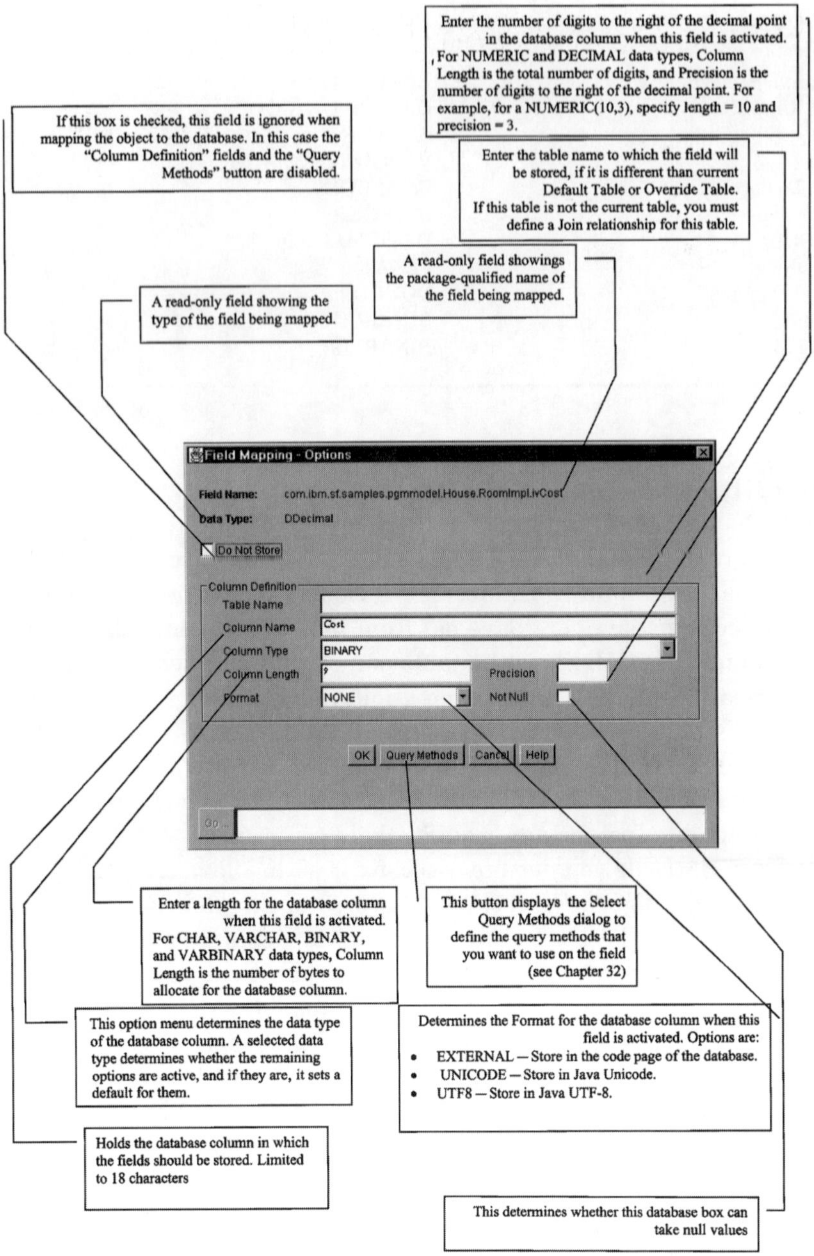

Figure 31-7
Schema mapping tool: mapping a primitive data type.

TABLE 31-1

Default mappings for primitive datatypes

Java Type	Default Mapping
Boolean, DBoolean	BINARY(1)
char, DCharacter	CHAR(2) UNICODE
byte	SMALLINT
String	VARCHAR(128) UNICODE
Short, DShort	SMALLINT
int, DInteger	INTEGER
long, Dlong	DECIMAL(19,0)
float, DFloat	FLOAT
Double, Ddouble	DOUBLE
DTime	BINARY(16)
DDecimal	BINARY(9)

Working with SML Files

Once you are done with the schema mapping of the objects, you should save the mapping to an SML file. As previously mentioned, you can do that by selecting “Save” or “Save as” from the “File” menu. The default name used for the SML file is the table name (non-qualified, i.e. the low-order part of the default table name), followed by the `.sml` extension. This suffix is required for the proper use of SML files. It is important to point out that SML files are not intended to be edited by users or developers, because of their sensitivity to changes; instead, you should use the Schema Mapping Tool for any modifications you require.

To use an SML file you need to associate it with a Java class using the SanFrancisco Configuration tool (as described in Chapter 34). Then, you need to connect the data source to the appropriate container, as described in the same chapter. When performing these operations you should keep in mind that a class may only be configured to a single SML file.

Once you perform these two operations SanFrancisco can load the SML file at runtime to generate the code that is needed for accessing the database. This does not incur any significant overhead because interpreting the SML files is quite efficient.

Using the “Open” option from the “File” menu (or from the Schema Mapping—Startup dialog), you may edit the schema mapping of an object already mapped, the editing process itself is identical to the one described above for new mappings.

CHAPTER 32

Advanced Mapping Issues

The previous chapter introduced the Schema Mapping Tool. In this chapter, we address the issue of mapping objects that contain embedded objects, as well as other mapping techniques supported by the Schema Mapping Tool. This chapter concludes our presentation of RDB persistency in SanFrancisco.

The first section in this chapter elaborates on the different kinds of object mapping you can use. The following sections discuss additional steps that can optionally be taken when mapping an object. These steps include mapping subclasses of the object being mapped, assigning a primary key, joining tables, and mapping multiple rows.

Object Mapping

As we saw in the previous chapter, for each object (actually each level in the mapping of an object), you can select the mapping method, which can be one of the following:

- *Stream Object*. This option stores the whole object into a single column in a database table. This is the default type of mapping for array and handle objects, and for other objects containing a field map that cannot be mapped. The field types that cannot be mapped are:
    - Objects that are abstract classes
    - Interfaces without any matching `Impl` class
    - Objects that include in them other objects which are not supported by SanFrancisco (e.g. multi-dimensional arrays, `HashTable`).

  Streaming an object to a column in a table is an easy alternative to mapping each individual field. The object is streamed to the column that you define under "Column Definition." You can stream an object only to columns of type BINARY, VARBINARY, or LONGVARBINARY.

- *Map Fields*. This option allows you to specify the mapping for each of the object attributes to a database table. The "Field Mapping" table has a row for each field and embedded object, which contains the field name, the current mapping (under "Column Definition") and the Java data type. An example can be seen in Figure 30-2. If the "Column Definition" is blank, the row is associated with an embedded object, i.e. a Dependent object, a Handle, or an array.

- *Reference to SML File*. This option is enabled when mapping certain embedded objects (usually dependents). Using this option you can use an existing schema map for the object. This is useful when you have Dependent objects that get mapped to the database frequently, and always in the same way. The only input you need to provide when selecting this option is the full path
- *Not Stored*. As mentioned in the previous chapter, this type of mapping is used when you do not want to store the object or field in the table. If you select this option, the object will not have a corresponding column in the database table.

When mapping embedded objects (of type `Dependent`, `Handle`, or `array`), the actual procedure depends on the type of the embedded object. When mapping a `Dependent`, you may select the query methods (as we will soon discuss query methods), if there are any, they can either map individual fields or use a reference to an SML file if this `Dependent` already has such a file.

Mapping Arrays

When mapping arrays with one dimension of Handles, Dependents, Strings, or primitive Java data types, the default mapping is to stream the entire array to a single column in the database table. However, you may also map an array element that is a Dependent or a Handle to a separate column or columns. Array elements must all be of the same type or class, but can be a mixture of subclasses. In order to do field mapping of an array, you must specify in advance the number of elements in the array (since you must know how many columns you need). For large arrays (e.g. arrays with more than 10 to 20 elements) this obviously is not very efficient. Actually, arrays having 100 elements or more cannot be mapped this way. The "Data Type" column for an array shows the array type and, if it is field mapped, its size (e.g. int[10]).

Mapping Handles

Handles are used to associate Entities with one another, essentially acting as references. An embedded Handle includes one or more fields that hold the unique identity of another object. A "Handle type" determines the type of field (or fields) in the embedded Handle. This means that different types of Handles may use different definitions of the object represented by the Handle.

Typically, an embedded Handle in SanFrancisco is stream-mapped to a foreign key in a table. This is pretty obvious because a foreign key in a relational database is the database's equivalent to an object reference. The SML also allows you to map an embedded Handle to a foreign key by figuring out the "container ID" and "class ID" that compose the Handle, instead of storing these as database columns.

To get hold of the "container ID", you may either assume it is the same as the one for the Entity that contains the Handle, or you can store the container name in the datastore. Another option is to use the Naming service to find out the default container for the class the Handle references (Chapter 17 has more details on how to do that). Once SanFrancisco conforms to EJB all these will need to be unified into a consistent framework.

To extract the "class ID", either store the class name (or class ID, where supported) in the data store or code the class name as a constant. Another possibility it to specify a logical expression similar to an "SQL WHERE" clause that checks column values to determine the class. For example, you can specify that the class is `myClass if mytable.column1 == ''ABC''`. Figure 32-1 shows an example of how a "WHERE" clause is defined. This is a code-based approach to class typing where a set of designated database codes are equivalent to our class structures.

A Handle that is mapped (shown in Figure 32-2) may either be streamed, not stored, or defined using the Handle types. If you stream it, then you just enter the column definitions, possibly after defining query methods. If you choose to define handle types, the column definitions section is replaced by fields allowing you to define handle types. Note that only one handle type can exist per Handle object. You have two options to choose from:

- *Default Handle*. You need to define a column in which to store the streamed Handle, or map the contents of the Handle, the object that the Handle references, and the Handle itself. If mapping the contents of the Handle, you need to specify how to get the class

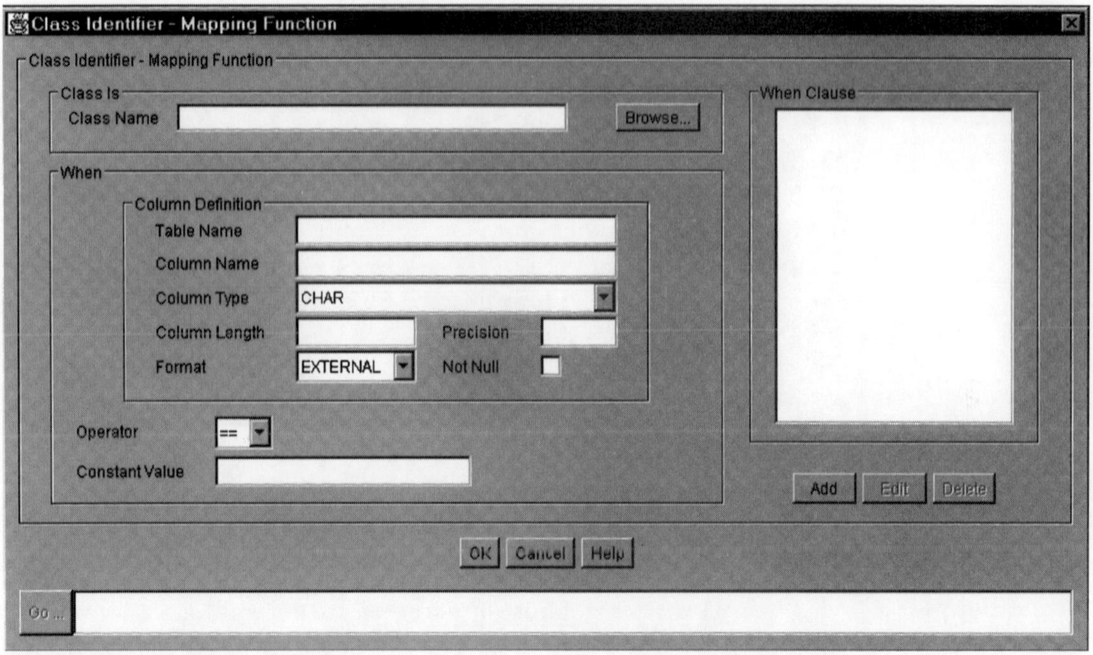

Figure 32-1
Definition of a "WHERE" clause.

name or class ID and the object ID of the referenced object. Figures 32-3–32-5 show examples of how this is done. When mapping the Handle itself you only need to specify how to get the Handle type.

- *User Defined Handle*. Here you need to define a column in which to store the streamed Handle, or map the content of the Handle, the object that the Handle references, and the Handle itself. To map the contents of the handle, you specify a Dependent class that represents the unique fields of the User Defined Handle. Then you map the fields of the Dependent class (or accept default data type mappings). Once you confirm your choice of the Dependent class and save the Handle mapping, it is impossible to change the Dependent class for this Handle type, unless you delete the Handle type and re-map it. Specify the Container that holds information about the object referenced by the Handle. You need to specify how to get the class name of the referenced object.

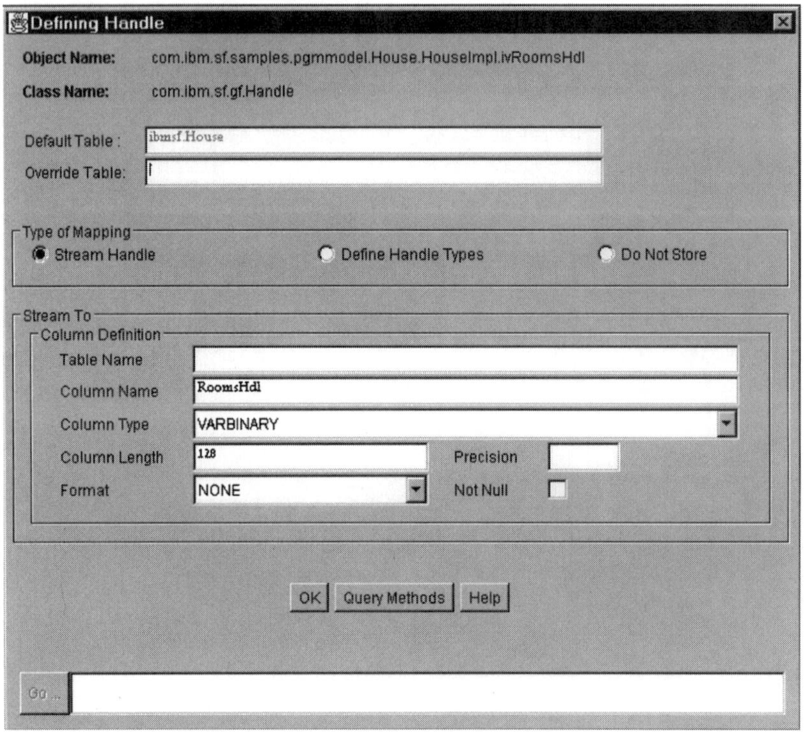

Figure 32-2
Mapping a Handle.

Default and Override Tables

The database table to which your schema-mapped object is stored is the "Default Table". You can override this and designate your own table by specifying an "Override Table". The "Default Table" can only be modified in the class level (i.e. top-level) "Object Mapping" interface. The default table should be the one that contains primary key columns, if there are any. The default table name for the class is of the form

```
<collection name>.<table name>
```

where the table name is the class name, truncated to 18 characters. As mentioned in the previous chapter the collection name (i.e. the high-order part of the default table name) can be specified when defining user preferences.

Note that any modification in the "Default Table" name in the top-most "Object Mapping" interface changes the "Default Table" for the whole schema mapping. However, it does not affect the preference file you are using. When you need to map a class to a specific existing table,

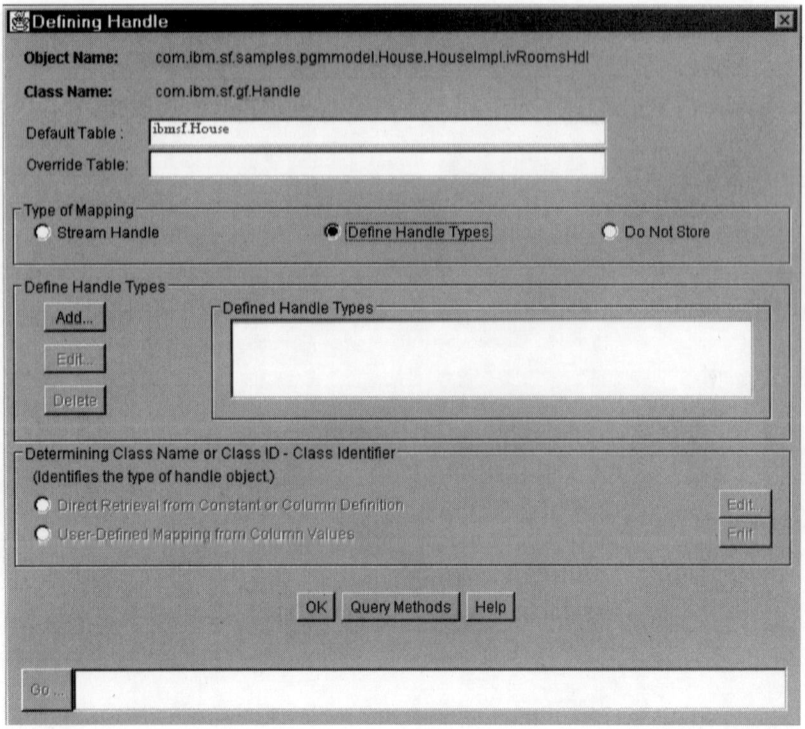

Figure 32-3
Define Handle types.

you should set the "Default Table" name to correspond (exactly) to the name of the existing table. This is useful when working with legacy data stored in a relational database. The "Default Table" cannot be changed in the lower levels of the "Object Mapping" (i.e. the ones below the whole class mapping). However, you can override it by specifying an "Override Table." If you specify such an "Override Table," it takes precedence over the "Default Table" for the specific mapping level and all the levels below it (i.e. the ones corresponding to this specific embedded object, subclass, or field). The "Override Table" can be specified in the corresponding field in the "Object Mapping" interface (for Dependents and arrays), in the various dialogs concerning Handles, and in the "Subclass Mapping" interface.

It is important to remember that once you specify the "Override Table" it becomes the "Default Table" for the levels of mapping below it.

You override the "Default Table" or "Override Table" for fields that are mapped to primitives (the ones listed in Table 32-1) by specifying a different "Table Name" in the "Column Definitions" panel.

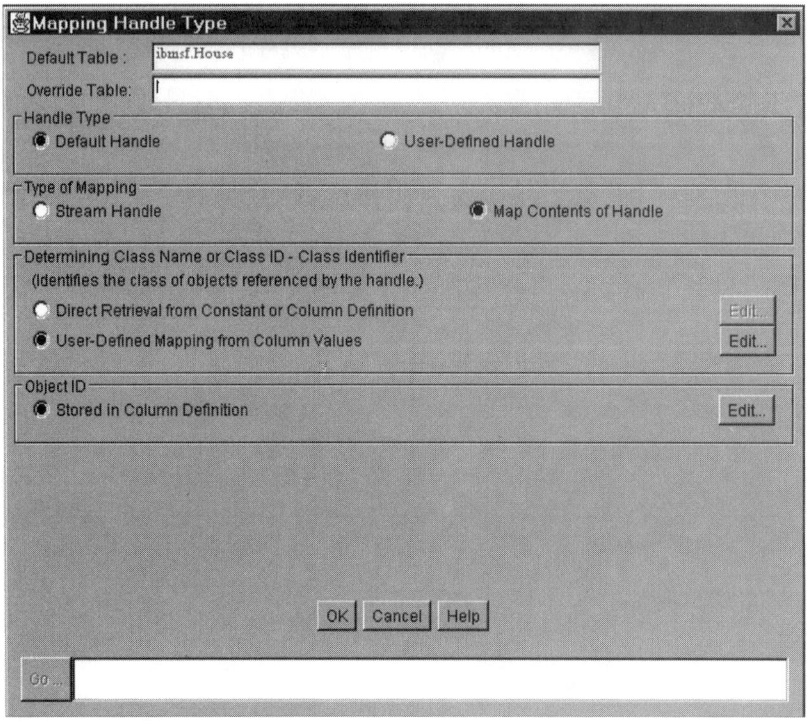

Figure 32-4 Mapping Handle types.

Primary Key

Each Entity has a network-wide identity used by the Foundation layer to locate it on the network, and this identity is essentially the content of a Handle to the Entity. A Handle may either be "independent," which means it is not contained in another object, or "embedded" in another object. Unlike an embedded Handle, an independent Handle is not a field in any object—it usually references an Entity after its creation. Independent handles are considered preferable in terms of object modeling because object identifiers should always be opaque and not part of the object model.

Embedded Handles are fields in objects that form the basis for associations between objects. A "Primary Key" is a unique table identifier that the Schema Mapping Tool can map to the unique identity portion of the independent Handle for an Entity. The SMT defines two types of primary keys: an Object ID and a Dependent class.

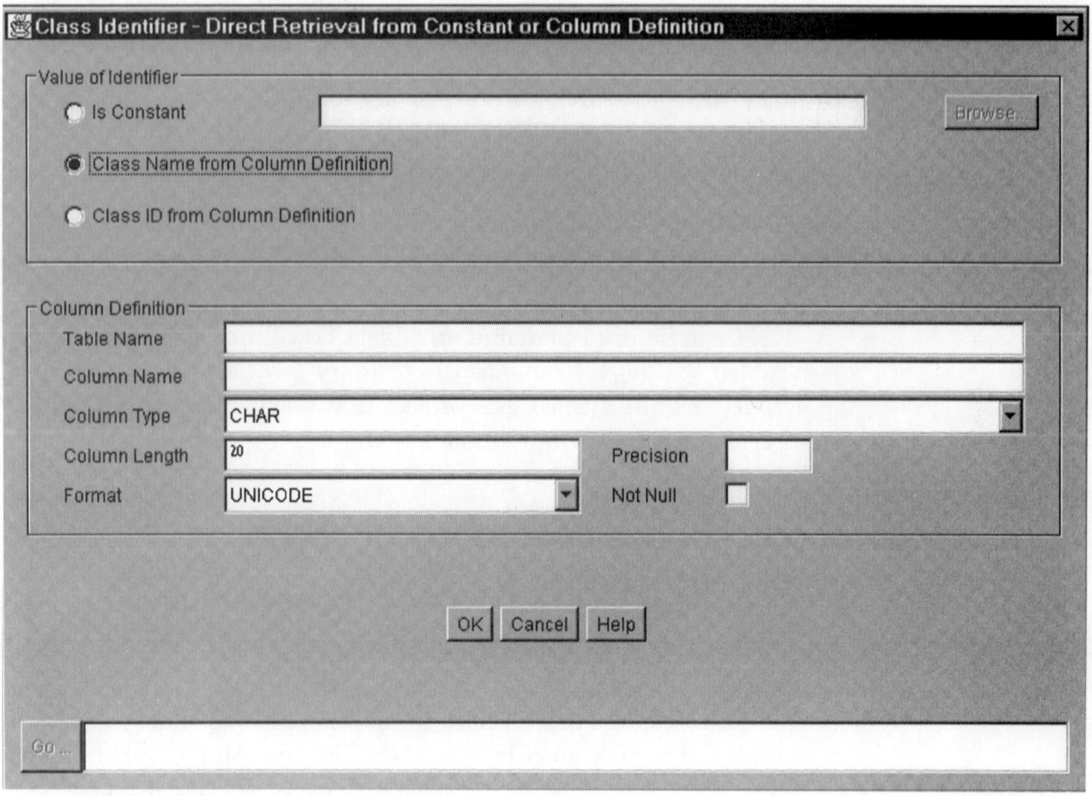

Figure 32-5
Class ID definition for Mapping Handle type.

TABLE 32-1

Schema mapping primitive data types and their default mappings

Java Type	Default Mapping
`Boolean, DBoolean`	`BINARY(1)`
`char, DCharacter`	`CHAR(2) UNICODE`
`byte`	`SMALLINT`
`String`	`VARCHAR(128) UNICODE`
`Short, DShort`	`SMALLINT`
`int, DInteger`	`INTEGER`
`long, Dlong`	`DECIMAL(19,0)`
`float, DFloat`	`FLOAT`
`Double, Ddouble`	`DOUBLE`
`DTime`	`BINARY(16)`
`DDecimal`	`BINARY(9)`

Object ID

At runtime, the ESM cannot automatically know about the primary key for the table. The database administrator must define a primary key for the table. This can be done in one of two ways.

- The SMT Create Table Assistant tool (available under the "Tools" menu) can be used to create a new table that has a primary key defined as the Object ID.
- The ESM can be used to define an Object ID column that has been added to a legacy table as the primary key. Note that such an activity is quite typical in a project that starts out with an existing schema but wants to move to an object model.

Dependent Class

A Dependent class used in this context must be derived like any other Dependent class from the `com.ibm.sf.gf.DependentImpl` class. You must map all attributes in this class to columns in the primary key, and each of these attributes must be one of the Schema Mapping Primitives (see Table 32-1). Defining the Dependent class as the primary key requires specifying it as the `identifyingKey` on the `createEntity` method of the object. You must not change the primary key in a database table if a Handle exists for the object that is to be mapped. If the primary key value of the table changes after creation of the Handle of the object, the Handle can no longer access the object.

Assigning a Primary Key

In order to assign a primary key to your object you first change the "Default Table" in the "Object Mapping" Interface to be the name of the table that contains the primary key column. Then click the "Primary Key" column at the top of the SMT interface. The interface allows you to select "None", "Use ObjectID," or "Use Dependent Class" as shown in Figure 32-6. The first option, "None" indicates that the object does not have a primary key. This is the default, unless the class is derived from `EntityImpl`.

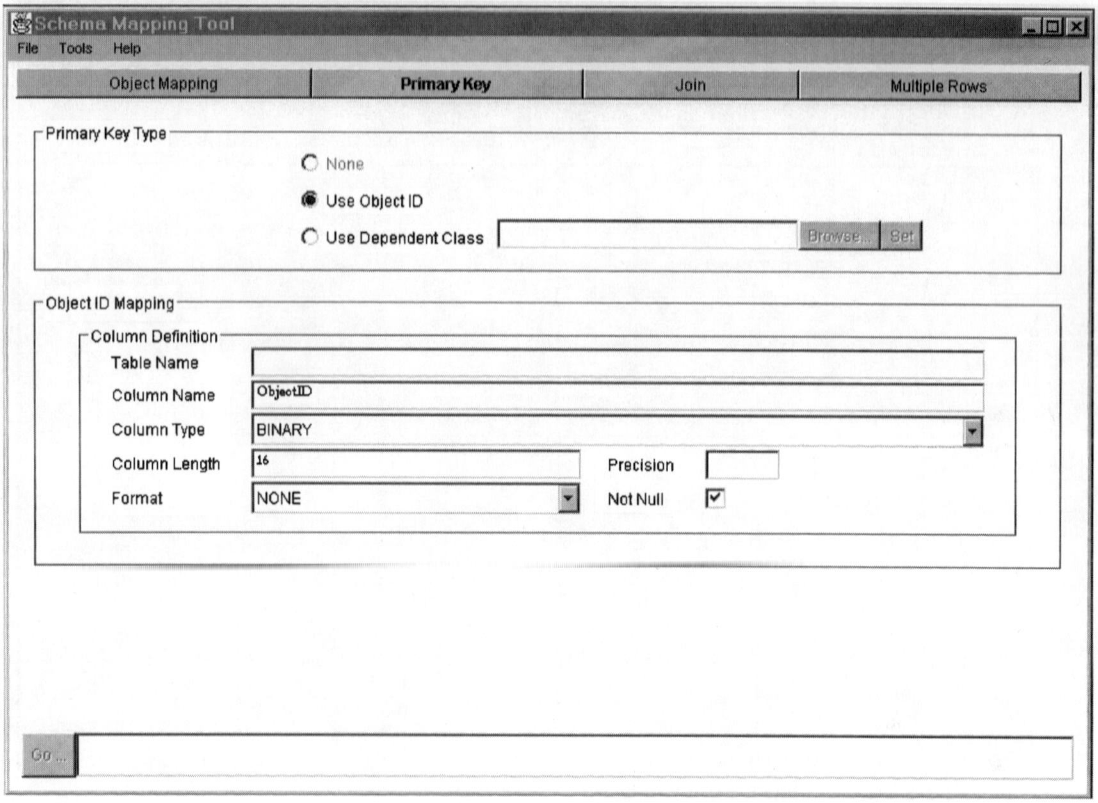

Figure 32-6
Primary key interface.

As mentioned above, select "Use ObjectID" when you want a primary key and you are either generating a new table or have added an ObjectID column to an existing table. This is the default when the class descends from `EntityImpl`. Complete the Object ID mapping by specifying the column name, column type, and column length.

Select "Use Dependent Class" to specify a user-defined primary key, which must match the primary key of the database table. Then you should specify a Dependent class to be used for mapping the unique Handle identity to the primary key. Then click "Set" to map the individual fields of the Dependent.

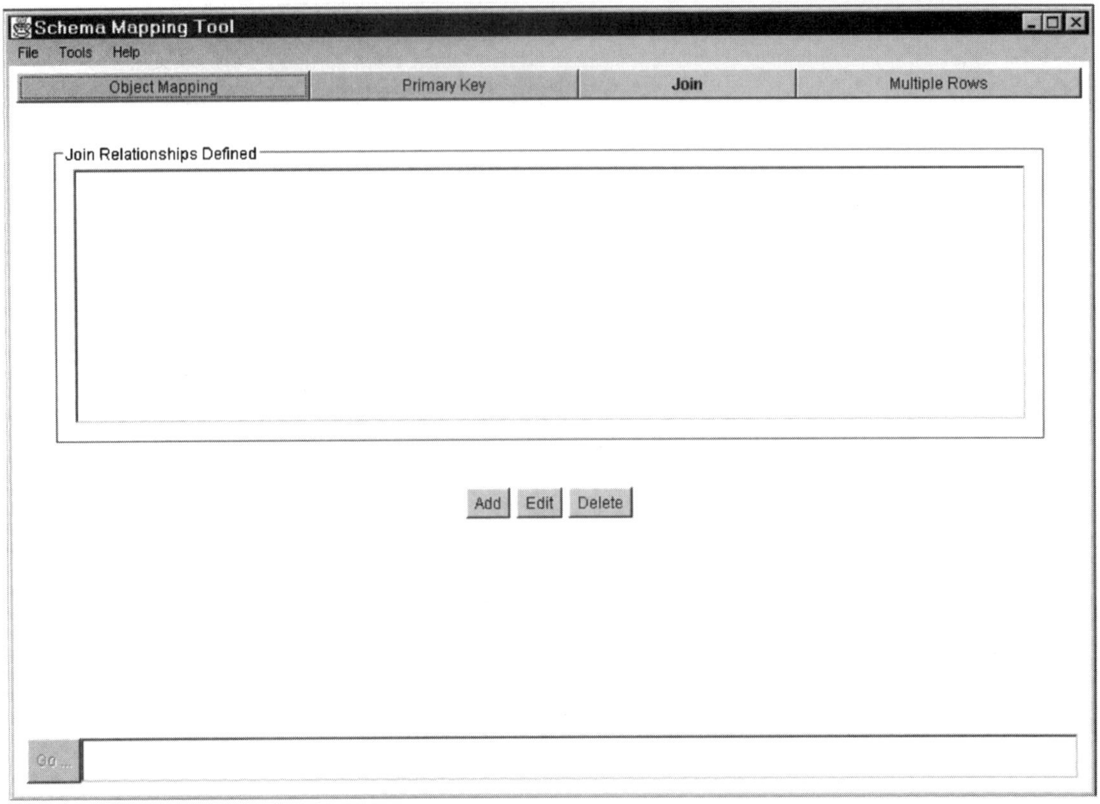

Figure 32-7
Join interface.

Joins

In order to map an object to multiple tables, you must define a join relationship between these tables. Since database tables are often normalized and object models are fairly complex in nature, joins are an important part of any object-to-relational mapping. In order to define joins press the "Join" button on the upper part of the Schema Mapping Tool window. The display changes to the one shown in Figure 32-7. When you perform a join operation, you define one or more join relationships. When building joins, you need to specify the relationship between column pairs: a column in a primary table associated with a column in a secondary table. The latter need not exist at the time of the definition, but of course, it must exist at runtime. The interface for pairing is shown in Figure 32-8.

After defining the column pairs, you can choose the join type and the primary key setting. The defined joins must ultimately chain back to the default table. Without full chaining of all tables to the primary table the runtime creation of objects from tables may end up using an SQL statement that is an external product of the tables—creating a mass of irrelevant objects.

An inner join returns only those rows in the primary table that have corresponding rows in the secondary table. An outer join returns all rows in the parent table. However, if no corresponding row exists in the secondary table, each column of the secondary table returns a null value. Outer joins are not supported by all databases, and the syntax for this

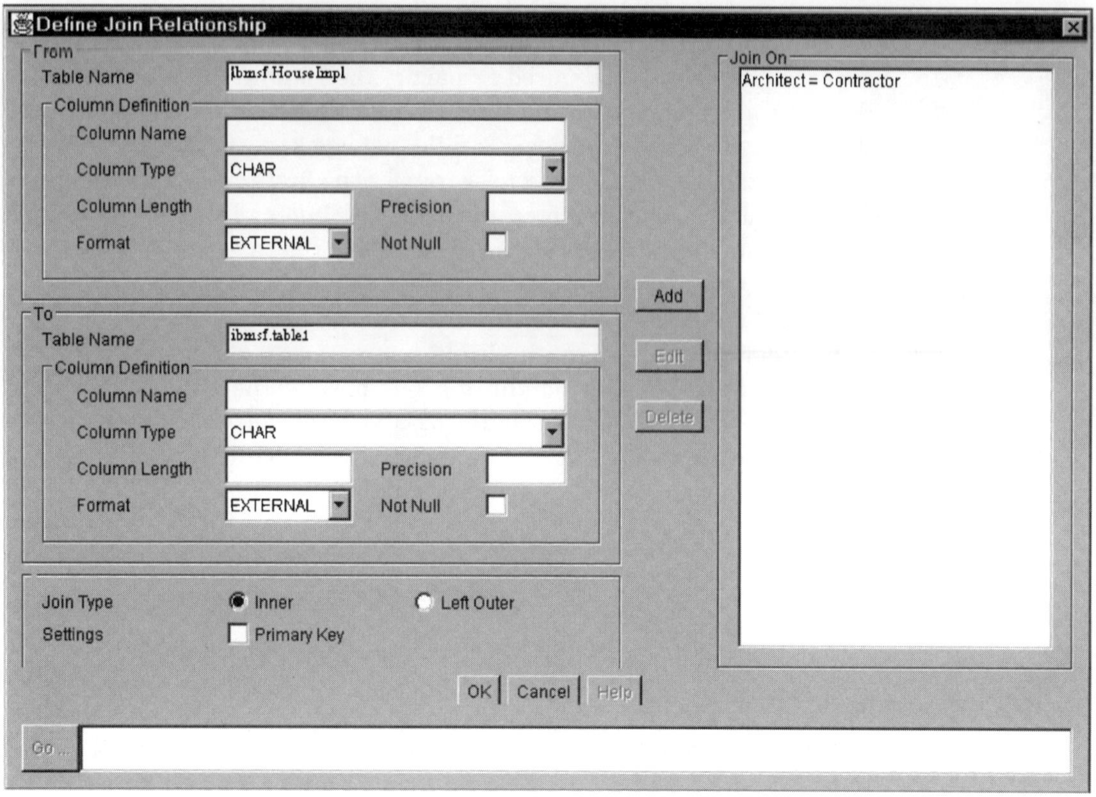

Figure 32-8
Defining a join relation.

join is not consistent in different databases. It is therefore problematic for a database-neutral tool to use.

Select "Primary Key" if all column pairs for this join constitute a primary key for the purposes of this particular join. Enabling the primary key setting requires that all columns of the join that are in the secondary table be primary key columns.

Multiple Rows

The Schema Mapping Tool has multiple row support that facilitates mapping large objects. Such large objects are mapped to multiple rows of a column in the primary table. When using multiple row support, a column needs to hold an integer sequence number. This sequence number determines the ordering of the rows corresponding to an object. The sequence number is not stored as part of the Handle state for the object that you are mapping to multiple rows. This is a little confusing, but there is a distinction, however subtle, between the primary key of the table and the key that is used to search for the first row of a multiple row object. You should never map the field attributes of any object to this special sequence number column. The values that are stored in this column must remain unchanged in order for schema mapping to work properly.

In order to activate the multiple row support you should click the "Multiple Rows" button on the top left part of the Schema Mapping Tool window. As shown in Figure 32-9 you can now enable or disable multiple row mappings, and if you select to enable it you only need to define the mapping for the sequence number.

Reference Columns

The Schema Mapping Tool allows you to map multiple fields of an object to the same database column. This happens whenever a column definition for a field matches another column definition for a different field. These fields can be either primitive mapping data types (shown in Table 32-1) or a field-mapped (i.e. non-stream mapped) Dependent, array, or Handle.

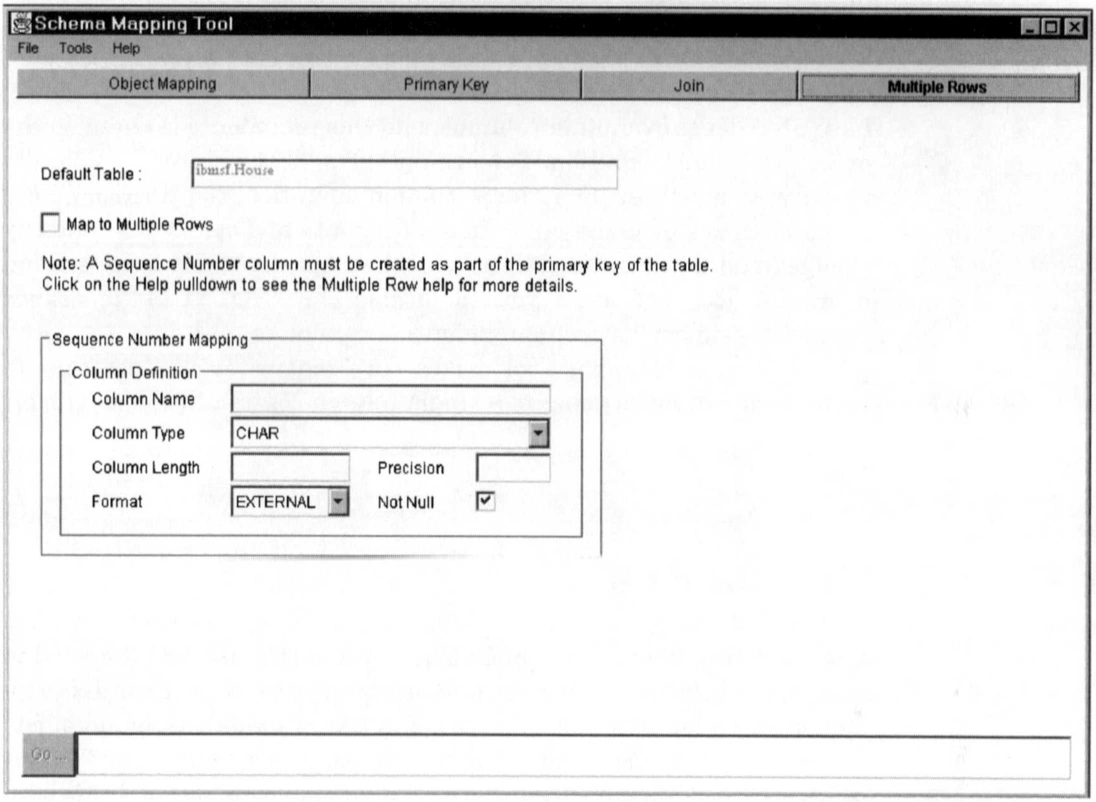

Figure 32-9
Multiple row interface.

The reasons for using this feature, and having the same column definitions for different fields might vary. One possibility is that you want to use the same column definition for an object attribute (which you defined using "Object Mapping"), and for a column corresponding to a unique identity field in the independent Handle of the object (defined using "Primary Key"). Another scenario is that the "WHEN" clause of a user-defined class ID mapping specifies a column definition that is already referenced elsewhere.

In general, specifying the same column name for different columns that have identical column definitions causes one of the columns to reference the other. Having the same column definition means that all the column attributes are the same in both column definitions (e.g. type, length, etc). Once you establish such a reference, a change in one column definition is reflected in the other column definition. The only exception is when this cannot be done because of precedence of the owning column. Columns that are primary keys, field maps, or part of a "WHEN" clause, have precedence over other columns, and this precedence is based on the order of column definition. For example if a "Primary Key" column is identical to a certain "Field Map" column definition, the "Primary Key" has precedence over the other column definition. This means that any change in either definition affects the other, but the "Field Map" column definition does not allow you to disable the "NOTNULL" checkbox because a primary key column definition cannot be null.

The Schema Mapping Tool makes sure that when you use column referencing, all fields going to a single column contain the same value.

Subclasses

When defining the mapping of an object, you might also be interested in mapping subclasses of this object (because often hierarchy-based mapping makes a lot more sense—either in terms of performance and indexing or in terms of modeling). This is done using the "Subclasses" button in the "Object Mapping" interface. The actual mapping of fields of a subclass is very similar to regular class mapping. The notion of subclass mapping is not recursive; that is, you cannot map the subclass of a subclass using subclass mapping. You must map the subclass of a subclass back to the original class using the class-level "Object Mapping" interface.

After clicking on the "Subclasses" button, you select a subclass of the object. Then you can map the fields of this subclass. This is done according to the same principles of mapping objects (described previously).

Enabling multiple row support for a class also enables that support for the defined and mapped subclasses. Deleting mapped subclasses can cause an automatic update of the Class ID for the base object.

Query Methods (Query Pushdown)

Chapter 19 describes the Query Mechanism that is part of the Foundation layer. Query methods provide a mechanism to associate a field of an object with a column in a database table. This mechanism enables SanFrancisco to "push down" a query (provided to the Foundation layer) to the underlying database engine. Two criteria must be met in order to allow such pushdown:

- "get" methods on the field must comply with certain restrictions and naming conventions; and
- the field must be used in the "WHERE" clause of the query.

Get methods that do not follow the prescribed naming conventions but conform to other restrictions can still be used as query methods for query pushdown from a list of defined candidates.

When selecting "Query Methods" you define the methods for query pushdown. You select the methods one by one into one of two lists. The "Defined Methods" list shows the candidate methods that only fully conform to the get method criteria. The "Selected Methods" list shows methods that meet both criteria. Figure 32-10 shows the interface for selecting "Query Methods".

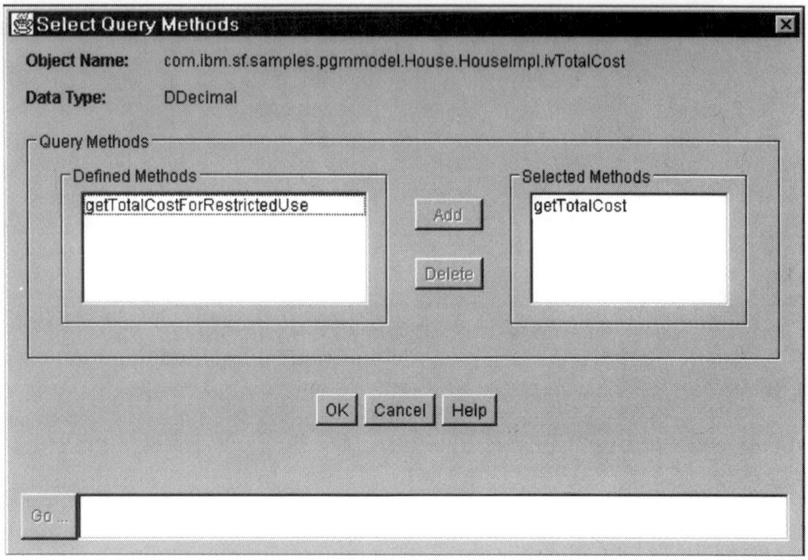

Figure 32-10 Query method selection.

Create Table Assistant

The Schema Mapping Tools allows creating a new table directly from an SML file. This is done using the "Create Table Assistant," which can be started from the "Tools" menu.

This tool interprets the current SML file in order to generate both a CREATE TABLE statement and a DROP TABLE statement. Executing the CREATE TABLE statement from within the tool creates a table that is needed to persistently store the class file that your schema mapped. Executing the DROP TABLE statement drops the table.

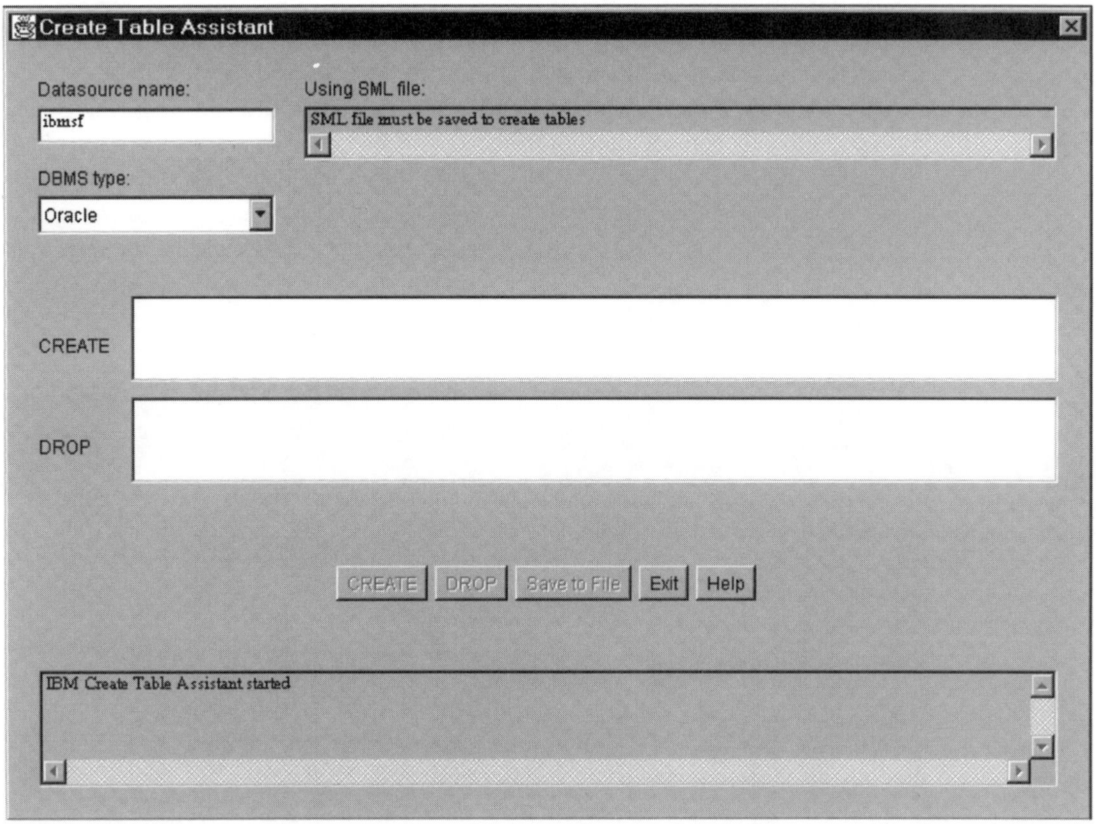

Figure 32-11
Create table assistant

The interface for this tool, shown in Figure 32-11, requires you to place the datastore name, and select the DBMS type. Once you do that, you can either create the table, drop it, or store the create statement to file, using the appropriate buttons.

PART 7

Deployment Issues

CHAPTER 33

The Logical SanFrancisco Network

SanFrancisco is aimed at developing distributed applications. As such, it facilitates multiple server processes to cooperate, each managing a different task or set of tasks. Server processes might run on the same computer or be distributed over a network of computers. The set of processes cooperating to perform a common set of tasks distributed over different servers is called a "Logical SanFrancisco Network," or LSFN.

The Composition of an LSFN

The LSFN is a group of clients and business object processes that share the same instance of the Global Server Manager (GSM) process. The GSM is the center of the LSFN. Processes in an LSFN can either reside in the same computer, or be located on separate computers. The SanFrancisco processes use TCP/IP in order to communicate. One LSFN consists of the following elements:

- One GSM Process
- Any number of Business Object Processes (BOPs)
- Any number of client processes

The GSM process contains several service objects that are critical to LSFN functioning. These service objects are:

- *GSM Service*. This service is in charge of all the BOP. It keeps all the BOP configuration information, tracks all the active and inactive BOPs, and is responsible for routing request from clients to specific BOPs
- *Global Distributed Process Manager (GDPM) Service*. This service tracks all active clients in the LSFN. It must be running before clients can run on the LSFN.
- *Global Name Server (GNS)*. This service is responsible for managing the name space of the LSFN. Specifically, it is responsible for:
  - Resolving user aliases
  - Identifying which classes have to be used to create instances of business objects
  - Determining where to create instances

- Implementing the definitions in the containers, security configurations and the transaction model used.

Another service running in the various BOP is the *Local Server Manager Service*. This is responsible for starting BOPs. One instance of this service must be running on each computer in the LSFN. It exists in one of the following processes:

- GSM Process of the Global Server computer
- SanFrancisco Server Manager (SFSM) Process for any other computer having BOPs.

Security management is handled by security-controlling services:

- *Master Security Service*. This service manages authentication for the LSFN. It exists in the GSM Process.
- *Server Security Service*. This service authenticates client requests. It exists in each BOP as well as in the GSM Process.

Business object instances are managed by the following services:

- *Factory Manager*. This service takes care of creating and holding instances of SanFrancisco business objects.
- *Transaction Service*. This service monitors transaction processing and coordinates recovery when needed. One instance of this service exists in each BOP that uses transactions (usually the same process that holds a Factory Manager).

Finally, some administrative tasks are managed by these two processes, which can run in any BOP, but should have only one instance in the whole LSFN:

- *Problem Service*. This service logs problems for internal services.
- *Conflict Control Service*. Manages conflict controlled actions (see Chapter 35)

Configuring an LSFN

The LSFN configuration is different depending on different approaches for locating clients and services. In general, there are three approaches for placing clients and services:

- *A Client and Server Residing in the Same Computer*. This is the simplest and easiest SanFrancisco configuration. It is usually unrealistic in real-life situations, but is very convienient during application development. When using this approach, the GSM, GNS, and Factory services all reside on the same physical machine as the client applications.
- *Multiple Clients Connecting to a Single Server*. In this case the GNS, GSM and Factory services all run on the same machine, but client services can be remote.
- *Several Factory Services Running on Several Computers* (this is the general case). In this approach, the GNS and GSM reside on one server, whereas Factory services and clients are distributed on different computers.

Using the Configuration Utility

After installation, use the IBM SanFrancisco Configuration Utility to define the following settings:

- Set the HTML browser you want to use to view the help files from within a GUI.
- Set the security policy.
- Specify the need for a required user-id. If this is not set to "required", the User Administration and the Access Right Administration cannot start.
- Set an initial administrator password if you want to set a required password.
- Specify any required password and the password rules.
- Change the persistence type. After installation and priming, the persistence for all containers is set to POSIX. You can change this to a database, if you want.

- Create new classes that distribute and access remotely.
- Create a new container.
- Assign classes to another container.
- Control the transaction operation.
- Change the stores where data persist. This is, database tables and databases for data with relational database persistence, or the directory for data with POSIX persistence.
- Append information to the current SanFrancisco configuration.

To start the configuration utility, follow these steps:

- Open the SanFrancisco folder.
- Open the Base Utilities folder.
- Double click on the IBM SanFrancisco Configuration icon

The configuration tools window appears, as shown in Figure 33-1. Figure 33-2 shows the "local data configuration" window that you reach by selecting "Local Machine" from the configure menu. Figure 33-3 shows the "transaction configuration" window. You reach this window by selecting "Transaction Execution" from the "Configure Menu." In this window, you can select the commit protocol you want to use. The commit protocol is either TWO_PHASE or MIXED_PHASE. See Chapter 16 for explanations about this parameter.

Other uses of the Configuration utility are described in the next two chapters.

Continuing the Configuration Process

In order to complete your configuration, you should take care of the following issues.

- Configuring servers—covered in Chapter 34
- Configuring containers—covered in Chapter 34
- Configuring classes—covered in Chapter 34
- Configuring users and access rights—covered in Chapter 35
- Configuring conflict control—covered in Chapter 35

Figure 33-1
The SanFrancisco configuration utility.

The Problem Manager

SanFrancisco provides the Problem Manager Utility as an interface that can be used to review problems and error messages recorded during the execution of the LSFN. It is important to analyze problems reported by this interface because they usually imply that there are either coding errors in your application, or that there are some configuration problems that should be resolved.

The Problem Manager Utility retrieves data from the SanFrancisco Problem Server (mentioned in Section 33.1) which is named *SFBOProcess3* by default. If the Problem Server is inactive, this utility attempts to start the server in order to retrieve the problem logs.

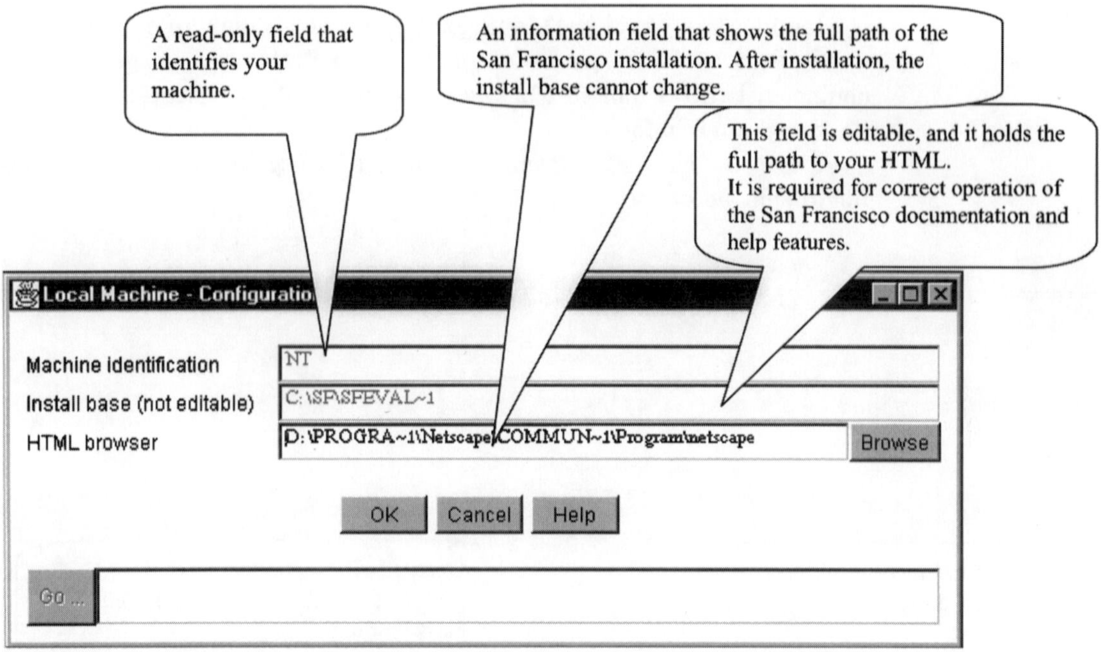

Figure 33-2
The SanFrancisco configuration utility: local machine configuration.

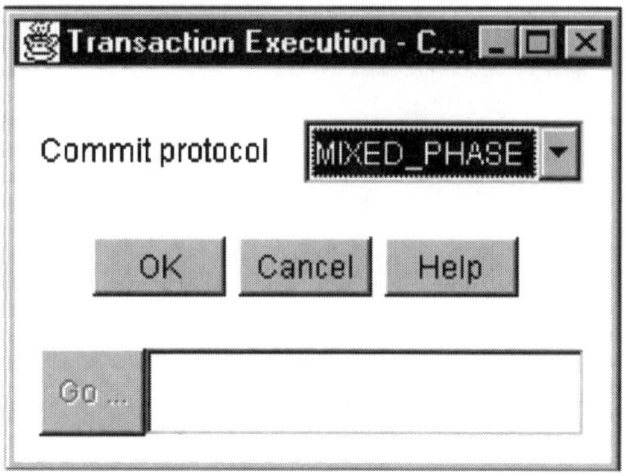

Figure 33-3
The SanFrancisco configuration utility: transaction configuration.

Starting the Problem Manager Utility is similar to starting the Configuration Utility. In order to start the Problem Manager Utility, double-click the Problem Manager icon in the Base Utilities folder in the SanFrancisco folder.

Figure 33-4 shows the Problem Manager Utility GUI and the information displayed on it.

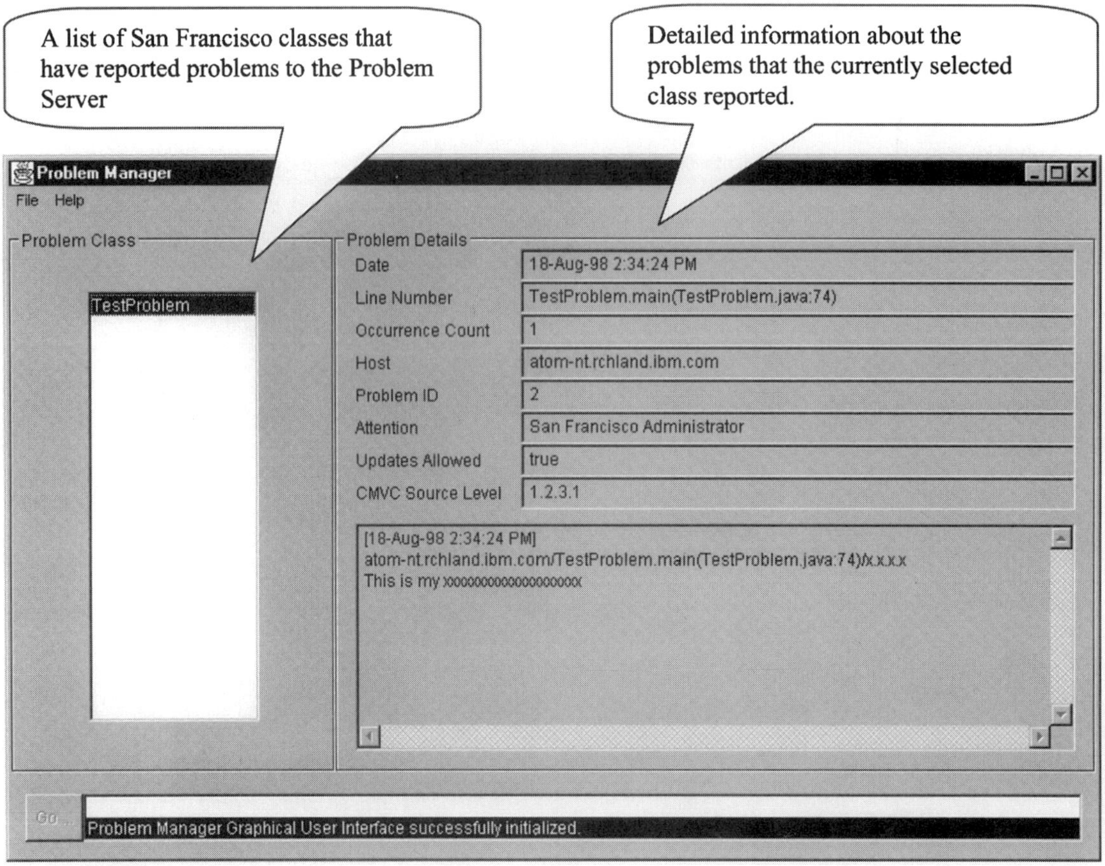

Figure 33-4
Problem manager GUI.

CHAPTER 34

Configuring Servers and Containers

A running SanFrancisco application involves multiple server processes that engage in different tasks relating to a pool of objects. These objects are of course application-specific, and they are held in repositories called "containers."

In order to configure the servers, and define the object containers, SanFrancisco offers a set of configuration tools, which are pretty straightforward to use.

Server Configuration

The SanFrancisco Default Configuration

Table 34-1 details the predefined server processes. Whenever a new host is added to the Logical SanFrancisco Network, it automatically starts a SFSMProcess, which contains the Local Server Manager for this machine.

These are just the default configurations, which can be modified according to your needs. The next section describes how you can do that. The only services whose location cannot be modified are the GSM, GNS, and Security Service, which are hard coded to exist in the SFGSMProcess.

TABLE 34-1

Predefined server configuration

Process Name	Content
SFGSMProcess	■ Global Server Manager (GSM) (hardcoded to live in this server process) ■ Global Name Service (GNS) (hardcoded to live in this server process) ■ Security Service (hardcoded to live in this server process) ■ Factory Service ■ Transaction Service
SFBOProcess1	■ Factory Service ■ Transaction Service
SFBOProcess2	■ Factory Service ■ Transaction Service
SFBOProcess3	■ Factory Service ■ Transaction Service ■ Problem Service
SFBOProcess4	■ Factory Service ■ Transaction Service ■ Conflict Control Service

Using the Server Management Configuration Console

The Server Management Configuration Console is used to configure services in the Logical SanFrancisco Network. As with other SanFrancisco tools, the LSFN must be running in order to use it. In order to start the SanFrancisco Server Management Configuration utility, double-click the "Server Management Configuration" icon in the "Base Utilities" folder, which is in the SanFrancisco program folder. Figure 34-1 shows the Configuration Console that comes up. This console has a tree view of the logical network hierarchy on its left side. The root of the tree represents the entire LSFN, and the next level in the hierarchy represents the

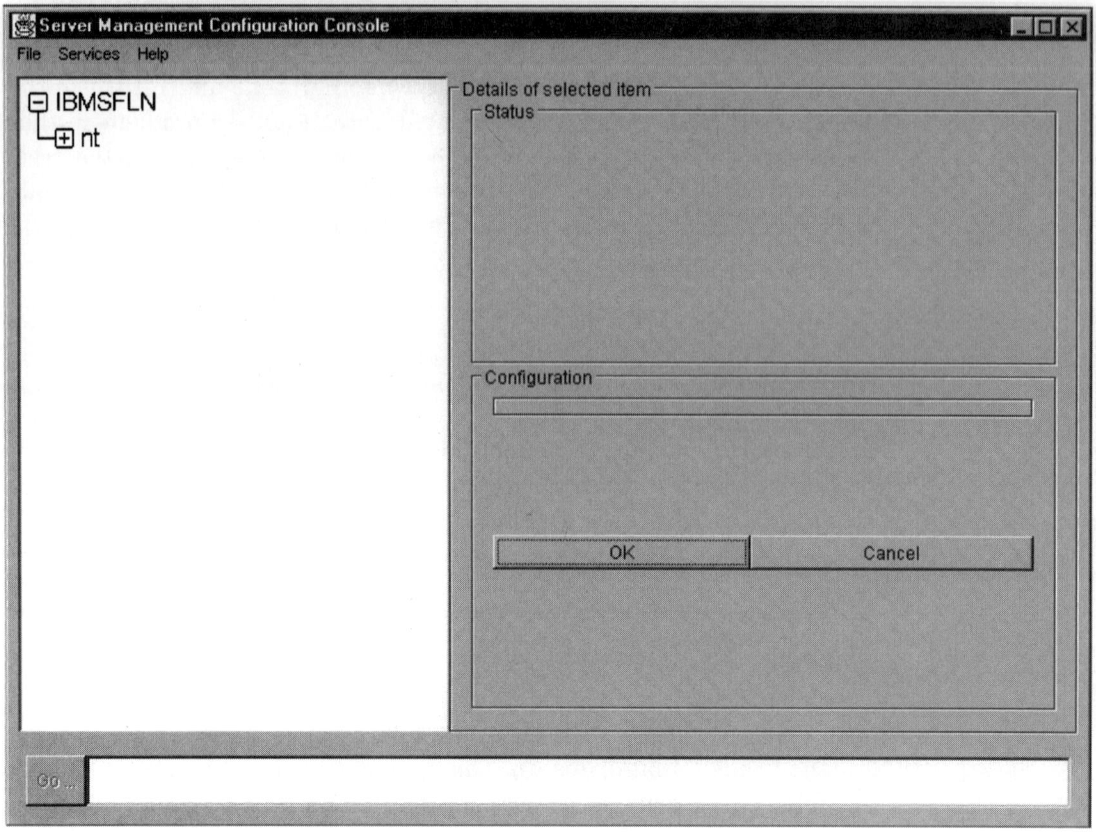

Figure 34-1
Server management configuration console.

various hosts that are presently configured. Under each host, you find nodes that represent the different processes that are configured to execute on that host. Finally, under each process node, you find the Service Objects that are configured to run in that process. The Service objects are "leaves" of the tree, so there is nothing below them. You can traverse this tree-like display in a manner that resembles the way you work with Windows Explorer. You may expand or collapse branches of the tree, and when you select a specific node, the right-hand side of the console will show the specifics of the selected node (i.e. its current configuration information).

A confusing feature of this console is that it never refreshes the display of the current node, but rather shows you the configuration information as it was defined when you started looking at the current node. In other words, any changes made to the node being inspected are not reflected on the display, unless they are made through this console. Specifically, any changes caused by the activities of other users are not reflected in the display. To bypass this, you just select another node and return to the current one, and you get the updated data. Another problem is that sometimes when you add a new node it does not appear in the tree. You can easily overcome this problem by contracting the parent node of the missing node and the expanding it right back.

Manipulating Host Configuration

As you probably figured out from the description in the previous section, to view the configuration of a specific host, you just select the host. The configuration data is displayed on the right-hand side of the window. To add a new host to the logical network, execute the following steps.

1. Highlight IBMSFLN, the topmost node (by clicking on it).
2. Select "New" from the "Services" pull-down menu. A dialog window appears (see Figure 34-2).
3. Type in a valid host name in the text field for "Host Name" in the window that opens up. This host name should include the full TCP/IP name of the host in the regular dotted notation (e.g. workstation1.salesdiv.mycompany.com).
4. Select the operating system on the specified host system in the option menu named "Platform Type."

Figure 34-2
Adding a new host to the LSFN.

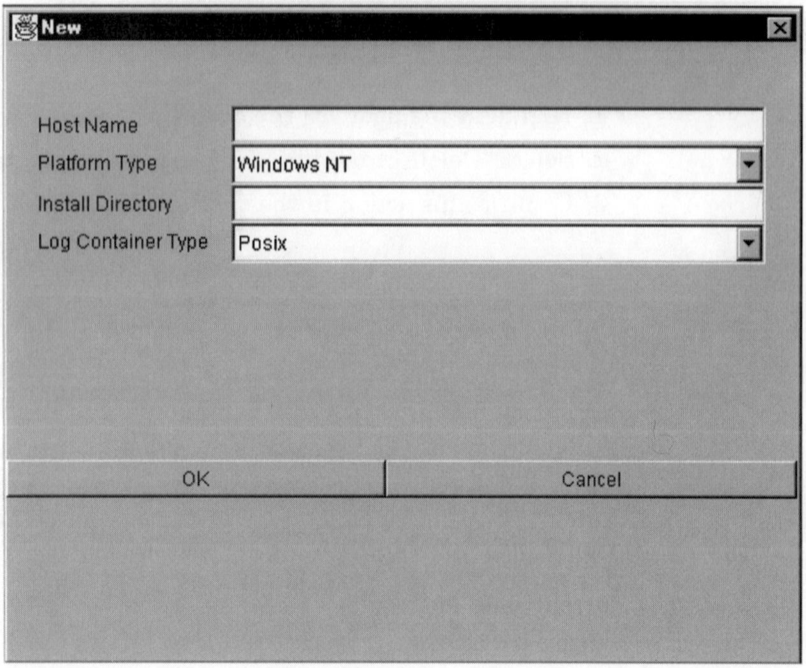

5. Type in the directory path of the SanFrancisco installation on the specified host in the text field "Installation Directory."
6. You may indicate what kind of log container you wish to use in this host, in the option menu titled "Log Container Type."
7. Finally, press the OK button to confirm

It is important to note that this console does not support altering the host data. So, after adding a host to the network, the host configuration data is fixed and cannot be edited. The only way to change the data is to delete the host and repeat the process of adding it, now with the new configuration data.

Once the host is created, you can expand its node to see the processes that are pre-configured to run on it. You may place your service objects in these processes or in new processes you create, as described in the next two sections.

A host can be removed from the LSFN. This can be useful for modifying its configuration or when it is really removed from the network. However, this option should be used carefully because there is no undo function for it, and it removes the host with all the components configured into it. To delete a host, perform the following steps:

1. Highlight the node for the host, by clicking it
2. Select "Delete" from the "Services" pull-down menu
3. Confirm this action in the special window that appears

Manipulating Process Configuration

Similar to hosts, you can view or change the settings for a process, just by clicking on the node representing this process. The data for the selected server shows in the right part of the window. The top line shows the Process Status, which is either active or inactive. The rest of the configuration data shown is explained in the following.

To add a new process, follow these steps:

1. Highlight the node for the host under which you want to add the process (by clicking on it).
2. Select "New" from the "Services" pull-down menu. A window appears in which you can specify the configuration data of the new process (as shown in Figure 34-3).
3. Type in the process name into the first text field. Note that this field cannot be changed for an existing process.
4. Specify the class path for this process in the text field titled "Class Path." If you leave this field empty, the default Java CLASSPATH is used.
5. If you wish, you may modify the initial and maximum heap size to be reserved in the JVM (Java Virtual Machine) for this process. The defaults are 16 000 KB and 64 000 KB, respectively. The maximum heap size is important because if the specified limit is exceeded, the JVM throws an out-of-memory exception to the running process.
6. You may specify a timeout value in the appropriate field. This value is used when an object is accessed with the Timeout value set to DEFAULT_WAIT (see Chapter 14). This value is 30 000 milliseconds by default.

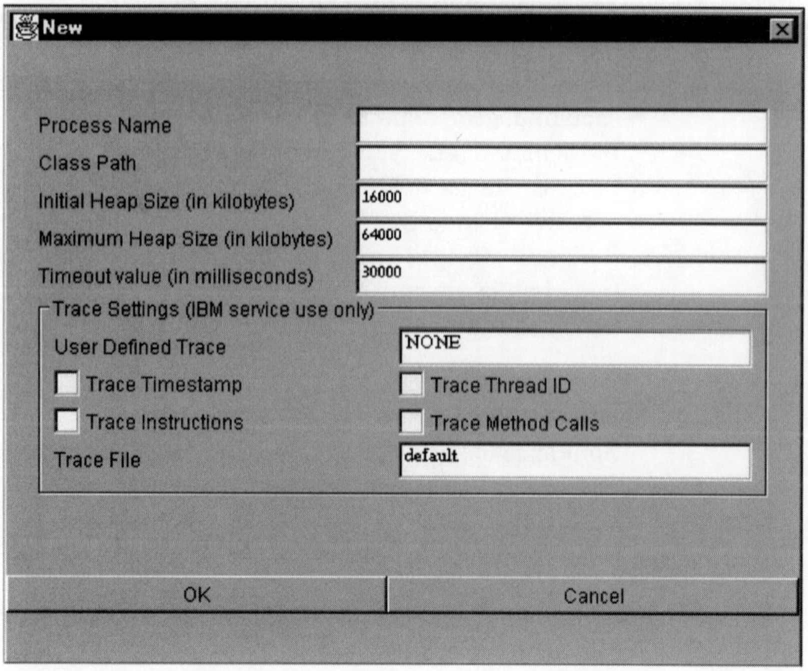

Figure 34-3
Adding a new Server Process.

7. The remaining fields relate to "Trace Setting" that are for use by SanFrancisco services, namely for debugging SanFrancisco. Usually, these are not used.
8. Finally, press the "OK" button to add the process.

A Process can be removed, and the procedure for doing that is almost identical to removing a host. What you have to do is select the services and then select "Delete" from the "Services" menu. You get a confirmation window just like in the case of deleting a host. You should remember to use this feature carefully because, like removing a host, this option does not have an undo function.

A running process can be stopped by pressing the "Stop Process" button. When stopping a process or server, the Server Management Console makes sure an orderly termination takes place, and it notifies other service objects, allowing them to perform any required cleanup actions. For this reason, this is the recommended way for stopping processes, and you should use it while avoiding killing the window that is running the process.

Manipulating Service Configuration

The setting of a certain service can be viewed by selecting the corresponding node. The data for the service is shown on the right side of the window, and you can view or edit it. At the top, you can see the Process Status field. This information field shows whether the service is active or inactive.

For all services except the transaction service, this is the only information that is shown. For a transaction service you also see other data fields, which are explained below in the procedure of adding a new service.

To add a new service, perform the following steps:

1. Select the process in which you wish to add the service, by clicking its node.
2. Select "New" from the "Services" menu. A dialog window appears, as shown in Figure 34-4.
3. Select a service type in the option menu titled "Service Object." As discussed above, this is the only configuration information

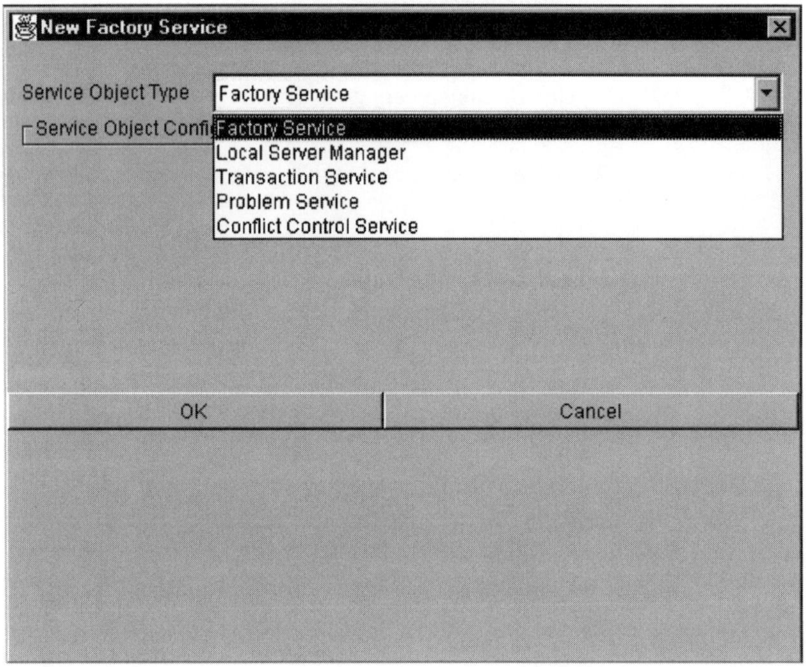

Figure 34-4
Adding a new Service.

you have to specify, for all services except for a Transaction service. Table 34-2 specifies the fields you can modify for a Transaction Service.

4. You may modify the field for "Maximum Retry Attempts", which is 10 by default. You may modify the "Retry Interval" which is 3 by default. You may select the "Heuristic Action," which is to be performed when a `HeuristicException` is thrown. The default is Rollback, but you may change it to Commit (e.g. when your database doesn't support rollback).

Similar to components, services can be deleted by selecting them and choosing "Delete" from the Services menu. A confirmation window appears before the service is removed. Take care when removing a service—this operation cannot be undone.

Container Configuration

The actual location of SanFrancisco (persistent) business objects is of no interest to the developer, as SanFrancisco offers transparency with

TABLE 34-2

Transaction service attributes

Parameter Name	Meaning	Default Value	Comments
Maximum Retry Attempts	The number of times that an application attempts to contact a server during transaction recovery.	10	You might like to have a different value in case your application is complex and runs on a large network
Retry Interval	The length of time (measured in minutes) between the retry attempts made to contact a server during transaction recovery.	3 Minutes	This interval should be changed in cases of complex applications that run on a large network because it might take some time for a new service to start. During development, you might like to reduce this value to 1 to speed up the recovery when testing it.
Heuristic Action	Defines the action taken when the outcome of a transaction cannot be determined.	Rollback	The other option is Commit. It should be used when your database does not support rollback (when a heuristic exception occurs).

respect to object location. However, each object must be placed somewhere. SanFrancisco places persistent business objects in business object containers (BOCs). The task of actual placement is left to an administrator responsible for the site. This person should have the appropriate knowledge of the specific computer and network hardware.

The factory service dynamically instantiates containers, as needed. The factory is responsible for keeping Java references to all active containers within the server process, and it is responsible for routing requests for object creation, deletion, and updates through the appropriate container.

SanFrancisco developers do not need to be concerned with containers, and do not require any information relating to them, other than having the ability to obtain a handle to a BOC (this is done using the Naming service described in Chapter 17).

However, during deployment and administration, you need to be intimately familiar with containers to be able to configure them according to the persistence requirements of the application and the users. Failing to correctly configure class and container information will cause runtime errors.

Before you get to configure containers, you must set the business class configuration data since Containers use it to get the actual class to create a new instance. You can configure all three kinds of business object classes: Entities, Dependents, and Commands.

Configuring Class Data

To configure business class data, you use the "SanFrancisco Configuration" program which resides in the "Base Utilities" folder of the SanFrancisco folder. Open the "Configure" menu, and select "Classes," then "General," and finally either "Entities," "Dependents," "Commands," or "Stores" (see Figure 34-5).

After selecting any of the first three options, you get to the respective class window that lists all classes of the selected type (i.e. all Entities, all Dependents, or all Commands). The "Stores" option is described in the next section. Now, after selecting either "New" from the "Item" menu, or selecting an Entity and then "Modify" from the "Item" menu in the list window, the specific Class Configuration window appears. In this window you can enter or edit the various fields of the class configuration, which are detailed in Table 34-3.

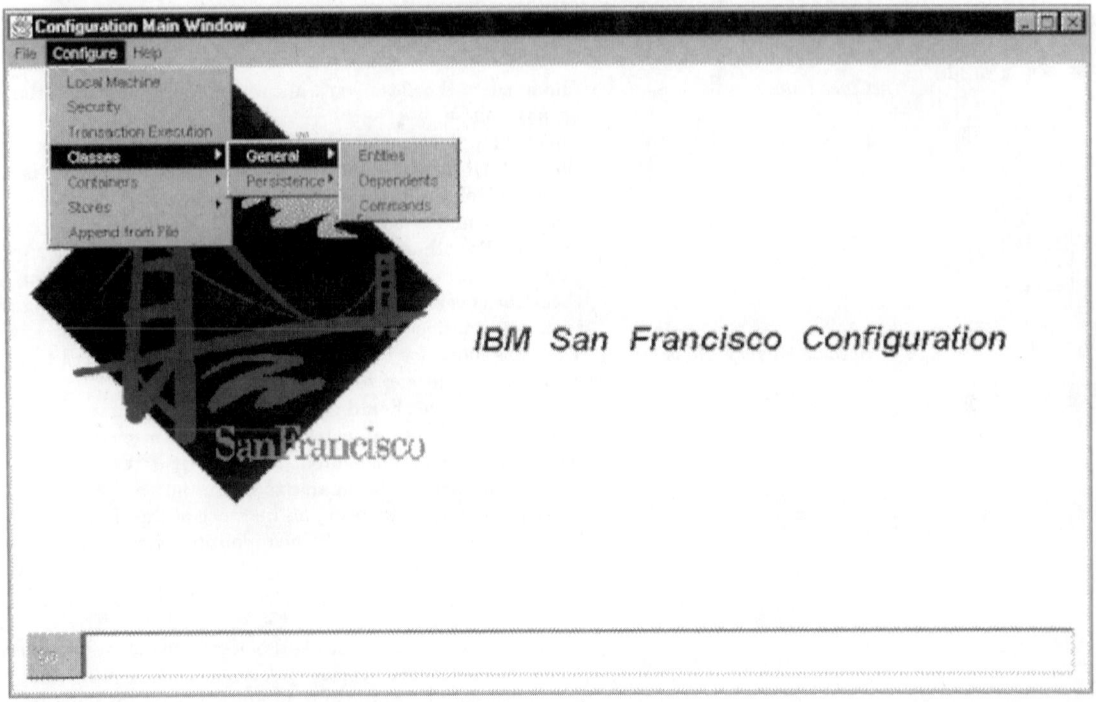

Figure 34-5
Class Configuration using the SanFrancisco Configuration Utility.

In addition to the class data, you need to define Persistence data. Persistence data defines class and container-specific persistence information. For each class, you can define more than one class and container relationship. This data determines which classes a container supports, and is used to provide the metadata that a specific container type needs in order to make instances of a given class persistent. Note that you must configure each and every class that a container will need to support.

To get to the class persistence configuration windows, go to the "Configure" menu, select "Classes" then "Persistence" and finally "RDB" or "POSIX." Now you get a window with a list of all classes with RDB or POSIX persistency, respectively (based on your last choice). Similar to the way class configuration data is edited, you get the configuration window for a specific class after selecting "New" from the "Item" menu or selecting a specific entity and then "Modify" from the same menu.

TABLE 34-3

Class configuration fields

Field Name	Meaning
Class Name	The name of the class you want to configure, including the package name.
Class is not Replaceable	This field indicates whether the class token points to another class, which means, the class is "replaceable." If a class is "replaceable" you can change the actual class for this configuration. For some classes, this field is checked and is inactive. For other classes, the field is active, which means that you can mark a class as not being replaceable. If you check the checkbox, this is irreversible, and the field changes to an information field where you specify the real class.
Special Factory Class Name	The class name for the associated special factory used to create an instance of the class. Again, this name should include the package name. This field is where the factory replacement mechanism of SanFrancisco is implemented. The `BaseFactory` uses this special factory class name to instantiate a special factory, used when creating an instance of the class.
Class Token	The class token is a user-defined identifier for a class. It passed on calls to `Global.factory().createEntity` or `Global.factory.createDependent ()` (depending on whether the class being edited is an Entity or a Dependent) to identify the class to be created. Any name can be selected here, the only limitation is that it must be unique.

If you are editing a class with RDB persistence, you need to fill in (or edit) the data in the fields that are listed in Table 34-4. An example of a window with these fields is shown in Figure 34-6.

Below those fields there is a table that lists the database and the table in which objects of this class are stored. You work with this table just like you would with any other components in the SanFrancisco Configuration application. You can use the "Item" menu to perform the following operations:

- *New*—add a new entry (database or table)
- *Modify*—modify a selected entry; a new window appears in which you modify the data
- *Delete*—delete an entry

Selection and deselection of specific databases or tables is done by clicking on the appropriate entry. You can use the "Edit" menu to "Select All," "Deselect All," and "Invert Selection."

TABLE 34-4

RDB persistent class configuration fields

Field Name	Meaning	Comments
Class Name	The Entity class to be assigned to this container	The same class can be assigned to several containers
Container Name	The RDB container for holding the Entity class.	This container must exist first (i.e. you should create it if it doesn't exist).
Schema Map	■ If the schema map type is DEFAULT, the Java class sets to `com.ibm.sf.gf.OdbcSchemaMapImpl` and is unchangeable. ■ If the schema map type is EXTENDED, this field should hold a Schema Map Language file (.sml file). You do not need to add the .sml suffix because it is added automatically.	The .sml file could be provided as a partial path (and then the full path is obtained by using the SML root path and using the full class name to generate the list of subdirectories). You are supposed to name sml files in the same name as the Java implementation file, and keep them in the same directory.
Schema Map Type	In this field you either set DEFAULT or EXTENDED. ■ DEFAULT—Default schema mapping is quite powerful in that it does not require any code to be written in order to support object persistency. Instead, the default schema mapping code dynamically creates tables and SQL statements that take care of persisting the object in the RDB. This is suitable for simple structures or for a testing environment, because it does have performance drawbacks (resulting from dynamic calculation of SQL statements) and you have no control over the names of tables and columns. ■ EXTENDED—Extended schema mapping still uses the default schema mapping code and, thus, has the same advantages as default. However, you cannot choose your own table and column name because the Schema Map Language file that you provide specifies them.	

Once you use the "New" or "Modify" entries from the "Item" menu when working on the databases table, you get to the RDB store configuration window. An example of this window is shown in Figure 34-7. The fields you can edit in this window are described in Table 34-5 along with their meaning. Note that the fields you can actually edit depend on the schema mapping type you select in the Class RDB Persistence window.

If you are editing a class with POSIX persistence, you need to fill in or edit the data fields that are listed in Table 34-6. An example of how a Class POSIX Persistence Configuration window looks is shown in Figure 34-8.

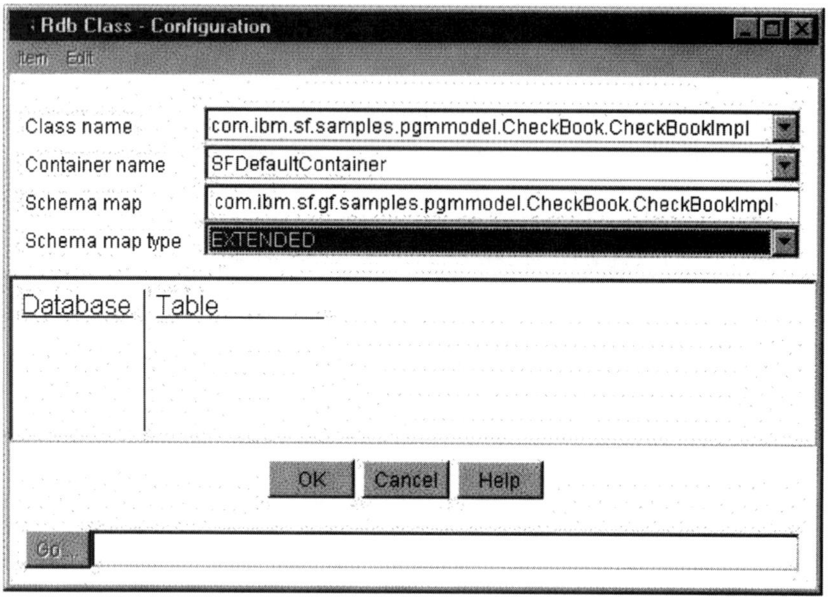

Figure 34-6 Class RDB configuration when using EXTENDED schema mapping.

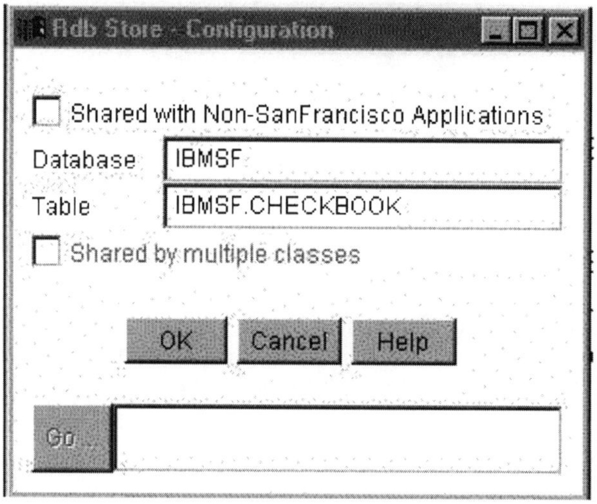

Figure 34-7 RDB store configuration window.

TABLE 34-5

RDB store configuration fields

Field Name	Meaning	Comments
Shared with Non-SanFrancisco Applications	This field indicates whether the store is shared by both SanFrancisco and non-SanFrancisco applications (e.g. legacy software)	
Database	This field holds the name of the database in which the objects of the current class will persist into.	
Table	This file holds the name of the database table in which the objects of the current class will persist into.	
Shared by Multiple Classes	This field indicates whether the data of the objects are persisted to a store that is shared by several classes.	This item is automatically determined by SanFrancisco, hence it is not editable

Viewing or Modifying Persistent Class Stores

You can view a list of all existing stores where classes are stored by going to the "Configure" menu, then selecting "Stores," and then either "RDB," or "POSIX." You select a store to view, or modify from the "Stores with RDB Persistence" window or the "Stores with POSIX Persistence" window by double-clicking on it.

Note that you cannot create new stores; these are created automatically when a class with either RDB or POSIX persistence is configured. You can only modify stores that already exist.

TABLE 34-6

POSIX store configuration fields

Field Name	Meaning	Comments
Class Name	The Entity class assigned to this container	One class can be assigned to several containers
Container Name	The POSIX container where the class resides	
Shared with Non-SanFrancisco Applications	This field indicates whether the store is shared by both SanFrancisco and non-SanFrancisco applications.	
Directory	This field holds the full path of a POSIX directory where the data persists.	

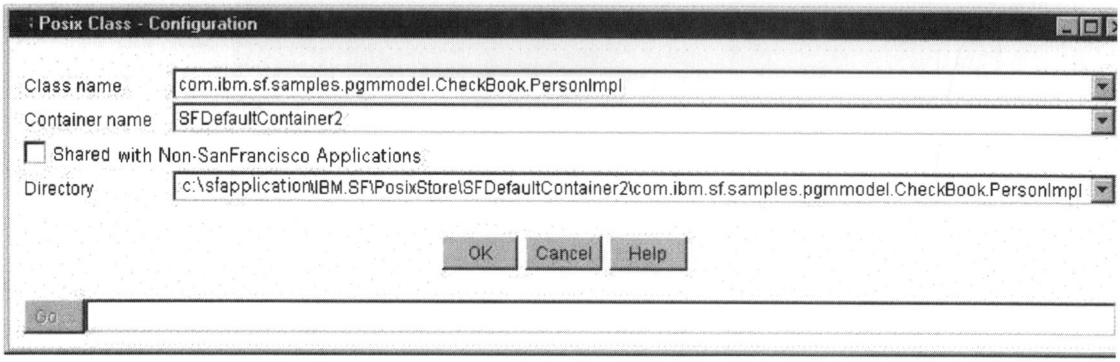

Figure 34-8
POSIX store configuration window.

Configuring Container Data

SanFrancisco supports two kinds of persistent containers:

- RDB containers. Allow storing (persisting) entities in a relational database using ODBC or native database access (see Figure 34-9)
- POSIX containers. Allows storing (persisting) entities in POSIX files. Each entity instance is stored in a separate file. These containers cannot be recovered, and are not very useful for real-world applications. They can be used for playing with SanFrancisco and for testing. See Figure 34-10.

To get to the Container Configuration windows, run the SanFrancisco Configuration application, then select from the "Configure" menu "Containers," and then either "RDB" or "POSIX."

You can then add or edit containers by selecting "New" or "Modify" from the item menu. The configuration data for containers is summarized in the following three tables:

- Table 34-7 shows the configuration data for all containers
- Table 34-8 shows configuration data for RDB containers
- Table 34-9 shows configuration data for POSIX containers

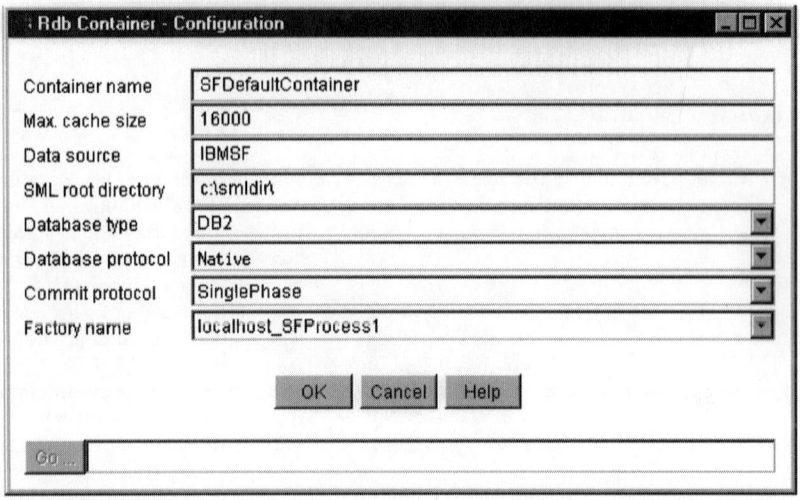

Figure 34-9 Configuration of container with RDB persistence.

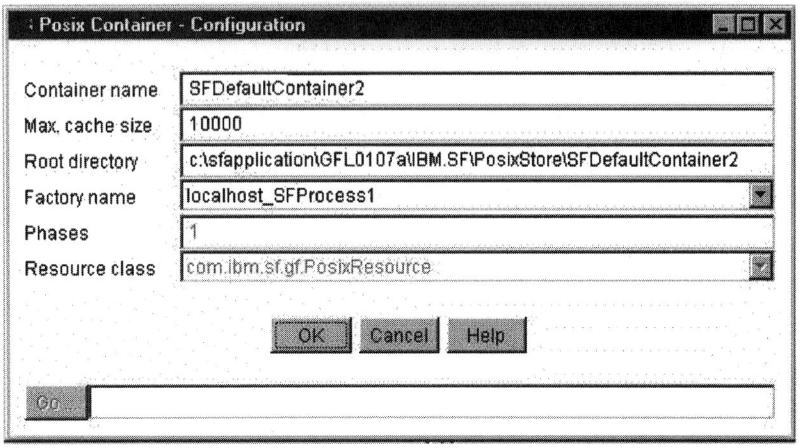

Figure 34-10 Configuration of container with POSIX persistence

TABLE 34-7

Configuration data for all containers

Field Name	Meaning	Comments
Container Name	The name of the container. For normal containers (i.e. non-log container), you can use any name.	Make sure that the log container's container name has the suffix "GBOFLogContainer," otherwise the system does not recognize it as a log container. When creating a container you cannot change a log container into a normal container (or the reverse).
makeCopy	This checkbox is currently inactive.	Reserved for use in future versions.
Max. Cache Size	The value in this field controls the number of objects that a container holds in its memory cache.	The higher this value is, the more main memory the container uses. The default value is 5000 entities. This value should be set according to the available physical memory (the rule of thumb here is to have about 5000 entities for each 64 MB you have; however, because Entity sizes can vary, these figures should be finely tuned according to the resulting amount of paging).
Factory Name	Select the factory server process where this container is defined.	
Resource Class	This is an information field for POSIX containers. The resource class is always com.ibm.sf.gf.PosixResource	Not used for RDB containers

TABLE 34-8

Configuration data for RDB containers

Field Name	Meaning	Comments
Data Source	The name of the ODBC data source that you configure for your database.	If no value is specified, the default value `ibmsf` is used.
SML Root Directory	This is the path where the sml files reside, excluding the path that makes up the package name.	The path should be specified according to the convention used in the specific platform (i.e. / for UNIX, \ for Windows). In any case, the schema map may use periods to separate directories, and at runtime the periods convert to the correct character for the platform.
Database Type	This field determines the database used (DB2 or Oracle).	The default is DB2.
Database Protocol	This field determines the required database access protocol to use. *Native* (i.e. use the native database APIs) appears automatically in this field if the Database type is set to *DB2*. "*Odbc*" (i.e. use ODBC APIs for database access) appears automatically in this field if the Database type is set to "*Oracle*".	This field is unchangeable unless the Database type is changed:
Commit Protocol	This field determines the required commit protocol, which is either *SinglePhase* or *TwoPhase*.	TwoPhase Commit is currently not available for Oracle. A single-phase container cannot ensure recovery in the case of system failures.

TABLE 34-9

Configuration data for POSIX containers

Field Name	Meaning	Comments
Phases	This field determines the required commit protocol. That is, the protocol for either a single-phase or a two-phase datastore.	For POSIX containers, this is always 1
Root Directory	This field holds the full path to the root directory of this POSIX container store. For each class that you configure to use, this POSIX container subdirectory is created under this root, and there the files storing specific objects are created.	If you do not specify this directory the default value is "<Installdir>/IBM.SF".

CHAPTER 35

Security and Conflict Configuration

This chapter explains two different aspects of SanFrancisco configuration, namely security and conflict control.

Security Configuration

In general, security in computer systems can be implemented at the application level or at the system level. SanFrancisco implements security at the level of the application. This way, the security administration is done centrally and is managed using a common interface for all platforms and, more importantly, is consistent across all platforms and applications. The SanFrancisco security mechanisms can be complemented by any external mechanisms working in the operating system level.

SanFrancisco provides the client programmer with low-level APIs that implement authentication, verifications, and an easy way to use this to present a complete out-of-the-box logon window, which can be used to establishing the identity of a user. In addition, an API is provided to define secure tasks that consist of security-sensitive actions. A typical use of this API is in the application's installation routine, where the administrator authorizes individual users or groups of users to perform specific operations that are considered to be secure tasks.

The configuration tools enable you to define the following components of the security configuration:

- security policy;
- users and user groups; and
- access rights.

The remainder of this section describes how to configure these components.

Security Policy Configuration

SanFrancisco requires that for each LSFN a security configuration be defined. This configuration determines the security policies for the LSFN. These do not affect and are unrelated to security policies in the data store or the operating system.

To view and edit the security configuration, you need to start the SanFrancisco Configuration program. To do that, follow these steps.

1. Open the SanFrancisco folder
2. Open the "Base utilities" folder
3. Double-click on the "SanFrancisco Configuration" icon

Once the configuration program is running, select "Security" from the configuration menu. The Security Configuration window appears, as shown in Figure 35-1. The various fields in this window are described in Table 35-1.

User Configuration

User configuration is managed through the User Administration tool. To start it, follow these steps.

1. Open the SanFrancisco folder
2. Open the "Base Utilities" folder
3. Double-click the "User Administration" icon

Once this utility is started, the "Edit—All Users" window appears, as shown in Figure 35-2. You can use this window to add or change the users and user groups to which you want to assign access rights. The actual assignment of these rights, however, is done in the "Access Rights Administration" tool described below.

In order to add or modify a user, use this window. Select a user group by clicking it, and then "Create member" or "Edit," respectively, from the "Selected" menu. A window appears in which you select whether you want to create a user or a further user group within the selected user group. Select "User" and press the "OK" button. Then, a window appears in which you can edit the following user data:

- *UserId*. A mandatory field for the user id is assigned to the user. This user id should be unique (within each LSFN).
- *First Name*. A mandatory field holding the first name of the user.
- *Last Name*. A mandatory field holding the last name of the user.
- *Description*. An optional field that holds any additional information about the user.

TABLE 35-1

Security configuration window fields.

Field Name	Meaning	Comments
Userid required	Indicates whether users need to go through a login process in order to run SanFrancisco programs.	This must be set (to be on) before you can use the User Administration, Access Rights Administration, or Server Rights Administration utilities. The values "Password required", "Secure task checking", and "Server authorization" are disabled if this option is not on. When setting this to on, you should specify the administrator userid (which is Administrator by default).
Password required	Indicates whether users should require passwords when logging in.	This field is disable if the "userid required" field is off. When setting this to on, you should specify the administrator password.
Max. Retries	Determines how many failed attempts at password entry are allowed before the application exits.	This is not a very effective security measure because the application can be restarted.
Number of password saves	Determines how many old passwords the system saves.	Old passwords cannot be used when changing the password.
Signing required	Indicates if you use digital signing to verify all security objects on your network.	This feature is supposed to make the system tougher to hack, but has some performance penalties.
Password life in days	Determines how many days a password remains valid until it expires, and the user is forced to change it.	
Allow repeating characters	Indicates whether the password is allowed to contain two consecutive identical characters.	
Password minimal length	The minimal number of characters a password must have.	
Password maximal length	The maximal number of characters a password can have.	
Forbidden characters	Specifies characters that are not allowed in passwords.	
Secure task check	Indicates whether the system should perform a check.	

If the security policy for your system includes password verification, password information is shown too. You can edit the following fields:

- *Password defined*. Indicates whether the user has a password defined for him
- *Number of Days Until Password Expires*. This field indicates how long it will take before the user must change their password.

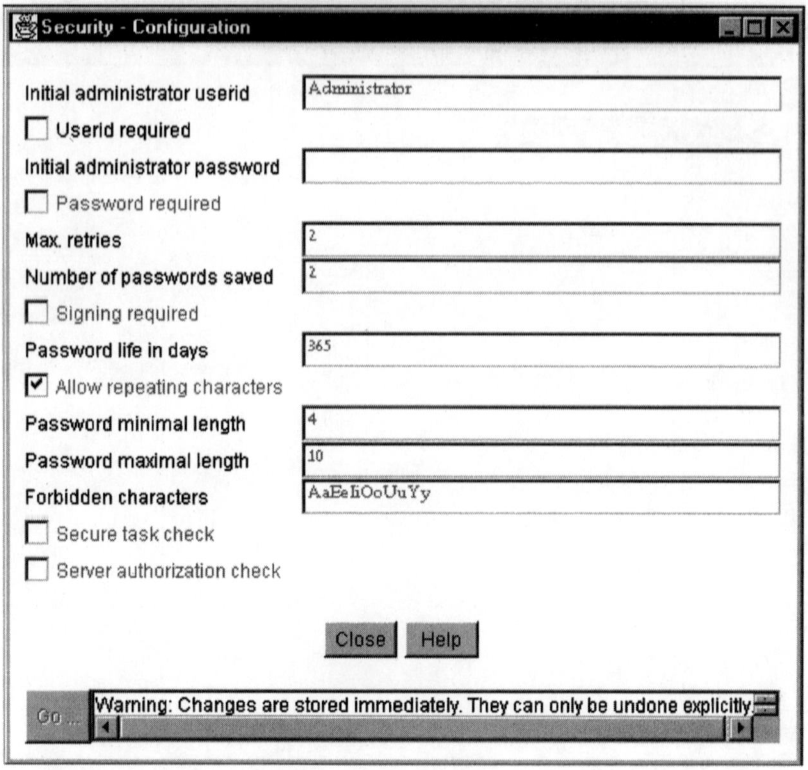

Figure 35-1
Security configuration window.

- *User Active*. This checkbox allows you to activate or deactivate the user. The user can log into the system if (and only if) the checkbox is marked.

To actually define a password for a user, press the "Set Password" button; a window appears in which you can set an initial password for a user. The "Set Password" button is only available if specified in the security configuration. In the window you can fill in the following fields:

- *Userid*. This field shows the user when the password is changed.
- *New Password*. The password is entered in this field.
- *Confirm Password*. The password is entered again.

In order to confirm your entry, press the "OK" button.

To create or modify a user group, you follow a similar procedure. Select a parent-user group, which may be "All users" or any other group in the User Administration window. "Create Member" from the "Selected"

Figure 35-2
Users configuration utility.

menu; a window appears in which you select whether you want to create a user or a user group within the selected user group. Select "User group" and press the "OK" button. Then, a window appears in which you can specify the appropriate values. If you wish to edit an existing group select "Edit" in the "Selected" menu. The following fields can be edited for a user group.

- *Name*. This mandatory field holds a unique name for the user group.

- *Description*. This optional field holds any details that describe the user group.

Introducing the concept of user groups simplifies the administration of access rights because you can manage access permissions collectively for a group of users performing a certain set of actions.

Inside the "Edit—All Users" window you are able to copy, move, and remove items and groups of items using the entries under the "Selected" menu. This menu offers you standard "Copy", "Cut," and "Paste" options. You can also use drag-and-drop to move items around. You can view items in separate windows using the "Open Sub-tree" and "Open List" commands under the "Selected" menu, which show you a hierarchical (tree-like) view of a specific group, and a flat view of all items and groups, respectively. The lists inside these windows can be expanded and collapsed using the appropriate entries in the "View" menu. Similar to the way Windows Explorer works, an entry marked with a plus sign ("+") can be expanded, and an entry with a minus sign ("–") can be collapsed.

When you close the "User Administration Configuration" without saving, or if you try closing the "User Administration Configuration" tool without closing properly from the "File" menu, a confirmation window appears. This window is shown in Figure 35-3 along with the meaning of its buttons.

Access Rights Configuration

Access rights are configured using the SanFrancisco "Access Right Administration Utility." You may define access rights either for specific users or for specific servers. This section deals with both kinds of access rights. To start the Access Rights Configuration tool, perform the following operations:

1. Open the SanFrancisco folder.
2. Open the Base Utilities folder.
3. Double-click on one of the following:
   - Access Rights Administration icon: to administer access rights that allow a user to perform certain actions for a set of objects.

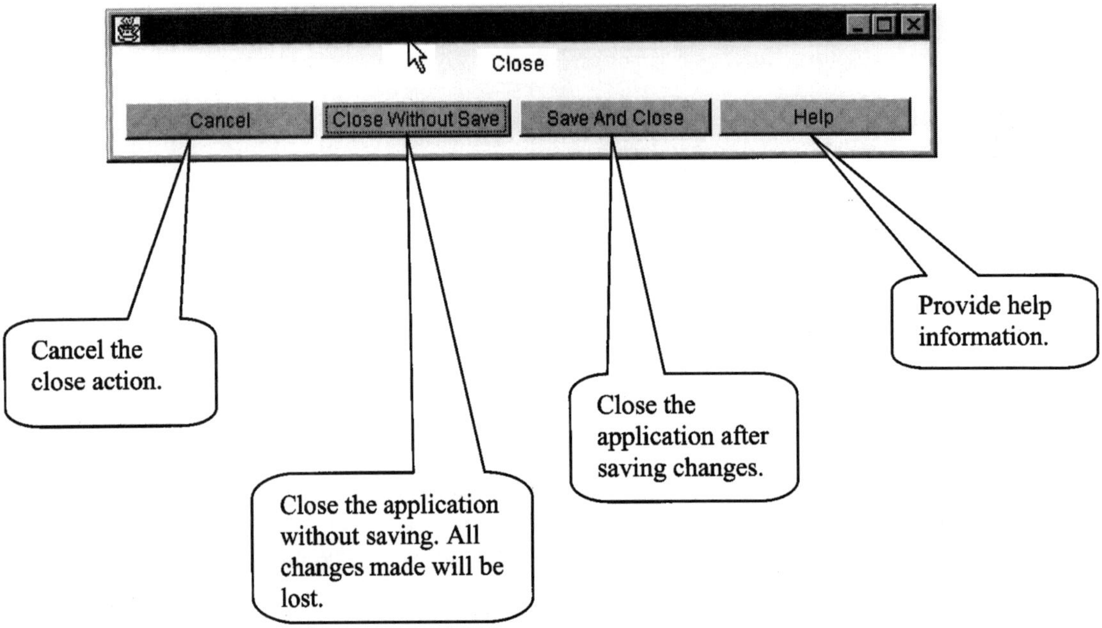

Figure 35-3
Buttons in warning dialog display upon unexpected "Close".

- Server Access Rights Administration icon: to administer access rights that allow a user to access objects that are stored on a specific server.

In order to start working with access rights, you first have to add in users and groups as described above. Set the "Userid required" checkbox in the Security section of the SanFrancisco Configuration utility (see Figure 35-1); this is a prerequisite for enabling access right verification in SanFrancisco. In other words, if this checkbox is not selected, the Access Right Administration utility will not start. If you also want to secure the actions by forcing the user to enter a password, enable this option in the same dialog.

After you start the Access Right Administration, you get to the main window. This main window consists of three data columns.

- *Users*. Shows all SanFrancisco users and user groups. All users and user groups are contained in the top-level group called "All users."

- *Actions*. Shows all actions that are performed within the application, for which you define the access rights.
  - Access Rights Administration. The application provides a list of actions, and cannot change. However, what you can do to ease the task of assigning access rights, is create action groups. You can then define access rights for a whole action group instead of defining this for each action individually.
  - Server Access Rights Administration. The only action is "Use"
- *Resources*. Shows all resources with which users can perform certain actions.
  - Access Rights Administration. The resource list is determined by the Foundation layer. Currently, the resources consist of companies only. In future, other kinds of resources might be supported. The application provides a list of resources that cannot be modified. This is in contrast to the actions.
  - Server Access Rights Administration. Shows all the servers that are configured.

If you want to enable authorization checking, based on the server access rights that you define, the *Server authorization* must be enabled. To do that, you need to enable *Server authorization* in the Security section of the SanFrancisco Configuration utility.

You create an access right by selecting data in each column. This way you define which user or user group is allowed to perform which action (or actions) with which resource (or resources).

You can also query the access rights from different points of view, by selecting "Open Access Rights" from the "Selected" menu.

- For a resource, you can see which user (or users) is allowed to perform which action (or actions) for this resource (or resources).
- For an action, you can see which user (or users) is allowed to perform this action for which resource (or resources).
- For a user, you see the action (or actions) this user is allowed to perform for which resource (or resources).

Once you select "Actions" from the edit menu, the "Edit—All Actions" window appears (see Figure 35-4). The list of actions shown is a complete list of actions for the specific applications. This list is totally dependent on the specific applications and you cannot modify it. What you can do is create and change action groups.

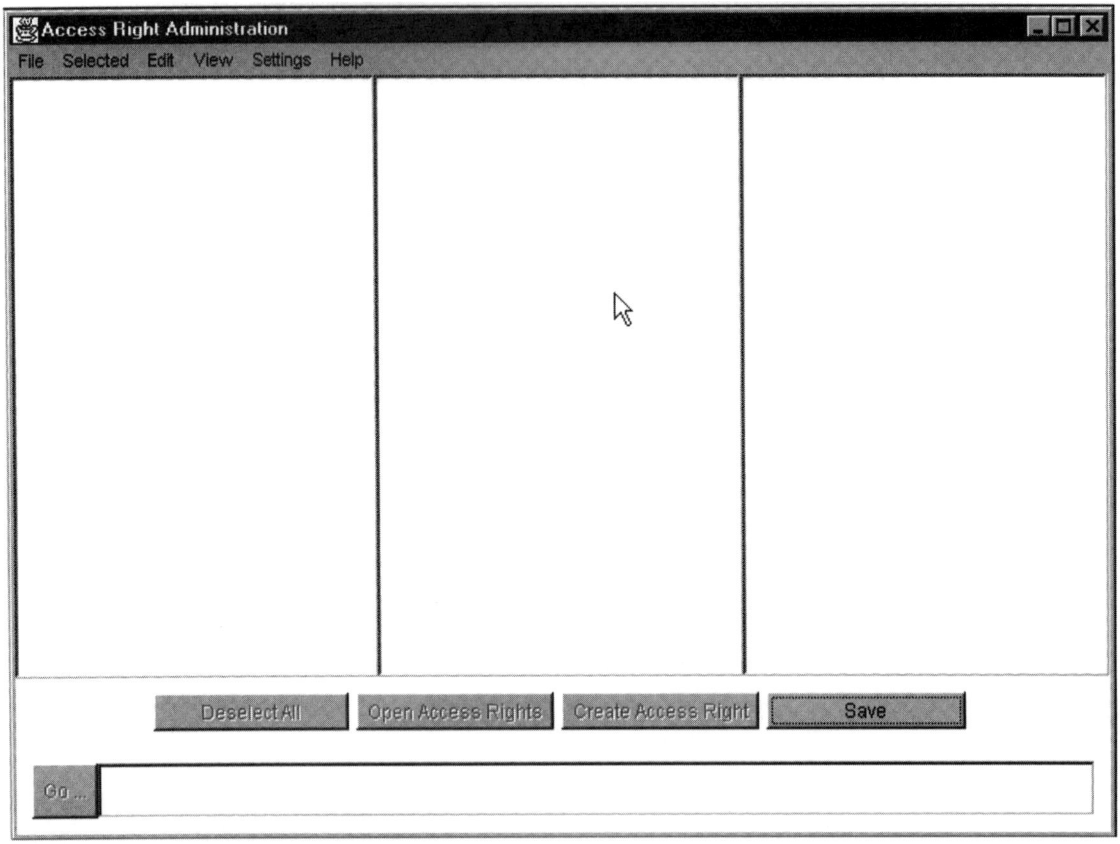

Figure 35-4
Access rights configuration utility: "Edit—All Actions" window.

To change action groups, select a group. This might be "All actions" or any other group. Then choose "Create Member" from the "Selected" menu, and a window will appear in which you specify an action group in the selected group. You may edit the following items (you can also get to this window for an existing group by selecting "Edit" from the "Selected" menu after selecting a group, or just by double-clicking on a group):

- *Name*. A mandatory field, holding a unique name for the action group you want to create or modify.
- *Description*. Holds an optional description of the action group.

In order to define which user is allowed to perform which operation on which resource, you define access rights. When creating an access right, you define who is allowed to do what for which resource. To do that you select a user or user group, an action or action group, and a resource you would like the user(s) to perform the selected action(s) upon. Now you choose "Creates Access Right" from the "Selected" menu (pushing the "Create Access Right" button has the same effect).

The status area now shows a message saying that the access right has been defined but not saved. If you are sure you want to keep the created access right, press the Save button or select "Save" from the "File" menu. As you can imagine, this will save your definition. If you want to discard this newly created access right, you can select "Reset" from the "File" menu. This restores the configuration data of the last save. You can also delete a specific Access Right.

This is done by using "Open Access Rights" from the "Selected" menu (or just pushing the "Open Access Rights" button), as mentioned above, this opens a list of actions, depending on the selected object (and whether it is a user, action, or resource). In this list you can remove entries using "Delete" from the "File" menu.

Conflict Control

In a business application, there are some actions that must not run concurrently because this might lead to erroneous or inconsistent results. Actions or groups of actions that must not be executed at the same time are referred to as "Conflicts." The Conflict Control service manages the execution of conflicting actions.

An action can conflict not only with another action or group of actions, it can also conflict with itself (e.g. end-of-quarter closing that must not be started twice). Parameters can qualify actions in order to determine when conflicts occur (for example, the action A for company X can be started while the action B for company Y is running).

The conflict control utility helps you define potential conflicts and makes sure that conflicting actions are not being run at the same time. For the purpose of our presentation of conflict control, consider an action to be synonymous with a method.

Conflict Control Administration Utility

The purpose of the Conflict Control Administration Utility is to create and maintain conflict definitions. To start this utility, you need to follow a similar procedure like the utilities described previously in this chapter. Namely, you need to double-click the “Conflict Control Administration” icon under the “Conflict Control” folder residing in the “Base Utilities” folder in the SanFrancisco folder.

With the conflict control administration utility you can create conflict definitions (called “conflicts” in the remainder of this chapter) between certain actions in your application. If predefined conflicts already exist in your application, you can use this tool to analyze and refine the conflict definitions. If no predefined conflicts are defined, the window shows a root category under which you can now add any conflicts you want to define. Figure 35-5 shows the Conflict Control Administration tool, along with an explanation of the two parts of its display.

Like in the Access Right Administration tool, user operation can be conducted either through the “File”, “Edit,” and “Help” entries in the menu bar, or by the buttons at the bottom of the window. Either way, you get the same functionality. The other menu-bar entries control the display.

For both the left and the right parts of the windows, you have a menu bar entry, named “Item definition and selection” and “Conflict definition,” respectively (Figure 35-6). In these menus you may define the type of view in the respective window. The types of views available are:

- *Tree View*. This view, which is the default view, shows hierarchical display of the actions and action categories. Each level can be collapsed and expanded, using the same menus corresponding to the two parts of the window (these menus have an entry for expanding and collapsing levels). In this view you only see the id of each action or category. This shows a graphical view of the categories and actions hierarchy.
- *Details View*. This view shows the actions and categories in a list. In this display, you may not expand or collapse levels, but you get to see a little more detail about items, namely the id and type (category or action), which are also shown in the tree view, and also the description of each item.

In order to create a new action or action category, select the respective entry from “New subitem” in the “Selected Menu”. You have the choice of

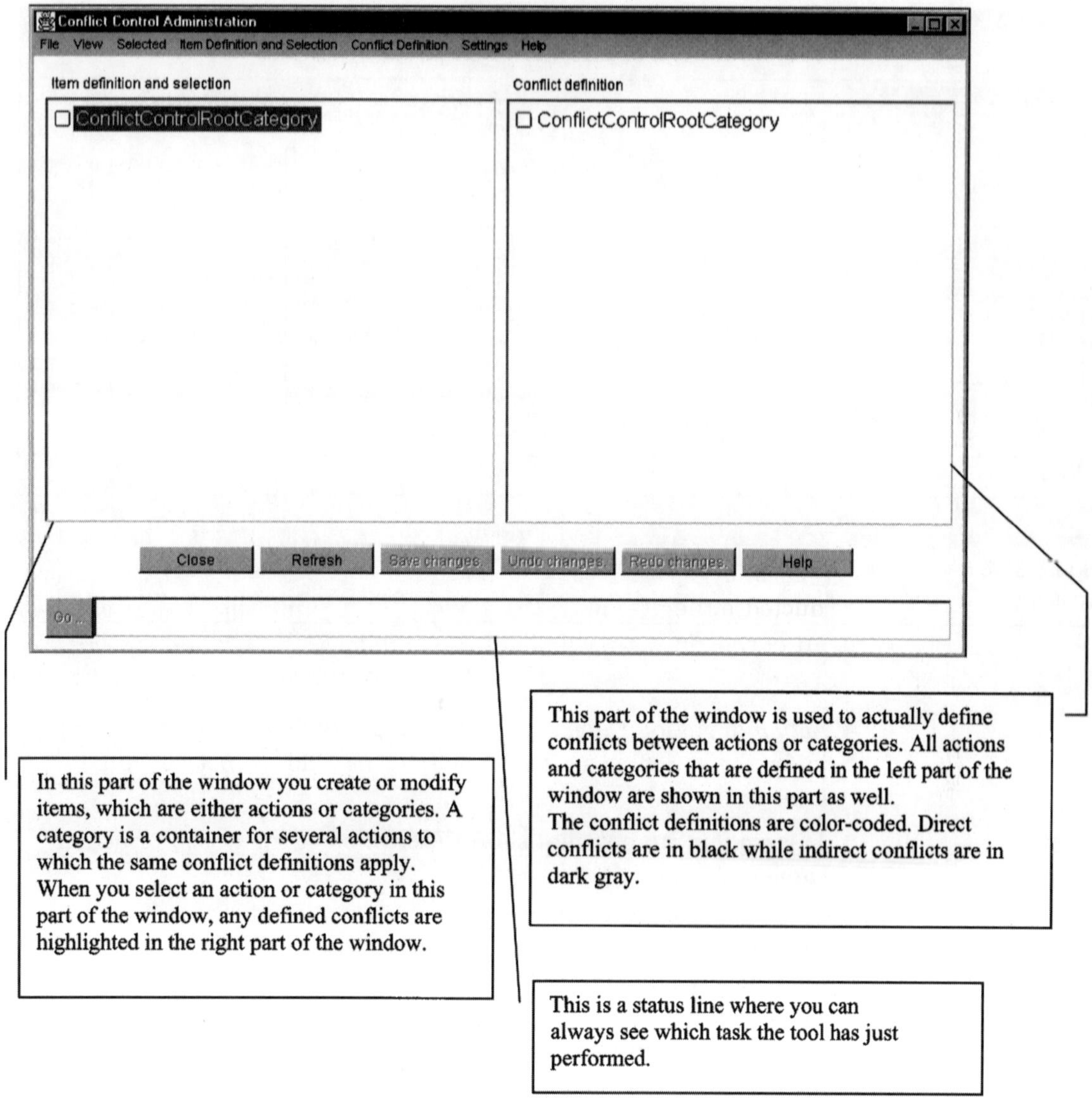

Figure 35-5
Conflict control administration tool.

"Action" or "Action Category." After selecting a parent, go to *Selected*, *New subitem*, and then *Action* or *Action category*. You get to a dialog where you can enter the data for a new action or category. In this dialog, you should provide the following fields:

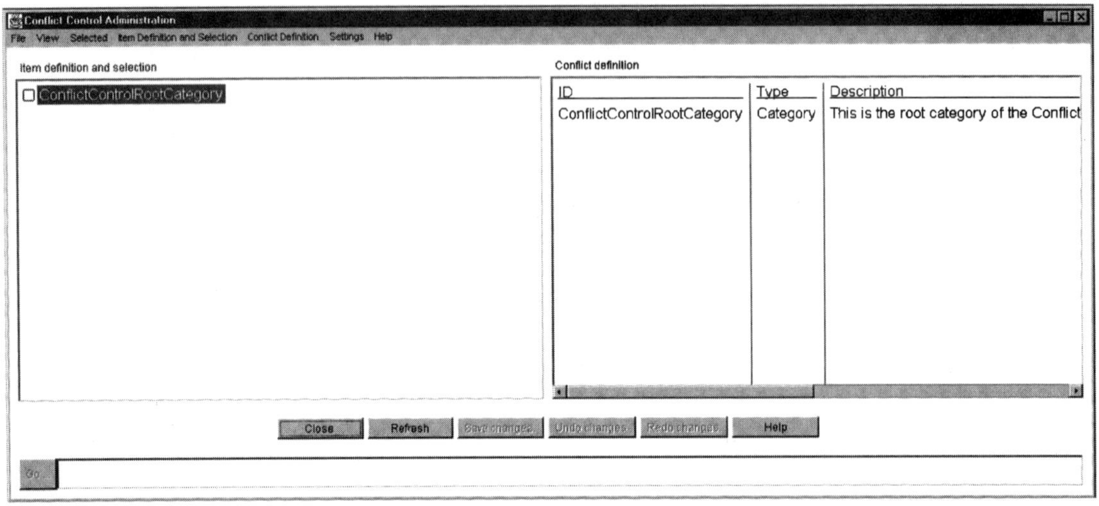

Figure 35-6
Conflict control administration utility with the details view for conflict definitions.

- *Action* or *Action Category id*. A mandatory field holding a unique id for the action or action category. This field cannot be edited later on.
- *Description*. An optional short description of the action or action category.

You may commit your edit by pressing the "OK" button on the bottom of the dialog window. Once you do that, the new action or action category is added to the parent you selected. If you wish to edit the action or action group you choose "Edit" from the "Select" menu. If you do that, you get a dialog similar to the last one described, only that the id field is read only, and you can only edit the "Description" field.

The main purpose of this application is to create conflict definitions. You can create a conflict definition between two actions, between two categories, or between an action and a category. The only exception is the root category for which you may not define any conflicts. To add a new conflict between actions or categories select an action or category on the left part of the window (titled "Item Definition"), and another action or category on the right part of the window (titled "Conflict Definition"). Once you perform the second selection, you've completed adding the new conflict. The status bar shows a message indicating that a conflict definition was created. Note that the action or category for which this conflict was created is highlighted in a folder that indicates the type of conflict. This color-coding, explained in Table 35-2 is applicable whenever you select an item that has conflicts defined for it (or when you add a new conflict).

As indicated in Table 35-2, you may query the cause of indirect conflict. This can be done using the "Conflicts Causing Indirect Conflicts" entry under "Show" from the "Selected" menu. Once you select a specific conflict and press "OK", you get to the Causing Conflicts View. This view shows the conflict you are interested in and, below it in a table, you see one or more categories that have direct conflicts; these are precisely the reason why an indirect conflict exists for the former conflict.

When working with this tool, especially when several people have access to the system, it is important to remember to occasionally use the "Refresh" button. This way you can see changes done by other users since the time that you started. The same effect can be achieved by selecting "Refresh" from the "File" menu.

Conflict Control Maintenance Utility

The purpose of the Conflict Control Maintenance Utility is to monitor active actions and enable troubleshooting if it is needed. The user interface is similar to the tool described in the previous section. In order to start this utility, you double-click the "Conflict Control Maintenance" icon in the "Conflict Control" folder.

You can use the maintenance utility for several purposes.

- Monitoring active actions
- Reloading new or changed conflict definitions

TABLE 35-2

Conflict color-coding.

Color	Meaning
Light gray	This item has only indirect conflicts, which do not result from your editing. You can query the cause of indirect conflicts.
Medium gray	This item has only direct conflicts, which are conflicts defined explicitly by your operations.
Dark gray	The item has both direct and direct conflicts.

- Troubleshooting in case an action has ended abnormally. It can happen that such an action is not automatically deleted from the active actions list and, thus, prevents other actions from being started. In such cases, you must manually delete the action.

The Conflict Control Maintenance Utility display is shown in Figure 35-7. The conflict control maintenance utility presents the list of active actions in a table. The information represents the state at the time when you started the utility, or when you last refreshed the list.

As with the Conflict Administration tool, the list of active actions does not automatically refresh and, therefore, does not represent the latest

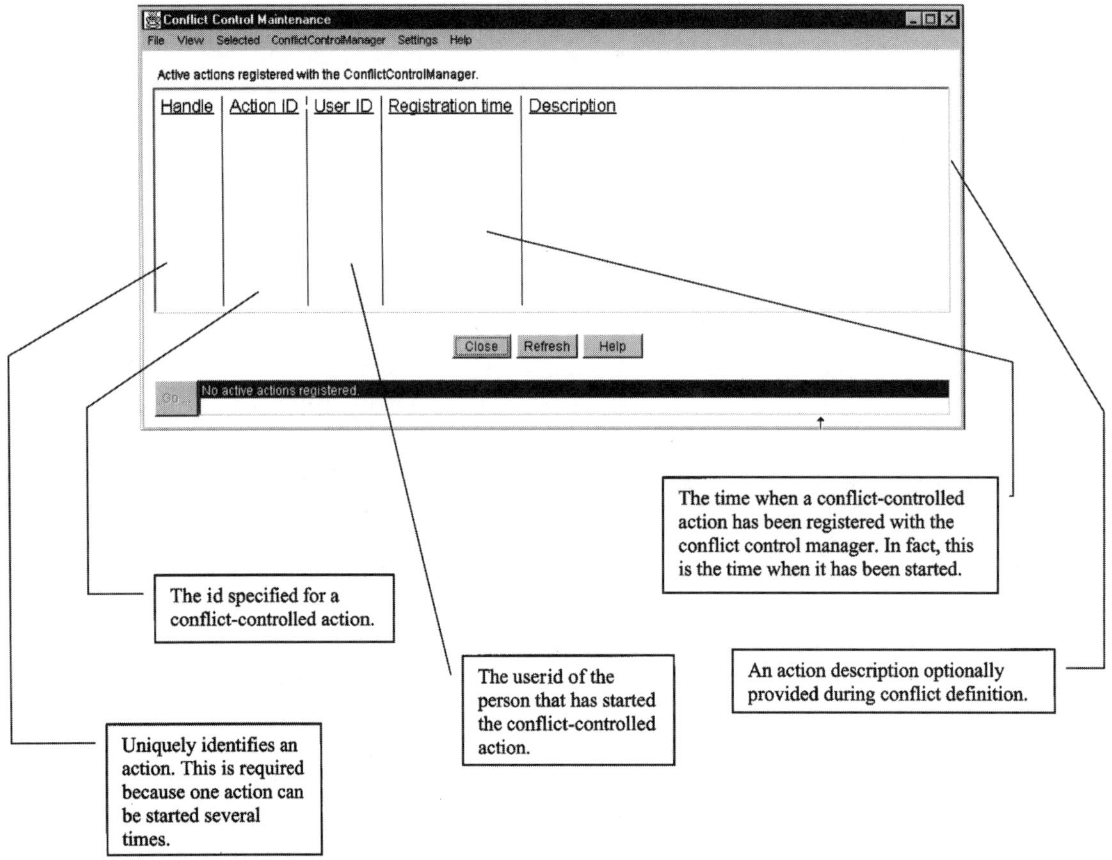

Figure 35-7
Conflict control maintenance utility

situation. The list can be manually refreshed either by selecting "Refresh" from the "File" menu or by pressing the "Refresh" button. "Refresh" is especially important before you start analyzing or solving potential problems.

Action parameters represent optional information that is supplied by the application during runtime. They provide additional information about an action. If you need to delete an active action and there are several actions with the same action id, the parameters help identify the action to be deleted. To query the parameters of an active action, select the action. Select "Show Parameters" from the "Selected" menu. If the "Show Parameters" option is inactive, this means there are no specified parameters for this action.

There might be situations where you might want to prevent any additional actions from starting. The most common situation will be that you want to load new or changed conflict definitions without interfering with any actions currently running. In some rare situations, you might also use this function to hunt down a hanging action that must be manually deleted. Disabling action registration means that no further conflict-controlled actions can start and register with the conflict control manager. Therefore, make sure that you enable action registration again as soon as possible because this has an adverse effect on users of your system. Any current running actions will not be affected. These actions can be completed normally, and only then can they be deregistered and removed from the list. To enable or disable registration of actions, select "Action Registration" from the "Conflict Control Manager" menu, and then "Enable" or "Disable," respectively.

Consider a case where for whatever reason an action terminates abnormally. It is possible that this action was not removed from the active actions list and not de-registered with the conflict control manager. As a result, any other actions that conflict with this action cannot start, and unless something is done to amend the situation, they will never be able to start.

In order to rectify the situation you must manually delete the hanging action. Find out which one of the actions is causing this deadlock situation. One indication is an extremely long duration since registration time (i.e. the difference between current time and the registration time). Then, you could contact the user who started this action to find out what is going on with this action. If this is not possible, the action description or the action's parameters could provide a clue as to why certain other actions cannot be started. Another possibility, which is a little extreme, is to disable registration of further actions. If you wait for enough time, all running actions will gradually disappear from the active actions list as they complete execution, while the hanging action will stay in the list. Obviously, this option should not be used on a running system with real users.

Once you manage to identify which action should be deleted, go ahead and select the action. You do that by selecting "Delete" from the "Selected" menu. The maintenance utility removes the action from the list, without presenting you with another confirmation window.

Conflict definitions can be created and modified in the Conflict Control Administration utility described in the previous section. When completed, the new definitions need to be activated at a certain point in time. Before you load the new conflict definitions, you are advised to make sure that, at this point in time, no conflict-controlled actions are running. Once you make sure of that you just disable the registration of new actions (as explained above), and repeatedly refresh the active actions list until you see it is empty (i.e. no actions are currently running), and finally select "Reload Definitions" from the "Conflict Control Manager" menu. As soon as the new definitions are loaded, you should re-enable action registration.

Tracing and Warning Settings

Both the Conflict Control tools and the Access Rights Administration tool provide tracing capabilities. These are turned off by default, but you may turn them on by selecting "Trace" from the "Settings" menu, then "On." Note that turning tracing on will have a certain (negative) effect on performance.

The Conflict Control Administration tool also has a warning facility that can be turned on or off from the "Settings" menu. This feature is on by default, and might be turned off to boost performance. You should do that only if you are quite sure you will not need these warnings.

CHAPTER 36

Packaging an Application

This is the final chapter, so the only thing left to discuss is how to package your application so that you can ensure a smooth installation.

SanFrancisco Application Packaging

The essential difference between packaging and deploying a SanFrancisco application and packaging and deploying any other Java program is that the SanFrancisco components must be first installed on the target machine before the application can be installed. Therefore, you must provide the SanFrancisco installation bundled with your own installation.

The main choice to be made is whether to package your own code together with the SanFrancisco code and use one installation program, or to use two separate installation programs. While it is quite straightforward to provide the user with the illusion of a single installation program, the latter method is a far better choice. By separating the installation of your own application from that of SanFrancisco you avoid a lot of potential headaches, especially when it comes to supporting multiple platforms.

There are quite a few products aimed at helping you create an installation file for your applications. For the 32-bit Windows platforms (Windows 95/98 and Windows NT), the most common installation in use is the InstallShield® product from the InstallShield Software Corporation (http://www.installshield.com). The 32-bit Windows version of SanFrancisco is installed using this product. You may modify the installation of SanFrancisco on these platforms using InstallShield. Note that InstallShield has a special version of their product that supports Java applications (http://www.installshield.com/java). On UNIX platforms, SanFrancisco is provided along with the installation scripts used for installing the frameworks.

SanFrancisco is provided as a set of separately installed components. The intent is for the developer to use the basic installation with minimal changes (e.g. deleting some components from the selection list) to create the final installation.

Messages Configuration

The notion of "Message Catalogs" was introduced in Chapter 20. One of the deployment considerations is where to place your messages files. You have the two options for defining where `StaticMessageCatalogs` initialization files are kept. They can be either kept on one machine (i.e. you have one centralized copy), or each machine running your application could have its own replicated copy of the message files. This is a tradeoff between the runtime performance for `StaticMessageCatalogs` and the effort in distributing the message files. The default is to have the files centralized. The way to specify your choice is through an entry in the *sfenv.ini* file (residing in Com\Ibm\Sf\etc under the SanFrancisco installation). In order to have the file on each machine add to the file `staticMessageFilesRemote = true`. Similarly, You have a few configuration options `DynamicMessageCatalogs`:

- First, you can decide whether you want your `DynamicMessageCatalogs` to be initialized from files. The default is to enable initialization from file. The way to specify your choice is again through an entry in the *sfenv.ini* file. To indicate you would like initialization from a file add to the *sfenv.ini* file the line: `fileLookupEnabled = true`
- You can define the location of the files that should be used to initialize `DynamicMessageCatalogs` with and to write the contents of `DynamicMessageCatalogs` to. The default location for these dynamic message files is the directory you started your application in. The way to specify a different location is once again through an entry in the sfenv.ini file; the form for this entry is, `DynamicMessageCatalogLocation = <directory>`. Note that for static message files there is no such option. These have to be placed in a subdirectory of a directory included in the CLASSPATH. That subdirectory is derived from the name of the `StaticMessageCatalog`. For example, the catalog name "resources.messages.MyMsgs" implies the relative subdirectory "resources\messages."

Bibliography

Aho, A.V., Hopcroft, E. and Ullman, J.D. (1985) *Data Structures and Algorithms*, Addison-Wesley.

Ames, A.L., Nadeau, D.R. and Moreland, J.L. (1995) *The VRML Sourcebook*, John Wiley.

Anuff, E. (1996) *The Java Sourcebook*, John Wiley.

Arnold, K. and Gosling, J. (1956) *The Java Programming Language*, Addison-Wesley.

Ayer, S. (1995) *Object-Oriented Client/Server Application Development*, McGraw-Hill.

Bernstein, T., Bhimani, A., Schultz, G. and Siegel C. (1996) *Internet Security for Business*, John Wiley.

Berners-Lee, T., Fielding, R. and Frystyk, H. (1995) *HTTP Working Group Internet Draft HTTP/1.0*, September.

Berners-Lee, T., Masinter, L. and McCahill, M. (1989) *Uniform Resource Locators*, RFC 1123, October.

Black, U. (1995) *TCP/IP and Related Protocols, Second Edition*, McGraw-Hill.

Black, U. (1995) *Network Management Standards: SNMP, CMIP, TMN, MIBs and Object Libraries*, McGraw-Hill.

Booch, G. (1991) *Object-Oriented Design with Applications*, Benjamin/Cummings.

Brockschmidt, K. (1994) *Inside OLE2*, Microsoft Press.

Cattell, R.G. (1992) *Object Data Management*, Addison-Wesley.

Cattell, R.G. (ed.) (1994) *The Object Database Standard: ODMG-93*, Morgan Kaufmann.

Coombs, T., Coombs, J. and Brewer, D. (1996) *The Netscape LiveWire Sourcebook: Create and Manage a Java Based Web Site*, John Wiley.

Cheswick, W.R. and Bellovin, S.M. (1994) *Firewalls & Internet Security – Repelling the Wily Hacker*, Addison–Wesley.

Cornell, G. and Horstmann, C.S. (1996) *Core Java*, Prentice Hall.

Daconta, M.C. (1996) *Java for C/C++ Programmers*, John Wiley.

Deep, J. and Holfelder, P. (1996) *Developing CGI Applications with Perl*, John Wiley.

Dean, D., Felten, E.W. and Wallach, D.S. (1996) "Java Security: From HotJava to Netscape and Beyond," *1996 IEEE Symposium on Security and Privacy*, Oakland CA, May 6–8, 1996.

Diffie, W. and Hellman, M.E. (1977) "New Directions in Cryptography," *IEEE Transactions on Information Theory*, June 1977, pp. 74–84.

Dixon, R. (1995) *Client/Server and Open Systems: Technologies and the Tools That Make Them Work*, John Wiley.

NIST FIPS 186 (1994) *Digital Signature Standard*, National Institute of Standards and Technology, May 1994.

Ellis, M.A. and Stroustrup, B. (1990) *The Annotated C++ Reference Manual*, Addison-Wesley.

Feather, S. (1996) *JavaScript By Example*, QUE.

Geary, D. and McClellan, A. (1996) *Graphic Java: Mastering the AWT*, Prentice Hall.

Gamma, E., Helm, R., Johnson, R. and Vlissides, J. (1995) *Design Patterns – Elements of Reusable Object-Oriented Software*, Addison Wesley.

Gosling, J. and McGilton, H., *The Java Language Environment: A White Paper*, `http://www.dipybird.com/java.html`.

Graham, I.S. (1996) *HTML Sourcebook*, John Wiley & Sons.

Grand, M. (1998) *Patterns in Java, Volume 1*, John Wiley & Sons.

Hare, C. and Siyan, K.S. (1996) *Internet Firewalls and Network Security*, New Riders Publishing.

Jackson, J.R. and McClellan, A. (1996) *Java By Example*, Prentice Hall.

[Java, JDK, JavaBeans] http://java.sun.com

[JAVAIDL] *IDL/Java Language Mapping*, OMG TC Document orbos/97-03-01, March 19, 1997.

[JB] Javabeans version 1.01 Graham Hamilton (Ed.), July 24, 1997.

[JOOP1_2] "Designing Reusable Classes," *The Journal of Object-Oriented Programming*, 1, (2), 1988.

[JOSS1] Joint Object Services Submission: Naming Service. OMG Technical Committee Document number 93-5-2. The Object Management Group.

[JOSS2] Joint Object Services Submission: Persistence Service. OMG Technical Committee Document number 93-5-5. The Object Management Group.

[JOSS3] Joint Object Services Submission: Overview. OMG Technical Committee Document number 93-7-1. The Object Management Group.

[JOSS4] Joint Object Services Submission: Event Service. OMG Technical Committee Document number 93-7-3. The Object Management Group.

[JOSS5] Joint Object Services Submission: Life Cycle Service. OMG Technical Committee Document number 93-7-4. The Object Management Group.

[JOSS6] Joint Object Service Specification: Compound Life Cycle Addendum. OMG Technical Committee Document number 94-5-6. The Object Management Group.

Khoshafian, S. (1995) *Object Orientation: Concepts, Analysis & Design, Languages, Databases, Graphical User Interfaces, Standards, Operating Systems*, John-Wiley.

Krawczyk, H. (1995) IETF Draft: "Keyed-MD5 for Message Authentication", November.

Krasner, G.E. and Pope, S.T. (1988) "A cookbook for using the Model-View-Controller user interface paradigm in Smalltalk-8," *Journal of Object Oriented Programming* 1(3): 26–49.

Lewis, G. (Ed.) *Object Services Roadmap (Final Draft)*, OMG Technical Committee Document number 92-8-5. The Object Management Group.

Lindholm, T. and Yellin, F. (1996) *The Java Virtual Machine Specification*, Addison-Wesley.

Lockhart, H.W., Jr. (1994) *OSF DCE*, McGraw-Hill.

Loomis, M.E.S. (1995) *Object Databases – The Essentials*, Addison-Wesley.

Naughton, P. (1996) *The Java Handbook*, McGraw-Hill.

Object-Oriented Programming and the Objective-C Language, NeXTSTEP Developer's Library, NeXT Computer Inc., Addison-Wesley, 1993.

[OMG1] *Object Management Architecture Guide*, The Object Management Group, 1992.

[OMG2] *The Common Object Request Broker: Architecture and Specification. Revision 1.1*, The Object Management Group and X/Open, John Wiley and Sons, 1992.

[OMG3] *The Common Object Request Broker: Architecture and Specification. Revision 1.2*, The Object Management Group, December, 1993.

[OMG4] *The Common Object Request Broker: Architecture and Specification. Revision 2.0*, The Object Management Group, July, 1996.

[PCT] http://pct.microsoft.com/pct/pct2.html

Peterson, M.T. (1995) *DCE: A Guide to Developing Portable Applications*, McGraw-Hill.

Pew, J.A. (1996) *Instant Java*, Prentice Hall.

[PKCS1] RSA Laboratories, "PKCS#1: RSA Encryption Standard" November, 1993.

[PKCS3] RSA Laboratories, "PKCS#3: Diffie-Hellman Key-Agreement Standard," Version 1.4, November, 1993.

[PKCS7] RSA Laboratories, "PKCS#7: Cryptographic Message Standard," November, 1993.

Postel, J. (1994) "Simple Mail Transfer Protocol", RFC-821, August, 1982. & Sons.

[SET] http://www.mastercard.com/set/set.htm

Siegel, J. (ed.) (1994) *Common Object Service Specification – Volume 1*, The Object Management Group, John Wiley & Sons.

Freier, A.O., Karlton, P. and Kocher, P.C. (1996) "The SSL Protocol Version 3", Internet Draft, April 1996.

Stevens, W.R. (1990) *Unix Network Programming*, Prentice-Hall.

Stevens, W.R. (1994) *TCP/IP Illustrated, Volume 1 – The Protocols*, Addison-Wesley.

Stevens, W.R. (1996) *TCP/IP Illustrated, Volume 3 – TCP for Transactions, HTTP, NNTP, and the UNIX Domain Protocols*, Addison-Wesley.

Goldberg, A. and Robson, B. (1983) *Smalltalk 80: The Language and its Implementation*, Addison-Wesley.

LaLonde, W.R. and Pugh, J.R. (1991) *Inside Smalltalk, vols. 1 and 2*, Prentice-Hall.

Thompson, C. (ed.) Object Services Architecture (6.0) OMG Technical Committee Document number 92-8-4, The Object Management Group.

Wakeman, L. and Jowett, J. (1993) *PCTE – The Standard for Open Repositories*, Prentice-Hall.

Wutka, M. et al. (1997) *Hacking Java: The Java Professional's Resource Kit*, QUE.

[X509] CCITT Recommendation X.509, "The Directory – Authentication Framework", 1988.

Index

D

E

F

G

H

I

J

N

O

P

Q

R

S

ABOUT THE AUTHORS

Ron Ben-Natan is currently Vice President, Product Development at RTS Software, where he is responsible for the technological direction of the firm and for delivering RTS's innovative e-ServiceSuite product line. Before that he was a consultant in a variety of industries including military, semiconductors, telecommunications, and especially the financial sector. He has a Ph.D. in Computer Science and over 15 years of experience with object-oriented software and distributed systems. His previous works include *CORBA*, *Objects on the Web*, and *CORBA on the Web*, all published by McGraw-Hill.

Ori Sasson is the co-founder and CEO of KS Software in Tel-Aviv, Israel. He has 11 years of experience in object-oriented technology. He has a M.Sc. in Computer Science from the Hebrew University of Jerusalem and extensive experience relating to Java and Internet computing.

SOFTWARE AND INFORMATION LICENSE

The software and information on this diskette (collectively referred to as the "Product") are the property of The McGraw-Hill Companies, Inc. ("McGraw-Hill") and are protected by both United States copyright law and international copyright treaty provision. You must treat this Product just like a book, except that you may copy it into a computer to be used and you may make archival copies of the Products for the sole purpose of backing up our software and protecting your investment from loss.

By saying "just like a book," McGraw-Hill means, for example, that the Product may be used by any number of people and may be freely moved from one computer location to another, so long as there is no possibility of the Product (or any part of the Product) being used at one location or on one computer while it is being used at another. Just as a book cannot be read by two different people in two different places at the same time, neither can the Product be used by two different people in two different places at the same time (unless, of course, McGraw-Hill's rights are being violated).

McGraw-Hill reserves the right to alter or modify the contents of the Product at any time.

This agreement is effective until terminated. The Agreement will terminate automatically without notice if you fail to comply with any provisions of this Agreement. In the event of termination by reason of your breach, you will destroy or erase all copies of the Product installed on any computer system or made for backup purposes and shall expunge the Product from your data storage facilities.

LIMITED WARRANTY

McGraw-Hill warrants the physical diskette(s) enclosed herein to be free of defects in materials and workmanship for a period of sixty days from the purchase date. If McGraw-Hill receives written notification within the warranty period of defects in materials or workmanship, and such notification is determined by McGraw-Hill to be correct, McGraw-Hill will replace the defective diskette(s). Send request to:

Customer Service
McGraw-Hill
Gahanna Industrial Park
860 Taylor Station Road
Blacklick, OH 43004-9615

The entire and exclusive liability and remedy for breach of this Limited Warranty shall be limited to replacement of defective diskette(s) and shall not include or extend to any claim for or right to cover any other damages, including but not limited to, loss of profit, data, or use of the software, or special, incidental, or consequential damages or other similar claims, even if McGraw-Hill has been specifically advised as to the possibility of such damages. In no event will McGraw-Hill's liability for any damages to you or any other person ever exceed the lower of suggested list price or actual price paid for the license to use the Product, regardless of any form of the claim.

THE McGRAW-HILL COMPANIES, INC. SPECIFICALLY DISCLAIMS ALL OTHER WARRANTIES, EXPRESS OR IMPLIED, INCLUDING BUT NOT LIMITED TO, ANY IMPLIED WARRANTY OF MERCHANTABILITY OR FITNESS FOR A PARTICULAR PURPOSE. Specifically, McGraw-Hill makes no representation or warranty that the Product is fit for any particular purpose and any implied warranty of merchantability is limited to the sixty day duration of the Limited Warranty covering the physical diskette(s) only (and not the software or in-formation) and is otherwise expressly and specifically disclaimed.

This Limited Warranty gives you specific legal rights, you may have others which may vary from state to state. Some states do not allow the exclusion of incidental or consequential damages, or the limitation on how long an implied warranty lasts, so some of the above may not apply to you.

This Agreement constitutes the entire agreement between the parties relating to use of the Product. The terms of any purchase order shall have no effect on the terms of this Agreement. Failure of McGraw-Hill to insist at any time on strict compliance with this Agreement shall not constitute a waiver of any rights under this Agreement. This Agreement shall be construed and governed in accordance with the laws of New York. If any provision of this Agreement is held to be contrary to law, that provision will be enforced to the maximum extent permissible and the remaining provisions will remain in force and effect.